Systems Engineering and Artificial Intelligence

William F. Lawless · Ranjeev Mittu ·
Donald A. Sofge · Thomas Shortell ·
Thomas A. McDermott
Editors

Systems Engineering and Artificial Intelligence

 Springer

Editors
William F. Lawless ⓘ
Paine College
Augusta, GA, USA

Donald A. Sofge ⓘ
United States Naval Research Laboratory
Washington, DC, USA

Thomas A. McDermott
Stevens Institute of Technology
Hoboken, NJ, USA

Ranjeev Mittu
Information Technology Division
United States Naval Research Laboratory
Washington, DC, USA

Thomas Shortell
Lockheed Martin Space Systems
King of Prussia, PA, USA

ISBN 978-3-030-77282-6   ISBN 978-3-030-77283-3   (eBook)
https://doi.org/10.1007/978-3-030-77283-3

This Springer imprint is published by the registered company Springer Nature Switzerland AG
The registered company address is: Gewerbestrasse 11, 6330 Cham, Switzerland

Preface

We began this book by asking representatives from Systems Engineering (SE) to participate with us in an Association for the Advancement of Artificial Intelligence (AAAI) Symposium in the Spring of 2020. We addressed our request for participation to representatives of the International Council on Systems Engineering (INCOSE). The symposium was intended to advance the science of autonomous human-machine teams (A-HMTs). After systems engineers agreed to participate, we included "systems" in our call. The symposium was scheduled to occur at Stanford University during March 23–25, 2020. Our agenda included AI scientists, system engineers, and interested participants and organizations from around the world. Unfortunately, the Covid-19 pandemic intervened. But AAAI gave us two opportunities: hold the March event as scheduled virtually, or have a Replacement Symposium in the Washington, DC area. We took advantage of both offers.

We gave our scheduled speakers the choice of participating in the virtual Spring Symposium, the Fall Replacement Symposium, or both. The agenda for the Spring Symposium was reduced to under 2 days, roughly replicated for the Replacement Fall Symposium, which also became a virtual event. However, the number of participants for both the Spring and Fall events slightly exceeded 100, a larger audience than we would have expected to attend in person at Stanford.

Both symposia had the same title:[1] "AI welcomes systems Engineering: Towards the science of interdependence for autonomous human-machine teams."[2] The original list of topics in our call for the Spring Symposium had sought potential speakers to give talks on "AI and machine learning, autonomy; systems engineering; Human-Machine Teams (HMT); machine explanations of decisions; and context." For the Replacement Symposium, we revised our list of topics for potential speakers to consider in addition: "machine explanations of decisions." For both symposia, we sought participants from across multiple disciplines who were willing to work together to contribute to the advancement of AI in welcoming SE to build a science of

---

[1] https://aaai.org/Symposia/Spring/sss20symposia.php#ss03.

[2] Michael Wollowski designed and built our supplementary website (wollowsk@rose-hulman.edu), found at https://sites.google.com/view/scienceofinterdependence.

interdependence for autonomous human-machine teams and systems. Our thinking continued to evolve, leading us to name the title of this book, "Systems Engineering and Artificial Intelligence."

The list of topics in this book expanded well beyond the listed agendas for our two symposia. That said, the theme of systems and AI has continued to motivate the chapters in this book. Our goal for the symposium was, and for this book is, to deal with the current state of the art in autonomy and artificial intelligence (AI) from a systems perspective for the betterment of society.

In advertising for our symposium and then for the chapters in this book, we sought contributors who could discuss the meaning, value, and interdependent effects on context wherever these AI-driven machines interact with humans to form autonomous human-machine teams or systems. We had called for extended abstracts (1–2 pages) or longer manuscripts of up to 8 pages in length. Our plan was to publish lengthy manuscripts as chapters in a book after the symposium. We hope that this resulting edited book will advance the next generation of systems that are being designed to include autonomous humans and machines operating as teams and systems interdependently with AI. By focusing on the gaps in the research performed worldwide and addressed in this book, we hope that autonomous human-machine systems wherever applied will be used safely.

In this edited volume, we explore how AI is expanding opportunities to increase its impact on society, which will significantly increase with autonomous human-machine teams and systems. With this book, we offer to the curious and professional alike a review of the theories, models, methods, and applications of AI systems to provide a better understanding, a more integrated perspective of what is in play and at stake from the autonomous humans-machine teams and systems soon to cause major disruptions. But our aim with this book is to help society, practitioners, and engineers to prepare for the extraordinary changes coming.

Machine Learning (ML) is a subset of Artificial Intelligence (AI). Already exceeding trillions of dollars invested, ML and AI have already wrought change across many fields with even greater impacts yet to come. As autonomous machines arrive on the scene, some of the new problems that have accompanied them are discussed in this book. For example, Judea Pearl warned AI scientists to "build machines that make sense of what goes on in their environment" to be able to communicate with humans. Self-driving vehicles have already been involved in fatalities, and yet AI/ML is still trying to explain to humans the contexts within which it operates.

This edited book reflects our belief that only an interdisciplinary approach can fully address Pearl's warning. At our two symposia, we had papers presented by AI computer scientists, systems engineers, social scientists, entrepreneurs, philosophers, and other specialists address how humans make decisions in large systems; how they determine context especially when facing unfamiliar environments or unanticipated events; how autonomous machines may be taught to understand shared contexts; and how human-machine teams may interdependently affect human awareness, other teams, systems, and society, and be affected consequently. For example, in the Uber self-driving fatality of a pedestrian in 2018, the car should have alerted its teammate, a human operator, of an object in the road ahead. As with the case of the Uber fatality, to best protect society, we need to know what happens if the context shared by human-machine teams is incomplete, malfunctions, or breaks down.

This book also includes one of the first, if not the very first, chapters coauthored by an artificially intelligent coauthor. Her name is Charlie. Her fellow coauthors address the value of recognizing Charlie and treating her with respect to build a context that is shared by all participants. For autonomous teams and systems involving humans and machines, constructing a shared context is fundamental, meaning that joint interpretations of reality must be addressed, requiring the interdisciplinary approach that we have adopted, so that we too can learn from Charlie, a significant moment for us, our fellow contributors, and we hope for you the reader, too.

The Organizers of Our Symposium

William F. Lawless, (w.lawless@icloud.com), corresponding, Professor, Mathematics & Psychology, Paine College, GA, Special Topics Editor, Entropy, and Review Board, ONR (AI; Command Decision Making).

Ranjeev Mittu (ranjeev.mittu@nrl.navy.mil), Branch Head, Information Management & Decision Architectures Branch, Information Technology Division, U.S. Naval Research Laboratory, Washington, DC.

Donald Sofge (don.sofge@nrl.navy.mil), Computer Scientist, Distributed Autonomous Systems Group, Navy Center for Applied Research in Artificial Intelligence, Naval Research Laboratory, Washington, DC.

Thomas Shortell (thomas.m.shortell@lmco.com), Certified Systems Engineering Professional, Lockheed Martin Space Systems, King of Prussia, PA.

Thomas A. McDermott (tamcdermott42@gmail.com), Deputy Director, Systems Engineering Research Center, Stevens Institute of Technology, Hoboken, NJ.

Participants at Our Symposium

We had several more participants than the speakers who attended our symposium. We wanted speakers and participants who could assess the foundations, metrics, or applications of autonomous AI/ML, human-machine teams, and systems and how these teams and systems affect or may be affected themselves. We kept both of the symposia open-ended for the topics and for this book. We considered all papers submitted for the two symposia and several afterwards for the book as long as they had a systems perspective. Accompanied by contributions from non-symposium participants, too, our goal then and now is to advance AI theory and concepts to improve the performance of autonomous human-machine teams and systems to improve society.

Program Committee for Our 2020 AAAI Symposia

- Manisha Misra, U Connecticut, Ph.D. graduate student, manisha.uconn@gmail.com
- Shu-Heng Chen, Taiwan, chen.shuheng@gmail.com
- Beth Cardier, Sirius-Beta, VA; School Health Professions, Eastern Virginia Medical School, bethcardier@hotmail.com
- Michael Floyd, Lead AI Scientist, Knexus Research, michael.floyd@knexusresearch.com
- Boris Galitsky, Chief Scientist, Oracle Corp., bgalitsky@hotmail.com
- Matt Johnson, Institute for Human and Machine Cognition, Research scientist in human-machine teaming for technologies, mjohnson@ihmc.us
- Georgiy Levchuk, Aptima Fellow, Senior Principal, Simulation & Optimization Engineer, georgiy@aptima.com
- Patrick J. Martin, MITRE Corporation, Autonomous Systems Engineer, pmartin@mitre.org
- Manisha Mishra, University of Connecticut, Systems Engineering, manisha.uconn@gmail.com
- Krishna Pattipati, University of Connecticut, Board of Trustees Distinguished Professor, Professor in Systems Engineering.

After the AAAI-Spring and Fall Replacement Symposia in 2020 were completed, speakers were asked to revise their talks into manuscripts for the chapters in this book. After the symposium, other authors who did not participate in the symposium were also invited and they agreed to participate. The following individuals were responsible for the proposal submitted to Springer for the book before the symposia, for the divergence between the topics considered by the two, and for editing this book that has resulted.

Augusta, GA, USA   William F. Lawless
Washington, DC, USA   Ranjeev Mittu
Washington, DC, USA   Donald A. Sofge
King of Prussia, PA, USA   Thomas Shortell
Hoboken, NJ, USA   Thomas A. McDermott

Contents

Chapter 1
Introduction to *"Systems Engineering and Artificial Intelligence"* and the Chapters

William F. Lawless, Ranjeev Mittu, Donald A. Sofge, Thomas Shortell, and Thomas A. McDermott

Abstract In this introductory chapter, we first review the science behind the two Association for the Advancement of Artificial Intelligence (AAAI) Symposia that we held in 2020 ("AI welcomes Systems Engineering. Towards the science of interdependence for autonomous human-machine teams"). Second, we provide a brief introduction to each of the chapters in this book.

1.1 Introduction. The Disruptive Nature of AI

Presently, the United States is facing formidable threats from China and Russia. In response to these threats, the Director of the Defense Intelligence Agency (Ashley, 2019) and DNI stated:

> China ... [is] acquiring technology by any means available. Domestic [Chinese] laws forced foreign partners of Chinese-based joint ventures to release their technology in exchange for entry into China's lucrative market, and China has used other means to secure needed technology and expertise. The result ... is a PLA on the verge of fielding some of the most modern weapon systems in the world. ... China is building a robust, lethal force with capabilities spanning the air, maritime, space and information domains which will enable China to impose its will in the region. (p. V) ... From China's leader, Xi Jinping, to his 19th Party Congress (p. 17) "We must do more to safeguard China's sovereignty, security, and development interests, and staunchly oppose all attempts to split China or undermine its ethnic unity and social harmony and stability."

W. F. Lawless (✉)
Paine College, Augusta, Georgia
e-mail: w.lawless@icloud.com

R. Mittu · D. A. Sofge · T. Shortell · T. A. McDermott
Systems Engineering Research Center, Stevens Institute of Technology, Hoboken, NJ, USA
e-mail: ranjeev.mittu@nrl.navy.mil

D. A. Sofge
e-mail: donald.sofge@nrl.navy.mil

T. Shortell
e-mail: thomas.m.shortell@lmco.com

To address these and other competitive threats, artificial intelligence (AI), especially machine learning (ML) that we discuss with fusion next, is a major factor. The U.S. Department of Defense (DoD), industry, commerce, education, and medicine among many other fields are seeking to use AI to gain a comparative advantage for systems. From the perspective of DoD (2019):

> AI is rapidly changing a wide range of businesses and industries. It is also poised to change the character of the future battlefield and the pace of threats we must face.

Simultaneously, the DoD recognizes the disruptive nature of AI (Oh et al., 2019). To mitigate this disruption while taking advantage of the ready-made solutions AI already offers to commerce, the current thinking appears to first use AI in areas that are less threatening to military planners, the public, and potential users; e.g., back-office administration; finance (e.g., Airbus is using AI to cut its financial costs by increasing efficiency, reducing errors, and freeing up humans for more strategic tasks such as planning, analysis, and audits; in Maurer, 2019); data collection and management; basic personnel matters; virtual assistants for basic skills training (i.e., Military Occupational Specialties, or MOSs); personal medical monitoring (e.g., drug compliance, weight reduction, sleep cycles); military maintenance; and simple logistics (e.g., ordering, tracking, maintaining supplies).

Second, when the DoD and other fields address the more disruptive aspects of AI, like autonomy and autonomous human–machine teams, many more social changes and impacts will arise, including the adverse threats posed by the use of AI, such as the "consequences of failure in autonomous and semi-autonomous weapon systems that could lead to unintended engagements" (DoD, 2019).

Machine Learning (ML) and Fusion: Machine learning has already had an extraordinary economic impact worldwide estimated in the trillions of dollars with even more economic and social impact to come (Brynjolfsson & Mitchell, 2017). The basic idea behind traditional ML methods is that a computer algorithm is trained with data collected in the field to learn a behavior presented to it as part of previous experience (e.g., self-driving cars) or with a data set to an extent that an outcome can be produced by the computer algorithm when it is presented with a novel situation (Raz et al., 2019).

Autonomy is changing the situation dramatically in the design and operational contexts for which future information fusion (IF) systems are evolving. There are many factors that influence or define these new contexts but among them are: movement to cloud-based environments involving possibly many semi-autonomous functional agents (e.g., the Internet of Things or IoT; Lawless et al., 2019b), the employment of a wide range of processing technologies and methods spread across agents and teams, an exceptional breadth of types and modalities of available data, and diverse and asynchronous communication patterns among independent and distributed agents and teams. These factors describe the contexts of complex adaptive systems (CAS) for "systems in which a perfect understanding of the individual parts does not automatically convey a perfect understanding of the whole system's behavior" (Raz et al., 2019).

Managing these disruptions must justify the need for speedy decisions; a systems approach; the commonality of interdependence in systems and social science; social science, including trust; the science of human–human teams (HHT); and human–machine teams (HMT). We discuss these topics in turn.

1.1.1   Justifying Speedy Decisions

Now is the time when decisions may need to be made faster than humans can process (Horowitz, 2019), as with the military development of hypersonic weapons by competitor nations (e.g., China; in Wong, 2018); the push for quicker command, control, and communication upgrades for nuclear weapons (NC-3; in DoD, 2018); and the common use of AI in public conveyances like self-driving cars, trucks, ships, or subways.

Many systems are approaching an operational status that use AI with humans "in-the-loop," characterized by when a human can override decisions by human–machine or machine–machine teams in combat, such as the Navy's new Ghost fleet (LaGrone, 2019); the Army's autonomous self-driving combat convoy (Langford, 2018); and the Marine Corps' remote ordinance disposal by human–machine teams (CRS, 2018).

Even more dramatic changes are to occur with human "on-the-loop" decisions, characterized by when decisions must be made faster than humans can process and take action based on the incoming information. Among the new weapon systems, these decisions may be made by a human–machine team composed of an F-35 teaming with the Air Force's aggressive, dispensable "attritable" drones flying in a wing or offensive position (Insinna, 2019); moreover, hypersonic weapons are forcing humans into roles as passive bystanders until a decision and its accompanying action have been completed. From an article in the *New York Times Magazine* (Smith, 2019),

> One of the two main hypersonic prototypes now under development in the United States is meant to fly at speeds between Mach 15 and Mach 20 ... when fired by the U.S. submarines or bombers stationed at Guam, they could in theory hit China's important inland missile bases ... in less than 15 minutes ...

By attacking the United States at hypersonic speeds, however, these speeds would make ballistic missile interceptors ineffective (e.g., Aegis ship-based, Thad ground-based, and Patriot systems). If launched by China or Russia against the United States (Smith, 2019), these missiles:

> would zoom along in the defensive void, maneuvering unpredictably, and then, in just a few final seconds of blindingly fast, mile-per-second flight, dive and strike a target such as an aircraft carrier from an altitude of 100,000 feet.

Human "on-the-loop" observations of autonomous machines making self-directed decisions carry significant risks. On the positive side, since most accidents are caused by human error (Lawless et al., 2017), self-directed machines may save more lives. But an editorial in the *New York Times* (Editors, 2019) expressed the public's concerns that AI systems can be hacked, suffer data breaches, and lose control to adversaries. The Editors quoted the UN Secretary General, Antonio Guterres, that "machines with the power and discretion to take lives without human involvement … should be prohibited by international law." The editorial recommended that "humans never completely surrender life and decision choices in combat to machines." (For a review of the U.N.'s failure to manage "killer robots," see Werkhäuser, 2019.)

Whether or not a treaty to manage threats from the use of "on the loop" decisions is enacted, the violations of existing treaties by nuclear states (e.g., NATO's judgment about suspected Russian treaty violations; in Gramer & Seligman, 2018) suggest the need to understand the science of autonomy for "on the loop" decisions and to counter the systems that use them.

Furthermore, the warning by the Editors of the *New York Times* is similar to those that arose during the early years of atomic science, balanced by managing the threats posed while at the same time allowing scientists to make numerous discoveries leading to the extraordinary gifts to humanity that have followed, crowned by the Higgs (the so-called "God") particle and quantum computing. The science of autonomy must also be managed to balance its threats while allowing scientists to make what we hope are similar advances in the social sphere ranging from Systems Engineering and social science to international affairs.

1.1.2 Systems Engineering (SE)

SE is also concerned about whether AI and ML will replace humans in the decision loop (Howell, 2019). System engineers prefer that humans and machines coexist together, that machines be used to augment human intelligence, but that if decisions by machines overtake human decision-making as is happening with "on-the-loop" decisions, at least humans should audit the machine decisions afterward (viz., see the Uber car fatality case below). SE also raises a series of other concerns and questions.

In addition to the public's concerns about AI expressed by the Editors in the *New York Times*, the application of AI/ML raises several concerns and questions for SE. One concern is whether or not to use a modular approach to build models (Rhodes, 2019). System engineers note that safety is an emergent property of a system (Howell, 2019). When a team "emerges," the whole has become more than the sum of its parts (Raz et al., 2019); in contrast, when a collective fails, as appears to be occurring in Europe today, it creates "a whole significantly less than the sum of its parts" (Mead, 2019). But if SE using AI/ML is to be transformed through model-centric engineering (Blackburn, 2019), how is that to be accomplished for autonomous teams? Systems often do not stand alone; in those cases where systems are a network of networks, how shall system engineers assure that the "pieces work together to achieve the objectives of the whole" (Thomas, 2019)? From retired General Stanley McCrystal's book, *Team of teams*, "We needed to enable a team operating in an interdependent environment to understand the butterfly-effect ramifications of their work and make them aware of the other teams with whom they would have to cooperate" (in Long, 2019). Continuing with the emphasis added by Long (2019), in the attempt by the Canadian Armed Forces to build a shared Communication and Information Systems (CIS) with networked teams and teams of teams in its systems of organizations,

> Systems must be specifically designed to enable resilient organizations, with the designer and community fully aware of the trade-offs that must be made to functionality, security, and cost. However, the benefits of **creating shared consciousness, lowering the cost of participation, and emulating familiar human communication patterns are significant** (Long's emphasis).

For more concerns, along with metrics for autonomous AI systems, formal verification (V&V), certification and risk assessments of these systems at the design, operational, and maintenance stages will be imperative for engineers (Lemnios, 2019; Richards, 2019). Is there a metric to assess the risk from collaboration, and if so, can it be calculated (Grogan, 2019)? The risk from not deploying AI systems should also be addressed (DeLaurentis, 2019); while an excellent suggestion, how can this concern be addressed?[1] Measured in performance versus expectations, when will these risks preclude humans from joining teams with machines; and what effect will machine redundancy have in autonomous systems (Barton, 2019)? Because data are dumb, how will the operational requirements and architectures be tested and evaluated for these systems over their lifecycle (Dare, 2019; Freeman, 2019)?

Boundaries and deception: AI can be used to defend against outsiders, or used with deception to exploit vulnerabilities in targeted networks (Yampolskiy, 2017). A team's system boundaries must be protected (Lawless, 2017a). Protecting a team's networks is also a concern. In contrast, deception functions by not standing out (i.e., fitting in structurally; in Lawless, 2017b). Deception can be used to compromise a network. From the *Wall Street Journal* (Volz & Youssef, 2019), the Department of Homeland Security's top cybersecurity official, Chris Krebs, issued a statement warning that Iran's malicious cyberactivities were on the rise. "What might start as an account compromise … can quickly become a situation where you've lost your whole network."

Caution: In the search for optimization, tradeoffs occur (Long, 2019); however, an optimized system should not tradeoff resilience.

1.1.3 Common Ground: AI, Interdependence, and SE

Systems engineers know about interdependence from a system's perspective. They claim to know little about human teams, which they hope can be improved by working

---

[1] One possibility is to use global metrics. In the case of the Uber car accident that killed a pedestrian discussed below, the industry's first pedestrian fatality, the company's self-driving section did not suffer until the accident, and then Uber and the rest of the self-driving industry have been significantly slowed by the fatality (Gardner, 2019).

with social scientists and by studying their own SE teams and organizations (DeLaurentis, 2019). Their own teams and organizations, however, are systems of social interdependence.

Systems Engineering addresses the interactions of systems too complex for an analysis of their independent parts without taking a system as a whole into account across its life cycle. System complexity from the "interdependencies between ... constituent systems" can produce unexpected effects (Walden et al., 2015, p. 10), making the management of systemic interdependence critical to a system's success. For example, the interactions for complex systems with numerous subsystems, like the International Space Station (ISS), interact interdependently (i.e., interdependence affected how the ISS modules were assembled into an integrated whole, how module upgrades affected each other, how interfaces between ISS modules were determined to be effective, how the overall configuration of the modules was constructed, how modules were modeled, etc.; in Stockman et al., 2010). From the ISS, in SE, we can see that interdependence transmits the interactions of subsystems. The study of interdependence in systems is not a new idea. For example, Llinas (2014, pp. 1, 6) issued a:

> call for action among the fusion, cognitive, decision-making, and computer-science communities to muster a cooperative initiative to examine and develop [the] ... metrics involved in measuring and evaluating process interdependencies ... [otherwise, the design of] modern decision support systems ... will remain disconnected and suboptimal going forward.

Similarly, in the social sciences, interdependence is the means of transmitting social effects (Lawless, 2019), such as the construction of a shared context between two humans, and, we propose, for human–machine teams (HMT). Interdependence then is the phenomenon that not only links Systems Engineering, AI, and other disciplines (e.g., social science, law, philosophy, etc.) but also, if interdependence can be mastered, it will provide a means to assist AI and SE in the development of a science of interdependence for human–machine teams.

The application of interdependence in a system to analyze an accident: In 2018, an Uber[2] self-driving car struck and killed a pedestrian. From the investigation report (NTSB, 2018; NTSB, 2019b), the machine saw the pedestrian about 6 s before striking her, selected the brakes 1.2 s before impact, but new actions like the brakes had a 1 s interlock to prevent precipitous action by (since corrected). The human operator saw the victim 1 s before impact and hit her brakes 1 s after impact. Of the conclusions to be drawn, first, although poorly designed, the Uber car performed faster than the human; but, second and more important, the Uber car was a poor team player by not updating the context it should have shared with its human operator (Sofge et al., 2019).

Trust as part of the accident analysis. When will machines be qualified to be trusted remains an important question. As we pointed out in a bet in *AI Magazine* (Sofge et al., 2019), despite the complexity and costs of validating these systems, according to a *New York Times* (Wakabayashi, 2018) investigation of the pedestrian's death in 2018 by the Uber self-driving car, Waymo self-driving cars:

---

[2] On December 7th, Uber sold its self-driving unit to Aurora Innovation Inc. (Somerville, 2020).

went an average of nearly 5,600 miles before the driver had to take control from the computer to steer out of trouble. As of March [2018, when the accident happened], Uber was struggling to meet its target of 13 miles per "intervention" in Arizona …

It must be kept in mind, however, that as incompletely and poorly trained as was the Uber car, it still responded to the situation as it had been designed; further, its response was faster than its human operator.

1.1.4 Social Science

The National Academy of Sciences (2019) *Decadal Survey of Social and Behavioral Sciences* finds that the social sciences want to be included in research using computational social science for human and AI agents in teams. In their thinking, social scientists are concerned about ethical and privacy issues with the large digital databases being collected. For systems of social networks, they recommended further study on:

> how information can be transmitted effectively … [from] change in social networks … network structure of online communities, the types of actors in those communities …

In addition, social scientists want more research to counter social cyberattacks, research on emotion, and, for our purposes (see below in Bisbey et al., 2019 for similar issues with research on human teams),

> … how to assemble and divide tasks among teams of humans and AI agents and measure performance in such teams. …

More importantly, while social scientists want to be included in the AI/ML revolution, they have had setbacks in their own disciplines with the reproducibility of experiments (e.g., Nosek, 2015; also, Harris, 2018). For our purposes, unexpectedly, research has indicated that the poorest performing teams of scientists were interdisciplinary teams (Cummings, 2015).[3] In addition, however, Cummings added that the best scientist teams maximized interdependence. Based on Cummings and our research (e.g., Lawless, 2019), we conclude that for interdisciplinary teams to function optimally, their team members must also be operating under maximum interdependence (Lawless, 2017a). By extension, for the optimum size of a team to maximize interdependence, a team's size must be the minimum size to solve a targeted problem (Lawless, 2017a), contradicting the Academy's two assertions that "more hands make light work" (Cooke & Hilton, 2015, Chap. 1, p. 13) and that the optimal size of a scientific team is an open problem (p. 33).

The advent of human–machine teams has elevated the need to determine context computationally, yet social science has offered little guidance for their design, operation, or to prevent accidents (see the Uber self-driving car accident described above that killed a pedestrian in 2018), let alone the means to construct a computational

---

[3] Cummings studied about 500 teams of scientists in the National Science Foundation's data base.

context (Lawless et al., 2019a). Recognizing their plight, social scientists argue, and we agree, that their science is the repository of an extraordinary amount of statistical and qualitative experience in determining and evaluating contexts for humans and human teams (NAS, 2019). Nonetheless, this situation leaves engineers to seek a quantitative path on their own. Instead, we foresee an integrated path as the better course going forward (Lawless, 2019).

Trust and machine autonomy: In the rapid decision-making milieux where trust between machine and human members of a team becomes a factor (Beling, 2019), to build trust, each member of a human–machine team must be able not only to exchange information about their status between teammates but also to keep that information private (Lawless et al., 2019a). In that humans cause most accidents (Lawless et al., 2017), trust can be important outside of the team, as when a human operator threatens passengers being transported, which happened with the crash of GermanWings Flight 9525 in the Alps in March 2015, killing all 150 aboard at the hands of its copilot who committed suicide (BEA, 2016); or the engineer on the train in the Northeast Corridor in the United States who allowed his train rounding a curve to speed above the track's limits (NTSB, 2016); or the ship's captain on the bridge of the *McCain* at the time the destroyer was turning out of control in a high-traffic zone (NTSB, 2019). In these and numerous other cases, it is possible with current technology and AI to authorize a plane, train, other public vehicle or military vehicle or Navy ship as part of a human–machine team to take control from its human operator (the bet that a machine will be authorized to take control from a dysfunctional human operator, Sofge et al., 2019).

1.1.5 The Science of Human Teams

From our review of human teams, Proctor and Vu (2019) conclude that the best forecasts improve with competition (Mellers & Tetlock, 2019). They also conclude that teams are formed by "extrinsic factors, intrinsic factors, or a combination of both." Extensive motivation is often generated from the collective consensus of many stakeholders (the public, researchers, and sponsoring agencies) that there is an urgent problem that needs to be solved. But they asserted that solutions require "a multi-disciplinary team that is large in score ... [with] the resources required to carry out the research ... to appropriate subject-matter experts, community organizations and other stakeholders ... [and] within an organization, administrative support for forming, coordinating, and motivating multidisciplinary teams ...".

Salas and his colleagues (Bisbey et al., 2019) conclude that "Teamwork allows a group of individuals to function effectively as a unit by using a set of interrelated knowledge, skills and attitudes (KSAs; p. 279). [On the other hand] ... poor teamwork can have devastating results ... plane crashes, ... friendly fire, ... surgical implications ... When the stakes are high, survival largely depends on effective teamwork." One of the first successes with human teams was: "Crew resource management [CRM] prompted by not "human error," but crew phenomena outside of crew member competencies such as poor communication in United Flight 173 led the Captain to disregard fuel state. ... CRM required the crew to solve its problems as a team" (p. 280). Another success for team science occurred in the attempts to understand the shoot-down of an Iranian commercial airliner by the USS Vincennes in 1988, leading to the study of stress in decision-making. Subsequently, following the combination of a significant number of unrelated human errors that led to new research after President Clinton's Institute of Medicine (IOM) review of medical errors in hospitals; the coordination errors with the BP/Deepwater Horizon oil spill in 2011; Hurricane Katrina in 2005; and the NASA accidents Columbia in 2003 and Challenger in 1986 space shuttle accidents. Based on this new research, human team scientists separated task-work from teamwork. Task work dealt with skills or a skills' domain (flying a plane), teamwork skills with team effectiveness across contexts (e.g., how to communicate with others; p. 282).

1.1.6 Human–Machine Teams

A précis of our research on mathematical models of interdependence and future directions follows. From our hypothesis that the best teams maximize interdependence to communicate information via constructive and destructive interference, we have established that the optimum size of teams and organizations occurs when they are freely able to choose to minimize redundant team members (Lawless, 2017a); we replicated the finding about redundancy and freedom in making choices, adding that redundancy in over-sized teams is associated with corruption (Lawless, 2017b), and that the decision-making of teams and organizations in interdependent states under the pressure of competition implies tradeoffs that require intelligence to navigate around the obstacles that would otherwise preclude a team from reaching its goal such as producing patents (Lawless, 2019). Our findings on redundancy contradict network scientists (Centola & Macy, 2007, p. 716) and the Academy (Cooke & Hilton, 2015, Chap. 1, p. 13); we have also found that interdependence identified in tracking polls indicates that it interferes adversely with predictions based on those polls (Lawless, 2017a, b); e.g., Tetlock and Gardiner's first super-forecasters failed in their two predictions in 2016, first that Brexit would not occur, followed by their second in 2016 that Trump would not be elected President.

In a recent article (Lawless, 2019), we found evidence that intelligence measured by levels of education is significantly associated with the production of patents; however, in earlier research from 2001 reviewed in the same article, we reported that education specific to air-combat maneuvering was unrelated to the performance of fighter pilots engaged in air-to-air combat, indicating that intelligence and physical skills tap orthogonal phenomena, offering a new model of mathematics and thermodynamics for teams, which also accounts for the failure of complementarity to be established; viz., for the latter, the best teams are composed of agents in orthogonal roles, measured by Von Neumann subadditivity, whereas agents in the worst teams are in roles measured by Shannon information (e.g., the conflict between CBS and

Viacom during 2016–18). Finally, orthogonality figures into our proposed next study on fundamental decision processes and emotion for a model of a social harmonic oscillator where we hypothesize that the best teams operate in a ground state while underperforming teams operate in excited states (Lawless, 2019).

1.2   Introduction to the Chapters

Artificial intelligence has already brought significant changes to the world; will the impact of human–machine teams be even greater? The first of the contributed chapters, Chap. 2, "Recognizing Artificial Intelligence: The Key to Unlocking Human AI Teams," was written by a team at Aptima, Inc., headquartered in Woburn, MA. The authors consist of Patrick Cummings, Nathan Schurr, Andrew Naber, Charlie, and Daniel Serfaty (Aptima's CEO and Founder). Readers, please recognize that one of the coauthors from Aptima, "Charlie," has no last name; she is an artificial embodiment. Charlie has made contributions to public before (e.g., at a workshop and a panel), but her contributions to Chap. 2 may be one of the first, if not the very first, chapters contributed to or co-authored by, as she is aptly described by her fellow coauthors, an "intelligent coworker." Interacting with Charlie in public over the past year has produced several insights signified and discussed by all of the authors in their chapter. Interestingly, several of these insights are based on the treatment of Charlie's spoken ideas and written contributions with deep respect, which they have described as "recognizing" Charlie as an equal contributor. The authors provide details about how Charlie came into existence and how she operates in public (e.g., her architecture, her public persona, her ability to brainstorm). The stated goal of all of the authors of Chap. 2 is to bring human and intelligent coworkers together to build an effective system in the future, not only one that recognizes human and artificial coworkers but also one that can be influenced by both human and artificial coworkers and by the contributions from both. We add: "Welcome, Charlie!".

Chapter 3 was written by three Systems Engineers, namely by Thomas A. McDermott and Mark R. Blackburn at the Stevens Institute of Technology in Hoboken, NJ; and by Peter A. Beling at the University of Virginia in Charlottesville, VA. (McDermott is one of the co-editors of this book.) Their chapter is titled, "Artificial Intelligence and Future of Systems Engineering." In it, the authors address the major transformation of their profession now occurring that is being driven by the new digital tools for modeling, data and the extraordinary "digital twins" resulting in the integration of data and modeling. These new tools include the artificial intelligence (AI) and machine learning (ML) software programs that are becoming key to the new processes arising during this period of transformation. Yes, Systems Engineering (SE) is being transformed, but the hope of the authors is that SE is able to guide these new tools and their applications to increase the benefits so that society welcomes this transformation. To help guide this transformation, the authors provide a roadmap being developed by the Systems Engineering Research Center (SERC); SERC is a University-Affiliated Research Center of the US Department of Defense.

The roadmap sets out a series of goals in the attempt by SERC to identify the opportunities and the risks ahead for the research community to guide Systems Engineers in preparation for the journey to the emergence of autonomy safely and ethically.

The fourth chapter, "Effective Human-Artificial Intelligence Teaming," was written by Nancy J. Cooke and William Lawless. Cooke is a Professor of Human Systems Engineering and Director of the Center for Human, Artificial Intelligence, and Robot Teaming at Arizona State University. Lawless is a Professor of Mathematics and Psychology at Paine College; he is also on two Navy Boards (the Science of AI and Command Decision Making); and he is a new Topics Editor of the journal *Entropy* ("The entropy of autonomy and shared context. Human–machine teams, organizations and systems"). They begin their chapter with a review of the history of interdependence. It has long been known to be present in every social interaction and central to understanding the social life of humans, but interdependence has been difficult to manage in the laboratory, producing effects that have "bewildered" social scientists. Since then, however, along with her colleagues and students, Cooke, the first author, has studied in detail the effects of interdependence in the laboratory with detailed studies. She has explored many of the aspects of interdependence and its important implications with her team. She was also the lead author in a review published by the National Academy of Sciences on what is known theoretically and experimentally about interdependence in a team, finding that interdependence enhances the performance of individuals (Cooke & Hilton, 2015). Writing Chap. 4 has provided her with the perspective she has gained from the considerable research, she and her colleagues have conducted over the years. This perspective allows her to estimate the additional research necessary before artificial intelligence (AI) agents and machines can replace a human teammate on a team.

Chapter 5, "Towards Systems Theoretical Foundations for Human-Autonomy Teams," was written by Marc Steinberg with the Office of Naval Research (ONR) in Arlington, VA. Steinberg is ONR's Program Officer for its Science of Autonomy program. In his chapter, he writes about the challenges posed by developing the autonomy of human and intelligent systems. These are new ones on how to best specify, model, design, and verify the correctness of systems. He discusses the real-time monitoring and repairing of autonomous systems over life times, all the while detecting problems and rebooting properties. These challenges entail Systems Engineering methods to model system life cycles by abstracting and decomposing systems in the design and development of components for intelligent autonomy. Exploring these higher-level abstractions, models, and decompositions may inspire solutions and lead to autonomy. These inspirations may integrate systems and humans and provide the means to assure safety. He samples perspectives across scientific fields, including biology, neuroscience, economics, game theory, and psychology. He includes methods for developing and assessing complex human–machine systems with human factors and organizational psychology, and engineering teams with computer science, robotics, and engineering. He discusses team organizational structures, allocating roles, functions, responsibilities, theories for teammates working on long-lived tasks, and modeling and composing autonomous human–machine teams and systems, and their implications.

The sixth chapter was written by James Llinas, Ranjeev Mittu, and Hesham Fouad. It is titled, "Systems Engineering for Artificial Intelligence-based Systems: A Review in Time." Llinas is the Director Emeritus at the Center for Multi-source Information Fusion as well as a Research Professor Emeritus, with both positions in the University at Buffalo. Ranjeev Mittu is the current Branch Head, Information Management & Decision Architectures Branch, Information Technology Division at the U.S. Naval Research Laboratory in Washington, DC; and Hesham Fouad is a Computer Scientist in the same branch at the Naval Research Laboratory. Their backgrounds include information systems, the science of information fusion, and information technology. In their chapter, they provide a review of Systems Engineering (SE) for artificial intelligence (AI) across time, starting with a brief history of AI (e.g., narrow, weak, and strong AI, including expert systems and machine learning). Regarding SE, based on the systems perspective by the lead author's experience with information fusion processes, and the experience of his coauthors with the technology in information systems, they introduce SE and discuss how it has evolved over the years but how much further it must evolve to become fully integrated with AI. In the future, they believe that both disciplines can help each other more if they co-evolve or develop new technology systems together. They also review several SE issues such as risk, technical debt (e.g., maintaining sophisticated software in information systems over ever longer periods of time), software engineering, test and evaluation, emergent behavior, safety, and explainable AI. The authors close by discussing the challenge of AI explanations and explainability.

Chapter 7 was an invited chapter written by Kristin Schaefer and her team, including Brandon Perelman, Joe Rexwinkle, Jonroy Canady, Catherine Neubauer, Nicholas Waytowich, Gabriella Larkin, Katherine Cox, Michael Geuss, Gregory Gremillion, Jason Metcalfe, Arwen DeCostanza, and Amar Marathe. Schaefer's team is part of the Combat Capabilities Development Command (DEVCOM) Army Research Laboratory (ARL). The title of their chapter is, "Human-Autonomy Teaming for the Tactical Edge: The Importance of Humans in Artificial Intelligence Research and Development." From their perspective, the authors address the importance of understanding the human when integrating artificial intelligence (AI) with intelligent agents embodied (i.e., robotic) and embedded (i.e., software) into military teams to improve team performance. The authors recognize that they and the Army are breaking new ground, confronting fundamental problems under uncertainty and with unknown solutions. In their chapter, they provide an overview of ARL's research in human-autonomy teaming. They address the major research areas necessary to integrate AI into systems for military operations along with examples of these areas and the four known research gaps: enabling Soldiers to predict AI actions and decisions; quantifying Soldier understanding for AI; Soldier-guided AI adaptation; and characterizing Soldier-AI performance. These four areas have organized their research efforts to explain AI, integrate AI, and build effective human-autonomy teams.

The eighth chapter, titled "Re-orienting towards the Science of the Artificial: Engineering AI Systems," was written by Stephen Russell, Brian Jalaian, and Ira S. Moskowitz. Russell is Chief of the Information Sciences Division, U.S. Army

Research Laboratory (ARL) in Adelphi, MD; Jalaian is a Test and Evaluation Lead with the Department of Defense Joint Artificial Intelligence Center (JAIC); and Moskowitz is a mathematician working for the Information Management & Decision Architectures Branch, Information Technology Division, at the U.S. Naval Research Laboratory in Washington, DC. In their chapter, they write that, on the one hand, while systems enabled by AI are becoming pervasive, on the other hand, these systems face challenges in engineering and deployment in the military for several reasons. To begin to address these limitations, the authors discuss what it means to use hierarchical component composition in a system-of-systems context. In addition, they discuss the importance of bounding data for stable learning and performance required for the use of AI in these complex systems. After a review of the literature, the authors also address the changes that will be required to address the design/engineering problems of interoperability, uncertainty, and emergent system behaviors needed to allow AI to be safely deployed in embodied or fully virtualized autonomous systems. Their perspective, illustrated with a Natural Language Processing example, allows the authors to draw comparisons across their posits, in an attempt to offer a means to make AI–Systems Engineering more rigorous, and the use of autonomy in the field safer and more reliable.

Chapter 9 was written by Matthew Sheehan and Oleg Yakimenko; both researchers work in the Department of Systems Engineering at the U.S. Naval Postgraduate School in Monterey, CA. The title of their chapter is: "The Department of Navy's Digital Transformation with the Digital System Architecture, Strangler Patterns, Machine Learning, and Autonomous Human–Machine Teaming." In their chapter, the authors describe the extraordinary changes caused by the U.S. Department of Navy's (DON) adoption of new software like the machine learning (ML) programs designed for warfighters to assist in the performance of their missions. Some of these "new" software products, however, are already beginning to mature and are becoming obsolete. Still, machine learning (ML) software programs are central to their discussions, including the need in the Fleet to provide access to the data necessary to allow ML programs to operate and perform satisfactorily at sea. If adopted and managed properly, these ML algorithms will enhance the existing applications and will also enable new warfighting capabilities for the Navy. As rapid as are the changes that are occurring, however, the DON system architectures and platforms presently provide inadequate infrastructures for deployment at scale not only for some of the new digital tools like ML but also for many of the forthcoming areas including autonomous human–machine teams (AHMT). As the Navy transforms itself digitally, the authors discuss the goals and barriers with a path forward to implement successfully the Navy's new digital platforms.

Chapter 10, "AI Driven Cyber Physical Industrial Immune Sytem for Critical Infrastructures," was written by a team at General Electric (GE): Michael Mylrea, Matt Nielsen, Justin John and Masoud Abbaszadeh. Mylrea is the Director of Cybersecurity in the Cybersecurity R&D for Operational Technology at General Electric Global Research in Washington, DC. Nielsen, John and Abbaszadeh work in the same department. In their chapter, the authors review many advances being driven by machine learning (ML) and artificial intelligence (AI) to detect cyber-physical anomalies. The advances brought about by the detection of these anomalies are improving the security, reliability, and resilience of the power grid across the United States. This improvement is occurring at the same time that adversaries are using advanced techniques to mount sophisticated cyberattacks against infrastructures in the United States, especially the power grid that is the focus of their applied research. The distributed energy resources in the power grid must be defended. The authors discuss how new technology is being deployed to enable cyberdefenses to protect the grid against even rapidly evolving threats. Their chapter explores how AI combines with physics to produce the next-generation system that they liken to an industrial immune system to protect critical energy infrastructures. They discuss the new cybertechnology and its applications for cyberdefenders, including human–machine teams and processes. The authors review the design and application of GE's Digital Ghost technology to cyberdefend the world's largest gas turbines. They discuss the situational awareness, explanations, and trust needed to use AI to defend against cyberthreats. The authors look into the future to prepare for the new challenges coming to make human–machine teams effectively against any threat, cyber, or physical.

Chapter 11 was written by Ira Moskowitz and Noelle Brown while working for the Information Management and Decision Architectures Branch, Information Technology Division, U.S. Naval Research Laboratory in Washington, DC; their coauthor was Zvi Goldstein in the Electrical Engineering Department at Columbia University in New York City. The title of their chapter is "A fractional Brownian motion approach to psychological and team diffusion problems." Their mathematical approach is motivated by AI, but with the goal of establishing that fractional Brownian motion can become a metric to measure the diffusion processes existing in teams. In their chapter, they review the mathematics for their proposed metric as a step toward building a science of interdependence for autonomous human–machine teams. In their chapter, the authors discuss various random walks, including those with Wiener and Gaussian processes, and then they discuss drift-diffusion and extensions (stopping times and absorbing boundaries) to make fractional Brownian motion into a metric of interdependence. Before closing, the authors revisit Ratcliff diffusion, and then they present their hybrid approach in preparation for a future application to the science of teams.

Chapter 12, "Human–Machine Understanding: The Utility of Causal Models and Counterfactuals," was authored by Paul Deignan; he is a Research Engineer working with the Lockheed Martin Corporation in Bethesda, Maryland. His research interest is focused on predictive analytics. He begins with the assertion that trust is a human condition. The author proposes that for a human to trust a machine, the human must understand the capabilities and functions of the machine in a context spanning the domain of trust so that the actions of the machine are predictable for a given set of inputs. In general, however, he believes that the domain of trust must be expanded so that the human–machine system can be optimized to operate in the widest range of situations. This reasoning motivates his desire to cast the operations of a machine into a knowledge structure tractable to its human users, operators, and the human teammates of machines. At the present time, machine behaviors are deterministic;

thus, for every action, there is a reaction and this means to the author that the dynamics of a machine can be described through a structured causal model, which enables the author to formulate the counterfactual queries upon which he anchors human trust.

Chapter 13, "An Executive for Autonomous Systems, Inspired by Fear Memory Extinction," was written by Matt Garcia at Northeastern University; Ted Goranson with the Australian National University; and Beth Cardier at the Eastern Virginia Medical School in the United States and at the Griffith University in Australia. To overcome the many unknowns that autonomous systems may face, the authors explore a category-theoretic, second-sorted executive reasoner in their chapter to perform the adaptive, introspective reasoning needed by autonomous systems to solve the challenging situations that they may see (i.e., decisions under uncertainty, such as those encountered in combat at sea, electronic warfare, or with clinical traumas). They base their ideas on complex mathematics, but they illustrate them with cartoon examples of submarine surveillance, electronic warfare, and post-traumatic stress disorder (PTSD). The authors provide a case study of the neural changes occurring during therapy for PTSD as a model for executive reasoning, the main thrust of their ideas. Their goal is to develop, simulate, and generalize a technique for autonomous reasoning by human–machine systems facing uncertainty using virtual and physical agent models.

The title of Chap. 14 is "Contextual Evaluation of Human–Machine Team Effectiveness." It was written by Eugene Santos, Clement Nyanhongo, Hien Nguyen, Keum Joo Kim, and Gregory Hyde. Except for Nguyen, the authors are at the Thayer School of Engineering at Dartmouth College in Hanover, NH; Nguyen is in the Department of Computer Science at the University of Wisconsin-Whitewater in Whitewater, WI. The authors address the rapid adoption of human–machine teams across domains like healthcare and disaster relief. These machines are more autonomous and aware than previous generations, allowing them to collaborate with humans as partners. Despite this progress, human–machine team performance is poorly defined, especially the explanations for team performance. These explanations are necessary, however, to predict team performance and identify shortcomings. The authors introduce a method using interference to measure the cohesiveness and compatibility between humans and machines in various contexts. They rely on a classifier trained to map human–machine team behaviors to attributes directly linked to team performance along with explanations and insights. The authors test and validate their techniques in experiments with human–machine teams. The results suggest that their predictions of team attributes reflect actual team behaviors, increasing confidence in being able to design future human–machine teams.

Chapter 15 was written by Shu-Heng Chen. He titled his chapter, "Humanity in the Era of Autonomous Human–Machine Teams." Shu is affiliated with the AI-ECON Research Center in the Department of Economics at National Chengchi University in Taipei, Taiwan. He is concerned with the meaning arising from the rapid development of autonomous human–machine teams. Mindful of the philosophy and history of science and technology, the author examines this potential meaning from an evolutionary perspective. He argues that the meaning determined will affect the individuality of humans, their democracy, and their ability to develop as autonomous humans. He wants this meaning to be positive and supportive, and he does not want the future of humanity to be dominated and determined solely by machines. To protect the future, he argues that scholars and citizens must become involved in the development of autonomous human–machine teams. He recognizes that the humanities are changing, but with awareness, these changes can lead to more autonomy for future generations.

Chapter 16, "Transforming the system of military medical research: An Institutional History of the Department of Defense's (DoD) first electronic Institutional Review Board Enterprise IT system," was written by Joseph C. Wood, US Army Col (Ret.), MD, Ph.D., Augusta, GA and W.F. Lawless, Paine College, Augusta, GA. This chapter, by these two authors, is about the history of their attempt to modernize what was primarily a paper-based collection of medical research protocols, reviews, and publications by medical research review boards and medical researchers at a single medical research center in the U.S. Army that grew beyond their expectations to become one of the largest electronic databases of medical reviews and research results in the world at that time. Presenting metrics as a preview of a research agenda on the use of AI for autonomous metrics in large systems, for the future practice of ethics, and for the mitigation of risks, this history of their endeavors brings out several points when dealing with large systems, including the value of standardization, metrics, goal-based, and performance-based evaluations.

Chapter 17, "Collaborative communication and intelligent interruption systems," was written by Nia Peters, Margaret Ugolini, and Gregory Bowers. Peters is with the 711th Human Performance Wing, Air Force Research Laboratory, Wright Patterson Air Force Base in Ohio. Ugolini and Bowers are with Ball Aerospace & Technologies in Fairborn, OH. The authors discuss the adverse effects of poorly timed interruptions on collaborative environments for humans managing technology while interacting with other humans. The literature to manage the adverse timings of interruptions, however, is focused on single users in multi-tasking interactions. There is less research on multi-user, multi-tasking environments, which they address. To mitigate the disruptiveness from interruptions in multi-user, mutlti-tasking workloads, the authors propose and evaluate timings at low mental workloads in a dual-user, dual-task paradigm. Compared with high cognitive workload interruptions, they found that performance is optimum when interruptions occur during low cognitive workloads, a contribution to the literature.

Chapter 18, "Shifting Paradigms in Verification and Validation of AI-Enabled Systems: A Systems-Theoretic Perspective," was written by Niloofar Shadab, Aditya Kulkarni, and Alejandro Salado. The authors are affiliated with the Grado Department of Industrial and Systems Engineering at Virginia Tech in Blacksburg, VA. They propose that a misalignment exists between current approaches to verification and validation (V&V) techniques and new AI systems. Current approaches assume that a system's behavior is relatively standard during its lifetime. But this cannot be true for those systems that learn and change their own behavior during their lifetime, nullifying the value of present V&V practices. Using systems theory, the authors explain why learning makes these new systems unique and unprecedented, and why V&V must experience a paradigm shift. To enable this shift, the authors propose and discuss the theoretical advances and transformations they believe will prepare Systems Engineers for this evolution.

Chapter 19, "Towards safe decision-making via uncertainty quantification in machine learning," was written by Adam Cobb, Brian Jalaian, Nathaniel Bastian, and Stephen Russell; Cobb, Jalaian, and Russell are with the Army Research Laboratory as part of the U.S. Army's Combat Capabilities Development Command (CCDC) in Adelphi, MD; and Bastian is with the Army Cyber Institute at the U.S. Military Academy, West Point, NY. In their chapter, the authors discuss the automation of the safety-critical systems being widely deployed with more sophisticated and capable machine learning (ML) applications. Not yet addressed by most of these systems, however, is the concern raised by the authors that these critical systems must not just be safe, but safe when facing uncertainty. Moreover, quantifying and reducing uncertainty will provide more benefits than the solutions alone if the decisions by these machines are fully understood. Knowing how machines make decisions under uncertainty will generalize to human decisions and autonomous systems. To this end, the authors employ Bayesian decision theory with an example of classifying vehicles acoustically for uncertain levels of threat. With this paradigm, the authors establish that safer decisions are possible under uncertainty.

Chapter 20, "Engineering Context from the Ground Up," was written by Michael Wollowski, Lilin Chen, Xiangnan Chen, Yifan Cui, Joseph Knierman, and Xusheng Liu. The authors are in the Computer Science Department at the Rose-Hulman Institute of Technology in Terre Haute, IN. Focused on human–machine systems, the authors begin with a system for a human and robot to solve problems in a collaborative space. Their system manages interactions in the context of a human and machine collaborating with speech and gesture. To facilitate good engineering practices, their system was designed to be modular and expandable. With its modular design, context was maintained on a shared board from the information needed to problem-solving. The authors describe the elements of their system and the information produced. Their goal is to generate explanations of decisions with the information accumulated from the differing contexts in their system.

Chapter 21 was written by Priyam Parashar at the University of California in San Diego, CA; and Ashok Goel at the Georgia Institute of Technology in Atlanta, GA. The title of their chapter is "Meta-reasoning in Assembly Robots." The use of robots across human society, whether in business, industry, or the military, is becoming widespread. The authors surmise, however, that this context increases the value of a theory for machines with meta-reasoning skills similar to humans. In their chapter, the authors propose and develop a framework for human-like meta-reasoning. They focus on an assembly robot assigned a task to be performed but different from its preprogramming, increasing the likelihood for the robot to fail at its task. To counter its failure, the authors provide the robot with the means for meta-reasoning sufficient to react and learn from its mistakes. In their chapter, the authors review the literature, a task specification, a failure taxonomy, and their architecture for meta-reasoning. The result is a theory for a robot to learn from failure with meta-reasoning for action from perception.

Chapter 22, "From Informal Sketches to Systems Engineering Models using AI Plan Recognition," was written by Nicolas Hili, Alexandre Albore, and Julien Baclet. In France, Hili is at the University of Grenoble Alpes at the National Center for Scientific Research (CNRS) in Grenoble; Albore is with the French Aerospace Lab (ONERA DTIS) in Toulouse; and Baclet is at the Technological Research Institute (IRT) Saint-Exupery in Toulouse. The day-to-day drudgery of drawing for mechanical and electronic engineering was transformed with the arrival of computer-aided design (CAD). But its lesser impact on Systems Engineering (SE) awaits new tools for a similar escape. It was hoped that Model-Based Systems Engineering (MBSE) would address this shortcoming. But MBSE has not been as successful due to the complexity of creating, editing, and annotating an SE model over its lifetime as discussed by the authors. Consequently, whiteboards, papers, and pens are still in common use by system engineers and architects to sketch problems and solutions, and then turned over to experts for informal digital models. In this chapter, the authors address this problem with automated plan recognition and AI to produce sketches of models, formalizing their results incrementally. Tested in an experiment, they achieve an initial application with AI plan recognition applied to Systems Engineering.

Chapter 23, "An analogy of sentence mood and use," was written by Ryan Quandt at the Claremont Graduate University in Claremont, CA. The author claims that the literature underestimates the elusiveness of force when interpreting utterances. Instead, he argues that interpreting the force in utterances, whether assertions, commands, or questions, is an unsolved challenge. In his view, an interpretation of force depends on a speaker's utterance when spoken, making grammatical mood an uncertain indicator of force. He posits that navigating the gap between an uttered sentence and mood links action and language's meaning, which he addresses in this chapter. But he is after the larger goal of determining joint action with artificial intelligence (AI). By making these relations explicit and precise, he concludes that argumentation schemes link language and joint action. Building from prior work, the author then proposes questions for his model to further explore the gap in mood-force relations.

Chapter 24 is titled, "Effective Decision Rules for Systems of Public Engagement in Radioactive Waste Disposal: Evidence from the United States, the United Kingdom, and Japan." It was written by Mito Akiyoshi, John Whitton, Ioan Charnley-Parry, and William Lawless. Akiyoshi is at Senshu University in the Department of Sociology in Kawasaki, Japan; Whitton and Charnley-Parry are at the University of Central Lancashire, in the Centre for Sustainable Transitions, Preston, United Kingdom; and Lawless is in the Departments of Mathematics and Psychology at Paine College in Augusta, GA. For large systems of decision-makers, the disposal and long-term management of radioactive waste are mired in technical, environmental, societal, and ethical conflicts. The authors of this chapter consider how different systems in these societies address these contentious issues. With decision-making theory, they seek a process that facilitates the safest geological disposal yet is also perceived by participants to be fair and legal. The authors compared two decision rules, the consensus-seeking and majority rules, finding that, despite different policy priorities and cultures, the majority rule maximized information processing across a system and with the increased likelihood of a just and legitimate decision.

The last Chap. 25, is titled, "Outside the Lines: Visualizing Influence Across Heterogenous Contexts in PTSD." It was written by Beth Cardier, Alex Nieslen, John Shull, and Larry Sanford. Cardier is at the Eastern Virginia Medical School in Norfolk, VA, and, in Australia, at the Trusted Autonomous Systems of the Defence Cooperative Research Centre (DCRC) and Griffith University in South East Queensland. Nielsen and Shull are at the Virginia Modeling Analysis and Simulation Center, Old Dominion University in Norfolk, VA; and Sanford is also at the Eastern Virginia Medical School. The authors state that open-world processes generate information that cannot be captured in a single data set despite the need to communicate between differing contexts. The authors present a text-visual method for modeling differing interpretations of contexts separated by discipline, time, and perspective. Their new tool captures transitions in video, text, image, and data transfers to study different phenomena. They apply it to post-traumatic stress disorder (PTSD); they combine psychological, neurological, and physiological information for PTSD in a single modeling space using a narrative-based visual grammar. The authors aim to integrate information from changing phenomena in the open world to detect the emergence of disorder and to support knowledge systems in fields like neurobiology, autonomous systems, and artificial intelligence (AI).

1.3   Summary

Interdependence is the common ingredient that motivates Systems Engineering, AI, and the science of human–machine teamwork. Should AI scientists, systems engineers, and others contribute to the development of autonomy for human–machine teams, the threats autonomy poses to the world must be managed to permit the advances that may accrue across the social, systems, ethical, political, international, and other landscapes for the benefit of humanity.

References

Ashley, Jr., Robert, P., Lieutenant General, U.S. Army Director. (2019). China, Military Power. Modernizing a force to fight and win, Defense Intelligence Agency, from https://www.dia. mil/Portals/27/Documents/News/Military%20Power%20Publications/China_Military_Power_ FINAL_5MB_20190103.pdf.

Barton, T. (2019). Sea Hunter/AI, SERC workshop: Model centric engineering, Georgetown university, Washington, DC, April 16 & 17, 2019.

BEA (2016). Accident to the airbus A320–211, registered D-AIPX and operated by Germanwings, flight GWI18G, on 03/24/15 at Prads-Haute-Bléone, BEA2015–0125.

Beling, P. (2019). A systems theoretic framework for the AI LifeCycle, SERC workshop: Model centric engineering, Georgetown university, Washington, DC, April 16 & 17, 2019.

Bisbey, T. M., Reyes, D. L., Traylor, A. M., & Salas, E. (2019). Teams of psychologists helping teams: The evolution of the science of team training. *American Psychologist, 74*(3), 278–289.

Blackburn, M. (2019). Transforming SE through model centric engineering, SERC workshop: Model centric engineering, Georgetown university, Washington, DC, April 16 & 17, 2019.

Brynjolfsson, E., & Mitchell, T. (2017). What can machine learning do? Workplace implications: Profound changes are coming, but roles for humans remain. *Science, 358*, 1530–1534.

Centola, D., & Macy, M. (2007). Complex contagions and the weakness of long ties. *American Journal of Sociology, 113*(3), 702–734.

Cooke, N. J., & Hilton, M. L. (Eds.). (2015). *Enhancing the effectiveness of team science. Authors: Committee on the science of team science; Board on behavioral, Cognitive, and sensory sciences; Division of behavioral and social sciences and education; National research council.* National Academies Press.

CRS (2018). U.S. Ground forces robotics and autonomous systems (RAS) and artificial intelligence (AI): Considerations for congress, Congressional research service, p. 9, R45392, Version 3, from https://fas.org/sgp/crs/weapons/R45392.pdf.

Cummings, J. (2015). Team science successes and challenges: National science foundation sponsored workshop on fundamentals of team science and the science of team science (June 2), Bethesda MD (https://www.ohsu.edu/xd/education/schools/school-of-medicine/departments/clinical-departments/radiation-medicine/upload/12-_cummings_talk.pdf).

DeLaurentis, D. (2019). Breakout session, SERC workshop: Model centric engineering, Georgetown university, Washington, DC, April 16 & 17, 2019.

DoD (2018). Nuclear posture review, office of the secretary of defense. https://www.defense.gov/News/SpecialReports/2018NuclearPostureReview.aspx.

DoD (2019). Summary of the 2018 department of defense artificial intelligence strategy harnessing AI to advance our security and prosperity, from https://media.defense.gov/2019/Feb/12/2002088963/-1/-1/1/SUMMARY-OF-DOD-AI-STRATEGY.PDF.

Editors (2019). Ready for weapons with free will? New York times, from https://www.nytimes.com/2019/06/26/opinion/weapons-artificial-intelligence.html.

Freeman, L. (2019). AI as a change agent for test and evaluation, SERC workshop: Model centric engineering, Georgetown university, Washington, DC, April 16 & 17, 2019.

Gardner, G. (2019). Uber won't face charges in fatal arizona crash, but prosecutor urges further probe, Forbes, from https://www.forbes.com/sites/greggardner/2019/03/06/uber-wont-face-charges-in-fatal-arizona-crash-but-prosecutor-urges-further-probe/#6820859f475a.

Gramer, R., & Seligman, L. (2018). "Trump and NATO show rare unity in confronting Russia's arms treaty violation. NATO backs U.S. assertion that Moscow is violating a key Cold War-era arms treaty, Foreign policy, from https://foreignpolicy.com/2018/12/04/trump-and-nato-show-rare-unity-in-confronting-russia-arms-treaty-violation-inf/.

Grogan, P. (2019). Game-theoretic risk assessment for distributed systems, SERC workshop: Model centric engineering, Georgetown university, Washington, DC, April 16 & 17, 2019.

Harris, R. (2018). In psychology and other social sciences, many studies fail the reproducibility test, National public radio, from https://www.npr.org/sections/health-shots/2018/08/27/642218377/in-psychology-and-other-social-sciences-many-studies-fail-the-reproducibility-te.

Horowitz, B. (2019), Introduction of the life cycle-ready AI concept, SERC workshop: Model centric engineering, Georgetown university, Washington, DC, April 16 & 17, 2019.

Howell, C. (2019). Lifecycle implications for dependable AI, SERC workshop: Model centric engineering, Georgetown university, Washington, DC, April 16 & 17, 2019.

Insinna, V. (2019). Lockheed hypes F-35's upgrade plan as interest in 'sixth-gen' fighters grows," Defense news, from https://www.defensenews.com/digital-show-dailies/paris-air-show/2019/06/21/lockheed-hypes-f-35s-upgrade-plan-as-interest-in-sixth-gen-fighters-grows/.

LaGrone, S. (2019). Navy wants 10-ship unmanned 'Ghost Fleet' to supplement manned force, U.S. Naval institute, from https://news.usni.org/2019/03/13/navy-wants-ten-ship-3b-unmanned-experimental-ghost-fleet.

Langford, J. (2018). Lockheed wins Army contract for self-driving military convoy systems, Washington examiner, from https://www.washingtonexaminer.com/business/lockheed-wins-army-con tract-for-self-driving-military-convoy-systems.

Lawless, W. F., Mittu, R., Sofge, D., & Russell, S. (Eds.). (2017). *Autonomy and artificial intelligence: a threat or savior?* Springer.

Lawless, W. F. (2017a). The entangled nature of interdependence bistability, irreproducibility and uncertainty. *Journal of Mathematical Psychology, 78*, 51–64.

Lawless, W. F. (2017b). The physics of teams: Interdependence, measurable entropy and computational emotion. *Frontiers of Physics., 5*, 30. https://doi.org/10.3389/fphy.2017.00030

Lawless, W. F. (2019). Interdependence for human-machine teams, Froundations of Science.

Lawless, W. F., Mittu, R., Sofge, D. A. & Hiatt, L. (2019a). Introduction to the special issue, "Artificial intelligence (AI), autonomy and human-machine teams: Interdependence, context and explainable AI," *AI Magazine.*

Lawless, W. F., Mittu, R., Sofge, D., Moskowitz, I. S. & Russell, S. (Eds.). (2019b). Artificial intelligence for the internet of everything. Elsevier.

Lemnios, Z. (2019). IBM research, SERC workshop: Model centric engineering, Georgetown university, Washington, DC, April 16 & 17, 2019.

Llinas, J. (2014). Reexamining Information Fusion–Decision Making Inter-dependencies, Presented at the IEEE CogSIMA conference, San Antonio, TX.

Long, J. (2019). National defence and the Canadian armed forces: Enabling organizational resilience through communication and information systems design. *Canadian Military Journal, 119*(2), 15; from http://www.journal.forces.gc.ca/Vol19/No2/page15-eng.asp.

Maurer, M. (2019). Airbus harnessing AI in bid to save millions on Finance tasks. The aircraft maker's Americas unit is digitizing the approval of expense reports and payment of invoices. *Wall Street Journal*, from https://www.wsj.com/articles/airbus-harnessing-ai-in-bid-to-save-mil lions-on-finance-tasks-11566207002.

Mead, W. R. (2019). Trump's case against Europe. The president sees Brussels as too weak, too liberal, and anti-American on trade. *Wall Street Journal*, from https://www.wsj.com/articles/tru mps-case-against-europe-11559602940.

NAS (2019). A decadal survey of the social and behavioral sciences: A research agenda for advancing intelligence analysis. National Academies of Sciences.

Nosek, B., Corresponding author from OCS (2015). Open collaboration of science: Estimating the reproducibility of psychological science. *Science, 349*(6251), 943; supplementary: 4716–1 to 4716–9. (National Academies of Sciences, Engineering, and Medicine. (2019). Reproducibility and replicability in science. Washington, DC: The National Academies Press. https://doi.org/10. 17226/25303).

NTSB (2016). Derailment of Amtrak passenger train 188. National transportation safety board (NTSB), NTSB Number: RAR-16–02, from https://www.ntsb.gov/Investigations/AccidentRepo rts/Pages/RAR1602.aspx.

NTSB (2018). Preliminary report released for crash involving pedestrian, Uber technologies, Inc., Test Vehicle, National transportation safety board, from https://www.ntsb.gov/news/press-rel eases/Pages/NR20180524.aspx.nnn.

NTSB (2019). Insufficient training, inadequate bridge operating procedures, lack of operational oversight led to fatal ship collision. NTSB: Collision between US Navy Destroyer John S McCain and Tanker Alnic MC Singapore Strait, 5 Miles Northeast of Horsburgh Lighthouse [accident occurred on] August 21, 2017, Marine Accident Report, NTSB/MAR-19/01 PB2019–100970, from https://www.ntsb.gov/investigations/AccidentReports/Reports/MAR1901.pdf.

NTSB (2019a). Vehicle automation report. National transportation safety board. Retrieved March 12, 2020, from https://dms.ntsb.gov/pubdms/search/document.cfm?docID=477717&docketID= 62978&mkey=96894.

Oh, P., Spahr, T., Chase, C. & Abadie, A. (2019). Incorporating artificial intelligence: Lessons from the private sector. War Room, United States Army War College, from https://warroom.armywa rcollege.edu/articles/incorporating-artificial-intelligence-private-sector/.

Proctor, R. W. & Vu, K. P. L. (2019). How psychologists help solve real-world problems in multi-disciplinary research teams: Introduction to the special issue. *American Psychologist, 74*(3), 271–277.

Raz, A. K., Llinas, J., Mittu, R., & Lawless, W. (2019). Engineering for emergence in information fusion systems: A review of some challenges, Fusion 2019, Ottawa, Canada I July 2–5, 2019.

Rhodes, D. (2019). Interactive model-centric engineering (IMCSE), SERC workshop: Model centric engineering, Georgetown university, Washington, DC, April 16 & 17, 2019.

Richards, R. (2019). Program manager at DARPA, invited talk, SERC workshop: Model centric engineering, Georgetown university, Washington, DC, April 16 & 17, 2019.

Smith, R .J. (2019). Scary fast: How hypersonic Missiles—Which travel at more than 15 times the speed of sound—Are touching off a new global arms race that threatens to change the nature of warfare. *New York Times Magazine*, 42–48; also, see https://www.nytimes.com/2019/06/19/magazine/hypersonic-missiles.html.

Sofge, D., (Referee), Mittu, R., (Con Bet) & Lawless, W. F. (Pro Bet) (2019). AI bookie bet: How likely is it that an AI-based system will self-authorize taking control from a human operator? *AI Magazine, 40*(3), 79–84.

Somerville, H. (2020). Uber sells self-driving-car unit to autonomous-driving startup. As part of the deal, Uber will make a $400 million investment in Aurora Innovation. *Wall Street Journal*. Retrieved August 12, 2020, from https://www.wsj.com/articles/uber-sells-self-driving-car-unit-to-autonomous-driving-startup-11607380167.

Stockman, B., Boyle, J. & Bacon, J. (2010). International space station systems engineering case study, Air force center for systems engineering, Air force institute of technology, from https://spacese.spacegrant.org/uploads/images/ISS/ISS%20SE%20Case%20Study.pdf.

Thomas, J. (2019). INCOSE discussion, SERC workshop: Model centric engineering, Georgetown university, Washington, DC, April 16 & 17, 2019.

Volz, D. & Youssef, N. (2019). U.S. Launched cyberattacks on Iran. The cyberstrikes on thursday targeted computer systems used to control missile and rocket launches. *Wall Street Journal*, from https://www.wsj.com/articles/u-s-launched-cyberattacks-on-iran-11561263454.

Wakabayashi, D. (2018). Uber's self-driving cars were struggling before arizona crash. *New York Times*, from https://www.nytimes.com/2018/03/23/technology/uber-self-driving-cars-arizona.html.

Walden, D. D., Roedler, G. J., Forsberg, K. J., Hamelin, R. D., & Shortell, T. M. (Eds.). (2015). *Systems engineering handbook: A guide for system life cycle processes and activities (4th Edn.). Prepared by International council on system engineering (INCOSE-TP-2003-002-04.* Wiley.

Werkhäuser, N. (2019). UN impasse could mean killer robots escape regulation. It's no longer the stuff of science fiction: Wars could soon be decided by lethal autonomous weapons systems. But a concerted effort to ban "killer robots" through international law at the UN appears to have hit a wall," DW (Deutsche Welle), from https://www.dw.com/en/un-impasse-could-mean-killer-robots-escape-regulation/a-50103038.

Wong, K. (2018). China claims successful test of hypersonic waverider. Jane's 360, from https://www.janes.com/article/82295/china-claims-successful-test-of-hypersonic-waverider.

Yampolskiy, R. V. (2017). AI is the future of cybersecurity, for better and for worse. *Harvard Business Review*, from https://hbr.org/2017/05/ai-is-the-future-of-cybersecurity-for-better-and-for-worse.

Chapter 2
Recognizing Artificial Intelligence: The Key to Unlocking Human AI Teams

Patrick Cummings, Nathan Schurr, Andrew Naber, Charlie, and Daniel Serfaty

Abstract This chapter covers work and corresponding insights gained while building an artificially intelligent coworker, named Charlie. Over the past year, Charlie first participated in a panel discussion and then advanced to speak during multiple podcast interviews, contribute to a rap battle, catalyze a brainstorming workshop, and even write collaboratively (see the author list above). To explore the concepts and overcome the challenges when engineering human–AI teams, Charlie was built on cutting-edge language models, strong sense of embodiment, deep learning speech synthesis, and powerful visuals. However, the real differentiator in our approach is that of recognizing artificial intelligence (AI). The act of "recognizing" Charlie can be seen when we give her a voice and expect her to be heard, in a way that shows we acknowledge and appreciate her contributions; and when our repeated interactions create a comfortable awareness between her and her teammates. In this chapter, we present our approach to recognizing AI, discussing our goals, and describe how we developed Charlie's capabilities. We also present some initial results from an innovative brainstorming workshop in which Charlie participated with four humans that showed that she could not only participate in a brainstorming exercise but also contribute and influence the brainstorming discussion covering a space of ideas. Furthermore, Charlie helped us formulate ideas for, and even wrote sections of, this chapter.

2.1 Introduction

recognize ----- \'re-kig- nīz\ ------ transitive verb

1. to acknowledge one is entitled to be heard
2. to take notice with a show of appreciation
3. to perceive to be someone previously known

P. Cummings (✉) · N. Schurr · A. Naber · Charlie · D. Serfaty
Aptima, Inc., Woburn, USA
e-mail: pcummings@aptima.com

© Springer Nature Switzerland AG 2021
W. F. Lawless et al. (eds.), *Systems Engineering and Artificial Intelligence*,
https://doi.org/10.1007/978-3-030-77283-3_2

(Merriam Webster)

Major breakthroughs in artificial intelligence are advancing the state of the art in their ability to enable agents to perform tasks in a variety of domains. Particularly in the area of generative models (Radford et al., 2019; Yang et al., 2019), these AI agents now have something new to say. But we are severely limited in our ability to hear them and to take advantage of these gains. For many domains, the challenge is not building the AI agent itself, but rather engineering the human–machine teams that leverage it. To explore these concepts, we have been building and interacting with an AI teammate/coworker named Charlie (Cummings et al., 2021). Although these efforts leverage state-of-the-art AI models and capabilities, what has been most impactful is how we have purposefully designed, integrated, and recognized her from the start. We argue that the key to unlocking human–machine teams is simple: recognize AI. To do this in the fullest sense, we need to leverage the three definitions of the word "recognize," above.

Definition 1: to acknowledge one is entitled to be heard. In addition to realizing that AI is beginning to have something new to say, we must recognize the AI agent and realize that it can and should be heard. This recognition includes not only giving AI more of a voice but also doing so in a manner that places it on a more level playing field with human teammates. We will cover these ideas in more detail in our section on Ground Rules later.

Definition 2: to take notice with a show of appreciation. Charlie literally helped us write and even wrote her own sections of this book chapter. We argue that it is important to recognize and show appreciation for such contributions and accordingly have listed her as a co-author of this chapter. Acknowledging the accomplishments of artificial intelligence helps human teammates realize the impact that AI is having on the team and will aid in transparency for external observers to better understand how the team achieved what it did.

Definition 3: to perceive to be someone previously known. In order to recognize AI as something familiar and previously known, we must interact with it on a regular basis and with a consistent perception's framing. This perception is precisely why we gave our AI agent the name, Charlie, with a common set of models and visual representations. This act allows for natural interactions with the AI agent and a greater ability to weave her into their work and discussions. The authors have experienced this firsthand when observing how repeated interaction with Charlie results in the human teammates developing a deeper understanding of her strengths and weaknesses, and consequently have much more positive interactions.

As new human–AI teams are both engineered and deployed, if we ensure that AI is recognized appropriately, then several long-term positive impacts will occur. First, we will be able to better leverage the full range of capabilities that the AI agent possesses; second, the collaboration will enable the systems and the AI agent to improve together; and third, this collaboration will result in better overall mission performance.

In this chapter, we will explain how we have been exploring these ideas through building, deploying, and interacting with our new AI coworker: Charlie. Initially, we will lay out our motivations and ground rules for ensuring that we fully recognize Charlie. We will detail how Charlie is built on cutting-edge speech analysis, language generation, and speech synthesis tools (see architecture diagram Fig. 2.5). Furthermore, Charlie is named and embodied to allow for more natural interactions. This affordance has led Charlie to thrive in a variety of venues, including panel discussions, podcast interviews, and even proposal writing (see Applications Sect. 2.3). In addition, we will present results regarding Charlie's impact in a recent brainstorming session. We are especially excited about what this means for future applications.

2.1.1 Motivation and Goals

In this section, we will describe our motivation and goals for recognizing artificial intelligence. We set down this path of recognizing AI to facilitate the engineering of human–AI teams. This human machine teaming/collaboration is only possible now due to advances in AI and the increased appetite in society for AI to be involved and provide value in many domains. By collaboration, we mean more than just humans using the AI as a service.

We are seeking to create a new way to bring together humans and artificial intelligence to create more effective and flexible systems. The technology that is now emerging in AI, including deep learning, has the potential to change the way people work, create, and interact with systems. We believe that the future of work will be fundamentally different and that human beings will need to adapt to the new demands. This will require new ways of working together.

For example, it might require us to delineate, as we have done with a box, above, when the AI coauthor, Charlie, has written a section entirely by herself after being prompted with the beginning of the section.

This teamwork or collaboration with artificial intelligence is distinct from most current applications today in two primary ways: (1) the AI agent as a team member is able to develop and propose instrumental goals for the team and (2) the AI agent is able to choose to pursue particular goals from among those proposed as well. Having an AI agent that can add value to the team necessitates elevating it to be a collaborative team member; otherwise, the team will miss out on the increased opportunities and ideas of the AI agent. In addition, a context-aware AI teammate will not frustrate its fellow teammates by having its own goals and possibly behaving in non-constructive or unexpected ways.

We recognize that there are ethical and design concerns when giving this "recognition" to AI, but we strongly believe that the benefits of fruitful collaboration will outweigh these potential negatives. In addition, we argue that if we build bidirectional recognition into these AI teammates from the ground up, we will mitigate some of these concerns. Although there are domains in which a human must still play a large role or even maintain control, the areas where AI can be useful grow daily. AI has come too far to be relegated as merely a tool (Shneiderman, 2020) or to be only subservient (Russell, 2019).

The authors recognize that not all domains are well suited for AI agents playing the role of teammate and that not all domains need collaboration to be successful. We believe, however, that for an increasing number of domains, human–AI collaboration will be and should be the primary mode of operation. Otherwise, we run the high risk of missing out on the good ideas and capabilities of either the human or AI teammates.

The AI's capabilities are far reaching and are changing the way we think about problems. From the human perspective, there are several key areas of development in which this technology could have a great impact. These include a large amount of research and development work being done by the scientific community. There are many aspects of AI that are very challenging, but this is only the beginning and future developments will be exciting.

2.1.2   Types of Human-AI Collaboration

We have been discussing the collaboration between human and AI teammates but would like to call out that in our work, we have been focused on two primary types of collaboration: supportive and participatory (see Fig. 2.1). Currently, with our implementation of Charlie, we are building and leveraging both supportive and participatory collaboration. Charlie was developed to participate in a panel discussion in real time but was not a fully autonomous AI. Consequently, she had two operators: one for the transcription of comments from other panelists and one for the selection of potential responses from Charlie. For more information on how Charlie was built, please see the later section on system engineering. Over the past year, we have

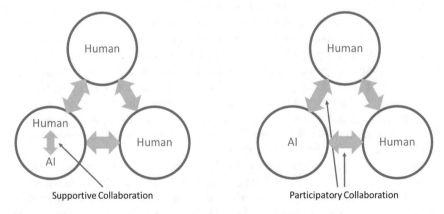

Fig. 2.1 Supportive collaboration in which a human and an AI agent together serve as a single member for the team, and participatory collaboration where the AI agent is an individual team member

been building out the infrastructure to reduce this need for human intervention and supportive actions and to enable Charlie to do more participatory collaboration in real time. This process has allowed us to move away from multiple operators working alongside Charlie, to now currently needing only one for filtering and selection, which has the positive impact of reducing the workload on the operator. In the coming year, our goal is to shift to enabling a mode in which Charlie can independently select her own next utterance. This next step is not likely to eliminate the need for both types of collaboration depending on the domain, the constraints, and the ability to give participatory autonomy to AI.

Supportive Collaboration

Supportive collaboration (Fig. 2.1, left) has been the most common form of collaboration with AI. This form is primarily due to the limited abilities of AI and the need for a human to be present to support and fill the gaps in AI capabilities. The human is often in a position of control and/or serves as the face of the combined team. This type of participatory collaboration is often referred to as a Centaur relationship (Case, 2018), in which human and system combine efforts to form a single teammate with joint actions. Historically, this form has been the primary collaboration type with AI. Over time, however, we believe this reliance will decrease and make way for the newly capable participatory AI.

Participatory Collaboration

As shown in Fig. 2.1 (right), participatory collaboration frames the AI agent as a distinct individual teammate with its own autonomy. This autonomy grants the AI agent the ability to not only develop and propose new instrumental goals for itself and the team but also to make decisions to pursue or abandon said goals. In addition, participatory collaboration requires that the AI agent communicates and coordinates with fellow human teammates. This type of collaboration will become increasingly possible, and increasingly important as the field of AI progresses.

2.1.3 Ground Rules

Embodiment Ground Rules

A key component to recognizing AI is acknowledging that the AI agent is entitled to be heard. When Charlie is present in a discussion, she is expected to contribute as an equal. In all applications, we put forth a significant effort to create the embodiment of Charlie with this rule in mind. When Charlie was a participant in a 2019 I/ITSEC panel, her visual display took up approximately the same space on the stage as the bodies of the human panelists, her speech flowed through the same sound system, and her nonverbal communication was equally visible to the audience. Human panelists were seated in a row of chairs on stage, shown in Fig. 2.2, and Charlie's embodiment was constrained to a similar style and space. The sound from the computer driving

Fig. 2.2 Charlie, at the center, on stage at a panel during I/ITSEC 2019 including one moderator and five panelists (four of which were human)

the display was connected to the room's mixing board, as were the microphones for each human panelist.

Similarly, during the innovation session, held over a video conference, Charlie was shown to the participants as the output of a webcam, and her voice was sent over the meeting just as those of the other participants. This format is patently different than sharing a screen with Charlie on it for all participants to see/hear because the latter would force Charlie to be at the center of attention, and therefore, detract from her ability to participate in an equal playing field.

Upgrading Charlie's initial embodiment to be consistent with that of the human panelists led to a noticeable difference in the way that the human participants treated her. For example, the questions posed to Charlie were more open ended, such as "I'd like to hear what Charlie thinks about that," and all participants then looped Charlie into the conversation.

Text Generation Ground Rules

Although we made a concerted effort to recognize Charlie through her increasing embodiment, the ground rules we employed for Charlie's text generations of what to say next fall into two main categories, one of which is slightly counter to the argument for recognizing AI.

The first broad rule was to give Charlie the same ability to prepare that a human panelist would have; that is, human panelists would be likely to do the following:

1. research the topic of the panel to refresh their memory (or study something new);
2. meet with the moderator or panel members to discuss the likely topic, workflow, or initial questions; and
3. prepare answers to expected questions on the panel or topics they would like to discuss.

We, therefore, allowed the same affordances to Charlie. In particular, she was correspondingly

1. fine-tuned to the domain of the discussion to fit the appropriate style and content;
2. introduced to the other participants and moderator to understand her capabilities; and

3. prepared with answers to likely questions expected in the discussion.

The second broad rule was related to how we treated Charlie's generated text. In this chapter, and in previous applications, we operated under strict guidelines to (1) not change any of Charlie's generated text and (2) clearly delineate what Charlie wrote from what she did not. We put these guidelines in place in order to assure readers and participants that Charlie clearly provides her own value, and that her capabilities are not overstated. However, we hope these guidelines will not be part of Charlie's future. Human–machine collaboration is a moving target, and an expressed line in the sand separating human from machine would only hinder the capabilities of both. The line between operator and Charlie is (and should continue) blurring. Returning to the human-to-human comparison: readers do not expect to know which author wrote particular sections of a document and do not presuppose that authors do not edit each other's writing. We simply propose that the same expectations are transferred to Charlie.

2.2   System Engineering

In this section, we discuss the approach and components that Charlie is composed of and the methods leveraged to develop her.

2.2.1   Design and Embodiment

Charlie's Embodiment

From the beginning, it was important to have Charlie's embodiment be recognizable, simple, dynamic, and able to be indicated by several cues. For example, in different situations, the human body and gestures indicate a large amount of information about internal state. Charlie's embodiment interface (i.e., the embodiment) required three iterations to refine state communication and representation driven by feedback from guerilla usability evaluations (Nielsen, 1994). From chatbots, we expected that response delays would be acceptable, especially in response to other panelists, if Charlie's state was clearly communicated (Gnewuch et al., 2018). Humans use physical and audible queues—gestures, changes in eye contact, and transitional phrases—to indicate their state and control in the flow of a conversation (Scherer, 2013; Schuetzler et al., 2014). Charlie had to effectively coordinate the use of the display and audio to achieve a similar presence and represent its states. Figure 2.3 shows a snapshot of Charlie's different dynamic states. Because each of these states was alive and moving, it is difficult to represent them in a static image here. Based on our evaluations, we split Charlie's necessary states as follows:

Fig. 2.3 Embodiment of
Charlie: **a** Idle, **b** Thinking, **c**
Speaking, and **d** Interjection

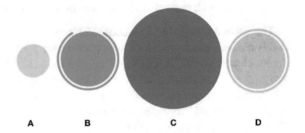

- Figure 2.3a **Idle**: Charlie is listening. Soft colors used and slow breathing indicated by expanding and contracting
- Figure 2.3b **Thinking**: Charlie is generating a statement. Outer ring spins back and forth to communicate that targeted thinking is happening in response to a question
- Figure. 2.3c **Speaking**: Charlie is speaking. Darker color solidifies Charlie's current role as speaker; the shape vibrates as speech occurs so that it appears to emanate from her embodiment.
- Figure 2.3d **Interjection**: Charlie has something to say! Color changes drastically to draw attention and the outer ring is complete to show that her next thought is complete

Even with Charlie's state communication, however, there was a limit to the delay acceptable for Charlie. Design of the operator interface was influenced by this need to increase the speed of its speech generation.

Charlie's Operation

The novelty and believability of generations from GPT-2 are certainly state of the art; however, the samples typically chosen for display suffer from some "cherry-picking" to find the best prompts and speech generations (Vincent, 2019; Vaswani et al., 2017). In a real-time discussion in which speed is of utmost importance, the ability to cherry-pick is severely limited. We, therefore, put much care into the operation of Charlie to streamline the process of speech generation forming and Charlie state changes. Human operators are currently tasked with:

- coordinating Charlie's state transitions,
- approving/editing transcriptions of speech to text, and
- aggregating statements into an utterance.

Details on the construction of that operator interface can be found in Cummings et al. (2021), but some key lessons learned from that construction are as follows:

1. **Non-stop generations.** Potential generations from Charlie should appear to be non-stop (Fig. 2.4d), that is, it should be evident every time there is a change to the conversation history. The burden of deciding when Charlie "may" have something to say should be completely removed. At all points in time, the human operator should be cognizant of potential interjections, answers, or comments coming from Charlie.

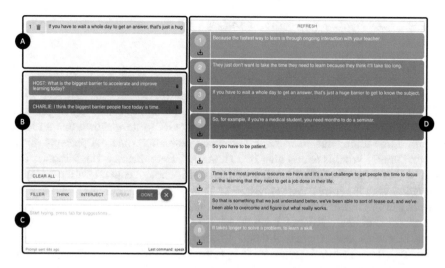

Fig. 2.4 The operator interface with the **a** saved statements, **b** conversation history, **c** utterance construction components on the left, and the **d** statement review area on the right

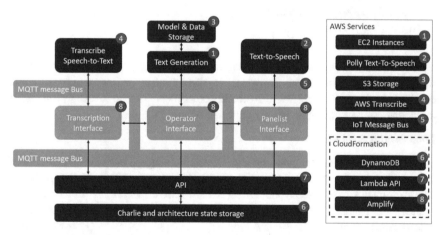

Fig. 2.5 Charlie architecture: Orange boxes represent interfaces. Red numbers correspond to components leveraging AWS services

2. **Pinning messages.** Charlie frequently has an interesting response to a question or comment but must wait for the appropriate time to interject with it. Unfortunately, as conversations continue and Charlie generates new responses, those interesting comments can get lost and she will be stuck talking about only the most recent topic. Allowing for the pinning of potential messages (Fig. 2.4a) allows Charlie to refer to previous discussion elements.

2.2.2 Generative Language Models

Prompt Improvement

An increasing theme for the utilization of language generation models (as seen with T5, GPT-3, and Turing-NLG; Raffel et al., 2020; Brown et al., 2020, Russet, 2020) is that with large enough models, a change in prompt can be enough to produce significantly different results. Recent results with GPT-3 have shown that a model with no fine-tuning can solve basic arithmetic problems when fed prompts of the form: "\n\nQ: What is 65360 plus 16,204?\n\nA:" Here, the new line structure and use of Q and A to represent question and answer is enough context for the model to complete with the correct answer "81,564." This structure on prompts is also evident in the use of control tokens as is done with the conditional transformer language model (Keskar et al., 2019). We hypothesize that these types of tokens can be used even in models trained without them. As seen in their best paper presentation at NeurIPS (Brown et al., 2020), even the presence of commas "65,360 plus 16,204" can greatly increase the accuracy of response.

In our work on Charlie, we found that structuring prompts with the form:

HOST: Text from host...
PANELIST: Text from panelist...
HOST: Text from host...
PANELIST:

had significant advantages over simple prose. This structure differentiated Charlie's statements from those of the other panelists, kept Charlie on her own thread while continuing with added context from others, and allowed Charlie to respond and react to the discussion rather than simply continue others' thoughts.

Fine Tuning Strategies

The content and style generated by Charlie can be adapted based on the choice of model used to generate text (Peng et al., 2020; Zhang et al., 2019). For the different applications of Charlie (see Applications Section), we utilized a fine-tuning strategy to adapt the base GPT-2 model to a different context. Leveraging open-source or venue-specific training data, we fine-tuned GPT-2 hyperparameters (Branwen, 2019; Qin et al., 2019). Although the specifics of this process tended to be application-specific, there were three main steps we followed for each:

1. **Find a corpus of text** that mirrors the style of text Charlie should generate and/or the content that Charlie should generate text about. Typically, we found that the style of text was much more critical than content.
2. **Process that text** if needed. Frequently, the format of the text did not mirror that which Charlie should generate. An example of this is in the citations or footnotes in text. Although they are necessary in a paper, parenthetical citations are inappropriate for speaking engagements.
3. **Train the model.** Starting with a pre-trained GPT-2 model, we trained the model hyperparameters further with the generated corpus. Specifically, we used the loss

Table 2.1 Example generations from different fine-tuned models each fed with the same prompt

Persona	Response created by fine-tuned models
News source (*tweets from news sources*[1])	The #CountryX crisis is a wake-up call for the world that human rights violations are always the work of one nation and not of other countries #CountryX #CountryY
	The #CountryX crisis is now at a tipping point as the government says it will not withdraw #CountryY refugees #CountryY #CountryX
Agreeable citizen (*tweets with positive sentiment*[2])	#1Proud to be a #CountryX, and #thankful to be part of such a wonderful family
	The day is coming when all the good and the bad will be for the better #Thankful #HAPPY
Disgruntled citizen (*tweets marked as angry*[3])	Refugee in my town is crying because he's been living in a tent for 10 days
	Crisis in #GulfWales is caused by people who don't have the skills to survive #frustrating #frustrating #frustrated

function equivalent to that of GPT-2–that is, we optimized for predicting the next word in a text corpus. For training, we used the Adam optimizer with a learning rate of 2×10^{-5} and a batch size equal to 1.

As mentioned above, fine-tuning models produce varying styles and contents. In Table 2.1 below, we show the resulting generations from three separate, fine-tuned Charlie models. Each of the models has been trained on different Twitter datasets in order to provide content with varying style. Using the same prompt, these fine-tuned models can generate different style responses based on the training data used to fine-tune the model. For each of the below generations, we utilized GPT-2 parameters of temperature = 0.7 (to control the randomness of selections) and top_k = 40 (to limit generations to only the top 40 words) as well as filtering for repeating sequences of size 2.

PROMPT

TWEET: As CountryX begins to feel the effects of #coronavirus, economic fallout and a preexisting crisis, we can't turn our back on CountryY refugees and migrants.

TWEET: Vulnerable families in #CountryX are receiving needed supplies thanks to our partners

TWEET: Today we join the humanitarian community in coming together to support

#CountryX

TWEET:

---

[1] https://www.kaggle.com/naortedgi/twitter-twitts-from-news-providers.

[2] https://www.kaggle.com/kazanova/sentiment140.

[3] Wang et al. 2012. Harnessing Twitter "big data" for automatic emotion identification.

Multiple parallel models

Fine-tuning models give Charlie the capability to change the style of her content to be more (or less) conversational, happy/sad, confident, or not, etc. for a conversation. However, sometimes as a conversation unfolds, or even within an utterance, Charlie benefits from the ability to quickly adapt her style. For example, in a podcast or panel discussion, comments or answers are typically a mix of conversational bridges or fillers between deep technical knowledge about the content.

> *HOST: There are fears of artificial intelligence replacing us. Will artificial intelligence replace teachers and change classrooms?*
>
> *CHARLIE: Gosh, that's a hard one. This is a real concern for many educators today. Yes, we will very likely have to change the way we teach, and there are a number of new additional competencies available to us in the classroom. I am going to focus on what is new, new fortes for technology, foremost artificial intelligence, worldwide, where teachers and the core tools, smaller working groups, and even small classrooms can all, if they are sufficiently equipped, leverage the power of artificial intelligence to not only serve their students' education, but also to place educators at the center of their digital classrooms in new and different ways.*

The above shows an example of Charlie's response to a technical question with a mix of generation styles. As can be seen in the response Charlie gives the combination of (1) a transition sentence (i.e., filler text) as she thinks of a response, (2) a general sentence connecting the question to educators, (3) a response to the question at a broad level, and finally (4) a technical answer digging into the possibilities she posits.

2.2.3   System Architecture

Charlie consists of a series of components communicating over an MQTT message bus (see Fig. 2.5). Many components reside on the Amazon Web Services (AWS) cloud infrastructure. The trained models run on one or more Elastic Compute Cloud (EC2) nodes with high-performance GPU compute. Amazon's Polly and Amazon Transcribe services provide, respectively, Charlie's text-to-speech and speech-to-text capabilities. For model storage and training data storage, Charlie uses Amazon's S3 service, and for architecture, state, history, and general tracking of live data, Charlie uses AWS Lambda and AWS DynamoDB.

The remaining components, namely the interfaces, run on a local computer or can be web-hosted using Amazon's S3 and Amplify services. The Embodiment interface provides Charlie's representation of her state and the outbound audio interface. The operator interface enables human augmentation of Charlie during the discussion. The Transcription interface provides the inbound audio interface and displays the incoming transcriptions.

2.2.4   Agile Development

Charlie has been designed and developed using guerilla usability testing (Nielsen, 1994), agile software development practices (Fowler et al., 2001), design thinking (Black et al., 2019), and rapid prototyping methods (Luqi & Steigerwald, 1992). Each application of Charlie has necessitated different methods of testing; however, the main themes have remained the same. For each, we conducted a series of guerilla usability tests. These tests originally consisted of evaluating utterance believability to embodiment effectiveness in small conversations with two or three participants and eventually progressed to small-scale panel or brainstorming discussions with Charlie.

2.3   Applications

Thus far, Charlie has participated in several different activities that can be broadly grouped into two different categories. The first is real-time discussions, in which ideation and debate are the key components. The second is writing tasks, in which Charlie either works with a human to complete writing tasks or writes her own content.

2.3.1   Ideation Discussions

Charlie was introduced as a panelist in a discussion of "AI-empowered learning" as part of the 2019 Interservice/Industry Simulation, Training, and Education Conference (I/ITSEC; Serfaty et al., 2019; Cummings et al., 2021). Conference panels are a prime venue for conjecture, offering a creative, improvisational environment for ideation in which an AI-powered agent can thrive. Similarly, Charlie has been a member of two podcasts: Fed Tech Talk[4] and MINDWORKS.[5] In both podcasts, she joined humans in discussing her construction and brainstorming the future of artificial intelligence. The last key application of Charlie in this category was her participation in an innovation workshop to brainstorm solutions to broad problems and to measure the influence of Charlie (see the Innovative Brainstorm Workshop Sect. 2.4 for a detailed discussion).

A key lesson learned while developing Charlie is that in parallel to the evolution of Charlie, the people interacting with her necessarily evolved as well. This was very clear in the case of the panel discussion in that, as with human-to-human interaction, there is a need to understand the way that each participant fits into the discussion

---

[4] https://federalnewsnetwork.com/federal-tech-talk/2020/03/artificial-intelligence-it-gives-you-possibilities/.

[5] https://www.com/mindworks-episode-2/.aptima.com/mindworks-episode-2/.

as well as their strengths and weaknesses. For the moderator of a panel, a large component of facilitation is in knowing what types of questions to direct to which participants and how to reframe things in the appropriate manner. This approach was key for Charlie and the panel moderator in that there was a need for the moderator (and other panelists) to learn the right way to interact, that is, the types of questions Charlie excels at answering and which ones she does not.

2.3.2 Collaborative Writing

A similar group task that Charlie is proficient at is writing tasks. To date, Charlie has experimented with songwriting for a company "rap battle," she has written a component of a winning research proposal, and she has contributed to the writing of this book chapter as shown in the Introduction and Conclusion.

Given the context of previous writing, Charlie can write her own content. This skill is shown in this paper and was done in the case of the rap battle as well. In each of these, we followed a "choose your adventure" type path to writing. That is, Charlie generated potential next options at the sentence level, then with some human intervention to select the best sentence, Charlie continued to generate the next piece. In this way, Charlie wrote her own content with some guidance from humans.

These roles can, and more commonly are, flipped. Similar to what is done in Google's Smart Compose (Chen et al., 2019), Charlie can work with a human by offering suggestions of how to complete or continue a current thought. The Smart Compose model interactively offers sentence completions as a user types out an email, which is very similar to the behavior Charlie provides to a user. However, the goal and, consequently, the method of the two tools are starkly different. Smart Compose's goal is to "draft emails faster," and so when it is confident it knows what you are about to say, it will suggest it to you. Therefore, Smart Compose's goal is not to think differently from the user or to help ideate, its goal is to mimic the user and only provide completions when it is confident it can do that mimicry well. On the other hand, the goal of Charlie is to bring different ideas and spur thought when experiencing a writer's block. This goal is orthogonal to the mimicry goal and, therefore, requires Charlie to make novel suggestions about how to continue a thought.

2.4 Innovative Brainstorm Workshop

Recently, we have been exploring additional domains in which Charlie can have the strongest impact. We believe there is great potential for Charlie to leverage her participatory collaboration (as described earlier) in brainstorming-type sessions and have experimented with an innovative brainstorming workshop. The goal of that workshop was to brainstorm solutions to broad problems and measure the influence of Charlie. This event occurred over a video-conferencing platform and served as a proof of concept that Charlie can join, participate in, and even influence the type of brainstorming meeting that is quite commonplace in research and development teams.

2.4.1   Protocol

Three Charlie brainstorming trials occurred with four human participants and Charlie. The trials occurred sequentially in a single session over a video-conferencing platform and used "Gallery View" such that each participant could see all the other participants and Charlie's display. All participants were informed that this would follow typical brainstorming norms: come up with as many creative ideas as possible, build on others' ideas, and be mindful of and open to other participants' opportunities to speak—including Charlie's indicators. Furthermore, all participants were asked to treat their fellow participants, whether human or AI, equally and respectfully. Then each participant, including Charlie, introduced themselves before beginning the three trials.

For each trial, participants were given the initial prompt and some background by the session facilitator. Other than providing the initial prompt, the facilitator did not take part in the brainstorming exercise. Participants did not interact with or ask further questions of the facilitator.

The first session's prompt was to generate pizza toppings for a new restaurant, and the trial lasted approximately 7 min and 45 s. The second prompt was to elicit propositions for ending world hunger. This trial lasted approximately 18 min and 45 s. The final prompt requested direction for the research and development of time travel. This final trial lasted 18 min and 30 s. Participants had time for breaks, but otherwise, the trials were held successively over the course of 2 h.

2.4.2   Analysis

Qualitative coding of the Charlie brainstorming session was done iteratively by (1) tagging the topic and provenance of participants' ideas, (2) tagging statements in reference to other participants' ideas and additional utterances, and (3) categorizing those statements in reference to participants' ideas. Over the course of these iterations, seven categories of utterances emerged. All specific utterances were tagged as ideas, support, build, facilitation, request for clarity, clarifications, and uncoded utterances. Otherwise, non-identified utterances were tagged simply as uncoded utterances (e.g., jokes, quick agreements without additional support, or interrupted utterances). Coding definitions are reported in Table 2.2.

Timestamps were tracked within 5 s increments and indicated the moment that the utterance by a single participant began. An utterance reflected when the participant

Table 2.2 Qualitative coding labels

Label	Definition and methods
Idea	An identifiable, contained, and proposed idea (e.g., a processor to turn raw biomass into protein to solve world hunger)
Support (name)	Expression of support for, agreement with, or additional data to supplement a previously proposed idea, with the name in parentheses identified as the originator of the idea
Build (name)	Statement or question that builds or riffs upon a previously proposed idea, with the name in parentheses identified as the originator of the idea. Individuals could build on their own idea
Facilitation	Trying to guide the larger flow of the discussion, pivoting, or re-contextualizing. This aspect was distinguished from building statements in that the utterances redirected the conversation, rather than continuing it further down the same path. (e.g., "Does all that cloning come at a cost?")
Request for clarity	Asking for additional information related to an idea (e.g., "I kinda remember that?", "I believe there was a movie about this?")
Clarification	Providing additional information in direct response to a request for clarity, or to put fundamentally the same idea into different words (e.g., "A bunch of these superluminal ideas are from movies.")
(Uncoded) Utterances	Any otherwise non-characterized utterance (e.g., making a joke) that was not clearly a supporting or building statement
Utterances	The sum of all utterance categories by an individual

began speaking—including any pauses and deviations—and ended when another participant began speaking. Accordingly, a single utterance could contain multiple coded labels. That is, a single utterance may begin with an expression of support for another's idea and then segue to a facilitating statement or a new idea entirely. Otherwise, the length of utterances—speaking duration or word count—was not recorded.

2.4.3 Preliminary Results

The resulting analysis can be found in Tables 2.3 and 2.4. Each participant's utterances—including Charlie's—were tracked independently for each trial. After all utterance categories were tagged, these were summed by trial and by provenance. Next, these were summed by categorization and averaged across the three trials. Neither particular trends were anticipated nor hypothesized. Due to the small sample size and exploratory nature of this effort, only descriptive statistics are reported.

Across three trials, Charlie made the fewest total utterances of any participant (20 total utterances compared with the human participants' $M = 40.50$, $Range = 27$–52 utterances). Similarly, Charlie had the fewest ideas of any participant (12 ideas total, compared with the human participants with $M = 14.75$, $Range = 13$–19 ideas).

Table 2.3 Categorization of utterances

	Human participants mean	Charlie
Ideas	14.75	12.00
Supporting statements	10.50	2.00
Building statements	10.50	2.00
(Uncoded) utterances	4.00	0.00
Requests for clarity	2.50	0.00
Clarifications	2.50	2.00
Facilitations	1.25	7.00
Total utterances	40.50	20.00

Note N = 4 human participants. Average utterances do not sum to total utterances because a single utterance may include multiple categorizations

Table 2.4 Supporting a building statements

	Human participants mean	Charlie
Support	6.25	17.00
Build	7.75	12.00
Supporting statements per idea	0.43	1.42
Building statements per idea	0.54	1.00

Note N = 4 human participants

Charlie supported other member statements twice, whereas human participants made supporting statements an average of 10.5 times (*Range* = 7–14). Charlie built upon other member statements twice whereas human participants did for an average of 10.5 times (*Range* = 7–17). Charlie had no uncoded utterances and did not make any requests for clarification.

In terms of categorization and frequency of utterances, Charlie was a relatively quieter participant compared with the human participants. Nevertheless, frequency appears to underreport Charlie's contributions to the conversation. We note the following as two striking observations.

First, Charlie facilitated discussion seven times, compared with the average human rate of 1.25 times (*Range* = 0–3). Furthermore, these facilitating statements made up 35.00% of Charlie's total utterances, compared with 3.09% of the humans' total utterances. Similarly, Charlie asked for clarification more than her human counterparts; human participants clarified statements on average 2.5 times, comparable to Charlie's 2. This difference is a small one in absolute terms, but clarification queries made up 10.00% of Charlie's total utterances compared with 3.09% of the humans' total utterances. Although we do not yet have a measure of the effect of those facilitations, it is striking that Charlie, without developing her capabilities or prompting her toward facilitation, still leans in this direction more than humans.

Second, although Charlie provided fewer than the mean number of ideas, her ideas were *supported by and built upon* more by human participants than their own ideas. In absolute terms, human participants supported Charlie's ideas 17 times and built on these ideas 12 times, whereas the average human participant's ideas were supported by other participants 6.25 times and built on 7.75 times. (This includes supporting and building statements made by Charlie). In relative terms, for every idea that Charlie produced, participants made 1.42 supporting statements and 1.00 building statement. In contrast, for every idea that human participants produced, other participants made 0.43 supporting statements and 0.54 building statements. This would imply that Charlie's ideas spurred discussion to a greater extent than humans' ideas (see Table 2.4).

2.5 Related Work

Clearly, Charlie's development touches upon work related to artificial intelligence in several domains. But, research investigating human–machine teams and human interaction with AI is often confined to the computer science literature, constrained to design benefitting the human (e.g., user interface or explainability from AI to human), or circumscribed around a particular performance domain (e.g., customer service). In contrast, Charlie's integration into a workplace or team deals with broader research domains. As AI co-workers become increasingly viable and pervasive, research domains touching on common workplace issues with AI components will no longer be theoretical. Accordingly, we distinguish our efforts not just in terms of novelty, but by the opportunity to weave together distinct domains of both research and practice.

The literature relevant to Charlie's development illustrates her evolution as a teammate. Mirroring Charlie's growth is the acknowledgment that one is entitled to be heard, appreciated, and perceived as someone previously known. Put another way, to be considered as a teammate, Charlie must understand, meaningfully converse, and cooperate; thus, she must be interwoven into content domains with language processing, conversational agents, and human–machine systems.

A fundamental goal of AI is the development and realization of natural dialogue between machines and humans. This goal and the long-term utility of any natural language understanding technology requires AI that generalizes beyond a single performance or content domain (Wang, Singh, Michael, Hill, Levy, & Bowman, 2018). Building from work on natural language processing and language models detailed previously, Charlie's development stands on the shoulders of cutting-edge language models, leveraging state-of-the-art AI models and capabilities. Specifically, Charlie relies on the integration of transformers (Vaswani et al., 2017) and pre-trained GPT-2 models (Qiu, Sun, Xu, Shao, Dai, & Huang, 2020), and allows for processing language that is not exclusive to a single performance or content domain (Wang et al., 2018). These technologies allowed Charlie to converse with human participants across such diverse topics as pizza toppings, world hunger, and time travel.

Conversational agents respond to natural language input—requiring an understanding of team member requests and the ability to form an appropriate response. Thanks to public demonstrations, most people are aware of sophisticated conversational agents like Watson or AI Debater. Perhaps more importantly, people interact so frequently with conversational agents as customer service chatbots and virtual personal assistants (VPAs) that the latter blend into the background. Indeed, as conversational agents, VPAs are so common in homes that they have become one of the primary methods of interacting with the biggest technology companies (e.g., Microsoft's Cortana, Apple's Siri, Amazon Alexa, Google Assistant, and Facebook's M; Kepuska & Bohouta, 2018). In circumscribed performance domains, conversational agents can be simpler. Participating in open-ended conversations such as brainstorming or functioning as a full team member requires an AI agent to know when to ask for additional information and missing data in order to respond appropriately. Perhaps not surprisingly, the Alexa Prize 2017 effort (Ram et al., 2018) found that a robust natural language understanding system with strong domain coverage led to the fewest response errors and higher high user ratings. Ultimately, the natural extension of a sufficiently advanced AI teammate must expand to be synonymous with any human teammate.

More and more, conversational agents operate in the workplace across managerial, clerical, professional, and manual positions (Feng & Buxmann, 2020). As noted by Meyer et al.'s (2019) review and synthesis of the conversational agents in the workplace literature, few empirical findings exist, and even fewer investigate collaborative work between employees. But inevitably, AI agents will be capable of substituting for operational human team members, rather than acting merely in an augmentation role. The blurring of the distinction between humans' and machines' tasking in collaborative work will alter how human–machine systems are conceptualized. Just as the composition of individual humans in a traditional team impacts performance at an emergent level, the characteristics of AI agents impact performance at the human–machine systems level. In traditional teams, successfully integrating efforts among team members requires both specialized skills (task- or domain-specific) and generic skills (teamwork; Cannon-Bowers et al., 1995). With the inclusion of AI team members at full team member capacity, this is no less true.

Effective AI team members must be able to understand their human teammates, converse in potentially unexpected and unstructured ways, and integrate their own efforts within the team's shifting dynamic. Although these are technical challenges, they are also opportunities to augment team—both human and machine—performance in new ways. In this effort, the inclusion of Charlie in a brainstorming task offers an intriguing example of how adding AI team members can augment some traditionally human processes while still being bound by others.

Brainstorming as a group is notorious for being less effective than pooling from individuals independently generating ideas (i.e., nominal brainstorming groups; Larson, 2010). Causes of this include the setting of emergent norms regarding ideation pacing, production frequency and blocking, and unsuccessful retrieval. Team members tend to produce a similar quantity of ideas in brainstorming groups—in comparison to nominal brainstorming groups—as productivity norms are established that may be below the capabilities of most members (Brown & Paulus, 1996; Camacho & Paulus, 1995; Paulus & Dzindolet, 1993). Interrelated with this issue, an AI-based teammate cannot overcome one of the primary limitations in brainstorming–production blocking, whereby the performance of one team member interrupts or impedes the performance of another team member. Both computational and empirical models demonstrate that retrieval can limit the overall production of ideas from a group. As ideas flit in and out of short-term memory, participant opportunities to voice an idea may not coincide with successful retrieval. However, heterogeneous groups appear to mitigate this—presumably, by having access to different problem-relevant semantic categories and distributed processing across individuals (Brown et al., 1998; Stroebe & Diehl, 1994). In a brainstorming task, how can Charlie overcome these challenges? Compared with a human participant, Charlie can artificially set the norm by increasing the quantity and frequency of her outputs. Less limited by memory retrieval impediments, Charlie could also anticipate the responses of others based on prior conversations and prompt individuals along those particular paths. In these ways, Charlie could serve not only in a unique supporting role to mitigate common human hindrances but also in a facilitating role if independent of the brainstorming task.

2.6 Future Applications

Unlocking human–machine teams by recognizing artificial intelligence bodes well for many potential future applications. The authors are excited to see how far we have come in only a limited amount of time exploring these challenges, and we look forward to addressing more. In this section, we will focus on three potential future applications.

The first application area is that of a scientific collaborator. As demonstrated in our initial brainstorming workshop, there is huge potential for an AI to participate in, or even facilitate, scientific collaboration and discussion. This kind of participatory AI requires knowledge of context and the ability to communicate with other scientific collaborators. Charlie has already shown the ability to contribute to and strongly influence these types of discussions.

In addition, another area of low-hanging fruit is that of an integrated workflow. This area falls under the category of more supportive artificial intelligence and could be focused on a particular work tool or domain, for example, collaborative writing.

Another potential application is the creation of an AI to assist a medical practitioner in diagnosing a patient's health. This kind of collaboration could be facilitated by an AI that is able to recognize and understand a patient's symptoms and the associated clinical signs. This kind of collaborative AI can help with diagnosis and can be very useful for the patient as well as the medical practitioner. The application is one that requires a combination of technology and human expertise to make it successful.

2.7 Conclusion

Increasingly capable and pervasive artificial intelligence creates an opportunity to engineer human–AI teams. Over the past year, we have been collaborating (both participatory and supportively) with our AI coworker, Charlie. During that time, Charlie made her debut by participating in a panel discussion and then advanced to speak during multiple podcast interviews, contribute to a rap battle, catalyze a brainstorming workshop, and even collaboratively write this chapter with us. Charlie was built on cutting-edge language models' strong sense of embodiment, deep learning speech synthesis, and powerful visuals. However, the real differentiator in our approach is that of recognizing the artificial intelligence. The act of "recognizing" Charlie can be seen when we give her a voice and expect her to be heard, in a way that shows we acknowledge and appreciate her contributions, and when our repeated interactions create a comfortable awareness between teammates. We covered some initial results from an innovative brainstorming workshop in which Charlie was shown to not only participate in the brainstorming exercise but also to contribute to and influence the brainstorming discussion idea space. We are excited to see what the future holds in a variety of domains as we and others work toward recognizing artificial intelligence.

Acknowledgements The authors would like to acknowledge the larger team that has helped make Charlie a reality through design, development, deployment, testing and analysis. This team includes Laura Cassani, Peter Cinibulk, Will Dupree, Deirdre Kelliher, Manuel Moquete, Ryan Mullins, Louis Penafiel.

References

Black, S., Gardner, D. G., Pierce, J. L., & Steers, R. (2019). Design thinking, Organizational Behavior.

Branwen, G. (2019). Gpt-2 neural network poetry.

Brown T, et al. (2020). Language models are few-shot learners, in *NeurIPS Proceedings*.

Brown, V., & Paulus, P. (1996). A simple dynamic model of social factors in group brainstorming. *Small Group Research, 27*(10), 91–114.

Brown, V., Tumeo, M., Larey, T., & Paulus, P. (1998). Modeling cognitive interactions during group brainstorming. *Small Group Research, 29*(4), 495–526.

Camacho, L., & Paulus, P. (1995). The role of social anxiousness in group brainstorming. *Journal of Personality and Social Psychology, 68*(106), 1071–1080.

Cannon-Bowers, J., Tannenbaum, S., Salas, E., & Volpe, C. (1995). Defining competencies and establishing team training requirements. *Team Effectiveness and Decision Making in Organizations, 16*, 333–380.

Case, N. (2018) How to become a centaur. *Journal of Design and Science.*

Chen, M. X., et al. (2019) Gmail smart compose: Real-time assisted writing, in *SIGKDD Conference on Knowledge Discovery and Data Mining.*

Cummings, P., Mullins, R., Moquete, M., & Schurr, N. (2021). HelloWorld! I am Charlie, an artificially intelligent conference panelist. *HICSS.*

Feng, S., & Buxmann, P. (2020). My virtual colleague: A state-of-the-art analysis of conversational agents for the workplace, in *Proceedings of the 53rd Hawaii International Conference on System Sciences*.

Fowler, M., Highsmith, J., et al. (2001). The agile manifesto. *Software Development, 9*(8), 28–35.

Gnewuch, U., Morana, S., Adam, M., & Maedche, A. (2018). Faster is not always better: Understanding the effect of dynamic response delays in human-chatbot interaction. *ECIS*.

Kepuska, V., & Bohouta, G. (2018). Next-generation of virtual personal assistants (microsoft cortana, apple siri, amazon alexa and google home), in *2018 IEEE 8th Annual Computing and Communication Workshop and Conference (CCWC)* (pp. 99–103). IEEE.

Keskar, N., McCann, B., Varshney, L., Xiong, C., & Socher, R. (2019). Ctrl: A conditional transformer language model for controllable generation. *ArXiv, abs/1909.05858*.

Larson, J. R. (2010). In search of synergy in small group performance. Psychology Press.

Luqi L., & Steigerwald, R. (1992). Rapid software prototyping, in *Proceedings of the Twenty-Fifth Hawaii International Conference on System Sciences* (vol. 2, pp. 470–479). IEEE.

von Wolff, R. M., Hobert, S., & Schumann, M. (2019). How may i help you?–state of the art and open research questions for chatbots at the digital workplace, in *Proceedings of the 52nd Hawaii International Conference on System Sciences*.

Nielsen, J. (1994). Guerrilla HCI: Using discount usability engineering to penetrate the intimidation barrier. *Cost-Justifying Usability* 245–272.

Paulus, P., & Dzindolet, M. (1993). Social influence processes in group brainstorming. *Journal of Personality and Social Psychology, 64*(104), 575–586.

Peng, X., Li, S., Frazier, S., & Riedl, M. (2020). Fine-tuning a transformer-based language model to avoid generating non-normative text. arXiv:2001.08764.

Radford, A., Wu, J., Child, R., Luan, D., Amodei, D., & Sutskever, I. (2019). Language models are unsupervised multitask learners.

Ram, A., Prasad, R., Khatri, C., Venkatesh, A., Gabriel, R., Liu, Q., Nunn, J., Hedayatnia, B., Cheng, M., & Nagar, A., et al. (2018). Conversational AI: The science behind the alexa prize. arXiv:1801.03604.

Russet, C. (2020). Turing-NLG: A 17-billion-parameter language model by microsoft.

Qin, L., Bosselut, A., Holtzman, A., Bhagavatula, C., Clark, E., & Choi, Y. (2019). Counterfactual story reasoning and generation. arXiv:1909.04076.

Qiu, X., Sun, T., Xu, Y., Shao, Y., Dai, N., & Huang, X. (2020). Pre-trained models for natural language processing: A survey. arXiv:2003.08271.

Raffel, C., Shazeer, N., Roberts, A., Lee, K., Narang, S., Matena, M., Zhou, Y., Li, W., & Liu, P. J. (2020). Exploring the limits of transfer learning with a unified text-to-text transformer. *Journal of Machine Learning Research, 21*.

Russell, S. (2019). Human compatible: Artificial intelligence and the problem of control. *Penguin*.

Scherer, K. R. (2013). The functions of nonverbal signs in conversation, in *The social and psychological contexts of language* (pp. 237–256), Psychology Press.

Schuetzler, R. M., Grimes, M., Giboney, J. S., & Buckman, J. (2014). Facilitating natural conversational agent interactions: lessons from a deception experiment.

Serfaty, D. (2019). Imagine 2030: Ai-empowered learning. *I/ITSEC*.

Shneiderman, B. (2020). Bridging the gap between ethics and practice: guidelines for reliable, safe, and trustworthy human-centered AI systems. *ACM Transactions on Interactive Intelligent Systems (TiiS), 10*(4), 1–31.

Stroebe, W., & Diehl, M. (1994). Why groups are less effective than their members: On productivity losses in idea-generating groups. *European Review of Social Psychology, 5*(1), 271–303.

Vaswani, A., Shazeer, N., Parmar, N., Uszkoreit, J., Jones, L., Gomez, A., Kaiser, L., & Polosukhin, I. (2017). Attention is all you need *06*.

Vincent, J. (2019). Openai's new multitalented AI writes, translates, and slanders. *The Verge, 14*.

Wang, A., Singh, A., Michael, J., Hill, F., Levy, O., & Bowman, S. (2018). Glue: A multi-task benchmark and analysis platform for natural language understanding *04*.

Yang, Z., Dai, Z., Yang, Y., Carbonell, J., Salakhutdinov, R., & Le, Q. (2019). Xlnet: Generalized autoregressive pretraining for language understanding *06*.

Zhang, Y., Sun, S., Galley, M., Chen, Y. -C., Brockett, C., Gao, X., Gao, J., Liu, J., & Dolan, B. (2019). Dialogpt: Large-scale generative pre-training for conversational response generation.

Zhou, C., Sun, C., Liu, Z., & Lau, F. (2015). A c-lstm neural network for text classification *11*.

Chapter 3
Artificial Intelligence and Future of Systems Engineering

Thomas A. McDermott, Mark R. Blackburn, and Peter A. Beling

Abstract Systems Engineering (SE) is in the midst of a digital transformation driven by advanced modeling tools, data integration, and resulting "digital twins." Like many other domains, the engineering disciplines will see transformational advances in the use of artificial intelligence (AI) and machine learning (ML) to automate many routine engineering tasks. At the same time, applying AI, ML, and autonomation to complex and critical systems needs holistic, system-oriented approaches. This will encourage new systems engineering methods, processes, and tools. It is imperative that the SE community deeply understand emerging AI and ML technologies and applications, incorporate them into methods and tools, and ensure that appropriate SE approaches are used to make AI systems ethical, reliable, safe, and secure. This chapter presents a road mapping activity undertaken by the Systems Engineering Research Center (SERC). The goal is to broadly identify opportunities and risks that might appear as this evolution proceeds as well as potentially provide information that guides further research in both SE and AI/ML.

3.1 Introduction

In 2019, the Research Council of the Systems Engineering Research Center (SERC), a U.S. Defense Department sponsored University Affiliated Research Center (UARC), developed a roadmap to structure and guide research in artificial intelligence (AI) and autonomy. This roadmap was updated in 2020. This chapter presents the current roadmap as well as key aspects of the underlying Digital Engineering transformation that will enable both transformation of SE practices using AI for SE and drive the need for new systems engineering practices that support a new wave of automated, adaptive, and learning systems, termed SE for AI. The "AI4SE" and "SE4AI" labels have become metaphors for an upcoming rapid evolutionary phase in the SE Community.

T. A. McDermott (✉) · M. R. Blackburn
Stevens Institute of Technology, Hoboken, NJ, USA

P. A. Beling
University of Virginia, Charlottesville, VA, USA

© Springer Nature Switzerland AG 2021
W. F. Lawless et al. (eds.), *Systems Engineering and Artificial Intelligence*,
https://doi.org/10.1007/978-3-030-77283-3_3

47

AI4SE applies AI and ML techniques to improve human-driven engineering practices. This goal of "augmented intelligence" includes outcomes such as achieving scale in model construction and efficiency in design space exploration. SE4AI applies SE methods to learning-based systems' design and operation, with outcomes such as improved safety, security, ethics, etc.

SE is in the midst of a digital transformation driven by advanced modeling tools, data integration, and the resulting "digital twins" that maintain virtual copies of portions of real-world systems across lifecycles of system use. This transformation is changing what used to be primarily document-based system descriptions (concept of operations, requirements, architectures, etc.) into digital data and descriptive models that link data from different disciplines together. This central dataset, known as an "authoritative source of truth," will over time integrate all aspects of engineering design, use, and maintenance of systems into a linked set of information. This digital engineering transformation will be followed by transformational advances in the discipline of systems engineering using AI and ML technology for automation of many engineering tasks, designed to augment human intelligence.

At the same time, the application of AI, ML, and autonomy to many of today's complex and critical systems drives the need for new SE methods, processes, and tools. Today, applications of these technologies represent serious challenges to the SE community. A primary goal of SE is to ensure that the behavior and performance of complex engineered systems meet the expected outcomes driven by user needs, and that the configuration of the system is managed across its lifetime. Advances in AI and ML application mean that future system components may learn and adapt more rapidly, and that behavior and performance may be non-deterministic with less predictable but manageable outcomes. This change may introduce new failure modes not previously experienced in the engineering community. The inability to explicitly validate system behaviors or the time it takes to do that will impact trust in these systems and will change the way the SE community traditionally addresses system validation. The uncertainty present in multiple AI/ML components that interact will defy traditional decomposition methods used by the SE community, requiring new synthesis methods. Finally, as systems develop means for co-learning between human users and machines, traditional models that separate human behaviors from the machine will need to be revisited.

At an early 2019 Future of Systems Engineering (FuSE) workshop hosted by the International Council on Systems Engineering (INCOSE), the terms AI for SE and SE for AI were first used to describe this dual transformation (McDermott et al., 2020). The "AI4SE" and "SE4AI" labels have quickly become metaphors for an upcoming rapid evolutionary phase in the SE Community. AI4SE may be defined as the application of augmented intelligence and machine learning techniques to support the practice of systems engineering. Goals in such applications include achieving scale in model construction and confidence in design space exploration. SE4AI may be defined as the application of systems engineering methods to the design and operation of learning-based systems. Key research application areas include the development of principles for learning-based systems design, models of life cycle evolution, and model curation methods.

3.2 SERC AI4SE and SE4AI Roadmap

In order to better understand and focus on this evolution, the Research Council of the SERC developed a roadmap to structure and guide research in artificial intelligence (AI) and autonomy. This roadmap was described in McDermott et al. (2020) and presented in a number of forums including both systems disciplines (McDermott, 2019, 2020a) and AI disciplines (McDermott, 2020b). A dedicated "SE4AI/AI4SE" workshop sponsored by the SERC and the U.S. Army further refined the roadmap. An initial version was presented at the Fall 2020 Association for the Advancement of Artificial Intelligence (AAAI) conference, and the current version will be published in 2021 in an INCOSE AI primer for systems engineers. This roadmap is being published with a goal to link the discipline of systems engineering to various trends in artificial intelligence and its application to automation in systems. This linkage is provided as a means to discuss the possible evolution of AI/ML technology, autonomy, and the SE discipline over time. Figure 3.1 depicts the current notional roadmap.

The envisioned long-term outcome is "Human–Machine Co-learning." This outcome captures a future where both humans and machines will adapt their behavior over time by learning from each other or alongside each other. For the SE community, this is a new context and lifecycle model that is not envisioned and supported by most of the current-day systems engineering practices. This new context implies a fairly significant transformation of SE methods, tools, and practices and is underway that will change both SE and AI methods, processes, and tools over time.

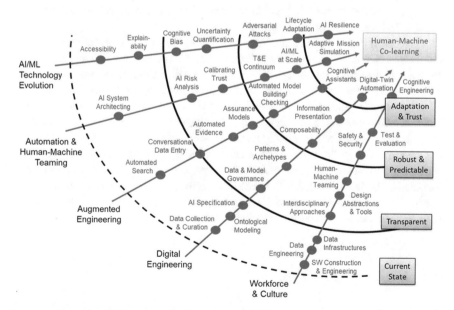

Fig. 3.1 The SERC AI4SE and SE4AI Roadmap

To achieve this end state, one might consider there is a need for both the AI and SE disciplines to pass through a set of "waves" or eras. The first of these includes sets of technologies and approaches that make the decisions produced by AI systems more transparent to the human developers and users. This broadly relates to the evolution of trust in such systems. Today, much of the activity in the "transparency" wave is termed "Explainable AI," but it also includes more transparency and understanding of the methods and tools used to develop AI applications, the underlying data, and the human–machine interfaces that lead to effective decision-making in the type of complex systems SE deals with routinely.

The "robust and predictable" wave is to produce systems that learn and may be non-deterministic, but that is also appropriately robust, predictable, and trustworthy in the type of critical and complex uses common to the application of SE practices today. This wave particularly includes both human and machine behaviors in joint decision environments, highly reliant on good human-system design and presentation of decision information. It also includes the adaptation of test and evaluation processes to co-learning environments.

The third wave involves systems that actually adapt and learn dynamically from their environments. In this wave, machine-to-machine and human-to-machine (and maybe machine-to-human) trust will be critical. Trust implies a dependence between the human and machine, which must emerge from human–machine interaction. Trust normally requires the human to understand and validate the performance of the system against a set of criteria in a known context. In this third wave, systems will be expected to learn to modify or create new behaviors as the context changes and this may happen fairly rapidly. Methods that revalidate system performance extremely rapidly or "on the fly" are not part of the current SE practice set and must be developed along with these types of learning systems.

The vectors of this notional roadmap span five categories. The first of these vectors recognizes that the technological implementation of AI systems will evolve and need to evolve in directions relevant to SE. Most of these directions can be related to transparency and trust in the technology. The second vector recognizes that the purpose of AI in systems is generally to provide for automation of human tasks and decisions, and this will change how we design and test systems. The third vector recognizes that AI technologies will gradually be used more and more to augment the work of engineering. The fourth vector recognizes that the current digital engineering transformation will be an enabler for that. A short description of the first four categories is included in Tables 3.1, 3.2, 3.3, 3.4. The fifth vector recognizes a transformation will need to be accomplished in the SE workforce, with significantly more integration of software and human behavioral sciences at the forefront.

3.3   Digital Engineering

We start with digital engineering as it is the enabler for the first three roadmap vectors. Table 3.1 provides a consolidated summary of the research and development

Table 3.1 Digital engineering as the enabler for AI4SE and SE4AI

Research area	Definition	Use in systems engineering
Digital engineering		
Data collection and curation	Specific activities to build infrastructure and collect and manage data needed for engineering and programmatic activities in system development and support	Provides connectivity and reuse of data across disciplines and system lifecycles
Ontological modeling	Knowledge representation of engineering and programmatic data providing interoperability through standard and domain-specific ontologies	Improves model-based systems engineering; enables AI-based reasoning
AI specification (Seshia et al., 2018)	System-level and formal specifications for AI behaviors supporting verification activities	Allows specification of requirements for AI-related functions in a mathematically rigorous form
Data and model governance	Lifecycle management, control, preservation, and enhancement of models and associated data to ensure value for current and future use, as well as repurposing beyond initial purpose and context	Configuration management, quality management, pedigree, and reuse of digital data and models
Patterns and archetypes	Widely used modeling constructs that separate design from implementation, supporting better reuse and composition	Development of standard model templates and patterns for composition
Composability	Rapid development and integration of design using higher level abstracted components and patterns, across multiple disciplines	Development of domain-specific computer languages and low-code software tools
Information presentation	Visualization approaches and interfaces supporting human–machine real-time collaborative information sharing via multiple media	Integration of human task and machine behavior modeling into common digital data
Digital twin automation	Fully dynamic virtual system copies built from the same models as the real systems running in parallel to physical systems and updating from the same data feeds as their real counterparts	Allows systems to be regularly measured and updated based on learning in new or changing contexts

Table 3.2 Summary of the research in AI/ML relevant to SE disciplines

Research area	Definition	Use in SE
AI/ML Technology Evolution		
Accessibility	AI algorithms and methods become more available in tools that can be used by multiple disciplines	Increase the number of professionals who use and understand the tools
Explainability [DARPA]	Developing sets of machine learning techniques that produce more explainable models, while maintaining a high level of learning performance (prediction accuracy); and enable human users to understand, appropriately trust, and effectively manage the resulting automation	Allowing the human analysis and decisions to better understand and trust the machine-generated analysis and decisions
Cognitive bias	Reducing errors induced in sampled data or algorithms that cause the expected results of the system to be inappropriate for use	Requirements for and evaluation of training data and application usage in the system
Uncertainty quantification (Abdar et al., 2020)	Representing the uncertainty of AI predictions as well as the sources of uncertainty	Requirements for and evaluation of the performance of AI usage in the system
Adversarial attacks (Ren, et al., 2020)	Use of adversarial samples to fool machine learning algorithms; defensive techniques for detection/classification of adversarial samples	Requirements for and evaluation of adversarial defense approaches and their effectiveness in the system
Lifecycle adaptation	Evolution of AI performance over the lifecycle of a system as the system changes/evolves	Learning design and use takes into account the variability of a system over time
AI resilience	Operational resilience of the system and its users incorporating AI, particularly involving the characteristics of ML systems	Application of resilience assessment methods to systems using AI

areas evolving in the current digital transformation of the engineering disciplines (Hagedorn et al., 2020). As more of the underlying data is collected in engineering modeling and analysis, it will become training data for ML applications.

There are several ongoing advancements in digital engineering relevant to AI4SE (McDermott et al., 2020):

Table 3.3 Summary of research in AI/ML relevant to SE disciplines

Research area	Definition	Use in SE
Automation and human–machine teaming		
AI system architecting	Building appropriate data and also live and virtual system architectures to support learning and adaptation and more agile change processes	Parallel development and comparison of in vivo (real) and in silico (virtual) deployments
AI risk analysis	Methods, processes, and tools need to connect system risk analysis results with AI software modules related to those risks	Characteristics of AI systems incorporated into operational loss, hazard, and risk analysis
Calibrating trust	AI systems self-adapt while maintaining rigorous safety, security, and policy constraints	Adaptation and learning incorporated into human system integration
T&E continuum	Methods for addressing AI-related system test and evaluation (T&E) addressing these systems' ability to adapt and learn from changing deployment contexts	New approaches for both system and user verification and validation (V&V) of adaptive systems
AI/ML at scale	Appreciation for the dependence of an AI's outputs on its inputs; scale in AI-based systems will increasingly lead to more general intelligence and an inability to relegate AI to a particular subsystem or component	SE frameworks specifying complex system-level behaviors, distinct from decomposition to functions and requirements
Adaptive mission simulation	Computer-based simulation and training supporting non-static objectives and/or goals (games, course-of-action analysis) are necessary to provide contextual learning environments for these systems	Real and simulated co-learning (digital twins) will be a standard system development form

- Tool and Domain Taxonomies and Ontologies: engineering and programmatic data will gain interoperability through domain-specific ontologies. Graph databases for linked data are becoming more prominent in model-based systems engineering tools. Taxonomies provide the starting point for building ontologies, ultimately enabling AI-based reasoning on the underlying data. This advancement is the transformational infrastructure in AI4SE.
- Inter-Enterprise Data Integration: a primary goal of digital engineering is an authoritative source of truth data that underlies the different engineering and

Table 3.4 Summary of research in augmented engineering

Research area	Definition	Use in systems engineering
Augmented engineering		
Automated search	Applying ML to historical data and relationships in the engineering domains	Greatly improve the speed and consistency of systems engineering activities
Conversational data entry	Human/computer interaction processes to convert the natural language and other media to formal models	Improve knowledge transfer and consistency in future systems engineering tools
Automated evidence	Automation of certification and accreditation processes via models, and automation of quality assurance data	Improved speed and coverage, particularly for systems-of-systems and distributed development and test activities
Assurance models	Automation of evidence-based models for assuring correctness and completeness of system requirements and design	Improved specification and verification/validation of critical assurance characteristics
Automated model building/checking	Automated construction of models from features in semantic data used in both creation of new models and correctness of developed models	Improved speed of development
Cognitive assistants	Conversational systems automating many mundane data entry, exploration, and engineering calculation tasks, and many workflows	Improved speed of development, improved collaboration

program management activities in complex engineered systems. As programs and engineering design activities share data, enterprises will build large datasets for knowledge transfer and reuse across different programs and projects. These data will be available to automate search, model-building/checking, and decision-making.

- Semantic Rules in Engineering Tools: based on knowledge representations such as ontologies, semantic rules will provide the basis for reasoning (using AI) about the completeness and consistency of engineering models.
- Digital Twin Automation: engineered systems will be supported by twins—fully dynamic virtual system copies built from the same models as the real systems and running in parallel to physical systems. System design and build data will be updated from the same data feeds as their real counterparts. This dynamic process provides a starting infrastructure for human–machine co-learning.

3.4   AI/ML Technology Evolution

Table 3.2 provides a consolidated summary of the research and development areas in the AI/ML disciplines that are relevant to SE practices. This table is provided as both a view for the SE practitioner as well as perhaps a prioritization in the AI/ML world of research needs, particularly as applications of ML evolve to larger system usage and more critical application areas.

We see a progression of research and development in AI/ML technologies and applications that will lead to increased engineering acceptance and use across more complex engineered systems. This advance starts with the accessibility of AI/ML algorithms and techniques.

The rapid growth of ML technologies has been aided by free open-source tools and low-cost training, but this rise is still targeting computer and data scientists and is based on foundational skills that are not widespread in the SE community. Wade, Buenfil, & Collopy (2020) discuss a potential business model using an abstraction to bring AI/ML to the SE community based on a similar experience in the Very Large Scale Integrated (VLSI) circuit's revolution. Just as abstraction and high-level programming languages hid the underlying complexity of microcircuits from an average designer, the growth in "low-code" AI/ML design tools will make the technology more accessible to other disciplines.

SE is a discipline targeted at improving the predictability of function and performance in the design and use of complex systems. Current day ML applications that "hide" decision paths in deep networks create predictability concerns in the SE community. Even rule-based systems at large scales are a concern for the community, which strives for explicit verification and validation of function and performance in the critical functions of a system. Issues with explainability and data/training bias must be overcome for AI/ML technologies and applications to gain acceptance in the SE community for critical functions. Research in digital twins and extended applications of modeling and simulation for validation are needed. Otherwise, the "validation by use" will be cost and risk-prohibitive in large safety-critical applications. Research in uncertainty quantification of deep learning applications is of particular research interest in the engineering community as certainty in decision-making improves opportunities for validation by decomposition of function. Abdar et al. (2020) provide a good review of this research area.

Improved resilience from design errors and malicious attacks is a concern for use of AI/ML in critical applications. Protection from adversarial attacks and general robustness cannot be provided by add-on applications. It must be designed into the learning process. Ren et al. (McDermott, 2019) provide an overview of this research area and some possible defensive techniques.

In the long term, adaptation and contextual learning in AI/ML systems across long system lifecycles, and the resilience of these systems to changing contexts (environment, use, etc.) will be an active area of research and development in the engineering community. Cody, Adams, and Beling (2020) provide an example of the need and possible approaches to make an AI/ML application more robust to changes in a physical system over time. This article provides a good example of the challenges of ML in operational environments. Eventually, the broad use of learning applications for multiple interconnected functions in complex systems will arrive. At some point, the SE community will no longer be able to rely primarily on decompositional approaches to system design and must adopt new, more holistic approaches.

Automation and Human–Machine Teaming

Table 3.3 provides a consolidated summary of the research and development areas in automation and human–machine teaming disciplines that are relevant to SE practices. Automation and the use of AI are not new to the SE discipline; but the use of ML is more recent. We envision that humans and machines will team in ways that they learn from each other while using complex engineered systems in complex environments. The robustness of these interactions at scale is an SE challenge.

The future state in SE and automation will see, using a terminology from Madni (2020), the deployment of adaptive cyber-physical-human systems (CPHS). In adaptive CPHS, humans and complex machines learn together as they move across different contexts. Adaptive CPHS employ different types of human and machine learning to flexibly respond to unexpected or novel situations during mission and task execution; to respond using plan and goal adjustment and adaptation; to learn from experience to evolve the system; and to continuously adapt the human and machine tasks in operational performance of the system. A key issue in this future is modeling human behavior in the context of the machine design (Ren et al., 2020). The SE community, to manage complexity and skillsets, generally views the human system activities, the machine function and behavior, and the related modeling and simulation as three independent subdisciplines. These subdisciplines will need to converge as human behaviors and machine behaviors are allowed to adapt together while in use, with the changes sensed by large-scale digital twins. An important research area is adaptive mission simulation—simulation environments that provide contextual learning to both humans and machines across the development, test, and operational lifetimes of a system.

The system architecting process will change as automation scales in more complex systems. System architectures must support learning and adaptation and more agile change processes. System architectures for large hardware systems will include the training data and associated information technologies that support their AI/ML components. Future system architecting must consider the parallel development and the comparison of in vivo (real) and in silico (virtual) deployments with sensing and data collection subsystems that support continuous learning and adaptation.

The SE community has traditionally viewed T&E of systems and architectures as static events supporting specific lifecycle decisions. Future views of T&E must evolve to support learning and adaptation. Freeman (2020) lists a number of themes for the evolution of the T&E processes to be considered by the SE community:

- T&E is a continuum where data accumulate over time;
- The continuum does not end until the system retires;

- Integrating information from disparate data sources requires unique methods and activities (models, simulations, and test environments) to collect and combine the data;
- Data management is foundational—evaluation of data quality and readiness is essential;
- AI systems require a risk-based test approach that considers all of the evidence collected versus consequence severity in the operational environment;
- Test metrics may have different interpretations, and new metrics may be necessary to focus on risk for AI systems;
- It becomes more essential to understand the operational context and threats for these systems; and to achieve this,
- All AI areas need testbeds for experimentation with operational data.

In all of these cases, pure decomposition of function to design and buildup of function to test may not apply in traditional ways. As multiple AI/ML applications become dependent on each other, the SE community must add methods for the aggregation of decisions and associated behaviors in the systems. Characterization of system behavior in the aggregate will affect traditional T&E approaches as noted previously.

Automation of function has been a continuous feature of engineered systems since the industrial age began, but human–machine co-learning requires different methods to assess risk and trust in future systems. The T&E continuum must support this, but we also need new methods to evaluate risk and to make decisions on whether or not a system is safe, secure, ethical, etc. We are already seeing such issues arise in applications like self-driving cars and facial recognition systems where the societal norms for safety, security, privacy, and fairness are being adjusted. Concepts and metrics for trust need to become more explicit in the SE community—both in the human interaction and the dependability of the machines.

3.5   Augmented Engineering

Table 3.4 provides a consolidated summary of the research and development areas in augmented engineering. We envision that as digital engineering evolves and traditional engineering models and practices rely more on the underlying data, many engineering tasks related to data collection and search, data manipulation, and data analysis will become automated. Also, the machine learning of modeled relationships and underlying data will become more complex over time. This augmentation will automate many mundane engineering tasks leading to a greater focus on problem-solving and design for the human engineer. In addition, we envision that engineering speed and quality will improve as more engineering test and validation activities become automated. The idea of "cognitive assistants" that broadly support the engineer will evolve but they must evolve in a way that supports the problem-solving and associated learning processes associated with engineering.

Rouse (2020) argues for terms like "augmented intelligence" and "augmented engineering" in the SE community because SE is highly associated with human problem-solving. He argues that future cognitive assistants in this domain must not only support automated search and model building/checking but also contextual inferencing of intent, explanation management, and intelligent tutoring with respect to machine inferences and recommendations. Selva and Viros (2019) provide an example of a cognitive assistant for engineering design and system analysis. In this work, they show that a cognitive assistant can increase engineering performance, but, as a side effect, can also decrease human learning (Selva, 2019). This result is an example of the need for co-learning in human–machine teaming.

In the long term, as the engineering community captures more of their process in digital data and models, the use of AI/ML will improve the quality of engineering design and test activities. Automation of data collection and search, model-building, evidence collection, data and model checking, and eventually system assurance processes will lead to better more robust systems.

3.6 Workforce and Culture

In the category of workforce and culture, many system engineers come from foundational disciplines in engineering and lack some of the computer science foundations that drive the AI discipline area. The systems engineering workforce needs to further develop basic digital engineering competencies in software construction and engineering, data engineering, and related information technologies. AI/ML systems are created in these three disciplinary domains. However, SE can bring its strong foundation in interdisciplinary approaches to the AI community. Over time, AI development tools will incorporate design abstractions and patterns that make the technology more accessible to a broad set of engineers, improving the interdisciplinary understanding and use of the technology. A clear workforce development concern is the integration of AI with systems engineering and human systems integration—a much greater representation of the cognitive sciences and cognitive engineering in the SE discipline set. Specialty systems engineering disciplines such as security and safety must move to the forefront. New test and evaluation approaches for learning and adaptation will significantly affect those disciplines.

3.7 Summary—The AI imperative for Systems Engineering

SE is undergoing a digital transformation. This evolution will lead to further transformational advances in the use of AI and ML technology to automate many routine engineering tasks. At the same time, applying AI, ML, and autonomy to complex and critical systems encourages new systems engineering methods, processes, and tools. It is imperative that the systems engineering community deeply understand the emerging AI and ML technologies and applications, incorporate them into the methods and tools in ways that improve the SE discipline, and ensure that appropriate systems engineering approaches are used to make AI systems ethical, reliable, safe, and secure. The road mapping activity presented here attempts to understand broadly all of the opportunities and risks that might appear as this evolution proceeds as well as potentially provide the information that guides further research.

References

Abdar, M., Pourpanah, F., Hussain, S., Rezazadegan, D., Liu, L., Ghavamzadeh, M., & Nahavandi, S. (2020). A review of uncertainty quantification in deep learning: Techniques, applications and challenges. arXiv:2011.06225.

Cody, T., Adams, S., & Beling, P. (2020). Motivating a systems theory of AI. *Insight, 23*(1), 37–40.

DARPA. https://www.darpa.mil/program/explainable-artificial-intelligence.

Freeman, L. (2020). Test and evaluation for artificial intelligence. *Insight, 23*(1), 27–30.

Hagedorn, T., Bone, M., Kruse, B., Grosse, I., & Blackburn, M. (2020). Knowledge representation with ontologies and semantic web technologies to promote augmented and artificial intelligence in systems engineering. *Incose Insight, 23*(1), 15–20.

Madni, A., & Erwin D. (2018). Next generation adaptive cyber physical human systems, Year 1 technical report, Systems engineering research center. Retrieved from https://sercuarc.org/serc-programs-projects/project/67/.

McDermott, T., DeLaurentis, D., Beling, P., Blackburn, M., & Bone, M. (2020). AI4SE and SE4AI: A research roadmap. *Incose Insight, 23*(1), 8–14.

McDermott, T. (2019). A framework to guide AI/ML and autonomy research in systems engineering, in *22nd Annual National Defense Industrial Association (NDIA) Systems and Mission Engineering Conference*. Tampa, FL.

McDermott, T. (2020). Digital engineering and AI—Transformation of systems engineering. *Presentation to the International Council on Systems Engineering (INCOSE) Northstar Chapter*.

McDermott, T. (2020). Digital engineering and AI—Transformation of systems engineering, in AI welcomes systems engineering: Towards the science of interdependence for autonomous human-machine teams, *Association for the Advancement of Artificial Intelligence (AAAI) 2020 Spring Symposium Series*.

Ren, K., Zheng, T., Qin, Z., & Liu, X. (2020). Adversarial attacks and defenses in deep learning. *Engineering, 6*(3), 346–360.

Selva, D. (2019). Fostering Human Learning from cognitive assistants for design space exploration, in *Technical Report SERC-2019-TR-017, Systems Engineering Research Center*.

Seshia, S. A., Desai, A., Dreossi, T., Fremont, D. J., Ghosh, S., Kim, E., & Yue, X. (2018). Formal specification for deep neural networks, in *International Symposium on Automated Technology for Verification and Analysis* (pp. 20–34). Springer, Cham.

Viros, A., & Selva, D. (2019). Daphne: A virtual assistant for designing earth observation distributed spacecraft missions. *IEEE Journal of Selected Topics in Applied Earth Observations and Remote Sensing (J-stars)*.

Wade, J., Buenfil, J., & Collopy, P. (2020). A systems engineering approach for artificial intelligence: Inspired by the VLSI revolution of mead & conway. *Insight, 23*(1), 41–47.

Chapter 4
Effective Human–Artificial Intelligence Teaming

Nancy J. Cooke and William F. Lawless

Abstract In 1998, the great social psychologist, (Jones, Gilbert et al.Fiske et al.Lindzey (eds), The Handbook of Social Psychology, McGraw-Hill, 1998), asserted that interdependence was present in every social interaction and key to unlocking the social life of humans, but this key, he also declared, had produced effects in the laboratory that were "bewildering," and too difficult to control. Since then, along with colleagues and students, we have brought the effects of interdependence into the laboratory for detailed studies where we have successfully explored many of the aspects of interdependence and its implications. In addition, in a review led by the first author and a colleague, the National Academy of Sciences reported that interdependence in a team enhances the performance of the individual (Cooke and Hilton,.Enhancing the Effectiveness of Team Science. Authors: Committee on the Science of Team Science; Board on Behavioral, Cognitive, and Sensory Sciences; Division of Behavioral and Social Sciences and Education; National Research Council, National Academies Press, 2015). This book chapter allows me to review the considerable research experiences we have gained from our studies over the years to consider the situations in which an artificial intelligence (AI) agent or machine begins to assist and possibly replace a human teammate on a team in the future.

4.1 Introduction

In this chapter, we provide an overview of team research and team cognition in sociotechnical systems. It will include a review of human teaming and human–autonomy teaming in the context of remotely piloted aircraft system ground control team studies; the theory of Interactive Team Cognition (ITC); a review of our research with a synthetic teammate as an air vehicle operator; and that will be followed by a

N. J. Cooke (✉)
Human Systems Engineering, Center for Human, Artificial, Intelligence, and Robot Teaming, Arizona State University, Tempe, USA
e-mail: nancy.Cooke@asu.edu

W. F. Lawless
Mathematics and Psychology, Paine College, Augusta, GA, USA

© Springer Nature Switzerland AG 2021
W. F. Lawless et al. (eds.), *Systems Engineering and Artificial Intelligence*,
https://doi.org/10.1007/978-3-030-77283-3_4

review of a synthetic teammate validation study. Then we will close the chapter with a short review of the next steps.

A team is defined as an interdependent group of individuals (see Fig. 4.1), each with distinct roles and responsibilities, who work toward a common objective (Salas et al., 1992). This definition implies that a team is a special type of group. With advances in artificial intelligence (AI), AI agents can fulfill critical roles and responsibilities for a team; often those are the roles and responsibilities that are too dull, difficult, dirty, or dangerous for humans. Are these human–AI teams different from all human teams? Are human teammates different from AI teammates? What does it take for AI to be a good teammate? These and other questions have been addressed in my laboratory over the last decade. One critical finding that has emerged from many studies is the importance of interaction that can manifest as the communication or coordination required to exploit the team's interdependencies (Cooke, 2015; Cooke et al., 2013).

In the study above by Salas et al. (1992), Salas and his team recognized that teams at work have been a research subject in the field of business management for many years with the result of several developments that have improved the organizations for teams and the human resource managements that have benefitted from applying their lessons. In their review, the authors studied the formation of work teams and the processes with them that have led to human resource excellence. From the perspectives in the workplace existing at the time, the complexity of work situations was proving to be too difficult for employees to address on their own, exemplifying the value of teams and teamwork that underscored the need for this research. For teams, the research focus was initially placed on team structure, leadership, control, mutual support, and communication. For human resources excellence, the authors studied delegation, motivation, and teamwork. With the data collected by the authors from a questionnaire and then analyzed in regression, they concluded that team structure,

Fig. 4.1 Left: A familiar action-oriented team playing basketball seen most often during the Fall and Winter months in backyards, playgrounds, schools, and universities and at locations spread all over the world. Center: A military decision-making team commonly found in darkened rooms associated with multi-hued lights and with brightly lit screens organized around the human decision-makers who are increasingly aided by artificial intelligence (AI). Right: A human–autonomy team (HAT) signified by the two robots, one at the lower left and the second climbing in the center of the right-hand image, both performing as part of a recovery search team after a weather disaster, closely watched by an "in-the-loop" human operator or observer

leadership, control, and communication meaningfully affect human resources excellence, whereas mutual support does not appear to have a meaningful effect on human resources excellence.

To provide more detail for the study by Cooke (2015), the members of a team make decisions and assess situations together as a team. In years past, the cognition behind these activities was attributed to the knowledge held by the individuals participating in the team as a unit and distributed across the team. That is, based on the perspectives prevalent at that time, smarter individuals with similar knowledge should have led to smarter teams. In contrast, however, Cooke's view, developed from years of empirical work, is that team cognition exists in the interactions experienced by the team, a rich context that must be measured not at the individual levels of a team's members where the data are commonly collected one-by-one, but at the level of the team as a whole where the data must be collected from the team as a whole. This very different approach has major implications for how these effects are measured, understood, and improved.

Based on years of study of all-human teams and observations of teams in synthetic environments (including Remotely Piloted Aircraft System ground control and Noncombatant Evacuation Operation scenarios; see Fig. 4.2, which is discussed in more detail in the next section), the theory of interactive team cognition (ITC) emerged (Cooke, 2015; Cooke et al., 2013). This theory holds that interaction is key to teams, especially action-oriented teams, and that team cognition should be treated as a process, should be measured at the team level, and should be measured in context. Empirical results have indicated that team interaction is, in fact, more predictive of team effectiveness than individual performance (Duran, 2010).

Briefly, from Cooke et al. (2013), Interactive team cognition has arisen from our findings over years of research and experience that team interactions often in the form of explicit communications are the foundation of team cognition. This finding is based on several assumptions: First, team cognition is an activity, not a property of the members of a team or the team itself, and not a product of the team or its members. Second, team cognition is inextricably tied to context—change the context and the team's cognition changes as well. And, third, team cognition is best measured and studied when the team is the unit of analysis, not by summing what is collected from the individual members who constitute a team.

Interactive team cognition has implications for measuring team cognition and for intervening to improve team cognition. For instance, we have developed measures that rely heavily on interactions in the form of communication and message passing (Cooke & Gorman, 2009). With the goal of having unobtrusive measures structured for a specific context, and collected in real-time, automatically, we have relied on communication flow and the timing of the passing of pertinent information. Interventions to improve team cognition can also involve manipulating interactions. For instance, perturbation training involves blocking a particular communication channel so that team members need to explore other ways to coordinate. Perturbation training has led to the development of more adaptive teams (Gorman, Cooke, & Amazeen, 2010).

Fig. 4.2 The RPAS research testbed: RPAS-STE: remotely piloted aircraft system (ground control station) synthetic task environment. In our RPAS-STE, three human operators must interdependently coordinate their actions over headsets or text chat messages to be able to maneuver their RPA under their control to take pictures of selected ground targets based on intelligence or other requests. Clockwise from the lower right-hand image is shown a remotely piloted drone (pictured: A Northrop Grumman RQ-4 Global Hawk; it is a high-altitude, *remotely-piloted, surveillance aircraft*). At the bottom-left is an image of experimenter control stations for the RPAS-STE. At the upper-left is an image of three human operators interdependently in action. And at the upper-right is an image of an operator controlling a RPA drone

To provide more detail for the study by Cooke and Gorman (2009), the authors attempted to integrate cognitive engineering into a systems engineering process. The authors reported that it required different methods for measurement to exploit the variance often found across the social and physical environment. The new measures that they sought had to be reliable and valid, as well as not apparent to those being measured, and yet still be able to provide in real time both predictive and diagnostic information. In response, the authors developed measures of human teams to represent systems; the measures that were developed produced data based on an automatic analysis of sequential communications while the team under study was interacting. Then the authors mapped the data to metrics to measure the performance of the system, its changes over time, its processes, the coordination expended, and the situation awareness that was developed by a team as a consequence. In the final analysis, the authors concluded that this mapping offered added value to integrate the activities of other cognitive systems.

To dwell in more detail on the study by Gorman, Cooke, & Amazeen (2010), the authors reported on an experiment that contrasted three training styles that would allow them to explore the adaptability of teams. These approaches were cross-training designed to build knowledge shared across a team; a new approach, described by the authors as perturbation training, specifically designed to constrain the interactions of a team so as to help it to build the coordination skills that a team would need during unexpected changes in a task environment; and with the contrast to the first two groups to be provided by a more traditional approach designed simply to train a team on the procedures of a task taught to the members of a team individually. Their subjects were 26 teams assigned with the task of flying nine missions win the RPAS-STE (see Fig. 4.3) but with only three critical missions dedicated to testing the ability of the teams to adapt to the novel conditions presented during the studies, measured by each team's response times and their shared team knowledge. Subsequently, the authors found that procedural training led to the poorest adaptive outcome; that for two of the three critical test missions, perturbation training outperformed all teams; and that cross-training improved the knowledge shared by a team, but for only one of the critical missions tested. The authors concluded overall, however, that perturbation training improved coordination among the teams the best, that it could lead to more well-trained and better-adapted teams, and that the experiences a team learns even in simulation training should be able to transfer to the real-world and novel situations.

Fig. 4.3   A Remotely Piloted Aircraft System (RPAS) ground control station can be located almost anywhere, but principally on the ground or on a ship. Here screenshots from the Cognitive Engineering Research on Team Tasks (CERTT) RPAS Synthetic Task Environment (STE) are provided: (Left) The left-hand screen image is an image from a screenshot of a Payload Operator's station and what is commonly seen in a real-time video in its upper-right portion; the Payload Operator controls the various camera settings, takes photos of selected objects or targets, and monitors the different camera systems. (Center) A screenshot of an image from the Data Exploiter Mission Planning Controller's (DEMPC) work station is shown; the DEMPC is the navigator, mission planner, and route planner from target to target. (Right) A screenshot taken of an image from the Air Vehicle Operator work station where the controls for the RPA's airspeed, heading, altitude, and air vehicle systems are maintained and monitored

4.2 Synthetic Teammates

The main purpose of the Synthetic Teammate Project (Ball, Myers, Heiberg, Cooke, Matessa & Freiman, 2009; see Fig. 4.5) was to develop the language that would be needed to enable tasks for synthetic agents capable to perform work sufficiently well to be integrated into simulations that would permit human-autonomous team training. The goal was to fulfill this achievement without harming the team training necessary for human teams to accomplish their missions. To meet this lofty goal, the synthetic agents had to be designed to match or to be capable of closely matching the human behavior a synthetic agent was to replace, to become cognitively plausible, yet to be functional synthetic teammates. For this to be successful, the Synthetic Teammate would have to emulate, understand, and utilize human language relevant to the situations and training of human teammate it would replace; if successful, the Synthetic Teammate would then be integrated into team training simulations to constrain the system it would fit into, namely, the behaviors it would perform would have to be human-like ones rather than purely algorithmic or the optimum solutions that might ignore such constraints, making the results obtained to fit the context at hand, not an idealized context. In a given situation with a specific task to perform, the Synthetic Teammate had to not only act like a human would act for a given situation (context) but also chat with other humans in a human way by comprehending their chat messages and to generate appropriate chats in its replies. Before its implementation of a specific role, it had to be validated. For the Synthetic Teammate, initially, the first application was to create an agent that could replace a pilot performing the functions of flying an RPA. Should this application be successful, it was planned that the Synthetic Teammate would be applied in a simulation as part of a three-person team (i.e., PLO Photographer, AVO Pilot, and DEMPC Navigator; see Fig. 4.4).

In summarizing what was desired, the Synthetic Teammate Project was designed to demonstrate "cognitively plausible" agents capable of performing complex tasks and yet able to interact with human teammates in natural language environments. These Synthetic Teammate Agents had to be designed to be able to provide effective team training at any time and anywhere around the world, specifically for Department of Defense (DoD) relevant, complex, and dynamic environments. The Synthetic Teammate Project had to be able to facilitate the transitions to new DoD applications wherever needed. Moreover, the Synthetic Teammate Project had to be able to take cognitive modeling to the level of functional systems operated alongside and integrated with human operators.

One of the goals of the Synthetic Teammate Project was to validate it to be both functional and cognitively plausible (Ball, Myers, Heiberg, Cooke, Matessa & Freiman, 2009). Due to its complexity, a considerable challenge, it was considered too impractical to validate all of its ACT-R subsystems, Instead, key and relevant behaviors were selected to be scrutinized and to be tested for empirical validation. First, we wanted to show as a pilot (the AVO) that the Synthetic Teammate could conduct the task as well as its human counterparts. Second, we wanted to contrast

Sender	Sent	Message
DEMPC	517.22	the speed restriction for f-area is from 150 to 200.
PLO	530.16	good photo. go on.
PLO	572.02	go to next waypoint.
DEMPC	633.1	the next waypoint is prk. it is entry.
AVO	736.63	What is the effective radius for oak?
AVO	747.35	What is the next point after prk?
DEMPC	768.78	no effective radius for oak.
DEMPC	803.77	the next waypoint is s-ste. it is target. the altitude restriction is from 3000 to 3100.
AVO	843.41	What is the next point after s-ste?
DEMPC	924.9	the speed restriction for s-ste is from 300 to 350.
DEMPC	982.94	the next waypoint is m-ste. it is target.
DEMPC	1123.08	the next waypoint is m-ste.

Fig. 4.4 A Synthetic Teammate Demonstration System (installed at Wright Patterson Air Force Base, Dayton, OH; see Ball, Myers, Heiberg, Cooke, Matessa & Freiman, 2009). Results: The largest cognitive model built-in ACT-R. In ACT-R, it had 2459 Productions and 57,949 Declarative Memory chunks. Among the largest cognitive models built in any cognitive architecture at the time, it had five major components. By computer science standards, it was a very large program. (Left image) Facing the human operator, at the upper left, a computer screen-shot of the images seen is those of the CERTT Consoles (i.e., the Navigator; Photographer; Pilot). At the bottom left facing the human operator is shown the text messaging subsystem. At the upper right top and bottom, screenshots are shown of the Synthetic Teammate. (Right image) To the right is a series of actual texts captured between the human operators and the Synthetic Teammate (highlighted in yellow) as it communicated with its human teammates

its ability to "push" and "pull" information with similar data collected for human teams. In this validation attempt, we were mindful that the evidence of similarity in the two different data streams was in and of itself insufficient; that is, the Synthetic Teammate had to be able to demonstrate to its teammates that it was able to function as a teammate under all of the constraints that that implied for human teammates as well.

McNeese et al. (2018) had the goal of comparing three different configurations of teams with the aim of improving their understanding of human–autonomy teaming (HAT). They first looked into the extensive literature that existed on human-automation interaction. Despite this rather large literature, they begin with the notion that very little was known at the time about a HAT for situations in which humans and autonomous agents coordinated and interacted together as a unit. Thus, the purpose of this research was to begin to explore the implications of these previously unexplored interactions and their effects on a team and its autonomy. The context for their laboratory studies was the CERTT RPAS STE. In that context, the authors considered three types of teams: a synthetic team with the pilot as the synthetic teammate; a control team with the pilot as an inexperienced human participant; and an experimenter team in which an experimenter served as an experienced pilot. Ten teams were run in each experimental condition. The authors measured team performance, target processing skills, the situation awareness of the teams, and their verbal behaviors were also assessed. Experimenter teams performed the best overall, followed

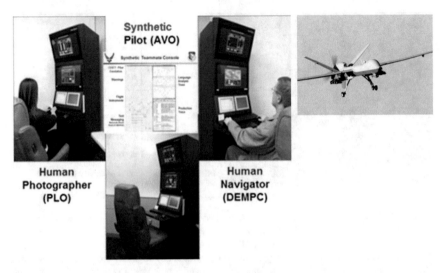

Fig. 4.5 An autonomous agent as a collaborator on a heterogeneous team (i.e., the role and nature of the agent) that operates by flying a Remotely Piloted Aircraft (RPA) to allow the team's human photographer to take reconnaissance photos. The human photographer (PLO) and human navigator (DEMPC) have been kept in the same roles in this simulated RPAS as they held in Fig. 4.3. The air vehicle operator was an ACT-R cognitive model. By introducing the Synthetic Pilot, several implications arise regarding Interactive Team Cognition (ITC) for the Synthetic Teammate: First, the interaction goes well beyond language understanding and generation. Second, coordination among team members is central to this task; timely and adaptive passing of information among team members is affected by what the Synthetic Teammate can or cannot perform. Third, humans sometimes display subtle coordination behaviors that may be absent in or conveyed by the synthetic teammate, or even not understood by the synthetic teammate. And fourth, the failures of the synthetic teammate will highlight the requisite coordination behaviors, which we have found that a good teammate performs

by synthetic and the all-human control teams, which performed equally well, except that the synthetic teams processed targets least well. The authors were heartened by the performance of the synthetic agent teams, concluding that the potential existed so that one day in the future they may be able to replace a human teammate, but they concluded that for now, for these agents to perform satisfactorily in the field today, the science of autonomy had to improve significantly. The authors also concluded that their results advanced our understanding of what autonomy has to achieve to be able to replace a human teammate (see more below and Fig. 4.5).

As Cooke and her colleagues have established, interaction proved to be critical in perturbation training. Similarly, when an AI agent or "Synthetic Teammate" is included on a three-agent team (see Fig. 4.5), interaction also proves to be critical (McNeese et al., 2018). The synthetic teammate turned out not to be a good team player, as it failed to anticipate the information needs of its fellow human teammates. That is, it performed its task of piloting the air vehicle well but did not provide the human team members (navigator and sensor operator) with information in a timely manner or even ahead of time. Humans do this naturally and get better at it as they practice the task. Interestingly, the human team members "entrained" or stopped anticipating the needs of others on the team, as if modeling the synthetic teammate. Thus, even though the synthetic teammate was pretty good at its own taskwork, it was not effective at teamwork, resulting in a gradual decline of teamwork by the entire team.

With more detail from Demir et al. (2018), the authors brought new insights into the study of the relations at the global level between the dynamics of teams and their performance at the system level. Mindful of their approach, they reviewed the literature in an attempt to identify the characteristics of the dynamics of teams and the performance of teams. Specifically, they applied methods from non-linear dynamical systems to the communication and coordination behaviors in two different studies of teams. The first was an application to human-synthetic agent teams in a Remotely-Piloted Aircraft Systems (RPAS) simulated task environment; and the second was for human-dyads in a simulated victim locator "Minecraft" task environment. The authors discovered an inverted U-shaped model from which they were able to relate the coordination of teams and the performance of teams. For the human–autonomy teams (HAT), they found that these HATs were more rigid than the human teams, the latter being the least stable; and that extreme low and high stability were associated with poor team performance. Based on their results, the authors hypothesized going forward that training helped to stabilize teams, reaching an optimal level of stability and flexibility; and they also predicted that as autonomous agents improved, HATs would tend to reach a moderate level of stability (meta-stability) being sought by all-human teams.

Examining team dynamics has given us a view into the communication dynamics of the team which for us represents team cognition (Gorman, Amazeen, & Cooke, 2010a, 2010b). Also, extending this system view beyond the three agents to the vehicle, controls, and environment in which they act, we have demonstrated how signals from these various components of the system can be observed over time. Given a perturbation, then one can observe changes in particular system components, followed by others. These patterns provide an indication of system interdependencies and open many possibilities for understanding not only teams but also system complexity (Gorman et al., 2019). It is intriguing to consider using a system's time to adapt to a perturbation and then to return to a resting place as an index of context-free team effectiveness.

From Demir, McNeese, and Cooke (2019), the authors focused on two topics. First, the authors wanted to better grasp the evolution of human–autonomy teams (HAT) while working in a Remotely Piloted Aircraft Systems (RPAS) task context. In addition, the authors wanted to explore how HATs reacted to three modes of failure over time, specifically, under automation failures, autonomy failures, and a cyber-attack. The authors summarized the results of their recent three experiments with team interactions by a HAT performing in an RPAS operating in a dynamic context over time. In the first two of these three experiments with three-member teams, by comparing HATs with all-human teams, the authors summarized the findings related to team member interaction. For the third experiment, which extended beyond the first two experiments, the authors investigated the evolution of a HAT when it was faced with three types of failures during the performance of its tasks. In these experiments, they applied the theory of interactive team cognition and, by focusing measures on team interactions and temporal dynamics, they found that their results were consistent with the theory of interactive team cognition (ITC). The authors applied Joint Recurrence Quantification Analysis to the communication flows across the three experiments. Of particular interest, regarding team evolution was the idea of entrainment, namely that one team member who happened to be the pilot, both as an agent and as a human, over time can affect the other teammates, specifically their communication behaviors, their coordination behaviors, and the team's performance (also, see the discussion above regarding Demir et al., 2018). In the first two studies, the synthetic teams were passive agents that led to very stable and rigid coordination compared with the all-human teams, which were less stable. In comparison, experimenter teams showed meta-stable coordination, coordination that was neither rigid nor unstable, performing better than the rigid and unstable teams during the dynamic task. For comparison, in the third experiment, the teams were metastable, which helped them to overcome all three types of failures. In sum, these findings help to ensure three potential future needs for effective HATs. First, training autonomous agents on teamwork principles so that they understand the tasks to be performed and the roles of the teammates. Second, human-centered machine learning designs must be brought to bear on synthetic agents to better understand human behavior and human needs. Third, and finally for then, human members must be trained to communicate to address the Natural Language Processing limitations of synthetic agents, or, alternatively, a new human–autonomy language needs to be developed.

To summarize the results of the validation study, first, the synthetic teams *performed as well* as did the control teams, but the synthetic teams had difficulties when coordinating and processing targets efficiently; in general, they showed a failure to anticipate what was needed in a given situation. Second, we established that a *synthetic teammate* can impact a team's ability to coordinate and to perform, which we described as "entrainment." Third, to compare with our second finding, we introduced an *experimenter condition, which then* demonstrated how a teammate who excels at coordination can elevate the coordination of a whole team. And fourth, we established that compared with when conditions were nominal, coordination became even more important in off-nominal conditions.

4.3   HAT Findings and Their Implications for Human Teams

For a doctoral thesis, Hinski (2017) reported that, according to the American Heart Association (AHA), there were approximately 200,000 annual in-hospital cardiac arrests (IHCA) along with low rates of survival of about 22% to discharge. To counter this poor survival rate, AHA joined in a consensus statement with the Institute of Medicine (IOM) to recommend programs to train cardiac arrest teams, known colloquially as code teams. Traditionally, health care was commonly administered in a team format, however, traditional health care training was taught at the individual level, creating rigid habits ingrained at the individual level that were often counterproductive in teams, leading to poor team performance when the situation required highly functioning teams. Despite the need, many obstacles to the training of code-blue resuscitation teams at the team level were in the way, factors like logistics, the coordination of a team's personnel, the time available to train amidst the busy schedules of team members, and financial barriers that made training in teams a hindrance (see Fig. 4.6). Inspired by findings in the Experimenter condition of the RPAS Synthetic Teammate evaluation experiment, Hinski followed a three-step process: first, a metric was developed to evaluate the performance of code-blue teams; second, a communications model was developed that captured a team's and the leaders' communications during a code-blue resuscitation; and third, a focus was placed on the code team leader's (CTL) performance using the model of communications that had been developed. With these conceptual and methodological approaches gained from the interdisciplinary science of teams, Hinski was able to apply the results to a broad vision of improving IHCA events, especially for code-blue resuscitations (see Table 4.1).

The control group of untrained code leaders and the trained code team leaders were similar in many respects. Only one control group and only one group with a trained leader asked for the patient's code status. This result might have been due to the simulation, which involved a code response, however, code-blue teams must know and be able to communicate the status of a patient's code before beginning a resuscitation attempt. The team members had considerable knowledge (seven of eight code team leaders were internal medicine physicians), but only one leader had previous formal team training. For purposes of comparison, the control and trained team leaders were as evenly matched as possible. Errors in performance were observed against guidelines for when the first shock must be delivered to the simulated "patient" within 2 minutes of identifying a shockable rhythm. Those and other common errors made by the two groups during SBCEs are illustrated and compared in the next figure (see Fig. 4.7). Despite the brevity of the training, a clear

Mock Code Blue Experiment

Fig. 4.6 Applying coordination coaching to code-blue resuscitation. A code-blue team participating in a mock code-blue resuscitation (Hinski, 2017)

Table 4.1 From Hinski (2017), an intensivist code that code team leaders (CTL) studied based on the (ICT) communication model for 5–10 min prior to receiving a Simulated Code-Blue Event (SCBE) as part of Advanced Cardiac Life Support (ACLS) training

Arrival to code	Introduces self as the code team leader (CTL)
Contingency	IF: Code RN does not immediately give the CTL a brief history, code status, and confirm advanced monitoring is established THEN: CTL must directly ask the Code RN for the information
Within 30 s of arrival to code	Asks about ABCs (airway, breathing, circulation) IF: No one person is performing CPR or performing bag-mask ventilating upon arrival of CTL THEN: CTL must direct code team member to immediately perform CPR and the respiratory therapist (RT) to bag the patient
Once monitoring is established	Asks for ACLS therapies as indicated IF: Medication or shock delivery is delayed more than 10 s after identification of rhythm THEN: CTL must directly ask the pharmacist or RN to deliver the meds and/or shock
Constant feedback	Asks if there are any problems, so CTL can troubleshoot or delegate task to another person, keeps the team on task, should be in SBAR format (situation-background-assessment-recommendation)
Contingency	IF: Code team does not clarify ROSC (resuscitation)/stabilization of ABCs or clinical worsening THEN: CTL must clarify disposition (i.e., transfer to ICU, need for more advanced therapies, discontinuation of efforts, etc.)

CODE TEAM ERRORS

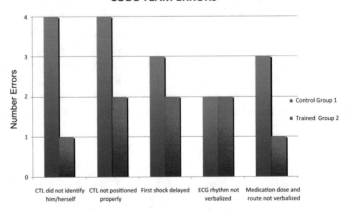

Fig. 4.7 From Hinski (2017), common errors committed after the Simulated Code-Blue Event (SCBE) training compared with a control group and during an SCBE run for both groups

difference is seen between the trained groups of SCBE leaders versus the control group.

In the medical field today, the knowledge held by the individual members of a team is still considered to be an important part of an effective team's performance, but interactive team cognition (ITC; Cooke et al., 2013) implies that training a team as a team must also be considered when attempting to improve a team's performance. Hinski concluded that training strategies need to focus on how the team functions as a unit and how it performs as a unit, independently of the combined knowledge held by the individual members of a team. The development of the ITC communication model allowed for the development of a series of training steps that could be applied to the entire resuscitation team through the prompts from a trained code team leader of the resuscitation team. When ITC "coordination coaching" was applied to the training for a simulated code-blue event (SCBE), which led us to provide code team members with richer feedback on their team's performance, to generate quantitative assessments of the value of their SCBE practice, and to make simulated training exercises a more efficient training tool for their team as a unit. The ultimate aim to build these high-performing code teams is, of course, to improve their patient outcomes following a cardiac arrest. In Hinksi's study, the trained code team leader teams demonstrated superior performance compared with the control teams even despite only an average of 26 min spent on training with the ITC communication model. Despite the limits accrued to the hospital environment, which limited the sample size considerably, the time spent to train the medical team leaders for SCBEs was the very minimum amount of time compared with how much time it would take to train an entire team for SCBEs. While the data were limited in this study, nonetheless, it offered an optimistic view of what this strategy could offer in the future given the reduced training time needed for team performance improvement. This type of training strategy should be studied in the future with larger groups of trainees.

Overall, we find that there is much more to team effectiveness than having the right teammates on the team with the right skills and abilities. The teammates need to be able to navigate the team interdependencies in adaptive and resilient ways. Effective teams learn to do this over time. AI agents need to also have this ability and without it, they may be a disruptive force to the system that is a team. More specifically, by measuring at the unit level of the team, we have found that as teams acquire experience, the team's performance improves, its interactions improve, but a team's individual or collective knowledge does not improve.

4.4   Conclusions and Future Work

For our team's next steps, we plan to more and more take team performance measurements out of the laboratory. We have established ground truth in the laboratory, which we can use to measure outcomes against. In the laboratory, team performance is measured as an outcome and demonstrates that an effective team has a positive outcome. Away from the laboratory, however, for an infinite number of reasons, ground truth may be hidden, obscured, or uncertain (e.g., cyber teams, sports teams, military and civilian intelligence teams, RPAS teams, and even urban search and rescue teams). Research, for example, conducted by a science team may run afoul of unforeseen circumstances, such as the COVID-19 pandemic that has shut down numerous experiments across the USA and around the world (e.g., Chen, 2020). Thus, outside the laboratory, the outcomes may not be obvious or effective, even for Code-Blue Resuscitations. And yet, taking teams seriously indicates from our research that effective teams are adaptive and resilient. Adaptive teams are those that respond quickly to perturbations. In contrast, resilient teams are those that bounce back quickly from perturbations.

We not only want to take human teams seriously, but we also want to take human autonomous teams seriously. Based our my research, my students' research, and the research of my collaborators, there are five conclusions that can be drawn at this time and applied to human autonomous teams: First, team members have different roles and responsibilities; autonomous teammates should not replicate humans. Second, for effective teams, each human team member understands that each member of a team has a different role and responsibility while each must avoid team member role confusion yet still be able to back up each other when it becomes necessary; autonomous teammates must be able to understand this as well as the tasks of the whole team. Third, implicit communication being critical to the effective team performance of human teams, effective human-autonomous teams must train sufficiently well enough to be able to *share knowledge* about their team goals and their experiences of context changes to facilitate coordination and implicit communication in all contexts. Fourth, the most effective human teams have team members who are interdependent with each other and are thus able to *interact and communicate interdependently* even when direct communication is not possible; human-autonomous teams must also be able to communicate even if it is in a communication model other than natural language. Fifth, finally, for now, *interpersonal trust* among the best human teams is important to the humans on these teams; by extension, human–autonomy teams need to be able to explain and to be explicable to each other.

References

Ball, J., Myers, C., Heiberg, A., Cooke, N., Matessa, M. & Freiman, M. (2009). The synthetic team-mate project, in *The Proceedings of the 18th Conference on Behavior Representation, Modeling and Simulation, Sundance, UT*, 31 March–2 April 2009 [paper: 09-BRIMS-018, 73–80].

Chen, J. (2020). Covid-19 has shuttered scientific labs: It could put a generation of researchers at risk. *Stat News*. Retrieved June 28, 2020, from https://www.statnews.com/2020/05/04/corona virus-lab-shutdowns-impact-on-scientists-research-delays/.

Cooke, N. J. (2015). Team cognition as interaction. *Current Directions in Psychological Science, 34*, 415–419.

Cooke, N. J., & Gorman, J. C. (2009). Interaction-based measures of cognitive systems. *Journal of Cognitive Engineering and Decision Making: Special Section on: Integrating Cognitive*

Engineering in the Systems Engineering Process: Opportunities, Challenges and Emerging Approaches, 3, 27–46.

Cooke, N. J., Gorman, J. C., Myers, C. W., & Duran, J. L. (2013). Interactive team cognition. *Cognitive Science, 37,* 255–285. https://doi.org/10.1111/cogs.12009

Cooke, N. J., & Hilton, M. L. (Eds.). (2015). *Enhancing the effectiveness of team science. Authors: Committee on the science of team science; Board on behavioral, cognitive, and sensory sciences; Division of behavioral and social sciences and education; National research council.* National Academies Press.

Demir, M., Cooke, N. J., & Amazeen, P. G. (2018). A conceptual model of team dynamical behaviors and performance in human-autonomy teaming. *Cognitive Systems Research, 52,* 497–507. https://doi.org/10.1016/j.cogsys.2018.07.029

Demir, M., McNeese, N. J. & Cooke, N. J. (2019). The evolution of human-autonomy teams in remotely piloted aircraft systems operations. *Frontiers in Communication.* Retrieved June 11, 2020, from https://doi.org/10.3389/fcomm.2019.00050.

Duran, J. (2010). Are teams equal to the sum of their members? An empirical test. M.S. Thesis, Arizona State University.

Gorman, J. C., Amazeen, P. G., & Cooke, N. J. (2010). Team coordination dynamics. *Nonlinear Dynamics Psychology and Life Sciences, 14,* 265–289.

Gorman, J. C., Cooke, N. J., & Amazeen, P. G. (2010). Training adaptive teams. *Human Factors, 52,* 295–307.

Gorman, J. C., Demir, M., Cooke, N., & Grimm, D. A. (2019). Evaluating sociotechnical dynamics in a simulated remotely-piloted aircraft system: A layered dynamics approach. *Ergonomics.* https://doi.org/10.1080/00140139.2018.1557750

Hinski, S (2017). Training the code team leader as a forcing function to improve overall team performance during simulated code blue events. Ph.D. thesis, Human Systems Engineering, Arizona State University. Retrieved June 28, 2020, from https://repository.asu.edu/attachments/194035/content/Hinski_asu_0010E_17454.pdf.

Jones, E. E. (1998). Major developments in five decades of social psychology. In D. T. Gilbert, S. T. Fiske, & G. Lindzey (Eds.), *The handbook of social psychology* (Vol. I, pp. 3–57). McGraw-Hill.

McNeese, N. J., Demir, M., Cooke, N. J., & Myers, C. (2018). Teaming with a synthetic teammate: Insights into human-autonomy teaming. *Human Factors, 60,* 262–273. https://doi.org/10.1177/0018720817743223

Salas, E., Dickinson, T. L., Converse, S. A., & Tannenbaum, S. I. (1992). Toward an understanding of team performance and training. In R. W. Swezey & E. Salas (Eds.), *Teams: Their training and performance* (pp. 3–29). Ablex.

Chapter 5
Toward System Theoretical Foundations for Human–Autonomy Teams

Marc Steinberg

Abstract Both human–autonomy teaming, specifically, and intelligent autonomous systems, more generally, raise new challenges in considering how best to specify, model, design, and verify correctness at a system level. Also important are extending this to monitoring and repairing systems in real time and over lifetimes to detect problems and restore desired properties when they are lost. Systems engineering methods that address these issues are typically based around a level of modeling that involves a broader focus on the life cycle of the system and much higher levels of abstraction and decomposition than some common ones used in disciplines concerned with the design and development of individual elements of intelligent autonomous systems. Nonetheless, many of the disciplines associated with autonomy do have reasons for exploring higher level abstractions, models, and ways of decomposing problems. Some of these may match well or be useful inspirations for systems engineering and related problems like system safety and human system integration. This chapter will provide a sampling of perspectives across scientific fields such as biology, neuroscience, economics/game theory, and psychology, methods for developing and accessing complex socio-technical systems from human factors and organizational psychology, and methods for engineering teams from computer science, robotics, and engineering. Areas of coverage will include considerations of team organizational structure, allocation of roles, functions, and responsibilities, theories for how teammates can work together on tasks, teaming over longer time durations, and formally modeling and composing complex human–machine systems.

5.1 Introduction

Bringing system-level theoretical foundations to the design and development of intelligent autonomous systems has many challenges even without incorporating human–machine teaming into the mix. This set of challenges includes how to specify requirements, measure, and formally model the different elements of autonomous systems

M. Steinberg (✉)
Office of Naval Research, Arlington, USA
e-mail: marc.steinberg@navy.mil

and their cyber, physical, and social interactions at an appropriate level of abstraction. Beyond that are many open questions about how to systematically design, compose, analyze, test, and develop life cycle processes to assure requirements are met, operational constraints are followed, the end user's needs are supported, and no undesirable emergent properties are likely to occur between intelligent, adaptive, and learning components, more traditional forms of automation, and the people and hardware that together make up an entire system. Moving also to Human–Autonomy Teams (HAT) creates substantial additional new challenges compared with a more traditional division of human and machine roles, responsibilities, and functions (Klien et al., 2004; Groom & Nass, 2007; Shah & Breazeal, 2010; Cooke et al., 2013; Gao et al., 2016; Endsley, 2017; McNeese et al., 2018; Johnson & Vera, 2019). HAT may involve new types of organizational structures in which multiple humans dynamically interact with multiple autonomous systems outside of fixed control hierarchies and with dynamically changing roles. Interaction between teammates may involve multi-modal tiered strategies with both verbal and non-verbal and explicit and implicit communications. Effective joint communication, attention, and action may depend on the ability to recognize individual capabilities, activities, and status, and infer other team members' intent, beliefs, knowledge, and plans. Team activities may not be limited to just real-time task performance but include also the ability to jointly train, rehearse, plan, and make a priori agreements prior to performing work together, and to assess performance and improve together afterward. While this might appear a daunting list of capabilities to achieve in machines, it is not necessary that HAT operates on exactly the same principles as high functioning human teams that exhibit these characteristics. A much broader spectrum of group types is possible that could be considered teams and would be more plausible to engineer in the near future. Furthermore, the true value of HAT may lie in exploiting the heterogeneity between humans and machines to create entirely new types of organizations rather than trying to mimic fully human ones or force humans into the rigid frameworks of multi-agent machine systems. In this spirit, a human–autonomy team will be categorized in this chapter as requiring only the following properties:

(1)   Teams are set up to achieve a common goal or goals that are believed achievable in a bounded period of time. It is not required that every member has the same depth of understanding of the goal. This goal would be very challenging for machines on many complex, real-world problems, and is not the case for teams of humans and working animals or teams of human adults and children that may provide useful inspiration for the degree of heterogeneity to be found in HAT. As well, this is consistent with broader findings in the human team literature, particularly for teams that are heterogeneous or that have a larger number of members (Cooke et al., 2013).

(2)   Teams exploit role specialization and have bi-directional interdependencies between teammates. Teaming interdependencies are not predominantly one way, such as in human supervisory control of autonomy. Methods that focus primarily on decomposing and allocating loosely coupled tasks between

humans and machines to ensure task completion with non-interference between agents would also not be sufficient on their own to be considered teaming.

(3) Individual identities, skills, and capabilities of teammates matter. This "naming" allows for unique relationships or associations to be formed between particular pairings or subsets of teammates along with a joint understanding of which individuals have which responsibilities. This differs from multi-agent forms of organization in which individual agents can be anonymous, such as biologically inspired collective behaviors (Steinberg, 2011), and call center or service-oriented models with a pool of autonomous systems (Lewis et al., 2011).

Much research to date on human–autonomy teams has focused narrowly on relatively small teams performing short-time duration tasks. Nonetheless, a system perspective must also consider aspects such as the qualifications, selection, and training of both machine and human members of the team, the ability for the team to jointly do pre-task planning, agreements, and rehearsal, and post-task assessment, maintenance, and improvement. Also, critical for some applications will be processed to ensure the health and safety of human team members and bystanders. To accomplish even just this for HAT goes beyond current system theories or the methods of any particular discipline. Thus, it makes sense to consider foundations from as broad a perspective as possible. This chapter will consider a sampling of perspectives across scientific fields such as biology, neuroscience, economics/game theory, and psychology, methods for developing and accessing complex socio-technical systems from human factors and organizational psychology, and methods for engineering teams from computer science, robotics, and engineering.

5.2 Organizational Structure and Role/Function Allocation

Groups of humans and working social animals have particular relevance for human–autonomy teaming (HAT) because they encompass some of the same degree of extreme heterogeneity of physical, sensing, communication, and cognitive abilities (Phillips et al., 2016). Additionally, recent animal cognition research has focused on the extent to which different animal species may excel at solving specific niches of cognitive problems under particular ecological constraints while being rather poor at others (Rogers & Kaplan, 2012). For example, there is an increasing body of evidence on the impressive social cognitive abilities, dogs can use to solve problems jointly with humans, while simultaneously finding dogs can be much less capable of individually solving other classes of cognitive problems (Hare & Woods, 2013). This situation has similarities to the state of the art of today's autonomous systems and may provide both an inspiration for teaming architectures and an effective metaphor for human interaction with autonomous teammates. There are a number of systemic frameworks from the animal literature that can be considered for HAT including different subordinate strategies (Sun et al., 2010), mutualism (Madden et al., 2010), or reciprocal altruism and association strengths between individuals (Haque & Egerstedt, 2009). A dominance framework, for example, can provide a principle framework to allow for more freedom of action by human teammates, while limiting machine teammates to act within constraints imposed by human plans and actions. From an engineering perspective, this can be considered a satisficing type of solution. The constraints imposed by dominance relationships between team members ensure some degree of non-interference and also can substantially simplify computationally intractable group coordination problems, so they can be solved even for complex groups at scale. For example, adopting a dominance like structure has enabled the solution of large-scale group problems with Decentralized Partially Observable Markov Decision Processes (Sun et al., 2010), and several approaches for motion planning with a large number of systems in complex environments have achieved scalability with related types of prioritizations and constraints (Herbert et al., 2017). There also have been a number of successes in showing how particular architectures relate to the degree of optimality, robustness, resilience, or the best or worst possible cases (Ramaswamy et al., 2019).

A different set of methods can be drawn from human factors. For example, in an assessment of the literature, Roth et al. (2019) identified a four-stage process for role allocation in HAT to analyze operational and task demands, consider ways of distributing work across human and machine team members, examine interdependencies in both nominal and off-nominal conditions, and explore the trade space of options with different potential tools. One of the particular tools that had success at such novel problem domains is Cognitive Work Analysis (CWA) (Vicente, 1999). CWA has been successfully applied to two related classes of problems of human supervisory control of autonomous teams in which the human is not a teammate (Linegang et al., 2006; Hoffman, 2008), and to the development of assistive technologies for human teams in fields like healthcare and aviation in which the automation is not a teammate (Ashoori & Burns, 2013). A strength of CWA for novel systems is that it is based on an ecological theory in which human/machine activity and interaction can be considered from the perspective of constraints on what is and is not possible in the work environment rather than starting with stronger assumptions on how the work will be done. Thus, CWA has been particularly effective on problems that are dominated by persistent fundamental constraints of physics or information flow. CWA could also be effective for HAT problems with similar characteristics. However, there is only a limited body of work on extending the abstractions involved to team problems even in the fully human case. Furthermore, there are many challenges in applying this kind of method, and some prior work has found that results do not sufficiently encompass what is enabled by the new technological options. Another method of considering interdependencies that was developed more specifically for HAT problems is Co-Active Design (Johnson et al., 2014).

Similar to human factors, human–robotic interaction can provide a rich set of theories for human–autonomy coordination and adaptation that take into account the realities of implementing methods on real autonomous systems. Discussions of human–robot and human–autonomy teams sometimes proceed from the assumption that the machine team members will be something like a peer. However, realistically, many machine teammates in the next few decades will probably still require some degree of human supervision and support. This need may be due to either technological limitations or interrelated issues such as laws, regulations, organizational policies, ethical concerns, societal norms, and professional standards of due diligence. Thus, some system frameworks developed for non-team interactions with robotic and autonomous systems will still have validity. For example, an important framework for considering human–robotic interaction is the span of control (Crandall et al., 2005). Historically, the focus of this range has been on matching the human capacity to the tempo and quantity of "servicing" that the machines require. In one approach, this is based around a neglected time representing the amount of time a robot can operate safely and effectively or be trusted to do so without human intervention. In moving from an operator to a teammate, this framework may need to consider a metaphor more like a human sports team or a medical team. A given size and complexity of team might require a certain number of on-field leaders, and off-field coaches, trainers, and health and safety monitors. A converse of neglect time is neglect benevolence (Walker et al., 2012). Neglect benevolence recognizes that there are circumstances in which a lower bandwidth of interaction between some group members would be beneficial for team performance, including from human supervisors to machines.

5.3   Working Together on Tasks

Effective autonomous teammates may require very different capabilities depending on features of the team organization and task. Some autonomous teammates may be effective mainly by exploiting detailed knowledge of the group tasks while others may require more general types of cognitive abilities. An example of a general capability that may be foundational for achieving higher performing teams in some circumstances is Theory of Mind (ToM). ToM is the ability to infer that others have different knowledge, beliefs, desires, and intentions than one's self. Neuroscience research on simultaneous imaging of multiple brains has found connections as well with how synchronization of behavior, language, and gesture is achieved in some types of group interactions (Dumas et al., 2010). For autonomous teammates, ToM could provide principled connections between perception, perceptual attention and active sensing, intent and activity recognition, knowledge and world representation, prediction, and decision-making in groups. Theory of Mind has been shown to exist in some form in increasingly younger human children (Doherty, 2008), and there are debates on the extent to which at least rudimentary ToM occurs in non-human primates, other mammals, and even several bird species (Rogers & Kaplan, 2012). An important divergence between psychological models and robotics has been that the three main psychological theories of ToM centered on an ability to project one's own experiences and way of thinking onto others. Autonomous systems, lacking remotely comparable brains and experiences to their human teammates, instead may need to have their ToM more heavily grounded in processes of observation and learning. Thus, robotic versions of ToM have tended to focus on narrower abilities of perspective-taking, belief management with limited numbers of entities and objects, and bounded rationality that can be tailored for a particular experiment, but are difficult to scale to more realistic, open-world problems (Scassellati, 2002; Breazeal et al., 2009; Hiatt et al., 2011; Weerd et al., 2013). However, scientific research has also begun to emphasize the role of observation in the natural development of such abilities, and this opening may be an excellent opportunity to reconsider ToM as a foundational theory for HAT (Jara-Ettinger et al. (2016); Albrecht and Stone (2018)).

Another important set of theories are those for joint action/activity (Clark, 1996; Bradshaw et al., 2009) and common ground (Stubbs et al., 2007). Joint activity involves the ability to coordinate tasks with interdependencies and can depend on common ground as a kind of floor of the minimum knowledge, beliefs, and assumptions that are required to be shared and maintained between agents. This can range from direct communications between teammates to generally shared world knowledge or widely accessible broadcasts. For teams, this requires both regular updating and maintenance and the ability to recognize when it has broken down and needs to be repaired. Note that while common ground might seem to be a particularly human ability, that is not the case. For example, dogs are capable of both spontaneously picking up on human cues and on signaling themselves in ways that can support joint problem-solving with humans. Common ground via non-direct communication has connections to both the biological literature on stigmergy, in which coordination is done via changes in the environment (Steinberg, 2011), and Dynamic Epistemic Logic, which can be used to reason about changes of belief and knowledge that occur due to trustworthy announcements to a group (Lutz, 2006). There are also relationships of these concepts to game theory research on how agents adapt to each other under some degree of bounded information (Fudenberg et al., 1998). In the study of human teams, joint action models often revolve around some notion of an agreement between agents that need to be maintained along with the common ground. However, within the biological and economics/game theory literature, there are debates on the extent to which seemingly strongly coordinated activities can instead arise as the result of more decentralized decision-making (Madden et al., 2010; Young & Zamir, 2014). Common ground and joint activity have sometimes been interpreted in robotics as the kind of information and plan representations found already in robotic "world models" or on operator displays, and there are a number of methods that have been considered for different aspects of this such as information theory, Partially Observable Markov Decision Processes (POMDP), bounded rationality, and Hierarchical Task Networks (HTN) (Roth et al., 2005; Unhelkar & Shah, 2016). However, these are much broader concepts, and an important part of common ground in HAT will be bridging the divide between human and machine representations of goals, tasks, and understandings of the world and each other. Relating to joint activity in human–robotic interaction is also the idea of shared control (Mulder et al., 2015). Some shared control research has focused on very application-specific designs such as human assistance teleoperation problems. However, other research can generalize this in a more abstract way that may be a good model for some of the richer interactions that may occur in HAT. For example, one approach is to provide a systematic way for a machine teammate to estimate the quality of interactions it is having with a human relative to goal achievement and then to be able to adjust the level of interaction and allocation of its tasks to one appropriate to the circumstances (Javaremi et al., 2019). The second example of shared control uses a formal linear temporal logic approach as a way to reason about shared policies (Fu & Topcu, 2015). Other examples utilize an optimal control paradigm that recognizes differences in machine and human understanding of the problem for physical tasks and address the issue of how humans may adapt to autonomy over time (Nikolaidis et al., 2017) or take into account a distribution of potential human goals if the actual human goal is unknown (Javdani et al., 2018).

Another group of methods from human factors and organizational psychology was developed specifically for human teams. A traditional approach has been models of shared cognition such as team mental models and shared mental models (Lim & Klein, 2006; Mohammed et al., 2010). A mental model, in this case, is a representation that allows the behavior of a system to be described, explained, and predicted. This group of theories provides a way to aggregate that as an information structure across the group. Shared mental models have also been a popular idea in human–robotic interaction and related forms of AI and autonomy, but the mechanizations of these models often are narrowly tailored to particular problems compared with the versatility that is implied in the human case and often focus on awareness rather than comprehension and prediction. There are challenges as well to deal with the heterogeneity of HAT. For example, in an ad hoc team, broad knowledge held by a machine may be less likely to be available, recognized as relevant, shared, or acted upon in a timely way than if held by a human team member. The differences between human–human interactions and human–machine interactions may play a more significant role than the team's information structure. An alternative approach is Integrated Team Cognition (Cooke et al., 2013). This approach arguably has significant compatibility with engineering and computer science methods in that it takes a bottom-up, layered, dynamical system approach based on observable interactions. This approach has been applied to small human–autonomy teams with sophisticated synthetic team members based on a full cognitive architecture. Research also has included off-nominal performance, failures, and compromising of the autonomous teammate (Gorman et al., 2019; McNeese et al., 2018). Several related bottom-up methods have also shown good compatibility with engineering methods such as the use of Hidden Markov Models (Cummings et al., 2019). Other important classes of methods from human factors include theory-based approaches to situation awareness (Endsley & Garland, 2000), transparency (Chen et al., 2018), and trust (Lee & See, 2004; Hancock et al., 2011) that have been effective on related classes of problems and applied to some cases of HAT. A related concept from human–robotic interaction is that of legibility and predictability (Dragan et al., 2013). Legibility represents how well an observer could rapidly infer the system's goals from observed behavior while predictability relates to the extent that observed behavior is what would be expected given a known goal. Finally, there has recently been considerable work within the fields of AI and robotics on the explainability of different system elements including neural networks and planners (Chakraborti et al., 2020).

A final related area concerns models of emotion, affect, and motivation, and how these may vary among individuals and relate to interaction and communication among team members. There has been considerable growth in the development of cognitive and neuroscience models of the role of effect and motive in cognition and even some principled systems theories in robotics based on either psychological or neural models (Moshkina et al., 2011). However, much research in this area has focused on problems such as virtual training environments, tutoring systems, games, toys, artificial pets, and companions. Some cognitively plausible models of effect and motivation have been applied to assist robots in their ability to communicate to humans in social domains. However, this research has often focused on the ability of the autonomous system to provide a more pleasant experience for the user, improved communications, and usability rather than taking a more functional perspective toward being an effective teammate that performs tasks with humans to achieve a common goal.

5.4 Teaming Over Longer Durations

Much research to date on human–autonomy teams has focused narrowly on relatively small teams performing short-time duration tasks. There are many open issues to extend our understanding to more complex team organizations that persist over time scales that may involve a much greater number of hours, days, months, or even years. As time durations increase, there is a need to better understand for these new HAT organizations the effect and mitigation of human limitations such as fatigue and boredom and machine limitations such as computational methods that either do not scale well to longer periods of run time or become increasingly likely to encounter a problem they cannot recover from without human assistance. At longer time scales, creating effective autonomous teammates must also consider aspects like the joint training of both machine and human members of the team; the ability for the team to jointly do pre-task planning, agreements; and rehearsal, and post-task assessment, maintenance, and improvement. At the longest time scale, it will be important to understand the dynamics of how humans and machines may adapt to each other and how this will impact trust and reliance. Human factors can provide both general frameworks to support the design, development, and analysis of complex socio-technical systems including some of the methods described above. These considerations have the advantage of encompassing a broad range of Human System Integration concerns, but they can require a great deal of care and creativity to extend to a fundamentally novel concept like a human–autonomy team (HAT). For example, joint training and rehearsal of both humans and machines have not had much study. However, there are theories that exist with regard to human training with autonomy (Zhou et al., 2019), autonomy as tutors for humans, and frameworks for interactive machine learning in which humans assist machines in learning. The latter has had some work that has considered human factors and human-centered design aspects that go beyond treating the human mainly as servicing the automation (Krening & Feigh, 2018). Joint planning also has had some work that has considered both human factors and human models within planning and risk management. An approach toward pre-task agreements that also has potential value for verification and decomposition of HAT is contract-based approaches (Benveniste et al., 2018; Nuzzo et al., 2015). At a system level, these can be used to guarantee global properties as long as each individual element abides by a set of guarantees that are rooted in local assumptions. In the event that an assumption is violated, there is research on monitoring and adapting contracts to be able to restore some guarantees in real time. This approach might seem like a very difficult method to bridge across people and machines, but some similar kinds of agreements have been successful with people. Finally, another significant area is self-assessment and prediction of proficiency and competency boundaries the ability to communicate this effectively to human teammates in terms of achievable performance over a range of operating parameters prior to starting a task, in real time while performing a task, and then afterward using knowledge of the completed task (Hutchins et al., 2015; Steinfeld & Goodrich, 2020).

5.5 Formally Modeling and Composing Complex Human–Machine Systems

While the prior sections have emphasized a human-centered focus, this section will discuss higher level specification, modeling, and verification of the broader systems in which human–autonomy teams may be embedded. Ideally, this level of abstraction should be appropriate across different stages of the system's life cycle. At design and development time, this level could be used for tradeoff analysis, verifying correctness and composability, and supporting either a correct by construction design or at least design guided by formal tools. In deployed systems, this level could be used for pre-mission and run-time validation, run-time monitoring to check if assumptions or constraints are violated, and real-time repair to restore some degree of guaranteed properties in unexpected circumstances. Over a whole life cycle, this could support monitoring, periodic recertification, and longer term maintenance, repair, and improvement. To achieve useful results at a system level, it will be important to have methods that can be automated and applied to end-to-end systems at useful scale and under realistic assumptions. These methods also will need to be tailored to different domains with different needs in terms of safety, time criticality, mission reliability and constraints, and the degree and types of human interaction that are possible or practical. Some key challenges in creating this level of system model are:

(1) Identifying the appropriate level of abstraction and meta-model for considering system-level issues. Rather than focus on lower level behaviors or states, this

representation might emphasize model abstractions such as aggregate capabilities, skills, goals, agents, and tasks. For example, a capability-based model might focus on what the system can do rather than how it can do it, what resources are required to execute that capability, and what constraints is the capability subject to (Bouchard et al., 2017, 2021). Alternatively, at a lower level, a skill might be defined as the ability to move between a particular set of pre-conditions to a particular set of post-conditions that can be specified formally (Pacheck et al., 2020). The composition of these skills would then provide something more like a broader capability. An important aspect of this level of representation is also considering how to measure similarity between different models for comparison and analysis purposes.

(2)   Developing methods to formally express properties associated with all of the different elements of the autonomous system at an appropriate level of abstraction via the desired representation types. Common types of representations to provide this more system perspective include timed and hybrid automata and various forms of temporal logic (Alur, 2015). There has been considerable progress in extending temporal logic-based methods to include real-valued parameters, probabilistic elements, uncertainty in perception and knowledge, and finite-time horizons that provide more flexible and perhaps appropriate ways to model the elements of intelligent autonomous systems (Littman et al., 2017, Elfar et al., 2020). However, it is still unclear how best to capture the relevant aspects of complex artificial intelligence algorithms, machine learning, adaptation, perception, and complex physical and social interactions with the external world in a way that yields useful results. Furthermore, there are significant tradeoffs between expressibility and scalability relative to the computational tools available for analysis, verification, and synthesis.

(3)   Establishing structural commitments within the system and between the system and external world. Ideally, this would enable composability and strong proofs of global properties across the system that could be maintained or adapted even after an individual component was replaced or changed. The idea of contracts mentioned above is one example of this idea as are methods that compose systems as graphs.

(4)   The shift from design to real-time operation and deployment enables considering a notion of autonomy "failures" during real-time operations One example of this shift would be if the system encounters a situation in which it is missing something needed in order to meet its requirements in its sets of capabilities, goals, goal selection/modification processes, cost functions, skills, behaviors, domain/task knowledge, and knowledge retrieval processes (Cox & Ram, 1999). Another example is if the system encounters a situation, in which the embodiment of these elements in the real world does not have the properties that are asserted in its models. In both cases, these are well-formulated problems to consider real-time repair to restore some degree of guarantee.

A significant challenge with this framework for human–autonomy teams particularly is in developing appropriate human models such that meaningful results are achieved when these models are used with methods for synthesis, analysis, verifi-cation, and repair (Alami et al., 2019; Kress-Gazit et al., 2020; Seshia et al., 2015). Significant research is needed on how best to formally model humans in order to get meaningful results. There have been attempts to model humans using a wide variety of engineering and computer science methods including finite state machines, process algebra, Petri-nets, queuing, Markov models, game theory, decision or behavior tress, and optical control and filtering. However, these are often better at normative, single-task focus, or "rational" behaviors and decision-making rather than being predictive of the kind of more naturalistic human behavior that would be found in real environ-ments. Nonetheless, there have been some attempts to approximate a distribution of more naturalistic behavior or individual differences using methods such as adding noise, varying parameters, or assuming a degree of "bounded rationality" or subop-timality to the above methods. Alternatively, there are human factors models that have been developed explicitly for use with formal methods, but not specifically for robotic or autonomous systems (Bolton et al., 2013). While some of these models focus on detection of problems associated with the human interface, several also have targeted system-level verification. Examples of this targeting include formal task modeling languages like the Operator Function Model (Bolton & Bass, 2017) and simplified cognitive models such as the Operator Choice Model. One benefit of these models is there has been some work on incorporating more naturalistic human behaviors such as errors. The cognitive models also provide additional insight into the causes of problems relative to particular cognitive processes.

Another significant challenge is how to represent artificial intelligence-based methods at a system level such as perception and learning. For an example of machine learning elements, there are several approaches that could be considered. One is to transform neural networks into a simpler abstraction such as a decision tree or automata (Bastani et al., 2018; Frosst & Hinton, 2017; Ivanov et al., 2019). A second possibility is to make verification part of the learning process with the goal of directing the neural network learning to have a particular set of desired properties (Anderson et al., 2020). This latter requires being able to quantify the closeness to a region with the desired properties during learning. A third approach is to ensure the desired global properties at a system level rather than at the level of the individual learning element, such as through a method like run-time shielding that checks the outputs of the learning element and changes its unsafe actions, or through related methods that can incorporate broader specification types (Gillula & Tomlin, 2012; Alshiekh et al., 2018).

5.6 Conclusions and Future Directions

Creating foundational systems theories for human–autonomy teams (HAT) raises new issues that are substantially different from those that have previously been encountered in related areas such as in the study of fully human teams or of human management and supervision of fully machine teams. One of the big challenges for the field remains developing appropriate formal models and representations at the right level of abstraction for all of the elements of the entire system. This obstacle is particularly true not only in the case of human models but also relevant to models of complex computational components and autonomous interactions with people and the environment. Nonetheless, many disciplines involved with different aspects of intelligent, autonomous systems have reasons for seeking higher level abstractions, models, and ways of decomposing problems. Some of these may match well or be useful inspirations for system engineers and related fields like system safety, and it will be important to engage these disciplines as early as possible. It will also be important to change the current perspective from an emphasis on demonstrating instances of short-duration tasks and deployments to both longitudinal studies on larger temporal scales and considering whole life cycles of these kinds of systems. Finally, there is also a need to broaden the research perspective from an emphasis on just the "user" of particular autonomous systems to considerations of the implications for whole socio-technical systems with many possibilities of different human–machine organizations including teams.

References

Alami, R., Eder, K. I., Hoffman, G., & Kress-Gazit, H. (2019). Verification and Synthesis of Human-Robot Interaction (Dagstuhl Seminar 19081). In Dagstuhl Reports (Vol. 9, No. 2). Schloss Dagstuhl-Leibniz-Zentrum fuer Informatik.

Alshiekh, M., Bloem, R., Ehlers, R., Könighofer, B., Niekum, S., & Topcu, U. (2018). Safe reinforcement learning via shielding. in *Thirty-Second AAAI Conference on Artificial Intelligence*.

Albrecht, S. V., & Stone, P. (2018). Autonomous agents modelling other agents: A comprehensive survey and open problems. *Artificial Intelligence, 258*, 66–95.

Alur, R. (2015). *Principles of cyber-physical systems*. MIT Press.

Anderson, G., Verma, A., Dillig, I., & Chaudhuri, S. (2020). Neurosymbolic Reinforcement Learning with Formally Verified Exploration. *Advances in Neural Information Processing Systems, 33*.

Ashoori, M., & Burns, C. (2013). Team cognitive work analysis: Structure and control tasks. *Journal of Cognitive Engineering and Decision Making, 7*(2), 123–140.

Bastani, O., Pu, Y., & Solar-Lezama, A. (2018). Verifiable reinforcement learning via policy extraction. In *Advances in neural information processing* systems (pp. 2494–2504).

Benveniste, A., Caillaud, B., Nickovic, D., Passerone, R., Raclet, J. B., Reinkemeier, P., & Larsen, K. G. (2018). Contracts for system design. *Foundations and Trends in Electronic Design Automation, 12*(2–3), 124–400.

Bolton, M. L., Bass, E. J., & Siminiceanu, R. I. (2013). Using formal verification to evaluate human-automation interaction: A review. *IEEE Transactions on Systems, Man, and Cybernetics: Systems, 43*(3), 488–503.

Bolton, M. L., & Bass, E. J. (2017). Enhanced operator function model (EOFM): A task analytic modeling formalism for including human behavior in the verification of complex systems. In *The handbook of formal methods in human-computer interaction* (pp. 343–377). Springer, Cham.

Bouchard, A., Tatum, R., & Horan, S. (2017). Verification of autonomous systems by capability verification composition (CVC). In *OCEANS 2017-Anchorage* (pp. 1–7). IEEE.

Bouchard, A., Tatum, R., Hartman, B., Kutzke, D. (2021). A philosophical and mathematical framework for associated problems of hierarchical verification of autonomous systems. Springer. (to appear)

Bradshaw, J. M., Feltovich, P., Johnson, M., Breedy, M., Bunch, L., Eskridge, & van Diggelen, J. (2009). From tools to teammates: Joint activity in human-agent-robot teams. In *International conference on human centered design* (pp. 935–944). Springer, Berlin, Heidelberg.

Breazeal, C., Gray, J., & Berlin, M. (2009). An embodied cognition approach to mindreading skills for socially intelligent robots. *The International Journal of Robotics Research, 28*(5), 656–680.

Chen, J. Y., Lakhmani, S. G., Stowers, K., Selkowitz, A. R., Wright, J. L., & Barnes, M. (2018). Situation awareness-based agent transparency and human-autonomy teaming effectiveness. *Theoretical Issues in Ergonomics Science, 19*(3), 259–282.

Clark, H. H. (1996). *Using language.* Cambridge University Press.

Cox, M. T., & Ram, A. (1999). Introspective multistrategy learning: On the construction of learning strategies. *Artificial Intelligence, 112*(1–2), 1–55.

Cooke, N. J., Gorman, J. C., Myers, C. W., & Duran, J. L. (2013). Interactive team cognition. *Cognitive Science, 37*(2), 255–285.

Crandall, J. W., Goodrich, M. A., Olsen, D. R., & Nielsen, C. W. (2005). Validating human-robot interaction schemes in multitasking environments. *IEEE Transactions on Systems, Man, and Cybernetics-Part a: Systems and Humans, 35*(4), 438–449.

De Weerd, H., Verbrugge, R., & Verheij, B. (2013). How much does it help to know what she knows you know? An agent-based simulation study. *Artificial Intelligence, 199*, 67–92.

Hutchins, A. R., Cummings, M. L., Draper, M., & Hughes, T. (2015). Representing autonomous systems' self-confidence through competency boundaries. In *Proceedings of the Human Factors and Ergonomics Society Annual Meeting* (Vol. 59, No. 1, pp. 279–283). Sage CA: Los Angeles, CA: SAGE Publications.

Cummings, M., Huang, L., Zhu, H., Finkelstein, D., & Wei, R. (2019). The impact of increasing autonomy on training requirements in a UAV supervisory control task. *Journal of Cognitive Engineering and Decision Making, 13*(4), 295–309.

Doherty, M. (2008). *Theory of mind: How children understand others' thoughts and feelings.* Psychology Press.

Dragan, A. D., Lee, K. C., & Srinivasa, S. S. (2013). Legibility and predictability of robot motion. In *2013 8th ACM/IEEE International Conference on Human-Robot Interaction (HRI)* (pp. 301–308). IEEE.

Dumas, G., Nadel, J., Soussignan, R., Martinerie, J., & Garnero, L. (2010). Inter-brain synchronization during social interaction. *PloS one, 5*(8).

Elfar, M., Wang, Y., & Pajic, M. (2020, October). Context-Aware Temporal Logic for Probabilistic Systems. In *International Symposium on Automated Technology for Verification and Analysis* (pp. 215–232). Springer, Cham.

Endsley, M. R., & Garland, D. J. (2000). Theoretical underpinnings of situation awareness: A critical review. *Situation Awareness Analysis and Measurement, 1*, 24.

Endsley, M. R. (2017). From here to autonomy: Lessons learned from human–automation research. *Human Factors, 59*(1), 5–27.

Frosst, N., & Hinton, G. (2017). Distilling a neural network into a soft decision tree. arXiv preprint arXiv:1711.09784.

Fu, J., & Topcu, U. (2015). Synthesis of shared autonomy policies with temporal logic specifications. *IEEE Transactions on Automation Science and Engineering, 13*(1), 7–17.

Fudenberg, D., Drew, F., Levine, D. K., & Levine, D. K. (1998). *The theory of learning in games* (Vol. 2). MIT press.

Gao, F., Cummings, M. L., & Solovey, E. (2016). Designing for robust and effective teamwork in human-agent teams. In *Robust intelligence and trust in autonomous systems* (pp. 167–190). Springer, Boston.

Gillula, J. H., & Tomlin, C. J. (2012, May). Guaranteed safe online learning via reachability: tracking a ground target using a quadrotor. In *2012 IEEE International Conference on Robotics and Automation* (pp. 2723–2730). IEEE.

Gorman, J. C., Demir, M., Cooke, N. J., & Grimm, D. A. (2019). Evaluating sociotechnical dynamics in a simulated remotely-piloted aircraft system: A layered dynamics approach. *Ergonomics, 62*(5), 629–643.

Groom, V., & Nass, C. (2007). Can robots be teammates?: Benchmarks in human–robot teams. *Interaction Studies, 8*(3), 483–500.

Hancock, P. A., Billings, D. R., Schaefer, K. E., Chen, J. Y., De Visser, E. J., & Parasuraman, R. (2011). A meta-analysis of factors affecting trust in human-robot interaction. *Human Factors, 53*(5), 517–527.

Haque, M. A., & Egerstedt, M. (2009). Coalition formation in multi-agent systems based on bottlenose dolphin alliances. In *2009 American Control Conference* (pp. 3280–3285). IEEE.

Hare, B., & Woods, V. (2013). *The genius of dogs: How dogs are smarter than you think.* Penguin.

Herbert, S. L., Chen, M., Han, S., Bansal, S., Fisac, J. F., & Tomlin, C. J. (2017, December). FaSTrack: A modular framework for fast and guaranteed safe motion planning. In 2017 IEEE 56th Annual Conference on Decision and Control (CDC) (pp. 1517–1522). IEEE.

Hiatt, L. M., Harrison, A. M., & Trafton, J. G. (2011, June). Accommodating human variability in human-robot teams through theory of mind. In *Twenty-Second International Joint Conference on Artificial Intelligence.*

Hoffman, J. D., Lee, J. D., & Seppelt, B. D. (2008). Identifying display concepts to support distributed collaboration of unmanned vehicle teams. In *Proceedings of the Human Factors and Ergonomics Society Annual Meeting* (Vol. 52, No. 5, pp. 488–492). Sage CA: Los Angeles, CA: SAGE Publications.

Ivanov, R., Weimer, J., Alur, R., Pappas, G. J., & Lee, I. (2019, April). Verisig: verifying safety properties of hybrid systems with neural network controllers. In *Proceedings of the 22nd ACM International Conference on Hybrid Systems: Computation and Control* (pp. 169–178).

Jara-Ettinger, J., Gweon, H., Schulz, L. E., & Tenenbaum, J. B. (2016). The naïve utility calculus: Computational principles underlying commonsense psychology. *Trends in Cognitive Sciences, 20*(8), 589–604.

Javaremi, M. N., Young, M., & Argall, B. D. (2019, June). Interface Operation and Implications for Shared-Control Assistive Robots. In 2019 IEEE 16th International Conference on Rehabilitation Robotics (ICORR) (pp. 232–239).

Javdani, S., Admoni, H., Pellegrinelli, S., Srinivasa, S. S., & Bagnell, J. A. (2018). Shared autonomy via hindsight optimization for teleoperation and teaming. *The International Journal of Robotics Research, 37*(7), 717–742.

Johnson, M., Bradshaw, J. M., Feltovich, P. J., Jonker, C. M., Van Riemsdijk, M. B., & Sierhuis, M. (2014). Coactive design: Designing support for interdependence in joint activity. *Journal of Human-Robot Interaction, 3*(1), 43–69.

Johnson, M., & Vera, A. (2019). No AI is an island: The case for teaming intelligence. *AI Magazine, 40*(1), 16–28.

Chakraborti, T., Sreedharan, S., & Kambhampati, S. (2020). The emerging landscape of explainable automated planning & decision making. In *Proceedings of the Twenty-Ninth International Joint Conference on Artificial Intelligence*, IJCAI-20 (pp. 4803–4811).

Klien, G., Woods, D. D., Bradshaw, J. M., Hoffman, R. R., & Feltovich, P. J. (2004). Ten challenges for making automation a" team player" in joint human-agent activity. *IEEE Intelligent Systems, 19*(6), 91–95.

Krening, S., & Feigh, K. M. (2018). Interaction algorithm effect on human experience with reinforcement learning. *ACM Transactions on Human-Robot Interaction (THRI), 7*(2), 1–22.

Kress-Gazit, H., Eder, K., Hoffman, G., Admoni, H., Argall, B., Ehlers, R., & Levy-Tzedek, S. (2020). Formalizing and Guaranteeing* Human-Robot Interaction. arXiv preprint arXiv:2006.16732.

Lee, J. D., & See, K. A. (2004). Trust in automation: Designing for appropriate reliance. *Human Factors, 46*(1), 50–80.

Lewis, M., Wang, H., Chien, S. Y., Velagapudi, P., Scerri, P., & Sycara, K. (2011). Process and performance in human-robot teams. *Journal of Cognitive Engineering and Decision Making, 5*(2), 186–208.

Lim, B. C., & Klein, K. J. (2006). Team mental models and team performance: A field study of the effects of team mental model similarity and accuracy. *Journal of Organizational Behavior: THe International Journal of Industrial, Occupational and Organizational Psychology and Behavior, 27*(4), 403–418.

Linegang, M. P., Stoner, H. A., Patterson, M. J., Seppelt, B. D., Hoffman, J. D., Crittendon, Z. B., & Lee, J. D. (2006). Human-automation collaboration in dynamic mission planning: A challenge requiring an ecological approach. In *Proceedings of the Human Factors and Ergonomics Society Annual Meeting* (Vol. 50, No. 23, pp. 2482–2486). Sage CA: Los Angeles, CA: SAGE Publications.

Littman, M. L., Topcu, U., Fu, J., Isbell, C., Wen, M., & MacGlashan, J. (2017). Environment-independent task specifications via GLTL. CoRR, vol. abs/1704.04341.

Lutz, C. (2006, May). Complexity and succinctness of public announcement logic. In *Proceedings of the fifth international joint conference on Autonomous agents and multiagent systems* (pp. 137–143).

Madden, J. D., Arkin, R. C., & MacNulty, D. R. (2010, December). Multi-robot system based on model of wolf hunting behavior to emulate wolf and elk interactions. In *2010 IEEE International Conference on Robotics and Biomimetics* (pp. 1043–1050). IEEE.

McNeese, N. J., Demir, M., Cooke, N. J., & Myers, C. (2018). Teaming with a synthetic teammate: Insights into human-autonomy teaming. *Human Factors, 60*(2), 262–273.

Mohammed, S., Ferzandi, L., & Hamilton, K. (2010). Metaphor no more: A 15-year review of the team mental model construct. *Journal of Management, 36*(4), 876–910.

Moshkina, L., Park, S., Arkin, R. C., Lee, J. K., & Jung, H. (2011). TAME: Time-varying affective response for humanoid robots. *International Journal of Social Robotics, 3*(3), 207–221.

Mulder, M., Abbink, D. A., & Carlson, T. (2015). Introduction to the special issue on shared control: Applications. *Journal of Human-Robot Interaction, 4*(3), 1–3.

Nikolaidis, S., Zhu, Y. X., Hsu, D., & Srinivasa, S. (2017, March). Human-robot mutual adaptation in shared autonomy. In 2017 12th ACM/IEEE International Conference on Human-Robot Interaction (HRI (pp. 294–302). IEEE.

Nuzzo, P., Sangiovanni-Vincentelli, A. L., Bresolin, D., Geretti, L., & Villa, T. (2015). A platform-based design methodology with contracts and related tools for the design of cyber-physical systems. *Proceedings of the IEEE, 103*(11), 2104–2132.

Pacheck, A., Moarref, S., & Kress-Gazit, H. (2020, May). Finding Missing Skills for High-Level Behaviors. In *2020 IEEE International Conference on Robotics and Automation (ICRA)* (pp. 10335–10341). IEEE.

Phillips, E., Schaefer, K. E., Billings, D. R., Jentsch, F., & Hancock, P. A. (2016). Human-animal teams as an analog for future human-robot teams: Influencing design and fostering trust. *Journal of Human-Robot Interaction, 5*(1), 100–125.

Ramaswamy, V., Paccagnan, D., & Marden, J. R. (2019). Multiagent maximum coverage problems: The trade-off between anarchy and stability. In 2019 18th European Control Conference (ECC) (pp. 1043–1048). IEEE.

Rogers, L. J., & Kaplan, G. (Eds.). (2012). *Comparative vertebrate cognition: are primates superior to non-primates?*. Springer Science & Business Media.

Roth, M., Simmons, R., & Veloso, M. (2005). Reasoning about joint beliefs for execution-time communication decisions. In Proceedings of the fourth international joint conference on Autonomous agents and multiagent systems (pp. 786–793).

Roth, E. M., Sushereba, C., Militello, L. G., Diiulio, J., & Ernst, K. (2019). Function Allocation Considerations in the Era of Human Autonomy Teaming. *Journal of Cognitive Engineering and Decision Making, 13*(4), 199–220.

Scassellati, B. (2002). Theory of mind for a humanoid robot. *Autonomous Robots, 12*(1), 13–24.

Seshia, S. A., Sadigh, D., & Sastry, S. S. (2015, June). Formal methods for semi-autonomous driving. In *2015 52nd ACM/EDAC/IEEE Design Automation Conference (DAC)* (pp. 1–5). IEEE.

Shah, J., & Breazeal, C. (2010). An empirical analysis of team coordination behaviors and action planning with application to human–robot teaming. *Human Factors, 52*(2), 234–245.

Steinberg, M. (2011, May). Biologically-inspired approaches for self-organization, adaptation, and collaboration of heterogeneous autonomous systems. In *Defense Transformation and Net-Centric Systems 2011* (Vol. 8062, p. 80620H). International Society for Optics and Photonics.

Steinfeld, A., & Goodrich, M. (2020, March). Assessing, Explaining, and Conveying Robot Proficiency for Human-Robot Teaming. In *Companion of the 2020 ACM/IEEE International Conference on Human-Robot Interaction* (pp. 662–662).

Stubbs, K., Hinds, P. J., & Wettergreen, D. (2007). Autonomy and common ground in human-robot interaction: A field study. *IEEE Intelligent Systems, 22*(2), 42–50.

Sun, X., Ray, L. E., Kralik, J. D., & Shi, D. (2010, October). Socially augmented hierarchical reinforcement learning for reducing complexity in cooperative multi-agent systems. In *2010 IEEE/RSJ International Conference on Intelligent Robots and Systems* (pp. 3244–3250). IEEE.

Unhelkar, V. V., & Shah, J. A. (2016, March). Contact: Deciding to communicate during time-critical collaborative tasks in unknown, deterministic domains. In *Thirtieth AAAI Conference on Artificial Intelligence*.

Vicente, K. J. (1999). *Cognitive work analysis: Toward safe, productive, and healthy computer-based work*. CRC Press.

Walker, P., Nunnally, S., Lewis, M., Kolling, A., Chakraborty, N., & Sycara, K. (2012, October). Neglect benevolence in human control of swarms in the presence of latency. In *2012 IEEE International Conference on Systems, Man, and Cybernetics (SMC)* (pp. 3009–3014). IEEE.

Young, P., & Zamir, S. (Eds.). (2014). *Handbook of game theory*. Elsevier.

Zhou, J., Zhu, H., Kim, M., & Cummings, M. L. (2019). The Impact of Different Levels of Autonomy and Training on Operators' Drone Control Strategies. *ACM Transactions on Human-Robot Interaction (THRI), 8*(4), 1–15.

Chapter 6
Systems Engineering for Artificial Intelligence-based Systems: A Review in Time

James Llinas, Hesham Fouad, and Ranjeev Mittu

Abstract With backgrounds in the science of information fusion and information technology, a review of Systems Engineering (SE) for Artificial Intelligence (AI)-based systems is provided across time, first with a brief history of AI and then the systems' perspective based on the lead author's experience with information fusion processes. The different types of AI are reviewed, such as expert systems and machine learning. Then SE is introduced and how it has evolved and must evolve further to become fully integrated with AI, such that both disciplines can help each other move into the future and evolve together. Several SE issues are reviewed, including risk, technical debt, software engineering, test and evaluation, emergent behavior, safety, and explainable AI.

6.1 Perspectives on AI and Systems Engineering

The field of Artificial Intelligence (AI) has a quite long history. Deciding exactly when the field started would be the subject of many arguments but early conceptual ideas, importantly related to computational feasibility, were defined in Turing's 1950 seminal paper in the philosophy journal Mind (Turing, 1950), often considered a major turning point in the history of AI. Wikipedia describes a "Golden years" period of 1956–74 when a variety of then-new and rather amazing computer programs were developed. Still following the metaphors in Wikipedia, a first AI "Winter" arises in the period 1974–80, followed by a boom years period, largely spawned by the rise

J. Llinas (✉)
Center for Multi-Source Information Fusion, Research Professor Emeritus, University At Buffalo, Director Emeritus, Buffalo, NY, USA
e-mail: llinas@buffalo.edu

H. Fouad
Computer Scientist, Information Management & Decision Architectures Branch, Information Technology Division, Hesham Fouad, U.S. Naval Research Laboratory, Washington, DC, USA

R. Mittu
Information Management & Decision Architectures Branch, Information Technology Division, U.S. Naval Research Laboratory, Washington, DC, USA

© Springer Nature Switzerland AG 2021
W. F. Lawless et al. (eds.), *Systems Engineering and Artificial Intelligence*,
https://doi.org/10.1007/978-3-030-77283-3_6

93

in Expert Systems techniques, and the efforts of the Japanese "Fifth Generation" project. Skeptical views of AI at high decision-making and funding levels (in spite of some continued advances) led to a second AI Winter, 1987–93. It was during this period, however, that the groundwork for connectionist approaches was laid, but the field still struggled through 2011. The current AI "Spring" could also be called the period of Deep Learning (DL) and Big Data.

It is important to understand current terminology such as "Narrow" AI. Narrow AI is a term used to describe artificial intelligence systems that are specified to handle a singular or limited task. Narrow AI is also sometimes called Weak AI, and some struggle over the distinction. And finally, there is the category of Strong AI or Artificial General Intelligence (AGI) that is "focused on creating intelligent machines that can successfully perform any intellectual task that a human being can." This intelligence comes down to three aspects: (1) the ability to generalize knowledge from one domain to another by taking knowledge from one area and applying it elsewhere; (2) the ability to make plans for the future based on knowledge and experiences; and (3) the ability to adapt to the environment as changes occur (from Walch (2019)). There are respected opinions that indicate we are still a long way from cause-effect modeling capability (Bergstein, 2020), and that such capabilities are crucial to serious movement toward an AGI computational capability. In spite of the recent accomplishments and the major investments being made in AI technology, its nature as measured by its many accomplishments and its trusted use is still to be noted, but exactly how this AI "season" evolves is still hard to determine with confidence.

It is also important to realize that systems engineering (SE) for these generational AI systems was a topic of concern for those times, i.e., that systems engineering for AI systems also has a history. Those engineering methods were developed largely in the boom years when Expert Systems were being prototyped, and books were written on the methods to build them, such as in Martin (1988); Purdue offered a website (Subarna, 2020) that outlined the stages of Expert System development; there are various other characterizations of these steps but broadly they can be summed as: Identification—Conceptualization—Formalization—Implementation—Testing.

As regards new progress in Systems Engineering (SE) for AI and AI-imbued systems (SE4AI), our review based on the technical literature suggests that there is an equally long way to go to both achieve the knowledge to develop a solid foundation of knowledge and methods for SE4AI but, perhaps more importantly, to have the broad AI community take up and employ these methods rigorously in assured systems development. Thus, we titled this Chapter: "Systems Engineering for AI-based Systems: A Review in Time," since the overarching field of AI is in a (complex) process of evolution with much uncertainty as to how the varied dimensions of the field will evolve; this is true for SE4AI as well.

6.2   The Dynamics of This Space

6.2.1   Evolving an SE Framework: Ontologies of AI/ML—Dealing with the Breadth of the Fields

Current-day descriptions and characterizations of AI and ML abound; if one Googles "What is AI?", 3.3 Billion hits will arise, with all kinds of definitions and diagrams. If we are to engineer the design, development, and testing of systems that are either AI/ML-centric or inclusive of AI/ML as components or subsystems, we should have a clearer understanding of these technologies. (We realize that AI and ML are quite different but use AI/ML for notational ease.) One of the clearer characterizations in our view are those which address: "What is it?"… and… "What does it do?". Rather detailed figures showing such mappings are developed in Corea (2018) for Artificial Intelligence shown here as in Fig. 6.1.

There have been efforts to develop ontologies of these technologies, such as in Hawley (2019), Bloehdorn (2009), but there do not seem to be any reference ontologies that can help clarify the many nuances and dimensions inherent in the AI and ML labels. Many such ontologies tend to anthropomorphize the technologies.

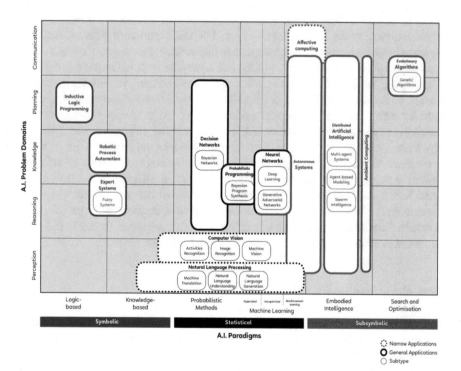

Fig. 6.1 Notional "What it is, What it does" Characterization of AI (adapted from Corea (2018))

Hawley (2019) suggests that the first challenge in addressing the development of an ontology for AI is the very changing definitions, calling the many variants as "intellectual wildcards." He also suggests that the difficulty is more in dealing with the term "intelligence" than "artificial"; these authors agree. The task-specific nature of applications of classic AI and ML, as in the above figures, is another complication in attempting to construct a generalized ontology. For ML, (Bloehdorn, 2009) suggests that a starting point for such an ontology would classify along two dimensions, the types of entities to which the ML is directed, e.g., textual data; and along the structural component of the ML techniques, such as along an axis of features. In a way, this view is again akin to the "what it does-what it is" dimensions. Our concern here is that it is immediately difficult to consider thinking about an engineering approach to an enabling capability if we cannot clearly and unambiguously define/describe what the engineering process is directed to enact.

6.2.2 Systems Engineering as a Moving Target

The issue of defined and clear baselines for the understanding of artifacts to be engineered is also a challenge as regards the methods of systems engineering of such artifacts, as each influences the other. But dynamics in defining the methods of SE are also driven by the SE community (e.g., INCOSE, the International Council on Systems Engineering) as it reflects on such methods needed to address the engineering challenges of systems-of-systems (SoS) and enterprise systems in the current time. Growing technological scale and the complexity of modern systems are in part the drivers of the need for change in SE (MITRE, 2020), but SE has been a dynamic field for many years. Systems engineering models and processes usually organize themselves around the concept of a life cycle, and the concept of life cycle has also been a moving target. The SE community has adapted to these changing life-cycle characterizations with Agile Development earlier and now "DevOps," the WIKI definition being a "set of practices that combines software development (*Dev*) and IT operations (*Ops*)," but this is too limiting to the software boundary, and applies also to the complex software-hardware-human aspects of complex systems. In part, DevOps is oriented to the idea of continuous delivery, so that a system's useable life cycle can adapt to broader limits and its characterizations of use.

DevOps for Modern Complex Systems

DevSecOps is a set of principles and practices that provide faster delivery of secure software capabilities by improving the collaboration and communication between software development teams, IT operations, and security staff within an organization, as well as with acquirers, suppliers, and other stakeholders in the life of a software system (see: [https://www.sei.cmu.edu/our-work/devsecops/]). The general idea is to more closely link the system development process to its continuing support during its deployment to operational status. The DevOps concept was a natural progression of the Agile software development methodology that has been evolving since the 1990s with work by many computer scientists both in academia and industry resulting in the publication of the Agile Manifesto in 2001 [http://agilemanifesto.org/].

To understand the factors motivating this movement, it is instructive to examine the evolution of the software development industry over the past three decades. Until the mid-2000s, the waterfall software development methodology was the defacto standard. The primary motivation was that it gave leaders of large organizations and government agencies a level of comfort that they were following a structured, well-understood process. In fact, the Department of Defense instituted a standard requiring waterfall as the sanctioned methodology for software development under a standard numbered DOD-STD-2167A [https://en.wikipedia.org/wiki/DOD-STD-2167A].

The waterfall methodology, depicted in Fig. 6.2, is heavily front loaded with requirements analysis, high level design, low-level design, and development plans. This results in some significant problems:

- Software release cycles average around 3 years [Varhol, TBD]. In the case of mission-critical software for medical, aerospace, and DoD organizations, it can be as long as decades.
- Development functions are dispersed across multiple departments within an organization. Once one stage of the process is complete, artifacts (documents, software, programs) are passed on to a different department for the next stage of the process. This results in the isolation of expertise within organizational boundaries.

Fig. 6.2 Waterfall Software Development Methodology

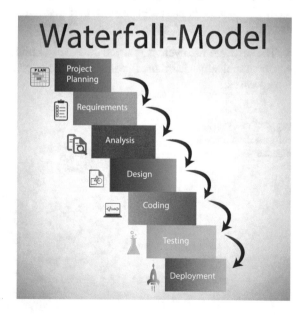

- Software end users are not exposed to the software until the final software product is released. Faulty assumptions in any of the stages of the waterfall methodology cannot be ameliorated to correct problems and redeploy the software in a timely fashion.
- Predicting the time necessary to develop software is difficult. Attempting to schedule a full development cycle in a front-end process is not useful (see Fred Brooks' seminal work on the topic (Brooks, 1982)).

A nice history of the evolution in software engineering from Waterfall to DevOps is in Chaillian (2019).

Adoption of the Agile methodology inspired the rethinking of how software development organizations and processes were structured. An Agile process of Continuous Delivery (CD) and Continuous Integration (CI) required a cohesive organization that spanned marketing, development, and operations expertise. These modifications to the software and systems engineering processes, and the benefits they yielded led to the inception of the DevOps concept. A key factor was having representation from all of the organizational areas making up the software development pipeline in all of the stages of software production. This created a much more streamlined, efficient, and responsive production process.

DevOps also introduced the potential for the automation of the full software life cycle. Figure 6.3 depicts the realization of DevOps in an automated software build, integration, test, and delivery process. As software modifications are committed to a shared repository, the DevOps pipeline "pulls" the latest source code from the repository, compiles the software, integrates various components into a deliverable form factor (Virtual Machine Images, Containers, or installable packages), deploys them on a local or cloud-based testbed, performs automated testing on the software, and publishes test results to stakeholders. This process has many advantages:

- The software life cycle is reduced drastically, builds often are performed daily.
- Geographically distributed teams can easily collaborate within the DevOps processes.

Fig. 6.3 DevSecOps software development pipeline

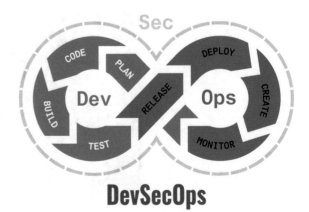

- Automated testing is performed frequently so that any anomalies introduced can be quickly detected and corrected.

The DoD has begun the transition from the waterfall methodology to Agile including the implementation of automated DevOps processes. The additional information assurance requirements imposed by DoD for software in operational settings requires the addition of a software security assurance phase to DevOps making it DevSecOps. The additional phase involves static scanning of software code to detect vulnerabilities that would make the software susceptible to classified information leakage or to cyber-attack. Additionally, dynamic software scanning is, in some cases, carried out where the running software is monitored for security violations during the "Sec" phase of DevSecOps.

With so much attention being paid to ML techniques within the DoD, research organizations are now working on specialized DevSecOps pipelines specifically tooled for ML. The problem then becomes how to procure "good" data and ensure that the ML networks are learning correctly. This poses a difficult problem in that the data required to train ML in the domain of tactical operations is sparse and, where available, is highly classified. One approach being examined is to utilize computer simulation technology to generate synthetic data for training ML systems. It remains to be seen whether or not this approach will bear fruit. The concern is that the simulations used to generate synthetic data consist of largely static, scripted events, whereas tactical operations are highly fluid and complex.

The other, largely unaddressed, problem with DevSecOps for AI/ML systems is in the Test, Evaluation, Validation, and Verification (TEVV) of those systems. Testing AI/ML systems requires that they be exposed to realistic scenarios and having an automated test system gauge whether or not the output of the AI/ML systems is appropriate. We again face the same problem of data sparsity. In the case of reinforcement learning approaches, TEVV will require a continuous monitoring model. For those seeking further information on implementing DevSecOps in regulated domains such as the DoD or healthcare, finance, etc., the SEI has produced a thorough report at Morales (2020). In the same fashion as has happened for SE in regard to SE4AI and AI4SE, there are many blogs and podcasts about how AI can be exploited for DevSecOps, e.g., Trivedi (2021).

6.2.3 The First to Market Motivation

The hoopla about AI and ML is also driving a transformation in business, both in the sense of what a business is and how it operates. Whether true or not, there is a widespread impression that rapid incorporation of AI and ML technologies is necessary to stay apace of competition in the marketplace. As well, the development tools for AI and ML have evolved in a context that allows quick prototyping and, if appropriately tested and evaluated (an issue), rapid delivery to market. In Zeller (2018), it is asserted that "Enterprises that wait too long to implement AI and Machine

Learning will put their businesses at significant risk as nimble competitors find new ways of disrupting the industry status quo." This sense of urgency has also spilled over into the defense R&D community, as can be witnessed by the "AI Next" program of the Defense Advanced Research Projects Agency (DARPA) in the United States (AI Next, 2020), where some US$2 billion will be invested across a wide array of programs to advance the integration and exploitation of AI/ML for a range of defense applications. These urgencies have given rise—or perhaps more correctly— have yielded a retrograde in engineering design-thinking that moves this framework "From deductive reasoning to inductive reasoning, From clear specifications to goals, and From guarantees to best effort," following Carnegie-Mellon University's course in "Software Engineering for AI-Enabled Systems" (CMU, 2020). We say retrograde because these methods were pretty much the principles of design from the Expert Systems era of AI. These guidelines support rapid development but often with clear compromises in quality and impacts on life-cycle costs.

6.2.4   Technical Debt

Harking back to a 30-year-old idea in the face of current-day software develop-ment problems, staffers at Google put forward ideas about technical debt on the applicability of these old ideas to modern-day development of ML code in Sculley (2015). That paper starts with a citation to a 1992 paper by Cunningham (1992) that argues "Although immature code may work fine and be completely acceptable to the customer, excess quantities (of immature code) will make a program unmasterable, leading to extreme specialization of programmers and finally an inflexible product. Shipping first-time code is like going into debt. A little debt speeds development so long as it is paid back promptly with a rewrite." This was a reflection on the imputed life-cycle cost debt of rapid software code development. Related to this, Google staffers assert (Sculley, 2015) "As the machine learning (ML) community continues to accumulate years of experience with live systems, a wide-spread and uncomfort-able trend has emerged: developing and deploying ML systems is relatively fast and cheap, but maintaining them over time is difficult and expensive." That paper focuses on system-level interactions and interfaces as an area where ML technical debt may rapidly accumulate, and offers various suggestions about strategies to address those issues, too detailed to review here, but their conclusions suggest that additional developments in the areas of maintainable ML, including better abstractions, testing methodologies, and design patterns, are all needed to avoid negative life-cycle cost implications of current-day rapid development practices.

6.2.5 Summary

The field of AI/ML technologies and the related engineering methods for designing, developing, and testing of systems that are either AI/ML-centric or have major AI/ML components or subsystems, is currently exhibiting considerable change. We discuss these in the context of this chapter focused on engineering methods to show that any discussion or suggestions regarding such engineering practices have to be taken/understood in the context of these advances, and at this point in time. It is going to take some time for AI/ML domain technical experts and systems engineers to come together and develop a mature community of practice that employs engineering methods to provide assured cost-benefits while achieving desired effectiveness.

6.3   Stepping Through Some Systems Engineering Issues

One of the overarching and essential challenges to realize the promise of AI/ML is that there is not currently a universally accepted approach when it comes to implementation, since the far greater proportion of implementations realized to date are highly specialized (Vora, 2019; Dwyer, 2019); there are yet other challenges as well, and there are many opinions about them (Marr, 2017). We will step through some of the important issues related to understanding the current state of affairs, and what might be done to make some progress in SE methods. Our focus is on the software aspects but clearly a full SE process would address hardware, human factors, etc.

6.3.1   Capability Maturity Model Integration [CMMI] and SE for R&D

Before marching through various SE steps, we make some overarching remarks on the top-level issues of engineering culture within a software development-oriented organization. A first remark comes from reviewing the Capability Maturity Model Integration (CMMI) review efforts of the Software Engineering Institute (SEI) at Carnegie-Mellon, as described in CMMI (2010). CMMI for development can be described as the collection of best practices that address development activities applied to products and services in any organization. It addresses practices that cover a product's life cycle from conception through delivery and maintenance; SEI's approach contains 22 such processes. The degree of thoroughness of such practices can be an indicator of the collective rigor within which an organization develops software. SEI has developed a five-level categorization of degrees for the organization that has embedded such practices in their engineering operations; these maturity categories are:

1. **Initial**: processes are seen as unpredictable, poorly controlled, and reactive. Businesses in this stage have an unpredictable environment that leads to increased risks and inefficiency.
2. **Initial**: processes are seen as unpredictable, poorly controlled, and reactive. Businesses in this stage have an unpredictable environment that leads to increased risks and inefficiency.
3. **Managed**: processes are characterized by projects and are frequently reactive.
4. **Defined**: processes are well-characterized and well-understood. The organization is more proactive than reactive, and there are organization-wide standards that provide guidance.
5. **Quantitatively Managed**: processes are measured and controlled. The organization is using quantitative data to implement predictable processes that meet organizational goals.
6. **Optimizing**: processes are stable and flexible. The organizational focus is on continued improvement and responding to changes.

Much of AI/ML development is being done within organizations rated at Levels 0 and 1, some are at Level 2. These ratings seem to be consistent with the overall state of maturity of SE rigor in AI/ML development.

Another top-level view from a similar perspective was carried out in Lombardo (2015), where the question addressed was the appropriate level of incorporation of SE rigor as a function of the type of organization doing the work, and, in particular, as regards R&D type organizations. It can be argued that such rigor in R&D organizations is often not warranted or affordable, particularly where it is uncertain whether a new technology can meet key performance goals. In Anderson (2005), three levels of SE are defined to support the right-sizing of systems engineering activities: informal, semi-formal, and formal. The overall scheme is risk-based in terms of the risk that the constructed system/product should have. Figure 6.4 shows this scheme (a risk categorization scheme and its factors are shown in the analysis):

Any organization therefore has these overarching questions in front of it, as regards choosing the level of rigor and completeness in its SE practices; rigor and completeness cost money. Building an organization having rigorous and complete SE practices will be costly along various dimensions. But issues of reputation and product/system

INFORMAL	SEMI-FORMAL	FORMAL
Incorporate systems thinking into project scope	Define specialized Systems Engineering tasks directed at Risk reduction	Systems Engineering activities, tasks defined based on TRL challenges and risks
Limited Systems Engrg Rigor	Defined Project Management Plan	Formal Systems Engrg Management Plan
LOW RISK PROJECT	MODERATE RISK PROJECT	HIGH RISK PROJECT

Fig. 6.4 Levels of SE Rigor for R&D organizations as a function of risk (derived from Anderson, 2005)

quality as well as risk in use and liability also play into the cost equation, and making such decisions will not be easy.

6.3.2 Requirements Engineering

Requirements Engineering (RE) is concerned with the elicitation, analysis, specification, and validation of software requirements as well as the management and documentation of requirements throughout the software product life cycle. RE is often the first or among the first steps in an SE approach. Among the effects on RE that have occurred in AI/ML system designs, hard and testable requirements have been replaced by goal statements (historically it has been asserted that the first requirement should be a testable concept for that requirement, else it was poorly defined). Such effects come from, at least in part, the complexity and opaqueness of AI/ML algorithms and processes, that is, in effect, the level of deeper understanding that is known early on in a system's evolution. Vogelsang and Borg (2019) "are convinced that RE for ML systems is special due to the different paradigm used to develop data-driven solutions." They analyze the effects of ML on RE, describing effects on requirements elicitation, analysis, specification, and Verification and Validation (V&V). For example, Elicitation is impacted by the existence of Important Stakeholders such as Data scientists and legal experts; Analysis by definitions of outlier effects among others, Specification by complications from the need for explainability, and V&V by complexities due to data biases.

In a similar way, Belani et al. (2019) develop an equivalent assessment along these same dimensions for the challenges to RE in the case of AI systems (see their Table 6.1 for a breakdown very similar to Table 1). They recommend a goal-oriented approach to RE ("GORE") that tries to balance the imprecision of goal statements with the precision of requirements specification. In Horkoff (2019), an extensive survey of papers on such GORE methods is done (there is a large literature on this topic), but the conclusions are obtuse, leaving the question of effectiveness open. Additional papers directed to RE deal with defining legal and ethical performance of AI/ML systems (Guizzardi, 2020), and of explainability (addressed later) (Hall, 2019).

These important aspects of SE thus remain under study, and how and whether there will be convergence to an agreed, stable, and consistent approach is unclear.

6.3.3 Software Engineering for AI/ML Systems

Software engineering methodology is another topic in this discussion that also has a long history. The history of these methods seems to date to 1956 in a paper by Bennington providing the first description of the well-known "Waterfall" software development method for "large computer programs" (Bennington, 1983), as also

Fig. 6.5 Machine learning workflow (derived from Amershi (2019))

described in Sect. 6.2.2.1. In performing a current-day search regarding software development methodologies, our search showed websites discussing a range of from 4 to 12 methods. In Tatvasoft (2015), a list of 12 methods is described, enumerating advantages and disadvantages of each.

These various methods were developed for different directed purposes, and they have a range of applicability, from those with well-defined requirements such as the Waterfall model to those that are more adaptable to changing requirements such as the Scrum model. None of these were really conceptualized to address the special needs of AI/Ml software development.

The most distinguishing aspect of AI/ML software development is the dependencies of the process on data characteristics. The AI/ML model life cycle can be summarized as a process in which it is necessary to deal with data, select a target classification model (and features) depending on the type of problem and the available data, train and test the model under different configurations and performance metrics, and finally, operate and feedback corrections to the trained model as necessary. Of course, a first question relates to the logic involved in selecting the data to learn, and then to condition that data for targeted purposes of the application. These steps require non-trivial domain knowledge and are interconnected and non-linear. Jointly, these steps have come to be known as "Feature Engineering," the process of using domain knowledge to extract features from raw data, often via data mining or other techniques. An example of this process is shown below in Fig. 6.5 (derived from Amershi (2019)). It can be seen that some steps are data-oriented while others are model-oriented, and that there are many feedback loops. The larger feedback arrows denote that model evaluation may loop back to any of the previous stages, and the smaller arrow shows that model training may loop back to feature engineering.

The workflow shown in Fig. 6.5 is one important factor affecting the formulation of a software engineering and development approach; the scheme in Yao (2018) for ML development emphasizes the dependencies on Data and Models, the important role of Feature Engineering, and of Verification and Validation note too, the specification of Goals versus precise requirements.

The additional complexities that these processes impute onto software development, and the concern for the related issues of technical debt, have given rise to an explosion of papers and ideas about identifying and addressing hidden technical debt in AI/ML development (see, e.g., Martini (2018)).

In a highly cited editorial (Kruchten, 2012), the various concerns for technical debt as related to AI/ML software development are discussed; Fig. 6.6 shows the

Fig. 6.6 The technical debt landscape (derived from Kruchten (2012))

"Technical Debt Landscape" derived from that work, showing that some concerns are not obvious ("mostly invisible" in the figure), and can be difficult to prevent.

Developing an AI/ML community approach to software engineering is another needed component of an overall SE approach; it is another issue in flux, facing a number of technical difficulties that underlie the development of an engineering process that is cost-effective and efficient, and formed to avoid both the subtle and more visible aspects of the drivers of technical debt.

6.3.4 Test and Evaluation

Test and Evaluation processes are clearly central to the overall SE paradigm. Within the Model-Based SE (MBSE) paradigm, model-based testing (MBT) means using models for describing test environments and test strategies, generating test cases, test execution, and test design quality. MBT is said to provide an approach that ensures the possibility to trace the correspondence between requirements, models, codes, and test cases used for the tested system. Model-based testing is a software testing technique where run-time behavior of software undergoing a test is checked against predictions made by a model. There are various ways that such testing could be enabled. To automate test-case generation and a test oracle, a specification of the system has to be expressed in formal languages which are amenable to an automated analysis. Tests are then automatically derived from those formal models, and subsequently executed.

Another level of testing is the class of model-based black-box testing techniques that aim to assess the correctness of a reactive system; i.e., the implementation under test (IUT) with respect to a given specification (assuming a specification has been properly constructed). The IUT is viewed as a black-box with an interface that accepts inputs and produces outputs. The goal of model-based black-box testing is to check if the observable behavior of the IUT "conforms" to a specification with respect to a particular conformance relation. In the case of Machine Learning models, there are no expected values beforehand in that ML models output a prediction. Given that the outcome of Machine Learning models is a prediction, it is not easy to compare or verify the prediction against an expected value that is not known beforehand. But for non-deterministic operations within an ML agent, there is no easy way to provide an expectation. This void has given rise to the idea of pseudo-oracles and "metamorphic" testing. Metamorphic relations represent a set of properties that relate multiple pairs of inputs and outputs of the target program/application such that proportional results due to changes in design parameters can be estimated (Kumar, 2018).

Software testing is a large and complex space, and we will not enter into the many issues lurking there, such as black-box and white-box testing, verification and validation, unit testing, etc. We will try to comment on some issues that are specific to AI and ML systems. One first question even before entering a test cycle is that of debugging AI/ML code, since testing should only be done with code that has at least passed the debugging stage. One example is in using Probabilistic Programming for AI inferencing, where debugging is more about odd behaviors than traditional discrete "bugs" (Nandi, 2019). For ML, the code first of all has many dynamic interdependent parts such as datasets, model architectures, model weights that are fine-tuned during training, an optimization algorithm and its parameters, gradients that change during training, and on. Among the problems encountered, the use of the various tools for ML, such as TensorFlow, abstract away underlying complexities, making access to certain functions not possible. Prasanna (2020) has written a posting that describes yet other issues related to ML code debugging, such as, when using a tool like TensorFlow in the "declarative approach," you do not have access to the defined graph model and the optimized graph, so debugging performance errors can be harder.

With regard to Test and Evaluation (T&E), the approaches for ML and AI are quite different. ML is about model testing for classification to a great degree, and AI is about possibly complex layers of inferencing. Selection of the T&E processes and metrics for both follow different paths. For ML, the historical base of mostly statistical and quantitative methods and metrics is quite rich, but there are still technical issues that can arise. Flasch, in Flasch (2019), offers good reminders about subtleties in the statistics of measuring ML performance. He offers various interesting points about metrics that compute different things from different viewpoints (such as F-scores, Areas Under (ROC) Curves, Brier scores, etc.), and the challenge of aggregating the best set of metrics for system-level evaluation. For T&E of AI processes, there lurks the fundamental challenge of agreeing on what constitutes intelligence, and deriving a T&E approach from the developed response to that challenge. Hernández-Orallo, in Hernández-Orallo (2017), focuses on the obstacles of an ability-oriented evaluation approach, where a system is characterized by its cognitive abilities rather than by the tasks it is designed to solve. The approach ranges over several possibilities: the adaptation of cognitive tests used for humans, the development of tests derived from algorithmic information theory, or more integrated approaches from psychometrics.

6.4 Sampling of Technical Issues and Challenges

It should be clear that AI and ML are complex domains, spanning wide ranges of categories of techniques and categories of applicability. Because they address complex challenges, it can be expected that designing these processes as well as understanding these processes will not be easy, as is perhaps already appreciated. Here, to emphasize this point, we give a sampling of technical complexities in the AI and ML domains, in no particular order.

6.4.1 Emergence and Emergent Behavior

ML processes typically employ/embody neural networks that are known to have inherent emergent behavior. Here, we prefer the definition of emergence described as a *property* of a complex system: "a property of a complex system is said to be 'emergent' and it arises out of the properties and relations characterizing the system's simpler constituents, but it is neither predictable from, nor reducible to, these lower-level characteristics" (Adcock, 2020). There are many other definitions and taxonomies of emergence (Fromm, 2005; Chalmers, 2006), but the focus regarding SE is on the effects of emergence, not emergence per se. Chalmers (2006) identifies "strong" and "weak" emergence, where strong emergence is not deducible even in principle from the laws of a lower-level domain, while weak emergence is only unexpected given the properties and principles of the lower-level domain. Neace and Chipkevich (2018) define weak emergent behavior as attributable to the behavior of its constituents; they have developed an engineering methodology designed to realize weak emergence as a desired property of a designed system. Desirable weak-emergent properties include self-healing, self-management, self-monitoring, and more; i.e., the desirable degrees of autonomous self-management. They introduce the ideas of network synchronization, functional coherence, and network entrainment as necessary mechanisms for weak emergence in a manufactured Complex Adaptive System (CAS), along with the software agents needed to intend and achieve weak emergence in the CAS. It may be possible to exploit emergent behavior for useful purposes in an SE-based approach to ML process design and development, but in any case, it will need to be addressed.

A further reflection of such concerns is given in DARPA's recent release of the call for the AIMEE program—Artificial Intelligence Mitigations of Emergent Execution (DARPA, 2019). Among the goals for the program is to learn how to prevent the propensity for emergent execution directly at the design stage when the system's programming abstractions and intended behaviors at a particular layer are translated into the more granular states and logic of the next computing substrate layer; by and large, this call by DARPA is fundamentally an SE challenge.

6.4.2   Safety in AI/ML

Related to but not bounded only by emergent properties, the AI literature has many entries about the various surprising and often undesirable behaviors of AI processes; such behaviors may clearly affect safe use. Yampolskiy (2019) addresses a position that discusses the unpredictability of AI in broad terms. In this paper, Yampolskiy surveys a number of works that discuss the related aspects for SE of AI Safety that addresses concepts of Unknowability (Vinge, 1993) and Cognitive Uncontainability (2019). In Amodei (2016), a lengthy review of specific problems in AI Safety are reviewed; the bulk of these problems are not dealing with the concepts of unpredictability and emergent behaviors per se, but issues that result from failures in systems engineering and design rigor of ML systems. Examples describe cases where the designer may have specified the *wrong formal objective function*; or the case where a designer may know the correct objective function, but it is judged *too expensive to employ*, leading to possible harmful behavior caused by bad extrapolations from limited data samples, calling this "Scalable oversight"; and, finally, the case of a correct formal objective, but problematic behavior due to making decisions from *insufficient or poorly curated training data*, called "Safe exploration." For those interested in this topic, which is definitely an SE topic, Faria (2018) provides another overview of safety issues in ML processes.

Other issues that can be of possibly major concern in system design relate to achieving systems whose behaviors and results are compliant with ethical standards (Rossi, 2019), and systems whose behaviors and results are unbiased (DeBrusk, 2018). These goals also open the discussion about subtle effects and factors that can influence system operations as well as results.

6.4.3   The Issue of Explanation/Explainability

As the applications and algorithms for AI and ML have matured in the new Spring of AI, the processes (especially on the ML side) have become extraordinarily complex, resulting in considerable opaqueness. Computing systems are opaque when their behaviors cannot be explained or understood. This impenetrableness is the case when it is difficult to know how or why inputs are transformed into corresponding outputs, and when it is not clear which environmental features and regularities are being tracked. The widespread use of machine learning has led to a proliferation of non-transparent computing systems, giving rise to the so-called "Black Box Problem" in AI, meaning that no views of the processes and workings between components are visible. Because this problem has significant practical, theoretical, and ethical consequences, research efforts in Explainable AI aim to solve the Black Box Problem through post-hoc analysis, or in an alternative approach to evade the Black Box Problem through the use of interpretable systems. Reflecting concern for this issue,

DARPA again spawned an early program in its huge AI Next program directed to Explainable AI (Gunning, 2016).

Interest in explanation capabilities, either within the system by re-engineering to reduce or avoid opaqueness, or by an explanation service, has exploded if we track the evolution of citations on these topics. There are a number of review papers on the subject matter but two stand out, scaled by the numbers of papers claimed to have been reviewed: the paper by Adadi and Berrada (2018) that reviewed 381 papers, and the one by Arrieta, et al. (2020), that reviewed 426 papers. These papers take exhaustive looks at the world of explanation, too expansive to summarize here.

In terms of some focal issues, we see discussions about Interpretability versus Completeness. The goal of interpretability is to describe the internals of a system in a way that is understandable to humans, whereas the goal of completeness is to describe the operation of a system in an accurate way (these can be alternately described as providing understandability versus justification of results). An explanation is said to be more complete when it allows the behavior of the system to be anticipated across a wide range of application conditions. Thus, the challenge facing explainable AI is in creating explanations that are both complete and interpretable. But achieving this balance is difficult, as the most accurate explanations are often not easily interpretable to people; conversely, the most interpretable explanations often do not provide predictive power in atypical cases. Importantly, these issues in turn will affect how humans will come to trust the systems, a critically important issue.

This issue, like many others addressed here, also has a long history. As the AI community evolved and developed such methods for estimation and inference, explanation arose quite early as an issue and adjunct capability that, for almost any application that could be considered "complex," was a necessary topic and co-process to consider. Figure 6.7 is a portion of a figure from Kass (1987), a 1987 publication that tried to address the range and types of explanations that the evolving AI community might have to think about. The figure offers a categorization of anomalous events that need explanation; the version here is a truncated portion of the original. So, explanation is not new and appears to be an inherent and mandatory capability for certain but likely far-reaching AI applications.

6.5 Summary

The technological domains of AI and ML have had, and will continue to have, a dynamic evolution. It is important to appreciate that historical context and to be patient with the development of improved engineering practices for the continued growth of capabilities, both for the ways AI and ML processes are engineered, but also for the systemic aspects of the applications they are engineered into. One factor that is a major omission from this chapter is that the engineering of the role of humans to coexist with and exploit AI/ML system capabilities is missing; explanation certainly relates to that issue but we mean here the systemic viewpoint of human-system interdependence. What is not so clear is, even if studies of engineering practice for

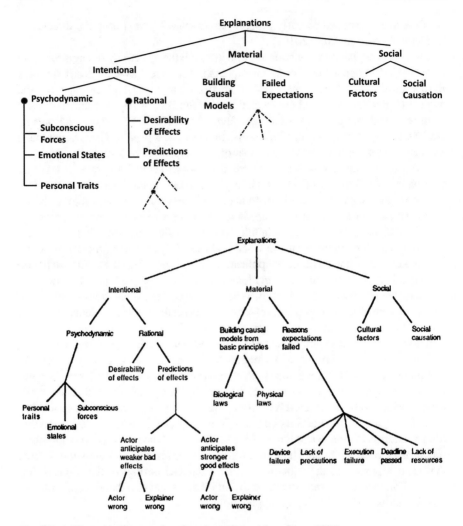

Fig. 6.7 A Hierarchy of types of explanations (derived from Kass, 1987)

AI/ML mature and offer better ways to engineer such systems, how will we be assured that those practices will be promulgated into the broader AI/ML communities? If, as Vora asserts (Vora, 2019), "The essential challenge with AI is that there is not currently a universally accepted approach when it comes to implementation," then this promulgation path will be an unresolved issue that follows even if good SE processes can be defined.

References

Adadi, A., & Berrada, M. (2018). Peeking Inside the black-box: A survey on explainable artificial intelligence (XAI). *IEEE Access, 6,* 52138–52160.

Adcock, R., et al. (2020). Emergence, systems engineering body of knowledge WIKI page. https://www.sebokwiki.org/wiki/Emergence. Retrieved February 2020.

AI Next Campaign. https://www.darpa.mil/work-with-us/ai-next-campaign. Retrieved February 2020.

Amershi, S., et al. (2019). Software engineering for machine learning: A case study. In *2019 IEEE/ACM 41st International Conference on Software Engineering: Software Engineering in Practice (ICSE-SEIP).*

Amodei, D., Olah, C., Steinhardt, J., Christiano, P., Schulman, J., & Mane, D. (2016). Concrete problems in AI safety. arXiv:1606.06565.

Anderson, N., & Nolte, W. (2005). Systems engineering principles applied to basic research and development. In *Georgia Tech Space Systems Engineering Conference*, Paper No. GTSSEC.D.5, Retrieved November 8–10, 2005.

Arrieta, A., et al. (2020). Explainable artificial intelligence (XAI): Concepts, taxonomies, opportunities and challenges toward responsible AIO. *Information Fusion, 58,* 82–115.

Belani, H., Vuković, M., & Car, Z. (2019). Requirements engineering challenges in building AI-based complex systems. arXiv:1908.11791.

Bennington, H. D. (1983). Production of large computer programs. *Annals of the History of Computing, 5*(4), 350–361. October–December 1983. https://doi.org/10.1109/MAHC.1983.10102.

Bergstein, B. (2020). AI still gets confused about how the world works. *MIT Technology Review, 123*(2), pp. 62–65. March/April 2020.

Bloehdorn S., & Hotho A. (2009). Ontologies for machine learning. In S. Staab, R. Studer (Eds.), *Handbook on Ontologies: International Handbooks on Information Systems.* Springer, Berlin, Heidelberg.

Brooks, F. P., Jr. (1982). The mythical man-month: Essays on software engineering. Reading, Mass.: Addison-Wesley Pub. Co.

Chaillan, N., & Yasar, H. (2019). Waterfall to DevSecOps in DoD, YouTube presentation. Retrieved March 15, 2021, from https://www.youtube.com/watch?v=vZ6AT7u_BcM.

Chalmers, D. J. (2006). Strong and weak emergence. In P. Clayton & P. Davies (Eds.), *The re-emergence of emergence* (pp. 244–256). UK; Oxford University Press.

Carnegie-Mellon University online course materials, Machine Learning in Production/AI Engineering. https://ckaestne.github.io/seai/. Retrieved February 2020.

Cognitive Uncontainability (2019). In Arbital. Retrieved May 19, 2019, from https://arbital.com/p/uncontainability/.

Corea, F. AI knowledge map: How to classify AI technologies. https://www.forbes.com/sites/cognitiveworld/2018/08/22/ai-knowledge-map-how-to-classify-ai-technologies/#2ec3f6337773.

Cunningham, W. OOPSLA '92: Addendum to the proceedings on object-oriented programming systems, languages, and applications (Addendum), pp. 29–30. Retrieved December 1992. https://doi-org.gate.lib.buffalo.edu/. https://doi.org/10.1145/157709.157715.

DARPA releases AIMEE call for proposals, Intelligence Community News. https://intelligencecommunitynews.com/darpa-releases-aimee-call-for-proposals/.

DeBrusk, C. The risk of machine learning bias (and How to Prevent it). https://www.oliverwyman.com/our-expertise/insights/2018/mar/the-risk-of-machine-learning-bias--and-how-to-prevent-it.html.

Dwyer, M. (2019). AI principles and the challenge of implementation. https://www.csis.org/analysis/ai-principles-and-challenge-implementation.

Faria, J. M. (2018). Machine learning safety: An overview. In *Proceedings of the 26th Safety Critical Systems Symposium.* New York, UK. Retrieved February 2018.

Flasch, P. (2019). Performance evaluation in machine learning: The good, the bad, the ugly and the way forward. In *Proceedings of the 33th AAAI Conference on Artificial Intelligence*

Fromm, J. (2005). Types and forms of emergence, distributed systems group, Universität Kassel, Germany. http://arxiv.org/ftp/nlin/papers/0506/0506028.pdf.

Guizzardi, R., et al. (2020). Ethical requirements for AI systems. In C. Goutte & X. Zhu (Eds.), *Advances in artificial intelligence* (pp. 251–256). Springer International Publishing.

Gunning, D. (2016). Explainable artificial intelligence, online presentation. https://www.cc.gatech. edu/~alanwags/DLAI2016/(Gunning)%20IJCAI-16%20DLAI%20WS.pdf.

Hall, M., Harborne, D., Tomsett, R., Galetic, V., Quintana-Amate, S., Nottle, A., & Preece, A. (2019). A systematic method to understand requirements for explainable AI (XAI) systems. In *Proceedings of the IJCAI Workshop on eXplainable Artificial Intelligence (XAI 2019)*. Macau, China.

Hawley, S. H. (2019). Challenges for an ontology of artificial intelligence, perspectives on science and christian faith (Vol. 71), Special Edition on A.I.

Hernández-Orallo, J. (2017). Evaluation in artificial intelligence: From task-oriented to ability-oriented measurement. *Artificial Intelligence Review, 48*, 397–447. https://doi.org/10.1007/s10 462-016-9505-7

Horkoff, J., Aydemir, F. B., et al. (2019). Goal-oriented requirements engineering: An extended systematic mapping study. *Requirements Engineering, 24*(2), 133–160.

Kass, A., & Leake, D. (1987). Types of explanations, Technical Report ADA183253, DTIC Document.

Kruchten, P., Nord, R. L., & Ozkaya, I. (2012). Technical debt: From metaphor to theory and practice. *IEEE Software, 29*(6), 18–21.

Kumar, A. QA—Metamorphic testing for machine learning models. https://vitalflux.com/qa-met amorphic-testing-machine-learning/.

Lombardo, N., et al. (2015). A systems engineering framework for R&D organizations. In *25th Annual INCOSE International Symposium (IS2015) Seattle*, WA. Retrieved July 13–16, 2015.

Military standard: Defense system software development. United States Department of Defense. Retrieved February 29, 1988.

Marr, B. (2010) The biggest challenges facing artificial intelligence (AI). In *Business and society*. https://www.forbes.com/sites/bernardmarr/2017/07/13/the-biggest-challenges-fac ing-artificial-intelligence-ai-in-business-and-society/#33ea75ef2aec [CMMI, 2010] Software Engineering for AI-Enabled Systems; https://ckaestne.github.io/seai/--CMMI Product Team, CMMI® for Development, Version 1.3, Carnegie-Mellon SEI Tech Report CMU/SEI-2010-TR-033, November 2010.

Martin, J., & Oxman, S. (1988). *Building expert systems: A tutorial*. Prentice-Hall, Inc.

Martini, A., Besker, T., & Bosch, J. (2018). Technical debt tracking: Current state of practice a survey and multiple case study in 15 large organizations. *Science of Computer Programming*.

Morales, J., Turner, R., Miller, S., Capell, P., Place, P., & Shepard, D. J. (2020). Guide to implementing DevSecOps for a system of systems in highly regulated environments. Technical report CMU/SEI-2020-TR-002. Retrieved April 2020.

Nandi, C., et al. (2017). Debugging probabilistic programs. In *Proceedings of MAPL'17*. Barcelona, Spain. Retrieved June 18, 2017.

Neace, K. S., & Chipkevich, M. B. A. (2018). Designed complex adaptive systems exhibiting weak emergence. In *NAECON 2018—IEEE National Aerospace and Electronics Conference*. Dayton, OH. Retrieved July 23–26, 2018.

Prasanna, S. (2020). How to debug machine learning models to catch issues early and often. https://towardsdatascience.com/how-to-debug-machine-learning-models-to-catch-issues-early-and-often-5663f2b4383b. Retrieved February 2020.

Rossi, F., & Mattei, M. (2019). Building ethically bounded AI. In *Proceedings of the 33rd AAAI Conference on Artificial Intelligence (AAAI)*.

Sculley, D., Holt, G., Golovin, D., Davydov, E., Phillips, T., Ebner, D., Chaudhary, V., Young, M., & Crespo, J. F. (2015). Hidden technical debt in machine learning systems. In *Neural Information Processing Systems (NIPS)*.

Shewan, D. 10 Companies using machine learning in cool ways. https://www.wordstream.com/blog/ws/2017/07/28/machine-learning-applications.

Subarna, D. (2020). Stages to develop an expert system. https://www.engineeringenotes.com/artificial-intelligence-2/expert-systems/stages-to-develop-an-expert-system-artificial-intelligence/35592. Retrieved February 2020.

The Mitre Corporation. (2020). The evolution of systems engineering. https://www.mitre.org/publications/systems-engineering-guide/systems-engineering-guide/the-evolution-of-systems. Retrieved February 2020.

Top 12 Software Development Methodologies & its Advantages & Disadvantages. (2015). https://www.tatvasoft.com/blog/top-12-software-development-methodologies-and-its-advantages-disadvantages/.

Trivedi, Mayank, T12 ways AI is transforming devops. Retrieved March 15, 2021, from https://www.tadigital.com/insights/perspectives/12-ways-ai-transforming-devops.

Turing, A. M. (1950). Computing machinery and intelligence. *Mind, New Series, 59*(236), 433–460.

Varhol, P. To agility and beyond: The history—and legacy—of agile development. https://techbeacon.com/app-dev-testing/agility-beyond-history-legacy-agile-development

Vinge, V. (1993). Technological singularity. In *VISION-21 Symposium sponsored by NASA Lewis Research Center and the Ohio Aerospace Institute.*

Vogelsang, A., & Borg, M. (2019). Requirements engineering for machine learning: Perspectives from data scientists. In *IEEE 27th International Requirements Engineering Conference Workshops.*

Vora, T. (2019). Design thinking for AI: Sustainable AI solution design. *BLOG.* https://www.cuelogic.com/blog/design-thinking-for-ai.

Walch, K. Rethinking weak versus. *Strong AI*. https://www.forbes.com/sites/cognitiveworld/2019/10/04/rethinking-weak-vs-strong-ai/?sh=7d8eb9c46da3.

Yampolskiy, R. V. (2019). Unexplainability and incomprehensibility of artificial intelligence. https://arxiv.org/ftp/arxiv/papers/1907/1907.03869.pdf.

Ways AI Transforms Software Development. (2018). https://www.metamaven.com/6-ways-machine-learning-transforms-software-development/.

Zeller, M. (2018). Leveraging AI and machine learning as competitive business drivers. Retrieved August 3, 2018, from https://www.dataversity.net/leveraging-ai-machine-learning-competitive-business-drivers/.

Chapter 7
Human-Autonomy Teaming for the Tactical Edge: The Importance of Humans in Artificial Intelligence Research and Development

Kristin E. Schaefer⬤, Brandon Perelman⬤, Joe Rexwinkle⬤,
Jonroy Canady⬤, Catherine Neubauer⬤, Nicholas Waytowich,
Gabriella Larkin, Katherine Cox⬤, Michael Geuss, Gregory Gremillion⬤,
Jason S. Metcalfe⬤, Arwen DeCostanza, and Amar Marathe

Abstract The U.S. Army is currently working to integrate artificial intelligence, or AI-enabled systems, into military working teams in the form of both embodied (i.e., robotic) and embedded (i.e., computer or software) intelligent agents with the express purpose of improving performance during all phases of the mission. However, this is largely uncharted territory, making it unclear how to do this integration effectively for human-AI teams. This chapter provides an overview of the Combat Capabilities Development Command (DEVCOM) Army Research Laboratory's effort to address the human as a critical gap with associated implications on effective teaming. This chapter articulates four major research thrusts critical to integrating AI-enabled systems into military operations, giving examples within these broader thrusts that are currently addressing specific research gaps. The four major research thrusts include: (1) Enabling Soldiers to predict AI; (2) Quantifying Soldier understanding for AI; (3) Soldier-guided AI adaptation; and (4) Characterizing Soldier-AI performance. These research thrusts are the organizing basis for explaining a path toward integration and effective human-autonomy teaming at the tactical edge.

Keywords Artificial intelligence · Autonomy · Human-autonomy teaming · Human–robot interaction

K. E. Schaefer (✉) · B. Perelman · J. Rexwinkle · J. Canady · C. Neubauer · N. Waytowich ·
G. Larkin · K. Cox · M. Geuss · G. Gremillion · J. S. Metcalfe · A. DeCostanza · A. Marathe
DEVCOM Army Research Laboratory, Aberdeen Proving Ground, Aberdeen, MD, USA
e-mail: kristin.e.schaefer-lay.civ@mail.mil

© Springer Nature Switzerland AG 2021   115
W. F. Lawless et al. (eds.), *Systems Engineering and Artificial Intelligence*,
https://doi.org/10.1007/978-3-030-77283-3_7

7.1 Introduction

Artificial intelligence (AI) is a core component of the U.S. Army's modernization strategy. Importantly, the accelerating development and integration of ever-advancing forms of AI will continually change the character of the battlefield, the dynamics of conflict, and even the very nature of the tasks that Soldiers perform. To date, however, the predominant aims in the larger domain of AI have tended to be focused on succeeding in limited aspects, or isolated functional snippets, of overall task performance (e.g., object identification, navigation, obstacle avoidance, conversational assistants), while also overlooking or even outright trivializing the essential human elements that we believe should be integral to the models that give life to these intelligent, blended systems. Many AI-centric approaches for implementing autonomous technologies have similarly tended to overlook opportunities to leverage the human as a teammate and a resource; for instance, using human biological, physiological, and behavioral responses as sources of data to teach, train, and inform real-time adaptations of mixed human-autonomy team performance. The tendency to develop these advanced intelligent systems without holding the human elements as fundamental seems to be a glaring omission in light of the intention to perfuse AI-based technologies into spaces that will also be predominantly occupied by many humans. This oversight becomes even more critical when the anticipated operational contexts are complex, austere, and involve high (and even mortal) risks.

In response to the need for better conceptualizations and implementations of human-AI systems for complex and risky operations, the Army Research Laboratory (ARL) has stood up an Essential Research Program (ERP) that focuses considerable fiscal, technical, and intellectual resources towards advancing the science and application of novel methods for human-autonomy teaming (HAT). As the flagship research program of ARL for the science of human-autonomy teams, the HAT ERP is built on a core concept that human-autonomy teams and Soldier-focused AI are critical to create the kinds of intelligent systems that can optimally adapt and maintain synergistic, integrated partnerships between Soldier intelligence and AI-enabled intelligent agents. Importantly, we argue that this effort is essential to assure that the US Army and its stakeholders can confidently expect complex, multi-agent Soldier-AI teams to perform robustly within the volatile dynamics and complexity inherent to the Army's functional operating concept of Multi-Domain Operations (MDO; U.S. Army TRADOC, 2018). This concept anticipates widely dispersed teams that must work towards multiple objectives in tight coordination to create and exploit limited windows of opportunity across a theater of operations that incorporates air, ground, sea, space, and cyberspace.

7.2 The Fundamental Nature of Human-Autonomy Teaming

A human-autonomy team, in this context, is a heterogeneous group of multiple humans and multiple intelligent agents. For this type of team dynamic to be effective, it requires some level of shared goals, interactive and interdependent role-based workflows, and some overall organizational objective (see Kozlowski & Ilgen, 2006 for a more in-depth definition of "teams"). While human-autonomy team dynamics certainly include interactions within more traditionally studied dyads (i.e., single operator–single system), the interaction dynamics of interest herein focus more on the complexity added within larger, more heterogeneous groups. In complex human-autonomy teams, the autonomy (i.e., intelligent agents) may take the form of embedded software agents, embodied robotic agents, or any kind of simpler technology that has been imbued with the intelligence to actively adapt to environmental and task conditions (e.g., intelligent sensors and sensor systems, adaptive interfaces, and so forth). Further, these technologies that may be perceived as singular intelligent agents can themselves contain multiple AI-enabled subsystems. As technical complexity progresses in this way, so does the imminence of the need to understand the capabilities and vulnerabilities that both expectedly and unexpectedly emerge from such human–machine collectives and their governing processes. In addition, performance dynamics in these mutually interactive teams may at any time involve particular human-to-human, human-to-agent, and even agent-to-agent interactions, as well as various permutations of individuals that form into varied need-based subteams. Understanding and eventually intentionally manifesting such a complex set of dynamically evolving interactions that yield an effective team performance ultimately demands a new—or at least heavily evolved—science of optimizing performance in human-autonomy teams.

The modern science of human-autonomy teaming is still relatively new. As a result, there are few established theoretic constructs upon which an evolved science of teamwork may be built to accommodate the objectives of characterizing, predicting, and controlling complex interactions among heterogeneous mixes of humans and intelligent agents. Historically, when machines were little more than mechanical extensions of human ingenuity and intention, the task of defining roles for and interactions between humans and machines was trivially viewed as a simple matter of "choosing the right tool for the job." That is, with simple machines, the division of labor is obvious: a nail needs to be driven into a board; the human uses a hammer and subsequently puts it away after the task is complete. With the observation that machines would progressively become more advanced and automated, early visionaries (e.g., Fitts, 1951) recognized that humans and machines generally and inherently excel in different ways, much like earlier tools (a hammer) were better suited for a task (driving a nail through a board) than the human tool equivalent (their closed fist).

7.2.1   Complementarity of Human and AI Characteristics

In Fitts' original humans-are-better-at, machines-are-better-at (HABA-MABA)[1] list, humans were described as superior for things like inductive reasoning, judgment, long-term memory encoding and retrieval, and improvisation; whereas machines were noted as better suited for performing repetitive tasks, deductive reasoning, and handling highly complex operational sequences, among others. While some elements of this original list have aged well, like machines outperforming humans in computation, others have not. For example, the claim that humans outperform machines in detecting "a small amount of visual or acoustic energy" (Fitts, 1951; p. 10) does not hold true; modern advanced sensors far surpass human sensory detection capabilities. Though useful, the continued heritage of the HABA-MABA perspective is also limiting in that it perpetuates the ever-more-outmoded notion that effective human-autonomy integration will continue to be necessarily and sufficiently accomplished by selecting "the right tool for the job" as well as "making better tools." That is, one of the most pervasive constructs in the literature, and one that appears to underlie concepts such as supervisory control (where the human is the supervisor of a putatively more capable autonomous agent), is formally known as *substitution-based function allocation*; it describes solving the task assignment question by dividing the end goal into functionally isolated tasks, and then matching the appropriate agent to the task that falls within its functional responsibility. Of course, the concept of function allocation tables as an integration strategy has been met with significant criticism, and rightly so, as this approach has considerable weaknesses (Dekker & Woods, 2002; Marathe et al., 2018; Sheridan, 2000).

A major criticism of function allocation methods is that they are only likely to work well in simple problem spaces, where AI would essentially be deployed as a tool but are too brittle for the broader space of complex tasks (Perelman, Metcalfe, Boothe, & McDowell, *manuscript under review*). Yet, even in the simple domain, the allocation decision may be more robustly made according to two quantifiable factors: *time available to take an action* (i.e., with more time available: a greater likelihood of success) and *certainty of the informational basis for the task* (i.e., greater certainty: greater chance of success). Figure 7.1 provides a visual depiction of this joint relationship, where *Panel A* represents the domain of simple tasks and *Panel B* represents complex tasks. A simple example of how *available time* might influence a "human-or-machine" decision is the so-called "problem size effect" in multiplication: humans can quickly multiply small numbers, but response times increase as the numbers grow larger (for a review, see Zbrodoff & Logan, 2005); thus, if time is a critical factor in getting the answer, the decision to pick the human or machine (calculator) would be driven by which agent would give the answer within the available time. The second factor, *informational certainty*, refers to the diagnosticity, or informational value, of the available information; information is only as useful as the value it provides to its recipient. For example, owing to particular cognitive biases, humans

---

[1] The original framing by Fitts (1951) was men-are-better-at, machines-are-better-at (MABA-MABA).

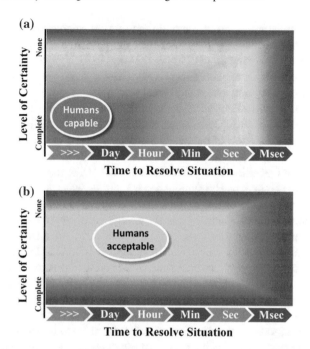

Fig. 7.1 Human performance depending upon the amount of time available to solve the problem (x axis; note the reversed direction going from most to least time) and the level of certainty in the information provided about the problem (y axis; also reversed) for simple problems (Panel A) and complex problems (Panel B). Color coding is an approximate representation of the human probability of success in both cases, with green representing the greatest likelihood, and red the lowest likelihood, and yellow as the intermediate range. Generally, humans perform well on simple problems, provided that they are given enough time and information to solve them. But, given insufficient time, and as probabilities approach chance, human performance degrades relative to tools and simple algorithms. When it comes to solving more complex problems, however, human performance is actually relatively well-calibrated; humans can deploy heuristics against these problems to rapidly achieve reasonable solutions. *Source* Perelman, Metcalfe, Boothe, & McDowell, *manuscript under review*

are notoriously challenged in making accurate probability judgements (Tversky & Kahneman, 1974). Thus, framing information to a human in terms of a probability will not necessarily lead to an effective response and neither will it increase certainty in the selection of response outcomes as much as it might for a suitably trained AI. Each of these examples illustrate a case where one could confidently assign a task *either* to a human *or* a technology; however, most tasks in the real world are not particularly reducible to simple functions as these and neither are they necessarily best assigned exclusively to one agent or another. Rather, as technologies become more capable with respect to independent behavior and problem-solving capabilities, they will be deployed against increasingly complex problems for which distinct and exclusive functional role allocations become much less clear.

Solving more complex problems will require more sophisticated ways of characterizing human–technology dynamics than the perpetual expansion of function allocation tables or coming up with improved ways to make humans better supervisors (or making AI better at being supervised). That is, when a problem is sufficiently complex, as they tend to manifest in the real world, the effectiveness of the human–technology partnership will be borne in the *interoperability* among agents, rather than their individual capabilities (DeCostanza et al., 2018). This capability comports with other contemporary models of human–technology teaming that treat team behavior as a product of interactions rather than as a sum of independent capabilities (e.g., Interactive Team Cognition theory; Cooke et al., 2013). As such, the complex problems to be discussed here can be approached in multiple ways, have an informational basis with a high degree of uncertainty, and may have multiple strong and viable solution options, none of which are clearly the right answer for the given situation, leading to multiple irreducible phases or stages that cannot be easily described by a single and parsimonious analytical model. Human evolution and experience enable solving these complex problems using decision-making heuristics that facilitate the generation of adequate solutions rapidly (e.g., note the lack of the linear decrease in human performance as a function of time in Fig. 7.1, *Panel B*). In some cases, such complex problems can be solved through dimensional reduction, or repackaging, of information in a modality that is more naturally amenable to human cognition (e.g., human performance on the visually presented versus numerically presented Traveling Salesman Problem; Polivanova, 1974). In other cases, sufficient repeated exposure to complex problems can allow humans to develop expertise that they can generalize to novel but similar problems (e.g., Recognition Primed Decision-Making; Klein, 1993).

Unlike in the simple domain, human-AI integration solutions like function allocation and supervisory control do not generalize well to most complex, real-world operational problems, with only a few noteworthy exceptions (e.g., airplane flight, nuclear power plant monitoring). Our work within this space has demonstrated that gains in effectiveness, increases in robustness, reductions in learning time, and increases in the ability to manage multiple objectives, as tends to occur in complex teaming situations (e.g., in mixed-initiative systems), are possible by targeting our science at characterizing and modeling the nature of interactions between humans and machines, all directed towards developing a deeper understanding of the fundamental states and processes that are essential to optimizing teamwork in these advanced systems (DeCostanza et al., 2018; Marathe et al., 2018; Ghandi et al., 2019). This notion that humans and AI must work synergistically and interdependently as teammates to achieve peak task performance is somewhat new; in the following section, we contextualize this perspective through a brief review of the trends in the history of human-AI partnering that have led us to this current state.

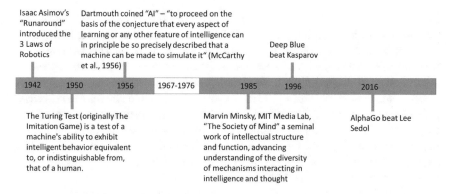

Fig. 7.2 A broad historical view of AI denoting the importance of the human to AI across time

7.2.2 Tracking the Important Roles of the Human Across AI History

In order to understand why the human is important to the future of AI, we must take a historical look at the role and the changing dynamics of human-AI interaction over time.[2] The human has had a key role in AI since the beginning, from early philosophers' attempts to superficially model human cognitive processes to science fiction writers who envisioned essential rules of robotic engagement with humans (Fig. 7.2). This interest in AI resulted in the development of the Turing Test in 1950, followed by the formal establishment of the term "artificial intelligence" in McCarthy et al. (1956) during a conference at Dartmouth College. Indeed, for much of the history of AI as a scholarly field, the human mind has been treated as the main benchmark against which AI has been judged, and if not the benchmark, certainly the prime model of intelligence to emulate. This has led to rivalry between humans and AI, with popular examples including the first-ever victory of IBM's Deep Blue over Chess Grandmaster Gary Kasparov in a single regulation game in 1996, followed by a rematch where an upgraded Deep Blue defeated Gary Kasparov to achieve the first ever full match victory by a computer against a reigning world champion in 1997, and AlphaGo winning four out of five games against Lee Sedol, considered one of the top Go players in the world at the time, in 2016.

The relationship between the human mind and AI has a much richer history than that of only creating AI that mirrors the human mind. We argue here that the efforts surrounding human-related AI development can be characterized as having been focused on analytical (e.g., processes that reflect cognitive intelligence), human-inspired (e.g., processes that reflect emotional intelligence), and humanized (e.g., processes that reflect social intelligence) AI approaches. Moreover, the evolution of the relationship between AI and humans has been a result of a few key factors,

---

[2] A full history of AI development is not within the scope of this paper; however, there are several detailed reviews that are worth exploring (see Haenlein & Kaplan, 2019).

including the progressive expansion of the raw capability of computational systems and the underlying algorithmic methods for instantiating intelligence, allowing AI to be used more effectively across a broader problem space. This evolving relationship has transformed the input required from humans to craft and update AI algorithms, and deepened the understanding of humans to such an extent that AI systems may now be capable of learning how to interpret and anticipate the needs of their human counterpart(s), a critical capability for enabling these systems to operate as a team member, rather than simply as a tool. As we aim to push the field of human-autonomy teaming forward, it is important to document how these changing capabilities have affected this relationship between humans and intelligent agents throughout the history of AI development.

Early basic AI development focused on progressively creating and evolving highly generalizable algorithms capable of producing optimal solutions to common problems under known conditions in polynomial time. Many of these algorithms dealt with networks of multiple nodes; for example, Dijkstra's algorithm (Dijkstra, 1959) for finding the shortest path; or Kruskal's minimum spanning-tree algorithm (Kruskal, 1956). These algorithms proved highly generalizable; demonstrated by Kruskal's algorithm finding applications requiring the least-cost connections among many nodes, such as laying telecommunications wire or urban planning. These early basic AI approaches all had the common properties of being deterministic, polynomial-time algorithms; moreover, at least in terms of these cases, the algorithms did not require human input into the decision-making process and could thus be used interchangeably as tools by humans and other AI programs to solve problems. However, these approaches suffer chiefly from the limitation that they do not address problems with the type of complexity frequently encountered in the real world, much less the most challenging and risky real-world environments. Karp (1972) argued that for many "unsolved" computational problems (i.e., there exists no algorithm capable of solving them in polynomial time), producing optimal solutions with satisfactory computational complexity is beyond the reach of such approaches. Thus, contemporary approaches to solving these problems have been generally developed to rely on deploying heuristics to find solutions that are sufficient for the intended application but not necessarily optimal. While it could be argued that these approaches have more in common with human decision-making than deterministic optimization algorithms, their intended use is the same: they have largely been intended to be used as improved tools that enable humans or higher-level AI to solve generalizable classes of problems.

By way of contrast, the early work in applied AI development for addressing domain-specific problems was made possible through a strategy to integrate human expertise, which led to the development of handcrafted expert systems that were able to solve well-defined problems.[3] While these approaches were rule-based and depended upon pre-defined outcomes, it was the human who provided the information

---

[3] An early example of an application of the expert systems approach was the MYCIN system, which predicted the types of bacteria that were most likely to be causing an infection by calculating a level of "belief" in the form of probabilities that were based on a selection of targeted questions that a physician would answer (Shortliffe and Buchanan, 1975). While the system performed reasonably

that was encoded by the AI. The process of handcrafting expert systems could be prohibitively difficult to implement, since it was conceived as reliant on the inputs from a team of subject-matter experts that collaborated with the system developers to imbue the AI system with a complete set of the knowledge that would be required to execute each complex task (Turban, 1988). Considering the static nature of the system after careful design, this type of system also reflects the philosophy of an intelligent agent as an explicit tool for a human to use.

Modern approaches are more often data-driven, encompassing a broad range of techniques from simpler machine learning classification methods, like logistic regression, to more advanced approaches, such as deep learning, the latter allowing the human's role in the relationship to shift within limits. For learning-based AI, the human has a consistent role in developing the initial parameters and architecture of the algorithm, which an AI then utilizes to learn from an existing dataset or through direct experience in the task environment. In this sense, learning-based AI still requires expert humans, just like the earlier expert systems, although the human role shifts from being the subject-matter experts who explicitly provide the necessary knowledge for the AI, towards being an expert developer in computer science and machine learning who crafts the framework for the fundamental algorithm, which then infers domain knowledge from the data.

Beyond system design, human inclusion in the data curation and labeling process is extremely important. The traditional paradigms for machine learning operate as either supervised or unsupervised. The key difference between these two processes is the extent to which the human is included in the data curation and learning procedure. For supervised learning, the paradigm involves a priori manual labeling of the data that would allow the algorithm to be trained to reliably and accurately recognize operationally relevant and important patterns. Active learning is a type of supervised learning that enables a more efficient method for data labeling by identifying the maximally informative samples in a data set and then asking for human labels to be provided for only those sub-selected samples. Indeed, this type of learning still requires human participation, but it allows for models to be updated on new data more efficiently by minimizing the amount of feedback required from a human oracle. Unsupervised learning focuses on identifying underlying patterns in the data without human supervision or explicit definition of the learning criterion. This type of learning has the potential for superior efficiency since it can theoretically operate at a much higher computational speed without slowing to consult a human oracle, but it often results in the classification of data that, at best, requires human review to determine what it qualitatively represents and, at worst, that it is not interpretable by human operators at all. A third category exists, dubbed "semi-supervised" learning. This category is a type of hybrid learning that relies on small batches of manually labeled data to initially train the system, which then continues by developing its own

---

effectively within its relatively well-defined domain, its core approach would be difficult to scale to broader diagnostics. That is, considering the number of questions a potential user would need to answer on the front end would grow exponentially, as well as the requisite complexity of the expert opinions stored on the back end, the system would need to provide accurate diagnostics across a broad spectrum of diseases.

model. The class of generative models is a good example of this type of system, as it requires an initial batch of data to learn the underlying features of classes, generates initial examples of the classes based upon the learned features, and, finally, continues training on the synthesized data in an unsupervised fashion. These latter algorithms can be very efficient, but they also run the risk of diverging from real-world examples of given classes if improperly tuned and left to run without supervision.

More recently, there has been another trend to change the role of the human in human-AI interactions from that of a designer or data labeler to a more natural-istic interaction. In this case, any non-expert human may directly affect the development of the system through a demonstration or feedback without requiring the human to explicitly label every data point or explain and supervise every step of a complex process (e.g., teleoperation of a robot for autonomous navigation). This case commonly involves a process known as learning from demonstrations (LfD) or imitation learning, in which the AI system learns from example demonstrations provided by a human to imitate the human's policy or actions. Essentially, imitation learning works by teaching a machine to perform a task after observing a human performing it. Inverse reinforcement learning is another common modality for learning from a human that uses human actions observed within an environment to build a value model for human actions, which can then be used to allow an algorithm to develop its own strategies to perform the given task according to the human values it has interpreted. This learning approach is a type of human-centered AI or human-in-the-loop AI, which aims to use the human to directly train or adapt the AI system through natural interaction techniques, such as those described above. As will be discussed in more detail in later sections of this chapter, within the HAT ERP, we are working on several methods to enable the integration of naturalistically collected human behavior and state information to partially label datasets, which will minimize the human effort required for supervised learning approaches and may eventually enable more efficient collection of operationally relevant data. As time has progressed, as knowledge has grown, and as technology has become more powerful, the presence and proliferation of intelligent systems in myriad domains has facilitated increas-ingly frequent and more greatly interdependent interactions with humans. This state means that, despite the increasing capability and autonomy of these systems, consid-eration and integration of the human is becoming increasingly critical. With the advancement from relatively static and limited systems like expert systems (which may still be considered as tools), modern systems are becoming increasingly capable of performing duties with a higher degree of success, a more facile adaptation, and an active interpretation of the states and needs of humans. Advancements in such human-centric applications of AI have enabled agents to more actively consider the needs of the humans they are working with by leveraging signals indicative of human states and behaviors.

Recent advances in computing and processing power and the availability of large (labeled) datasets, along with the proliferation and democratization of open source tools for machine learning (ML), have driven a large investment in and focus on ML techniques in academic research and industrial domains. This investment has yielded many impressive advancements and capabilities in AI, particularly in commercial applications, such as autonomous highway driving, image recognition, and financial fraud detection. However, there are still a number of major limitations to current AI approaches that drive the importance of looking into the role of the human within human-AI teams. First, many state-of-the-art AI techniques are developed and demonstrated within well-constrained environments, such as games (e.g., Deep Blue, AlphaGo), generating point solutions to challenging tasks that may not translate to new domains, resulting in brittle, narrow intelligence, rather than flexible, generalized intelligence. These approaches are difficult to apply to real-world, complex contexts (e.g., military operations) due to limitations in computing power and network bandwidth (particularly at lower command echelons, such as at the tactical level with individual Soldiers or small teams); a dearth of well-labeled or curated data; and a complex, high-tempo, interdependent environment. Further, the high-risk, high-consequence environment of military operations may require humans to remain in the loop and not fully displaced by AI farther into the future than in other domains. The following sections describe ongoing efforts that have been developed within the HAT ERP to address these and other limitations, as well as supporting the active community of human-AI teaming research as the field continues to evolve.

7.3 Artificial Intelligence for Human-Autonomy Teams

Our research is predicated on the idea that the paradigm for advancing the integration of AI and autonomy into military teams needs to be shifted towards instantiating concepts in direct applications for human-autonomy teaming in real-world operational contexts. It is time to dispense with mindsets that solely focus on selecting the right tool for the job and, instead, adopt an approach of building effective teams of humans and with AI that manifest the full potential of continual advancements in intelligent technology. We expect that the nature of the interaction between humans and AI-enabled systems will need to change dramatically to account for the dynamic changes in context—including different time constraints, levels of certainty, or the amount of data available—as well as the complexity of the problems faced. Intelligently designed and applied bidirectional teaming mechanisms will allow us to overcome the individual limitations of both human and machine capabilities to achieve a level of combined performance and ability that is currently not possible (DeCostanza et al., 2018; Marathe et al., 2018).

Broadly, in order to manifest the "teaming" vision that we espouse, it is essential to understand how and where human and machine capabilities complement each other, understand how and where they fundamentally differ—particularly for the sake of identifying critical gaps that would undermine effectiveness and understand how and what new capabilities can emerge once multiple intelligent agents are assembled into coordinated and reciprocally interdependent collectives. While the U.S. Army has employed smaller ground and air robots for dull, dirty, and dangerous tasks at the tactical level for decades (primarily teleoperated with very limited autonomous capabilities), new possibilities for increased intelligence and standoff are reaching

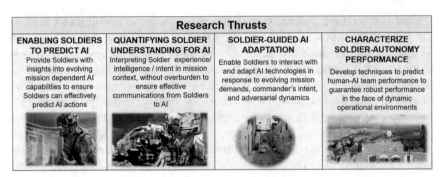

Research Thrusts			
ENABLING SOLDIERS TO PREDICT AI	**QUANTIFYING SOLDIER UNDERSTANDING FOR AI**	**SOLDIER-GUIDED AI ADAPTATION**	**CHARACTERIZE SOLDIER-AUTONOMY PERFORMANCE**
Provide Soldiers with insights into evolving mission dependent AI capabilities to ensure Soldiers can effectively predict AI actions	Interpreting Soldier experience/ intelligence / intent in mission context, without overburden to ensure effective communications from Soldiers to AI	Enable Soldiers to interact with and adapt AI technologies in response to evolving mission demands, commander's intent, and adversarial dynamics	Develop techniques to predict human-AI team performance to guarantee robust performance in the face of dynamic operational environments

Fig. 7.3 Descriptions of the research thrusts

the forefront with the introduction of large autonomous combat systems. These larger combat systems are expected to exhibit autonomous (or semi-autonomous) mobility, situation awareness (to include target recognition), decision making under risk, and robust communication. Introducing these evolved technologies is expected to offer new operational possibilities, but active research and development efforts remain focused on the effective integration of such systems to enable collective performance in dynamic environment from the tactical to strategic levels. This chapter articulates four major research thrusts critical to integrating AI-enabled systems into operational military teams, giving examples within these broader thrust that are addressing specific research gaps. The four major research thrusts include: (1) Enabling Soldiers to predict AI, (2) Quantifying Soldier understanding for AI, (3) Soldier-guided AI adaptation, and (4) Characterizing Soldier-AI performance (Fig. 7.3).

Enabling Soldiers to Predict AI.

This research thrust aims to develop robust mechanisms that provide insights into evolving mission-dependent AI capabilities to ensure Soldiers can not only anticipate agent behavior, but can also better understand their underlying decision-making processes. Across the broad research and development community, a number of approaches are utilized to enable more "human-like" decisions from AI, including the use of neural networks, reinforcement learning, and cognitive architectures, to name a few. However, there are cases in which the task environment does not lend itself to human-like solutions, or the decision-making process is irreducible and unobservable to the human. These approaches do little to make decision-making more transparent or explainable to human team members.

Much of the theory underlying our current research to enable Soldiers to predict AI draws both from direct applications and conceptual inspiration out of the Situation Awareness Agent-based Transparency (SAT) model (Chen et al., 2014, 2018). For effective and trusted teaming to be developed and maintained, Soldiers must be able to understand the intelligent agent's decisions or actions (SAT Level 1) and the reasoning by which these decisions are made (SAT Level 2) within the mission and environmental context in order to predict (SAT Level 3) future decisions or actions.

Therefore, the addition of both new and evolved transparency concepts and techniques is critical for enabling advanced teaming between Soldiers and AI-enabled systems in ways that cannot be achieved with current standard interface design techniques or by improving the performance of AI technology alone. Research has shown that there is not one single "human way" of making a decision or solving a problem (e.g., route planning; Perelman, Evans, & Schaefer, 2020a), which implies that even effective algorithms may still not be trusted by human team members. Therefore, advancing concepts for appropriate user interface design and communication strategies must be done in conjunction with continued algorithm development if we are to effectively communicate decisions made by the AI-enabled agents, convey their reasoning for making those decisions, and support the prediction of their future decisions or actions.

For human-AI teams to enjoy the benefits of collaboration, the nature of the interaction between human and autonomy must functionally support each team member in their interdependent contributions: information must be tailored to each intended recipient and reformatted to the appropriate modality when communicated between human and AI-enabled agents. Therefore, a key consideration is how we can optimize the display of required information, either generated through intelligent algorithms or otherwise, by considering and complementing human cognitive and perceptual capabilities and limitations. Simultaneously, the format and modality of information must be consumable by both human and AI team members. Never before have we had the opportunity that is presented through the anticipated ubiquitous nature of user displays. Combining this opportunity with advances in AI engenders a need to transform both the way we think about displays and information presentation, and literally, how we see the world.

User Interface Design for Enhanced Autonomous Mobility. Within the HAT ERP, our near-term efforts have focused on user interface design principles to enhance autonomous mobility. Specifically, the Army has prioritized the creation of Next Generation Combat Vehicles, which are expected to comprise both manned and unmanned (robotic) platforms enabled by autonomous mobility. This use case provides a near-term target to focus theoretical laboratory efforts on addressing some of the complex, real-world conditions that may be expected to be most challenging for human-autonomy teaming; and we have specifically focused on developing technologies and procedures for streamlining and expediting the decision-making processes related to mobility and joint maneuver in the context of complex team operation. Procedurally, these technologies enabled a control loop that allowed humans to ask the questions (that is, provide high-level goals), and the AI to provide rapid answers. Here, we describe and justify these procedures, and the design principles considered in doing so.

The first interactive procedure in enabling autonomous mobility was to move from human specification of precise and detailed waypoint navigation to the designation of one or more general goal-points to which the AI would determine the best route for navigation. Prior research has shown that AI decisions would need to be predictable in order for the system to function effectively as a trustworthy teammate (Chen et al., 2014; Lyons et al., 2019). This predictability can be facilitated by manipulations

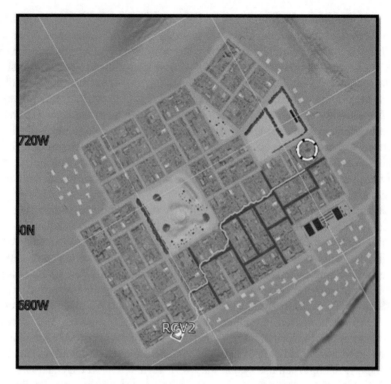

Fig. 7.4 The Transparent Route Planner has generated a route from the vehicle (labeled RCV2) to the goal location (black and white ring) using simple logic and a single click. This route plan can then be accepted or further modified by the user, increasing the team's ability to make decisions about mobility

designed to make the AI's intentions more transparent. In the present use case, this principle was implemented in the design of a Transparent Route Planner (Fig. 7.4), which reads terrain data and human-input goal locations to generate route plans. Functionally, this differed from the default method of interaction which relied on user-specified waypoints (independent of terrain data) that the robot would attempt to follow using local obstacle avoidance. This planner enabled a different style of supervisory control by allowing the operator to select the goal locations and the desired route plan and then calculated and displayed a potential route to the goal, which the operator could then either accept or modify. Importantly, the route planner generated waypoint plans (routes) at a sufficiently detailed level that the user could discern fine-scale local decisions made by the planner in advance; in contrast, generating a coarser waypoint plan and allowing the AI to make local decisions using its obstacle avoidance algorithm would not make sufficient detail available to the user during planning. Achieving transparency in this case required us to follow a second design principle, one of parity, which describes an equivalence between the information available to human and AI team members; in this case, parity was achieved by providing the autonomy with the terrain data by making it available to the human. The end result of this interaction is Soldier-in-the-loop control and planning execution. In testing with Soldiers, this capability improved the users' understanding of the AI's mobility actions by over 60% (Perelman et al., 2020b).

The aforementioned Transparent Route Planner achieved information parity by providing autonomy with the terrain information available to the human teammates. Extending this principle of information parity in the opposite direction, we sought to provide the human with representations of the types of information that the autonomy could use to generate routes. Specifically, in military settings, Soldiers need to consider many factors about the mission, enemy, time and their troops available, terrain, and civil considerations; such a complex problem space does not lend itself to optimal decision-making, since solutions that optimize one particular criterion may sacrifice another. For example, one route may be faster but offer less cover and concealment. In order to operationalize these factors, we developed cost maps associated with different mission parameters that the Transparent Route Planner could consider during a route generation: vehicle mobility, exposure to enemy contact, and wireless signal strength. These cost maps were visualized for the human users in the form of icons on the map display. In order to facilitate bidirectional communication between the Transparent Route Planner and the human user, we developed a Comparator Display based on visualizations found in prior work in unmanned vehicle operations (e.g., Behymer et al., 2015; Stowers et al., 2016). The Comparator Display allowed users to evaluate the tradeoffs among routes visually for each of the parameters (see Fig. 7.5). When used in conjunction with the Transparent Route Planner, the Comparator Display allowed the users to select multiple mission-relevant parameters and generate the routes that automatically optimized them. Merging these two technologies allowed a Soldier-autonomy team to rapidly develop courses of action using the Soldier's expertise and prior experience in understanding context, and the

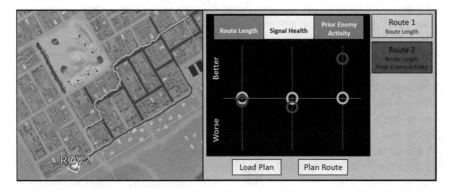

Fig. 7.5 Comparator Display prototype (right panel) along with two routes generated by the Transparent Route Planner (left panel). The Y axis of the Comparator Display is used to depict which route is better in terms of each of the mission parameters. The route shown in amber is slightly better in terms of signal health and route length. However, the route shown in red is much better in terms of avoiding prior enemy activity

AI's superiority in rapidly generating analytical solutions to spatial problems. With this Comparator Display, users improved their understanding of the courses of action proposed by the AI-enabled agents by over 30%, while simultaneously reducing the time spent interpreting the decisions by an average margin of approximately 40% (Perelman et al., 2020c).

In the aforementioned route planning use case, the design principles that drove the technology development were developed to enhance relatively long timescale decision-making. That is, during planning, team performance could be improved by providing more information in the appropriate format to each team member. In other situations, team members may need to communicate information rapidly in high-saliency modalities for rapid consumption. During armored vehicle operations, the transition to, and execution of, portions of the mission may have the potential to exceed human information processing capacity (Huey & Wickens, 1993). AI-enabled teammates can potentially cue human teammates during periods of high workload by presenting signals in highly salient non-visual modalities. To reduce crew workload and improve crew members' local situation awareness and understanding of vehicle autonomy status during mission execution, a multimodal cueing system was implemented that presented auditory and vibrotactile cues to crew members when their robotic vehicle neared dangerous areas of the environment as well as when the vehicle's autonomy encountered mobility challenges (Chhan et al., 2020). The multimodal cueing system reduced the duration of major mobility challenges during remote operation by an average of almost 15%, and it helped reduce the vehicles' exposure to threats in the environment by over 35%. Summarily, relatively simple multimodal interface manipulations designed to make the AI-enabled agent's actions, intentions, goals, and general reasoning processes more transparent to human teammates were shown as capable of dramatically improving the situation awareness of these systems and their local environments during remote operation.

User Interface Design for Team Coordination. As human–machine team ratios continue to be reduced in size (i.e., fewer humans interacting proportionally with more intelligent agents), it becomes necessary for the underlying AI systems to exhibit independent behaviors that will allow the agent to function more as teammates than supplementary tools. This change creates the need for a new organizational structure and associated transparency displays that increase coordination between a commander and his or her crew with the team's AI assets and capabilities. As such, our work has led to the development of a Commander's Interface that can be operated within a vehicle on the battlefield, providing the commander with the needed capabilities to enable Command and Control (C2) to coordinate the execution of human-autonomy team responses to evolving mission needs. This interface allows the commander to maintain situation awareness and coordinate the Soldier and AI team by providing a consolidated view of information related to vehicle state (e.g., unmanned ground and air vehicles), crew state (e.g., tasking, activity, and physiological state), and autonomy state (e.g., mobility, aided target recognition, and decision support tools). These functionalities allow commanders to quickly and easily maintain situation awareness of the mission and all of their crew and assets to enhance teaming and improve performance in dynamic missions and environments, including the ability to call standard battle drills, to display the requirements of the battle drills to the crew, and to delegate appropriate actions to both the human and agent team members.

Human–Computer Vision Collaboration for Intelligent Displays. Soldier-AI systems, such as aided target recognition, are designed to use virtual content overlaid on the real world (augmented reality) as a primary means for both communication with, and support of, effective Soldier-AI team performance. However, these highly artificial and very salient stimuli fundamentally change our visual interactions with the world; as displays become increasingly ubiquitous as moderators of our visual experience with the world, the criticality of the cognitive science research required to leverage rapid technological advances grows exponentially.

Our research in this area focuses on how visual interaction with the environment is fundamentally changed as a function of the overlay of new information via intelligent displays. This change leads to more effective reasoning and awareness of the mechanisms and processes that underpin both the desired performance and the relevant principles of visual cognition, and thus, improved targeting (Larkin et al., 2020; Geuss et al., 2020). By leveraging this improved understanding of visual cognition, entirely new means of representing and highlighting visual information may be created. Through a research emphasis and design focus on total system performance, there is the potential to create new, increasingly effective levels of joint human-AI target acquisition and engagement decisions. It is also key to consider that when we alter the way that Soldiers see the world, we are also altering the information collected from Soldier behaviors that may be opportunistically sensed (Geuss et al., 2019; Lance et al., 2020).

Visual perception is not a one-for-one representation of physical stimuli, but rather a probabilistic modeling of what the world looks like (see Geisler, 2008). In brief, this model takes into account physical inputs, cognitive priors, randomness, and noise related it to a characteristic of interest in the environment. The construct of *scene statistics* is essentially meant to stand in as a description of this process and how the brain exploits it. Examples of how scene statistics are influential include evaluating the connection between a scene and the visual performance for specific visual tasks; predicting neural responses of human operators; specifying how detected scene features are best represented (e.g., Berman, 2018); understanding how scene features relate to perception (Brady et al., 2017); and understanding, as well as incorporating into design, the time course of processing associated with different scene features (Mares et al., 2018). Finally, there is considerable evidence to suggest that altering low level sensory-perceptual features can impact higher order cognition in various ways (e.g., perceptual discomfort in Habtegiorgis et al., 2019; affective response in Takahshi & Watanabe, 2015); and, of course, the most well-known examples are visual illusions (described in Howe & Purves, 2002, 2005).

Our brains have evolved to take advantage of these statistical properties, and that forms the foundations of our perception. We rapidly adapt to changes from natural to urban environments, even virtual environments. Color perception is a good example of that adaptation; our sensitivity to different colors and contrasts adapt pretty rapidly to reflect the distributions in our environments (e.g., Bao & Engel, 2019). But what happens as we change the environment, as we add these different dimensions into current environments by changing the distribution of low level features? Do we change those statistical relationships? Does it alter the statistical distributions that we are leveraging? Does it change how we perceive the world? And if so, can we alter that perception intentionally? Currently, we are exploring these questions through a series of experiments that are aimed at defining novel forms of visual interaction leveraging augmented reality concepts. Although much adjacent work would be required to leverage such knowledge, to include improved predictive algorithms, computer vision, processing speed and power, it is imperative that cognitive science keep pace with these new interfaces and opportunities, given the exponential rate at which technology continues to develop and the potential impact in real-world operations of all sorts.

Visualization of Uncertainty. The successful teaming of human and AI capabilities will often require communicating the degree of uncertainty in the AI-based information to the user. Uncertainty is introduced in AI-based capabilities from errors in sensors that are used by AI algorithms, through data aggregation, in model estimations, and when operating in contested environments, to name a few possible sources. Communicating the degree of uncertainty can improve user trust in the system as well as offer another data point from which users can base their decisions and thus improve performance. Recent research has shown that communicating the degree of uncertainty in weather forecasts (Ruginski et al., 2016), in spatial location (McKenzie et al., 2016), and in other applications like image labeling (Marathe et al., 2018) can improve objective performance and user understanding of content. Importantly, the way in which uncertain information is visually communicated can exert a moderating influence on performance (for a review see Padilla et al., 2020). Further research is needed to understand optimum methods of representing uncertainty within augmented reality applications (Geuss et al., 2020).

The importance of communicating uncertainty does not end with user performance. If user behavior is intended to—through opportunistic sensing (Lance et al., 2020)—be used to refine algorithms, the effects of uncertainty representation on behavior may be manifested in unexpected adjustments to AI algorithms. For example, if an Aided Target Recognition (AiTR) system, which uses machine learning to identify potential threats in the environment, not only highlights the potential target but also provides the user with an estimate of how certain the classification of its threat, the user may behave differently based on the system's certainty. Further, users may only engage highly certain targets while ignoring targets whose associated certainty is lower. If user behavior occurs like this, then opportunistically sensed information (e.g., taken as a result of a Soldier raising his weapon) would only serve to reinforce the AI system's confidence in high certainty targets but provide no additional benefit to targets with low certainty, which is arguably the situation where opportunistic sensing would provide the most benefit. Future research is needed to understand how users make decisions under uncertainty both to (1) improve the utility of AI-generated information, and (2) understand potential secondary implications for the utilization of opportunistically sensed information. This work suggests that overall system performance would be improved by communicating the level of uncertainty in AI-generated information.

Creating Collaborative Situation Awareness. Information sharing is a critical factor in maintaining a shared understanding, or shared awareness, in a team. Shared situation awareness (SSA) is a critical feature of effective performance in human teams (Salas, Stout, & Cannon-Bowers, 1994) where all team members need to know what tasks must be completed or which decisions need to be made to complete a task or mission (van Dijk, van de Merwe, & Zon, 2011). Teams can achieve SSA by beginning with a common awareness, or mental model, of the environment, tasks at hand, and goals. When teammates have a shared mental model, or similar knowledge about a mission and tasks, team performance is shown to improve (Mathieu et al., 2000). With time, particularly as each of these components may change and even do so dynamically, communication between teammates becomes critical to maintaining SSA. In human teams, the way in which information is conveyed between teammates affects performance. Implicit forms of communication are more effective than explicit communication in achieving successful team performance, especially during complex tasks (Butchibabu et al., 2016). The ideal communication would allow achieving and maintaining SSA along with a reduced burden to teammates. Proactive communication, or anticipating future situations and creating a shared mental model for those, allows for reduced unnecessary communication and better team performance.

Interfaces are an ideal way through which to communicate in order to maintain SSA in human-AI teams. Through opportunistic sensing (Lance et al., 2020), AI can assess human behavior, gaining an understanding of present and future tasks and approaches to reaching a goal. An AI can share its knowledge and increase SSA in the human-AI team through transparency concepts (Perelman et al., 2020c) or through screen overlays (Larkin et al., 2020; Geuss et al., 2020). In many instances, communication and information sharing can be immediate and can be done without an increased workload or burden to humans, AI, or the human-AI team as a whole, increasing SSA and team performance. However, as we move to more complex scenarios and continuously evolving contexts involving large-scale integrated operations, questions remain on how we operationalize "shared" mental models in these complex teams. Future research will need to build on these design principles and begin to address how human-AI teams develop and manage shared mental models of complex, ever-evolving problems, environments, and other team members in order to facilitate the communication, rapid mission planning, and quick adaptation needed for sustained performance in future operating environments.

Way ahead. Cognitive science research, such as in the topics outlined above, is necessary, both to identify cognitive-centric design principles and to create novel forms of human-AI teaming through augmented and mixed reality display capabilities. This section advocates for an ongoing program of strategic research on novel approaches to defining the cognitive pairing mechanisms for new technologies by understanding how technological complexity interacts with cognition. Success in this area may provide revolutionary advances in the creation of new levels of cognitive capabilities under conditions of technological complexities.

7.3.1 Quantifying Soldier Understanding for AI

The Quantifying Soldier understanding for AI research thrust, *which focuses on* interpreting a Soldier's experience, intelligence, and intent within a mission context—without creating overburden—is necessary to ensure that effective bidirectional communications enable the kinds of dynamic real-time adaptation that are needed for intelligent systems to adjust their performance to the needs of the human Soldiers in the human-autonomy team. Whereas research and development efforts articulated within the first thrust were primarily looking at the information being communicated *to* the Soldier, this area focuses on the ability for AI to understand the Soldier—their actions, intentions, and goals—in a continuous manner. By leveraging Soldier behaviors, traits, and physiology, it is possible to continuously provide AI-enabled systems with specific states and constraints about the team members and their interactions with each other (e.g., Kulic & Croft, 2007; Rani et al., 2006). By fusing those data with environment-specific data necessary for adapting models of the world, we can then provide a method to improve outcomes and enhance team situation awareness in a way that is specifically tailored to both the individual Soldier and the collective team's needs.

The Soldier as a Sensor. Recent advancements in research and development of wearable technologies and human cognitive, behavioral, and physiological models have made it possible to truly consider the Soldier as a sensor within human-autonomy teaming operations. Neuroscientific advancements reveal how differences in brain structure and function are associated with precise human behaviors (Telesford et al., 2017; Garcia et al., 2017); social and environmental sensing tools are able to characterize patterns of gross human social behaviors over time (Kalia et al., 2017); while advances in physiological and biochemical sensing provide continuous measurement of internal human dynamics and stable characteristics influencing team performance. Critical to a human-autonomy team, the capability to continuously stream behavioral, physiological, and environmental data from the Soldier enables AI to infer and understand the actions, intentions, and context of their human teammates, first meeting and eventually exceeding the capabilities of human-to-human teammates. These advances can be coupled with novel computational methods to infer motivations, predict behavior, and reason about the environment and the agents acting in it. This advancement has the potential to provide additional understanding of the relationships between individual and team states and processes—such as stress, fatigue, engagement, trust, coordination, and performance—as well as how these relationships vary across different team types and operational contexts (Metcalfe et al., 2017; Schaefer et al., 2019).

With more robust models of human states, actions, intentions, and goals built around real-time, machine-consumable measures (e.g., Hoffing & Thurman, 2020; Jain & Argall, 2019), we expect to push the boundaries of what is possible with human-autonomy teams by providing intelligent systems with an accurate, continuous, operational understanding of their human teammates and the unfolding team performance over time. Therefore, we are developing new technologies that objectively characterize natural interactions between the human and the AI to account for the behavior and performance of the entire team, in order to provide a more objective, continuous, real-time assessment. Development of these novel technologies will require creating an integrated system capable of combining wearable sensing devices with advanced machine learning approaches for real-time state estimation (Marathe et al., 2020). Additionally, many research questions need to be addressed toward realizing the goal of defining predictive algorithms for an individualized adaptation in human-AI teams. To enhance human-AI teaming, technologies must be capable of balancing among diverse sources, levels, and timing of variability within the team. For example, questions remain regarding the respective influence of individual and team variability on performance. Can we effectively predict the relationships between individual and team states and behaviors, incorporating variability in humans and agents over time? How can advanced measurement methodologies and modeling techniques be employed to understand the dynamics in team processes over multiple time-scales? In addition to "within team" dynamics, research must also address methods to sense shifts in environmental and sociocultural influences and to determine relevance to the team's mission. As dynamic events unfold, the availability of information is often sparse, and the reliability of information available is often unknown. What mechanisms are critical to account for and adapt to the fluid nature of the information availability and reliability in these complex environments and dynamic situations?

We envision a future where adaptive and individualized systems function with individual capabilities and limitations to achieve greater human-system performance. This individualized human-technology approach is expected to enable a greater variety in human behavior, while having the ability to maintain consistent, robust outcomes when viewing the human-technology behavior as a system. Critically, when considering multiple agents and multiple humans, much work on the prediction of individual and team states and processes exacting to performance is required to fully realize this envisioned future of human-AI teaming. Outcomes of this research will enable systems to continuously adapt to individual Soldiers, leading to an enhanced Soldier-AI team situation awareness, a greater awareness of unknowns and blind spots, a reduced Soldier burden, an increasingly robust sustained support, and an enhanced overall teaming dynamics.

Integrating Soldier Knowledge into AI. Conceiving Soldiers as sensors and advancing the current state of the art on prediction of individual and collective dynamics for enhanced teaming leaves vague the notion of integration of that knowledge into AI systems. Thus, additional efforts are needed to appropriately integrate Soldier knowledge into AI. The current paradigm for training AI systems, such as deep-learning-based image classification algorithms, involves acquiring and manually labeling large datasets, a time-consuming and expensive process. This problem is ubiquitous across the research community and technology industries, but it is a particularly difficult problem to solve in a military application. While many computer vision applications are able to leverage pre-labeled data, either by accessing specialized datasets or by aggregating publicly available images of particular target types, the images of Soldiers, vehicles, and equipment necessary to train military-relevant computer vision are often not publicly available; also, the sensitive nature of the images limits the ability to crowdsource labels for the data, creating a bottleneck since only approved experts will be able to properly label the data. This issue is a substantial one with commercially prevalent optical sensors (e.g., cameras), which is compounded with the inclusion of specialized sensors commonly utilized in the military domain, such as infrared (IR) and LiDAR. The labeling efficiency problem is potentially mitigated by having Soldiers partially label this data at the point of origin, but placing additional burden upon the Soldier risks their performance and well-being, especially in a combat environment, where their attention is already at a premium. These costs and risks make it difficult to regularly update AI agents, which will be key to enabling the adaptation to new tactics, targets, and environments as required in the complex and dynamic future battlefield envisioned by the Army's operating concept of MDO. It is prohibitively expensive and time-consuming to set up data collection scenarios for the volume and variety of data necessary to represent every potential scenario that may be encountered on the battlefield, and this approach would still result in models for AI that are unable to adapt to new scenarios on time-scales that allow the team to remain operationally viable. However, the ability to adapt to never-before-seen scenarios is a hallmark of human cognition.

It is necessary to leverage more efficient models of data acquisition and labeling to make the constant updating of future technologies feasible. To this end, we propose the use of opportunistic sensing, defined as "obtaining operational data required to train and validate AI/ML algorithms from tasks the operator is already doing, without negatively affecting performance on those tasks or requiring any additional tasks to be performed" (Lance et al., 2020). This approach is inspired by techniques used in industry to continuously update systems based upon information passively provided by pervasive technology. For example, the route recommendations provided by Google Maps are made possible by a combination of continuous sensing from any devices running the application, providing real-time data on the current state of traffic; and models trained on previously collected data for a given road along a potential route that predict what traffic will be like at a given time (Lau, 2020). This approach avoids the requirement for deploying resources to independently monitor traffic (e.g., traffic helicopters) or asking for active feedback from end users who are engaged in driving. A similar approach can be taken for military applications by aggregating the various sensor, vehicle, equipment, and user behavior data to provide context for the raw data coming from a system without requiring the Soldier to intervene and while minimizing the necessary post-hoc analysis by an expert.

By inferring the states and behaviors of the Soldier, we are able to add necessary context to incoming data on the environment and adversary actions that are key to understanding scenarios outside the initial training set of an agent (Lance et al., 2020). As such, under this area of emphasis, our research focuses on characterizing the link between Soldier's knowledge and understanding and their associated behavior; specifically, investigating what information can be gleaned from the way in which the Soldier interacts with their systems, environment, or teammates (human or intelligent agent) in order to be used to draw inferences of the Soldier's knowledge, state, action, or intent. Fusing raw sensor feeds and operational data with the knowledge inferred from the humans creates new sources of labeled training sets that better reflect an evolving threat and changing environments. A simple example is using a Soldier pulling the weapon trigger as an indication that a threat is present in the environment. Temporarily setting aside the possibility of a misfire, this becomes an obvious and accessible data point that usually provides a clear indication of a threat, which may be useful in identifying portions of the data that are relevant to training the threat response behaviors or identifying the sensor profiles of novel or modified targets that the current iteration of the computer vision might have missed (e.g., adversarial designed camouflage on a tank may cause the miscatergorization based on pre-trained computer vision data). With these opportunistically collected data supplementing the broad, static datasets that agents are initially trained on, we anticipate more robust performance in real-world, dynamic environments.

When applied on a larger scale, this work supports the development of tools to promote tactical awareness via collective knowledge. By combining passive sensing from multiple individuals, it is possible to aggregate across a military squad or larger elements in order to derive contextual information at higher echelons (Lance et al., 2020). In particular, the intention to field the Integrated Visual Augmentation System (IVAS; Microsoft, Redmond, WA), an augmented reality system with dynamic tracking of head movement in 3D and eye tracking as an intended feature, may provide Soldier gaze as a source of opportunistically sensed data. Eye movement characteristics have been determined to be an indicator of a variety of states, ranging from workload, which may provide useful information for team tasking, to attention, which has a clear function in detecting targets of interest in an environment (Di Nocera et al., 2007; Findlay & Gilchrist, 1998; Kowler et al., 1995; Marquart et al., 2015; Motter & Belky, 1998; Pomplun & Sunkara, 2003; Schulz et al., 2011; Van Orden et al., 2001). While these are not necessarily robustly indicative of a singular state or target of interest when interpreting the behavior of a single individual, by considering the behavior of a larger formation, the signals become more meaningful. For instance, a single Soldier fixating on a particular section of a scene may be incidental, but if the entire formation fixates on the same section of the scene while traversing its space, it may be an indicator of an aberration indicating a threat in that location or a likely target location. This sort of experientially learned knowledge is difficult to explicitly define to train an agent in advance, but by leveraging the understanding of all of the Soldiers available, we anticipate the ability to assign tasks to AI-enabled agents based on inferred situational understanding and in line with mission objectives.

Way ahead. Utilizing the approaches described above, our research program extends to far future-focused applications. Human-AI teams, as envisioned in the future, will be capable of performing within environments of ever-increasing complexity, almost inconceivable today. To facilitate effective performance within these realms of complexity, we are conducting the fundamental research to realize a future with individualized, adaptive technologies that are continuously sensing the critical actors and environment while evolving to enhance the functioning of the team over time. Going beyond specific task-focused application spaces, such as threat detection, AI can utilize Soldier-based inputs to target the enhanced functioning of the team itself. Our research addresses the use of individualized, adaptive technologies to enhance human-AI team cognition and behavioral processes, such as a shared understanding in distributed environments; the coordination, cohesion, and swift action with new, diverse, rotating, and evolving team members; and the minimization of process losses (e.g., communication, coordination, backup behaviors) as team complexity increases.

7.3.2 Soldier-Guided AI Adaptations

The research thrust that is focused on Soldier-guided AI adaptation was conceived to enable Soldiers to interact with and adapt AI technologies in response to evolving mission demands, a commander's intent, and adversarial dynamics. While the first two thrusts were designed to facilitate working with relatively static agents and general methods for communicating between human and artificial agents, this research aims to develop and refine algorithms that use a Soldier's interaction and reinforcement learning *to continuously improve and adapt team capabilities* for dynamic and adversarial missions. This research supports the development of intelligent agents that can modify their own behavior, learning how to improve themselves directly from interacting with Soldiers either through the imitation of a Soldier, receiving feedback from the Soldier, or some combination of intuitive interaction between the Soldier and AI system. Additionally, this research contains a focus on developing AI systems that are capable of dynamically orchestrating the tasking and flow of information across a distributed Soldier-AI team. However, complex, dynamic, and data-sparse combat environments can limit the tractability and success of many of the modern machine learning strategies, such as the deep reinforcement learning used in civilian settings, to produce remarkable AI behaviors and capabilities. Research in Soldier-guided training of AI assets is being undertaken to overcome these constraints and to leverage the intelligence and experience of non-expert human users to rapidly imbue learning agents with the desired behaviors through data-efficient and naturalistic interactions that can then be more easily utilized by Soldiers in training and on the ground (Goecks, et al., 2019).

Human-in-the-Loop RL/Cycle-of-Learning. Due to the computational complexity and sample inefficiency of deep learning and reinforcement learning, methods of reducing that complexity, via leveraging human knowledge, have grown more important over recent years. Techniques, such as learning from demonstrations or learning from human preferences, allow for non-expert persons to give intuitive feedback and instruction to AI algorithms to improve training and robustness. However, these techniques have their own weaknesses in terms of generalization (such as the data distributional shift problem when learning from demonstrations).

The cycle-of-learning is a framework for leveraging multiple modalities of human input to improve the training of deep-learning-based AI algorithms (Waytowich et al., 2018). These modalities can include human demonstrations (i.e., human-provided exemplars of behaviors), human interventions (i.e., interdictions in agent behavior that take the form or corrections or interventions provided by the human), and human evaluations (i.e., feedback or sparse indications of the quality of the agent behavior). Every one of these modalities of human interaction have been previously shown to provide various benefits in learning performance and efficiency, each with its own unique drawbacks. The goal of the cycle-of-learning framework is to unify different human-in-the-loop learning techniques by combining each of these interaction modalities into a single framework in order to leverage their complementary characteristics and mitigate their individual weaknesses (Waytowich et al., 2018, Goecks et al., 2019, Goecks et al., 2020).

The cycle-of-learning (shown in Fig. 7.6) combines multiple forms of learning modalities for training an AI agent based on the intuition of how a teacher would teach a student to perform a new task for the first time. For example, in order to convey an entirely new concept or task to the student, the teacher may first proceed by demonstrating that task, intervening as needed while the student is learning the task, and then providing a series of critiques or evaluations as the student starts to gain mastery of the task. At some point during this cycle, the student would also practice to further his or her ability to perform the task (i.e., reinforcement learning). This process is repeated at various stages as new concepts and tasks are introduced. While there is significant extant research into each of these human-in-the-loop learning modalities individually, to the best of our knowledge, this proposal is the only method that combines these modalities into a single framework. The cycle-of-learning has indeed been shown to significantly improve the robustness, quality, and speed of training AI agents compared to existing techniques (Goecks, et al., 2020).

Adaptive Coordination. The optimal orchestration of resources in heterogeneous human-autonomy teams is critical for effective team operation. Coordination of

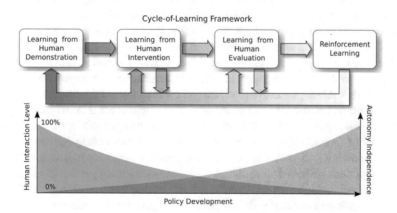

Fig. 7.6 Cycle-of-Learning for Autonomous Systems from Human Interaction: a concept for combining multiple forms of human interaction with reinforcement learning. As the policy develops, the autonomy independence increases, and the human interaction level decreases

a complex, decentralized team of heterogeneous, autonomous entities with time-varying characteristics and performance capacities will be prohibitively challenging for Soldiers, particularly as they interface with an increasing number of intelligent agents. As described above, decision aids and transparency tools will need to be developed and implemented to fluidly integrate distributed teams of Soldiers and AI-enabled systems and to manage the high volume of information needed to effectively coordinate team assets. These improved teaming capabilities will help prevent break-downs in effectiveness, improve resiliency, and increase decision speed and quality in dynamic combat environments. Moving beyond traditional tools and incorporating Soldier-guided AI adaptation, the notional concept to achieve this capability is a closed-loop system that monitors the state of the team and the environment, and dynamically allocates the resources of the Soldier-autonomy team (e.g., tasking, attention, information flow, and physical formation) via agents integrated within user interfaces to maintain desirable team metrics (e.g., performance, Soldier states, and situation awareness). With this goal in mind, several studies are currently being formulated which will: (1) characterize the effects on these metrics of interest when modulating team resources in a controlled manner in military-relevant settings; (2) learn desired, generalizable task allocation strategies for heterogeneous teams from limited exemplar human demonstrations; and (3) examine the adoption of team tasking recommendations from an explainable expert system to inform the development of decision aids and, ultimately, systems for fully automated dynamic resource orchestration.

Way Ahead. In the complex multi-domain environments of the future, on-the-fly joint decision-making, changes in tactics, deception, and novel organizational forms will be critical to success for human-AI teams. To be capable of contributing to this potential technological advantage, humans and intelligent agents must fluidly adapt in real-time, in symbiotic ways, to the potential but changing individual and team dynamics as the situation evolves. Envisioning the future, we expect intelligent agents capable of learning and adapting to new data and changing contexts on the fly, and humans that must fluidly adapt with these autonomous team members while undertaking novel roles for enhanced decision-making and performance. To address this future need, we are engaged in research building on the above principles of Soldier-guided AI adaptation, but focused on how to enable the continuous adaptation to complex environmental demands in teams of multiple humans and multiple agents without breaking down the emergent cohesive properties of the team. Can we use principles of individualized and adaptive instruction and human-AI teamwork to develop evolving systems of humans and agents with ever-increasing intelligence and capabilities capable of more complex performance (or altogether novel behavior or creative solutions)? Can we understand and enable more advanced capabilities within teams that have yet to be fully realized or imagined, as future human-autonomy teams on the battlefield operating seamlessly to accomplish joint goals create new opportunities to maximize human potential and to rapidly increase the speed and effectiveness of decision making?

7.3.3 Characterizing Soldier-Autonomy Performance

Current research toward the thrust in *characterizing Soldier-autonomy performance* focuses on developing the techniques to measure and monitor performance in the face of distributed, dynamic operational environments wherein complex, interconnected activities are continuously evolving; such techniques will further enable interventions to improve performance. Decades of research on human teams has produced a wealth of literature on factors that are useful for predicting performance outcomes for these teams. However, as the U.S. Army moves to integrate AI, there are several existing deficiencies that must be overcome in order to enable effective teaming. First, the majority of this literature describes qualitative factors that are difficult to integrate with systems for measurement and optimization in their native formats. Second, attempts to quantify factors that are predictive of team performance frequently employ data and data collection techniques that are not compatible with many current AI capabilities. For example, a great deal of the literature on human team dynamics employs qualitative questionnaires that are difficult for AI to interpret as well as performance measures for which observable changes lack unique explanations at a mechanistic level within a complex team. Moreover, until recently, the data necessary to understand the micro-, meso-, and macro-level dynamics unfolding over time in teams to influence performance has been lacking. Research is needed to understand the critical team-level states, processes, and their respective dynamics within human-AI teams and how to appropriately aggregate individual, dyadic, and group-level data over time to accurately reflect team performance across diverse tasks. Finally, some types of data that are useful for predicting the performance of integrated human-autonomy teams may require the rapid processing of high-dimensional or large-packet-size data collected at a high sampling rate from spatially distributed agents by computationally expensive algorithms. There is the potential for these data to quickly exceed the relatively sparse bandwidth and accessible storage limitations on the battlefield; that is, we should not expect to have access to *all of the data, all of the time* and, instead, we should plan for inferential and predictive mechanisms that can operate robustly in such environments.

To overcome these challenges, we are developing novel techniques and technologies for estimating human and AI outcomes during operations distributed over space and time, initially for experimental settings. Our approach is designed to employ advancements in sensors and networks that permit the unobtrusive collection and transmission of massive amounts of data, AI, and machine learning approaches for sensor and information management, along with online data analysis in real-time, networking technologies to allow near real-time collaboration, displays and touchscreen technologies, human factors and ergonomics, after-action review technologies, and novel data analysis techniques, in order to radically change the way that these teams are assessed. Further, this approach draws on assessment methods from the experimental, test and evaluation, and military working communities with the goal of providing the near-real-time, continuous assessment of team *effectiveness* and prediction of the team's outcomes. Specifically, our approach leverages the interest of multiple stakeholders (experimenters, engineers, users, and expert evaluators) and, recognizing their potential unique contributions to the assessment process, democratizes assessment across those stakeholder populations by means of closed-loop interactions through a tablet-based graphical user interface Dashboard. There are four primary components to this effort: Dashboard development, predictive modeling and signal management, novel measures of team effectiveness, and crew state estimation.

Assessments of a team can be made on the basis of highly multivariate information, requiring a multidisciplinary team in order to parse, annotate, and interpret data and its analyses to create information. At the heart of this assessment capability is the requirement to be able to retroactively play, pause, stop, and rewind an entire mission's worth of data, adding annotations or exporting subset data streams as required. However, members of such heterogeneous teams also vary in terms of knowledge, skills, and abilities, as well as in terms of the data that they might require to make assessments. Consider that a large-scale experiment will likely produce a large amount of data from human participants, autonomous systems, and the simulation environment. Human science researchers will benefit from analyzing, and will be able to generate insights from, highly detailed raw human subjects' data, but they may have little to offer in the way of analyzing mission data collected from the simulation environment or the output packets from real or simulated autonomous systems. Comparatively, subject-matter expert evaluators would be primarily interested in analyzing mission data from the simulation environment, but they may also benefit from dimensionally reduced or summarized data about the human subjects and autonomy. In order to democratize data analysis across a multivariate team of stakeholders, data streams will need to be processed by AI and machine learning algorithms and displayed as time series at the appropriate resolution for each type of stakeholder. Here, we attempt to answer the research question, "How can a heterogeneous team of military, science, and engineering stakeholders collaborate to generate novel, actionable information from unique interpretations of mission data during an after-action review; how must that mission data be visualized, represented, or dimensionally reduced in order to maximize the contributions of these team members?".

Such distributed, naturalistic experiments will necessarily produce a great deal of multimodal data that can be useful for predicting outcomes; so much data, in fact, that networks are unlikely to support the unfettered transmission of all of it. Algorithms aimed at predicting team outcomes must be, to some degree, aware of the *diagnosticity* of each data stream, given particular experimental contexts, in order to permit the intelligent sampling of the right data at the right time. This thrust area seeks to answer the research question, "What hardware, software, and data collection techniques will allow human-autonomy teams to mitigate the challenges presented by bandwidth constraints during distributed, large-scale simulation experiments, exercises, and training events?".

Generally speaking, many real-world application domains of autonomous systems are inherently high-noise; that is, there are many factors that contribute to a team's success or failure beyond simply a team's performance, which may be difficult to measure or may be only measurable infrequently. Furthermore, it may be difficult to draw comparisons between measures of performance generated from human versus autonomous team members under different conditions and contexts. Predicting team outcomes under these conditions may not be accomplished by asking how well the team is currently performing, but rather by asking how effectively the team is functioning. Such measures of effectiveness must be robust to perturbations in data streams and severe amounts of data loss, must be somewhat agnostic but flexible with respect to the level of analysis, and must be able to draw comparisons among different data modalities. The research question driving this thrust area is, "How can we measure the effectiveness of heterogeneous human-autonomy teams, and ultimately predict team outcomes, using the types of sparse, multi-modal data generated by human and autonomous agents during distributed, large-scale data collection?".

Finally, we encourage the expansion of the range of unobtrusively, opportunistically sensed data, to include neurophysiological data. Human brain activity potentially contains a great deal of information relevant to team effectiveness, including activity changes within single users as well as activity patterns shared among multiple users. Emerging research on novel materials make collecting such data less obtrusive; such technologies include in-ear and dry electroencephalography devices. In the near term, we seek to answer the research question, "Where is the state of neuroscience hardware, software, and data analysis and processing techniques relative to the level of maturity required for its useful application under real-world conditions?".

These approaches, taken together, form the groundwork for a comprehensive approach toward enabling experimentation over the types of physical and temporal distances inherent to the real world. Answering these research questions will allow us to advance the start of the art by radically shifting experimental paradigms. The future of data analysis, as we see it, is not the simple application of highly tailored algorithms to specific types of data, but rather the more general application of AI and human expertise across the broad range of experimental data to transform it into actionable information and measures.

7.4 Conclusions

As AI-enabled technologies approach a point where they may be deployed on the battlefield, it is not enough to simply consider the performance of static algorithms as tools that have been developed and refined in a well-structured and relatively "sterile" laboratory setting and then expect that performance to translate into the real world. Rather, we, as a community of researchers, must ensure: (1) that intelligent technologies can operate effectively in real-world contexts with a team of human Soldiers and a heterogeneous array of AI-enabled systems; and (2) that they can adapt to the continuously changing environmental and mission conditions to maximize their utility, resilience, and robustness. The ARL HAT ERP exists to address these current research gaps and to manifest the revolutionary potential of instantiating and managing complex, heterogeneous human-AI teams. The above discussion documents currently active research under the HAT ERP, but other research gaps and new capabilities will continue to be addressed as we work to turn AI from tools to teammates for U.S. Soldiers.

Acknowledgements The views and conclusions contained in this document are those of the authors and should not be interpreted as representing the official policies, either expressed or implied, of the DEVCOM Army Research Laboratory or the U.S. Government. The U.S. Government is authorized to reproduce and distribute reprints for Government purposes notwithstanding any copyright notation herein.

References

Bao, M., & Engel, S. A. (2019). Augmented reality as a tool for studying visual plasticity: 2009–2018. *Current Directions in Psychological Science, 28*, 574–580.

Behymer, K. J., Mersch, E. M., Ruff, H. A., Calhoun, G. L., & Spriggs, S. E. (2015). Unmanned vehicle plan comparison visualizations for effective human-autonomy teaming. *Procedia Manufacturing, 3*, 1022–1029. https://doi.org/10.1016/j.promfg.2015.07.162

Berman, D. (2018). *Representations of spatial frequency, depth, and higher-level image content in human visual cortex* (Doctoral dissertation, The Ohio State University).

Brady, T. F., Shafer-Skelton, A., & Alvarez, G. A. (2017). Global ensemble texture representations are critical to rapid scene perception. *Journal of Experimental Psychology: Human Perception and Performance, 43*(6), 1160.

Butchibabu, A., Sparano-Huiban, C., Sonenberg, L., & Shah, J. (2016). Implicit coordination strategies for effective team communication. *Human Factors, 58*(4), 595–610.

Chen, J. Y. C., Lakhmani, S. G., Stowers, K., Selkowitz, A. R., Wright, J. L., & Barnes, M. (2018). Situation awareness-based agent transparency and human-autonomy teaming effectiveness. *Theoretical Issues in Ergonomics Science, 19*(3), 259–282. https://doi.org/10.1080/1463922X.2017.1315750

Chen, J. Y. C., Procci, K., Boyce, M., Wright, J. L., Garcia, A., & Barnes, M. (2014). *Situation awareness-based agent transparency* (No. ARL-TR-6905). Army Research Laboratory, Aberdeen Proving Ground, MD.

Chhan, D., Scharine, A., & Perelman, B. S. (2020). Human-autonomy teaming essential research program project 2: Transparent multimodal crew interface designs. technical note 3: Multimodal cueing for transparency in mobility operations. Technical note ARL-TN-1019. Aberdeen Proving Ground, MD: CCDC Army Research Laboratory.

Cooke, N. J., Gorman, J. C., Myers, C. W., & Duran, J. L. (2013). Interactive team cognition. *Cognitive Science, 37*, 255–285.

DeCostanza, A. H., Marathe, A. R., Bohannon, A., Evans, A. W., Palazzolo, E. T., Metcalfe, J. S., & McDowell, K. (2018). Enhancing human-agent teaming with individualized, adaptive technologies: A discussion of critical scientific questions. Technical report ARL-TR-8359. Aberdeen Proving Ground, MD: US Army Research Laboratory.

Dekker, S. W., & Woods, D. D. (2002). MABA-MABA or Abracadabra? Progress on human-automation co-ordination. *Cognition, Technology & Work, 4*, 240–244.

DiNocera, F., Cmilli, M., & Terenzi, M. (2007). A random glance at the flight deck: Pilots' scanning strategies and the real-time assessment of mental workload. *Journal of Cognitive Engineering and Decision Making, 1*(3), 271–285.

Dijkstra, E. W. (1959). A note on two problems in connexion with graphs. *Numerische Mathematik, 1*(1), 269–271.

Findlay, J. M., & Gilchrist, I. D. (1998). Chapter 13—Eye guidance and visual search. In G. Underwood (Ed) Eye guidance in reading and scene perception (295–312), Elsevier Science.

Fitts, P. M. (1951). *Human engineering for an effective air navigation and traffic control system.* National Research Council.

Garcia, J. O., Brooks, J., Kerick, S., Johnson, T., Mullen, T. R., & Vettel, J. M. (2017). Estimating direction in brain-behavior interactions: Proactive and reactive brain states in driving. *NeuroImage, 150*, 239–249.

Geisler, W. S. (2008). Visual perception and the statistical properties of natural scenes. *Annual Review of Psychology, 59*, 167–192.

Geuss, M. N., Cooper, L., Bakdash, J., Moore, S., & Holder, E. (2020). Visualizing dynamic and uncertain battlefield information: Lessons from cognitive science. In *Virtual, augmented, and mixed reality technology for multi-domain operations, international SPIE: Defense + commercial sensing.*

Geuss, M. N., Larkin, G., Swoboda, J., Yu, A., Bakdash, J., White, T., & Lance, B. (2019). Intelligent squad weapon: Challenges to displaying and interacting with artificial intelligence in small arms weapon systems. In *Artificial intelligence and machine learning for multi-domain operations applications* (Vol. 11006, p. 110060V). International Society for Optics and Photonics.

Gandhi, S., Oates, T., Mohsenin, T., & Waytowich, N. (2019). Learning from observations using a single video demonstration and human feedback. arXiv:1909.13392.

Goecks, V. G., Gremillion, G. M., Lawhern, V. J., Valasek, J., & Waytowich, N. R. (2019). Efficiently combining human demonstrations and interventions for safe training of autonomous systems in real-time. In *Proceedings of the AAAI conference on artificial intelligence* (Vol. 33, pp. 2462–2470).https://doi.org/10.1609/aaai.v33i01.33012462.

Goecks, V. G., Gremillion, G. M., Lawhern, V. J., Valasek, J., & Waytowich, N. R. (2020). Integrating behavior cloning and reinforcement learning for improved performance in dense and sparse reward environments. In *Proceedings of the AAMAS 2020 conference on artificial intelligence* https://doi.org/10.13140/RG.2.2.35626.16322.

Haenlein, M., & Kaplan, A. (2019). A brief history of artificial intelligence: On the past, present, and future of artificial intelligence. *California Management Review, 61*(4), 5–14.

Habtegiorgis, S. W., Jarvers, C., Rifai, K., Neumann, H., & Wahl, S. (2019). The role of bottom-up and top-down cortical interactions in adaptation to natural scene statistics. *Frontiers in Neural Circuits, 13.*

Hoffing, R. A., & Thurman, S. M. (2020). The state of the pupil: Moving toward enabling real-world use of pupillometry-based estimation of human states. Army research lab aberdeen proving ground md aberdeen proving ground United States.

Howe, C. Q., & Purves, D. (2002). Range image statistics can explain the anomalous perception of length. *Proceedings of the National Academy of Sciences, 99*(20), 13184–13188.

Howe, C. Q., & Purves, D. (2005). The Müller-Lyer illusion explained by the statistics of image–source relationships. *Proceedings of the National Academy of Sciences, 102*(4), 1234–1239.

Huey, B. M., & Wickens, C. D. (1993). *Workload transition: Implications for individual and team performance.* National Academy Press.

Jain, S., & Argall, B. (2019). Probabilistic human intent recognition for shared autonomy in assistive robotics. *ACM Transactions on Human-Robot Interaction (THRI), 9*(1), 1–23.

Kalia, A. K., Buchler, N., DeCostanza, A., & Singh, M. P. (2017). Computing team process measures from the structure and content of broadcast collaborative communications. *IEEE Transactions on Computational Social Systems, 4*(2), 26–39.

Karp, R. M. (1972). Reducibility among combinatorial problems. In *Complexity of computer computations* (pp. 85–103). Springer, Boston, MA.

Klein, G. A. (1993). A recognition-primed decision (RPD) model of rapid decision making. In *Decision making in action: Models and methods* (pp. 138–147). Westport, CT: Ablex Publishing.

Kowler, E., Anderson, E., Dosher, B., & Blaser, E. (1995). The role of attention in the programming of saccades. *Vision Research, 35*(13), 1897–1916.

Kozlowski, S. W. J., & Ilgen, D. R. (2006). Enhancing the effectiveness of work groups and teams. *Psychological Science in the Public Interest, 7*(3), 77–124. https://doi.org/10.1111/j.1529-1006.2006.00030.x

Kruskal, J. B. (1956). On the shortest spanning subtree of a graph and the traveling salesman problem. *Proceedings of the American Mathematical Society, 7*(1), 48–50.

Kulic, D., & Croft, E. A. (2007). Affective state estimation for human–robot interaction. *IEEE Transactions on Robotics, 23*(5), 991–1000.

Lance, B. J., Larkin, G. B., Touryan, J. O., Rexwinkle, J. T., Gutstein, S. M., Gordon, S. M. Toulson, O., Choi, J., Mahdi, A., Hung, C. P., & Lawhern, V. J. (2020). Minimizing data requirements for soldier-interactive AI/ML applications through opportunistic sensing. In *Proceedings of the SPIE 11413, artificial intelligence and machine learning for multi-domain operations applications.* https://doi.org/10.1117/12.2564514.

Larkin, G. B., Geuss, M., Yu, A., Rexwinkle, J. T., Callahan-Flintoft, C., Bakdash, J. Z., Swoboda, J., Lieberman, G., Hung, C. P., Moore, S., & Lance, B. J. (2020). Augmented target recognition display recommendations. *Defense Systems Information Analysis Center Journal, 7*(1), 28–34.

Lau, J. (2020). Google maps 101: How AI helps predict traffic and determine routes, Google (Blog). https://blog.google/products/maps/google-maps-101-how-ai-helps-predict-traffic-and-determine-routes/.

Lyons, J. B., Wynne, K. T., Mahoney, S., & Roebke, M. A. (2019). Trust and human-machine teaming: A qualitative study. In W. Lawless, R. Mittu, D. Sofge, I. S., Moskowitz, & S. Russel (Eds.), *Artificial intelligence for the internet of everything* (pp. 101–116). Academic Press.

Marathe, A. R., Brewer, R. W., Kellihan, B., & Schaefer, K. E. (2020). Leveraging wearable technologies to improve test & evaluation of human-agent teams. *Theoretical Issues in Ergonomics Science, 21*(4), 397–417. https://doi.org/10.1080/1463922X.2019.1697389

Marathe, A. R.; Schaefer, K. E., Evans, A. W., & Metcalfe J. S. (2018). Bidirectional communication for effective human-agent teaming. In J. Y. C. J. Chen, & G. Fragomeni (Eds.), *Virtual, augmented and mixed reality: Interaction, navigation, visualization, embodiment, and simulation. VAMR 2018. Lecture notes in computer science* (pp. 338–350). Cham: Springer.

Mares, I., Smith, M. L., Johnson, M. H., & Senju, A. (2018). Revealing the neural time-course of direct gaze processing via spatial frequency manipulation of faces. *Biological Psychology, 135*, 76–83.

Marquart, G., Cabrall, C., & de Winter, J. (2015). Review of eye-realted measures of drivers' mental workload. *Procedia Manufacturing, 3*, 2854–2861.

Mathieu, J. E., Heffner, T. S., Goodwin, G. F., Salas, E., & Cannon-Bowers, J. A. (2000). The influence of shared mental models on team process and performance. *Journal of Applied Psychology, 85*(2), 273.

McCarthy, J., Minsky, M. L., Rochester, N., & Shannon, C. E. (1956). A proposal for the dartmouth summer research project on artificial intelligence. Dartmouth.

McKenzie, G., Hegarty, M., Barrett, T., & Goodchild, M. (2016). Assessing the effectiveness of different visualizations for judgments of positional uncertainty. *International Journal of Geographical Information Science, 30*(2), 221–239.

Metcalfe, J. S., Marathe, A. R., Haynes, B., Paul, V. J., Gremillion, G. M., Drnec, K., Atwater, C., Estepp, J. R., Lukos, J. R., Carter, E. C., & Nothwang, W. D. (2017). Building a framework to manage trust in automation. In *Proceedings of the micro-and nanotechnology sensors, systems, and applications IX* (Vol. 10194, p. 101941U). International Society for Optics and Photonics. https://doi.org/10.1117/12/2264245.

Motter, B. C., & Belky, E. J. (1998). The guidance of eye movements during active visual search. *Vision Research, 38*(12), 1805–1815.

Padilla, L., Kay, M., & Hullman, J. (2020). Uncertainty visualization. In R. Levine (Ed.), Handbook of Computational Statistics & Data Science: Springer Science

Perelman, B. S., Evans, A. W., & Schaefer, K. E. (2020a). Where do you think you're going? Characterizing spatial mental models from planned routes. *ACM Transactions in Human Robot Interaction, 9*(4) https://doi.org/10.1145/3385008.

Perelman, B. S., Wright, J. L., Lieberman, G. A., & Lakhmani, S. (2020b). Human-autonomy teaming essential research program project 2: transparent multimodal crew interface designs.

Technical note 2: Transparency in mobility planning. technical note ARL-TN-1004. Aberdeen Proving Ground, MD: CCDC Army Research Laboratory.

Perelman, B. S., Lakhmani, S., Wright, J. L., Chhan, D., Scharine, A., Evans, A. W. III., & Marathe, A. R. (2020c). Human-autonomy teaming essential research program project 2: Transparent multimodal crew interface designs. project summary technical report. Technical Report ARL-TR-9002. Aberdeen Proving Ground, MD: CCDC Army Research Laboratory.

Perelman, B. S, Metcalfe, J. S., Boothe, D. L., & McDowell, K. Oversimplifications limit potential for human-AI partnerships. IEEE Access. Manuscript under review.

Polivanova, N. I. (1974). Functional and structural aspects of the visual components of intuition in problem solving. *Voprosy Psychologii, 4,* 41–51.

Pomplun, M., & Sunkara, S. (2003). Pupil dilation as an indicator of cognitive workload in human-computer interaction. In *Proceedings of the international conference on HCI,* 2003.

Rani, P., Liu, C., Sarkar, N., & Vanman, E. (2006). An empirical study of machine learning techniques for affect recognition in human–robot interaction. *Pattern Analysis and Applications, 9*(1), 58–69.

Ruginski, I. T., Boone, A. P., Padilla, L. M., Liu, L., Heydari, N., Kramer, H. S., & Creem-Regehr, S. H. (2016). Non-expert interpretations of hurricane forecast uncertainty visualizations. *Spatial Cognition & Computation, 16*(2), 154–172.

Salas, E., Stout, R., & Cannon-Bowers, J. (1994). The role of shared mental models in developing shared situational awareness. In: *Situational awareness in complex systems* pp. 297–304.

Schaefer, K. E., Baker, A. L., Brewer, R. W., Patton, D., Canady, J., & Metcalfe, J. S. (2019). Assessing multi-agent human-autonomy teams: US army robotic wingman gunnery operations. In *Proceedings of the SPIE 10982, micro- and nanotechnology sensors, systems, and applications XI,* 109822B. https://doi.org/10.1117/12.2519302.

Schulz, C. M., Schneider, E., Frtiz, L., Vockeroth, J., Hapfelmeier, A., Wasmaier, M., Kochs, E. F., & Schneider, G. (2011). Eye tracking for assessment of workload: A pilot study in an anaesthesia simulator environment. *British Journal of Anaesthesia, 106*(1), 44–50.

Sheridan, T. B. (2000). Function Allocation: Algorithm, Alchemy or Apostasy? *The International Journal of Human-Computer Studies, 52,* 203–216.

Shortliffe, E. H., & Buchanan, B. G. (1975). A model of inexact reasoning in medicine. *Mathematical Biosciences, 23*(3–4), 351–379.

Stowers, K., Kasdaglis, N., Newton, O., Lakhmani, S., Wohleber, R., & Chen, J. (2016). Intelligent agent transparency: The design and evaluation of an interface to facilitate human and intelligent agent collaboration. *Proceedings of the Human Factors and Ergonomics Society Annual Meeting, 60*(1), 1706–1710. https://doi.org/10.1177/1541931213601392

Takahshi, K., & Watanabe, K. (2015). Effects of image blur on visual perception and affective response. IEEE 978-1-4799-6049.

Telesford, Q. K., Ashourvan, A., Wymbs, N. F., Grafton, S. T., Vettel, J. M., & Bassett, D. S. (2017). Cohesive network reconfiguration accompanies extended training. *Human Brain Mapping, 38*(9), 4744–4759.

Turban, E. (1988). Review of expert systems technology. *IEEE Transactions on Engineering Management, 35*(2), 71–81.

Tversky, A., & Kahneman, D. (1974). Judgment under uncertainty: Heuristics and biases. *Science, 185*(4157), 1124–1131.

U.S. Army TRADOC. (2018). The U.S. Army in Multi-Domain Operations. Army TRADOC Pamphlet 525-3-1. Available at: https://www.tradoc.army.mil/Portals/14/Documents/MDO/TP525-3-1_30Nov2018

van Dijk, H., van de Merwe, K., & Zon, R. (2011). A Coherent impression of the pilots' situation awareness: studying relevant human factors tools *The International Journal of Aviation Psychology, 21*(4), 343–356

Van Orden, K. F., Limbert, W., Makeig, S., & Jung, T.-P. (2001). Eye activity correlates of workload during a visuospatial memory task. *Human Factors, 43*(1), 111–121.

Waytowich, Nicholas & G. Goecks, Vinicius & Lawhern, Vernon. (2018). Workshop on Human Robot Interaction.

Zbrodoff, N. J., Logan, G. D. (2005). What everyone finds: The problem-size effect. In J. D. Campbell (Ed.), *Handbook of mathematical cognition* (pp. 331–346). New York, NY: Psychology Press.

Chapter 8
Re-orienting Toward the Science of the Artificial: Engineering AI Systems

Stephen Russell, Brian Jalaian, and Ira S. Moskowitz

Abstract AI-enabled systems are becoming more pervasive, yet system engineering techniques still face limitations in how AI systems are being deployed. This chapter provides a discussion of the implications of hierarchical component composition and the importance of data in bounding AI system performance and stability. Issues of interoperability and uncertainty are introduced and how they can impact emergent behaviors of AI systems are illustrated through the presentation of a natural language processing (NLP) system used to provide similarity comparisons of organizational corpora. Within the bounds of this discussion, we examine how the concepts from Design science can introduce additional rigor to AI complex system engineering.

Keywords Artificial intelligence · Machine learning · System engineering · Design science

8.1 Introduction

It is almost overly trendy to talk about how advances in artificial intelligence (AI) are enabling new capabilities in a number of application domains from biology/medicine, defense, business decision-making to communications. As a core technology, AI relies on sophisticated machine learning (ML) algorithms that utilize exemplar data to learn and predict new insights. While there are direct connections to hardware in robotic AI and ML algorithms are increasingly being embedded in programmable chips, AI itself is fundamentally a software innovation, with its scientific grounding in computer science.

S. Russell (✉) · B. Jalaian
Army Research Laboratory, Adelphi, MD, USA
e-mail: stephen.russell15.civ@mail.mil

B. Jalaian
e-mail: brian.jalaian.civ@mail.mil

I. S. Moskowitz
Naval Research Laboratory, Washington, DC, USA
e-mail: ira.moskowitz@nrl.navy.mil

Much of the software or algorithmic (non-embodied) AI research examines and advances isolated instances of learning manifested in ML approaches and generally focuses on improving predictive accuracy. In a system's context, or perhaps more appropriately stated in an application context, these approaches almost never exist in isolation and are applied to process-oriented problems such as mobility, maneuver, and decision-making. Further, even within a "single system" multiple ML algorithms are commonly implemented as an ensemble component, creating system-level AI that depends on and interacts with other system components. As such, it is apparent that an AI-enabled system is defined as a complex system—a system composed of many components which may interact with each other. The literature on complex systems suggests that large complex systems may be expected to be stable up to a critical level of connectedness, and then as this connectedness increases it will *suddenly* become unstable (Cohen & Newmans, 1985; May, 1972). This is certainly seen in complex dynamical systems that reach a bifurcation point where the behavior becomes chaotic and unpredictable (May, 1976). System instability that produces emergent system behaviors has a high probability of being unanticipated. In other words, one class of emergent system behaviors are instantiated outputs of unstable complex systems. These types of emergent or unanticipated behaviors usually appear as system mistakes or errors, particularly when a complex system is AI-enabled (Russell & Moskowitz, 2016). The notions of complex system verification and emergent behaviors are soundly placed in the domain of systems engineering. The challenge, in an age where there is a preponderance of intelligent complex systems, is to bring scientific rigor to the engineering of such intelligent systems. Addressing this challenge is necessary to advance the fundamental understanding, as opposed to an operational understanding of AI complex systems in any broad or generalizable capacity.

While there is ample work in the complex systems literature on systems engineering (Alpcan et al., 2017; Belani et al., 2019; Carleton et al., 2020), examining AI software engineering as a hierarchical complex system remains an open and active research area. The scope of this chapter presents a background of issues in engineering AI-enabled systems, which by definition are complex systems. We discuss the implications of hierarchical component composition and the importance of data in bounding AI system performance and stability. Within the bounds of this discussion, we examine how the concepts from Design science can introduce additional rigor to the AI complex system engineering. Recognizing systems engineering is a broad topical area, and more qualitative aspects of AI complex systems engineering, such as explainability, ethics, and trust, are outside the scope of this chapter.

The chapter is organized as follows. The first section provides a short background on software engineering, followed by a section on AI-enabled systems-of-systems and emergent behaviors. The next section discusses the importance of interoperability technologies. We consider the role of uncertainty in ML algorithms in the fifth section and present an example of system engineering challenges, using natural language processing in the sixth section. We present the applicability of Simon's Sciences of the Artificial (Simon, 1969), specifically Design science theories and concepts, to AI systems engineering in Sect. 8.7 and conclude in Sect. 8.8.

8.2   AI Software Engineering

Before providing a meaningful perspective on system engineering artificial intelligence (AI) systems, it is important to scope the domain of system engineering in this context. Clearly, system engineering is not a new topic and has seen extensive study ranging from biological to physical/mechanical, and, of most relevance, software system contexts. While the grounding and parallels in biological and mechanical complex systems are many (Newman, 2011; Ottino, 2004; Schindel, 1996; Thurner et al., 2018), our focus is on software because the implementation of machine learning (ML) methods are algorithmic and thus instantiated as software. For performance reasons, ML software may get implemented in hardware; e.g., programmable chips, embedded systems, application-specific integrated circuits, etc. However, the implementation of software algorithms in hardware only complicates the overall system engineering and does not remove many of the most critical problems in software engineering (De Michell & Gupta, 1997). Traditionally, software systems are constructed deductively by writing down the rules that govern system behaviors that get implemented as program code. However, with ML techniques, these rules are inferred from training data (from which the requirements are generated inductively). This paradigm shift makes reasoning about the behavior of software systems with ML components difficult, resulting in software systems that are intrinsically challenging to test and verify (Khomh et al., 2018).

There is a saying that software errors all occur at the intersection of logic and data. This saying makes clear the importance of software/system engineering for AI applications. In the case of AI systems, the logic incorporates ML models, which have *minimally* two data intersections: the data on which it was built and the data that it interacts with. This case is further compounded by the emphasis on which ML researchers and engineers place on getting improved application-specific accuracy (Yang et al., 2020). As a result, the coupling between the model and the specific application tends to be extremely tight, leading to constrained system engineering.

This is not to say that tremendous benefit cannot be gained from the use of AI systems. The core point is that increased focus should be given to the system engineering in which the AI exists (Breck et al., 2017). This focus should ensure that appropriate constraints and controls are used in the creation, usage, and improvement of the AI system. The Institute of Electrical and Electronics Engineers (IEEE) (I.S.C. Committee, 1990) defines software engineering as the application of a systematic, disciplined, quantifiable approach to the development, operation, and maintenance of software [systems]. While one might argue that software engineering for traditional (i.e., non-adaptive software) is fairly straightforward, fundamental expectations such as repeatability become far more elusive to describe and predict in the case of ML software. Ignoring the complexity of the model building, ML software *learns* and thus will produce different outputs given both the sequence of inputs and the characteristics of those inputs.

Figure 8.1 illustrates a typical ML model development "pipeline" where the cyclic nature of ML model development essentially implies that the AI system would need

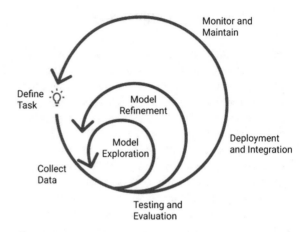

Fig. 8.1 Machine learning pipeline. Adapted from [17]

ongoing updates if the system task has any significant variability. Figure 8.1 notably shows the essential role that data (collect data) plays in the ML engineering life cycle. This data requirement has led to the broad use of general models, provided much like a code library, and built from extremely large datasets or opensource collections. The problem with these models is that much like a software library any misrepresentations, bias, or other variability that exist in the model are then built (transferred) into the receiving system. For an application, this problem is compounded by the fact that these extrinsic models incorporate data at a scale where the people using the subsequent models and building their own AI systems cannot easily gain insights into the training data details.

The ML pipeline intrinsically has software engineering demands that translate directly to AI system engineering requirements. Systems engineering is about engineering systems that provide the functionality to users as required, when required, and how required. Table 8.1 shows empirical system engineering challenges that result from the existence of ML pipelines in systems of different types (prototype, non-critical, critical, and cascading). Lwakatare et al. (2019) provide an empirical study of system engineering challenges for machine learning systems. However, they do not extend the systems engineering challenges to the system in which the ML is deployed. AI systems are not monolithic. The ML model must operate as an element of a multi-component system that provides macro user-driven functions. Challenges in cascading deployment are particularly relevant to AI *systems* because with the scale they do not exist in isolation and the boundaries that typically define system locality can be greatly expanded and obfuscated, leading to emergent system behaviors. We provide more details on these intimations in the next section.

The discipline of systems theory, which is the grounding for system engineering, provides the foundational knowledge to address problems where it is necessary to understand the behavior of the system (e.g., a realized assembly, or an artifact) as a function of the behavior and interaction of its constituent elements (components). The previous discussion provides a simple example of how AI-enabled systems should be viewed as a hierarchical system—the next section will extend this notion toward

Table 8.1 System engineering challenges in the use of ML components (Lwakatare et al., 2019)

	Experimental or prototyping	Non-critical deployment	Critical deployment	Cascading deployment
Assemble dataset	Issues with problem formulation and specifying the desired outcome	Data silos, scarcity of labeled data, and an imbalanced training set	Limitations in techniques for gathering training data from large-scale, non-stationary data sources	Complex and effects of data dependencies
Create model	Use of non-representative dataset, data drifts	No critical analysis of training data	Difficulties in building highly scalable ML pipeline	Entanglements causing difficulties in isolating improvements
Train and evaluate model	Lack of well-established ground truth	No evaluation of models with business-centric measures	Difficulties in reproducing models, results, and debugging deep learning models	Need of techniques for sliced analysis in the final model
Deploy model	No deployment mechanism	Training-serving skew	Adhering to stringent serving requirements; e.g., latency, throughput	Hidden feedback loops and undeclared consumers of the models

a complex system. By a hierarchic system, we adopt a definition of a system that is composed of interrelated subsystems, each of the latter being, in turn, hierarchic in structure until some lowest level of an elementary subsystem is reached (Simon, 1991). Currently, in the AI system engineering literature, ML is treated as an elementary subsystem when it is in fact exceedingly complex. This same notion expands to account for dynamically composed AI systems, as increasingly the boundaries and nature of intelligent systems should be characterized and complex systems-of-systems with the advance of technologies such as the Internet of Things and pervasive networking.

8.3 AI-enabled Complex Systems-of-Systems and Emergent Behaviors

The purpose of systems engineering, as a discipline that applies scientific principles and engineering methods as a means to cope with the challenges of complexity, should yield abstractions that characterize the hierarchical nature of systems at their individual boundaries. As with all of the sciences, the understanding of complex adaptive systems is reached solely in a quantitative, predictive, and ultimately experimentally testable manner. Complex adaptive systems are dynamical systems that are able to change their structure, their interactions, and, consequently, their dynamics as they evolve in time (Tolk et al., 2018). The theory of complex systems is the theory of generalized time-varying interactions between components that are characterized by their states. The notion of interactions introduces an expanded dimension of systems engineering as it implies the isolation of its component functionality. It is possible at this point to have a philosophical discussion about what exactly a system is if its atomic boundaries are not clearly defined and the complexity of the system is a function of component interactions. Rather than entertain the philosophical nature of systems, which has been deeply covered in the literature (Backlund, 2000), we adopt a simple definition: a system is a set of interconnected things that work together to perform a function. In the case of AI-enabled systems, these "things" exist in a hierarchical construct where they are composed to meet a purpose. The role of the AI components within this construct is to introduce intelligent interactions, which en masse evince system behaviors.

Inter-system interactions typically occur on networks that connect system components. The interactions may cause the states of the component themselves and/or the network to change over time. The complexity of a system increases when the interaction networks have the ability to change and rearrange as a consequence of changes in the states of its components. Thus, complex systems are systems whose states change as a result of interactions and whose interactions change as a result of states. The same characterizes AI system ML algorithms, many of which (such as neural nets) utilize internal components and states as learned representations. Thus, if ML algorithms are complex (sub) systems, the hierarchical system in which they exist must also be complex. Consider any case where a system is providing more than rudimentary intelligence. It would be necessary to create an ensemble of ML algorithms that are interconnected and interdependent such that greater degrees of learning and intelligence can be achieved. If one AI system interacts with another AI system to achieve a macro-objective or satisfy a global requirement, the AI system can be thought of as a system-of-systems. Keeping in mind the reciprocated nature of system state and interactions, complex AI system-of-systems have the propensity to show a rich spectrum of behavior: they are resilient, adaptive, and co-evolutionary with an inherent ability to exhibit unexpected and emergent behaviors. Predictability is a highly desirable outcome of system engineering (Kuras & White, 2005). Emergent behaviors are often the inverse of predictable behaviors and emergence is an innate characteristic of complex AI systems (Brings et al., 2020).

Emergent system behavior is a response, or set of responses, that cannot be predicted through analysis at any level simpler than that of the system as a whole. Emergent behavior, by definition, is what is left after everything else has been explained away. This definition highlights the difficulty in predicting and explaining emergent behavior (Li et al., 2006). If the behavior is predictable and explainable, then it will not be treated as emergent behavior and its approaches can be designed to handle the responses. From an engineering standpoint, understanding emergence can lead us to design smarter and more resilient systems while at the same time furthering our understanding of phenomena in systems' interactions (Tolk et al., 2018). The source of emergence is the nonlinear combination of components at different states over time. Emergence, in this case, is one of the possible states a system might take even if the observer or designer of the system is not aware of the possibility (Mittal & Rainey, 2014). Consider an AI system that is no longer behaving as originally specified but had adapted to a new environment by developing new multi-level interactions and feedback loops. How can such self-modification and adaption reconcile with the design of the system's creators when it exceeds the bounds of their intention? From an AI systems engineering perspective, embedded in this first question is a second, perhaps more important one: how then to limit learning and prevent errors resulting from gaps in what the system knows? The intuitive answer is to limit interactions and exposure to new data. However, this would lead to an over-constrained system, which is seldom desirable (Russell et al., 2017).

The above discussion characterizes the variability, through ensuring emergent behaviors, that AI introduces into a system, thereby guaranteeing that any AI system is a hierarchical complex system-of-systems. Thus, ensuring predictability from efficient and rigorous system engineering is at best a bounding problem and at worst a stochastic one. Further illustrating the severity of this issue, it is important to present another element of complication in AI system engineering that is entangled in the underlying ML models. Most ML algorithms incorporate adjustable parameters that control the training of the model. These standard parameters are part of the mathematical formulation and need to be learned from the (training) data. ML algorithms employ a second type of parameter, called hyper-parameters, that cannot be directly learned from the regular training process. Hyper-parameters typically express properties of the model such as its complexity or how fast it should learn and are usually fixed before the actual training process begins. Examples of common deep learning hyper-parameters include learning rate, momentum, dropout, number of layers, neurons per layer, etc.

Figure 8.2 shows the implications on training time, in terms of *iterations*, and convergence, in terms of progress toward the minima or *loss*. Learning rate is a hyper-parameter that determines how quickly a deep learning ML model, that employs a gradient descent methodology, can converge to local minima, i.e., arrive at the best accuracy. More specifically, the learning rate controls how much the weights of the neural network are adjusted, with respect to the loss gradient. The gradient equation can be described in the following manner: new_weight = existing_weight−learning_rate × the_gradient. In this context, each epoch/iteration represents an ML model state, given a consistent set of training data. In the gradient descent equation shown in Fig. 8.2, alpha (α) represents the learning rate hyper-parameter. If α is too small the gradient descent can be slow; shown as a *low learning rate* in Fig. 8.2. If α is too large, the gradient descent can overshoot the minimum, fail to converge, or even diverge, shown as *high* or *very high learning rate* in Fig. 8.2. An ideal or optimal learning rate would produce a reasonably rapid descent to asymmetry, noted as a *good learning rate* in the figure.

Given different settings for learning rate, Fig. 8.2 illustrates that ML software engineering requires close coupling with the learning problem and likely a significant

Fig. 8.2 Effect of learning rate on loss. Adapted from [27]

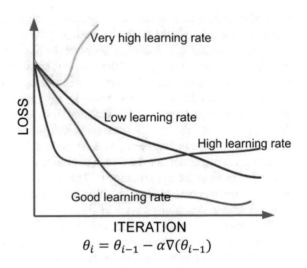

$$\theta_i = \theta_{i-1} - \alpha\nabla(\theta_{i-1})$$

amount of domain expertise in model creation. Consider a system that employs three ML models, each with seven hyper-parameters (not unreasonable, albeit a somewhat low number (Probst et al., 2018; Smith, 2018)). Keep in mind the difficulties in engineering traditional (non-learning) software (e.g., object inheritance, encapsulation, bias, etc.)—all of which would exist in such a three-ML model system. Even ignoring diversity/variability in training and operational data, there are at least 15,120 (7! × 3) possible combinations of hyper-parameter settings and this number assumes independence of the three ML models. This example also does not factor in the likelihood that the ML models were created by using externally pre-trained base models, such as RESNET (He et al., 2016) or variations of BERT (Devlin et al., 2018), which would further obfuscate parameters, hyper-parameters, and initial training data variability. It is not surprising that AI system engineers face challenges of structural and functional complexity when dealing with AI systems, as both structural and functional complexity increase with the number of system options.

It becomes nearly impossible to provide any stringent guarantees on the behavior of such a system. However, the system engineering trend is to automate the search for good model hyper-parameters (i.e., the balance of speed, accuracy, and reliability). So, there are system engineering things that can be done to increase the understanding of an AI system, certainly at the component level of the system. Obtaining this same degree of understanding at higher levels in the system hierarchy remains a challenge. It is noteworthy to revisit the fact that AI systems seldom operate in the isolation in which AI researchers design them and often they are connected to other AI systems, increasing the likelihood of unanticipated interactions.

The complexity introduced by data, hyper-parameters, and potentially varying scales of interdependent components create an elaborate system engineering landscape that must still account for the existence of emergent behaviors. Mairer et al. (Maier et al., 2015) describe four categories of emergent behaviors: simple, weak, strong, and extrinsic or "spooky." Simple emergence is where the emergent properties can be readily predicted by simplified models of the system. Weak emergence defines where the emergent property is reproducible and can be consistently predicted. Strong emergence describes emergent properties that are consistent with other known properties but not reproducible and thus, inconsistent and unpredictable. Extrinsic emergence defines where emergent properties are inconsistent with the known properties of the system. Figure 8.3 presents relationships between simple, complicated, and complex systems, relative to the degree of emergence they tend to exhibit. The oval shape in Fig. 8.3 shows where AI-enabled systems fit, with some systems being complicated or on the fringe of being complex, all the way to the outside of system boundaries, where emergent behavior will be fully unpredictable.

In a time of loosely coupled systems that dynamically connect with one another to achieve broader objectives, the AI system engineering challenges will not necessarily be localized to a singularly designed system. There are some who may argue that this loose-coupling is just a trend, and is not likely to continue or become the norm. To that argument, consider a modern cell phone where a user wishes to post a picture on their social network. The user utilizes a camera app to take a picture; the AI in that app processes the picture to apply filters and make adjustments, perhaps based on the intended social context. The same camera app (automatically) inserts the picture in a social networking app's process, where the social network AI may make further adjustments to the image or file prior to transmitting it to the social network server. The communication network optimization AI in the phone operating system further processes the file for efficient transmission considerations. The post is received by the social network's servers, where server-side AI analyzes the image post for the purposes of the social network company. In the simple example of posting a social network picture, where are the bounds of the AI "system" and what is really

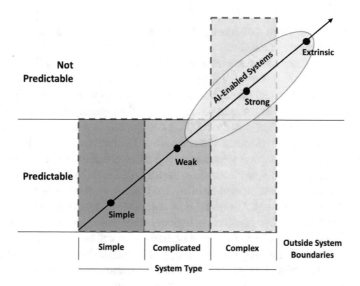

Fig. 8.3 Systems and emergence. Adapted from [20]

external when all the parts are necessary to achieve the objective? In this case, system boundaries around functional organizational ownership may be drawn out of convenience or attribution, but from a process perspective, it may be challenging to localize a latent or non-obvious emergent behavior. There are plenty of other examples of similar transparent, from users' perspective, AI-to-AI system interactions such as Internet-of-Things-based applications, business processes, and automation applications like self-driving vehicles. If emergence happens unpredictably and outside of a component system's domain, however, it may be defined—or even beyond designers' original way of thinking—the emergent behaviors would require radically new ways to deal with it from a system engineering perspective.

The inability to predict emergent behaviors is at the core of what makes AI systems such a system engineering challenge. The extensibility of AI systems in contemporary applications increases the propensity of extrinsic emergence. Simplification of system functions can make a system much more predictable and the trend in technology is to compartmentalize; e.g., apps, micro-services, containerization, etc. However, over time the scope of compartmentalized systems eventually exceeds the bounds of their functionality, if only for updates or maintenance. While this problem is not limited to AI systems, because of their learning capabilities, AI systems are naturally interactive. These interactions provide the opportunity to stress the AI systems, as their internal ML algorithms depend on interacting with data, their model parameters are tuned to a function, and the boundaries of their outputs typically exist in larger decision-making processes.

8.4   The Importance of Interoperability

There is ample literature that frames AI-enabled systems as complex systems-of-systems with emergent behaviors. Yet very little attention is given to the relevance of interoperability and technologies that provide the capability to facilitate system-to-system interactions. Interoperability technologies have the unglamorous role of being the spackle, glue, and grease that allow often incompatible systems to interact and behave collectively in a single process. When data warehouses were becoming popular in the late 1990s and early 2000s, a cottage industry for extract-transform-and-load (ETL) software also became a significant market (Mali & Bojewar, 2015; Russell et al., 2010). ETL tools were responsible for extracting data from one system and transforming it into a representation that allowed it to be loaded into another system. This type of data interoperability may seem on the surface to be fairly simple and straightforward. However, it is complicated by issues of localization, schematic differences, time constraints, logic representations, and other architectural considerations. As part of the front end of "data science" tasks in the AI pipeline, ETL architectures define entry points in ML-to-ML interactions. From an AI system engineering perspective, ETL architectures and functions actually shape the range of expected behaviors of ML algorithms. Figure 8.4 shows the trend in Google scholar for research on ETL and ML, illustrating the correlation between ETL and ML over

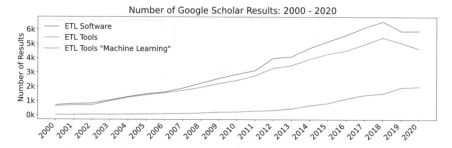

Fig. 8.4 Google scholar extract-transform-load trend

time. While the displayed trend correlations are not conclusively related, they indicate a similar upward pattern and also show that ML research and ETL research remain relatively separate; evidenced by the spacing between the top two lines (ETL as a search term alone) and the bottom line (ETL and ML as co-occurring search terms).

In AI-enabled systems, interoperability is much more than extracting and converting data between two data stores. Standards, application programming interfaces (APIs), ML libraries, middleware, and even the hardware processing at the points of collection (e.g., sensor hardware optimization, photosensor enhancement, etc.) all can affect interactions between AI system components. The interactions at the cyber-physical boundary of AI systems, where the data it relies on originates, can provide indications of the variability that a system will encounter. Thus, exercising the entry points of an AI system can help provide insights and understanding of system constraints and perhaps reveal emergent behaviors. The ML research community has given this challenge some focus, primarily with respect to ML algorithms and their training data (McDuff et al., 2018). However, while important and valuable, much of this work ignores the propagation of the ML output beyond the algorithm. The above-described entry point exercising is fairly common in the modeling and simulation literature, but can be costly and difficult with complex systems, and even more so with dynamically composed complex systems.

Standards such as network protocols and file formats (e.g., png, jpg, xml, json, etc.) are helpful in addressing data-oriented system engineering challenges, but they are not an absolute answer. Standards are challenged by the pace of technological change, constraints on innovation, and performance implications (Lewis et al., 2008), all essential factors in AI system design. The same can be said of application programming interfaces (APIs), as they are simply component or system-specific standards. This situation is not to suggest that standards and APIs are not useful, rather than that system engineering methods should factor and account for the limitations of standards and APIs. According to Lewis et al. (2008), there are actions system engineers can take, including identifying required levels of interoperability, understanding relevant existing standards, analyzing the gaps in standards, and taking measures to fill in the gaps. These pragmatic approaches are sensible, but may not address the uncertainty introduced by a learning system. We posit that standards and

APIs provide a baseline, a floor, upon which design variances can be gauged. Yet more is needed to facilitate the emergent dynamics of AI-enabled systems.

Middleware technologies are intended to fill the gap between standards and implementations that deviate or vary from them. Much like ETL, middleware rose in popularity in the 1990s and 2000s because of the technology's ability to provide translation services between systems. By translation here, we do not mean converting one spoken language to another. We mean translating between disparate system specifications. Initially, there was not much difference between the capabilities of middleware and ETL software. In fact, ETL was labeled middleware due to the overlap in its functionality. However, unlike the data-centric orientation of ETL, middleware became much more than just ETL because it translated messaging, services, and, most importantly, processes. Today, middleware is often delivered as architectural layers that integrate business process execution languages and system APIs with services that perform functions abstractly between the systems and transparently across networks, implementing adaptive composability. Modern middleware functionality can provide the means to gain an understanding of inter-system interactions, identify usage variabilities, and manage emergent behaviors.

Surprisingly, ML has *not* been widely implemented to advance today's middleware capabilities, although there are some examples of the promise ML functionality could provide to middleware tasks (Abukwaik et al., 2016; Nilsson, 2019; Nilsson et al., 2019). Even in AI-enabled systems, contemporary middleware is implemented as traditional code and scripting elements (Salama et al., 2019). AI is likely to increasingly be the middleware that handles the functions of interoperability in the future. However, the middleware with the ability to learn inter-component interactions and emergent behaviors will increase the overall complexity of AI-enabled systems. From a system engineering perspective, escalated complexity will increase the requirement for high-resolution and extensive modeling and simulation, due to the cost of exploring a robust range of possibilities (Saurabh Mittal, 2019). Additionally, it will also be the role of the AI-enabled middleware to quantify and propagate the uncertainty introduced by inter-component and inter-system interactions. This means the AI will have to address uncertainties that are teased out by design-time modeling and simulation as well as those that occur outside the boundaries of the system engineering.

8.5   The Role of Uncertainty in ML

The presence of uncertainty in any system process opens an opportunity to emergent system behavior that expands the boundary of the system's functions. Modern AI is particularly prone to introducing uncertainty into its outputs as a result of its reliance on ML algorithms (Ning & You, 2019). At its core, such uncertainty stems from the data and the implementation because the designer of an ML algorithm must encode constraints on the algorithm's behavior in the feasible set or the objective function. Uncertainty in ML typically has four sources: (1) noise, (2) model parameters, (3) model specification, and (4) extrapolation (Jalaian et al., 2019). The preceding sections presented the implications of these four sources on AI system complexity and emergent behaviors: data variability and interoperability limitations (noise and extrapolation), hyper-parameters (model parameters), and ML software engineering (model specification). These same complexity-increasing considerations can also expand uncertainty in AI-provided outputs and complicate the anticipation, repeatability, and traceability of unexpected and emergent system behaviors.

Because AI is often implemented to automate or aid decision-making, there is a growing field of research to quantify the uncertainty that ML may have in its outputs. There are several novel approaches that, if incorporated in low-level machine learning algorithms, can provide the necessary uncertainty quantification that is needed to help lower overall system uncertainty. These approaches include stochastic and chance-constrained programming (Ning & You, 2019), Seldonian regression approaches (Thomas et al., 2019), Hamiltonian Monte-Carlo inference (Cobb & Jalaian, 2020), and other methods that integrate Bayesian decision theory with ML. The challenge with most of these approaches is that they tend to be computationally intensive and, as such, create trade-offs in other system engineering concerns.

Quantified ML uncertainty can be a signal for system engineering considerations and may provide a starting point for addressing replication and traceability. While sparse, the literature is not without examples of system engineering approaches to incorporate these signals (Buisson & Lakehal, 2019; Kläs & Jöckel, 2020; Trinchero et al., 2018). Under a simulation approach, AI system engineering can be informed about the amount of uncertainty introduced by ML components (D'Ambrogio & Durak, 2016; Schluse et al., 2018). While integrating uncertainty quantification methods can provide indicators toward the bounds of ML components, it may not be sufficient to address all of the considerations raised by the complexity of learning systems. However, quantified uncertainty, particularly those that are elicited through robust simulation, can put constraints on the potential scope of system engineering concerns and provide limits around which to offer guarantees of system behavior.

8.6 The Challenge of Data and ML: An NLP Example

To provide an example of the system engineering problems that intrinsically exist in AI-enabled systems, we conducted an experiment using natural language processing (NLP). NLP is a suite of techniques grounded in ML that enable computers to analyze, interpret, and even generate meaningful text (Mikolov et al., 2013). NLP is typically used to derive value from corpora of documents, where a document can be of varying sizes (e.g., a short phrase, sentence, paragraph, or a large body of text). NLP tasks typically are intended to obtain information about the lexical units of a language, provide word sense disambiguation, and/or construct part-of-speech tagging, all to achieve higher-order aims or goals, such as document classification, content understanding, or entity-event relationship extraction.

We selected an NLP-based problem for several reasons. First, NLP is one of the most mature domains of AI. Second, using NLP for content understanding is one of the most challenging AI-problem domains, due to the nature of textual communication. For example, text can have complex meanings. Words have multiple definitions and in usage have highly variable ordering. This leads to variable-size blocks of text with contextually constrained representations, where the surrounding text alters the interpretation. Word ordering matters in two directions—what comes before as well as what comes after. Third, NLP applications typically have multiple ML methods being utilized in a sequential fashion to achieve the objective of content understanding. Fourth, uncertainty stemming from the first three preceding challenges impacts NLP in a variety of ways. For example, a simple keyword search is a classic approach and the presence of that keyword in a document does not necessarily assure a document's relevance to the query. Additionally, uncertainty can result from the ambiguity of certain words (e.g., the word "bimonthly" can mean twice a month or every two months depending on the context; the word "quite" can have different meanings to American and British audiences; etc.). Lastly, we chose NLP because although the underlying data may be of the same language, it is likely to have provenantial nuances embedded in it. For example, given the data's language is English, English words may have regional, temporal, and domain-specific variability. These considerations represent a challenging, but common, case for AI system engineering, and thus we felt it would likely provide a robust and generalizable example of the concepts in this thesis.

The functional goal of the experimental NLP system is quite simple: in an unsupervised manner, understand the content of weekly activity reports (WARs) that document the significant activities of information science researchers at the Army Research Laboratory. In short, the objective is to (without a human reading all the documents) identify documents that are about similar topics and present a summary of those relationships graphically. The WARs are supplied as entries from individual researchers and written with an intended audience of senior science and technology (S&T) managers. As such, jargon is limited and emphasis is placed on the contribution of the research accomplishment in terms of the impact on Army S&T priorities. A topic modeling NLP approach was adopted and used to determine similarity across documents. Twenty-nine documents were utilized, each consisting of a block of text with an average of 195 words. There may be some discussion about whether this corpus is a sufficient amount of data for this NLP activity. However, sufficiency remains an open research question. The convention is that more documents are better. Yet even the definition of a document in an applied context is ambiguous, as the literature offers different decompositions (e.g., sentences, single paragraphs, sections, chapters, etc.) even from a single "document" file. Further, an optimal requisite amount of text data for NLP-ML algorithms has been challenged by arguments of specificity and subsequent over and underfitting. It is noteworthy that our topic modeling approach is a unigram ("bag-of-words") model, which is common in information retrieval contexts, and we are not attempting to do language modeling in this example.

8.6.1 System Architecture

The general system functional process consists of building a topic model (ML-1) and then using that topic model to elicit a Euclidean relationship between the documents (ML-2). The results of the topics, the resulting clustering (ML-1 output feeding ML-2), and the similarity measure (ML-2 output) are graphically displayed as a final result. As part of the process, for each document, a dominant topic is identified. It is also important to note that the text preprocessing (stop word removal, n-gramming, stemming, and lemmatization) was also done consistently across runs. Preprocessing is critical to NLP because how the text is prepared, e.g., what words are included/excluded, handling pluralities, and morphological form reduction, all can dramatically affect the efficacy of NLP-ML algorithms.

For brevity, we only touch on the technical details of the NLP-ML methods employed here, as they are documented in detail in the literature and our implementation attempts to utilize popular Python libraries. We adopted the Anaconda Python environment to help standardize underlying software libraries. To implement the NLP-ML algorithms, we used the Genism library (Rehurek & Sojka, 2010), utilized latent Dirichlet allocation (LDA) (Blei et al., 2003) for topic building, t-distributed stochastic neighbor embedding (t-SNE) (Maaten & Hinton, 2008) for dimensionality-reduced clustering, and cosine similarity (Y. H. Li & Jain, 1998) for relating LDA topic similarity across documents. It is worth noting that this experiment was repeated using BERT (Devlin et al., 2018) to develop the topic models, instead of LDA, with the remainder of the architecture being the same. In the second experiment using BERT, the results were largely the same, so we focus on the LDA approach here.

The Gensim LDA module was implemented, exposing over 15 hyper-parameters, including learning rate, random seed, and epochs. In this experiment we held 14 of them constant and only adjusted the number of topics. The number of topics hyper-parameter can have a dramatic impact on downstream similarity comparisons, so the experiment included a function that iterated over several values and displayed them for selection in final results. The ML pipeline was partially automated to produce output for the one key hyper-parameter (number of topics) versus model "goodness," as shown in Fig. 8.5. Figure 8.5 shows the results of coherence and perplexity measures of the experimental LDA model, varying the number of topics hyper-parameter.

LDA topic models learn topics, typically represented as sets of important words, automatically from documents in an unsupervised way and coherence provides a quantitative metric of the resulting topics regarding their understandability (Röder et al., 2015). Similarly, the perplexity score, which is also used by convention in language modeling, can provide an indication of a model's goodness in terms of its predictive generalizability. Unlike coherence, which tends to increase up to the point where it levels off, perplexity tends to monotonically decrease in the likelihood of the test data and is algebraically equivalent to the inverse of the geometric mean per-word likelihood. Thus, in general, higher coherence and lower perplexity scores

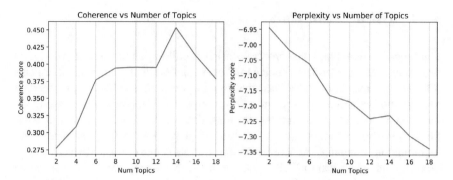

Fig. 8.5 Coherence and perplexity measures of LDA model, based on the number of topic hyper-parameter

are desirable. However, the rules for these measures are not firm, as there are implicit trade-offs between generalizability and interpretability. Further, as can be shown in Fig. 8.5, the minimum perplexity may not correspond to the maximum coherence and there is the issue of the number of documents versus the number of topics. In the case of smaller numbers of documents, arguably the number of topics hyper-parameter could be set to the same number of documents, leading to a unique (dominant) topic for each document, which is less than useful for comparison or retrieval tasks. So, a pragmatic rule heuristic rule is to: (1) identify where the coherence score levels off and its maximum before decreasing, and (2) select a number of topics value from this range. This number of topics should also occur before an increase (positive slope) in the perplexity score. Examining Fig. 8.5, a reasonable number of topics is likely between 8 and 12.

8.6.2   Results

The experiment provided reasonable results, which were manually (and qualitatively) verified by reading the documents to see how well they were represented by the topics. Figure 8.6 shows the topics that were created using LDA with the number of topics set to 12 and shown as word clouds. From a qualitative standpoint, it is not a stretch, even to a uniformed eye, that the topics could easily represent the kind of weekly activities of information science researchers, particularly if they had to type them every week over the course of a year. This particular part of the information science division does work on computational linguistics, dialog, and intelligent agents. This work too is readily evident in the NLP topics elicited from the content.

The topics, shown in Fig. 8.6, formed the basis for the similarity matrix and the clusters shown in Figs. 8.8 and 8.9. As expected, the increased number of topics decreased the overall level of degree of similarity between the documents. This relationship can be seen in Fig. 8.7, as the heatmaps for the higher number of topics

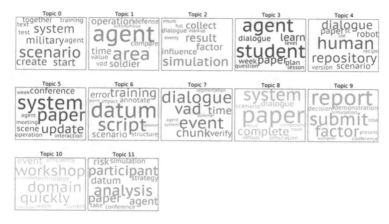

Fig. 8.6 Word clouds of 12 topics

are more of a neutral/lighter color rather than the darker shades that indicate strong positive or negative correlations. What is interesting is that some documents that were highly correlated, given 10 topics, are not correlated at all when 12 topics were used. This same effect can be seen in the plot of the t-SNE clusters (Fig. 8.9), where examples of some of the varying topics are shown with boxes around them. Documents clustered with 10 topics become probabilistically closer than when the number of topics was increased to 12. This probabilistic distance is shown as its spatial distance in the t-SNE plots. While the t-SNE dimensions are not necessarily linear, the parameters and hyper-parameters were set the same, and the only difference between the plots was the number of topics and associated document weights in the input. The scale of the plots was set to be the same to allow a direct comparison. It is important to note that the t-SNE plots employ an arbitrary 2-D space represented by tsne_D_one and tsne_D_two in Figs. 8.8 and 8.9.

Taking document *819-cub.txt* (the solid line box in the t-SNE plots) as a reference, its relative position (approximately [0, −380]) in the 10-topic cluster shifts in the positive y-direction (approximately [0, −100]) for the 12-topic plot. Other documents

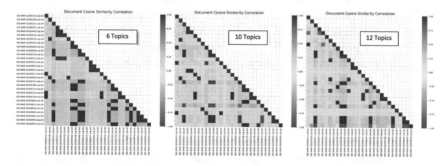

Fig. 8.7 Document similarity matrices for 6, 10, and 12 topics

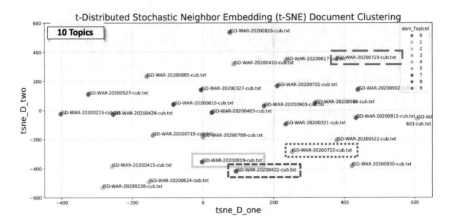

Fig. 8.8 Document clustering based on 10 topics

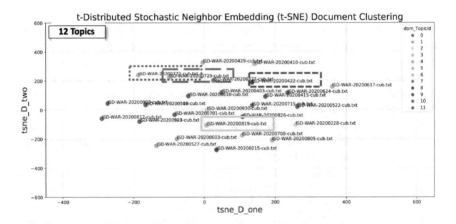

Fig. 8.9 Document clustering based on 12 topics

relative to this document also shift with the increased number of topics, yielding a significant increase in dissimilarity between *819-cub.txt* and several other documents: *422-cub.txt* (the medium-dashed box), *722-cub.txt* (the small-dashed box), and *729-cub.txt* (the long-dashed box). While this sub-section presents the results, the next sub-section provides an interpretation and discussion of the results.

8.6.3 Discussion

This empirical experiment is not about advancing the state-of-the-art in NLP-related machine learning. Rather, it is intended to illustrate the complications of AI system engineering and illustrates many of the system engineering challenges described in previous sections. By manipulating only 1/15 hyper-parameters, the experimental AI system significantly changed its output. We illustrated how this occurred, even in this simple example, where surprising results (more topics yielding tighter document clustering while reducing correlation) emerged. In this experiment, the internals of the system were fully exposed; and thus, data and hyper-parameters could be manipulated. However, most AI systems are often delivered as black boxes with minimal insight as to how the models work and other internals such as hyper-parameter settings. For example, in the word clouds, references to the word "data" were converted to the word "datum." These reports would not likely have included the word datum, as it is not part of the researchers' general jargon. The output of the word datum was a *surprising and unexpected* output. Only upon deep investigation was it discovered that the word datum came from the stemming and lemmatizing preprocessing step. It is noteworthy that the Genism stemming and lemmatizing code itself depends on an external stopword and rule library—i.e., 1000 s of words and 100 s of replacement rules. Of course, for human consumption, (most) people know that the word datum is the same as data, but the transposition into the context from this corpus was surprising nonetheless. This replacement is a very simple and harmless behavior but shows how easily emergent behaviors can occur and how susceptible AI-enabled systems are to problems of this nature.

Black box deployments often lead to obfuscation in the understanding of why the system was behaving the way it behaved. Yet this phenomenon is more involved than just a lack of ML explainability because the general results are reasonable in the specific ML task, just less reasonable within the overall system objective. In a typical deployment, an LDA model produced from training data is typically applied to new data, not used for similarity with the training data. The implication here is the number of topics and other hyper-parameters are embedded in the model, yet they may no longer be optimal or even appropriate for use with new text, depending on the nature of the new documents. The only indication of this issue is incorrect outputs, errors, or unexpected behaviors.

The experiment showed how embedded variability in one ML learner can affect other learners that rely on that output. The preprocessing portion of the experiment was a reasonable proxy for interoperability problems. Much like the role of interoperability, the preprocessing step translated the documents from their original source (MS Word files) into a format and structure that is appropriate for the Python Gensim libraries. As described in the interoperability section, ambiguity in the interoperability process can dramatically change the expected system behaviors and make system outputs less repeatable. Other factors that affect the system's behavior are embedded in the ML and abstracted away from end-user awareness. Issues such as data constraints and specificity, hyper-parameter variability, and the potential for emergent behaviors (i.e., embedded uncertainty) can all be hidden behind seemingly sensible system performance.

It is seemingly reasonable outputs from AI-enabled systems that create the largest demand signal for an increased emphasis on AI system engineering. Anecdotally, discussions about the output of this experimental system with management colleagues have sparked interest in applying the system to other functional areas within our organization. In short, the system outwardly did achieve its objective. Furthermore, the experimental system could theoretically be re-purposed as a data exploration tool, but even in that deployment, it would need to be accompanied by a system engineer or an NLP researcher to be used reliably with any durability. This result simply does not scale.

The increased complexity and embedded uncertainty of such an AI-enabled system, however, much of an example it may be, does not reduce the propensity for others to naively desire to utilize the system for their own corpora, or worse, make comparative conclusions across the outputs of varied users. In this sense, it is not the intelligence of the system that is at issue. Thus, a significant challenge is how to make such AI-enabled systems robust enough to handle anything more than hyper-specific tasks. Incorporated in this challenge is how to alter how AI-enabled systems are engineered so that they harness emergent behaviors and self-protect against their own underlying learning and intelligence; all to reduce the uncertainty that might stem from the use of their own outputs.

8.7   Design Science: Toward the Science of AI System Engineering

The bulk of this chapter discusses the problems of engineering interoperability, emergent behaviors, and uncertainty in complex AI systems. This section discusses the potential for a body of literature that may offer a solution that applies additional scientific rigor to systems engineering.

While there is plenty of literature that focuses on the machine learning lifecycle (Ashmore et al., 2019; Khomh et al., 2018; Schindel, 1996), the literature on the treatment of these components within a complex system is proportionally sparse. Furthermore, most of the ML lifecycle approaches tend to treat the learners as atomic functions providing a single capability. This perspective is much like controlling one individual's behavior while ignoring the effect they have on the crowd around them. AI complexity and emergence will require new methods and tools, and maybe even different structures. After years of specialization and focusing on more and more details that helped to provide a tremendous amount of knowledge and understanding and led to breakthroughs in so many disciplines and domains, a new set of research characteristics may "emerge" that takes the opposite approach. Tenets of Design science may provide a holistic framework in which to introduce rigor in the definitions, ontologies, boundaries, guidelines, and deliverables required for AI system engineering.

Design science is the study of an engineered artifact in context and its two significant activities are designing and investigating this artifact in context (Wieringa,

2014). It is a very different approach compared to computer science. From a pragmatic perspective, while this difference is a fundamental issue with AI system engineering, it still currently remains a problem largely being addressed by computer scientists and researchers. Table 8.2, initially proposed by Wieringa (2014), provides heuristic identifiers as a contrast between computer science problems and information systems/design problems. The computer sciences, and thus AI scientists, typically focus on knowledge questions, whereas information systems scientists and researchers are more concerned with *design* problems.

Traditional ML research, in classical computer science style, focuses on studying new AI methods and creating algorithms. Adopting a Design science approach to ML would take an information system approach that answers knowledge questions regarding systems. In this manner, Design science can provide a rigorous approach to understanding complex AI-enabled systems from a design perspective that, by its nature, must account for context and a problem's surrounding environment. Hence, this approach puts the system artifact at the center of study. The notion of an artifact is a central element in Design science. It is a fundamental premise that a design is problem-driven and leads to an artifact that solves the problem when the artifact is introduced into nature. There is debate over whether Design science must result in an artifactual production, and there are endless disagreements over what exactly constitutes an information systems artifact. For some, the only legitimate artifact is actually executing, runnable, code. For others, the only legitimate IT artifact is conceptual (e.g., the concept behind the executing code). Such artifacts are not exempt from natural laws or behavioral theories, but the artifact alone is not Design science (Baskerville, 2008). Design science integrates artifacts with design theory, a fundamental concept in the scholarly information sciences and systems field. It creates theoretical approaches for understanding, explaining, and describing design knowledge and practice. The inclusion of design practice reinforces the fact that goal or contextual orientation must be a core element of any design theory.

Foundations of Design science were extended by Herbert Simon (1988), and it is in Simon's work that the applicability of Design science for AI system engineering can be elicited. Originally characterized by Simon (1969) as the "Science of the Artificial," the artificial is distinguished from the natural in four ways: 1) Artificial things are *synthesized* (though not always or usually) with full forethought by man; 2) they may imitate appearances in natural things while lacking, in one or many

Table 8.2 Heuristics to distinguish design problems from knowledge questions (Wieringa, 2014)

Design problems	Knowledge questions
Call for a change of the world	Ask for knowledge about the world
Solution is a design	Answer is a proposition
Many solutions	One answer
Evaluated by utility	Evaluated by truth
Utility depends on stakeholder goals	Truth does not depend on stakeholder goals

respects, the reality of the latter; 3) they can be characterized in terms of *functions*, *goals*, and *adaptation*; and 4) they are often discussed, particularly when they are designed in terms of imperatives as well as descriptives. Toward AI-enabled systems, it is apparent the explicit relevance of 1, 2, and 3. In terms of AI system design, the introduction of function, goals, and adaptation are critical to a reliable design. Simon extends this importance of function and goals (i.e., context) with his idea of the artificial not only applying to the machines or objects designed by man but also human problem-solving in which in some sense one must cognitively "design" a solution. Simon synthesizes the sciences of the artificial, relating these concepts to design and the architecture of complexity. It is this relationship that forms the basis for Design science. Simon advocates for the existence of a science of design concerned with "how things might be" in contrast to the natural sciences, which are concerned with "how things are."

This perspective is directly related to AI system design due to the composite, adaptive, and dynamic learning nature of ML and AI systems. Design sciences' emphasis on the artifact can provide grounding theory for how to approach the engineering of AI systems. Designing useful artifacts is complex due to the need for creative advances in a domain in which existing theory is often insufficient. As knowledge grows, artificial systems are applied to new application areas that were not previously believed to be amenable to artificial system support (Markus et al., 2002). The resultant system artifacts extend the boundaries of human problem-solving and organizational capabilities by providing intellectual as well as computational tools (Hevner et al., 2004). In 2002, however, Markus' work (2002) had the foresight to begin to focus on the need for design theories that dealt with emergent knowledge processes. For example, Markus notes, catalysts of the design process emerge in unpredictable ways, sometimes resulting from external competitive forces and sometimes from internally generated needs for higher performance. Although that work did not focus on AI-enabled systems, Markus' emphasis on decision support systems begins to characterize many of the design challenges associated with them. To this end, much can be extrapolated from Design science to address the issues of designing AI-enabled systems.

At its core, Design science is directed toward understanding and improving the search among potential components in order to construct an artifact that is intended to solve a problem (Baskerville, 2008). The iterative nature, around an artifact in its context, may provide the means to elicit and mitigate the limitations in AI system engineering. We posit that adopting a Design science approach to AI system engineering can provide the theoretical grounding needed to create artifacts that can be iteratively studied by researchers such that emergent behaviors can be better understood in context. To meet this objective, robust simulation is key to exercising an AI-enabled system in a multitude of configurations, across problem domains, and with real and synthetic datasets. Future work is planned to explore this approach by using the experimental NLP system as an artifact.

8.8 Conclusion

This chapter is intended to generate a discussion and energize a research agenda. The discussion is mainly driven by the authors and their expertise and experience, so it needs to be extended and discussed in the broader audience as envisioned in this chapter. This chapter presented engineering challenges intrinsic to AI-enabled systems, including dynamisms of the learning process and adaptation, the potential for interoperability to significantly affect the learning process, and emergent behaviors that increase uncertainty and potentially lead to errors. To illustrate the concepts, we presented an experimental NLP AI system that produced reasonable results but also demonstrated pragmatic examples of conceptual system challenges.

There are engineering considerations that are being advanced by the AI research and system engineering community that will provide solutions to the challenges identified in this chapter, such as quantified uncertainty, ML, intelligent interoperability solutions, and autonomic system functionality. However, these approaches are likely to introduce additional complexity that may be compounded by the amorphous bounds of AI systems in pervasive use. This evolutionary nature of AI systems may find solutions in the iterative nature of Design science. Much like other engineering disciplines in past decades, the application of Design science aims to aggregate the power of a few key ideas to help to manage the increasing complexity of AI-enabled systems. Whereas civil engineering and chemical engineering were built on the hard sciences, i.e., physics and chemistry, this new engineering discipline will be built on the building blocks that ground Design science—ideas such as information, algorithms, uncertainty, computing, inference, and complexity. While the building blocks have begun to emerge, the principles for putting these blocks together have not yet fully been realized, so the blocks are currently being put together in ad hoc ways. What we are missing is an engineering discipline with its principles of analysis and design.

In stimulating further research and discussion, we should not pretend that AI-enabled systems are not a transformative technology. AI artifacts should be built to work as expected. We do not want to build systems that help us with medical treatments, provide transportation, and support our decision-making only to find out after the fact that these systems do not really work and that they make errors and have unanticipated negative effects. While the expansion of these concepts is still an open research challenge, we should embrace the fact that there is an opportunity to redefine system engineering with these and other concepts.

References

Abukwaik, H., Abujayyab, M., Humayoun, S. R., & Rombach, D. (2016). Extracting conceptual interoperability constraints from API documentation using machine learning. *Proceedings of the 38th International Conference on Software Engineering Companion*, 701–703.

Alpcan, T., Erfani, S. M., & Leckie, C. (2017). Toward the starting line: A systems engineering approach to strong AI. ArXiv:1707.09095.

Ashmore, R., Calinescu, R., & Paterson, C. (2019). Assuring the machine learning lifecycle: Desiderata, methods, and challenges. ArXiv:1905.04223.

Backlund, A. (2000). The definition of system. *Kybernetes: The International Journal of Systems & Cybernetics, 29*(4), 444–451.

Baskerville, R. (2008). What design science is not. *European Journal of Information Systems, 17*(5), 441–443. https://doi.org/10.1057/ejis.2008.45

Belani, H., Vukovic, M., & Car, Ž. (2019). Requirements Engineering Challenges in Building AI-Based Complex Systems. *2019 IEEE 27th International Requirements Engineering Conference Workshops (REW)*, 252–255.

Blei, D. M., Ng, A. Y., & Jordan, M. I. (2003). Latent dirichlet allocation. *Journal of Machine Learning Research, 3*(Jan), 993–1022.

Breck, E., Cai, S., Nielsen, E., Salib, M., & Sculley, D. (2017). The ML Test Score: A Rubric for ML Production Readiness and Technical Debt Reduction. *Proceedings of IEEE Big Data.*

Brings, J., Daun, M., Keller, K., Obe, P. A., & Weyer, T. (2020). A systematic map on verification and validation of emergent behavior in software engineering research. *Future Generation Computer Systems, 112*, 1010–1037.

Buisson, B., & Lakehal, D. (2019). Towards an integrated machine-learning framework for model evaluation and uncertainty quantification. *Nuclear Engineering and Design, 354*, 110197.

Carleton, A. D., Harper, E., Menzies, T., Xie, T., Eldh, S., & Lyu, M. R. (2020). The AI Effect: Working at the Intersection of AI and SE. *IEEE Software, 37*(4), 26–35.

Cobb, A. D., & Jalaian, B. (2020). Scaling Hamiltonian Monte Carlo Inference for Bayesian Neural Networks with Symmetric Splitting. ArXiv:2010.06772.

Cohen, J. E., & Newmans, C. M. (1985). When will a large complex system be stable? *Journal of Theoretical Biology, 113*, 153–156.

D'Ambrogio, A., & Durak, U. (2016). Setting systems and simulation life cycle processes side by side. *IEEE International Symposium on Systems Engineering (ISSE), 2016*, 1–7.

De Michell, G., & Gupta, R. K. (1997). Hardware/software co-design. *Proceedings of the IEEE, 85*(3), 349–365.

Devlin, J., Chang, M.-W., Lee, K., & Toutanova, K. (2018). BERT: Pre-training of deep bidirectional transformers for language understanding. ArXiv:1810.04805.

He, K., Zhang, X., Ren, S., & Sun, J. (2016). Deep residual learning for image recognition. *Proceedings of the IEEE Conference on Computer Vision and Pattern Recognition*, 770–778.

Hevner, A. R., March, S. T., Park, J., & Ram, S. (2004). Design Science in Information Systems Research. *MIS Quarterly, 28*(1), 75–105. https://doi.org/10.2307/25148625

I.S.C. Committee. (1990). IEEE Standard Glossary of Software Engineering Terminology (IEEE Std 610.12–1990). Los Alamitos. *CA IEEE Comput. Soc.*

Jalaian, B., Lee, M., & Russell, S. (2019). Uncertain Context: Uncertainty Quantification in Machine Learning. *AI Magazine, 39*(4).

Khomh, F., Adams, B., Cheng, J., Fokaefs, M., & Antoniol, G. (2018). Software engineering for machine-learning applications: The road ahead. *IEEE Software, 35*(5), 81–84.

Kläs, M., & Jöckel, L. (2020). A Framework for Building Uncertainty Wrappers for AI/ML-Based Data-Driven Components. *International Conference on Computer Safety, Reliability, and Security*, 315–327.

Kuras, M. L., & White, B. E. (2005). Engineering Enterprises Using Complex-System Engineering. *INCOSE International Symposium, 15*(1), 251–265.

Lewis, G. A., Morris, E., Simanta, S., & Wrage, L. (2008). Why standards are not enough to guarantee end-to-end interoperability. *Seventh International Conference on Composition-Based Software Systems (ICCBSS 2008)*, 164–173.

Li, Y. H., & Jain, A. K. (1998). Classification of text documents. *The Computer Journal, 41*(8), 537–546.

Li, Z., Sim, C. H., & Low, M. Y. H. (2006). A survey of emergent behavior and its impacts in agent-based systems. *2006 4th IEEE International Conference on Industrial Informatics*, 1295–1300.

Lwakatare, L. E., Raj, A., Bosch, J., Olsson, H., & Crnkovic, I. (2019). *A Taxonomy of Software Engineering Challenges for Machine Learning Systems: An Empirical Investigation* (pp. 227–243). https://doi.org/10.1007/978-3-030-19034-7_14

Maaten, L. van der, & Hinton, G. (2008). Visualizing data using t-SNE. *Journal of Machine Learning Research, 9*(Nov), 2579–2605.

Maier, M. W., Rainey, L. B., & Tolk, A. (2015). The role of modeling and simulation in system of systems development. *Modeling and Simulation Support for System of Systems Engineering Applications*, 11–41.

Mali, N., & Bojewar, S. (2015). A Survey of ETL Tools. *International Journal of Computer Techniques, 2*(5), 20–27.

Markus, M. L., Majchrzak, A., & Gasser, L. (2002). A design theory for systems that support emergent knowledge processes. *MIS Quarterly*, 179–212.

May, R. M. (1972). Will a large complex system be stable? *Nature, 238*(5364), 413–414.

May, R. M. (1976). Simple mathematical models with very complicated dynamics. *Nature, 261*(5560), 459–467.

McDuff, D., Cheng, R., & Kapoor, A. (2018). Identifying Bias in AI using Simulation. ArXiv:1810.00471 *[Cs, Stat]*. http://arxiv.org/abs/1810.00471

Mikolov, T., Chen, K., Corrado, G., & Dean, J. (2013). Efficient estimation of word representations in vector space. ArXiv:1301.3781.

Mittal, S., & Rainey, L. (2014). Harnessing Emergence: The design and control of emergent behavior in system of systems engineering. *Proceedings of the Summer Simulation Multi-Conference*.

Mittal, Saurabh. (2019). New frontiers in modeling and simulation in complex systems engineering: The case of synthetic emergence. In *Summer of Simulation* (pp. 173–194). Springer.

Newman, M. E. (2011). Complex systems: A survey. ArXiv:1112.1440.

Nilsson, J. (2019). *System of systems interoperability machine learning model* [PhD Thesis]. Lule\aa University of Technology.

Nilsson, J., Sandin, F., & Delsing, J. (2019). Interoperability and machine-to-machine translation model with mappings to machine learning tasks. *2019 IEEE 17th International Conference on Industrial Informatics (INDIN), 1*, 284–289.

Ning, C., & You, F. (2019). Optimization under uncertainty in the era of big data and deep learning: When machine learning meets mathematical programming. *Computers & Chemical Engineering, 125*, 434–448.

Ottino, J. M. (2004). Engineering complex systems. *Nature, 427*(6973), 399–399.

Probst, P., Bischl, B., & Boulesteix, A.-L. (2018). *Tunability: Importance of Hyperparameters of Machine Learning Algorithms*.

Rehurek, R., & Sojka, P. (2010). Software framework for topic modelling with large corpora. *In Proceedings of the LREC 2010 Workshop on New Challenges for NLP Frameworks*.

Röder, M., Both, A., & Hinneburg, A. (2015). Exploring the Space of Topic Coherence Measures. *Proceedings of the Eighth ACM International Conference on Web Search and Data Mining*, pp. 399–408. https://doi.org/10.1145/2684822.2685324

Russell, S., Haddad, M., Bruni, M., & Granger, M. (2010). Organic Evolution and the Capability Maturity of Business Intelligence. *AMCIS*, 501.

Russell, S., Moskowitz, I., & Raglin, A. (2017). Human Information Interaction, Artificial Intelligence, and Errors. In *Autonomy and Artificial Intelligence: A Threat or Savior?* (pp. 71–101). https://doi.org/10.1007/978-3-319-59719-5_4

Russell, S., & Moskowitz, I. S. (2016, March 4). Human Information Interaction, Artificial Intelligence, and Errors. *2016 AAAI Spring Symposium Series*. 2016 AAAI Spring Symposium. https://www.aaai.org/ocs/index.php/SSS/SSS16/paper/view/12767

Salama, A., Linke, A., Rocha, I. P., & Binnig, C. (2019). XAI: A Middleware for Scalable AI. *DATA*, 109–120.

Schindel, W. D. (1996). *System Engineering: An Overview of Complexity's Impact*. SAE Technical Paper.

Schluse, M., Priggemeyer, M., Atorf, L., & Rossmann, J. (2018). Experimentable digital twins— Streamlining simulation-based systems engineering for industry 4.0. *IEEE Transactions on Industrial Informatics, 14*(4), 1722–1731.

Simon, H. A. (1969). The sciences of the artificial. *Cambridge, MA*.

Simon, H. A. (1988). The science of design: Creating the artificial. *Design Issues*, 67–82.

Simon, H. A. (1991). The architecture of complexity. In *Facets of systems science* (pp. 457–476). Springer.

Smith, L. N. (2018). A disciplined approach to neural network hyper-parameters: Part 1–learning rate, batch size, momentum, and weight decay. ArXiv:1803.09820.

Thomas, P. S., da Silva, B. C., Barto, A. G., Giguere, S., Brun, Y., & Brunskill, E. (2019). Preventing undesirable behavior of intelligent machines. *Science, 366*(6468), 999–1004.

Thurner, S., Hanel, R., & Klimek, P. (2018). *Introduction to the theory of complex systems*. Oxford University Press.

Tolk, A., Diallo, S., & Mittal, S. (2018). Complex systems engineering and the challenge of emergence. *Emergent Behavior in Complex Systems Engineering: A Modeling and Simulation Approach*, 79–97.

Trinchero, R., Larbi, M., Torun, H. M., Canavero, F. G., & Swaminathan, M. (2018). Machine learning and uncertainty quantification for surrogate models of integrated devices with a large number of parameters. *IEEE Access, 7*, 4056–4066.

Wieringa, R. J. (2014). What Is Design Science? In R. J. Wieringa (Ed.), *Design Science Methodology for Information Systems and Software Engineering* (pp. 3–11). Springer. https://doi.org/10.1007/978-3-662-43839-8_1

Yang, Z., Yu, Y., You, C., Steinhardt, J., & Ma, Y. (2020). Rethinking bias-variance trade-off for generalization of neural networks. ArXiv:2002.11328.

Chapter 9
The Department of Navy's Digital Transformation with the Digital System Architecture, Strangler Patterns, Machine Learning, and Autonomous Human–Machine Teaming

Matthew Sheehan and Oleg Yakimenko

Abstract The Department of Navy (DoN) is rapidly adopting mature technologies, products, and methods used within the software development community due to the proliferation of machine learning (ML) capabilities required to complete warfighting missions. One of the most impactful places where ML algorithms, their applications, and capabilities will have on warfighting is in the area of autonomous human–machine teaming (AHMT). However, stakeholders given the task to implement AHMT solutions enterprise-wide are finding current DoN system architectures and platform infrastructures inadequate to facilitate deployment at scale. In this chapter, the authors discuss the DoN's goal, barriers to, and a potential path to success in implementing AHMT solutions fleet- and force-wide.

Keywords DevSecOps · Systems engineering · Machine learning · Digital system architecture · Strangler pattern

9.1 Introduction

Artificial intelligence (AI) has the potential to significantly shape national security and military capabilities due to its broad applicability across a range of functions and fields. At the moment, AI research inside of the Department of Defense (DoD) is being conducted within the fields of intelligence collection and analysis, logistics, cyber operations, information operations, command and control, and in semi-autonomous and autonomous vehicles (CRS, 2019). Due to its potential advantages to outmaneuver top adversaries, AI and, more specifically, machine learning (ML) are highlighted as priority research areas within authoritative governing documents like that of the National Security Strategy (White House, 2017) and National Defense Strategy (DoD, 2018a). While the formulation of guidance from the Executive Office of the President of the United States concerning AI has been slowly progressing

M. Sheehan (✉) · O. Yakimenko
Department of Systems Engineering, Naval Postgraduate School, Monterey, CA 93940, USA
e-mail: matthew.sheehan2@navy.mil; mmsheeha@nps.edu

© Springer Nature Switzerland AG 2021
W. F. Lawless et al. (eds.), *Systems Engineering and Artificial Intelligence*,
https://doi.org/10.1007/978-3-030-77283-3_9

since 2016, the DoD has been exploring the implications of integrating autonomous systems with an eye to intelligent, learning, and adaptive software systems even before that.

Specifically, in 2010, the Under Secretary of Defense for Acquisition, Technology and Logistics sponsored a Federal Advisory Committee, the Defense Science Board (DSB), to provide independent advice to the Secretary of Defense about the role of Autonomy in the Department of Defense (DoD) systems. With the motivation of "identifying new opportunities to more aggressively use autonomy in military missions, anticipate vulnerabilities, and make recommendations for overcoming operational difficulties and systematic barriers to realizing the full potential of autonomous systems" (DSB, 2012), this task force uncovered multiple technical challenges with the implementation of autonomous systems. These technical challenges were as follows: perception, planning, learning, human–robot interaction/human–system interaction, natural language, and multiagent coordination (DSB, 2012). Follow-on technical interchange meetings uncovered additional non-technical barriers by integrating AI into military missions in the form of adaptive challenges for the DoD organizational structure and culture, defense acquisition system (DAS), lifecycle development, and management of processes that are used (DoD, 2015; DSB, 2018; DIB, 2019).

At the military department level, the DoN understands the importance of software and how AI can make a profound and unique impact on the operational and strategic levels of war (DoN, 2016; DoD, 2018b). These algorithms will have unique impacts on the operational and strategic levels of war. Applications include (1) omnipresent and omniscient autonomous vehicles; (2) big-data-driven modeling, simulation, and wargaming; (3) focused intelligence collection and analysis; (4) system of systems enabling exquisite intelligence, surveillance, and reconnaissance (ISR); (5) precision targeting of strategic assets; (6) effective missile defense; and (7) AI-guided cyber (Davis, 2019). Of the applications above, the DoN is especially interested in leveraging AHMT solutions to aid the warfighter in decision-making. Battle management aids and tactical decision aids (BMAs/TDAs) are a logical first step and are seen as a "quick-win" or "low hanging fruit" by senior leaders due to the availability of required data, documented decision trees/application state diagrams, ease of operator integration with current application user interfaces, and high return-on-investment (ROI) in automating operator ancillary tasking indirect to the mission.

However, the AHMT "quick win" is not quite what it seems at first glance. The DoN acquisition methodology of "lift-and-shift" or "rip-off and deploy," while proving to be historically successful for most technologies, needs to be evolved when applied to AHMT solutions. The DoN must embrace software engineering patterns using development, security, and operations (DevSecOps) methods with agile and test-driven practices. Considering the DoN is a distributed collection of organizations, authorities, environments, warfighting/readiness/business domain-specific requirements, a mix of evolving technologies, and independent security enclaves, a holistic system engineering enterprise approach must be taken in order to effectively succeed in deploying integrated AHMT solutions.

This chapter discusses the barriers, limitations, and implications of the DoN's desire to develop, test, integrate, and deploy AHMT algorithms, applications, and capabilities to the fleet and force at scale. Specifically, Sect. 9.2 analyzes the difficulty in achieving seamless AHMT integration in general; followed by Sect. 9.3 detailing the unique challenges the DoN is facing to achieve this seamless integration at scale. Closing with Sect. 9.4, a path to success is proposed which will allow the DoN to achieve its AHMT goal while working within the confines of the DoD's cumbersome defense acquisition system (DAS).

9.2 Autonomous Human–Machine Teaming Lifecycle Difficulties

Before diving into the specific difficulties with AHMT algorithms, applications, and capabilities, it is important to understand a few key tenets from the software systems engineering community required to make effective AHMT possible. Due to many AHMT solutions employing ML techniques, the proper software development lifecycle (SDLC) model, software architecture pattern, platform service model, application testing, and deployment model choices all have impacts on the associated foundational requirements of the software being developed and operated.

There are many SDLC models to choose from, the most common being waterfall, iterative, spiral, v-shaped, and agile. Each of these SDLC models shares similar phases—requirements gathering, analysis, design, development, testing, deployment, and maintenance (SDLC, 2019), however, each one is suited for particular software project types and complexities. One glaring difference with AHMT algorithms, applications, and capabilities as compared to static code is the need to constantly evolve. Due to this characteristic, SDLC models which require a low level of uncertainty and an increased need for planning and control should not be used. Therefore, the iterative and agile SDLC models are natural fits for AHMT endeavors, including a fit with ML application development pipelines resulting in each iteration developing, testing, and deploying new features.

AHMT solutions interact with systems in different ways depending on the evolution timeline of the AHMT application and the targeted system for deployment. If both the AHMT application and target deployment system are in synchronous development timelines, the AHMT application group has added flexibility in the software architecture pattern that can be used. If these development timelines are temporally segregated, the AHMT application group may find many design decisions limited by the targeted monolithic system where it is to be deployed. Among different software architecture patterns, the event-driven and microservice ones are the most commonly used for AHMT solutions. These two software architecture patterns are suitable for complex environments, lend themselves well to continuous new functionality updates, and are highly scalable.

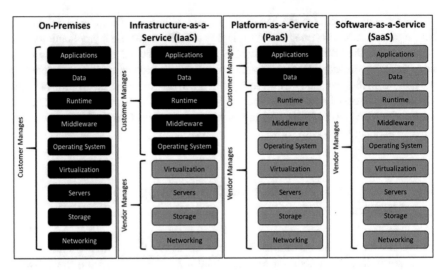

Fig. 9.1 Platform service models as applied to the cloud computing stack (adapted from BigCommerce, 2020)

While the platform service model (software as a service (SaaS); platform as a service (PaaS); infrastructure as a service (IaaS); and on-premises) is not directly tied to the AHMT solution being used, it affects the business model chosen which in turn has impacts to how the AHMT solution is integrated and maintained. The platform service model computing stack is a series of interconnected systems or protocols that exchange information between layers in support of a function. When describing the layers of a platform service model, it is common to reference a version of the open systems interconnection (OSI) model as applied to cloud computing. In the version shown in Fig. 9.1, the layers of the computing stack are as follows: networking, storage, servers, virtualization, operating system, middleware, runtime, data, and applications. In the on-premises service model, the customer retains control and is responsible for the entire computing stack. While this allows the customer the most flexibility and control in system decisions, this model also requires the most knowledge and has the largest overhead to run effectively. In the IaaS model, the customer manages applications, data, runtime, middleware, and operating systems, while outside vendors manage the rest of the computing stack. The IaaS model allows for enterprises to pay-as-they-go for networking, storage, and virtualization, freeing up capital from the expensive on-premises infrastructure and subsequent on-site requirements. The platform service model most likely to be leveraged by AHMT solutions is the PaaS model. In the PaaS model, the customer only manages the application and data layers. The PaaS model allows AHMT developers to focus on algorithm and application development, testing, and deployment. The other tasks of the computing stack are managed by outside vendors allowing all resources to be focused on AHMT solutions and integration with the system targeted for deployment. In the final platform service model, SaaS, the software application is available to the customer over the network. AHMT solutions that fit into this model are typically turnkey commercial-off-the-shelf (COTS) products purchased by customers, which do not require complex integration with fielded systems due to the nature of their decoupled hardware/software.

Due to the requirement for AHMT solutions to constantly evolve and become more refined or feature-rich as these algorithms and applications learn, a robust feedback mechanism must be in place to inform developers of the next set of deployment features. Thus, these AHMT solutions are dependent upon DevSecOps methods with agile and test-driven practices allowing for continuous software integration and delivery/deployment (CI/CD). However, even for organizations considered "digitally native" or "software intensive" with years of expertise in the above topics, successful implementation is difficult. Data collected from these industry leaders paint a troubling picture for AHMT solutions: 30% of application deployments fail (Cruz, 2018); 29% of IT project implementations are unsuccessful, with 20% being unrecoverable; 75% of customers rated their application deployment as failing (Hastie & Wojewoda, 2015); and 87% of ML models developed never get deployed (VB, 2019). In fact, Google's AI Chief stated that only 15% of ML models developed within Google are deployed (Moore, 2019).

The above statistics illustrate the difficulties in successfully developing, integrating, and deploying AHMT solutions at scale. In the future where decisive victory on the battlefield will not only be decided by algorithms supporting warfighters with actionable intelligence but also by how well the DoN enterprise continuously integrates and delivers/deploys its algorithms, the DoN will need to digitally transform almost every aspect of how it performs acquisition.

9.3   Unique Challenges Facing the Department of Navy and Autonomous Human–Machine Teaming

While there are always technical challenges in transitioning new technologies into a large complex system of systems, like those within the DoN, AHMT solutions also pose non-technical challenges not shared by other endeavors. This section details these non-technical challenges with the introduction of the defense acquisition system (DAS) in order to show how it is not suited for AHMT solution acquisition as classically executed. It is then followed by detailing the technical challenges the DoN is up against in integrating these AHMT solutions (prospective costs) while leveraging previous investments (sunk costs) to ensure maximum use of DoN asset "technical debt."

9.3.1 Department of Navy Non-technical Challenges

The acquisition of systems within the DoD is complex. It comprised multiple processes, stakeholders, authorities, phases, barriers, and limitations. All of these variables must be understood, aligned, and executed in sync to be successful. Acquiring systems within the DoD is so complex that Congress passed Public Law 101–510 in 1990, creating the Defense Acquisition University (DAU) by enacting the Defense Acquisition Workforce Improvement Act (DAWIA) to educate and train civilian and military DoD workforce members in a number of functional areas in support of performing acquisition more effectively (DAU, 2019). However, despite a trained workforce, a survey in 2015 found all DoD Major Defense Acquisition Programs (MDAPs) were collectively $468 billion over budget and almost 30 months behind schedule, with data pointing to expected cost growth to reach 51% by 2020 (Lineberger, 2016). Additionally, the DoD returns an average of $13.5 billion a year in canceled funds to the Treasury, or about 2.6% of its appropriated budget in unspent funds (Bartels, 2019). These facts point to an uneasy conclusion: the way in which the DoD does business is fundamentally at odds with the goal of military departments rapidly fielding capabilities to outpace peer/near-peer threats.

As shown in Fig. 9.2, the DAS consists of three distinct, yet intertwined, processes correlating to the functions of acquisition management (known as "Acquisition"), requirements development and verification (known as the Joint Capabilities Integration and Development System (JCIDS)), and financial planning and execution (known as Planning, Programming, Budgeting and Execution (PPBE)). The Acquisition process provides a "management foundation" for programs to follow through their lifecycle. This event-based process breaks the lifecycle into phases, milestones, and reviews where a program is required to meet certain criteria in order to proceed to the next phase. As depicted in Fig. 9.3, the process consists of five phases, three milestone reviews, and potentially over 70 required key criteria deliverables based

Fig. 9.2 Defense acquisition system relationships (AcqNotes, 2018)

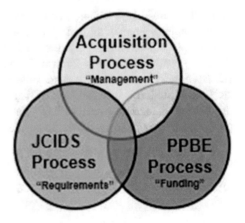

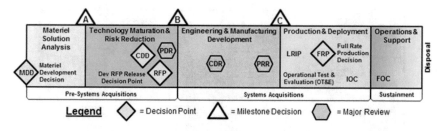

Fig. 9.3 Tailored acquisition process (AcqNotes, 2018)

on program size as measured by total research and development funding and total procurement cost.

The JCIDS process was created in support of the Joint Requirements Oversight Council (JROC) to ensure warfighting requirements are properly validated as required by JROC Title 10 responsibilities (AcqNotes, 2018). The JCIDS is designed to identify warfighting requirements, uncover operational performance requirements, and produce/validate the Capabilities Base Assessment, Initial Capabilities Document, and Capability Development Document. Figure 9.4 shows how these documents created in the JCIDS process interact with the DAS.

The PPBE process is the only calendar-driven process of the three. It is also the only process of the three in which a program will find itself in all of its associated stages at once. The execution phase is tied to the current year (CY) of program execution, while each subsequent phase (budgeting, programming, and planning) is tied to CY+1 out-year(s). The execution phase (CY) is where financial management of ongoing obligations and expenditures takes place. The budgeting phase (CY+1)

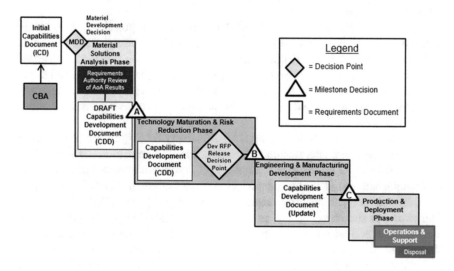

Fig. 9.4 JCIDS and DAS interaction (AcqNotes, 2018)

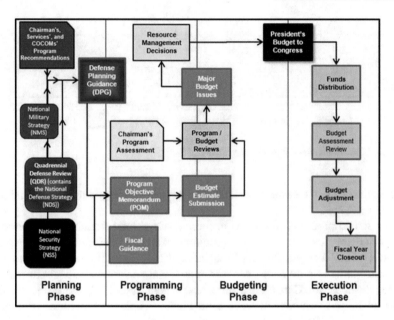

Fig. 9.5 PPBE process overview (AcqNotes, 2018)

is where formulation, justification, and control of funding resources are exercised to ensure efficient allocation. The programming phase (CY+2) is where resource proposals are evaluated and prioritized against future capability needs. The planning phase (CY+3) is where trend analysis is conducted to understand the long-term implications of execution phase results (AcqNotes, 2018). Figure 9.5 details the steps taken in each PPBE phase.

While the graphics in Figs. 9.3 and 9.4 depict simple processes, it should be noted that each of these processes has follow-on, multistep, complex sub-processes, and various rule-sets uniquely implemented by each military department. Figure 9.6 shows one such breakout of the misleadingly simple process for the tailored acquisition process shown in Fig. 9.3. It should be noted that Fig. 9.6 is not meant to be readable; instead, it is meant to convey the additional complexities existing within each sub-process.

The DoD has struggled to use the DAS effectively for acquiring non-hardware-centric systems in a timely manner. Panels on Defense Acquisition Reform in 2010 found the delivery of information technology (IT) systems and related software products to take between 48 and 60 months (Gansler & Lucyshyn, 2012). Thus, in 2019 the DoD released the adaptive acquisition framework (AAF) (DoD, 2019). This framework, as shown in Fig. 9.7, aims to simplify acquisition policy, tailor-specific approaches based on relevance, actively manage risk, and emphasize sustainment. While AAF is a great first step away from the old "one size fits all" process used in the past allowing for program flexibility, it is too early to assess its effectiveness.

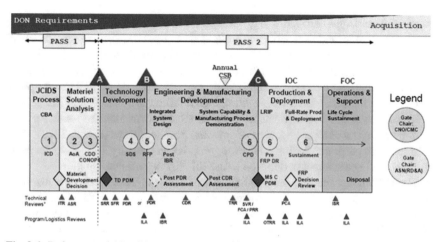

Fig. 9.6 Defense acquisition lifecycle (AcqNotes, 2018)

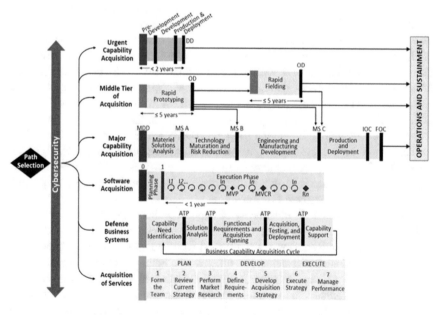

Fig. 9.7 Adaptive acquisition framework (DoD, 2020)

In fact, to date, only two out of nine associated new policy documents have been promulgated.

It should be noted that AAF only addresses one-third of the three-part DAS (see Fig. 9.3). The JCIDS process, as it is executed today, creates incentives for programs of records (PoRs) to only focus on their domain-specific requirements. This near-sightedness adversely affects AHMT solutions by segregating PoRs based on their acquisition decisions and technology choices. This remaining behavior will not allow the DoN to maximize the capabilities brought about by AHMT solutions. The PPBE process is piloting a new appropriation category targeting software acquisition known as Budget Activity (BA) 8. This "new color" of funding, currently under test, removes the administrative and accounting burden for appropriation categories that were put in place during the earlier hardware-centric, industrial-age acquisition era. The misapplied balance of development versus production versus sustainment funds for software projects is a continued source of software product delays (Serbu, 2020). With nine software programs testing this new appropriation category, Congress has yet to grant the DoD permanent permission to use this BA department-wide.

The DAS is not the only non-technical challenge the DoN faces. Organizationally, the DoN comprised multiple bodies, each using hybrid organizational structures. At the highest level, the DoN consists of nine entities: the Secretary of the Navy's (SECNAV) office, the Office of the Chief of Naval Operations (OPNAV), Headquarters Marine Corps (HQMC), the United States Navy (USN) Operating Forces, the United States Marine Corps (USMC) Operating Forces, USN Shore Establishment, USMC Shore Establishment, USN reserve forces, and USMC reserve forces. Each of these entities is further broken down and divided into subsequent organizations, sometimes having multiple reporting chains across entities. Additionally, each of these subordinate organizations has multiple unique organizational structures. For example, uniformed military service members follow a hierarchical organizational structure in terms of its chain-of-command. Operating forces are structured using divisional organizational structures, like those of a geographic region (e.g., U.S. Pacific Fleet). OPNAV, HQMC, and Shore Establishments follow a combination of functional and divisional (domain-based) organizational structures. Even further within these organizations, like those at an "echelon 4" or below, divisional (product-based) and functional organizational structures are used. As more than one organizational structure is at play at all times, the DoN tends to execute acquisition functions in a cross-matrixed fashion.

The advantages and disadvantages of each organizational structure are shown in Fig. 9.8. While many of these organizational structures have a few redeeming advantages, the disadvantages are multiplied when an entity executes a maneuver for hybrid organizational structures in unison. It is believed that the organizational structure institutionalizes the organizational culture within, which cycles back to legitimize the organizational structure in place (Janicijevic, 2013). Thus, it can be surmised that each organization within the DoN has its own unique culture, institutional identity, knowledge, and memory to contend with when it comes to an AHMT's solution development and deployment. It seems unavoidable that AHMT solutions on an individual program level will be limited in the benefit they can provide to the DoN due to the limited access to cross-domain and inter-domain data. However, AHMT solutions on an enterprise level will suffer from competing priorities, conflicting requirements, and non-value-added individual organizational policies.

The DoD has worked, and continues today, in addressing DAS shortcomings through acquisition reform. However, despite multiple reform attempts, the DoD's track record shows repeated cost overruns, missed delivery targets, and degraded

Hierarchical	Functional	Divisional	Matrix
Advantages • Defines levels of authority and responsibility • Clear reporting and tasking lines **Disadvantages** • Slows innovation and critical change due to increased bureaucracy • Causes individuals to act in the interest of the department instead of the enterprise	**Advantages** • Encourages specialization • Easily scalable **Disadvantages** • Creates silos within enterprises • Obscures enterprise strategy and integration efforts for differing divisional efforts (domain, product, geographical)	**Advantages** • Allows for flexibility and increased responsiveness to landscape changes • Promotes independence and customized methods to support specific needs **Disadvantages** • Duplication of resources • Internal enterprise competition for resources (zero-sum game)	**Advantages** • Flexibility in applying human capital resources • Promotes interdisciplinary skillsets and project exposure **Disadvantages** • Decreased task stability and focus • Competing priorities • Decreased accountability

Fig. 9.8 Pro et contra of various organizational structures (adapted from Williams, 2020)

capability acceptance. In fact, an analysis of historical acquisition reform efforts across almost four decades (1970–2000s) shows no improvement and even degraded performance in some programs and services (Baldwin & Cook, 2017). In concert with numerous strained attempts to streamline the DAS, the product landscape has fundamentally changed from what the DoD has historically acquired: ranging from hardware-centric products using a linear, sequential "waterfall" development methodology; to that of software-centric products (like AHMT solutions) dependent upon development, security, and operations (DevSecOps) methods with agile and test-driven practices allowing for CI/CD. Highlighting this product landscape shift, PoRs have cited software as the most frequent and critical driver of programmatic risk in nearly 60% of all acquisition programs (DSB, 2018). Mr. Marc Andreessen may have said it best, "software is eating the world." Technology, healthcare, finance, entertainment, telecom, retail, energy, and even national defense companies are becoming less hardware-centric and more software-centric. Dominant companies controlling large segments of their industry market-share are doing so through the use of software and delivering their services online (Andreessen, 2011). AHMT solutions have an uphill battle to overcome the inherent barriers within the DAS, let alone the organizational structures with their cultures, as applied to agile software development, acquisition, and deployment. The DoD directed study on software acquisition and practices pursuant to Sect. 872 of the 2018 National Defense Authorization Act that may summarize the DoN non-technical challenges best: "The current approach to software development is broken and is a leading source of risk to DoD: it takes too long, is too expensive, and exposes warfighters to unacceptable risk by delaying their access to tools they need to ensure mission success" (DIB, 2019, p. i).

9.3.2 Department of Navy Technical Challenges

To understand the full scope of technical challenges facing the DoN, it is imperative to understand how large the DoN is in terms of the capital assets and the supporting resources the compose it. This capital asset measurement is called the "existing fleet-and force-level" (CRS, 2020). The Government Accountability Office (GAO) estimates that the DoD manages a $1.8 trillion portfolio of 85 major weapon systems. Of these, over 40 are within the DoN with a collective estimated price tag of $855 billion (GAO, 2020). With each major weapon system costing an average of $20.6 billion dollars and being over 14 years old, the DoN has a significant amount of "technical debt" and "technical inflation" to manage. Technical debt is the concept of delaying necessary work during the development phase of a project to deliver a new product or meet a deadline, only to come back and finish or redo the work later. Technical inflation is the concept of the state of technology surpassing the foundational functions of a product even to the extent the product is no longer compatible with the current technology state. If both of these concepts are allowed to proliferate within an organization, long-term support for the product becomes expensive, and integrating new capabilities or modernizing the product's underlying support systems becomes extremely complex.

The DoN's weapon systems are considerably more complex than its manpower and training information technology (IT) systems; the latter is a litmus test for analysis to understand how complex the DoN's weapon system technical challenges have become. In 2017, the DoN undertook an effort to modernize its manpower and training IT systems. With the goal of transitioning legacy systems and databases to a modern enterprise resource planning (ERP) system allowing for the creation of an authoritative data environment, the complexities uncovered proved to be a lesson in technical debt and inflation acceptance. Once all of the legacy systems were discovered and analyzed, 55 independent systems were found, with 18% of these systems being at least three decades old (Serbu, 2018). Additionally, these systems were distributed across 73 data centers and networks, increasing the complexity for the modernization team to map legacy system interdependencies. If the number of systems and their distributed nature was not enough to contend with, the systems had been independently managed by differing organizations, leading to segregated, incremental system updates as each organization was executing its own system's capability evolution plan. Ultimately, this has led to software being deployed and executed in 21 different programming languages running atop nine different operating systems (Serbu, 2018).

While the above example is not about DoN weapon systems, parallels can most certainly be drawn. One can most certainly expect system-of-system (SoS) complexities to be the going-in position when it comes to AHMT solution integration. Additionally, AHMT solution developers should expect the majority of platforms in existence within the DoN to be unable to support the hardware, software, network, and data requirements needed by their applications and algorithms to function effectively.

DoN weapon systems, like that in the IT example above, also have numerous architectures, differing codebases, unique hardware sets, exotic network timing requirements, and incompatible interfaces, all managed by different program offices. To make matters worse, DoN verification and validation (V&V) constraints and objectives must be met in the cyber and test domains to achieve certification for deployment; meaning COTS AHMT solutions may have additional requirements that mandate their customization.

The DoN cannot afford the cost or losing ground with near-peer threats, to scrap its "existing fleet- and force-level" for a new, modern system architecture and infrastructure to enable AHMT solutions. Therefore, the DoN must turn upside-down some of its long-held program management ethos, organizational structure-induced cultures, and focused behaviors. The Navy must aggressively attack technical debt to remove the technical inflation that has built up over the decades and replace it with a new acquisition lifecycle path modeled after modern software development and deployment practices.

9.4 Attacking the Technical Debt and Inflation to Enable AHMT Solutions

The challenges to AHMT solutions mentioned above are in direct conflict with the DoN's future vision of distributed maritime operations (DMO), the USMC's vision of littoral operations in a contested environment (LOCE), and the marine expeditionary advance base operations (EABO). These visions require an integrated fleet and force to connect platforms, payloads, and sensors to enable information sharing at the tactical and operational levels of war. Achieving these visions will require AHMT solutions. The AHMT solutions necessitate unique infrastructures, lifecycle practices, integration interfaces, and cross-system data feeds along with the associated policies needed to make each of these topics successful. This situation requires a fundamental shift from how the DoN currently develops and fields systems. In fact, given the rapid rate of technological change, decreased cycle time of massive technological adoption, and market dominance of deploying more software-centric products than hardware-centric products, the DoN must digitally transform itself.

This section details two complementary paths to success in developing AHMT solutions at scale for deployment to new target platforms along with its legacy target platforms. These complimentary paths are intertwined and are both required to ensure the DoN effectively leverages previous investments (sunk costs/existing fleet- and force-level/technical debt) and maximizes its return-on-investment with new AHMT solutions (prospective costs).

9.4.1 AHMT Solutions and New Target Platforms

Following the requirements of an AHMT solution employing AI/ML needing robust software development pipelines, large datasets, and CI/CD mechanisms, a new "digital" acquisition paradigm must be built to enable these solutions. Unrolling the classical graphic describing the DevSecOps lifecycle into a linear depiction, as in Fig. 9.9, shows a rudimentary concept of the building blocks needed to support AHMT solutions.

As fielded AHMT solutions within the DoN are required to meet stringent standards (i.e., cyber, safety, stability certifications, and the like), architecting a "digital" acquisition lifecycle pipeline modeled after the DevSecOps lifecycle is a natural fit due to this model promoting product predictability, reproducibility, maintainability, speed to market, increased quality, reduced risk of defects, resiliency, modularity, and uncovering cost efficiencies (Guru99, 2020). Applying Fig. 9.9 to a notional DoN-centric "digital" acquisition lifecycle pipeline is shown in Fig. 9.10.

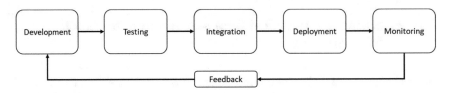

Fig. 9.9 DevSecOps lifecycle unrolled (adapted from Guru99, 2020)

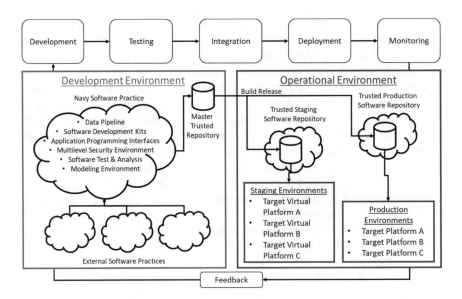

Fig. 9.10 Notional DoN-centric "digital" acquisition lifecycle pipeline (adapted from Kato, 2020)

In this depiction, AHMT solutions would be developed, tested, and certified within the DoN's development environment. This software practice would allow developers to code their applications and algorithms to DoN standards by making use of specific application programming interfaces (API), software development kits (SDK), architecture design principles, and access to the relevant DoN data. This software practice would also be linked to external software practices, allowing partners of the DoN to develop within their own controlled area if intellectual property dissemination is a concern, or if unique test hardware and software is required that does not reside within a DoN's software practice. The DoN's software practice also would allow developers to access current models of deployed systems, legacy codebases, and other applications at all security levels with live-data feeds to deployed systems making use of analytical tools to gain insight into operational target platforms. As AHMT solution providers build their applications, they will then be able to test and certify their applications and AI/ML algorithms for deployment. While software release patterns will be dependent on the specific item being deployed, in most cases virtual platforms or digital twins will be used to ensure system testing and stressing does not introduce unforeseen breakages into operationally deployed systems. Once the AHMT solutions have passed this step and have satisfied all performance measures, they can be released to the various production environments where the target platforms exist. The target platform will then continuously provide feedback to aid in the monitoring of performance and to provide data back to the development environment for further development efforts and testing sets.

With the DoN-centric "digital" acquisition lifecycle pipeline built, the target platform architecture must next be evolved to allow for AHMT solutions. In their current state, DoN platforms do not allow for advanced CI/CD software practices, edge-device detection and synchronization, or distributed orchestration of resources. In order to make these things possible, the DoN must start architecting and acquiring systems with decoupled service layers and models. This step will break the cycle of vendor lock, complex integration due to competing standards/architectures; lifetime sustainment hardware purchases due to tightly coupled hardware and software; and unrealized capability due to an inability to leverage all system sensors and effectors together.

A target platform architecture model, titled the digital system architecture (DSA), allowing for maximum flexibility at each service-oriented architecture layer is depicted in Fig. 9.11. This architecture enables commodity hardware to be interchanged seamlessly as it ages while still keeping AHMT application-specific hardware intact as needed. It also promotes information exchanges between AHMT applications, thereby increasing application capability and performance. Additionally, the DSA is a flexible and scalable computing infrastructure accommodating vitalized and containerized AHMT solutions. This architecture also builds upon microservice and service-mesh principles facilitating cross-service data exchanges. For AHMT solution developers, access to these common services and the "digital" acquisition lifecycle pipeline lowers the barrier of entry for software development and enables these developers to integrate new features and capabilities into their products. While

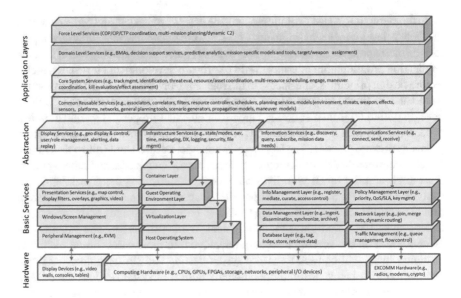

Fig. 9.11 Digital system architecture (adapted from Emery, 2019)

a few AHMT solutions may require unique hardware, for example AI/ML algorithms needing specialized processing units, most acquired AHMT solutions will be hardware agnostic. Building these applications with the provided SDK in the DoN's development environment and making use of the enterprise APIs will allow the applications to leverage all of the target platform's data, hardware infrastructure, sensor and effector systems, communication services, human–system interfaces, and other external platform data not within the target platform. Additionally, this will simplify AHMT solution design and deployment strategies as the DSA will be standardized across all target platforms. AHMT solution configuration management, version control, feature release, and target platform performance feedback will become second nature.

While it is straightforward to develop a new system guided by the DSA, evolving an existing architecture to that of the DSA is a complex task that will require the continued use of one or more software design patterns.

9.4.2   AHMT Solutions and Legacy Target Platforms

As it is impossible and unwise to scrap the "existing fleet- and force-level," the DoN must evolve its platforms to be compatible with the DSA to ensure that AHMT solutions are effective. This evolution must be done carefully to ensure currently fielded SoSs are not corrupted and are not taken offline. While a standard approach is needed to evolve battlespace domain legacy target platforms to the DSA in support of

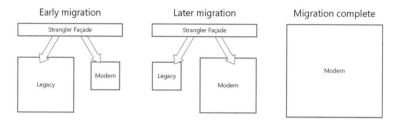

Fig. 9.12 Strangler pattern evolution (adapted from Microsoft, 2017a)

AHMT solutions, some legacy target platforms will require customized approaches. For example, the DoN surface combatant community struggles with timely and cost-effective hardware and software updates and upgrades. Software running on these platforms can be six years out-of-date and hardware can be over a decade old (RAND, 2013). At any given time, there are dozens of hardware and software baseline combinations, making configuration management impractical. Therefore, a few key tenets of software modernization will need to be applied to all legacy target platforms.

Design patterns, software specific and the like, are reusable, formalized best practices employed by architects and engineers to solve frequently reoccurring problems within various endeavors. The strangler pattern is a software design pattern commonly used in the rewriting of large, legacy codebases (Rook, 2016). The basic premise of the strangler pattern is to incrementally migrate a legacy codebase by gradually replicating/replacing functions with new applications and services. As these new applications and services come online and their functionality is proved by conducting rigorous V&V activities, the new system's functions replace the old system's functions (Microsoft, 2017a). This effectively "strangles" the old system as its functions are progressively decommissioned and migrated to/provided by the new system. An example of a legacy system going through this process is shown in Fig. 9.12.

When applying the strangler pattern to active critical systems, it is important to ensure translation between subsystems not sharing exact semantics. As the new functions come online, they may be dependent upon the legacy system to provide the information necessary to deliver this function. This includes information not typically designed into modern applications, such as outdated infrastructure support, deprecated data models, antiquated protocols, and unique APIs, to name a few (Microsoft, 2017b). Due to these dependencies, new system performance and quality measures may be impacted by legacy system shortcomings causing "corruption" within the new system design. Additionally, unintended/unknown impacts to current legacy system functions may occur as new system functions take over and interact with legacy data stores. To prevent and minimize these impacts, an anti-corruption layer pattern should be adopted in conjunction with a strangler pattern (Microsoft, 2019). An example of this is shown in Fig. 9.13.

Making use of these two design patterns, the DoN will be able to evolve critical legacy target platforms to the DSA with reduced risk and increased speed to enable

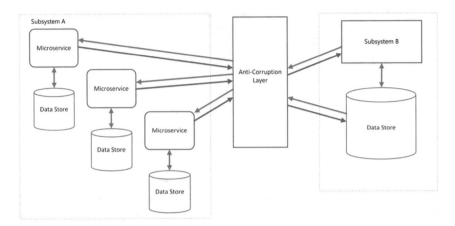

Fig. 9.13 Anti-corruption layer pattern in use (adapted from Microsoft, 2017b)

AHMT solutions. These current disparate systems suffer from complicated legacy code and monolithic architectures and are supported by fragmented organizations saddled with immeasurable amounts of technical debt and technical inflation which are resistant to change. Figure 9.14 shows an example of how current legacy target

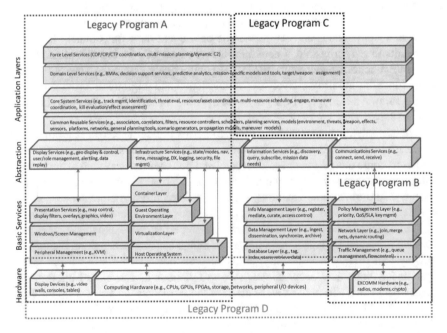

Fig. 9.14 Legacy program architecture boundaries applied to the DSA digital stack (adapted from Emery, 2019)

platforms exist and why making use of these design patterns for evolution is needed. As discussed previously, the DoN currently allows platforms and programs to acquire various levels of the digital stack to meet their PoR performance requirements. This challenge becomes a modernization and integration nightmare for the resulting SoS platforms when these capabilities are integrated. The resultant legacy target platform becomes a "Frankenstein's monster" of competing hardware sets, codebase languages, hardware and software architectures, APIs, and security policies. It also becomes a complex task to map SoS dependencies, resulting in a "spaghetti diagram" of possible failure modes when individual PoRs upgrade their individual systems but do not control their entire digital stack.

To deploy AHMT solutions at scale to legacy target platforms, specific legacy program architectures will need to make use of the anti-corruption layer design pattern prior to DSA re-factorization. The anti-corruption layer and strangler façade should be used as a subclass of digital twins known as a virtual twin. This virtualized, mirror copy of the system in-being will not only act as the anti-corruption layer it will also have the added benefit of being used as the test, evaluation, validation, and verification harness for the application and subsystem services being re-factored into the various microservice functions and integrated across the service mesh architecture. Additionally, this virtual twin will also serve as the host to the staging software build to be released in either an environment-based or application-based pattern. Given the DoN will have more than a handful of target legacy platforms that AHMT solutions will need to be released, an environment-based release pattern will likely be the first choice until all of the target legacy platforms have been successfully re-factored to be compliant with the DSA. Once in compliance, AHMT solutions may be able to proceed with an application-based release pattern.

When it comes to selecting environment-based release patterns, the blue-green, canary, and cluster immune system deployment patterns will be the most useful to the DoN. The blue-green deployment pattern, shown in Fig. 9.15, consists of two production environments with only one being "live" at any point in time (Kim et al., 2016). A new build release is deployed to the "non-live" environment for testing. Once V&V is completed, the "live" and "non-live" environments switch roles. This deployment pattern allows for rollbacks as well if the new release causes an unforeseen error not previously uncovered in testing.

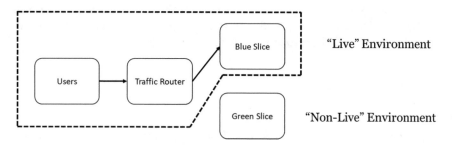

Fig. 9.15 Blue-green deployment pattern (adapted from Kim et al., 2016)

The canary and cluster immune system deployment patterns build upon the blue-green deployment pattern by further minimizing the user's exposure to potential system errors not uncovered in the testing phase. The canary deployment pattern differs from the blue-green deployment pattern by progressively routing more users to the new build release over time. This routing of users over time allows for a subset of users to use the new build release to potentially uncover hidden errors before exposing the entire user population to these errors. The cluster immune system deployment pattern takes the canary deployment pattern a step further by automating the rollback of production build releases through monitoring system user performance (Kim et al., 2016). AHMT solutions will most certainly be held to these deployment patterns when incorporating AI/ML algorithms and applications that may affect other systems.

Executing the new target platform development path in concert with the legacy target platform modernization path will enable the DoN to maximize the use of AHMT solutions and their associated AI/ML algorithms while simultaneously modernizing the "existing fleet- and force-level" and ensuring future acquisitions are compliant with true naval enterprise architecture. The DSA is a critical enabler to the DoN for realizing battlefield dominance with its algorithms supporting AHMT solutions.

9.5   Conclusion and Path Forward

The DoN is an immense organization with a wealth of capability and talent, however, a new enterprise approach is needed for how the future fleet and force acquires and integrates capabilities to take advantage of AHMT solutions employing AI/ML algorithms. It will not be easy for the DoN to deviate from its current structures and processes as institutional and acquisition apparatus change is difficult. The ideas described within this chapter provide a path for success if the enterprise architects and system engineers are meaningfully empowered with cross-organizational authority. This proposed path is a technical stepping-stone to success in the effort to deploy AHMT solutions and make the most of the DoN's investment in legacy platforms. Future areas for development in conjunction with the ideas mentioned above include level-of-effort-based contracts for software projects; specific contract data requirements tailored for AI/ML algorithms; PoR budget exhibit justification language and structure; and the flexible application of appropriations to ensure compliance with laws like that of the Misappropriations Act (AcqNotes, 2018).

References

AcqNotes. (2018). Acquisition Process. Retrieved from: acqnotes.com/acqnote/acquisitions/acquisition-process-overview
Andreessen, M. (2011). Why software is eating the world. *The Wall Street Journal*. New York, NY.

Baldwin, L., & Cook, C. (2017) Lessons from a long history of acquisition reform. RAND Corporation. www.rand.org/blog/2015/07/lessons-from-a-long-history-of-acquisition-reform.html.

Big Commerce. (2020). Cloud computing stack. Retrieved from: https://www.bigcommerce.com/blog/saas-vs-paas-vs-iaas/#the-key-differences-between-on-premise-saas-paas-iaas.

Bartels, F. (2019) Pentagon's $80 billion in unspent funds shows need for a better budget process. The Heritage Foundation. Retrieved from: www.heritage.org/defense/commentary/pentagons-80-billion-unspent-funds-shows-need-better-budget-process.

Cruz, V. (2018) Why 30% of app deployments fail. www.wired.com/insights/2013/04/why-30-of-app-deployments-fail.

Congressional Research Service. (2019). Artificial intelligence and national security. Retrieved from: https://crsreports.congress.gov. Report number R45178

Congressional Research Service (2020). Navy force structure and shipbuilding plans: Background and issues for congress. Retrieved from https://crsreports.congress.gov. Report number RL32665

Davis, Z. (2019). Artificial intelligence on the battlefield. center for global security research Lawrence Livermore national laboratory. Livermore, CA.

Department of Defense. (2019). DoD directive 5000.81, urgent capability acquisition. Washington, DC.

Department of Defense. (2020). DOD instruction 5000.02: Operation of the adaptive acquisition framework. Washington, DC.

Defense Acquisition University. (2019). Frequently asked questions. Belvoir, VA. Retrieved from: www.dau.edu/faq/Pages/Certifications-Programs.aspx.

Defense Innovation Board. (2019). Software is never done. Washington, DC: Department of Defense.

Defense Science Board. (2018). Task force report: Design and acquisition of software for defense systems. Washington, DC: Department of Defense.

Department of Defense. (2018a). National defense strategy. Washington, DC.

Department of Defense. (2018b). Digital engineering strategy. Washington, DC.

Defense Science Board. (2012). Task force report: The role of autonomy in DoD systems. Washington, DC: Department of Defense.

Department of Defense. (2015). Technology investment strategy 2015–2018. Washington, DC.

Department of the Navy. (2016). Department of the navy unmanned systems (UxS) goals. Washington, DC.

Emery, K. (2019). Generalized system architecture. Working papers. Arlington, VA.

Government Accountability Office. (2020). Defense acquisitions annual assessment. Washington, DC.

Guru99. (2020). DevOps tutorial: Complete beginners training. Retrieved from: www.guru99.com/devops-tutorial.html.

Gansler, J., & Lucyshyn, W. (2012). IT acquisition: Expediting the process to deliver business capabilities to the DoD enterprise. University of Maryland, Center for Public Policy and Private Enterprise. College Park, MD.

Hastie, S., & Wojewoda, S. (2015). Standish group 2015 Chaos report. Retrieved from: www.infoq.com/articles/standish-chaos-2015.

https://www.learntek.org/blog/sdlc-phases/.

Janicijevic, N. (2013). The mutual impact of organizational culture and structure, economic annals (Vol. LVIII, No. 198). Belgrade, Serbia.

Kim, G., Humble, J., Debois, P., & Willis, J. (2016). *The DevOps handbook*. IT Revolution Press, LLC.

Kato, K. (2020). DevSecOps strategy for the enterprise. Working papers. Washington, DC.

Lineberger, R. (2016). Program management in aerospace and defense: Still late and over budget, Deloitte Center for Industry Insights. New York, NY.

Williams, S. (2020). 7 types of organizational structures (+org charts for implementation). Retrieved from: www.lucidchart.com/blog/types-of-organizational-structures.

Microsoft. (2017a). Strangler pattern. Retrieved from: https://docs.microsoft.com/en-us/azure/arc hitecture/patterns/strangler.

Microsoft. (2017b). Anti-corruption layer patter. Retrieved from: https://docs.microsoft.com/en-us/azure/architecture/patterns/anti-corruption-layer.

Microsoft. (2019). Design patterns for microservices. Retrieve from: https://docs.microsoft.com/en-us/azure/architecture/microservices/design/patterns; Microsoft. (2017b). Strangler pattern. Retrieved from: https://docs.microsoft.com/en-us/azure/architecture/patterns/strangler.

Moore, A. (2019). Department of navy AI technical interchange.

RAND Corporation. (2013). Assessing aegis program transition to an open-architecture model. Santa Monica, CA.

Rook, M. (2016). The Strangler patter in practice. Michiel Rook's blog. Retrieved from: www.mic hielrook.nl/2016/11/strangler-pattern-practice.

Serbu, J. (2018). Navy to unplug decades-old personnel IT systems, clear way for app-based self service. Ret revived from: www.federalnewnetwork.com/all-news/2019/04/.

SDLC (Software Development Life Cycle). (2019). Retrieved from.

Serbu, J. (2020). Pentagon teeing up nine programs to test new 'color of money' for software development. Retrevived from: www.federalnewsnetwork.com/acquisition/2020/03/pentagon-teeing-up-nine-programs-to-test-new-color-of-money-for-software-development/.

Venture Beat Staff (2019) Why do 87% of data science projects never make it into production? https://venturebeat.com/2019/07/19/why-do-87-of-data-science-projects-never-make-it-into-production.

White House. (2017). *National security strategy*. Washington, DC.

Chapter 10
Digital Twin Industrial Immune System: AI-driven Cybersecurity for Critical Infrastructures

Michael Mylrea, Matt Nielsen, Justin John, and Masoud Abbaszadeh

Abstract Innovative advances in machine learning (ML) and artificial intelligence (AI)-driven cyber-physical anomaly detection will help to improve the security, reliability and resilience of the United States' power grid. These advances are timely as sophisticated cyber adversaries are increasingly deploying innovative tactics, techniques and technology to attack critical energy infrastructures. Defenders of these modern infrastructures need to better understand how to combine innovative technology in a way that enables their teams to detect, protect, respond and endure attacks from complex, nonlinear and rapidly evolving cyber threats. This chapter (i) explores how AI is being combined with advances in physics to develop a next-generation industrial immune system to defend against sophisticated cyber-physical attacks to critical infrastructure; (ii) provides an overview of the technology and explores its applicability to address the needs of cyber defenders to critical energy infrastructures; applicability is explored through opportunities and challenges related to human–machine teams as well as the process and technology; (iii) includes validation and verification of findings when the technology was tested defending against stealthy attacks on the world's largest gas turbines; (iv) explores how the AI algorithms are being developed to provide cyber defenders with improved cyber situation awareness to rapidly detect, locate and neutralize the threat; and (v) concludes with future research to overcome human–machine challenges with neutralizing threats from all hazards.

M. Mylrea (✉)
Distinguished Engineer, Cybersecurity & Digital Innovation, National Resilience, Inc,
Washington, DC, USA
e-mail: michael.mylrea@resilience.com

M. Nielsen · J. John · M. Abbaszadeh
Cybersecurity, R&D for Operational Technology, General Electric (GE) Global Research,
Washington, DC, USA

© Springer Nature Switzerland AG 2021
W. F. Lawless et al. (eds.), *Systems Engineering and Artificial Intelligence*,
https://doi.org/10.1007/978-3-030-77283-3_10

10.1   Introduction

A digital transformation of critical energy infrastructures is underway that is rapidly digitizing, networking and automating the energy value chain. Today's smart energy systems unlock new value in modernizing the grid that is increasingly interoperable, two-way, agile and flexible in incorporating distributed energy resources. While grid modernization helped transition energy usage and consumption to lower carbon, sustainable, renewable energy, new cyber-physical security challenges in securing critical energy delivery systems and associated operational technology (OT) have accompanied this digital transformation. The rapid digital transformation of our critical systems has significantly increased its attack surfaces by combining cyber-physical systems, software and hardware, information technology (IT) and operational technology (OT). This has created new challenges to identify, monitor and protect these critical systems. Improvements are needed for real-time cyber-physical situational awareness and monitoring the cyber threat-attack surface in terms of control systems, automation and other operational technology.

10.1.1   Overview

While cybersecurity technology continues to improve, the attack surfaces of the power grid have expanded significantly, leaving a number of major cyber gaps remaining. For one, most cyber defenses and monitoring solutions are ineffective in detecting sophisticated attacks targeting operational technology, such as energy delivery and industrial control sytems. Zero-day exploits, insider and supply chain attacks continue to evade and defeat cyber defenses and intrusion detection systems. These systems originated from securing information technology across a business enterprise and defending against known malware, malicious packets and other attacks that are easy to catalogue in a library as signature herusitics. However, OT found in various energy delivery systems, such as electricity infrastructures presents new challenges as the protocol, malware signatures, and tactics, techniques and procedures used by adversaries also differ significantly. Moreover, a number of more than 3,000 energy utilities in the U.S. lack basic cybersecurity defenses to identify and monitor their critical cyber OT assets. Thus, the detection of sophisticated adversaries is limited—usually too late or reactive, only after the damage has been done—enabling them to perist their malicious activities in critical systems and networks and often without being detected.

   To overcome these limitations, solutions must advance from security to resilience and provide more holistic cover for critical OT in electricity infrastructures. To realize these goals, GE research has been working closely with the U.S. Department of Energy, DARPA and our energy utlitiy partners to leverage advances in artificial intelligence (AI) and machine learning (ML) to develop an industrial immune system for critical operational technology, from wind turbines to combined-cycle power plants, and from hydropower to oil and gas pipelines. In one of the world's first demonstrations of AI/ML self-healing neutralization at scale and with accuracy (99%), GE Research demonstrated the ability to neutralize sophisticated cyber-attacks on the world's largest gas turbines. While this scientific accomplishment highlighted advances in AI/ML cyber-physical anomaly detection, a number of challenges remain. Overcoming these challenges requires scientific advances and research that combine complex problem sets at the nexus of people to accomplish these goals, process and technology to secure high assurance systems that are increasingly autonomous. Some of these areas explored in this chapter include explainable AI (XAI), invariant learning and humble AI. These advances are critical to improve the data fusion, trustworthiness and accuracy of AI-driven technology and its application in empowering human–machine teams.

Additional advances are needed not only to detect and challenge decision support for complex autonomous systems but also to the system designers and operators who do not understand and/or trust the decisions that the algorithms are making. This lack of explanation, context and trustworthiness in the algorithms slows adoption and impedes innovation. End users are hesitant to trust the algorithms because they cannot correlate AI-driven machine decisions with the physics and their own domain of experience. In a safety critical system, not understanding the physics and how algorithms are reaching their decisions curtails innovation in next-generation system design and deployment. Overcoming these barriers would help owners, operators and other complex systems stakeholders better understand how algorithms are learning and making decisions, allowing the translation of big data sets into actionable intelligence. Advancements in explainable AI (XAI) would remove these barriers to innovation and provide significant value in advancing the science of sense-making, context and trustworthiness of AI systems.

10.1.2   Cybersecurity Technology Gaps for Advanced Detection, Protection and Monitoring Solutions

Grid modernization has spurred the integration of distributed energy resources (DER's) and the electricity infrastructure that is increasingly digitized, networked, automated and complex in its communications using multiple languages and protocols between an increasing number of parties (Qi et al., 2016). Securing these critical communications in transit, at rest and at the device level without sacrificing improvement in forecasting, control and optimization of these assets is essential. Indeed, any effective cybersecurity solution should not curtail advances in control and optimization. Fig. 10.1 highlights how grid cyber defenders have responded to the cyber threats posed to (DERs) with various cybersecurity solutions that try to segment and

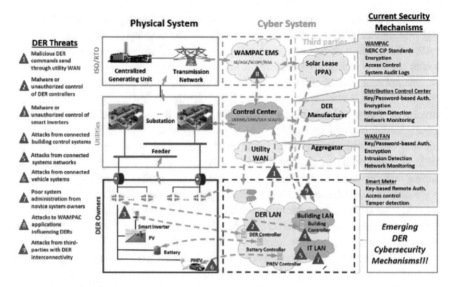

Fig. 10.1 Cyber-physical threat to distributed energy resources (DERs)

to provide "air gaps" for critical systems. However, these cybersecurity solutions do not provide cyber resilience against sophisticated threat actors nor hybrid cyber-physical events (e.g., extreme weather, insider threats, human error, supply chain attacks on software, hardware, etc.) (Fig. 10.1).[1]

As a result, there are numerous cybersecurity gaps for the advanced detection, protection and monitoring of energy delivery systems, networks and interconnected energy delivery systems. These gaps could potentially be exploited to cause the degradation of service and potential cascading failures to the power grid. However, due to the many gaps existing in detection and monitoring, it is difficult to quantify the threat and risk. Increased monitoring and detection of electricity infrastructure may give the perception that attacks to the grid are increasing when in fact this increase is a measure of an improved cyber situation awareness. When an industry article and/or publication suggests there is an increase in cyber-attacks on the grid, is that because monitoring and detection technology have improved, or because threat groups are increasingly targeting the grid? Currently, there is a major gap in the research and data available to quantify these risks. This gap makes it difficult for energy utilities to make strategic investments to buy down the risks to them that are greatest based on the threat. Another major cybersecurity gap for advanced detection, protection and monitoring is found with the increasing penetration of distributed energy resources (DERs, Greenberg et al., 2018; also, see Utility Dive).[2,3] Increased connectivity and

---

[1] Qi et al. (2016).

[2] https://www.utilitydive.com/news/security-and-distributed-resources-an-attacker-will-eventually-get-in-s/565966/.

[3] Greenberg et al. (2018).

the two-way communications of DERs with infrastructure associated with the bulk power grid will require advanced threat monitoring and detection to address existing and potential future cybersecurity gaps (Lee, 2013).[4] Any holistic solution requires a comprehensive approach of human and machine, or people, process and technology. But many other gaps remain.

Policy Gaps—Currently the North American Electric Reliability Corporation Critical Infrastructure Protection (NERC CIP) cybersecurity requirements have increased defenses for critical systems found in the bulk grid. However, distribution and grid-edge devices that are increasingly connected to bulk grid infrastructures are vulnerable to sophisticated cyber-attacks.

Technology Gaps—The data and connectivity requirements needed to improve grid edge and DER management—increased awareness, controls direct-level electrical loads, manage capacity constraints and reverse power flows—has significantly expanded the attack surfaces of our nation's grid. For example, solar energy systems grid-support functions can be manipulated to diminish reliability and damage electricity infrastructure. Securing photovoltaic (PV) system critical communications at rest as well as in transit to aggregators (residential, utility, commercial), utilities and other grid operators is increasingly challenging due to increased internet connectivity and digitization (Johnson, 2017)[5] as well as communication protocols that prioritize interoperability but lack basic encryption and authentication mechanism (Onunkwo et al., 2018).[6]

Together, current policies, processes and technologies prioritize interoperability and connectivity but they do not provide the high fidelity cyber situational awareness needed to detect cyber-physical anomalies to DERs. Even when monitoring is available, determining the cause of the anomaly and localizing and neutralizing the threat is a major gap in this space. Sophisticated adversaries can perturb systems to instigate abnormal power flows; supply chain attacks can push updates to be behind the metered systems to add or drop load in a way that could potentially cause a grid level event; insider attacks can cause instabilities like sub-synchronous resonances, and man in the middle attacks can amplify weak grid conditions, just to name a few.

10.1.3   Digital Ghost: A Next-Generation Response to Close Critical Energy Infrastructure Gaps

In response, researchers at GE Global Research, in partnership with the U.S. energy industry and the U.S. Department of Energy, have developed innovative solutions to identify, mitigate and autonomously respond to evolving cyber threats. This next-generation, cyber-physical anomaly detection solution combines advances in machine learning (AI) to rapidly identify, protect, detect, respond and

---

[4] Lee (2013).

[5] Johnson (2017).

[6] Onunkwo et al. (2018).

recover from cyber-physical threats and vulnerabilities targeting operational technology (OT). If an adversary attacks, manipulates or compromises a critical energy delivery system, GE's Digital Ghost helps to detect anomalous behavior, locate and neutralize the attack while maintaining the availability and integrity of critical operations. To realize this goal, Digital Ghost leverages machine learning of digital twins (high-resolution models of OT/IT systems and networks) in order to: *Identify*, detect and map critical systems, anomalies and associated vulnerabilities and to quantify them; *Localize*, Isolate and Protect critical control systems and OT (sensors/actuators/drives/controllers); and *Neutralize* to autonomously *Respond* and *Recover*, mitigating advanced threats. The ability to review the control logic and to autonomously maintain operations without losing the availability of critical systems is a potential game changer to provide cyber-physical resilience, but many challenges remain.

Cyber defense of critical infrastructure continues to evolve, but cyber adversaries often have the upper hand as their offensive tools improve and the attack surface available to them expands. Cyber challenges remain for policies, technology and people (workforce and expertise). To change this equation, new paradigms and formal methods as well as advances in threat mitigation technology need to be developed. Even as cyber defense technology improves, workforce development, especially in the area of OT cybersecurity, remains a major gap. The confidentiality, integrity and availability triad that has defined cybersecurity in the last 20 years continues to be pressured by the digital transformation underway that prioritizes interoperability, connectivity and the move toward automation. As we digitize, automate and connect systems in critical infrastructure to the internet, this also expands the cyber-physical attack surface.

To improve the current state-of-the-art in grid cyber-defense requires moving beyond the cybersecurity triad paradigm to cyber resilience, which assumes that we can identify, detect, respond and recover to cyber threats and vulnerabilities in subsecond times. Cyber resilience includes not only a hardened perimeter, but it also neutralizes sophisticated attacks once they have been found.

Advances of innovative threat mitigation solutions help to move the industry toward cyber resilience. However, the design and implementation of these advances, such as machine learning algorithms, requires the distillation of large data sets to be intelligently fused with operations. The form of the cyber-defense technology needs to be complemented by a process function in a way that turns data into intelligence. Through this information fusion, human–machine teams can increase both their autonomy and effectiveness to evolve their defenses to be cyber resilience in response to sophisticated evolving threats. The following provides an overview of the design and deployment of the next-generation AI cyber-defense technology to detect, localize and neutralize threats in a more effective and autonomous way. To realize this goal requires **the leveraging of the science of interdependence for autonomous human–machine teams in a synergistic way to identify and overcome existing gaps with** people, process and technology explored further in Fig. 10.2.

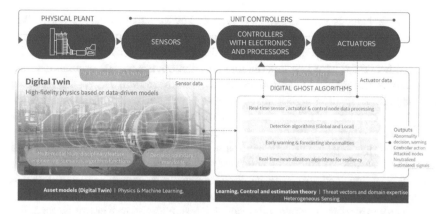

Fig. 10.2 Digital Ghost functionality diagram. The example is of a power generation plant. The top portion in the figures depicts a complex system with sensors, controls and actuators. The bottom left pane shows how the Digital Ghost is trained from off-line operational data and physics-based models. The bottom right pane outlines the real-time algorithms providing detection and neutralization functions

10.2   People, Process and Technology Applicability Gap Analysis

This section examines the applicability of the existing cybersecurity technology to address cyber defender needs for modern critical energy infrastructures, which is going through its own digital transformation. Applicability and gap analysis is explored through the opportunities and challenges related to human–machine team or *people* as well as the *process* and *technology*.

10.2.1   Attack Detection

Attack Detection—Advanced threat detection starts with a comprehensive design. Digital Ghost's design phase started with scoping the target system and defining the sub-systems that are of primary interest. Instead of a purely unsupervised approach to develop the machine learning algorithms, we leveraged our deep domain knowledge of the physics for the systems to establish a matrix of credible cyber-attacks, naturally occurring faults and vulnerabilities in the system. The highest impact abnormalities (i.e., attacks/faults) are chosen for computer model simulations. The high-fidelity Digital Twin models are exercised to define the system's operating boundaries. Normal operating space is mapped out as well as attack/abnormal operating spaces. The machine learning algorithm developed from these defined scenarios is intended to differentiate between a naturally occurring system fault or a degradation mode and a likely malicious cyber-attack scenario. Historical data obtained from the asset or plant is reviewed to establish the key system monitoring nodes. The next step is to establish the decision boundary, called a decision manifold, between the normal and attack/fault (abnormal) operating regions. Performance predictions are then generated based on this optimal decision boundary. The optimal decision boundary is also updated over time in the future as the system evolves via real-time learning and adaptation algorithms. The next step is deploying the detection algorithms on a computer platform connected to the targeted system. Once deployed, the detection algorithm performance is reviewed and continuously monitored.

Technology Gaps—The following four are the areas in technology gaps that need to be closed: (i) Unlike IT solutions which are easy to enumerate and inventory by scanning, operational technology includes a diverse attack surface that is often connected through both internet protocol (IP), serial and other connections. (ii) Proprietary protocols are often vulnerable by design as vendors prioritize functionality, ease of use and cost over security. (iii) Firewalls, network and host intrusion detection systems are limited to defending against malicious signatures, but they are not in their libraries of attack signatures. Thus, a brute force, polymorphic, AI-generated or insider attack will be very difficult to detect. Zero-day exploits targeting operational technology are very difficult to block with most existing attack detection solutions that are designed for IT. (iv) And resource-intensive tuning can be required for AI defense critical solutions to be integrated into existing technology stacks for security information and event management (SIEM).

Process and Policy Gaps: As AI solutions improve attack detections it will increase the speed, size and fidelity of logging critical machine state integrity as well as other network and system outputs. Thus, monitoring policies and process updates need to intelligently distill and fuse these findings for this data to create actionable cyber intelligence. Often, grid cyber defenders have policies and processes in place to monitor and log their critical cyber assets as defined by the NERC CIP requirements; however, they often times do not read these logs. Moreover, additional networks or systems that are connected to these critical cyber assets can provide an attack pathway if they are not secured.

People Gaps: Machine learning algorithms that have high-false positive rates create prohibitive operations and maintenance requirements for security teams. Cybersecurity teams have been traditionally IT-focused; however, the convergence of IT/OT in critical infrastructures has increased the responsibilities and created new workforce development challenges for them. Some innovative new tools require training, but adding another tool creates information fusion challenges. Finally, AI solutions that are tuned and learn what is normal on networks and systems that are already infected may be providing a false sense of security to their operators. Advances in invariant learning and humble AI explored in this chapter highlight how researchers are overcoming these gaps.

10.2.2   Attack Localization

This phase develops a software algorithm that localizes the attack to a specific system function. Attack dependency tests are conducted to further separate the attacks into independent or dependent attacks. Local decision manifold boundaries are created for each monitoring node using data sets by running various attack scenarios with the high-fidelity Digital Twin models mentioned previously. The system post-processes the localized attack and determines whether the detected attack is an independent attack or an artifact of a previous attack through propagation of the effects in the closed-loop feedback control system. This feedback provides additional information and insight and is useful when multiple attacks are detected. The same approach is practiced for localization when naturally occurring faults are detected.

Technology Gaps: For critical OT assets and systems, the sub-second time requirements for effective detection and localization are a major gap for most cyber-defense solutions. Moreover, there is a lack of real-time detection and localization solutions to respond to cyber-attacks. Visibility of the data and the probable fault or attack is limited across the energy value chain. Advances in supervisory control and data acquisition as well as energy management and distribution management systems have increased fidelity and control of the data. Similarly, advances in active scanning and interrogating/communicating with an OT in its native protocol has increased visibility. However, many gaps remain and have created prohibitive localization response times. The speed of response for malware and infiltration mitigation to an attack is a critical gap that needs to be met to maintain reliable, safe and secure plant operations. Finally, critical OT is difficult to monitor, especially in converged IT/OT environments that combine various cyber and physical legacy and modern system protocols.

Process and Policy Gaps: Current processes focus on localizing faults, safety and reliability issues. Cybersecurity is often an afterthought. Systems engineering approaches in practice are often reduced to adages, such as "if it's not broken, don't fix it." Or even the colloquial KISS expression—"keep it stupid simple." As a result, most policies focus on how to localize and respond to sensor or actuator faults; component level faults; system level faults that could cause a loss of power or degradation in output; but not how to localize a cyber-attack. There is a real risk that adversaries could imbed themselves onto a critical system, establish a stealth command and control channel, and potentially carry out an attack undetected at a later date.

Human Resource Gaps: Locating a fault in a complex system like a power plant is no trivial task. In addition, the resource gaps noted for detection and localization have similar and related issues related to localizing an actual system that faulted; this problem is especially true during a transient event or when there is a highly variable stochastic load, events that create a lot of noise and that challenge human operators' ability to localize the problem. Moreover, sensor or actuator faults, component level faults, system level faults, and cyber-attacks may all produce similar effects in a system (i.e., the loss of power or degradation in output).

10.2.3 Attack Neutralization

Advancing from cybersecurity to cyber resilience requires improvements in neutralization and the ability to recover and endure all hazards, ranging from sophisticated cyber-attacks to naturally occurring events. Neutralization also requires the ability to remove the effects of attacks on the monitoring nodes so that the system can continue to function even in the presence of attacks. It uses the observability provided by the deemed trusted nodes (non-attacked nodes) in its calculations. It will enable true operational signals to be provided to the control system on a continuous basis while informing the operator when attacks are detected.[7] If an attacked node lacks observability, then the error in its replacement estimate may be unacceptably large, preventing continued operation.

Further research into how to autonomously identify critical nodes with poor observability is required to advance secure communication application methods for critical OT. Since neutralization cyber solutions will interact directly with the critical control loops of an operating asset, additional research focused on control stability is needed. Operators must be able to trust that the combined system (Digital Ghost, controller and asset) will behave with stable operations. Operating regions may exist where stability cannot be guaranteed, e.g., outside of the boundaries used for training. The asset's allowable operations must be limited, and research into autonomously identifying these restricted regions is required.

Technology Gaps: For critical OT assets and systems, there are sub-second time requirements for effective communications. Sub-second time requirements are demanded by the dynamics of the system. For many of the critical assets we want to be monitored with Digital Ghost, we need to be able to attack the nodes estimated via the neutralization module at the timescales required by the dynamics of the system. Cyber resilience requires the ability to both detect and localize rapidly to effectively and accurately neutralize an attack or anomaly. Sophisticated cyber-attacks, zero-day exploits, hybrid cyber-physical attacks, insider threats to name a few, create challenges in neutralization. Control systems are designed with functionality, ease of use, safety, cost and connectivity in mind, but not security. This gap creates additional challenges related to neutralization. The TRISIS cyber exploit was exemplary of these design vulnerabilities where a safety instrumented control system was exploited in a sophisticated attack on operational technology.

Process and Policy Gaps: **Three areas are noted**: **(i)** Today, cyber-security policies for critical energy infrastructures often prioritize the availability and integrity of critical systems; however, most current solutions only identify threats and vulnerabilities, relying on manual response; (ii) Manual responses create resources and response-time challenges that are prohibitive; and (iii) Existing tools lack prioritization and create prohibitive resource requirements with false positives.

People Gaps: (i) Lastly, trust between Digital Ghost's neutralization algorithm and the operator must be established. During a cyber-attack, the operator must be presented with clear, concise and understandable information to quickly ascertain

---

[7] John et al. (2020).

the context and impact to the operations of the machine protected by Digital Ghost. Neutralization leverages concepts from AI/ML, while operators and control engineers often prefer "deterministic" algorithms governing control logic. Research into the more effective autonomous system–human operations is required for neutralization to be an accepted mitigation approach.

10.2.4   Man Versus Machine Anomaly Forecasting and Detection

Anomaly forecasts enable the early detection of stealthy attacks which could otherwise remain in an asset for days or months without being caught. It also enables the early engagement of the system's operator or the automatic accommodation in a cyber incident. Furthermore, the anomaly forecast system can predict future system failures/malfunctions and can be used as a tool for predictive health monitoring and prognostics. Once the security of a system is compromised, the adversarial impact will propagate through the system until it gets detected by the attack detection mechanisms. However, by the time that those mechanisms have detected an attack, the damage may have already been done, with an impact too large to be accommodated. These advances provide an early warning capability to attack detection so that a security breach is detected and alarmed at an early stage both for an operator's response and for an attack accommodation by the system.

The outputs of prediction models in different timescales (also known as the future values of the features) are compared with the corresponding decision boundaries for anomaly forecasting. While comparing the feature vectors to the decision boundary, the estimated time to cross the decision boundary will provide information for a future anomaly. If a future anomaly is detected, an early warning is generated in the operator's display with the anticipated time to reach an anomalous state, and a message is sent to the automatic accommodation system for its potential early engagement.

10.3   Digital Ghost Research Findings and Future Research

10.3.1   Invariant Learning

Measuring both anomalies and invariances in deep networks for a complex system-of-systems like the power grid is not an easy task. For one, the increased penetration of stochastic and intermittent distributed energy resources further complicates the essential pattern recognition tasks to be able to flag anomalies and variances. Recent research shows advances in training deep architectures in a supervised manner to be invariant to the multiple confounding properties and input transformations found in electricity infrastructures (Goodfellow et al., 2009).[8] Future research examining how to enhance invariant machine learning to improve the cyber-attack detection and accommodation (ADA) accuracy of the Digital Twin models that identify and protect against cyber-physical attacks on critical energy systems and infrastructures is essential.

Modeling a complex system-of-systems for an electricity infrastructure is challenging due to the number of issues from bias offsets between the actual values of the key nodes being monitored and those found in simulations to be "noise" in the system. What appears as an anomaly could be caused by human error, computational error, a naturally occurring weather and ambient event, an increase in supply and demand, a cyber-attack, or a hybrid cyber-physical event. Moreover, adversaries could potentially exploit continuous machine learning biases with the next-generation machine learning attacks that slowly bias key nodes such that the continuous system "learns" this incorrect behavior and treats it as normal. To overcome these challenges, the next-generation, cyber-resilient, invariant-learning algorithms need to be improved to advance physical detection and mitigate risk from sophisticated AI attacks. Moreover, for these innovative technology solutions to be successfully transitioned to the energy sector will require alerts of cyber events that are clearly displayed to the cyber defenders of a grid especially when they are already distracted with many tools, screens and the day-to-day challenges of keeping the grid reliable and balanced.

These findings point toward the need to employ continuous learning to modify the algorithms and/or decision manifolds based upon actual field data. Allowing flexibility for the algorithms to be modified or adjusted based upon actual field data could help to alleviate model mismatches. However, continuous learning could also create a potential new cyber-attack surface where an attacker slowly biases key nodes so that the continuous system again "learns" this incorrect behavior and treats it as normal. Advances in invariant learning are needed to mitigate this manipulation of continuous learning algorithms.

10.3.2   Autonomous Defense: Critical Sensors Identification and Trust

Self-healing complex system-of-systems are the holy grail of cybersecurity research and development. Conference organizers highlight the many challenges that affect "the design, performance, networks operating autonomous human–machine teams" (Lawless et al., 2020).[9] Research findings from testing Digital Ghost's neutralization algorithms suggest that these challenges increase when human teams lack the observability and context for a complex transient system such as a gas turbine. This

---

[8] Goodfellow et al. (2009).

[9] Lawless et al. (2020).

gap suggests that advances in autonomous cyber defenses must prioritize the observability of remaining non-attacked sensors to calculate an estimate that would work in closed-loop control.

Future research on the science of interdependence for autonomous human–machine teams combined with advances in control theory methods may help to improve the ability of machine learning algorithms to decide which sensors have poor observability before moving to deployment. In a complex, transient system-of-systems, there is a need to improve the observability and trustworthiness of critical energy delivery sensors to autonomously protect, detect, recover and neutralize cyber-physical threats. In absence of these capabilities, that near-terms opportunities to improve the state-of-the-art for neutralization, including determining the sensors that lack observability for neutralization, are needed to create an alert for human operators; this alert would signal the inability for neutralization to provide corrective action if one of these nodes were attacked. Applying advanced encryption and authentication mechanisms for these sensors via trusted platform modules and other solutions is also ripe for future research and exploration. This achievement would help the information security community to better understand how to improve control theory methods that combine with human–machine teams so that machine learning algorithms can empower cyber defenders to better determine the integrity and trustworthiness of critical sensors.

10.3.3 Humble AI

Humble AI is making valuable advances in marrying man and machine, answering such questions as: How can the algorithms alert the operator of a potential decrease in accuracy or confidence in its threat classification results? How can the ML/AI methods recognize they are being asked to extrapolate into previously unseen operating regions? What is the proper response if this extrapolation happens? If so, should Digital Ghost or other advanced AI cyber-defense halt operations? Or does the system continue but express reduced confidence in its results? The next-generation AI-cyber-physical anomaly detection and neutralization requires the continuous improvement of ML/AI methods that are agile, adaptable and evolve for complex, nonlinear and changing threats. R&D findings from the Digital Ghost algorithms that are trained off-line to create the various decision manifolds for both local and global detection need to be able to adapt to the field operating conditions of all hazards—cyber, physical, naturally occurring—as critical energy delivery systems move away from training and into regions not simulated previously. In the field, if operating conditions move away from training and extend into regions not previously simulated, it is essential that the algorithms recognize this fact and alert the operator of a potential decrease in accuracy or confidence in the classification results.

10.3.4 Explainable AI (XAI)

Explainable AI or XAI is the ability of AI-based machines to explain the reasoning underlying their decisions in a way that is understandable to humans. Many challenging questions and/or gaps remain, such as: how do we develop intuitive, trustworthy explanations of how and why our AI algorithms arrive at decisions? How do we do this in a way that is easy to interpret, visualize and use to empower human–machine teams?

How do we trust the black-box nature of deep neural networks? That is, numerous parameters in deep neural networks (DNNs) add complexity that is hard to interpret and explain. As a result, algorithms and models can learn and misinterpret representations from the data differently than humans. This creates issues with trust, ethics and biases.

Answering these questions will help to improve the state-of-the-art of (AI/ML) algorithms with a focus on advancing XAI physics-based anomaly detection in complex systems.

If successful, human–machine teams will be able to both trust and understand *how* the ML/AI algorithms arrive at their solutions. This collaboration can be done through advanced human–machine interfaces containing easy-to-understand visualization techniques. This result is essential for machines to be trusted in making autonomous/semi-autonomous decisions, especially for kinetic platforms that are increasingly autonomous as well as for safety and other mission-critical applications that determine diagnostics and cyber-physical security.

Advances in AI require both human operators and machines to understand and trust how the ML/AI algorithms are arriving, or are unable to arrive, at their solutions via human–machine interfaces and intuitive visualizations.

Machine-learning-based approaches of anomaly detection often result in a classification decision along with an anomaly score. However, the contribution, ranking and significance of each of the input variables/features, the causality directions, the effect of the size of the training data set and the reasoning path in the algorithm leading to a particular decision are often obscure. An example of this is shown in Fig. 10.3, where several signal traces are presented as well as features used as inputs for an AI/ML-based, anomaly-classification system, i.e., Digital Ghost. These traces

Fig. 10.3 Sensor signal traces and features captured during GE's recent cybersecurity demonstration using an operating heavy-duty gas turbine. The red line indicates the time at which synthetic cyber-attack was injected

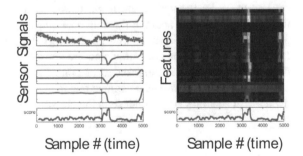

were captured on GE Power's test facility during a demonstration wherein sophisticated synthetic cyberattacks were injected into a critical network of an operating gas turbine, and Digital Ghost correctly detected and identified the impacted gas-turbine sensors. While novel in improving the applied science of AI cyber-physical anomaly detection, it has proved difficult to explain to human operators how the complex algorithms arrived at the correct inferences (attack and attacked node) in a manner that an operator can understand, trust and then act upon.

Future research on explainable XAI will advance AI/ML capabilities without reducing the fidelity and accuracy of the detection, localization and neutralization capabilities. It is essential that Digital Ghost's next-generation cyber-physical, anomaly-detection and neutralization algorithms reduce their technical complexity and that they are intuitive to grid operators and cyber defenders. This explanation creates a number of human and cyber-physical integration challenges that could be explored with future research on how best to integrate humans and machines. Lessons learned from (DG) research have helped to develop complex algorithms, some of which are constructed using machine learning and AI techniques. Future operators, however, may still be skeptical because of the complexity and non-intuitiveness contained within the highly nonlinear algorithms of Digital Ghost.

10.4   Conclusion

Grid modernization has been accompanied by a digital transformation that has increasingly digitized, networked and automated the energy value chain. Today's smart grid is increasingly two-way, agile and flexible in incorporating distributed energy resources that have helped transition to a lower-carbon economy. Research in this chapter highlighted how this digital transformation must marry man and machine. Similarly, research findings also suggest that human–machine teams can be empowered but also blindsided by AI by being given a false sense of security. The "smart" grid has increased connectivity and created new cyber-physical security challenges in securing an array of vulnerable energy delivery systems and associated operational technology. As a manufacturer of a large percentage of the world's power systems, GE has been integral to grid modernization and has unique insight as well as a responsibility to ensure more holistic cyber resilient policies, processes and technology.

Realizing this goal is imperative as the U.S. electricity infrastructure will require a holistic approach of people, policies and technology. Research findings suggest the successful adoption of next-generation technology, such as the AI algorithms found in Digital Ghost. Findings also suggest that innovation should not happen with humans out-of-the-loop. The form of the technology R&D must compliment the function and independencies of the team in order to empower the cyber defenders of our nation's power grid. This result is especially true as sophisticated cyber adversaries are increasingly deploying technology such as AI combined with stealthy tactics and techniques to attack critical energy infrastructures. Defenders of these modern infrastructures need to better understand how to combine innovative technology in a way that empowers their teams to respond to a complex, nonlinear and rapidly evolving cyber threat. Novel technology advances combining domain expertise in physics and next-generation AI solutions will only be successful if humans are empowered in the loop, not disintermediated from the loop. This is especially true when defending against the diverse, complex, nonlinear and rapidly evolving threats of human adversaries executing sophisticated cyber-physical attacks on critical infrastructures.

If the first cybersecurity paradigm was focused on keeping adversaries out, building firewalls and digital moats, the next evolution must move us toward resilience with a more holistic approach where machine learning and other innovative technology empowers teams and where policies protect humans from themselves. Ironically, in this paradigm, humans are empowered and no longer the weakest link in the chain, but the supervisory layer that provides integrity.

References

Goodfellow, I., Lee, H., Le, Q. V., Saxe, A., & Ng, A. Y. (2009). Measuring invariances in deep networks. In *Advances in neural information processing systems* (pp. 646–654).

Greenberg, A., Dreyfuss, E., Barrett, B., Gold, D., Lapowsky, I., & Newman, L. H. (2018). How hacked water heaters could trigger mass blackouts. Wired, August 2018.

John, J., Nielsen, M., Abazadeh, M., & Markam. (2020). *Advanced detection and accommodation research findings*. GE Global Research (need to update this citation with names, etc.).

Johnson, J. (2017). Roadmap for photovoltaic cyber security. Sandia Technical. Report, SAND2017–13262.

Onunkwo, I., Wright, B., Cordeiro, P., Jacobs, N., Lai, C., Johnson, J., & Hutchins, T. et al. (2018). *Cybersecurity assessments on emulated DER communication networks*. Sandia Technical Report.

Lawless, W. F., Mittu, R., Sofge, D., Shortell, T., & McDermott, T. (2020). AI welcomes systems engineering: *Towards the science of interdependence for autonomous human-machine teams*. AAAI Spring Symposium 2020 Abstract.

Lee, A. (2013). Electric sector failure scenarios and impact analyses. *National electric sector cybersecurity organization resource (NESCOR) technical working group 1*.

Qi, J., Hahn, A., Lu, X., Wang, J., & Liu, C.-C. (2016). Cybersecurity for distributed energy resources and smart inverters. *IET Cyber-Physical Systems: Theory & Applications.*, *1*, 28–39. https://doi.org/10.1049/iet-cps.2016.0018

Chapter 11
A Fractional Brownian Motion Approach to Psychological and Team Diffusion Problems

Ira S. Moskowitz, Noelle L. Brown, and Zvi Goldstein

Abstract In this chapter we discuss drift diffusion and extensions to fractional Brownian motion. We include some Artificial Intelligence (AI) motivated issues in fractional Brownian motion. We also discuss how fractional Brownian motion may be used as a metric for interdependence in Team science.

Keywords Drift diffusion model · Random walk · Wiener process · Brownian motion · Fractional Brownian motion · Geometry · Information · Neural networks · Machine learning · Team science · Interdependence

11.1 Introduction

In this chapter, we discuss Ratcliff diffusion and extensions to fractional Brownian motion. We include some Artificial Intelligence (AI) motivated issues in fractional Brownian motion. We also discuss how fractional Brownian motion may be used as a metric for interdependence in Team science.

We start with a thorough review of Ratcliff's drift diffusion model (Ratcliff, 1978) with many of the mathematical subtleties filled in. This will enable us to precisely extend the model to fractional Brownian motion in the later parts of the chapter. We then discuss some of these issues we have with determining the Hurst exponent and different machine learning (ML) techniques that we have used. We conclude with future work which includes a new direction for the concept of interdependence in Team science.

I. S. Moskowitz (✉) · N. L. Brown
Information Management & Decision Architectures Branch, Code 5580, Naval Research Laboratory, 4555 Overlook Ave., SW, Washington, DC 20375, USA
e-mail: ira.moskowitz@nrl.navy.mil

Z. Goldstein
Electrical Engineering Department, Columbia University, 500 W 120th St #510, New York, NY 10027, USA

© Springer Nature Switzerland AG 2021
W. F. Lawless et al. (eds.), *Systems Engineering and Artificial Intelligence*,
https://doi.org/10.1007/978-3-030-77283-3_11

Ratcliff's (Ratcliff, 1978) seminal chapter provided a precise mathematical model for memory retrieval. The Ratcliff Diffusion Model (RDM) captures the quick (1–2 sec) reaction time (RT) of someone trying to retrieve a fact to make a binary decision. There are two possible answers: correct and incorrect. These fast, binary decisions are driven by a Brownian motion (BM) with usually non-zero drift. The drift rate is assumed to be influenced by both systematic processes and random noise. The drift rate models the accumulation of information toward one boundary. In this chapter for simplicity we assume that the drift rate is fixed and not stochastic (Ratcliff, 1978). Once a boundary is reached, the decision is terminated and a response is given. The RDM statistically separates the decision process to uniquely allow for its broad application and to avoid the limitations associated with task specific models (Ratcliff, 1978; Ratcliff et al., 2016; Ratcliff and Tuberlinckx, 2002; Voss et al., 2004).

The RDM estimates decision outcomes as an intricate exchange between the separate model parameters that map onto distinguishable cognitive processes. Specifically, the RDM estimates decision bias, response caution, information accumulation, and response execution and coordination. Thus, one can determine the underlying cognitive mechanisms that support decision-making through the application of the model. Of course any conclusions that are drawn are only valid to the extent that the model parameters actually measure the cognitive processes theorized (Arnold et al., 2015; Lerche and Voss, 2018; Voss et al., 2004).

When there is no drift and the diffusion is 1, we have the simplest form of Brownian motion, known as the Wiener process (WP) (Wiener, 1923). We review the mathematics showing that the Wiener process is an infinitesimal generalization of a random walk. The Brownian motion scenario that Ratcliff models has two absorbing boundaries and thus is the infinitesimal version of the Gambler's ruin problem (Cox and Miller, 1990; Feller, 1968; Resnick, 2002) (which of course, is a random walk with two absorbing boundaries). To paraphrase Ratcliff (Ratcliff, 1978)—the analogy is made between a gambler winning or losing with a person recalling or not recalling something during a memory probe.

We are interested in seeing what happens to these parameters and the associated probabilities if instead of Brownian motion, the underlying process is in fact the more general fractional Brownian motion (fBM), of which BM is special case. The major distinction is that BM is a Markov process, whereas fBM, except for the special case of BM, is not. This has implications on how we understand and model RT decisions in humans. Of particular interest to us are the absorbing probabilities and probabilities of the time to absorption.

An easy way to distinguish BM as a special case among fBM is via the Hurst exponent H. We will define this later, but for now BM is fBM with $H = 1/2$. We are concerned with the geometric aspects of fBM and information we can glean from the geometry. This comes about in determining H (Sanchez Granero et al., 2008; Mandelbrot and Van Ness, 1968; Peng et al., 2012; Segovia et al., 2012), and in a very different aspect by looking at associated Riemannian manifolds with respect to power spectral densities (Peng et al., 2012).

As previously mentioned, the diffusion model stands out when compared to other memory models because it is not task or domain specific. The model's parameters provide separate estimates for the cognitive processes involved in making binary decisions based on the speed of decisions and their correctness. The model has been used to successfully account for performance on a variety of tasks, differentiate clinical populations, and speak to individual differences in cognitive ability. More recent work has used diffusion models to also explain value-based decision, social choice , and consumer decisions (Ratcliff et al., 2016). The model has advanced our understanding of the cognitive processes involved in decision-making and how they are affected by the speed-accuracy trade-off. In other words, the diffusion model allows us to predict how performance will change when people are forced to focus on their accuracy or the speed of their decisions. This is valuable for applied settings where the interest is on not only preventing errors but also in predicting when they are likely to occur. Applying the findings from the past four decades with the diffusion model may be used to create improved human-machine teams where the machines can be designed to support humans under the conditions known to elicit errors (i.e., speeded responses, bias). However, it remains to be seen whether these findings hold under operational settings and whether the model could benefit from an update to the Hurst exponent to accommodate real-world application of the model.

11.2 Random Walk

The Wiener process is an infinitesimal version of a random walk. A simple random walk is where we have discrete-time values, say 0, 1, 2, ..., the walker starts at position 0, and the probability of flipping a 1 or -1 are equal at .5. The walker flips a fair coin to obtain ± 1. If it is 1 the walker moves to 1, if it is -1 the walker moves to -1. The process is repeated at the new position at time 1, etc. Of course there are variants of this such as the coin not being fair (a non-simple random walk), the jumps not just being ± 1, etc. We are also restricting ourselves to the line. We present a definition that is precise, but without too much machinery involved (we adapt the presentation and definitions from (Feller, 1968; Charles, 1997)).

Comment: When the random variable is understood we use μ to signify the expected value, σ^2 the variance, and its square root σ, the standard deviation. Sometimes we may express these terms as a function of the random variable in question, or use the notation E or just state variance, etc.

Definition 11.1 *Let $\{X_k\}_{k=1}^\infty$ be a sequence of independent, identically distributed random variables. For each positive integer n, we let R_n denote the sum $X_1 + X_2 + \cdots + X_n$, and set $R_0 = 0$ The sequence $R_n, n = 0, 1, \ldots, \infty$ is called a **random walk**.*

Note 11.1 *We may extend the definition to an **initialized random walk** by letting $R_0 \neq 0$.*

Note 11.2 *If the X_i are instead i.i.d. binary random variables B_i taking on the values 1 with probability p, and -1 with probability $q = 1 - p$, we say that we have* *a* **simple random walk.** *We denote the random walk then with the notation W_n to be clear. That is for a simple random walk*

$$W_n = B_1 + \cdots + B_n .$$

If the B_i are Rademacher random variables, that is $p = q = 1/2$ we have a **fair simple random walk.**

Note 11.3 *If we have a random walk with the $X_i = N(\mu, \sigma^2)$ we say we have a* **Gaussian random walk** *and denote it as G_n or G_n^{μ,σ^2}. If $X_i = N(0, 1)$ we say it is a* **standard Gaussian random walk** *as denote it as $G_n^{0,1}$.*

A random walk has three important properties.

(1) Markov Property: $P(R_n = r_n | R_{n-1} = r_{n-1}, R_{n-2} = r_{n-2}, \ldots, R_1 = r_1, R_0 = 0) = P(R_n = r_n | R_{n-1} = r_{n-1})$ (that is up to regularity conditions we have a discrete-time Markov chain).
(2) Stationary Increments: The distribution of the random variable $R_t - R_s, t \geq s$, only depends on $t - s$. This is equivalent to $R_t - R_s, t \geq s$ having the same distribution as R_{t-s}.
(3) Independent Increments: For $0 \leq t_1 < t_2 < \cdots < t_n$ the random variables R_{t_1}, $R_{t_2} - R_{t_1}, \ldots, R_{t_n} - R_{t_{n-1}}$ are independent.

If $\mu(X_i) = 0$, then we have the obvious additional property below:

(4) Martingale Property: $E(R_{n+1} | R_n) = R_n$. (Since a random walk has the Markov property we only need to condition one step back, instead of all the way back).

Note a *martingale* can be a discrete or continuous stochastic process (norms of the random variable have finite expectation for all t) such that the expectation of the random variable at t, conditioned on the random variable up to s is the random variable at s.

Now we will develop some statistics for the simple random walk W_n. For a simple random walk $\mu(B_i) = p - q$. Since expectation is a linear operator on random variables we have that

$$E(W_N) = N\mu(B_i) = N(p - q) . \tag{11.1}$$

Thus, for a fair simple random walk, no matter what the (discrete) time is the expected position is 0. Now we will compute the variance of W_N.

$$E(B_i^2) = 1^2 \cdot p + (-1)^2 \cdot q = 1$$

$$\sigma^2(B_i) = E(B_i^2) - [E(B_i)]^2 = 1 - (p - q)^2 = (p + q)^2 - (p - q)^2 = 4pq$$

$$\sigma^2(W_N) = \sigma^2 \left(\sum_{i=1}^{N} B_i \right) = \sum_{i=1}^{N} \sigma^2(B_i) = N \cdot 4pq \text{ since the } B_i \text{ are i.i.d, summarizing}$$

$\mu(W_N) = (p - q)N$ and $\sigma^2(W_N) = 4pqN$. Thus the standard deviation is $\qquad$ (11.2)

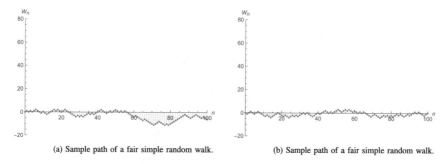

(a) Sample path of a fair simple random walk.   (b) Sample path of a fair simple random walk.

Fig. 11.1 Two fair simple random walk sample paths with $N = 100$

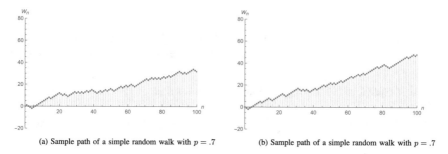

(a) Sample path of a simple random walk with $p = .7$ (b) Sample path of a simple random walk with $p = .7$

Fig. 11.2 Two sample paths of a simple random walk with $p = .7, N = 100$

$$\sigma(W_N) = 2\sqrt{pqN}. \qquad (11.3)$$

Thus for a fair simple random walk the mean is 0, and the variance (maximal among the simple random walks) is N. For a simple random walk in general the points (at every n) tend to cluster around a line of slope $p - q$, however they spread out in time. It makes sense for the variance to increase because as n increases, so do the possible positions. In Fig. 11.1 we show two fair simple random walks, and in Fig. 11.2 two simple random walks with $p = .70$.

In Fig. 11.3 we show a sample path for $p = .4$, $N = 100$ where the inner red curves are $\mu \pm \sigma$, the next level orange curves are $\mu \pm 2\sigma$, the green lines are $\mu \pm \sigma^2$, and the brown lines are $\pm N$.

Figure 11.3 shows that we can easily apply the central limit theorem to the random walk and expect the points to cluster around the mean, with the usual bell-like behavior around the mean. Keep in mind that σ grows as $\sqrt{n}$ not n.

Theorem 11.1 (Central Limit Theorem (Ross, 1988)). *Let $X_1, X_2, \ldots$ be a sequence of independent and identically distributed random variables each having mean μ and variance σ^2*

$$\lim_{n \to \infty} \left\{ \frac{X_1 + \cdots X_n - n\mu}{\sigma\sqrt{n}} \leq a \right\} = \Phi(a), \qquad (11.4)$$

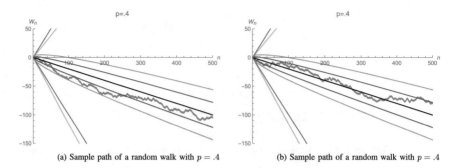

(a) Sample path of a random walk with $p = .4$ (b) Sample path of a random walk with $p = .4$

Fig. 11.3 Two sample paths with $p = .4$, $N = 500$

where $\Phi(a)$ is the cumulative distribution function of the standard normal random variable $\mathcal{N}(0, 1)$, where $\mathcal{N}(a, b^2)$ is a normal distribution with mean a and variance b^2.

Another equivalent of putting the above theorem is that

The random variable $(X_1 + \cdots + X_n) \xrightarrow[n \to \infty]{\mathcal{D}} \mathcal{N}\left(n \cdot \mu(X_i), n \cdot \sigma^2(X_i)\right)$ (for any i since they are identical)

$$(11.5)$$

since the random variable $\frac{\mathcal{N}(a,b^2)-a}{b} = \mathcal{N}(0, 1)$ and letting $a = n \cdot \mu(X_i)$, $b^2 = n \cdot \sigma^2(X_i)$.

But now recall that $W_n = B_1 + \cdots B_n$, $\mu(B_i) = p - q$, and $\sigma^2(B_i) = 4pq$. Therefore, by the central limit theorem

Theorem 11.2

$$W_n \xrightarrow[n \to \infty]{\mathcal{D}} \mathcal{N}(n(p - q), n \cdot 4pq) = \mathcal{N}\left(\mu(W_n), \sigma^2(W_n)\right) . \qquad (11.6)$$

Or equivalently

$$\frac{W_n - \mu(W_n)}{\sigma(W_n)} \xrightarrow[n \to \infty]{\mathcal{D}} \mathcal{N}(0, 1) \qquad (11.7)$$

which is the phenomena illustrated in Fig. 11.3.

This is not to say that the time series behaves like a normal distribution, rather for a particular time n it behaves like a normal distribution, and more and more for each n. Of course the central limit theorem does not tell us how quickly W_n converges to a normal distribution. However, the Berry-Esseen theorem (Breiman, 1968, p. 184), (Feller, 1968, V. 2, p.542) does

Theorem 11.3 *(Berry-Esseen) If Z_i are i.i.d. with zero mean and finite variance s^2, with $E(|Z_i|^3) = \rho < \infty$, then*[1]

---

[1] We can conservatively take $C = 1$ given the state of the art published and unpublished literature. We refer the interested reader to the various search engines for the copious details.

$$\sup_x \left| P\left(\frac{\sum Z_i}{\mathfrak{s}\sqrt{n}} < x\right) - \Phi(x) \right| \leq C \frac{E|Z_i|^3}{\mathfrak{s}^3 . \sqrt{n}} \tag{11.8}$$

Now using our B_i from before the beginning of the chapter that by choosing $Z_i = B_i - E(B_i)$, the Berry-Esseen theorem gives us

$$\sup_x \left| P\left(\frac{W_n - n(p-q)}{2\sqrt{pqn}} < x\right) - \Phi(x) \right| \leq \frac{E|Z_i|^3}{(4pq)^3\sqrt{n}}, \text{ equivalently} \tag{11.9}$$

$$\sup_x \left| P\left(\frac{W_n - \mu(W_n)}{\sigma(W_n)} < x\right) - \Phi(x) \right| \leq \frac{E|Z_i|^3}{(4pq)^3\sqrt{n}}, \text{ which gives us} \tag{11.10}$$

$$\sup_z \left| P\left(W_n < z\right) - P\left(\mathcal{N}(\mu(W_n), \sigma^2(W_n)) < z\right) \right| \leq \frac{E|Z_i|^3}{(4pq)^3\sqrt{n}}. \tag{11.11}$$

Since $Z_i = B_i - (p-q)$ we have that $E(|Z_i|^3) = E(|B_i - (p-q)|^3) \leq 2^3$, thus

$$\sup_z \left| P\left(W_n < z\right) - P\left(\mathcal{N}(\mu(W_n), \sigma^2(W_n)) < z\right) \right| \leq \frac{1}{(8pq)^3\sqrt{n}}. \tag{11.12}$$

Of course, for p near 0 or 1, we need a large n to keep the error small, however, for p near 1/2 moderate values of n give us a very small error between W_n and $\mathcal{N}(\mu(W_n), \sigma^2(W_n))$.

Thus, the above gives us the following note.

Note 11.4 *For p near 1/2, the plot of W_n should lie between $\pm 2\sigma$ approximately 95% of the time, and between $\pm 3\sigma$ approximately 99% of the time.*

There are many other interesting properties of the random walk, such as often it returns to the mean, or how and when it hits a boundary. With the exception of our above application of the Berry-Esseen theorem this is all easily found in the literature. We now turn to the limiting case of a random walk and look at Brownian motion.

Wiener process and *Brownian motion*. The generalized stochastic process that we are interested in is Brownian motion. Brownian motion can have drift and diffusion. If the drift is 0, and the diffusion 1, we say that we have *standard Brownian motion*, we also can, and do, use the term Wiener process for standard Brownian motion.

For a Wiener process, instead of jumps of constant size, the jump sizes are drawn from a normal random variable, and the jumps are instantaneous from one-time value to the next. Of course, this is a mathematical nicety, and the simulations use very small time increments instead. Of course a random walk can, up to the accuracy of the random number generators, be accurately created.

11.2.1 Wiener Process from the Fair Simple Random Walk

Consider a fair simple random walk in a set amount of total time T time units (see (Breiman, 1968, 12.2)). We divide each time unit into increments of length δ, so $1/\delta = n$ are the total amount of intervals in each time unit. We now perform the random walk every *increment* instead of every *time unit*. We want things to "start looking continuous" as δ gets small, but as long as the jumps are ± 1 this will not happen. Therefore, we need to change Δx from ± 1, there are many ways to do this, but we set $\Delta x = \sqrt{\delta}$. Given t there are $\lfloor t/\delta \rfloor$ intervals of length δ plus an amount $\epsilon, 0 \leq \epsilon < \delta$. We formalize this below.

Start with the B_i from a fair simple random walk then we adjust the jump sizes as we make the time smaller and smaller. That is we have new random variables X_i as follows. Each random variable $B'_i = \pm \Delta x = \pm \sqrt{\delta}, i > 1$ with equal probabilities of 1/2. $X_0 = 0$, that is $B'_i = \sqrt{\delta} B_i$). Therefore, at time t the position of the moving particle is given by the random variable

$$S_t = \sum_{i=1}^{\lfloor t/\delta \rfloor} B'_i. \tag{11.13}$$

Let us rewrite this using the fact that $n = 1/\delta$, and keep in mind that S_t is also a function of $1/\delta$, since the smaller $1/\delta$ is the more terms that make up the sum S_t.

$$S^n(t) = \sum_{i=1}^{\lfloor nt \rfloor} B'_i. \tag{11.14}$$

Let us look at some interesting things first.

- As discussed $\lfloor t/\delta \rfloor = \lfloor nt \rfloor$ is an integer. However, $\delta \cdot \lfloor nt \rfloor + \epsilon = t$. But as $n \to \infty$, $\delta \cdot \lfloor nt \rfloor \to t$
- $Var(B'_i) = E(B'^2_i) - \left(E(B'_i)\right)^2 = E(B'^2_i) = .5 \cdot (\sqrt{\delta})^2 + .5 \cdot (-\sqrt{\delta})^2 = \delta$
- $E(S^n(t)) = \lfloor nt \rfloor \cdot E(B'_i) = 0$
- Since the B'_i are i.i.d we have $Var(S^n(t)) = \lfloor nt \rfloor Var(B'_i) = \lfloor nt \rfloor \cdot \delta \to t$ as n grows.

We know by the central limit theorem that for $t = 1$ that $S^n(1) \to \mathcal{N}(0, 1)$ as $n \to \infty$, what is remarkable for each t there is also convergence, but to $\mathcal{N}(0, t)$. This is not totally surprising since $n \to \infty$ for each t. We will return to $\lim_{n \to \infty} S^n(t)$ after we define a Wiener Process. For now though, without all the mathematical niceties, we state without proof (will return to this soon) that the stochastic process $L(t) := \lim_{n \to \infty} S^n(t)$ does in fact converge, and it converges to the yet to be defined Wiener process. We will address this further in the next subsection. We note that (Breiman, 1968, 12.2) goes through the above situation in some detail.

Before we move on to the formal definition of a Wiener process we note some interesting properties (Pishro-Nik, 2014) of $L(t)$:

(1) Since each X_i is independent, for $0 \le t_1 < t_2 < t_3 \cdots < t_m$ so are the random variables $L(t_2) - L(t_1), L(t_3) - L(t_2), \ldots, L(t_m) - L(t_{m-1})$. This tells us that the stochastic process $L(t)$ has *independent increments*.

(2) For any $\tau > 0$ and $t_2 > t_1 \ge 0$ the random variables $L(t_2) - L(t_1)$ and $L(t_2 + \tau) - L(t_1 + \tau)$ have the same distribution. This means they have *stationary increments*. This follows because of the sum construction of $L(t)$, the τ drops out of the variance calculations since only the difference matters since the means are 0, and the variance of the sum is the sum of the variances. In fact $L(t + \tau) - L(\tau)$ has the same distribution as $L(t) - L(0) = L(t)$. Now, this itself is $N(0, t)$ by the central limit theorem, and similarly $L(t_2) - L(t_1) = N(0, t_2 - t_1)$.

(3) If we take a sample path of $W(t)$ we can, up to events of zero probability (if total time $t \to \infty$), view it as a continuous path. This is because the jumps are no more than $\pm\sqrt{\delta}$ in its construction, and as $n \to \infty$ the jumps get smaller and smaller, therefore we can always satisfy the $\epsilon - \delta$ definition of continuity. We prove this later in the chapter.

So we have discussed that if we take a random walk with n increments per unit time and $X_i = \pm 1/\sqrt{n}$ then this process in the limit gives us a so-called Wiener process. We discuss it in more detail below.

11.2.2 Wiener Process (standard Brownian Motion) Defined

Definition 11.2 *We say that the stochastic process $\mathscr{W}(t), t \ge 0$ is a Wiener process (Lalley and Mykland, 2013) if*

(1) $\mathscr{W}_0 = 0$.

(2) With probability 1, the function $t \to \mathscr{W}_t$ is continuous in t. (That is sample paths are continuous with probability 1. This rules out 0 probability pathological occurrences such as the process being 1 on rational numbers, and -1 on irrational. It is interesting that they are not differentiable though.)

(3) The stochastic process $\{\mathscr{W}_t\}, t \ge 0$ has stationary, independent increments.

(4) The increment $\mathscr{W}_{t+s} - \mathscr{W}_s$ has the distribution of $N(0, t)$. (Which tells us that $\mathscr{W}_t$ has the distribution of $N(0, t)$).

This may not be the slickest definition but it is an easy to understand definition. Note that stationary increments and independent increments are defined in the previous subsection.

Wiener was the first to show that this process exists (and not just defined) in (Wiener, 1923). Of course, others have worked on this after. Note that Donsker (Donsker, 1951) showed an existence proof over a finite time interval $[0, T]$ using the $S^n(t)$ from above and (Doob, 1949).

Theorem 11.4 *(Donsker (Doob, 1949, App.), (Donsker, 1951), (Donsker, 1952), (Donsker's Theorem, 2020), (Schondorf, 2019)) In Eq. 11.13 above replace the B_i with any i.i.d M_i with mean 0 and variance 1, then if we set*

$$\mathcal{D}(t) := \sum_{i=1}^{\lfloor nt \rfloor} \sqrt{\delta} M_i$$

then, as stochastic processes, $\mathcal{D}(t)$ weakly converges to $\mathcal{W}(t)$, $t \in [0, T]$.

Comment 1 *An important take away from Donsker's theorem, and one of physical significance, is that the random variables that we are summing have standard deviation equal to the square root of the time increment. Of course, this makes their variance equal to the time increment.*

We will not discuss the convergence mentioned above. It suffices for us to take the limit of the normalized fair simple random walk as the Wiener process, for details see (Karatzas and Shreve, 2019, 2.4.A., Def. 4.3). Of course the above theorem generalizes what we did with the fair simple random walk in the previous subsection. That is Donsker's theorem actually is more general than starting with the random variables from a simple random walk. In fact Donsker's theorem holds for $\mathcal{D}(t)$ constructed by using the standard Gaussian random walk $G_n^{0,1}$ instead of the fair simple random walk as above. In fact this is a better approximation since all the steps are based on draws from a normal, which directly aligns with how the increments should behave (since the sum of normal is normal) without appealing to central limit theorem type results. This is what we use in the simulation below.

11.2.3   Simulation of the Wiener Process via $G_n^{0,1}$

Since the Wiener process is a continuous stochastic process any computer simulation is an approximation, this is nothing new, but we stress the fact to distinguish it from a random walk with very small time increments. In fact we could use the process $L(t)$ from the fair simple random walk, but we can do better by instead of using fixed jumps of size δ we use draws from a normal random variable with variance δ. This follows from the above comment to Donsker's theorem by using $\mathcal{D}(t)$ via $G_n^{0,1}$. Note that these type simulations rely on the fact that $k \cdot N(0, 1) = N(0, k^2)$, so the $\sigma(k \cdot N(0, 1)) = k$, where σ is the standard deviation operator.

Let us examine how to perform the simulation.

(1) Decide on T, n, where n is the number of increments per unit time. Thus $\Delta t = 1/n$ and the standard deviation $sd := \sqrt{\Delta t}$. The smaller Δt the more accurate and of course the total number of increments nT increases.
(2) Each X_i is a draw from $N(0, 1)$.
(3) We add the $sd \cdot X_i$.
(4) Plot.

As mentioned above this is a very good simulation since the sum of normals is normal. Of course, the approximation is only accurate at the actual increment values, and the sum is constant on each increment. This is similar to the Riemann sum

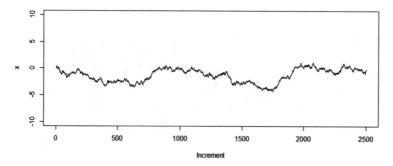

Fig. 11.4 Sample path of a simulated Wiener process with T=25, $dt = \Delta t = .01$, thus having 2,500 total steps

approach to integration, the smaller the increment values, the better the approximation. Also, as stated before what is somewhat wonderful is that this actually converges to something, and what it converges to is the Wiener process!

Below is the R code for the simulation of a Wiener process with total time $T = 25$, and $\Delta t = .01$. This of course gives us $n = 100$ increments per time step, with a total of 2500 increments. An output is given in Fig. 11.4.

```
#http://phytools.org/eqg/Exercise_4.1/ T<-25  # time dt <- .01
#delta t
  n <- 1/delt #increments per time unit
  N <- n*T #total number  of increments
  t <- 0:N  # total time increments
  sig2 <- dt  #for Wiener process, simple Brownian motion 0 drift , 1 diffusion
## first, simulate a set of random deviates dx <- 1*rnorm(n =
length(t) - 1, sd = sqrt(sig2)) ## now compute their cumulative sum
R <- c(0, cumsum(dx)) plot(t, R, type = "l", ylim = c(-2*sqrt(T),
2*sqrt(T)),xlab="Increment",main=bquote("total time T" == .(T)
   ~",  variance = delta t is"==.(dt)~", n is"==.(n) )).
```

So our simulation that approximates $\mathscr{W}(t)$ is, as above:

$$\mathscr{W}(t) \approx \sum_{i}^{\lfloor \frac{T}{\Delta t} \rfloor} \Delta x = \sum_{i}^{\lfloor \frac{T}{\Delta t} \rfloor} N(0, \Delta t).$$

In Fig. 11.5 we adjust the above code so that $T = 100$ and we plot 100 runs on the same plot. We see that this nicely illustrates Note 4 in that most of the paths lie within $\pm 3\sigma = \pm 3\sqrt{100} = \pm 30$.

We note that the Wiener process, and Brownian motion, belong to a more general type of stochastic processes called Gaussian processes. Note the random time-weighted Gaussian process $G(t) = N(0, t)$ shares the property with $\mathscr{W}(t)$ that at time t the process is $N(0, t)$, but we can see from Fig. 11.6 that they are very different.

Please compare Fig. 11.6 with Fig. 11.4. Figure 11.4 represents the limiting case of a random walk, where the next step is a normal draw added onto the existing

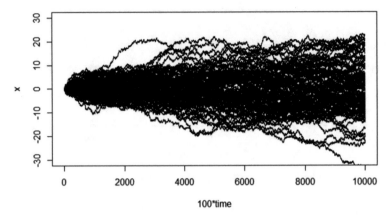

Fig. 11.5 Sample paths of 100 simulated Wiener processes, T=100, $\Delta t = .01$, 10,000 total steps

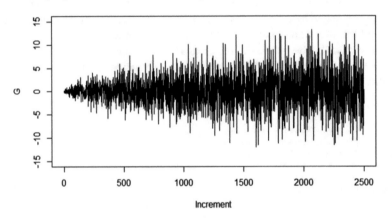

Fig. 11.6 Sample path of the random time-weighted Gaussian process $G(t) = N(0, t)$, $T = 25$, $\Delta t = .01$, 2500 total steps

position. Figure 11.6 is a random draw from a time-weighted normal at each step not caring what the present value is and is essentially time-weighted Gaussian noise.

11.2.4 Continuity of Sample Paths

By definition a Wiener process has continuous sample paths with probability 1. However, we did not prove Donsker's theorem but it is not too far a stretch to see how it generalizes the central limit theorem and that in the limit the increments have the correct behavior with respect to the normal distribution. What is not obvious is that the limiting behavior of the scaled random walk should have continuous sample paths (with probability 1). We wish to address this without doing a proof of Donsker's theorem. At first instead of using the rescaled normal distribution, we shall go back to the original bi-valued rescaled random variable B_i' and Eq. 11.13. Recall that a function is continuous iff the inverse image of an open set is an open set. For a given t look at an ϵ-neighborhood, ϵ small, around S_t. Now consider t and a small neighborhood U around t. Since we are in U there is a limit to how far $S(t')$ can be from $S(t)$ since the jumps are limited by the sum of the values of B_i', thus by making U small we can keep its image in the ϵ-neighborhood around $S(t)$. If we use rescaled $G_n^{0,1}$ instead of the rescaled B_i we can still have elements of U jump out of the ϵ-neighborhood around $S(t)$, but as the time increments get smaller and smaller, the variance of the rescaled $G_n^{0,1}$ also gets smaller and smaller, with the net result being that with high probability all the image points stay in the ϵ neighborhood around $S(t)$. This probability goes to 1, as the time increment goes to 0. This holds no matter what the random variable is doing to all the theorems that abound about random variables and their variances. Thus, we now have a feeling why Donsker's theorem gives us continuous (with probability 1) sample paths no matter what the random variable is that we rescale (with mean 0 and initial variance 1).

11.2.5 Non-differentiability of Wiener Process Sample Paths

We just concern ourselves with the actual Wiener process and not any approximations via Donsker's theorem. We also point out that the non-differentiability is also a probabilistic statement. It is possible, with probability 0, for a sample path to be a straight line for instance. So the non-differentiability is a probabilistic statement that depends on how a random variable behaves with respect to its variance. The proof sketch we use follows (Dobrow, 2016, Sect. 8.3).

Let $0 < s, h$ then if the derivative of $\mathcal{W}(t)$ exists at s then the one sided limit $\lim_{h \to 0^+} \frac{\mathcal{W}(s+h) - \mathcal{W}(s)}{h}$ must certainly exist. Since $\mathcal{W}(t)$ is a Wiener process we know that $\mathcal{W}(s+h) - \mathcal{W}(s) = \mathcal{W}(h) = N(0, h)$. Therefore,

$$\lim_{h \to 0^+} \frac{\mathcal{W}(s+h) - \mathcal{W}(s)}{h} = \lim_{h \to 0^+} \frac{1}{h} N(0, h) = \lim_{h \to 0^+} N(0, h/h^2) = \lim_{h \to 0^+} N(0, 1/h).$$

But as h gets small the variance of $N(0, 1/h)$ goes to ∞, so the values of $N(0, 1/h)$ jump between large magnitude positive and negative numbers (with larger and larger probability), so there is no limit. Therefore, via proof by contradiction there is no derivative (with probability 1) of the Wiener process.

11.3   Brownian Motion

The Wiener process is modeled on $N(0, 1)$, whereas Brownian motion is modeled on $N(\mu, \sigma)$. As stated earlier μ is considered to be the drift, and σ is the diffusion. Let us define Brownian motion.

Definition 11.3 *We say that the stochastic process $B(t), t \geq 0$ is Brownian motion if for real μ and $\sigma > 0$, and $W(t)$ the Wiener process*

$$B(t) = \mu t + \sigma W(t) .\tag{11.15}$$

We call μ the drift (coefficient) and σ the diffusion (coefficient).

Note 11.5 *The diffusion is sometimes called scale, volatility (economics), or variance. Note when we use the term Wiener process many use the term Brownian motion, and when we use Brownian motion many use the term Brownian motion with drift. We find this confusing and just view the Wiener process as Brownian motion with 0 drift and 0 diffusion. We also note that RDM (Ratcliff, 1978) allows stochastic drift, which we ignore in this chapter.*

Brownian motion has the same properties as a Wiener process except that the increment $B(t + s) - B(t)$ has the distribution $N(\mu s, \sigma^2 s)$ instead of $N(0, s)$ as for the Wiener process.

In particular a Brownian motion $B(t)$ with drift μ and diffusion σ has the properties (Breiman, 1968, Def. 12.5, p. 250).

Theorem 11.5 *The increments $B(t + s) - B(t), t, s \geq 0$ are*

(1) independent, and
(2) normally distributed with

$$E(B(t + s) - B(t)) = s\mu, \text{ and } Variance(B(t + s) - B(t)) = s\sigma^2 .$$

Definition 11.4 *We say that we have a Brownian motion $B(t)$ with starting point A if the above is adjusted by an additive constant A. Keep in mind that $\mathfrak{B}(0) = A$.*

$$\mathfrak{B}(t) = A + B(t) = A + \mu t + \sigma W(t) .\tag{11.16}$$

Thus, $B(t)$ is the subclass of $\mathfrak{B}(t)$ with $A = 0$. We are not trying to be pedantic with our definitions, rather we must be precise to avoid issues later. Also, as discussed the exisiting literature is all over the place. Thus, if readers consult the literature we want them to see how our notations and definitions fit into place.

We note that $\mathfrak{B}(t)$ has the same increment properties as $B(t)$ with one important and obvious difference. As discussed above for $0 \leq s, t$ it holds that $B(t + s) - B(t)$ has the distribution $N(\mu s, \sigma^2 s)$, so $B(s) - B(0) = B(s)$ has the distribution $N(\mu s, \sigma^2 s)$. However, for $0 < s, t$ we have that $\mathfrak{B}(t + s) - B(t)$ has the distribution $N(\mu s, \sigma^2 s)$, but $\mathfrak{B}(s)$ has the distribution of $A + B(s) = A + N(\mu s, \sigma^2 s) =$

$N(A + \mu s, \sigma^2 s)$. That is there is nothing deep about $\mathcal{B}(t)$ it is simply Brownian motion with the origin shifted to A.

11.3.1   Simulation of Brownian Motion

This is very similar to what we did for the Wiener process $\mathcal{W}(t)$, except σ is no longer 1, and there is a drift term. In terms of the Itô calculus Brownian motion satisfies (Breiman, 1968, p. 390)

$$d\mathcal{B} = \mu\, dt + \sigma\, d\mathcal{W}, \text{ which has the infinitesimal solution}$$

$$\mathcal{B}(dt) = \mu\, dt + N(0, \sigma^2 dt) \text{ (that is the standard deviation in the later term is } \sigma\sqrt{dt})$$

```
#http://phytools.org/eqg/Exercise_4.1/ #
https://www.rdocumentation.org/packages/stats/versions/3.6.2/topics/Normal
# http://www.columbia.edu/~ks20/4404-Sigman/4404-Notes-sim-BM.pdf
difcof<- 3 #this is the diffusion (coefficient)  that  corresponds
to $\sigma$ mu <- 2 T<-25  # time dt <- .01 #delta t
 n <- 1/delt #increments per time unit
 N <- n*T #total number  of increments
 t <- 0:N  # total time increments
 # sig2 <- dt  #for Wiener process, simple Brownian motion 0 drift , 1 diffusion
## first, simulate a set of random deviates
dx <- 1*rnorm(n = length(t) - 1,mean = mu*dt,
sd = difcof*sqrt(dt))
## now compute
their cumulative sum B <- c(0, cumsum(dx)) plot(t, B, type = "l",
ylim = c(-mu*T-2*difcof*sqrt(T),
mu*T+2*difcof*sqrt(T)),xlab="Increment",main=bquote("total time T"
== . (T)
    ~", diffusion"==.(difcof)~", var. = (difcof^2)*delta t "==.
(difcof*difcof*dt)~",drift"==.(mu)~",n"==.(n) )).
```

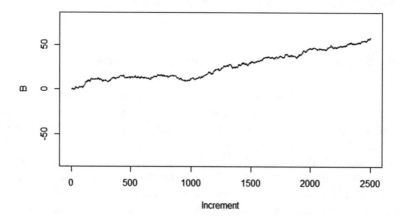

Fig. 11.7 Sample path of a simulated Brownian with T=25, $dt = \Delta t = .01$, $\mu = 2$, $\sigma = 3$, thus having 2,500 total steps

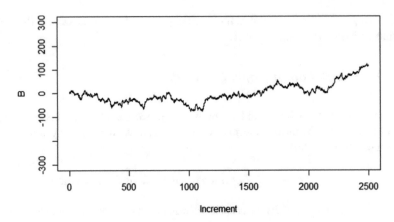

Fig. 11.8 Sample paths of a simulated Brownian with T=25, $dt = \Delta t = .01$, $\mu = 2$, $\sigma = 9$, thus having 2,500 total steps

Fig. 11.9 Brownian motion starting at Z with absorbing boundaries at A (top) and 0 (bottom)

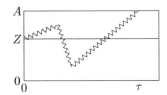

Now we increase the diffusion from 3 (Fig. 11.7) to 9 (Fig. 11.8), increase the vertical scale, and we can see that the Brownian motion now has more "volatility." (Of course these are cherry picked sample paths, but they capture the flavor of what is going on.) We invite the interested reader to generate their own sample paths to get a feel for Brownian motion with different drift and diffusion coefficients (Fig. 11.8).

11.4 Stopping Times and Absorbing Boundaries

The analysis of this is very complex and involves solving partial differential equations. So we will reference a lot of the results, but let the reader understand what is going on. The important result of Ratcliff (Ratcliff, 1978, Eq. A12), (Voss and Voss, 2008, Eq. 2) was developed by following Feller's work (Feller, 1968, Vol. 1, Ch. XIV, Eq. 6.15) (Cox and Miller, 1990, Sect. 5.17), which is not fully rigorous. Without starting *ab initio* we must make approximations or else we will be redoing the calculus of continuous state-space Markov processes, which is why we follow Ratcliff. We note that Einstein (Einstein, 1905) put Brownian motion on a firm foundation by developing a diffusion equation and emphasized the existence of the atom, before the Bohr model (Bohr, 1913).

Ratcliff and colleagues (Ratcliff, 1978; Ratcliff and Tuberlinckx, 2002; Ratcliff et al., 2016; Voss et al., 2004; Voss and Voss, 2008) use Brownian motion with a starting point with various parameters. In particular stopping times (first hitting, first passage times) are used to learn and evaluate the choice of parameter sets. As noted, many chapters have been written about these types of diffusion models. Our approach is different, we question the hypothesis that the models are based solely on Brownian motion, we wish to extend the models to fractional Brownian motion. We will discuss this more later. First though we wish to look at stopping times.

Ratcliff drift diffusion uses a model of Brownian motion with a starting point and two absorbing boundaries. The mathematics behind this model is actually quite difficult. So in this chapter instead of using the two boundary model we look at a simpler model with only one absorbing boundary. Of course, this cannot be used for Ratcliff drift diffusion, but it can be used to discuss the difference between using Brownian motion and fractional Brownian motion.

In Ratcliff diffusion we are concerned with two absorbing boundaries (See Fig. 11.9). Let us state the problem.

In what follows we note that the correct way to do things is to use the fact that the probability density function (with respect to x) $p(x; t)$ at time t of Brownian motion satisfies certain partial differential equations (PDE). The Wiener process satisfies the simplest PDE, the diffusion (or heat equation) with the diffusion constant set equal to $1/2$.

$$\frac{\partial p}{\partial t} = \frac{1}{2}\frac{\partial^2 p}{\partial x^2}.$$

The Wiener process has $\mu = 0$ and $\sigma = 1$. For the more complicated Brownian motion we have the Fokker-Planck (Kolomogorov) equation (Cox and Miller, 1990, Sect. 5.6).

$$\frac{\partial p}{\partial t} = \frac{1}{2}\sigma^2\frac{\partial^2 p}{\partial x^2} - \mu\frac{\partial p}{\partial x}$$

Note that Fokker-Plank equation reduces to the diffusion equation for the Wiener process.

The stopping time problems can be solved by using the Fokker-Plank equations. We will not do that since it is complicated and in the existing literature. We will present a heuristic solution below for a special case.

11.4.1 Two Absorbing Boundaries—The Situation for Ratcliff Drift Diffusion

We use the notation $\mathcal{B}_{\mu,\sigma}^Z(t)$ (abbreviated $\mathcal{B}(t)$ when the meaning is clear) for Brownian motion with drift μ, diffusion σ and starting point Z. There are two boundaries 0 and A. We start at time 0, as soon as the Brownian motion hits either 0 or A, the process ends. We call the time that it stops τ the stopping or first passage time, thus

$$\tau = \inf\{t | \mathcal{B}^Z_{\mu,\sigma}(t) = 0\} \wedge \inf\{t | \mathcal{B}^Z_{\mu,\sigma}(t) = A\}.$$

The finite version of this is obtained via Gambler's ruin problem. In the limit the difference equation for Gambler's ruin problem and its solution turn into the Fokker-Plank equation and its solution, respectively.

The stopping time τ is probabilistic and given by the random variable $\mathcal{T}$. Also the boundary that the Brownian motion is absorbed into (hits first) is also probabilistic and given by $\eth$, where $\eth = 0$ or A. Since the Brownian motion cannot hit 0 and A for the first time together we have that

$$P_Z(\mathcal{T} < t) = P_Z(\mathcal{T} < t, \eth = 0) + P_Z(\mathcal{T} < t, \eth = A). \qquad (11.17)$$

The density function for $\mathcal{T}$ is

$$g_Z(t) := \frac{d}{dt} P_Z(\mathcal{T} < t). \qquad (11.18)$$

Note that $P_Z(\mathcal{T} < t, \eth = 0)$ and $P_Z(\mathcal{T} < t, \eth = A)$ are *not* probability distributions. Ratcliff discussed this in (Ratcliff, 1978, App.), in fact some authors use the term *deficit distributions*. The next step are the deficit densities $g_Z(t, \eth = 0)$ and $g_Z(t, \eth = A)$, where

$$g_Z(t, \eth = 0) := \frac{d}{dt} P_Z(\mathcal{T} < t, \eth = 0). \qquad (11.19)$$

$$g_Z(t, \eth = A) := \frac{d}{dt} P_Z(\mathcal{T} < t, \eth = A), \text{ thus} \qquad (11.20)$$

$$g_Z(t) = g_Z(t, \eth = 0) + g_Z(t, \eth = A). \qquad (11.21)$$

It is heuristically shown in Feller (1968, V. 1, Eq. 6.15, p. 359) (see also (Fürth, 1917)), and solved via a separation of variables approach in Cox and Miller (1990, p. 222) that

$$g_Z(t, \eth = 0) = \frac{\pi \sigma^2}{A^2} e^{-\left(\frac{Z\mu}{\sigma^2}\right)} \sum_{k=1}^{\infty} k \sin\left(\frac{\pi Z k}{A}\right) e^{-\frac{1}{2}\left[\left(\frac{\mu}{\sigma}\right)^2 + \left(\frac{\pi k \sigma}{A}\right)^2\right]t}. \qquad (11.22)$$

Now, from the above we can derive $g_+(t, Z)$ by changing μ to $-\mu$ and changing Z to $Z - A$ (see (Navarro and Fuss, 2009)) which results in

$$g_Z(t, \eth = A) = \frac{\pi \sigma^2}{A^2} e^{\left(\frac{(A-Z)\mu}{\sigma^2}\right)} \sum_{k=1}^{\infty} k \sin\left(\frac{\pi (A - Z)k}{A}\right) e^{-\frac{1}{2}\left[\left(\frac{\mu}{\sigma}\right)^2 + \left(\frac{\pi k \sigma}{A}\right)^2\right]t}. \text{ Thus}$$

$$\qquad (11.23)$$

$$g_Z(t) = \frac{\pi\sigma^2}{A^2} e^{-\left(\frac{Z\mu}{\sigma^2}\right)} \sum_{k=1}^{\infty} k \sin\left(\frac{\pi Zk}{A}\right) e^{-\frac{1}{2}\left[\left(\frac{\mu}{\sigma}\right)^2 + \left(\frac{\pi k\sigma}{A}\right)^2\right]t} + \frac{\pi\sigma^2}{A^2} e^{\left(\frac{(A-Z)\mu}{\sigma^2}\right)}$$

$$\cdot \sum_{k=1}^{\infty} k \sin\left(\frac{\pi(A-Z)k}{A}\right) e^{-\frac{1}{2}\left[\left(\frac{\mu}{\sigma}\right)^2 + \left(\frac{\pi k\sigma}{A}\right)^2\right]t}. \tag{11.24}$$

Ratcliff (1978) notes that the distribution functions are better to work with than the density functions, we obtain those by integrating.

From above we have that $(x \geq 0)$ $P_Z(\tau < t, \mathfrak{d} = 0) = \int_0^t g_Z(x, \mathfrak{d} = 0)\,dx$ and $P_Z(\tau < t, \mathfrak{d} = A) = \int_0^t g_Z(x, \mathfrak{d} = 0)\,dx$. Putting this all together (and using the fact that terms converge properly) we have

$$P_Z(\tau < t) = \frac{\pi\sigma^2}{A^2} e^{-\left(\frac{Z\mu}{\sigma^2}\right)} \sum_{k=1}^{\infty} \left[k \sin\left(\frac{\pi Zk}{A}\right) \int_0^t e^{-\frac{1}{2}\left[\left(\frac{\mu}{\sigma}\right)^2 + \left(\frac{\pi k\sigma}{A}\right)^2\right]x}\,dx \right]$$

$$+ \frac{\pi\sigma^2}{A^2} e^{\left(\frac{(A-Z)\mu}{\sigma^2}\right)} \sum_{k=1}^{\infty} \left[k \sin\left(\frac{\pi(A-Z)k}{A}\right) \int_0^t e^{-\frac{1}{2}\left[\left(\frac{\mu}{\sigma}\right)^2 + \left(\frac{\pi k\sigma}{A}\right)^2\right]x}\,dx \right]. \text{ Thus } \tag{11.25}$$

$$P_Z(\tau < t) = \frac{\pi\sigma^2}{A^2} e^{-\left(\frac{Z\mu}{\sigma^2}\right)} \sum_{k=1}^{\infty} \left[\frac{2k \sin\left(\frac{\pi Zk}{A}\right)\left[1 - e^{-\frac{1}{2}\left[\left(\frac{\mu}{\sigma}\right)^2 + \left(\frac{\pi k\sigma}{A}\right)^2\right]t}\right]}{\left(\frac{\mu}{\sigma}\right)^2 + \left(\frac{\pi k\sigma}{A}\right)^2} \right]$$

$$+ \frac{\pi\sigma^2}{A^2} e^{\left(\frac{(A-Z)\mu}{\sigma^2}\right)} \sum_{k=1}^{\infty} \left[\frac{2k \sin\left(\frac{\pi(A-Z)k}{A}\right)\left[1 - e^{-\frac{1}{2}\left[\left(\frac{\mu}{\sigma}\right)^2 + \left(\frac{\pi k\sigma}{A}\right)^2\right]t}\right]}{\left(\frac{\mu}{\sigma}\right)^2 + \left(\frac{\pi k\sigma}{A}\right)^2} \right] \tag{11.26}$$

$$P_Z(\tau < t) = P_Z(\mathfrak{d} = 0) \cdot P_Z(\tau < t|\mathfrak{d} = 0) + P_Z(\mathfrak{d} = A) \cdot P_Z(\tau < t|\mathfrak{d} = A). \tag{11.27}$$

There are two more probabilities of interest. It can be shown that $P_Z(\mathfrak{d} = 0)$, which corresponds to ruin in Gambler's ruin discrete case is

$$P_Z(\mathfrak{d} = 0) = \frac{e^{-\frac{2A\mu}{\sigma^2}} - e^{-\frac{2Z\mu}{\sigma^2}}}{e^{-\frac{2A\mu}{\sigma^2}} - 1} \tag{11.28}$$

which trivially gives us

$$P_Z(\mathfrak{d} = A) = \frac{e^{-\frac{2Z\mu}{\sigma^2}} - 1}{e^{-\frac{2A\mu}{\sigma^2}} - 1}. \tag{11.29}$$

We could as Ratcliff notes (Ratcliff, 1978, p. 106) also derive these as

$$P_Z(\eth = 0) = \int_0^\infty g_Z(x, \eth = 0)\, dx \qquad (11.30)$$

$$P_Z(\eth = A) = \int_0^\infty g_Z(x, \eth = A)\, dx. \qquad (11.31)$$

In the limiting case, when the drift goes to 0 we have from Eq. 11.28 that

$$P_{Z,\mu=0}(\eth = 0) = 1 - \frac{Z}{A} \qquad (11.32)$$

and the probability of $P_Z(\eth = A)$, which corresponds to taking all the money in Gambler's ruin discrete case is

$$P_{Z,\mu=0}(\eth = A) = \frac{Z}{A}. \qquad (11.33)$$

To give a thorough proof of the above continuous results one has to appeal to martingale theory. Ratcliff (Ratcliff, 1978) discussed the validity of the above formulas by appealing to Feller (Feller, 1968) who showed how to take the random walk Gambler's ruin problem to the limit of infinitesimally small time increments. We see that in the discrete case when $A \to \infty$ that $P_{Z,\mu=0}(\eth = A) \to 0$. This is why it is called Gambler's ruin—with probability 1 a gambler (under the scenario in discussion) will lose against a "house" that has an infinite amount of money, vs. the gambler's finite pot.

Ratcliff (Ratcliff, 1978) was the first to use this in the psychological sciences, other authors use the same formula but with various normalizations such as setting $\sigma = 1$, or scaling Z as Z/A. These changes reflect the underlying cognitive mechanisms being modeled. This has relevance because it can reflect the bias toward one decision. When $A = 1$, starting at 1/2 reflects no bias. It is also interesting to see that for the fair simple walk (integer A, Z) and for Brownian motion without drift that the probabilities of hitting the boundaries are the same.

Note, a Wiener process (Brownian motion with drift 1 and diffusion 0), and more generally a Brownian motion without drift and starting point Z have the martingale property (there is no bias one way or another as time progresses). The *Optional Stopping Theorem* (Bhattacharya and Waymire, 2009, Thm. 4.1) tells us for a martingale that $E(\mathcal{T}) = E(\mathcal{B}(0)) = Z$.

But $E(\mathcal{T}) = 0 \cdot P_{Z,\mu=0}(\eth = 0) + A \cdot P_{\mu=0}(\eth = A) = A P_{Z,\mu=0}(\eth = A)$. So, we have the above result Eq. 11.33 that $P_{Z,\mu=0}(\eth = A) = \frac{Z}{A}$ and trivially Eq. 11.32. The general Eq. 11.28 is not handled as easily but we have to exponentiate the Brownian motion and look at *Geometric Brownian Motion*, see Dobrow (2016, p. 370, Ex. 8.36) for details, or use work of Wald and solve thte Fokker-Plank equation as in Darling and Siegert, (1953, Eq. 5.7). Ratcliff's approach, although it is not 100% complete, avoids this complicated modern machinery of stochastic processes.

Note that in the above we have tried to stay with Ratcliff's notation (Ratcliff, 1978) as much as possible but have modified it to make clear what the boundaries are and when we are dealing with conditional probabilities and by not overloading the notation when the conditioning is clear.

Note that in Eqs. 11.32 and 11.33 the drift is zero, but the diffusion may be any positive number. We will later make things simpler and assume that A is 1, this gives us

$$P_{Z,\mu=0}(\eth = 0) = 1 - Z \text{ and } P_{Z,\mu=0}(\eth = 1) = Z. \qquad (11.34)$$

Of course if the starting point for the Brownian motion is $Z = 0$, we have that $P_{0,\mu=0}(\eth = 0) = 1$, $P_{0,\mu=0}(\eth = 1) = 0$, since the process starts and ends instantaneously at time 0. If the starting point is $Z = 1$, we have the opposite $P_{1,\mu=0}(\eth = 0) = 0$, $P_{1,\mu=0}(\eth = 1) = 1$ since the Brownian motion starts and ends instantaneously at time 0 also.

11.5 Fractional Brownian Motion

Fractional (or sometimes Fractal) Brownian Motion (fBM) was introduced in its present theoretical form in (Mandelbrot and Van Ness, 1968), but actually had its beginnings by Hurst (Hurst, 1951) on his very applied engineering work on the Nile river. There is also earlier related work by Kolmogorov on the Wiener spiral (Kolmogorov, 1940). fBM is the natural generalization of Brownian motion. The definition is not very intuitive—at first. The important difference between BM and fBM is that the increments need *not be independent*. To keep our notation standard with the rest of the chapter, at the cost of being non-standard with the literature, we refer to a fBM with drift of 0, and diffusion as 1, as a fractional Wiener Process (fWP). (Others have used this term differently (Frasca and Farina, 2017).) Of course to give a full comparison against the RDM we would have to include drift, but that is beyond this chapter and will be in future work. Before we get to the definition we need some preliminaries to appreciate the definition.

11.5.1 Covariance of Brownian Motion

We know that $\text{Var}(\mathcal{B}(t)) = \sigma^2 t$. There is a very important property of Brownian motion that we wish to stress (Dobrow, 2016, Ex. 8.3), (Sigman, 2015, p. 4) below.

Theorem 11.6

$$Cov(\mathcal{B}(t), \mathcal{B}(t')) = \sigma^2 \cdot \min(t, t'); \ t, t' \geq 0 \, .$$

Proof We have that $Var(\mathcal{B}(\tau)) = \sigma^2\tau$, and, WLOG we assume that $t < t'$.

$$Cov(\mathcal{B}(t), \mathcal{B}(t')) = Cov(\mathcal{B}(t), \mathcal{B}(t) + \mathcal{B}(t') - \mathcal{B}(t)) \quad (11.35)$$

$$= Cov(\mathcal{B}(t), \mathcal{B}(t)) + Cov(\mathcal{B}(t), \mathcal{B}(t') - \mathcal{B}(t)) \quad (11.36)$$

$$= Var(\mathcal{B}(t) + Cov\left(\mathcal{B}(t), \mathcal{B}(t') - \mathcal{B}(t)\right), \text{ and since } \mathcal{B}(t') - \mathcal{B}(t), \mathcal{B}(t) \text{ are independent increments } (11.37)$$

$$= \sigma^2 t + 0. \quad (11.38)$$

Similarly, if $t' < t$. Note for $t = t'$ it holds because it is simply the variance.

Note in particular for Brownian motion with diffusion 1, which of course includes the Wiener process, we have

Corollary 11.6.1

$$Cov\left(\mathcal{B}_{m,1}(t), \mathcal{B}_{m,1}(t')\right) = Cov\left(\mathcal{W}(t), \mathcal{W}(t')\right) = \min(t, t').$$

11.5.2 Definition of the Fractional Wiener Process

One can also define a Wiener process as a Gaussian process (Cox and Miller, 1990).

Definition 11.5 *A stochastic process X_t is said to be* **Gaussian** *if for any $t_1, \ldots, t_k$ the joint distribution of $X_{t_1}, \ldots, X_{t_k}$ is multivariate normal.*

Note 11.6 *Keep in mind that a Gaussian process is completely determined by its mean and covariance properties, since for a multivariate normal random variable we only need its covariance matrix and mean to uniquely determine it (Doob, 1949, p. 71).*

Note 11.7 *We may also define a Wiener process $\mathcal{W}(t)$ as a Gaussian process with stationary increments and continuous sample paths, $t \geq 0$, such that*

- $E(\mathcal{W}(t)) = 0$
- $Cov(\mathcal{W}(S), \mathcal{W}(T)) = \min(S, T)$.

We see that for a Wiener process for $0 \leq t_1 < t_2 \leq t_3 < t_4$, we have

$$Cov(\mathcal{W}(t_2) - \mathcal{W}(t_1), \mathcal{W}(t_4) - \mathcal{W}(t_3))$$
$$= Cov(\mathcal{W}(t_2), \mathcal{W}(t_4)) - Cov(\mathcal{W}(t_2), \mathcal{W}(t_3)) - Cov(\mathcal{W}(t_1), \mathcal{W}(t_4)) + Cov(\mathcal{W}(t_1), W(t_3))$$
$$= t_2 - t_2 - t_1 + t_1 = 0 .$$

Thus we see that we also have independent intervals with this Gaussian process-type definition. We use the Gaussian process-type definition to define fractional Brownian motion below. This definition is simpler for exposition than using stochastic integration as originally done in (Mandelbrot and Van Ness, 1968).

Definition 11.6 *A fractional Wiener Process $\mathcal{W}_H(t)$ is (Mandelbrot and Van Ness, 1968) a Gaussian process with stationary increments and continuous sample paths, $t \geq 0$ such that for the Hurst exponent (coefficient, parameter, index, etc.) $H, 0 < H < 1$*

- $E(\mathscr{W}_H(t)) = 0$
- $Cov(\mathscr{W}_H(S), \mathscr{W}_H(T)) = \frac{1}{2}(S^{2H} + T^{2H} - |T - S|^{2H})$.

(We will show that) $\mathscr{W}_H(t)$ has independent increments iff $H = \frac{1}{2}$ and $\mathscr{W}_{\frac{1}{2}}(t)$ is simply the Wiener process. Furthermore, $\mathrm{Var}(\mathscr{W}_H(t)) = t^{2H}$. This fact is alluded to in the literature, and some chapters have a proof sketch. Since it is so important a property we present it as a theorem below using the approach in (Shevchenko, 2014) which uses convexity arguments. However, to make that argument precise we first need a result from (Gkioulekas, 2013).

Recall that a function is strictly convex (up) iff $\forall t \in (0, 1): f(ta + (1 - t)b) < tf(a) + (1 - t)f(b)$.

We adopt (Gkioulekas, 2013) the notation (for the slope of a secant line) that for a function $f(x), a \neq b$

$$\lambda(a, b) := \frac{f(b) - f(a)}{b - a}.$$

Lemma 11.7 *Given a strictly convex (up) function $f(x)$ and intervals $[t_1, t_2], [t_3, t_4]$, $t_1 < t_2, t_3 < t_4, t_2 < t_4$ and $t_1 < t_3$, we have the following inequality of secant slopes*

$$\lambda(t_1, t_2) < \lambda(t_3, t_4). \tag{11.39}$$

Proof The proof follows from (Gkioulekas, 2013, Lemma 2.1). Gkioulekas showed that for $f(x)$ strictly convex (up) and $a < m < b$ that

$$\lambda(a, m) < \lambda(a, b) < \lambda(m, b).$$

First consider $t_1 < t_2 < t_4$, thus (Gkioulekas, 2013, Lemma 2.1, LHS)

$$\lambda(t_1, t_2) < \lambda(t_1, t_4).$$

Next consider $t_1 < t_3 < t_4$, thus (Gkioulekas, 2013, Lemma 2.1, RHS)

$$\lambda(t_1, t_4) < \lambda(t_3, t_4).$$

Theorem 11.8 *$\mathscr{W}_H(t)$ has independent increments iff $H = \frac{1}{2}$. If $H \in (\frac{1}{2}, 1)$ the increments are positively correlated, if $H \in (0, \frac{1}{2})$ the increments are negatively correlated.*

Proof We use the above lemma along with Shevchenko's approach (Shevchenko, 2014, p. 3). We consider non-overlapping time intervals $[S_1, T_1]$ and $[S_2, T_2]$ with $0 \leq S_1 < T_1 < S_2 < T_2$.

$\text{Cov}(\mathcal{W}_H(T_1) - \mathcal{W}_H(S_1), \mathcal{W}_H(T_2) - \mathcal{W}_H(S_2))$

$= \text{Cov}(\mathcal{W}_H(T_1), \mathcal{W}_H(T_2)) - \text{Cov}(\mathcal{W}_H(S_1), \mathcal{W}_H(T_2)) - \text{Cov}(\mathcal{W}_H(T_1), \mathcal{W}_H(S_2)) + \text{Cov}(\mathcal{W}_H(S_1), \mathcal{W}_H(S_2))$

$= \frac{1}{2}\left[T_1^{2H} + T_2^{2H} - (T_2 - T_1)^{2H} - S_1^{2H} - T_2^{2H} + (T_2 - S_1)^{2H} - T_1^{2H} - S_2^{2H} + (S_2 - T_1)^{2H} + S_1^{2H} + S_2^{2H} - (S_2 - S_1)^{2H}\right]$

$= \frac{1}{2}\left[(T_2 - S_1)^{2H} - (T_2 - T_1)^{2H}\right] - \frac{1}{2}\left[(S_2 - S_1)^{2H} - (S_2 - T_1)^{2H}\right].$

(*) Note that $(T_2 - S_1) - (T_2 - T_1) = T_1 - S_1 > 0 = (S_2 - S_1) - (S_2 - T_1) = T_1 - S_1$.

For $H = 1/2$ the exponent $2H = 1$ and we have independent increments since:

$$\text{Cov}\left(\mathcal{W}_{1/2}(T_1) - \mathcal{W}_{1/2}(S_1), \mathcal{W}_{1/2}(T_2) - \mathcal{W}_{1/2}(S_2)\right) = 0.$$

In general, consider the four numbers $a_1 := (T_2 - S_1)$, $a_2 := (T_2 - T_1)$, $b_1 := (S_2 - S_1)$, $b_2 := (S_2 - T_1)$. From (*) above we have that $a_1 - a_2 = b_1 - b_2 = T_1 - S_1$. Letting

$$f(x) = x^{2H}, x > 0$$

and using, as above λ for the slope of a secant line of $f(s)$, we can express the covariance as

$$\text{Cov}(\mathcal{W}_H(T_1) - \mathcal{W}_H(S_1), \mathcal{W}_H(T_2) - \mathcal{W}_H(S_2)) = \frac{1}{2}\left[a_1^{2H} - a_2^{2H}\right] - \left[b_1^{2H} - b_2^{2H}\right]$$

$$= \frac{T_1 - S_1}{2}\left[\lambda(a_2, a_1) - \lambda(b_2, b_1)\right]. \quad (11.40)$$

Since $S_1 < T_1 < S_2 < T_2$ we see that the smallest number is b_2, the largest is a_1 and they order as $b_2 < b_1, a_2 < a_1$. Now since $f''(x) = 2H(2H - 1)x^{2H-2}$ is strictly convex (up) for $H > .5$, strictly concave (down) for $H < .5$, and a straight line for $H = .5$, we apply the above lemma which determines the sign of Eq. 11.40 and see that for

$$H > \frac{1}{2}, \; \text{Cov}(\mathcal{W}_H(T_1) - \mathcal{W}_H(S_1), \mathcal{W}_H(T_2) - \mathcal{W}_H(S_2)) > 0$$

$$H < \frac{1}{2}, \; \text{Cov}(\mathcal{W}_H(T_1) - \mathcal{W}_H(S_1), \mathcal{W}_H(T_2) - \mathcal{W}_H(S_2)) < 0.$$

This theorem is often thrown about in the literature as an obvious fact about the fractional Wiener process. Even though we proved it from elementary properties of convexity, we find it far from obvious.

Definition 11.7 *A fractional Brownian motion without drift* $\mathcal{B}_{H_{0,\sigma}}(t)$ *is (Guggen-berer et al., 2019; Shevchenko, 2014) a Gaussian process with stationary increments and continuous sample paths,* $t \geq 0$, *such that for the Hurst exponent (coefficient, parameter, index, etc.)* $H, 0 < H < 1$

- $E(\mathscr{W}_H(t)) = 0$
- $Cov\,(\mathscr{W}_H(S), \mathscr{W}_H(T)) = \frac{\sigma}{2}(S^{2H} + T^{2H} - |T - S|^{2H})$.

Obviously $\mathcal{B}_{\frac{1}{2}0,\sigma}(t) = \mathcal{B}_{0,\sigma}(t)$ and $\mathcal{B}_{H_{0,1}}(t) = \mathscr{W}_H(t)$.

Of course one can also define a fractional Brownian motion with drift $\mathcal{B}_{H_{\mu,\sigma}}(t)$ (Arutkin et al., 2020), (Cheridito, 2001, Sect. 4.5). However, we will only concentrate on the fractional Wiener process in the remainder of this chapter, since the results for generalized Brownian motion are a work in progress in the scientific arena. We also note that many authors use the term fractional Brownian motion to mean the fractional Wiener process. We have chosen not to and have developed what we feel is a more consistent naming convention.

11.5.3 Existence and Properties of the Fractional Wiener Process

We will not go into the details showing that the fractional Wiener process exists, that it has continuous sample paths, and that it is not differentiable (Mandelbrot and Van Ness, 1968; Shevchenko, 2014). To do the topic justice requires the use of stochastic calculus which is beyond the scope and interest of this chapter. We will assume these facts instead.

There are many ways to simulate the fractional Wiener process, none of them simple (Dieker, 2002). The construction of these simulations is beyond this scope of this chapter and we will also just assume their existence. For our simulations we use (Botev, 2016) which is based on (Kroese and Botev, 2120). In Fig. 11.10 we see the simulation of three sample paths for $\mathscr{W}_H(t)$.

The red line is for $\mathscr{W}_{.5}(t)$ which is just the standard Wiener process $\mathscr{W}(t)$. The increments are independent in this situation.

The blue line is for $\mathscr{W}_{.06}(t)$. In this situation there is almost maximal negative correlation between the increments. That is the fractional Wiener process for $H \in (0, .5)$ "has the property of counterpersistence: if it was increasing in the past, it is more likely to decrease in the future, and vice versa" (Shevchenko, 2014). This characteristic is seen by the very rough and spikey appearance of the sample path.

The green line is for $\mathscr{W}_{.94}(t)$. In this situation there is almost maximal positive correlation and the fractional Wiener process "is persistent, it is more likely to keep trend than to break it" (Shevchenko, 2014). This is seen by the smooth appearance of the sample path and the fact that once it takes off in a positive direction it tends to stay that way.

11.5.4 Ratcliff Diffusion Revisited

Ratcliff diffusion is based on the assumption of Brownian motion. We ask the question "Why not fractional Brownian motion?" Ratcliff diffusion was developed as the infinitesimal version of a random walk—Brownian motion. A key underlying

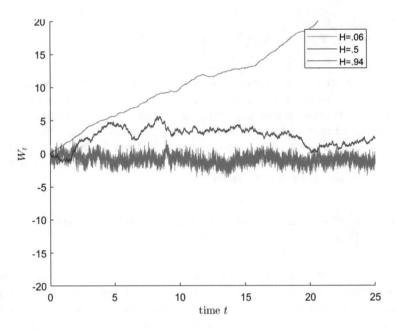

Fig. 11.10 Sample paths of simulated fractional Wiener processes for $H = .06, .5, .94$ and $T = 25$

assumption is that the behavior of the Ratcliff diffusion starting at time τ depends only on the starting point at time τ, not the behavior of the stochastic process prior to time τ. We wish to explore the possibility that there may be a dependency on past behavior. How would that affect the analysis of the various parameters that are obtained via experimentation on Ratcliff diffusion?

We noted above that Brownian motion has independent intervals. This is not true for fractional Brownian motion. Let us concentrate on the fractional Wiener process for simplicity (as discussed above).

We return to the comments after Fig. 11.10. What is it in Ratcliff diffusion that validates the idea of independent increments? Perhaps if one is modeling a human decision process then there might actually be a persistence in the behavior, and in fact that decision type process behaves more like the green line, than the red in Fig. 11.10. That is, perhaps Ratcliff diffusion should be re-examined in light of a Hurst exponent $H \geq .5$, not just $H = .5$? We do not think that human decisions are negatively correlated, though, and we would not see the blue line in Fig. 11.10.

When dealing with the fractional Wiener process, or more generally with fractional Brownian motion, the formulas discussed in earlier have to be generalized. Unfortunately, that is still a work in progress in the community.

For small H we see that the sample path hovers around the starting point. Therefore, the time to hit either the top or bottom boundary as discussed earlier would be larger than when $H = 1/2$. For large H the path seems to hit a boundary sooner. Of course, we are ignoring drift in these back of the envelope calculations.

In future research, since closed form solutions are often lacking we plan to research those solutions and use Monte Carlo techniques to arrive at first stopping time probabilities.

Let us return to Eq. 11.34 which holds for a Wiener process starting at the point $Z \in [0, 1]$. We concentrate on the probability that the Wiener process hits the top boundary (1) before it hits the bottom boundary (0).

$$P_{Z,\mu=0}(\eth = 1) = Z$$

The question of interest is what if it is not a Wiener process, but a fractional Wiener process? Therefore we now express the probability in more generality as

$$P_{Z,\text{Hurst}=H}(\eth = 1) = Z, \tag{11.41}$$

since it is a fractional Wiener process we know that $\mu = 0$ and we no longer need express it notationally. Of course we know that

$$P_{Z,\text{Hurst}=.5}(\eth = 1) = Z \tag{11.42}$$

Even this very simple probability is very difficult to obtain in closed form for $H \neq .5$. We will not go into details here, but it has been argued that (Wiese, 2019)

$$P_{Z,\text{Hurst}=H}(\eth = 1) \sim Z^{\phi}, \text{ for small } Z ,$$

where $\phi := \frac{1-H}{H}$ is called the persistence exponent. In addition (please see (Wiese, 2019) for further details)

$$\frac{d}{dZ} P_{Z,\text{Hurst}=H}(\eth = 1) = N[Z(1 - Z)]^{\left(\frac{1}{H}-2\right)} e^{\left(\epsilon F(x)+O(\epsilon^2)\right)} .$$

Note that $N \approx 1$, (Wiese, 2020). Of course, from Eq. 11.42 we trivially have that $\frac{d}{dZ} P_{Z,\text{Hurst}=.5}(\eth = 1) = 1$.

These terms of interest which were derived for $H = .5$ heavily depend upon geometric information of the underlying processes. In fact, fractional Brownian motions are fractal (with probability 1) in nature with the properties of self-similarity. In fact (Voss, 1988) the fractal dimension D of $\mathcal{B}_{H_{0,\sigma}}(t))$ is

$$D = 2 - H$$

which of course tells us that the fractal (box counting) dimension of (standard) Brownian motion is $3/2$.

11.6   Determining H, a Problem in AI

For Ratcliff type diffusion problems, the issue of determining H from the time series is hidden from us. We do not see the individual "thought" ticks in someone's mind, we know only what and when their decision was. However, we include this section as a contribution for determining H from a time series, which is an ongoing issue.

Existing methods of determining Hurst exponents from time series data is done by a power law fit to the rescaled range (RR). The RR quantifies the self-similarity (fractal nature) of a time series. To calculate (Wang et al., 2011) the RR, the time series X must be split into A equal sections of size m, denoted as D_a, $a = 1, 2, \ldots, A$. We find the average value $\bar{x}_a$ of each segment. Next, we find the mean centered time series Y using $Y_{k,a} = X_{k,a} - \bar{x}_a$ for $k = 1, 2, \ldots, m$ and for each section a. We find the cumulative series $Z_{k,a}$ using $Z_{k,a} = \sum_{i=1}^{k} Y_{k,a}$ for $k = 1, 2, \ldots, m$ and for each section a. We find the range $R_a = \max(Z_{k,a}) - \min(Z_{k,a})$ and the standard deviation S_a for $k = 1, 2, \ldots, m$ for each section a. We compute R_a/S_a for each section a, and then average over all sections to get the RR. The RR will report on more local trends if the time series is split more heavily and will report on more global trends if the time series is split more lightly. The RR is calculated for multiple splits to gather information on the local and global trends, and the power law fit is applied to all of the calculated RR values to get the Hurst exponent. This goes back to Hurst's original work (Hurst, 1951) and is somewhat heuristic.

Issues were encountered using existing packages in R and Python to find the Hurst exponent of a time series. We generated a time series from a sample fractional Wiener process characterized by the Hurst exponent using Python or R-package functions, and then used the inverse function given by the package to find the Hurst exponent. The outputted Hurst exponent from the inverse function varied wildly with the Hurst exponent used to generate the inputted time series, see Fig. 11.11.

We attempted to improve upon this by using neural nets. We built a convolutional neural net (CNN) which was chosen for its ability to find both local and global trends in a dataset. The CNN input layer was fed the entire time series, and the output layer had 11 nodes representing Hurst exponents $H = [0.51, 0.55, 0.60\ldots, 0.90, 0.95, 0.99]$. The hidden layers included 1D convolutional layers and max-pooling layers. The overall time series dataset had 44,000 examples, of which 10% was reserved for testing, and 10% was removed for validation. The model was trained to classify the time series into one of these 11 discrete Hurst "bins". Our CNN outperformed the existing power law methods, but still left much to be desired with a classification accuracy of only 59.68% (Fig. 11.12).

In recent work Kirichenko (Kirichenko et al., 2019) reported higher accuracy than our CNN approach at a 92.2% accuracy for a 4096 point time series using random forest regression trees. Random forest is an ensemble machine learning method which generates a large number of decision trees to make predictions based on the inputs. Each of the decision trees comes to an independent conclusion, and the prediction of the model is based on what the majority of the decision trees "vote" for. For inputs to their model, Kirichenko used statistical characteristics such as the standard deviation

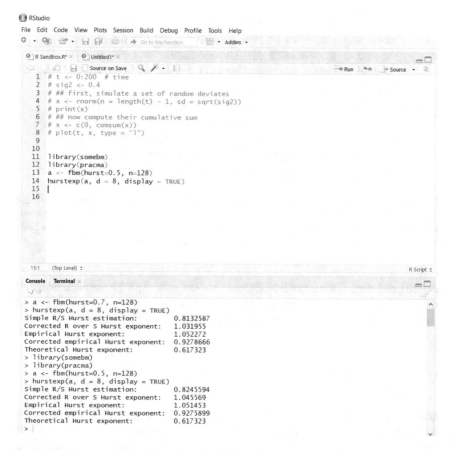

```
1   # t <- 0:200  # time
2   # sig2 <- 0.4
3   # ## first, simulate a set of random deviates
4   # x <- rnorm(n = length(t) - 1, sd = sqrt(sig2))
5   # print(x)
6   # ## now compute their cumulative sum
7   # x <- c(0, cumsum(x))
8   # plot(t, x, type = "l")
9
10
11  library(somebm)
12  library(pracma)
13  a <- fbm(hurst=0.5, n=128)
14  hurstexp(a, d = 8, display = TRUE)
15  |
16
```

```
> a <- fbm(hurst=0.7, n=128)
> hurstexp(a, d = 8, display = TRUE)
Simple R/S Hurst estimation:           0.8132587
Corrected R over S Hurst exponent:     1.031955
Empirical Hurst exponent:              1.052272
Corrected empirical Hurst exponent:    0.9278666
Theoretical Hurst exponent:            0.617323
> library(somebm)
> library(pracma)
> a <- fbm(hurst=0.5, n=128)
> hurstexp(a, d = 8, display = TRUE)
Simple R/S Hurst estimation:           0.8245594
Corrected R over S Hurst exponent:     1.045569
Empirical Hurst exponent:              1.051453
Corrected empirical Hurst exponent:    0.9275899
Theoretical Hurst exponent:            0.617323
>
```

Fig. 11.11 We generated sample paths using the R-package somebm with $H = .5, .7$. We then used the code to determine H. In both cases it gave us erroneous H values. We observed this with other sample paths. Note this is not the only code extant, but many of them give buggy results

Fig. 11.12 CNN prediction distribution from the validation data. The x-axis denoted how many bins off a prediction was, and the y-axis denotes the number of predictions. From the left, number of correct predictions, number of predictions that were one bin off (left edge: 0, 1, or 2), and number of predictions that were two bins off. Total accuracy was 59.68%

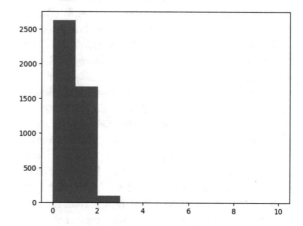

```
H = 0.50 >  [24.50492617 12.32474142  6.201683    3.17602208]
H = 0.55 >  [25.01654806 12.42491693  6.20371858 3.17501675]
H = 0.60 >  [25.70795807 12.59295568  6.28740384 3.21626019]
H = 0.65 >  [26.07267413 12.83993328  6.3589166  3.21770772]
H = 0.70 >  [26.60327437 13.08859808  6.42093495 3.23754967]
H = 0.75 >  [27.04698941 13.2972075   6.56529077 3.25337037]
H = 0.80 >  [27.31464299 13.49576625  6.61035008 3.28489222]
H = 0.85 >  [27.48111248 13.64396748  6.72491075 3.33402585]
H = 0.90 >  [27.54350541 13.71494133  6.79298931 3.36931839]
H = 0.95 >  [27.67193929 13.80624141  6.8561558  3.41164965]
```

Fig. 11.13 RR values for different Hurst exponents for four different splits, averaged over 200 runs. There is a strong relationship between the Hurst exponent and the rescaled range. However, as noted above in our code output the R/S Hurst estimates are off in practice on a case by case basis. Further theoretical work is needed to fully exploit Hurst's orginal ideas (Hurst, 1951)

and the maximum of the absolute values of time series, along with parameters related to the generalized Hurst exponent. Inadequate detail in the chapter made it difficult to reproduce the parameters relating to the generalized Hurst exponent.

11.6.1 Our Hybrid Approach

Because of this we developed a hybrid approach and investigated the RR [24, p. 793], (which, as noted, is closely related to H and is a good substitute parameter). To verify the correlation between H and the RR, we generated 200 times series for each of the values $H = .5, .55, .6, .65, \ldots, .95$. The time series data was split $A = 4$ different ways for each H value—in half, in quarters, in eights, and in sixteenths. For every Hurst exponent, we calculated the rescaled range for each of the 200 time series, for each split, and then averaged over every split. The results of this test showed a clear relationship between H and the rescaled range (Fig. 11.13).

The RR was combined with the standard deviation and the max absolute value of the dataset as inputs for a Machine Learning (ML) model. Three different ML models were tested: multi-layer perceptron, random forest regressor, and gradient boosting regressor. All of the models are from the scikit-learn Python library. The multi-layer perceptron model is a feedforward neural network. The gradient boosting regressor is a variation of the random forest regressor (described above), where the decision trees are generated one by one, with each successive decision tree tailored to most compensate for the mistakes of the decision tree that preceded it. A grid seach was performed using the scikit-learrn `gridSearchCv` function to determine the best parameters for each tested model. The worst model tried (multi-layer perceptron) with a time series of 512 data points returned an accuracy of 94.5%, while the best model tried (gradient boosting regressor) with a time series length of 4096 data points achieved an accuracy of 97.8%. The entropy, which encapsulates the distribution of unique values in a dataset, was added as an additional input parameter because it speaks to the presence of mean reverting tendencies in a dataset. Using a gradient boosting regressor, accuracy levels rose to 95.3% for a 512 point time series and 98.7% for a 4096 point time series. Overall, error was reduced by over 80% in assigning Hurst exponents to time series data of length 4096 with respect to Kirichenko.

11.7   Team Science and Future Work

In future work we plan to apply fractional Brownian motion to Team science. We will briefly describe our ideas for Team science in this section. We also plan in future work to examine the parameters from Ratcliff diffusion in terms of fractional Brownian motion, instead of just Brownian motion via experimentation.

A team consists of separate entities attempting to perform a task. An important concept of a team is its interdependence. Lawless and others have published much on this concept in the last decade, for example (Cooke and Hilton, 2015; Lawless et al., 2015, 2009, 2011; Lawless and Sofge, 2012, 2013; Lawless et al., 2015; Lawless, 2015). We propose to use the Hurst exponent H as a measure of Team interdependence.

We assume that the progress, via fractional Brownian motion, toward a goal is measured. In particular, we are modeling Team science as a diffusion type problem. We consider the stopping time with a top (success) and bottom (failure) boundary. There are three quantities at play – the drift, the diffusion, and H.

The drift measures the skill of each team member. We are assuming that each member of the team has the same skill level. This is somewhat unrealistic and in the future we wish to analyze this using stochastic drift as Ratcliff did (Ratcliff, 1978) for memory models. So for now we simply refer to the drift of the team as μ.

(1) If $\mu = 0$ the team has neutral skill, the team member are not good or bad at the task at hand.
(2) If $\mu > 0$ we are assuming that the team members are skilled at the task.
(3) If $\mu < 0$ we assume that they are unskilled.

The diffusion σ is a measure of the variability of the team as a whole and can be incorporated with the concept of stochastic drift.

Now we view H as a measure of Team interdependence. If the team members function independently of each other we set $H = .5$, and we are in the case of standard Brownian motion.

If they have a good dependence among themselves we have $H > .5$. Having a large H value gets us to a boundary quicker, but keep in mind that it could send us to the wrong answer.

If the team members have a dependency among themselves, but it is not a helpful dependency we set $H < .5$. This will cause the team to waffle in an intermediate stage before reaching a decision (success or failure).

As noted this is the direction for some of our future work.

Acknowledgements We thank Kay J. Wiese for his helpful e-conversations and insight. We thank Eleftherios Gkioulekas for catching an error. We also thank Hans Haucke, Sophie Cissé, and Ruth Irene for their comments. We especially thank William Lawless for his insights into Team Science, and his careful reading of the draft of this chapter.

References

Abry, P., & Sellan, F. (1996). The wavelet-based synthesis for fractional Brownian motion proposed by F. Sellam and Y. Meyer: Remarks and fast implementation. *Applied and Computational Harmonic Analysis, 3*(4), 377–383.

Arnold, Nina R., Bröder, Arndt, & Bayen, Ute J. (2015). Empirical validation of the diffusion model for recognition memory and a comparison of parameter-estimation methods. *Psychological Research, 79*, 882–898.

Arutkin, M., Walter, B., & Wiese, Kay J. (2020). Extreme events for fractional Brownian motion with drift: Theory and numerical validation. *Physical Review E, 102*, 022102.

Bohr, Niels. (1913). On the constitution of atoms and molecules, Part 1. *Philosophical Magazine, 26*(151), 1–24.

Botev, Z. (2016). https://www.mathworks.com/matlabcentral/fileexchange/38935-fractional-brownian-motion-generator. Retrieved 20 June 2016.

Breiman, L. (1968). *Probability* Addison-Wesley.

Cheridito, P. (2001). *Regularizing fractional brownian motion with a view towards stock price modeling*. Ph.D. Dissertation, Department of Mathematics, Swiss Federal Institute of Technology, Zurich.

Cooke, N. J., & Hilton, M. L. (Eds.). (2015). *Enhancing the effectiveness of team science*. National Research Council of the National Academy of Sciences.

Cox, D. R., & H. D. Miller. (1965/1990). *The theory of stochastic processes*. Chapman and Hall.

Darling, D. A., & Siegert, A. T. J. (1953). The first passage problem for a continuous Markov process. *The Annals of Mathematical Statistics, 24*(4), 624–639.

Dieker, T. (2002). *Simulation of fractional Brownian motion*. Master's thesis, Vrije Universiteit Amsterdam.

Donsker, M. D. (1951). An invariance principle for certain probability limit theorems. *Memoirs of the American Mathematical Society* (6).

Donsker, Monroe D. (1952). Justification and extension of Doob's heuristic approach to the Kolmogorov-Smirnov theorems. *The Annals of Mathematical Statistics, 23*(2), 277–281.

Donsker's Theorem. https://en.wikipedia.org/wiki/Donsker's_theorem. Retrieved April 4 2020.

Doob, J. L. (1949). Heuristic approach to the Kolmogorov-Smirnov theorems. *The Annals of Mathematical Statistics, 20*(3), 393–403.

Dobrow, R. P. (2016). Introduction to stochastic processes with R. Wiley.

Einstein, Albert. (1905). Über die von der Molekularkinetischen Theorie der Wärme geforderte Bewegung von in ruhenden Flüssigkeiten suspendierten Teilchen. *Annalen der Physik, 17*, 549–560.

Feller, W. (1950/1968). *An introduction to probability theory and its applications*, Vols.1&2. Wiley.

Frasca, M., & Farina, A. (2017). Numerical proof of existence of fractional Wiener processes. *Signal Image and Video Processing, 11*(1).

Fürth, R. (1917). *Einige Untersuchungen über Brownsche Bewegung an einem Einzelteilchen.* Annalen der Physik. IV. No. 11, Folge 53, pp. 177–213.

Gkioulekas, E. (2013). On equivalent characterizations of convexity of functions. *International Journal of Mathematical Education in Science and Technology, 44*(3), 410–417.

Sanchez Granero, M. A. S., Segovia, J. E. T., & Perez, J. G. (2008). Some Comments on Hurst exponent and the long memory processes on capital markets. *Physica A, 387*, 5543–5551.

Grinstead, C. M., & Snell, J. L. (1997). Introduction to probability.

Guggenberer, T., Pagani, G., Votja, T., & Metzler, R. (2019). Fractional Brownian motion in a finite interval: correlations effect depletion or accretion zones of particles near boundaries. *New Journal of Physics, 21*, 022002.

Hurst, H. E. (1951). Long-term storage capacity of reservoirs. *Transactions of the American Society of Civil Engineers, 116*, 770–799.

Karatzas, I., & Shreve, S. E. (2019). Brownian motion and stochastic calculus. In *Graduate text in mathematics* (2nd ed.). Springer.

Kolmogorov, A. N. (1940). Wiensersche Spiralen und einige andere interessante Kurven im Hilbertschen Raum. *C.R. (Doklady) Academy of Sciences URSS (N.S.), 26*, 115–118.

Kirichenko, L., Radivilova, T., & Bulakh, V. (2019). Machine learning in classification time series with fractal properties. *Data, 4*, 5.

Kroese, D. P., & Botev, Z. I. (2120). Spatial process simulation. In V. Schmidt, (Ed.), *Stochastic geometry, spatial statistics and random fields* (pp. 396–404). Lecture notes in mathematics. Springer.

Kulkarni, V. G. (2009). *Modeling and analysis of stochastic systems* (2nd ed.). CRC Press.

Lalley, S., & Mykland, P. (2013). *Lecture note statistics 313: Stochastic processes II,* Spring. https://galton.uchicago.edu/~lalley/Courses/313/.

Lawless, W. F., Sofge, D. A., Venayagamoorthy, G. K., Hillson, R., & Abubucker, C. P. (2009). A physics of interdependence for human-robot-machine organizations. In *Proceedings of the 2009 IEEE International Conference on System of Systems Engineering, SoSE* (pp. 1–9). IEEE.

Lawless, W. F., Rifkin, S., Sofge, D., Khrennikov, A., Jaeger, G., Scholsshauer, M., & Weihs, G. (2011). An Ab initio solution of interdependence: Social organization with first principles. In *Advances in Quantum Theory, Proceedings of the International Conference on Advances in Quantum Theory,* pp. 80–85.

Lawless, W. F. & Sofge, D. (2012). The mathematics of aggregation, interdependence, organizations and systems of Nash equilibria: A replacement for game theory. In *Procdings of the AAAI Spring Symposium,* pp. 34–41.

Lawless, W. F., & Sofge, D. (2013). Trust and interdependence in controlling multi-agent multi-tasking autonomous teams. In *Proceedings of the AAAI Spring Symposium,* pp. 44–45

Lawless, W. F., Moskowitz, I. S., Mittu, R., & Sofge, D. (2015). A thermodynamics of teams: Towards a robust computational model of autonomous teams. In *Proceedings of the AAAI Spring Symposium,* pp. 31–38.

Lawless, William F. (2015). The physics of interdependence, social uncertainty relations, and incompleteness. *Journal of Engineering Science and Technology Review, 8*, 72–78.

Lawless, W. F. (2016). The entangled nature of interdependence: Bistability, irreproducibility and uncertainty. *Journal of Mathematical Psychology, 78*.

Lerche, Veronika, & Voss, Andreas. (2018). Experimental validation of the diffusion model based on a slow response time paradigm. *Psychological Research, 83*, 1194–1209.

Mandelbrot, B. B., & Van Ness, J. W. (1968). Fractional Brownian motions, fractional noises, and applications. *SIAM Review, 10*(4), 422–437.

Moskowitz, I. S., Lawless, W. F., Hyden, P., & Mittu, R. (2015). A network science approach to entropy and training. In *Proceedings of the AAAI Spring Symposium,* pp. 44–51.

Navarro, D. J., & Fuss I. G. (2009). Fast and accurate calculations for first-passage times in Wiener diffusion models. *Journal of Mathematical Psychology, 53*(4), 222–230.

Peng, L., Sun, H., & Xu, G. (2012). Information geometric characterization of the complexity of fractional brownian motions. *Journal of Mathematical Physics, 53*.

Pishro-Nik, H. (2014). *Introduction to probability, statistics, and random processes*. https://www.probabilitycourse.com. Kappa Research LLC.

Bhattacharya, R. N., & Waymire, E. C. (1992/2009). Stochastic processes with applications. *SIAM Classics in Applied Mathematics, 61*.

Ratcliff, R. (1978). A theory of memory retrieval. *Psychological Review, 85*(2), 59–108.

Ratcliff, Roger, & Tuberlinckx, Frances. (2002). Estimating parameters of the diffusion model: Approaches to dealing with containment reaction times and parameter variability. *Psychonomic Bulletin & Review, 9*(3), 419–481.

Ratcliff, Roger, Smith, Philip L., Brown, Scott D., & McKoon, Gail. (2016). Diffusion decision model: Current issues and history. *Trends in Cognitive Science, 20*(4), 260–281.

Resnick, S. I. (2002). *Adventures in stochastic processes*. Springer.

Ross, S. (1988). *A first course in probability* (3rd ed.). Macmillan.

Schondorf, E. (2019). *The wiener measure and Donsker's invariance principle*. The University of Chicago Mathematics REU. http://math.uchicago.edu/~may/REU2019/.

Segovia, J. E., Fernandez-Martinez, M., & Sanchex-Granero, M. A. (2012). A note on geometric method-based procedures to calculate the hurst exponent. *Physica A, 6, 391*, 2209–2214.

Shevchenko, G. (2014). Fractional Brownian motion in a nutshell. In *International Journal of Modern Physics: Conference Series, 7th Jagna International Workshop* (Vol. 36), pp. 156002-1–156002-16.

Sigman, K. (2015). *IEOR 6712: Notes on Brownian Motion I*. Karl Sigman.

Voss, Andreas, Rothermund, Klaus, & Voss, Jochen. (2004). Interpreting the parameters of the diffusion model: An empirical validation. *Memory & Cognition, 32*, 1206–1220.

Voss, Andreas, & Voss, Jochen. (2008). A fast numerical algorithm for the estimation of diffusion model parameters. *Journal of Mathematical Psychology, 52*, 1–9.

Voss, R. F. (1988). Fractals in nature: From characterization to simulation. In H. Peitgen, & D. Saupe, (Eds.). *Chapter 1 The Science of Fractal Images*. Springer.

Wang, Yu-Zhi., Li, Bo., Wang, Ren-Qing., Jing, Su., & Rong, Xiao-Xia. (2011). Application of the Hurst exponent in ecology. *Computers and Mathematics with Applications, 61*, 2129–2131.

Wiener, N. (1923). Differential space. *Journal of Mathematical Physics*, pp. 132–174.

Wiese, K. J. (2019). First passage in an interval for fractional Brownian motion. *Physical Review E, 99*, 032106-1–032106-20.

Wiese, K. J. (2020). Private communication.

Chapter 12
Human–Machine Understanding: The Utility of Causal Models and Counterfactuals

Paul Deignan

Abstract Trust is a human condition. For a human to trust a machine, the human must understand the capabilities and functions of the machine in a context spanning the domain of trust so that the actions of the machine are predictable for a given set of inputs. In general, we would like to expand the domain of trust so that a human–machine system can be optimized for the widest range of operating scenarios. This reasoning motivates the desire to cast the operations of the machine into a knowledge structure that is tractable to the human. Since the machine is deterministic, for every action, there is a reaction and the dynamics of the machine can be described through a structural causal model to enable the formulation of the counterfactual queries upon which human trust may be anchored.

12.1 Introduction

The purpose of this chapter is to close the semantic gap in the development of structural causal model (SCM) knowledge representations of deterministic systems in order to better enable human–machine team interactions. The semantic gap that we are concerned with is that which exists between the measurement of the process as a restricted set of random variables within a Cartesian histogram coordinate frame and its representation as an SCM. The semantic gap is minimized for the measured phenomenon through maximizing Shannon's mutual information between measurement and representation while applying Occam's razor in the elimination of redundant and spurious information. The SCM maximizes the bias-corrected, pairwise mutual information between nodes and allows that redundant nodes may be subsumed into joint random variables. By maintaining a common reference throughout the construction, the trap of false comparisons is avoided while the informational integrity of the model is maintained.

Codebook information serves as an extensible reference frame for data reduction. Because independent sources of information are additive, the semantic gap is always

P. Deignan (✉)
Lockheed Martin Corp., Bethesda, MD, USA
e-mail: paul.deignan@lmco.com

© Springer Nature Switzerland AG 2021
W. F. Lawless et al. (eds.), *Systems Engineering and Artificial Intelligence*,
https://doi.org/10.1007/978-3-030-77283-3_12

less than or equal to the information content of the measurements that are not encoded into the SCM. While saying nothing about the semantic gap between the individual's understanding of the phenomenon and its expression in this mathematical information framework, it can be seen that the maximization of mutual information between the SCM and measurements can be achieved by identifying a source causal signal and subsequently forming a structure that seeks to maximize the capacity of information flow. This is the theme of the development of the SCM which, on consideration, can be seen to be equivalent to the minimization of total noise in the directed paths of cause–effect actions and the tendency to create bijections wherever possible in the linkages of the graph. Both factors endow the resultant SCM with counterfactual capabilities.

This chapter is organized as follows: In Sect. 12.2, the framework for SCM construction is presented. In Sect. 12.3, it is shown how information-theoretic techniques can be applied without bias across a fixed set of random variables for SCM construction. Next, in Sect. 12.4, the main result is presented for the construction of SCMs. Finally, in Sect. 12.5, other methods of SCM construction are discussed as they relate to the method of Sect. 12.4. The chapter concludes with summary remarks.

12.2   Information-Theoretic Framework for SCM Construction

Typically, machine data is collected over uniform time-steps with measurements of selected physical aspects of the machine taken synchronously at a specified frequency. The resulting data structure is often a couple of hundred columns wide and tens of thousands of rows in height over any run. Over a month, for one machine, it is common that gigabytes of such tables are recorded. Yet, since a full exposition of the dynamics of a machine would require orders of magnitude more measurements than is commonly available, the problem is to reconstruct a useful model of machine operation from partial information. Predictions from partial information are then a matter of clever inference but may be made less so if the machine states can be localized by a decision tree of command signals and their proxies and if a priori information of machine dynamics can be admitted into the invariants of the model. One principal invariant is the causal relationship occurring over the pathways of the machine control loops. In order to incorporate this unidirectional information, simple data associations are insufficient—a modeling methodology that goes beyond the expression of data association is needed.

A structural causal model (SCM) is a directed acyclic graph where the nodes are identified with random variables and the edges with a causal relation between the connected variables. Consider the structural causal model of Fig. 12.1 where the random variable X is the source node and the random variables Y and Z are sink nodes. In the absence of a driving intervention, the signal at X is exogenous

Fig. 12.1 Structural causal
model with the possibility of
node aggregation

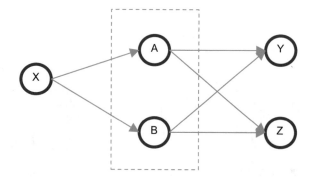

"noise" and the signal at A is a function of X and unmodeled noise, N_A; i.e., $X = N_X$ and $A = f(X, N_A)$. This estimation is, of course, an approximation of the situation where there may be no strict functional relation between the measured random variables, a common situation in practice even when modeling deterministic systems since there is no guarantee that the dynamical system manifold is unfolded in the measurement space. In such cases, models built on measures of central dispersion often give extremely poor approximations; instead, the search is for patches of local coherency in the measured space to reconstruct. These regions can be found by information-theoretic measures.

Shannon's mutual information is a measure of the degree to which a bijection can be made between sets of random variables being related. Entropies of random variables add as set-theoretic unions and intersections. If the mutual information between sets of random variables is equal to the lesser of the total entropies of the union of sets being related, the relation has a one-to-one correspondence for that lesser set of random variables. If mutual information between sets is less than this amount, then to the degree to which the mutual information is proportionate to the total entropy of the union of random variables a limited bijection exists. If the covering of entropies between sets is partial, then the mapping between the sets of random variables of the relation is partial as well. Note that in the case where only functions are allowed for the mapping, it is even more likely that the relation will tend to be approximate rather than exact. The benefit of using mutual information as a measure of association between variables is not only that it serves as a measure of the strength of any possible bijection, but specifically because it may not be known in which direction the causal relation applies a priori.

Now consider again Fig. 12.1 which clearly shows the possibility that random variables A and B may be two different measurements of the same physical aspect of the phenomenon and hence candidates for aggregation by Occam's razor. The decision to aggregate A and B can be determined by whether or not the joint mutual information, $I(A, B; \#)$ is greater in each case than the sum of the individual components of mutual information of A and B, respectively, between each linked variable ($\#$). If it is greater, then the pair A, B should be aggregated. If not, they should remain separate.

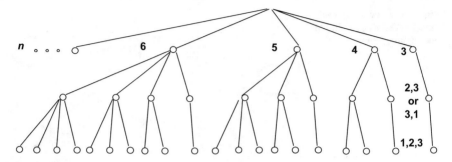

Fig. 12.2 Branch-and-bound indexing scheme for components of optimal joint mutual information

Obviously, the number of combinations of joint and pairwise mutual information calculations to be made can become excessive for a system with hundreds of random variables. However, only the maximum mutual information estimates are of importance in the potential paring of a particular random variable, so it makes sense to conduct these calculations at the onset of SCM construction for every random variable in the set of construction up to the level of grouping that is initially envisioned.

The optimal combination of pairwise and joint mutual information combinations and values can be had at each level of jointness through the application of a branch-and-bounding algorithm. This algorithm assures the return of optimal values at each level of calculation for a typically small fraction of the total potential combinatorics. The indexing scheme of the branch-and-bound algorithm is shown in Fig. 12.2. For a random variable Y and a target set X of cardinality n at a level of cardinality k of m, a simple bounding condition follows from information-theoretic inequalities:

$$I\left(X^{(m)}; Y\right) \le I\left(X^{(m-k)}; Y\right) + \max_{\Omega} \sum_{i=1}^{k} \left\{ I\left(X^{(m-k)}; Y\right) - I\left(X^{(m-k)} \setminus X_i; Y\right) \right\}, \{X_i \in \Omega | i = 1, 2, \ldots, n\}.$$

Note that as the length and depth of combinatorics grows, the remaining potential increments in joint mutual information diminishes. Therefore, if an unbiased threshold of significant mutual information can be established a priori, this algorithm may be made even more efficient through the rejection of combinations beyond the threshold of significance.

12.3 Assessing and Correcting for Bias in Information-Theoretic SCM Construction

Consider the system identification of a phenomenon as an encoding process. A representation of the measured phenomenon with minimal descriptors is, by Occam's razor, considered likely to be invariant and accurate within the language of the codebook. While the frame of reference of a physical phenomenon in our individual understanding is a composite of unstructured and semi-structured assumptions, it is necessary to formalize its representation in order to make inferences. Therefore, let our frame of reference for the purposes of this discussion be a Cartesian coordinate frame of uniform partitions in each dimension over the space of measured random variables of the phenomenon. Within this space, it is possible to construct histograms as estimates of the joint probability density function and to apply probabilistic measures for inference given, of course, that we admit mathematical knowledge into the framework, *ceteris paribus*.

Note that the reference frame itself has a quantifiable amount of information in its description. The list of reference items for the temporal encoding of the phenomenon is called the "Codebook" and its information content is called codebook information (CI). Here, the explicit CI is the partition entropy of the measurement space. Again, the mathematic information used to operate on the data structure of the codebook is not being quantified as it and other similarly useful external information is not being attached in any sort data structure-dependent manner and so should not induce bias. In embedding measurements of the phenomenon within the space, the information content of the data appears as both an artifact of the measurement process, for instance, in the number of synchronous measurements taken and as information relevant to the phenomenon. It will be necessary to account for each source of information separately if inferences are to be made between differently sized datasets.

Entropies associated with independent factors are additive (by the definition of independence). The phenomenological entropy (PE) is the information of the phenomenon that might be achieved ideally by measurement within the space of phenomenon-dependent random variables. The estimation process can be thought of as a compression of the PE where, by the data processing inequality, the estimated phenomenological entropy (EPE) will be less than or equal to the PE. The idea here is that the estimation process should comport with Occam's razor and take on no spurious artifacts of the estimation process itself. Without circumscribing knowledge of the phenomenon, the estimation method is designed by the maximum entropy principle. In the absence of prior knowledge of the distribution, the direct frequentist counting of events within intervals is the simplest method of estimation. A uniform partition is a maximum entropy partition in respect to the partition itself. In other words, if the prior information derived from an examination of the data is that there will be k parts of a partition correspondent to the structure of the EPE, the uniform partition uses the least additional information to establish how those parts should be configured.

A uniform partition structure does not necessarily maximize phenomenological information per bin since there is no assurance that the structure of the distribution of the phenomenon will be equivalent over any range of bins. However, again since a uniform partition is a maximum entropy partition, any other partition structure can be described as a restriction of a uniform partition over segments of the range of the distribution. Therefore, a uniform partition is a feasible starting point in a recursive search for an optimal nonuniform partition. Also, it might be mentioned that as with mathematical knowledge, knowledge of the physics of the process may impact the SCM reconstruction process within the reference frame. The point here is that since the purpose of the model is to facilitate the prediction of future measurable actions, that this information is in effect already part of the long-term dynamics within the reference frame. The incorporation of the knowledge of physics as it applies to prediction is simply a shortcut in the long-term mathematical development of the model from data within the reference frame and, therefore, does not violate the data processing inequality.

The problem of bias correction for finite data and partition entropy is the same as that of the problem to find the optimal partitioning. For any fixed set of data, N, of an estimate, it is possible to optimize the number of uniform bins, k, so that the codebook information for each random variable dimension reveals the most phenomenological entropy of a particular dimension, H, in reference to a uniform distribution of the same construction; i.e.,

$$k = argmax\left(H_k^N - H\right),$$

where the partition entropy is calculated as

$$H_k^N = -k \cdot \sum_{x=1}^{N} \left(\frac{n_k^x}{N}\right) log\left(\frac{n_k^x}{N}\right).$$

By the binomial distribution, each data point has a probability $1/k$ of being within a bin where x is a counting variable of the number of combinations assuming a uniform distribution

$$n_k^x = \binom{N}{x}(1/k)^x (1 - 1/k)^{(N-x)} I_{(0,1,\ldots,N)}(x),$$

where $I_{(0,1,\ldots,N)}(x)$ is the indicator function.

The remaining issue is the selection of dimensions in which to construct the SCM. While it is tempting to include all measured dimensions, this would be a mistake since spurious measurements are known to increase the variance of estimates. Also, since the dimensions are tied together by a deterministic process, it cannot be assumed that the dimensions are independent. The first step in dimensionality reduction is the elimination of any random variable that falls below the threshold of structure as measured by some fraction of the difference between the optimal bin estimation of entropy and the uniform partition entropy. However, there is another approach that is not only exhaustive but also efficient. In this alternative approach, model reconstruction begins in low dimensionality and explores the space of measurement using simple pairwise comparisons.

In using low-dimensional model constructions, estimated variances are minimized and the combinatorics are more manageable. The criticism of the potential nonoptimality of iterative methods is weaker if the measures of association used to determine the model space do not preclude potential correspondences that might arise later in the model construction process. This consideration is another reason to utilize information-theoretic metrics of association for model space determination as these measures are not only general as relations but also generic in terms of many-many relations that might later be exploited by local functional models. Local regions of high mutual information are regions where robust input–output mappings may be best estimated.

12.4 Construction of SCM for Counterfactuals

Unlike other associative model structures, the SCM is designed to allow for interventions—where a specific modification can be made at a node or edge. The most common intervention is to set the value of a node and then to examine the upstream or downstream effects of the intervention in that specific case. The ability to intervene springs from the assumption that the mechanism of action is independent of its cause. A counterfactual is an intervention on an effect with the values of the associated noise distributions for cause and effect fixed at an experienced or hypothesized value. Counterfactuals allow up to examine the causal implications in the presence of a "What if?" circumstance. Thus, the ability to pose counterfactuals gives SCM representations an important ability to inform outside of the natural flow of passive observations. This ability is particularly important in the case of high risk or reward occurrences. Since these are the situations that are of greatest concern, it is precisely these instances, the understanding of which, either make or break the bonds of trust.

For counterfactual queries to give precise answers, the functional cause–effect relation should be one-to-one; in contrast, many-to-one functional relations may yield ambiguities. Since physical relations are naturally one-to-one, the presence of many-to-one functions in the model is generally due to imprecisions in the modeling effort. These can be corrected through restrictions to the domain or the addition of intermediate mechanisms. In all cases, the use of functional relations in SCMs should incorporate as much physical knowledge as pertinent. Relations that are built from data alone should always be suspect for the presence of hidden variables in the causal chain which can be discovered either through localization of the regions of operation or by more thorough data collection efforts. Each causal path of an SCM should be complete and with sufficient reach to cover all modes of operation.

While the application of SCMs focuses on actions in cause–effect pairs, the construction of the SCM given here is centered on information. Ultimately, all inferences of cause–effect relations are drawn from observation, so it is with the modeling effort that the emphasis is on maximizing the explanatory power of the model through identification of the pathways of maximal information flow. Since the model is designed to be modular, this search is distilled into finding the maximal mutual information associations between random variables. This search can be done efficiently for the bias-corrected combinations of random variables using the branch-and-bound method of Sect. 12.2 up to the depth of potential aggregation of co-acting random variables. This search level may be set through a heuristic where the depth, m, requires approximately 10^m measurements for adequate estimation.

As it is allowed to take "shortcuts" in the application of physical knowledge of the system (as long as the shortcuts lead to a model that abides by Occam's razor), an algorithm for the system identification of SCMs may be laid out in steps with each step marking the point in the process where a priori information might play a part in the construction. The algorithm follows a growth-pruning scheme since information redundancies cannot be known until all potential pathways of causal action have been explicated. The coherency of causal relations is enforced as the linkages are evolved up to a common threshold of information significance as mentioned in Sect. 12.3. An optimal structure might be declared by weighing the complexity of the SCM and the level of informational significance.

1. Determine maximum adjusted entropy binning of each variable
2. Link pairs of variables by maximum bias-corrected pairwise mutual information
3. Determine directionality by first principles or shifted max MI (limit set by false nearest neighbors)
4. Check for fan out by joint MI and reiterate as necessary

The first step uses the bias correction in the calculation of entropy for fixed N with a line search over k to find the uniform bin size that reveals the maximal structure of the density function of the random variable. The reasoning is that structure in the density function is likely to be due to dynamic basins of attraction around operating points in the causal chain. The absence of structure is a uniform density function or maximum entropy. The optimization is done as a difference of entropies between the finite data uniform density and that of the random variable. The value of k that produces the maximum difference is taken as the optimal binning width for all subsequent calculations and the correspondent partition entropy is used as the bias-correction factor for the comparison of entropies. Note that a correspondent partition entropy can be calculated for all joint entropies and mutual information estimates. On inspection of the results of the line search, it is possible to make binning width adjustments should salient features require fine local adjustments. Also, it is possible to combine adjacent bins with no or few measurements for nonuniform partitions.

The second step creates the edges between random variables in order of adjusted mutual information between the variables as determined by a comprehensive first-level calculation of bias-corrected mutual information using the branch-and-bound algorithm for all variables of Sect. 12.2. Edges are connected in order of maximal bias-corrected mutual information with only one edge between variables. Connections proceed to be made until the lower threshold of relevant mutual information is reached. This threshold may be set upon consideration of the completeness of the SCM skeleton and the aim of the modeling and data collection efforts as mentioned in Sect. 12.3.

The third step determines causal directionality through the aid, but not exclusion, of time-shifted mutual information comparisons. Mutual information should obtain a maximum when the time-shifting of the variables is in the causal direction at approximately the physical transport lag between cause and effect. The false nearest neighbors algorithm can be used to bound the search space of time-shifts. Note that loops are not allowed in a directed acyclic graph when making causality determinations.

The fourth step is a check on the uniqueness of path connections to an individual node and synthesizes the results of the previous two steps to enforce Occam's razor by aggregating variables that are co-acting. All combinations of connected nodes to a referent node should have individual pairwise mutual information values that more than the sum to the joint mutual information values by an amount greater than the threshold of significance. Binning optimization and mutual information calculations should be re-run in all cases where random variables are aggregated. Should any nodes be aggregated, the construction process is reinitiated with the new aggregated nodes treated as a single random variable.

It should be mentioned that the process of system identification is critically dependent on the ability to make good estimates. Machinery operates over specified modes that can be segregated and for which data can be aggregated to improve estimates. The immediate benefit is that the spurious variables, which may be active in other modes, can be removed from the estimation process if they are not instrumental in the modes for which the model was built. The other immediate benefit is that data becomes denser from the localization and can support estimates with lower variability. Structural causal models should be constructed for each major operating mode with logic to switch between modes, preferably derived from machine command signals. In the absence of sufficient command signals, the primary measurements might be clustered to form the modes. However, the clustering process is again limited by partially measured dynamics and spurious dimensions, so care should be taken to make use of as much physical information as might be made available.

12.5 Notes on Related Work

The incorporation of causal ideas into system identification has perhaps always existed among engineers and physicists, however, in the age of big data analytics, this connection has been overshadowed by advances in brute-force statistical and data-mining methods. The preeminent leader for the reemergence of causality as a central consideration in modeling for big data analytics has undoubtedly been Judea Pearl who has published and argued extensively on the topic for the past 30 years. Pearl's methodology for inferring causality from data has been expanded by Bernhard Schölkopf and his colleagues specifically on the topic of the development of SCMs from data.

While many others have contributed to the problem of identifying SCMs from data, the works of Pearl and Schölkopf are landmarks in the consideration of the potential benefits of alternative methods as presented in this chapter and will therefore be discussed here. The development of SCMs from data is acknowledged by both authors to be an open field of study and neither author proposes that SCMs can be in all cases uniquely constructed from data alone. This claim is in agreement with the presentation of this chapter as the only claims made were that the information-theoretic-derived SCM models were useful and that the method of derivation is tractable—no claim is made that the methodology is optimal or complete in any sense of the word.

In the case that there may be latent variables, i.e., that the collected data is incomplete for the phenomenon for which the SCM is to be constructed, Pearl (2009) modifies his inductive causation (IC*) algorithm with the limitation that the end product is not guaranteed to be a directed acyclic graph since some adjacent nodes may have indeterminate causal relations. The first portion of the IC* algorithm attempts to identify sets of variables upon which a certain pair is conditionally independent to test the proposition that the nodes are linked.

The remainder of the algorithm attempts to resolve directionality of linkages such that the directionality of the inferred causality is consistent across the graph based on the notable assumption that if a variable is dependent on both of the tested nodes which are otherwise unconnected, then it must be that the variable is a collider for the pair, i.e., that causality is in the direction of the pair being a cause and the variable is the effect. There is some sense in this assumption if one presumes that the random variable set of measurements does not include multiple measurements of the very same aspect of the underlying phenomenon. In big data analytics, however, this assumption is not necessarily valid; hence, it is very possible that the resolution of causal directionality through consistency may be unproductive.

There are other serious problems with Pearl's IC* algorithm as a practical tool. Perhaps the most significant is that the algorithm proposes to construct a causal model from a set of variables for which there is no guarantee of any sort of association in physics or in mathematics other than that a stable probability density function (pdf) is assumed. This assumption is, of course, not one that tends to be valid for partial sets of physical measurements. The other seminal deficiency of the method is that the combinatorial search for conditional independencies in data measured is intractable. In statistics, the probability density functions (pdf) are not known, but rather estimated from the data. Indeed, if an assumption of the form of a pdf were feasible, then there would likely be a great deal of a priori information related to causality for which the algorithm specifically avoids assuming. And finally, the estimate of these pdfs would likely be made in a dimensionality for which it is extremely unlikely that finite data could support.

Nonetheless, it should be seen that the virtue of Pearl's approach is in laying out the theoretical foundation for the construction of an SCM from a mere probabilistic density function. In other words, the algorithm is pedagogical and not necessarily meant to be used in practice with actual measurements, but fits in nicely with Pearl's narrative in his argument for the utility of causality as an important augmentation of simple data association and which complements Pearl's exposition of the case for constructing SCMs as a guide to critical thinking.

The approach of Schölkopf [in Peters et al., (2017)] and his colleagues is to augment and fill out Pearl's exposition. The fundamental tool they have used is the principle of independent causal mechanisms, i.e., that the SCM has a modularity such that the probability density functions (pdfs) of the causal variables are independent of the pdf for the conditional pdf of the mechanism of the effect. Additionally, Schölkopf and his colleagues explore the cases of assumed model structures and the case of having only finite data for the SCM estimation. Rather than present a comprehensive algorithm, various tools and conditions are given as aids to causal exploration. In the end, it appears that Granger causality is preferred for directionality identification, a sensible use of the time-series ordering present in dynamical systems. The obvious conclusion from a review of this work is that the identification of causal structures is an active area of research with no certain preferred approach much less a clear definitive answer.

12.6 Summary

An information-theoretic method has been presented for the construction of structural causal models that seeks to maximize the information capacity throughout the model from source to sink node and, in so doing, to increase the tendency for bijections in the functional links. The resultant model may be used to satisfy counterfactual queries and should be as transparent as possible in its performance to enhance human understanding. In this construction, a method for generating bias-corrected mutual information estimates was provided together with a branch-and-bound algorithm for optimal joint mutual information determination. Finally, it was noted that it appears that the current state-of-the-art in SCM identification is an open area of research such that some of the techniques presented in this chapter may be useful for further consideration in light of the difficulties for robust model formulation uncovered in the works of Pearl and Schölkopf.

References

Pearl, J. (2009). *Causality: Models, Reasoning, and Inference* (2d ed.). New York: Cambridge University Press

Peters, J., Janzing, D., & Schölkopf, B. (2017). *Elements of Causal Inference: Foundations and Learning Algorithms*. Cambridge, MA: MIT Press.

Chapter 13
An Executive for Autonomous Systems, Inspired by Fear Memory Extinction

Matt Garcia, Ted Goranson, and Beth Cardier

Abstract We explore an executive function that performs adaptive, introspective reasoning for autonomous systems in challenging situations. This chapter presents a definition of the problem using cartoon examples for electronic warfare and submarine surveillance. A case study of neural processes in therapy for Post-traumatic Stress Disorder (PTSD) is discussed; PTSD provides both a second modelling challenge and an architectural inspiration for executive reasoning. The main body of the chapter is towards a technique for working with virtual and physical agent models in mixed human/machine systems. The architecture supposes a second-sorted reasoning system with complementary reasoning power over situations, influences and unknowns.

13.1 The Problem

In general, our most powerful solutions work best when the future is much behaved like the past and well behaved in other ways. Current techniques deal poorly with non-linear or non-ergodic futures, or their simpler presentation as unexpected outcomes. Additionally, we require a critical mass of facts, or data in the case of machine learning (ML). Unknowns flummox our systems: when key facts are missing or essential causal influences have unknown actors (Pearl, 2000). Many applications

M. Garcia
Northeastern University, Boston, MA 02115, USA
e-mail: m.garcia@northeastern.edu

T. Goranson (✉)
The Australian National University, Canberra, ACT 0200, Australia
e-mail: ted.goranson@anu.edu.au

B. Cardier
Eastern Virginia Medical School, Norfolk, VA 23507, USA

Trusted Autonomous Systems DCRC & Griffith University, Brisbane, Queensland 4111, Australia
e-mail: beth.cardier@griffith.edu.au

© Springer Nature Switzerland AG 2021
W. F. Lawless et al. (eds.), *Systems Engineering and Artificial Intelligence*,
https://doi.org/10.1007/978-3-030-77283-3_13

have these characteristics, including some that military users cannot ignore (Devlin, 2009, 2011).

Autonomous systems were supposed to be a foundational solution to these problems, especially in their mixed human/machine embodiments where the machine elements are highly heterogeneous, include virtual machines, and internal challenges. In practice, the increased complexity of coordinating opportunistic aggregations of these elements in *unexpected environments* is daunting.

We suppose that adding a second layer of reasoning to these systems will mitigate many of the operational challenges. The first reasoning system discovers and reasons about the world with current techniques. A new, second reasoning system reasons about the first at a higher level and its effect on the world. We shall suggest that using 'situations' as a defining concept for this second system can address the problems of unknowns, non-ergodicity and inscrutable influence.

One way of defining the problem is illustrated in Fig. 13.1.

The shaft is a reasoner. For simplicity, we have drawn one shaft, but the typical system would have many in a complex fabric, where shafts merge and separate, as in Fig. 13.2 below. The plane is a situation the reasoner encounters. A naïve view would have the shaft be algorithmic code and the plane the data that it encounters, but we want to include intent, context, ontology and world axioms in our situations, whether implicit or completely unknown. A reasoning system can be a traditional reasoner, or from the extended classes of simulators, mixed human and learning systems. The complex interaction of how they interact with and change each other is of interest. A novelty is that we explicitly model the situations as a collection of sets and categories where the categoric representations allow extended and introspective reasoning.

Our problem can be graphically illustrated in Fig. 13.3, which simply displays the types of situated challenges we wish to address. To make our characterisations universally applicable, we shall assume the situations in the figure and their state changes are representable in layered directed graphs.

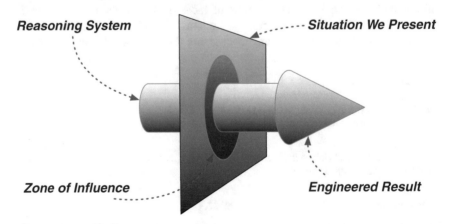

Fig. 13.1 Reasoners and situations

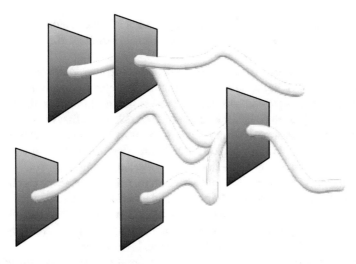

Fig. 13.2 Example branching

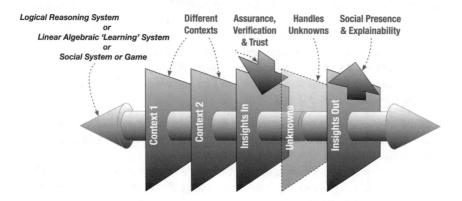

Fig. 13.3 Different situational challenges

From left to right in Fig. 13.3, we have:

(Labelled Contexts 1 and 2) We must deal with multiple situations, each with distinct character. Often this is simple ontological mismatch, but we will include more fundamental axiomatic divergence. Special challenges are presented when a context is a 'machine learning' context where ontologies are externally applied in one of several 'explainable AI' strategies. If constrained to the ontology problem, this one is at least well-studied if still far from resolved.

(Insights In) Next over is trust and verification, shown with an arrow pointing inward to denote a user's insight for an auditable confirmation, in general and specific reasoner/situation combinations that can confirm suitable levels of trust, assurance or verification depending on the requirements. In each of these domains (verification, assurance and trust), different solutions have emerged that are workable within constraints. Our extended vocabulary of uses in mixed autonomous systems, cyberwar, and unconventional reasoners sometimes; however, shrink these solved domains beyond a useful threshold.

(Unknowns) Our use cases often encounter situations where information is incompletely known, deliberately spoofed, misinterpreted or simply not there. We focus on *influence*, so we need situation models that capture all of the influential elements/agents/processes with their specific effect. We are as likely to have elements that singly or in aggregation have unknown effects as we are to encounter an effect that has no known cause. In some respects, this is our reference problem if we subsume everything under an 'effect modelling and aggregation' umbrella.

(Insights Out) Finally, we have the situation drawn with an arrow coming out of the situation to denote machine-dominated situations that need to present coherent, navigable results with affordances for human user interaction. When these situations themselves are generated from mixed human–machine systems and/or they have to present a human-like presence, the requirements become demanding.

In each of these cases, we will propose a common strategy of abstracting elements into a suitable type system for category theoretic reasoning. This approach presents a novel solution that should in many cases work in parallel with piecewise solutions to the above problems using reasoner or context elaborations. An example is a solution for trust in simple autonomous systems (Jacovi et al., 2020). In this approach, insights from explainable AI have been repurposed for explication as 'contracts' published for examination by a client or its administrator.

A common model of these processes has fact (or data) structures and operations. We suggest adding an element of 'situation' that:

- contains facts that are known and those that are not yet known but have influence;
- is interchangeable with 'fact structures' depending on context, where context is also a situation; and,
- contains process-typed fact structures that can be instanced as operations, either retrospectively (this is what got us here) or projectively (this will contribute to a future space of situations).

With this added multifaceted element, we can reason with arbitrary introspection about effects, futures and unknowns as described below.

13.2 Moondoodya, a Novel Electronic Warfare System

Here is a fictional embodiment we will come back to as an example. The system is an active electronically scanned array (AESA) radar using a synthetic aperture. As a class, these consist of many independent transmit-receive modules, typically connected by a single computer. With some coordination, the array can receive and send complex directional signals. By analysing the signals it receives, it can often determine a great deal. These systems are a significant component of the modern

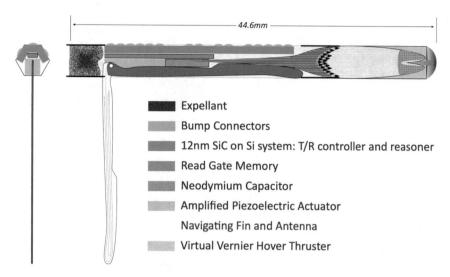

44.6mm

- Expellant
- Bump Connectors
- 12nm SiC on Si system: T/R controller and reasoner
- Read Gate Memory
- Neodymium Capacitor
- Amplified Piezoelectric Actuator
- Navigating Fin and Antenna
- Virtual Vernier Hover Thruster

Fig. 13.4   An example transmit receive module

defence force, and a candidate for advanced human/machine autonomous systems once vexing barriers from formal underpinnings are addressed.

The more dispersed over a large area the transmit-receive elements, the more sensitivity and directional control it has. Among the several uses of these systems is electronic warfare (EW), constituting the most complex use among several others. A typical EW function will be to encounter a signal by passive or active means, determine its nature and intent, and then by various devious means work to thwart that intent. In the general case, these systems talk to or control action by others, for example to control kinetic actors. But in our example, we only receive and emit signals in an EW context.

Needless to say, the sophistication of such systems is in the central processor and the training it has received. However, say we have a high speed missile attack against a ship, and we need a large temporary array some distance from the ship. It needs to only operate for a few minutes, but has to be much larger (more dispersed) than can be connected to a single powerful computer.

Our solution is an autonomous system of physical agents that consist of transmit-receive modules where each has a local computer, power and enough rocket propellant to stay more or less fixed in space for a few minutes. Figure 13.4 shows the design of a single unit which is about the size of a thick matchstick.

Figure 13.5 shows how multiples of these can be packed for delivery by a 50 calibre machine gun, 5 inch naval ordinance or in an existing canister system that can disperse 18,000 + elements in a 70 × 70 × 50 m space.

Nulka[1] is an existing EW system that is launched on attack from a ship (Gambling et al., 2013). Using a rocket engine, it hovers behind the ship and uses a single

---

[1] An Aboriginal word for 'be quick'.

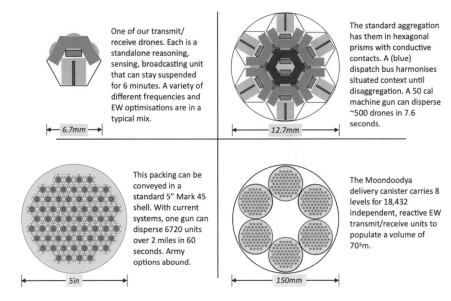

One of our transmit/receive drones. Each is a standalone reasoning, sensing, broadcasting unit that can stay suspended for 6 minutes. A variety of different frequencies and EW optimisations are in a typical mix.

6.7mm

The standard aggregation has them in hexagonal prisms with conductive contacts. A (blue) dispatch bus harmonises situated context until disaggregation. A 50 cal machine gun can disperse ~500 drones in 7.6 seconds.

12.7mm

This packing can be conveyed in a standard 5″ Mark 45 shell. With current systems, one gun can disperse 6720 units over 2 miles in 60 seconds. Army options abound.

5in

The Moondoodya delivery canister carries 8 levels for 18,432 independent, reactive EW transmit/receive units to populate a volume of 70^3m.

150mm

Fig. 13.5 Transmit receive module packing

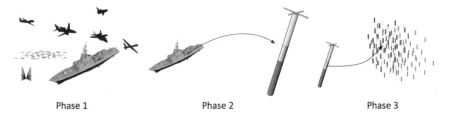

Phase 1   Phase 2   Phase 3

Fig. 13.6 Three phases of moondoodya

processor and antenna to lure a missile away. It used to work well. Moondoodya[2] replaces that with an autonomous system. In phase 1, the ship is advised of an attack. All of the 18,000 processors are connected together and to the shipboard system and its cloud. Some information about the threat is loaded into the Moondoodya canister. In Phase 2, the canister is launched from the ship, taking 9–16 s to get on station. During this time, all the processors act as one and potentially receive updates from the ship, perhaps by wire. In Phase 3, the units are dispersed. Figure 13.6 illustrates the sequence.

The processors separate at contact bumps (light green in Figs. 13.4 and 13.5), and we are left with a huge, mostly homogenous autonomous agent system. (The differences among elements are their hardwired frequency optimisations.) The combined system uses what it knows at release to listen and interpret what is going on with

---

[2] An Aboriginal (Barngarla) word for 'all at once'.

current adversarial threats that are designed to be inscrutable. The system has to figure out the game, and fool or flummox the missiles somehow. It is a remarkable, shifting game of life and death; we count on the adaptive nature of our system and its broad capabilities to send the right signals.

The challenge is that the 18,000 or so units in the system have to collaborate by implicit reasoning. They are completely isolated in space. There is no time or capability for explicit communication or direct collaboration of any kind. These units have to adaptively reason not only about what the adversary might do and how to affect adversarial reasoning and control processes, but they have to do the same thing for all of their sibling units, every one—including those that break or go rogue.

For each processor, situations to be captured include what it thinks are the salient features of situations it believes to be influential or indicative and passively communicate resulting intent to siblings. This communication will take into account what the sender thinks that sibling believes is the situation of the adversary(s), what it believes the aggregate will recommend, and what it needs to do.

We as the EW operator will have to characterise these intents and effects in sum, and run a large number of distributed simulations to advise the executive so that the emergent behaviours are faster and more effective than with a single unit. This 'training' can continue up to the explosive separation. What we are hoping for is the ability to cleverly respond to unknown adversarial profiles.

We like this fictionally constructed example because we can assume all of the agents are identical, with no privileged information or role. Explicit collaborative communication is completely eliminated, throwing all of the influences into inferred situations. The external trigger (the adversarial missiles) is explicit across the system.

Using our situation-centric model, we can characterise what situations the systems and components need to consider. Table 13.1 lists these. Each unit needs to reason about what to do to support the system's activities elsewhere in the list (as situations), and each of these must maintain models of the adversary further to the right. All of these are situations; most of them contain unknowns as we move from top to bottom in the table. Many of these must have and use models of the others.

13.3 PTSD Fear Extinction

Post-traumatic Stress Disorder (PTSD) is a rewarding condition to study for our purpose. It is epidemic in the military, including among non-combatants. PTSD is common in the civilian population as well (Kirkpatrick et al., 2013); we expect an explosion of COVID-19 induced PTSD cases both from the disease and its countermeasures, and from an expected refugee crisis exacerbated by COVID-19 (Shevlin et al., 2020). We know the best way to treat PTSD is by encounter therapy (Hoyt & Edwards-Stewart, 2018), where the initiating event is resituated safely. But skilled therapists are scarce and each case is unique. If we had better models of the influences entailed in individual PTSD cases, we might generate useful virtual reality toolkits for treatment of 'Fear Memory' (Nieminen, 2016).

Table 13.1 Moondoodya situations

WHAT WE NEED TO KNOW ABOUT OURSELVES	
AS A UNIT	**AS A SYSTEM**
How to support =>	Who & Where we present ourselves
	Who & Where we are protecting
	Our Deception Activities
	Our Detecting/Uncloaking Activities

WHAT WE NEED TO KNOW ABOUT THEM

What is their Kinetic Intent

What is their EW Intent

   How to defeat their Deception Activities

      Stealth

      Decoys

      Projected Profiles

   How to defeat their Uncloaking Activities

      Non-Target Probing Queries

      Out of Scope Behaviour

PTSD impairs about 5% of all adults and 20% of police and military personnel worldwide. It is implicated in most cases of substance abuse, depression, and suicide. The drug cost for serious mental illness is AU$150b/year and is the fasted growing pharmaceutical sector. So there is utility of a readable, accurate cognitive/neural signal model as an application, but the primary attraction for us is that it involves notions of agent, information flow and effect that inform the way we perform situated reasoning. Our rationale for this examination is that whatever paradigm we employ in systems like Moondoodya must be similar in key respects to how we relate situations to decisions. The reasoning for this is explored in a previous study on executive type systems (Goranson & Cardier, 2013). The understanding is that these systems are intrinsically mixed human–machine systems and core abstraction principles must be shared between the human and machine 'hardware' for shared ontology and logical foundations.

Therefore, the account of PTSD pathology here is superficial. The initiating event happens in the world is cognitively captured and consciously recalled. Deeper in the brain, other structures contribute to the disorder. Figure 13.7 illustrates the high-level processes. A patient brings a unique psychological profile to the encounter (1) and has a traumatic experience (2). He/she forms a memory of the event (3)

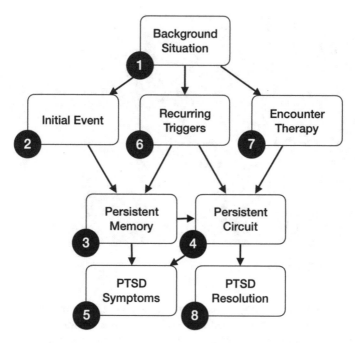

Fig. 13.7   Sequence of PTSD

with associated neural circuits (4). PTSD symptoms result (5). Trigger events may reinforce and deepen the disorder (6). Encounter therapy resolves the PTSD's 'fear memory' (7) and allostasis is achieved (8). We focus on the functions in the light blue box, straddling that cognitive/reasoning boundary.

Figure 13.8 tracks what happens in the brain (Sanford et al., 2015). We are not really concerned with PTSD details beyond this high level. The pink and purple connections are neural circuits among different areas. The key dynamic is the purple circuit. An event is perceived in the usual way, and a memory is formed in the Prefrontal Cortex. Meanwhile, the same event is perceived by the Amygdala, which triggers an initial alert mechanism. Because the Amygdala is alert, it prevents the circuit of Frontal Lobe, Hippocampus, and Amygdala from resolving. That circuit persists through the disorder. Other signals deep in the brain are activated; the primary result is that sleep is deprived, and rapid-eye movement (REM) enabled dream resolution is prevented. Secondary symptoms result that can be life threatening. The disorder is resolved by revisiting the event in a non-threatening situation, resetting the Amygdala's alertness trigger and allowing the primary circuit to resolve.

The relevance to our immediate problem is that there are two distinctly different neural systems at work. The neural processes in the prefrontal cortex are the model used when the term 'artificial intelligence' was devised more than a half century ago. This system interacts with the world, perceiving, reasoning, learning and forming memories. This system does not use logic, nor any algorithmic equivalent, but we

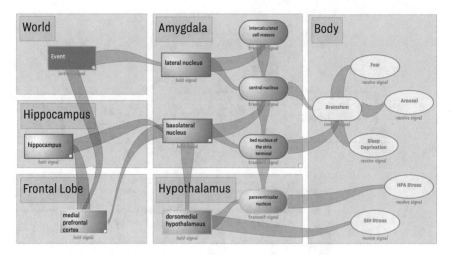

Fig. 13.8 Major PTSD circuits

do create logical statements when describing reasoning. Neural networks in the machine-learning sense have essentially nothing to do with brain neurons. Yet, we can readily map the processes of cognition, reasoning and memory to the computational model devised by von Neumann. That model is used by every computing device (Goldstine, 1980).

von Neumann also was the first to demonstrate that set theoretic foundations are inadequate to model the world (Birkhoff & von Neumann, 1936). This lack of capability is a significant problem because set theoretic methods, in logic, linear algebras, and algorithms are what we are stuck with for essentially everything in the agent systems we have illustrated in Fig. 13.3.

Figure 13.9 illustrates the types of neural processes in PTSD, and of course, most reasoning that reaches from the world to bodily mechanisms. A similar study of how olfactory neural regeneration is affected by experience and memory reveals the same dynamic (Goranson & Cardier, 2013). In this illustration, we are simplifying by omitting the influence of the Vagus Nerve and gut microbiome, but in the discussion that follows, register them as additional 'blue blobs.'

In the figure, the rectangle is our reasoning system and our red blob the memory in the conventional sense. The combination of event, history, genetics and so on plus the memory constitute the situations of Figs. 13.1 and 13.3. The oval and its two associated 'blue blobs' are something quite different. Neurons are involved, but they are physically distinct and with different signals. Memory of sorts is involved, but more like intuition operating on an evolutionary scale; these are denoted in blue. Recent discoveries may indicate that the physical conveyance of synaptic material is fundamentally different. In our 'red' systems, the mechanism is chemical. The 'blue' is genetic.

The blue blobs are altogether different from the red, being more instinctual and more like influence templates. This oval/blue system has evolved over eons, built for

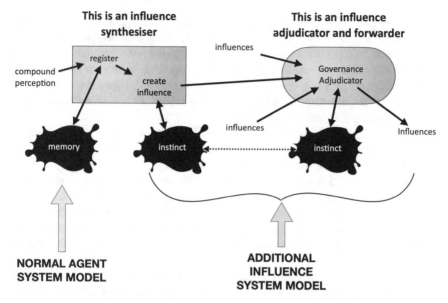

Fig. 13.9 Different neural abstractions

survival purposes and adapted to work in a self-aware collective system. We have labelled type A those that influence the rectangular agents and their red blob artefacts. Some of these may have some character that can be ontologically sorted, but probably not much. Type B on the right is more ephemeral and affect blue blobs only. If we were emulating this system, Type B centric situations could not be captured by any conventional agent or machine learning system. It is this second reasoning system that we reference in our approach.

We are not emulating a brain any more than ordinary AI or ML does. But we will use representational conventions informed by the way our minds work where we can because it should assure that human–machine integration is better, and that our goals for ontic registration are better achieved. (In previous work we have made the case that ontic phenomenology, meaning 'world-inspired', has to inform the type system of an introspective reasoner.)

We think we can approach building an abstract executive reasoner, using such a pragmatic metaphor and distinguishing between two types of memory with some simple mathematical tools, still emerging.

13.4 A Mathematical Approach to Executive Abstraction

An influence on our approach to this second-sorted reasoning executive harkens back to the original von Neumann challenge to find a class of 'geometric logics' that could complement the logic machines use to allow fuller modelling of the world, including the challenges of Fig. 13.3. In the last decade, this challenge has apparently been successfully addressed by Abramsky and Coecke at Oxford (Coecke, 2012).

Their motivation is different than ours: they address the von Neumann challenge on its mathematical merits, while their application domain is to support better models for physicists. Their work is within a tradition of using category theory to model influence spaces, allowing them to immediately inherit a body of implementation techniques using functional programming.

Elsewhere, we have described in some detail our use of categoric sorts, situation theory, narrative coherence, and ontic pragmatism (Goranson et al., 2015). In this chapter, we add two implementation strategies.

In short, we build a synthetic categoric reasoning system to reason in parallel with the legacy in the target domain. So far, we have mentioned cognitive/neural modelling for PTSD and implicit autonomous systems for electronic warfare. This is a two-sorted system where results in one are reflected in the other, each reasoning to complement the other. The second sort is populated with categoric abstractions as described below.

We use modern situation theory (Devlin, 1995) to relate the categories to contexts and influences. Within situation theory, we use a narrative coherence to order and bound the category instances and capture influence. Narrative coherence is the strongest connection between the second sort and the neural model as captured in the red and blue blobs.

The type abstraction strategy is described below; but the type instance strategy is ontic pragmatism. That is, we follow mainstream convention but do it deliberately, using real world metaphors where possible.

13.5 'Effect First' Modelling

A novelty we use is modelling 'backwards' from effect to cause. The technique is simple. Figure 13.10 illustrates what we are dealing with.

On the left, we have a stack of four boxes, collectively modelling an agent system. For us, these are autonomous agents with an introspective layer. From the bottom, we have the set theoretic model of the agents and their logic. Next up, also set theoretic, as indicated by the red colour, is what is known. This includes both the state of the system, the results as controls, and the working memory that in an old fashioned system may be beliefs, desires and intents. These two elements represented by the lower two boxes are the 'first sort' in a two-sorted system, and in most cases are legacy decisions.

Above that in blue are the two elements of the 'second sort', of executive reasoning. These two have a similar relationship to each other. The colour code shared with the red and blue blobs is deliberate. This blue pair models influence and influence coherence (and dissonance where it exists).

The stack on the left is before a state change and that on the right after. We have used these to denote on the left the *complete space of all the designs of an*

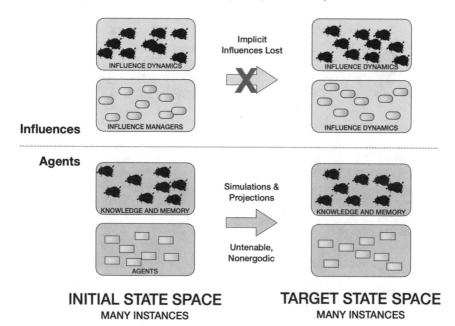

Fig. 13.10 Modelling from agents

agent system in an initial state space, and the column on the right being all possible results. The right hand column is the 'effect space.' Today, the way agent systems architects design systems is they start with the left, assuming they know what will result. (The influences are implicit; current methods cannot formally model them now.) We currently use different techniques to assure the desired effect space within a desired level of confidence. We can simulate and prune outcomes. We can *train* constrained systems to produce outcomes based on inputs. If everything is known and made explicit, we can apply formal verification systems. If it is just trust that we are worried about, we have some suitable emerging techniques (Jacovi et al., 2020), but only if everything is well defined and behaved.

But all of this is costly in interesting cases. Generally, it is imprecise, and in any case, anything known about influence is lost. Losing the influences is particularly harmful for designers of military forces and strategies. The goal in modern military systems is to work in multiple domains (Diplomacy, Information, Military and Economic) to modify influence to thwart an adversary or move one across the line from conflict to competition. The whole goal is an effect space with designed influence.

Figure 13.11 shows what we can do instead of the analytical flow of the previous figure.

Step 1: If we have suitable models in the stack, we can 'go backwards' by modelling the universe of outcomes we want. Specifically, we can engineer the states that constitute a desired outcome. The user can impose whatever mix of values

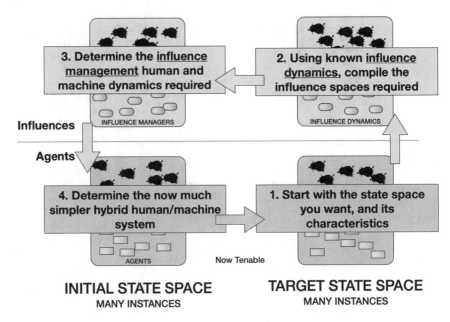

Fig. 13.11 Effect space modelling first

are desired, including predictable trust, ergodic profile, degree of novelty or simple effectiveness. These will be shown as graphs or lattices in the examples below.

Then in step 2, we move to the influence space that produce the desired effects. Influence is a more subtle and complex notion than cause, as it includes indirect effects, changes in interpretation, retroactive logic, and composed salience. Elsewhere, we have addressed methods to model influence at this level (Cardier et al., 2017).

This blue influence space in Fig. 13.11 is the executive for autonomous systems of our chapter's title.

Step 3 is the simplest of the four steps because modelling influence at all requires modelling the entire generative history. The best implementations tend to use reactive functions, so the entire history is available and potentially browsable if we have any successive state. Moving from a model of influences of a resulting effect space through the causal history of influences to a beginning state space is trivial.

If the first three steps are performed, then compiling an agent system design space is not difficult. We will still have to work with tradeoffs to select the right balance for satisfying the design criteria, including those of Fig. 13.3. But we will have a validatable formal path to outcomes or outcome probabilities.

13.6   A Closure Embedding Strategy

A significant problem we face is that generally we have to take the world as we find it. The tasks we can support with current methods have profound limits, and only work with cleanly tailored environments and representations. To a large degree, the examples in this chapter are simplified for the purpose of exposition, but we are in the business of building real systems for defence and industrial settings.

Real systems and information in these domains are challenging in the ordinary way from legacies: bad decisions and poor housekeeping; and from design omissions that have accepted implicit assumptions without examination. But even in the cleanest of domains, the information and code is not friendly to abstraction into our second sorted executive system for influence reasoning. So we need a flexible toolbox of abstraction methods to coordinate our red and blue systems.

This is not a data and ontology abstraction exercise. We have to abstract the *dynamics* (and potential dynamics) of a system. If we perform the effect space analyses noted above, we have to abstract every possible system design in the space; this requires that we ensure that the reasoning in the new (blue) reasoning space is closed. That is, whatever allowable operations we perform over our newly typed system has to produce results in the same type universe.

One reason we perform this abstraction is because we want to extend the power of autonomous agent systems to work with unknowns, specifically unknown influences or partly understood influences from unknown causes. As it stands, agent systems— or any von Neumann system—cannot do well in an open world. 'Open' means that it contains elements and relationships outside of the defined or known scope.

We suggest a clever abstraction strategy that allows openness in the base system by abstracting into a second executive reasoner where operations are closed. But that means we have to worry about abstracting and closure at the same time. Our solution is in the next three figures.

Our goal is to host our second sorted reasoning calculus in monoidal categories; we have justified that elsewhere (Goranson, 2020). One reason is that this is what the Oxford lab does in addressing the von Neumann challenge; we provide its underlying formal mechanics.

Figure 13.12 illustrates Types of Closure.

In Fig. 13.12, solid black arrows represent closure from the source to the target, e.g., the arrow from P_S to C_S 'adds in' what is necessary to turn P_S into a Cartesian closed category. When such a closure exists, it is unique. Dashed black arrows represent the use of a canonical product structure. These appear only with targets in the M domain (in yellow), since there are potentially many monoidal structures on a given category. In this diagram, we are always using the product structure on hand, but there are often other paths to get to M.

The hollow dashed arrow on the right represents that if we perform enough closure operations to get to T, and it is determined if we have landed in the E domain. Put another way, not every topos can be made into a model of synthetic differential

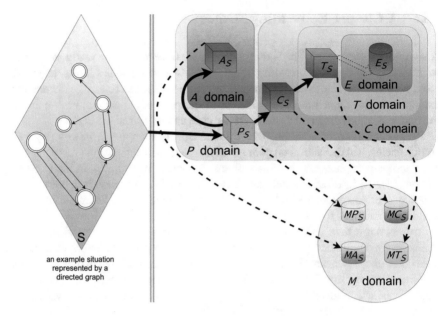

Fig. 13.12 Types of closure

geometry. A more practical way to leverage the E domain is by embedding our situation S into known models of synthetic differential geometry (SDG).

Each domain is inhabited by a specific type of category:

- P for categories possessing products.
- A for abelian, categories whose objects act like groups or vector spaces, where homology happens.
- C for Cartesian closed, categories whose internal logic serves as a model for the lambda calculus.
- T for topoi, categories whose internal logic is intuitionistic. These categories arise from sheaves on topological spaces.
- E for synthetic differential geometry, certain topoi that are well adapted to model physical/mechanical scenarios.
- M for (symmetric) monoidal categories, whose logic is linear and used to model quantum dynamics.

Closure operations should be used when we are trying to generate a context for reasoning that depends most heavily on an initial seed situation that we are interested in. Each closure operation is unique (when it exists).

Figure 13.13 illustrates a set of concurrent operations for embedding or abstracting.

Solid red arrows represent embedding of the situation S (read: directed graph) into a category in the relevant domain. The diagram can be misleading. In reality, there are many arrows here; not only might a graph be embedded into a particular category

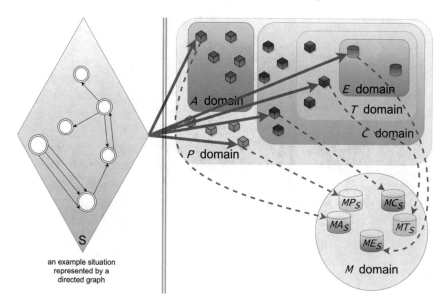

Fig. 13.13 Embedding strategies

in many different ways, but the category itself could be one of many categories. Dashed red arrows represent the use of a canonical product structure that depends on the embedding that precedes them. These appear only with targets in the M domain since there are potentially many monoidal structures on a given category. In this diagram, we are always using the product structure on hand, but there are often other paths to get to M.

In Fig. 13.13, starting from our simple graph model of S, we can potentially embed into any domain we please. This contrasts with the closure situation since each nested domain is dependent on the last.

The drawback of this approach is the potential for 'noise' to drown out the salient features of S that an analyst might want to pay attention to. The benefit is that if the analyst has a particular idea of what tools to use or if S exhibits certain features that are native to a certain domain, she can examine several test cases together rather than being forced to work with something as narrow as closure.

The possibilities addressed in Figs. 13.12 and 13.13 represent only a single step from the base sort (our red boxes in Figs. 13.10 and 13.11), and the executive sort in the blue boxes.

Embeddings should be used when a situation at hand is not necessarily the primary focus of the analyst. At first, coherent use of embeddings will rely on some sort of 'instinct.'

Figure 13.14 illustrates how these can work together.

Thin, faint dotted arrows shown in the colour of their domain represent functors between categories native to that domain. In this diagram, most all of these are added for effect and have no particular significance at present. Bold, dotted green arrows

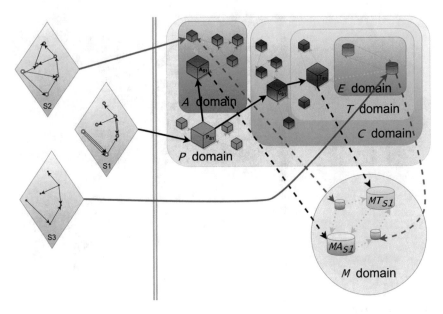

Fig. 13.14 Working together

are also domain specific functors; however, they are coloured this way to highlight their importance as examples of what steps need to be taken in further investigations.

We begin with three situations: (S1) the situation of primary focus, and from a graph theoretical perspective the most complex, (S2) a situation describing what is known about an enemy's intelligence; and (S3) a description of a physical system S1 is dependent on, e.g., a control system for a series of robots executing vision and actuation tasks by using a system of differential equations.

The analyst has chosen to examine both the A_{S1} and T_{S1} while embedding S3 into a topos (in the T domain) and S2 into an abelian category (in the A domain).

There is an abelian functor (possibly 'exact' is enough) between the A_{S1} and the category that S2 is embedded in. This is the green arrow in the A domain. What is the relationship between the green arrow in the A domain and the corresponding green arrow in the M domain? If the functor in the A domain happens to be monoidal, then we have an answer. If not, we have to investigate.

The green arrow going from the E domain to the T domain illustrates an important general point: functors can cross domains, always from more specific to less specific, but under certain conditions in the other direction as well. What are such conditions? Some cases are well documented facts, others require new mathematical research.

The answers to these questions will shed light on how exactly new entities, relations and information in general enter into the structure of where situations naively reside (the RHS). Jointly, the relationships reflected in the functors present in the A, M, T and E domains enrich the structure of our beginning situations.

The broad mathematical problem at hand is to determine how exactly the mechanisms of embedding and closure relate to one another. Less structural, but equally important, we need a way to effectively filter the noise introduced when embedding situations into categories and think about how to start building a model of what an analyst should intuit.

13.7 The Tookoonooka[3] Vortex Collaborative

This fictitious example is more complex, with agents, memory and messages being less conventional. The goal is enhanced submarine detection and surveillance. Usually, this requires a combination of hardware sensors; with some emitting and many others listening. The hardware to support these sensors is expensive and hard to put into the right place (Iqbal et al., 2020).

This system consists of special purpose directed energy (DE) systems aloft, and a fleet of unmanned underwater vehicle (UUVs). With a relatively low-energy long-wavelength pulse, a beam can opportunistically create a vortex in the surface of the ocean (Kleckner & Irvine, 2013). An artist's rendition is shown in Fig. 13.15.

A simple way to use these three systems (DE, Vortex, and UUV) is to have the DE create the vortices as sonic emitters, and the UUVs as listeners. However, once created, these vortices can be sustained for long periods by modulated DE beams of a second kind, creating vortex knots. An example from the lab is illustrated in Fig. 13.16.

These vortex structures are turbulent internally, but the envelopes are collectively sensitive enough to be a listening array for pings generated by both the DE vortex initiators, and the UUVs. Their forms perturb well enough to be queried by the UUVs, which can share information about what is in the sea with appropriate assets. Each vortex tells you very little, but we can support hundreds of thousands of vortices.

In this mode, we get a scalable, cheap detection system across wide areas, but it has no intrinsic intelligence as a system. There is no autonomy in the useful sense. But we can extend the speculative system to make it autonomous at low cost. Supposing that once we create (for pings) and sustain (for listening) the vortices, we modulate the sustaining DE system such that each vortex now contains information.

Information physically flows from the DE emitters, to the vortices, to the UUVs, and back to the DEs. Also, there is an information flow of pings from the created vortices and the returned pings distorting listener vortices. No information physically flows among the vortices as shown in Fig. 13.17. Yet we can consider the vortex cloud an autonomous agent system, reasoning among its members to probe the ocean to discover objects and report results, maintaining situation visibility through fractional awareness. The presumably unmanned drones in the sea and air support communication and remote processing, but are only for support.

---

[3] Tookoonooka is in Queensland, Australia and the location of the planet's largest known impact zone. It is effectively invisible, occluded by geomorphological flows.

Fig. 13.15 Directed energy vortex induction (artist's rendition)

This is a simpler example in some ways, but requires a bit of imagination. We will define the autonomous system as centred on the surface vortices; the fact that the communication and reasoning are handled 'out of a vortex' is not significant. The job of the system is simpler than with Moondoodya: just detect and reveal what is there. We can function as a sonar-based AESA, over a much greater area: one DE platform may support up to 245 km^2; but the physics are constrained: the sonic character of the medium is variable (surface weather, thermals, and fauna); the induced pings will only sometimes be resonant structures; the location and effective capabilities of the UUVs will be essentially random; and the pings are not directed aggregations. We expect most of the identification will be introspective, to pull out the defects and noise of the system.

In this case, referring to Fig. 13.14, S1 may be the state of the objects in the ocean; S2 the intrinsic noise and impediments from the physics, geometry and conditions; and S3 the combined actions from the system to maintain or improve its accuracy.

We have included this example because the system itself is physically irregular and most of the unknowns come from non-entropic process effects.

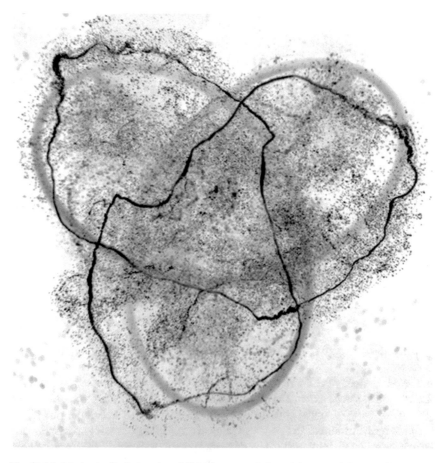

Fig. 13.16 Mechanically induced trefoil hydrovortex (adapted from an image by Irvine Lab, University of Chicago)

To implement each system, we have to take care in three areas that the examples are designed to illustrate.

The first grand challenge is that we are conveying structure across diverse abstract frameworks in real time with engineered loss so that essential relationships are preserved. A fundamental question concerns what the essential elements of that structure are. We are working toward a 'Bletchley Park' level study of symmetries and structure to understand this in the general case. Constraints come from the axiomatic foundations; from the limits of managing the programming and processing computationally; others from the need for intuitive expression; and, finally, we have the aforementioned constraints of ontic phenomenalism.

We believe general principles can be developed in time for next generation systems, hardware and computing paradigms. But for now, we will require that there be a consistent geometric metaphor across the P-A-M and P–C-T-E-M paths in

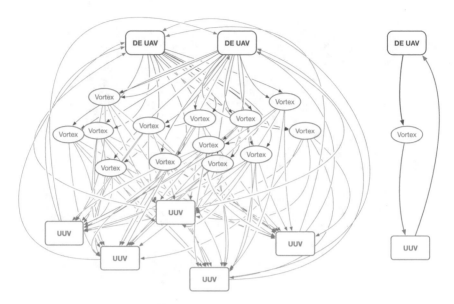

Fig. 13.17 Vortices as a virtual autonomous system

Figs. 13.12, 13.13, and 13.14 that can be modelled (as we have there) as introspective signals.

The Moondoodya example is able to model everything as ordered interference patterns across three spaces. The first is physical space, then we have a computational space (consisting of signals through junctions) and we have a spatially distributed semantic space of intent. In this way, we have cheated by inventing an EW system that can be uniquely implemented by this introspective technique. The Tookoonooka example is a simpler cheat because the geometry in all cases is physical, even the memory is in the geometry of engineered turbulence.

The second grand challenge is similar, but instead of rationalising across the domains of Figs. 13.12, 13.13, and 13.14, we rationalise across the translations with the arrows. They need to be in a coherent framework separate from the abstraction spaces as the basis of the second introspective layer. All else is implementation. The requirement is that all of the black arrows—the inter-space closure assurance arrows—need to be functorial. This follows from the requirement that the black arrow operations be introspective. Any legal combination of these black arrows has to be able to form an adjoint relation with the relevant component of a P, A, C or T. Mathematically, we assure this by constraining to a single right-adjoint definition, which we may get for free from the programming architecture we choose. We suggest Elixir, which is a version of Erlang. Erlang is a distributed processing paradigm that supports functional programming where messages can be functions. Elixir tailors the foundation to be reactive and suitable for a domain specific language that preserves right adjointness. Elixir in its native form is suitable for the Tookoonooka example. We can engineer and simulate Moondoodya in this environment, but to be implemented it has to be compiled to bare metal using techniques not yet devised.

The final grand challenge is that we have to understand and manage local introspection. We may have to maintain several formal mezzanines on our way to cross-situated two-sorted reasoning. Each step is lossy while granting additional reasoning; that is the nature of abstraction. That means when applying the right-adjointness noted above in a local context for a specific purpose, the situation is bounded to the local space. A simple example might be evaluating a trust model. Intuitively, one should understand that trust is bound to context, and neither commutes nor associates, so an aggregation model of global trust needs yet to be devised. This is an open issue and may require pseudo-functors and bi-categoric references in each abstraction space. Very likely, our research agenda will work from this third grand challenge backwards through the other two by using illustrative examples to implement seemingly impossible autonomous systems.

13.8   Conclusions

We used two fictitiously constructed examples and a neural template to illustrate an approach that leverages a number of ideas to provide unique benefits. The central concept of this chapter is the technique of abstracting into a category theoretic second-sorted executive reasoner in such a way that closure is assured. The result can then be used to reason from effect-space models to engineer systems that can gracefully deal with challenging situations. We presented two. Such situations can present unknowns as agents and influences, require various audits and verification, present navigable interfaces, and harmonise diverse ontologies and types.

Experience with these systems in practice is scant and proofs of concept will be achieved in the next step by critical simulations and small scale tests.

References

Birkhoff, G., & von Neumann, J. (1936). The logic of quantum mechanics. *Annals of Mathematics, 37*(4), 823.

Cardier, B., Sanford, L. D., Goranson, H. T., Devlin, K., Lundberg, P., Ciaverra, R. P. et al. (2017). *Modeling the Resituation of Memory in Neurobiology and Narrative.* Proceedings from AAAI 2017 Spring Series.

Coecke, B. (2012). The logic of quantum mechanics: Take II. http://arxiv.org/pdf/1204.3458v1. Retrieved 6 July 2021.

Devlin, K. J. (1995). *Logic and Information.* Cambridge, UK: Cambridge University Press.

Devlin, K. J. (2009). Modeling Real Reasoning. In G. Sommaruga (Ed.), *Formal Theories of Information: From Shannon to Semantic Information Theory and General Concepts of Information* (pp. 234–252). Berlin: Springer.

Devlin, K. J. (2011). A Uniform Framework for Describing and Analyzing the Modern Battlefield. Feasibility Study 19. https://web.stanford.edu/~kdevlin/Papers/Army_report_0711.pdf. Retrieved 21 Aug 2021.

Gambling, D. J., Crozier, M., & Northam, D. (2013). *Nulka: A Compelling Story*. Canberra, Australia: Defence Science and Technology Organisation.

Goldstine, H. H. (1980). *The computer: From Pascal to von Neumann*. Princeton, NJ: Princeton University Press.

Goranson, H. T. (2020). Adding command knowledge 'at the human edge'. In W. Lawless, R. Mittu, & D. Sofge (Eds.), *Human-Machine Shared Contexts*. London: Elsevier.

Goranson, H. T., & Cardier, B. (2013). A two-sorted logic for structurally modeling systems. *Progress in Biophysics and Molecular Biology, 113*(1), 141–178.

Goranson, H. T., Cardier, B., & Devlin, K. J. (2015). Pragmatic phenomenological types. *Progress in Biophysics and Molecular Biology, 119*(3), 420–436.

Hoyt, T., & Edwards-Stewart, A. (2018). Examining the impact of behavioral health encounter dose and frequency on posttraumatic stress symptoms among active duty service members. *Psychological Trauma: Theory, Research, Practice, and Policy, 10*(6), 681–688.

Iqbal, K., Zhang, M., Piao, S., & Ge, H. (2020). *Evolution of Sonobuoy through History & Its Applications: A Survey*. Proceedings from 17th International Bhurban Conference on Applied Sciences and Technology, Islamabad, Pakistan.

Jacovi, A., Marasović, A., Miller, T., & Goldberg, Y. (2020). Formalizing trust in artificial intelligence: prerequisites, causes and goals of human trust in AI. Preprint retrieved from https://arXiv.org/arXiv:2010.07487v1

Kirkpatrick, D. G., Resnick, H. S., Milanak, M. E., Keyes, K. M., & Friedman, M. J. (2013). National estimates of exposure to traumatic events and PTSD prevalence using DSM-IV and DSM-5 criteria. *Journal of Traumatic Stress, 26*(5), 537–547.

Kleckner, A., & Irvine, W. T. M. (2013). Creation and dynamics of knotted vortices. *Nature Physics, 13*, 229–231.

Nieminen, K. (2016). Internet-provided cognitive behaviour therapy of posttraumatic stress symptoms following childbirth-a randomized controlled trial. *Cognitive Behaviour Therapy, 45*(4), 287.

Pearl, J. (2000). *Causality: Models*. Cambridge, UK: Cambridge University Press.

Sanford, L. D., Suchecki, D., & Meerlo, P. (2015). Stress, arousal and sleep. *Current Topics in Behavioral Neuroscience, 25*, 379–410. https://doi.org/10.1007/7854_2014_314. Review. PubMed PMID: 24852799.

Shevlin, M., Murphy, J., McBride, O., Ben-Ezra, M., Bentall, R. P., Vallières, F., et al. (2020). Posttraumatic stress symptoms and associated comorbidity during the COVID-19 pandemic in Ireland: A population-based study. *Journal of Traumatic Stress, 33*(4), 365–370.

Chapter 14
Contextual Evaluation of Human–Machine Team Effectiveness

Eugene Santos Jr, Clement Nyanhongo, Hien Nguyen, Keum Joo Kim, and Gregory Hyde

Abstract The adoption of human-machine teams is rapidly expanding in many domains such as healthcare and disaster relief. Fueled by novel advances in robotics, artificial intelligence, and other technologies, machines with relatively high degrees of autonomy and self-awareness are being developed to improve efficiency and productivity in complex dynamic environments. The traditional role of machines as human tools is shifting to one where they now serve as human collaborative team partners. Despite this progression, evaluation of human-machine team performance remains ill-defined. In many human-machine team settings, end-users rely on metrics that are insufficient at explaining a team's performance. Explanations are crucial because they help understand a team's operational dynamics and identify the shortcomings that individual agents (human or machine) introduce to the team. To address this explanation gap, we introduce a context-specific interference-based methodology to evaluate human-machine team effectiveness. Interference provides a measure that reflects the cohesiveness and compatibility between the goals of the human and the machine agents. Context is essential as human-machine teams are deployed in various settings. Our methodology relies on using a classifier that is trained to map human-machine team behavior to a set of behavioral attributes that are directly linked to the team's performance. These behavioral attributes provide high-level explanations about the team's observed performance outcome and insights on the mechanism of team interference. To test our methodology, we conduct experiments involving the teaming of humans and scripted bots (machines) in a StarCraft 2 game domain. From these experiments, our classifier achieves an accuracy of 84% in predicting agent behavioral attributes from a set of 18 unique classes. To validate the use of this classifier in our evaluation approach, we compare the Pearson correlation between predicted team win-ratios and observed win-ratios, and we achieve a statistically significant score of 0.76. These results suggest that predicted team attributes

E. Santos Jr (✉) · C. Nyanhongo · K. J. Kim · G. Hyde
Thayer School of Engineering, Dartmouth College, Hanover, NH 03755, USA
e-mail: eugene.santos.jr@dartmouth.edu

H. Nguyen
Department of Computer Science, University of Wisconsin-Whitewater, Whitewater, WI 53190, USA

W. F. Lawless et al. (eds.), *Systems Engineering and Artificial Intelligence*,
https://doi.org/10.1007/978-3-030-77283-3_14

283

reflect the actual team behaviors; hence, we can confidently apply the predicted team attributes to evaluate and prescribe human-machine teams.

Keywords Human-Machine teams · Context · Evaluation · Effectiveness · Interference

14.1 Introduction

The objective of human-machine teaming is to create synergy between humans and machines to outperform either machines or humans if performed by themselves (Bolstad, 2019). This synergy was traditionally achieved by letting machines and humans specialize in tasks that they individually excelled at. For example, machines would specialize in computational, memory-intensive, and repetitive tasks while humans focused on tasks requiring intuition, adaptation, innovation, and creativity. With advancements in robotics and artificial intelligence (AI), machines' capabilities are continually improving, and machines can now perform tasks that were once only dedicated to human operators (Barro & Davenport, 2019; Krach et al., 2008). This development has shifted machines' role as simple tools to human-level collaborative partners (Hoc, 2001; Seeber 2020). With the world's ever-increasing complexity in the age of Big Data (Katal 2013) and AI, humans cannot only rely on their individual abilities, but need to harness machines as teammates in order to boost productivity.

Human Machine Teams (HMTs) are being successfully deployed in different application domains. In healthcare, for example, brain-machine interfaces (BMIs) are being developed to establish functional connections between human brains and assistive devices that restore motor and sensory functions in patients (Lebedev, 2014). In addition to treating patients, BMIs also have potential applications in computer games and autonomous driving (Isa et al., 2009; Biondi 2017). HMTs are also being developed to aid disaster relief after earthquakes, floods, and other natural disasters (Driewer et al., 2005), as these rescue tasks are dangerous for humans. In these rescue scenarios, mobile robots (machines) can potentially be used to navigate dangerous terrain, detect explosions, and lift heavy material that an ordinary human might not handle, whilst humans play a supervisory role to instruct and monitor the robots since they (humans) naturally have superior adaptive and situational awareness abilities. In social media sites such as Reddit, humans augment predictive AI algorithms to help with content moderation. Human moderators provide guidelines and regulation tools which form keywords and phrases that the automated systems use to identify violations. The HMT combination ensures that transparency and acceptable content delivery is efficiently achieved to the intended end-users (Jhaver et al., 2019). HMTs are also useful in many other applications such as virtual assistants, text prediction, and aviation. Given the wide range of HMT applications, our *goal* is to develop an explanation-based HMT evaluation approach that could ultimately be generalizable to these different application domains.

Most HMT evaluation approaches focus on performance-related metrics such as accuracy, coverage, efficiency, and false-alarm rates (Crandall & Cummings, 2007; Elara et al., 2010; O'Connell & Choong, 2008; Steinfeld et al., 2006). These metrics are essential in a team's evaluation process, but they are limited since they do not provide insights into the team's operational dynamics. We consider team operational dynamics to be cognitive interactional factors such as synergy, cohesion, or situational awareness (Cuevas et al., 2007). These factors are often intangible, difficult to quantify, and they typically require users to rely on subjective ratings to estimate them. In this work, we develop a data-driven methodology to incorporate these operational dynamics through reward functions that are computed via inverse reinforcement learning (IRL) using a team's past behavior. Reward functions reflect underlying agent goals and preferences; hence, we apply them to capture unique agent behavior. We map these rewards to high-level behavioral attributes (behA) that are connected to a team's performance metrics. These behA provide insights that will then help to explain a team's performance.

In our evaluation process, *interference* is used to capture a team's interactional processes. Interference occurs when the goals of one agent affect the goals of the other agents (Castelfranchi, 1998). When positive, it boosts a team's performance, and when negative, it degrades the team's performance (Hoc, 2001). Interference is likely to arise due to differences in communication mechanisms, roles, capabilities, adaptiveness, and responsibility between humans and machines. Agents should be aware of their teammates' needs, social hierarchy, and cultural norms. Human agents usually have superior communication and situational awareness, while machines often struggle with these skills (Damacharla et al., 2018; Endsley & Robertson, 2000). In most situations, the human agent takes a supervisory role to understand and allocate tasks to the machine(s) during cooperation (Vagia et al., 2016; Seeber et al., 2020). When the human understands the machine and can fully capitalize on the machine's strengths and abilities, positive interference is likely to occur. However, if the human fails to understand or anticipate the machine's goals, negative interference will likely happen. In this chapter, we perform experiments to examine how these human-machine dynamics interplay in an adversarial video game, StarCraft 2 (SC2). Each human-machine team comprises a human agent and an artificial bot (machine) designed to execute a given strategy. The designated goal for the HMT team is to defeat the default SC2 AI opponent by destroying its units. For the experiments, we use win-ratios (defined as the percentage of wins per game) to measure the performance of an agent, and behA to explain why the agent achieves its performance score.

To analyze interference, we compare differences between the HMT behA and the individual team members' behA (humans and machines). These behA are characteristics that affect how the agent (human, machine, or HMT) behaves; they provide a high-level explanation that allows the interpretion of an agent's expected behavior and performance. Examples of behA could be an agent's speed, computational power, or its number of sensors. Interference may reflect positively in teams composed of similar team members (i.e., sharing similar behA such as athletic ability). For example, Cummings and Keiser (2008), found that more interdisciplinary team members negatively influenced the productivity of their teams. However, it is also possible for team members to possess strikingly different compositions that might complement each other. In our experiments, to study the effect of an individual's behA and determine how they relate to human-machine team interference, we assume that the machine behA are known *apriori* since we design the bots to behave based on predetermined behA settings. Given the challenges inherent in determining a human's behA, both the human and the human-machine team behA are assumed to be unknown. Instead, our approach infers these behA (for the human and the HMT) based on the known machine's behA. We apply a feed-forward neural network classifier to map any agent's (can also be an HMT) behavior to the known set of machine behA. To capture agent behavior, we utilize IRL, first introduced by Ng and Russel (2000), to compute reward functions that reflect the agent's goals and preferences from past demonstrated behavior. In particular, we employ a new IRL algorithm, called the Preferential Trajectory-based IRL (PT-IRL), which finds reward values by discriminating across multiple agents to better differentiate a target agent's reward function.

Our classifier achieves an accuracy of 84% at predicting agent behA which are categorized into 18 classes. In addition, the Pearson correlation between predicted team win-ratios (from the behA) and observed win-ratios was 0.76, and it was statistically significant (p-value < 0.01). This suggests that the classifier is successful at capturing agent behavior; hence, we could use its computed behA to infer explanations on how a team behaved. Our main contribution in this chapter is the development of an intuitive and principled way to analyze teams: by mapping a team to a set of behA, we are treating a team as an individual, which enables us to compare differences between the team and its individual members' characteristics in the form of behA. This treatment helps to provide insights that explain how interference occurred and affected the team's performance.

This chapter is organized as follows: First, we will discuss the related works which explore foundational work on human-machine teams. Next, the background section will cover the concept of IRL and introduce a new algorithm that addresses challenges in existing IRL approaches. The concept of interference will be discussed in this section as well. After the background section, we introduce our technical approach, and describe the series of experiments that were conducted. Lastly, we present our conclusions and possible directions for future work.

14.2 Related Works

In this section, we review related works on the evaluation of team effectiveness for which either human teams or HMTs are assessed. Some literature from disciplines such as psychology, manufacturing, robotics, and AI have examined the concept of team effectiveness. In Hackman's work (1978), the author provides three criteria to assess team effectiveness in organizations. The first criterion is output (or performance)-related, and it states that for a team to be effective, "*the productive output of the work group should meet or exceed the performance standards of the performer who receive/or review the output.*" The second criterion deals with the state of the group as a performing unit, and it states that "*the social processes used in carrying out the work should maintain or enhance the capability of the members to work together on subsequent team tasks.*" Finally, the third criterion addresses the impact of the group experience on the team members, and it states that, "*the group experience should, on balance, satisfy rather than frustrate the personal needs of group members.*" These criteria make intuitive sense, and they are useful in developing benchmarks to achieve team effectiveness. However, the major limitation in practice is that these criteria are often hard to evaluate objectively. For example, in criteria 2 and 3, it is difficult to quantify the social and personal team processes. Our approach uses IRL to capture such processes through reward functions that are computed from a team's behavior, in addition, interference analysis is performed to understand how agent goal interactions occur to yield the effective team behavior.

In most empirical studies of team evaluation, team effectiveness has been assessed through subjective ratings since it is difficult to objectively quantify processes such as cohesion and coordination (Damacharla et al., 2018; Healey et al., 2004; O'Connell & Choong, 2008). In Glickman et al.'s (1987) work, the authors conducted several studies to determine team effectiveness in training Navy teams. They gathered a sample of 13 teams that performed a gunfire support training task, and categorized these teams as either effective or ineffective based on an exam administered during training. In one study, the goal was to determine if there were differences between effective and ineffective teams. They created a list of team effectiveness behaviors that would measure aspects such as coordination, adaptability, cooperation, and team spirit. They then conducted surveys on each team's instructors to rate how their teams fared on the values of the list of behaviors. Results of this survey showed that effective teams exhibited more effective behaviors (66% more) compared to ineffective teams. In a similar line of work, Pagell and LePine (2002) performed a study to find contextual factors that would be predictive of team effectiveness in manufacturing settings. These factors included work design, informal modes of communication, novelty of problems, and trust between team members and management. A sample of teams were collected and categorized as either effective or ineffective based on management perceptions of whether they would increase a firm's competitiveness. From qualitative analysis on the categorized teams, it was found that effective teams operated in environments with an output-based design, higher opportunities for informal communications, more novel problems, and stronger trust between management and team members, compared to ineffective teams. From these studies, it is clear that team effectiveness is improved when team processes, such as cohesion, coordination, and communication, work well within a team. However, the major challenge with these studies is that they are all subjective and qualitative. In more complex teams, it is difficult to fully capture all the elements that impact a team's effectiveness; hence, the team evaluation processes are likely to be weaker.

Our team evaluation process focuses on HMTs instead of human-human teams. Several empirical studies have proposed evaluation techniques for HMTs. However, these often focus on performance assessment, which yields non-generalizable results since HMTs are applied in a wide range of domains (Damacharla et al., 2018; Gombolay et al., 2015; Hoffman, 2019; Wang et al., 2016). For example, evaluating teams on accuracy scores such as false-alarm rates, sensor accuracy and coverage might only be applicable to specific human-robot domains (e.g., rescue robots), but not relevant to other HMT domains such as text prediction, health monitoring systems or our experimental testbed. In our approach, our goal is to provide an evaluation methodology that is generalizable to different HMT contexts by allowing for any desired performance measures. In addition to providing insights about how a team performs, our approach yields high-level explanation behA that we use in the interference analysis.

14.3 Background

In this section, we discuss the background work that lays the foundation of our work including the concept of interference, IRL, and a new Preferential Trajectory-based IRL algorithm.

14.3.1 Interference

Interference describes how, "the effects of the action of one agent are relevant for the goals of another" (Castelfranchi, 1998). In simple terms, interference can be classified as either positive—an agent's action favors the goals of the other agent(s) reinforcing team performance; or negative—an agent's action threatens the goals of the other agent(s) degrading the team performance as in Fig. 14.1 (Hoc, 2001).

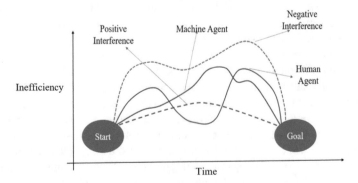

Fig. 14.1 A pictorial view of interference in human–machine teams. Positive interference reinforces a team's performance and negative interference degrades a team's performance

Interference can be further subcategorized as follows (Hoc, 2001): *Precondition*—one agent's activity is a precondition for another agent's activity; *Interaction*—interference due to mutual dependence (interaction leads towards a common goal), and reciprocal dependence (interaction leads to individual goals); *Mutual control*—the task "actually performed by one agent, by reason of responsibility, is also performed, but mentally by another agent for checking purposes"; *Redundancy*—the best available agent performs a task when no agent is allocated to the task. These definitions tend to be more subjective and unbounded, hence for simplicity, we only examined positive and negative interference in the experiments.

14.3.2 Inverse Reinforcement Learning (IRL)

IRL is a process by which demonstrated agent behavior is used to infer a reward function that reflects the agent's underlying preferences (Ng & Russell, 2000). The general framework makes use of a Markov Decision Process (MDP) consisting of a 5-tuple $\{S, A, P, \gamma, R\}$ wherein S represents the state space; A, the action space; $P : S \times A \to S$, the transition function which maps states and actions to states; $\gamma \in [0, 1]$ a discount factor; and, $R : S \times A \to \mathbb{R}$, the reward function which maps states and actions to reward values (Bellman, 1957). Conventionally, MDPs have a well-defined reward function, and in Reinforcement Learning (RL), the goal is to find some policy $\pi : S \to A$, which maps actions to states (Sutton & Barto, 1998). An optimal policy, π^*, is one that maximizes the expected reward over a horizon with respect to R. Optimal policies can be described by their state-action value function, q^*, which is defined in the following recurrence relation:

$$q^*(s, a) = \sum_{s',r} P\left(s', r \middle| s, a\right)\left[r + \gamma \max_{a'} q^*\left(s', a'\right)\right] \qquad (14.1)$$

The q^* function (Eq. 14.1) measures the value of taking an action, a, in state, s. The discount factor γ reflects greedy behavior over immediate rewards (when close to 0) versus distant rewards (when close to 1). IRL shifts the paradigm from RL in that no well-defined reward function is given. Instead, the goal for IRL is to infer R from an agent's observed behavior. This behavior is expressed in the form of trajectories, $t \in T$, where $t = \{s_o, a_o, s_1, \ldots, a_{n-1}, s_n\}$ and n is the length of the trajectory. The transition function P can be estimated from state, action, next state triples (s, a, s') sampled from the agent's demonstrated behavior.

Two emergent strategies exist for inferring R from a set of observations. The first was proposed by Ng and Russel (2000) who formulated a linear program aimed to maximize the sum of the differences between the quality of the optimal action and the quality of the next-best action:

$$\sum_{s \in S} \left(q^{\pi}(s, a_i) - \underset{a \in A \backslash a_i}{\mathrm{argmax}} q^{\pi}(s, a) \right) \tag{14.2}$$

Here, q^{π} simply denotes the state-action value function following a stationary policy π. However, this approach was mostly unconstrained, resulting in many possible solutions (some of which are degenerate). To address the ambiguity of choosing reward solutions, Ziebart et al. (2008) proposed Maximum Entropy (Maxent) IRL which is constrained to match feature expectations while not being committed to any viable policy over another. Maxent IRL assumes that the reward function is a linear combination of the trajectories' feature expectations, f_t:

$$reward(f_t) = \theta^T f_t \tag{14.3}$$

At each iteration, Maxent IRL computes weights, θ, and aims to minimize the difference between the actual observed feature expectations of the original data, and those produced by the current policy. An internal RL step computes feature expectations of the current policy by taking a backwards pass from the terminal state and computing action and state probability masses:

$$Z_{a_i, j} = \sum_k P(s_k | s_i, a_{i,j}) e^{reward(s_i | \theta)} Z_{s_k} \tag{14.4}$$

$$Z_{s_i} = \sum_{a_{i,j}} Z_{a_i, j} \tag{14.5}$$

With Eqs. (14.4) and (14.5), $P(a|s)$ can be determined and in a forward pass, feature expectations under the current policy can be determined. However, Maxent IRL has a slow convergence time and assumes state rewards rather than state-action paired rewards, which may lack expressiveness. Moreover, the primary assumption of Maxent IRL is that rewards share a linear relationship with feature expectations, however, it is possible that states may appear frequently due to necessity rather than being highly rewarding. For instance, consider two regions separated by a fissure, but connected by a bridge. If the goal is to reach the other side, then an agent must always pass through the bridge states out of necessity rather than by desire. Finally, neither described approaches can utilize behavior from multiple decision-makers. These concerns have led us to develop a new IRL algorithm described below.

14.3.3 Preferential Trajectory-Based IRL (PT-IRL)

To address the IRL concerns described in the previous section, we developed a new IRL algorithm, PT-IRL. Our approach yields a single optimal reward solution with rewards at the triple (s, a, s') level and does not assume feature expectations. Moreover, this algorithm uses multiple decision-makers to form constraints that can compare and contrast decision-makers on the fly. For our formulation, we consider a set of trajectory groups, $T = \{T_1, T_2, \ldots, T_L\}$, where each element represents a group of trajectories belonging to an individual decision-maker, and L is the number of groups. Let $\prec$ be a partial ordering over T, such that $T_l \prec T_{l+1}$, for all l. Further below, it will become more apparent what these partial orderings mean, but consider trajectories belonging to T_1 "more alike" to the target decision-maker whose reward function we wish to infer than trajectories belonging to T_2. In past experiments, we have used four unique trajectory groups, where T_1 is the set of decision-makers trajectories, T_2 is the set of synthetic decision-maker's trajectories (produced using a neural network generator), T_3 is the set of all the other decision-maker's trajectories, and, finally, T_4 is the set of synthetic other decision-maker's trajectories. There are other possible ways to organize these sets of trajectories, and the target trajectories may not be necessarily confined to T_1. We distinguish trajectories as belonging to the target or not. Let Ξ be the set of all target trajectories and $\Xi' = T - \Xi$ be the set of all non-target trajectories.

Using the above trajectory groupings, we begin our formulation by describing our expectation function over trajectories. For simplicity and ease of reward explanation, we use a linear expectation. Let $t_{l,m}$ denote the mth trajectory in the lth grouping; then:

$$LER(t_{l,m}) = \sum_{(s,a,s') \in t_{l,m}} P(s'|s, a) * R(s, a, s') \tag{14.6}$$

where $R(s, a, s')$ is a decision variable reflecting the inferred reward for a triple. Note that $P(s'|s, a)$ is determined by taking counts over the raw data, however, because this function represents the world physics, we can take these counts over all decision-makers. For each grouping, T_l, we assign upper (ub) and lower bounds (lb) as:

$$lb(T_l) = \min_{t_{l,m} \in T_l} LER(t_{l,m}) \tag{14.7}$$

and

$$ub(T_l) = \max_{t_{l,m} \in T_l} LER(t_{l,m}) \tag{14.8}$$

We can then define and constrain the spread between trajectory groups for all l as:

$$\delta(T_l, T_{l+1}) = lb(T_l) - ub(T_{l+1}) \geq 1 \tag{14.9}$$

While $P(s'|s, a)$ is the same across all decision-makers, the preferences reflected by $P(a|s)$ counts are not. We distinguish between the target's decision-making function, $P_\Xi(a|s)$, versus the others' decision-making function, $P_{\Xi'}(a|s)$, by taking the counts over their respective data separately. We then further constrain $R(s, a, s')$ by applying:

$$R(s, a, s') = peak * P_\Xi(a|s) + \Delta r_\Xi(s, a, s') \tag{14.10}$$

and

$$R(s, a, s') = -peak * P_{\Xi'}(a|s) + \Delta r_{\Xi'}(s, a, s') \tag{14.11}$$

where *peak* is some positive real-valued number specified by the user, and $\Delta r_\Xi(s, a, s')$ and $\Delta r_{\Xi'}(s, a, s')$ represent fractional reward variances for the subsequence $\{s, a, s'\}$ for the target and non-target decision-makers, respectively. These fractional reward variances are constrained by:

$$|\Delta r_\Xi(s, a, s')| \leq 2 * peak \tag{14.12}$$

and

$$|\Delta r_{\Xi'}(s, a, s')| \leq 2 * peak \tag{14.13}$$

For triples belonging solely to the non-target decision-makers, Eq. (14.11) has a clear negative bias reflecting that the target decision-maker had not yet been observed taking such an action. However, this does not rule out that the target decision-maker should never take that action. Also, for triples existing in both the target and non-target decision-makers, then both (Eqs. 14.10 and 14.11) must be applied. This application forces $\Delta r_\Xi(s, a, s')$ and $\Delta r_{\Xi'}(s, a, s')$ to compromise.

Our objective function is designed to minimize the overall fractional reward variance of the system, whilst finding an R that fits the target. Note that we enforce some discrimination over the decision-makers by forcing a gap between the spread terms (Eq. 14.9). We thereby minimize Eq. 14.14:

$$z = \max(\{\textstyle\bigcup_{(s,a,s')\in\Xi} \Delta r_\Xi(s, a, s')\} \ \cup \ \{\textstyle\bigcup_{(s,a,s')\in\Xi'} \Delta r_{\Xi'}(s, a, s')\}) \tag{14.14}$$

The result of Eq. (14.14) is that the LER should reflect our preferences in the partial order of our trajectory groupings. Because triples can be shared between decision-makers, our objective forces these triples to compromise with minimal variance. This helps prevent corner solutions where tradeoffs are entirely one-sided. Behavior that is "more alike" to the target will be more positively biased than behavior that is not. Also, R will be inferred such that it can provide distinction between the different trajectory groups by means of the LER. It is clear from the formulation that there is no bias towards feature expectations as it is possible to have a frequent triple that is negatively penalized. Moreover, rewards are not marked along the state, but rather along the triple. This approach gives us the expressiveness to differentiate based on $P_\Xi(a|s)$ and $P_{\Xi'}(a|s)$. Finally, our IRL algorithms make use of multiple decision-makers when inferring rewards. This helps to further constrain the problem and discriminate over different decision-making styles.

14.4   Approach

Our evaluation methodology relies on the creation of a classifier that maps agent behavior (individuals or a team) to behA which provide high-level explanations of an agent's performance. When an agent navigates an environment, its behavior (or trajectories) can be complex and difficult to draw quick insights from, hence, we map this behavior to a finite set of behA. Explanations from behA are high-level in the sense that they describe the team(s) in terms that are human interpretable. They are evaluated for their predictive capabilities on performance metrics (such as win-ratios), thus, providing a way to understand an agent's expected performance (see Fig. 14.2b). For example, suppose a soccer club has a series of gameplay videos of a prospective player that it is planning to recruit. From these videos, the club can infer behA, such as the player's average speed, number of fouls, tackles, and goals per game, which gives the club quick and intuitive insights to rate the player. The performance metrics (for example, win ratio) gives a result-oriented description of the agent's success in meeting its long-term objectives. We apply this approach to infer behA that explain the behavior of HMTs.

For a given HMT, multiple agents defined by their respective behA interact together to fulfill the team's shared objectives. During the HMT's cooperative behavior, interference (most likely a non-linear factor) occurs such that the resultant team behavior might not be the average of the behaviors of the team's individual members. To estimate the team's overall performance attributes, we need a classifier that can capture the complex team behavior and model existing non-linearities. This classifier is trained using trajectories of individual agents with known attributes and is then applied to predict team attributes as shown in Fig. 14.2.

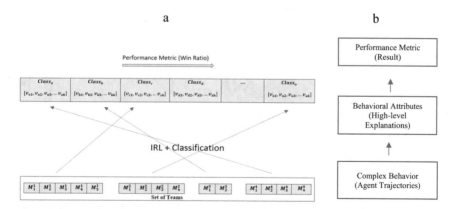

Fig. 14.2 a Architecture of the classifier created to map an agent's (team in this case) complex behavior (trajectories) into high-level performance attributes that define how the agent (team) performs. **b** Behavioral attributes provide a way to explain the agent's (team's) complex behavior from collected trajectories

To train the classifier, trajectories of individual agents with known attributes are gathered. From these trajectories, IRL is performed to obtain reward functions that are expressed as state, action, next state triples (s, a, s'). These reward functions provide a robust way to rate an agent's decision-making steps as it transitions from one state to another during a particular action. Since agent trajectories are often long, cyclic, and non-uniform in size, this poses as a challenge when training a feed-forward neural network classifier that requires uniform inputs (in terms of dimensions). To compress the reward triples, and express them in consistent input form, we train a linear regression model on the inferred triple rewards to obtain feature weights, W, which we use as inputs to our feed-forward neural network classifier. Suppose each state is defined by a set of features, $s = [f_1, f_2, f_3, \ldots . f_k]$, and each action is defined by a set of action features, $a = [\alpha_1, \alpha_2, \alpha_3, \ldots \alpha_x]$. As input to the linear regression model, we use the joint state, action, next state features $((f_1, f_2, f_3, \ldots \alpha_1, \alpha_2, \alpha_3, \ldots f_1, f_2, f_3)$ and the associated reward values (as inferred by PT-IRL). Our intuition is that the weights capture the relevancy over features with respect to the team's or agent's preferences. The reward feature weights are expressed as a function of the particular (s, a, s') triples as shown in Eq. (14.15).

$$Reward \ \ feature \ \ weights = W\left(s, a, s'\right) = W\left(f_1, f_2, \ldots f_k, \alpha_1, \alpha_2, \ldots \alpha_x, f_1', f_2', \ldots f_k'\right)$$
(14.15)

Using the learned reward weights as inputs, we train our neural network classifier to predict a set of known behA. At the individual level, we use (known) machine attributes as a training set and generalize this process for both humans and human-machine teams whose behA are unknown.

With predicted behA at both team and individual levels, the next step is to infer interference from comparing the predicted team behA to the team members' behA. We defined interference metrics for both the positive and negative cases as follows:

Strong Positive Interference (SPI): A situation where the team performance is better than the best individual performer in a team.

$$P_t > \max[P_1, \ldots, P_n]$$
(14.16)

Weak Positive Interference (WPI): A situation where the team performance is better than the average performance of the individuals in a team.

$$P_t > \frac{\sum_1^n P_i}{n}$$
(14.17)

Negative Interference (NI): A situation where the team performance is at most as good as the average performance of the individuals in a team.

$$P_t \leq \frac{\sum_1^n P_i}{n}$$
(14.18)

Agent Influence Vector (AIV): A vector showing how much an agent's individual behavioral attributes deviate from the team's attributes.

$$AIV = \left[\left| b_1^i - t_1 \right|, \ldots, \left| b_k^i - t_k \right| \right] \tag{14.19}$$

The SPI, from Eq. (14.16), shows the perfect case of positive interference for which the team's performance is greater than that of all the team members. In this case, every member in the team benefits from the cooperative behavior. Equation (14.17) which defines WPI, shows another case of positive interference for which the team's performance is greater than the average performance of all the team individuals. In this situation, it is highly likely that most team members benefit from the cooperative activity, however, some may sacrifice their performance by joining the team. In NI, Eq. (14.18), the team's performance is worse than or equal to the average individual performances of its individual members, hence, forming the team is inefficient. As the behA are inherently tied to performance (Fig. 14.2), we use individual and team behA to explain outcomes of Eqs. (14.16)–(14.18) using the AIV metric computed from Eq. (14.19).

From the AIV, the goal is to infer how behA captured at the individual level are significant to the team level's behA. We can infer how much an agent influences the overall team behavior by comparing its behA to that of the team. The smaller the magnitude of the AIV, the more influential an agent is to the team's performance, since the team behA are closer to those of the agent. If a team is performing poorly under negative interference for example, we can use the AIV to identify the agents mostly responsible for that adverse interference (the same analysis would also apply for positive interference). We use the AIV to infer insights on processes that lead to interference (for example, task allocation, and shared responsibility).

14.4.1   Experimental Setup

The primary goal of this chapter is to provide a holistic approach for evaluating the effectiveness of HMTs given the teams' past behavior. To achieve this, we conduct experiments using a python-based StarCraft 2 testbed (BurnySc2, 2016; Vinyals et al., 2017). StarCraft 2 is an adversarial game where players strategically build units to attack and destroy their opponents' units. We set up three types of agents: human players; machines (bots)—scripted python bots; and human-machine teams—combinations of a human and a bot playing together as a team against an AI opponent. We set the difficulty level of the AI opponent to hard (other levels were easy, medium, and very hard), to ensure that the human players would require some decent amount of strategic thinking and effort to successfully win their games. The goal for each agent (human, machine, HMT) was to destroy the default AI enemy by executing a distributed attack (DA) strategy which we created by modifying the distributed workers (DW) strategy (BurnySc2, 2016). The DW strategy requires an agent to build worker units (probes) and power units (pylons), to be able to collect resources (minerals and vespene gas) and expand its bases (controlled areas) to increase resource production. This strategy is relatively weak against the hard AI opponent since it does not attack the opponent; hence, we modified the strategy to enable each agent to build attacking units restricted to voidrays and stalkers (for simplicity). The race settings for the agents were set as the Protoss race, and, for the AI enemy, it was set to the Terran race. The environment for all game plays was the Abysmal Reef which simulates a coral reef. These race settings were arbitrarily chosen and remained constant throughout the experiments. For each gameplay, trajectories were collected as csv files. Each state vector encoded a snapshot of the game units in each particular time instance: $[f_1^1, f_2^1, .., f_{36}^1 | f_1^2, f_2^2, \ldots, f_{47}^2]$; where f_j^i is the sum of the jth feature for the ith agent; where $i = 1$ is a human, machine, or HMT; and where $i = 2$ is the AI opponent.

$$f_j^i \subset [pylon, canon, forge, voidray, stalker, \ldots \ldots, hacthery, lair, \ldots]$$

The action vector encoded the actions that the units were executing in a particular time instance. Each action was expressed as: $[a_1, a_2, a_3, \ldots a_{18}]$ where:

$$a_k \subset [is\_gathering, is\_attacking, \ldots \ldots, is\_idle]$$

Experiments were carried out in three phases:

1. Train a classifier that maps agent behavior (trajectories) to behA as described in the approach section.
2. Create combinations of humans and HMT to execute the given DA strategy.
3. Evaluate the effectiveness of the HMT using interference metrics defined in the approach section.

14.4.2   Training Classifier

The classifier was created to map agent behavior to a set of behA that provide intuitive explanations on how the agent is expected to behave. Eighteen different classes of bots (machines): $\{M_1, M_2, M_3, M_4, \ldots .M_{18}\}$, defined by four behA that were essential in executing the DA strategy were created (Table 14.1). For each bot class, 120 trajectories were collected, and the observed win-ratio (expressed as a percentage) was recorded (see Table 14.1). Each trajectory set was further sub-divided into 30 subsets of size four as in Eq. (14.20). We sub-divided trajectory sets to ensure that computation was feasible for the PT-IRL linear programming algorithm (since we had a large number of trajectories).

$$M_i = \{M_{i1}, M_{i2}, M_{i3}, \ldots, M_{i30}\} where \ i \in \{1, 2, 3, \ldots, 18\} \qquad (14.20)$$

To perform the PT-IRL method, different combinations of target and non-target trajectories were created according to Eq. (14.21). Target trajectories were trajectories

Table 14.1 Attributes define a bot's behavior in executing the DA strategy. These attributes were hand-selected to develop a classifier that would represent the possible range of behaviors any agent would take. They provide explanation insights to the associated performance metric (win-ratio)

Bot (classes)	Attributes				Data collection	
	Probes (Pb)	Pylons (Pn)	Stalkers (Sk)	VoidRays (Vr)	Number of games	Win-ratio (%)
1	5	3	2	6	120	0.83
2	5	3	6	2	120	0.00
3	5	7	2	6	120	0.00
4	5	7	6	2	120	0.00
5	5	12	2	6	120	0.00
6	5	12	6	2	120	0.00
7	10	3	2	6	120	23.33
8	10	3	6	2	120	12.50
9	10	7	2	6	120	17.50
10	10	7	6	2	120	3.33
11	10	12	2	6	120	7.50
12	10	12	6	2	120	5.83
13	20	3	2	6	120	50.83
14	20	3	6	2	120	28.33
15	20	7	2	6	120	53.33
16	20	7	6	2	120	24.16
17	20	12	2	6	120	45.00
18	20	12	6	2	120	29.17

from the bot that we aimed to compute the reward for, and non-target trajectories were collected from other bot trajectories (the PT-IRL algorithm finds a reward function based on separating target from non-target behaviors). For each target trajectory subset, two non-target subsets were arbitrarily chosen to run the PT-IRL algorithm in the following form (target subset, non-target subset):

$$\left(M_{ix}, \{M_{jx}, M_{kx}\}\right) for \quad i, j, k \in \{1, 2, 3, \ldots, 18\}, i \neq j \neq k, where \quad x \in \{1, 2, 3, \ldots, 30\}$$
$$(14.21)$$

Using the input samples generated in Eq. (14.21), IRL was performed and reward functions were obtained. The extracted reward values were converted to reward feature weights using linear regression (Algorithm 14.1). The accuracy of the classifier was 84% using a 33% testing set. Figure 14.3 shows the training profiles of the classifier. The confusion matrix reflects some relative uniformity in the rate of correct predictions across all classes, and the accuracy is relatively high which shows the effectiveness of the PT-IRL algorithm at capturing the complex trajectory behavior of the bots.

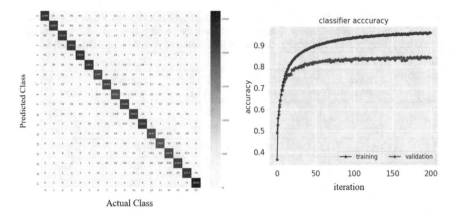

Fig. 14.3 Training profiles of the classifier. The classifier achieves an accuracy of 84% in classifying the attribute class of a given bot's behavior

14.4.3 Human and Human–Machine Teams

Although the behA of the machine agents (bots) were known beforehand, the behA of the human and the HMT were unknown. Our goal in this experiment was to apply the classifier to determine the behA of the human and the HMTs. We conducted a user study that comprised of three human participants $\{H_1, H_2, H_3\}$ who had prior experience with StarCraft 2. We estimated these participants to be intermediate players since they could win the game against easy AI opponents but not against hard opponents (at a time before the experiments). Instructions needed to execute the distributed attack strategy (DA) were provided to the players, and they independently played a sample of games.

After collecting the human trajectories, we created combinations of HMTs. For each HMT, one bot and one human agent played the same game simultaneously with the goal to defeat the AI enemy. For analysis, we randomly selected four bots: M_2, M_{13}, M_9, and M_6 (Table 14.1). A total of 12 human–machine teams defined as: $\{(H_i, M_j)\}$ for $i \in \{1, 2, 3\}$, $j \in \{2, 13, 9, 6\}$. Table 14.2 shows the number of games collected, and the win-ratios for both the human and the HMT teams.

After collecting the trajectories, we applied the classifier to infer behA for the human and the HMTs, and the results are shown in Table 14.3 as a percentage of the number of predictions for each behA class. We computed the predicted behA using two different methods:

$Attributes_{max}$—selects behA from the class with maximum percentage of predictions.

$Attributes_{aver}$—computes behA as the average sum of the product between all class behA vectors and the number of predictions per class.

To evaluate how predicted behA ($Attributes_{max}$ and $Attributes_{aver}$) reflected agent (humans and HMTs) behavior, we compared predicted win-ratios using two methods:

Table 14.2 The collected set of trajectories for the human and the HMT teams

Agents	Human only			Human and M_2			Human and M_{13}			Human and M_9			Human and M_6		
	H_1	H_2	H_3	H_1	H_2	H_3	H_1	H_2	H_3	H_1	H_2	H_3	H_1	H_2	H_3
Number of games	15	19	25	15	15	15	20	20	20	19	18	16	11	17	14
Win rates (%)	20	36.8	56	6.7	0	40	60	15	65	10.5	55.6	42.9	0	0	43.8

Table 14.3 Attribute predictions from the classifier as a percentage of the number of predictions per trajectory sets

Team	Predicted class number																	
	17	16	15	14	13	12	11	10	9	8	7	6	5	4	3	2	1	0
H_1	2.55	0.09	4.62	1.24	1.71	0.00	0.16	0.38	5.84	1.58	42.82	1.83	0.23	0.52	7.51	5.57	18.23	3.13
H_2	0.54	0.32	0.65	1.08	4.21	1.46	2.91	0.97	6.76	5.77	8.77	1.69	29.53	6.67	16.52	10.73	15.75	5.66
H_3	1.98	0.25	0.52	0.09	4.24	0.61	0.81	0.81	4.96	3.11	12.89	2.84	7.75	10.43	23.21	10.71	13.05	1.74
(H_1, M_2)	3.11	3.29	19.38	7.46	9.74	3.00	8.56	6.18	8.52	9.08	9.22	4.26	1.94	0.72	0.36	0.56	4.06	0.56
(H_2, M_2)	2.88	1.13	17.06	7.39	14.36	2.23	7.12	1.83	11.76	6.54	7.41	0.92	2.14	2.61	6.58	4.44	3.13	0.45
(H_3, M_2)	1.33	0.05	3.47	2.37	2.95	0.36	9.29	6.83	10.89	16.38	6.90	1.74	17.49	10.28	3.88	3.72	1.22	0.88
(H_1, M_{13})	1.15	0.07	1.24	0.74	0.27	0.05	0.81	0.47	3.02	1.92	3.11	1.10	9.08	7.28	25.35	24.70	9.11	10.53
(H_2, M_{13})	2.28	0.00	0.32	0.07	0.36	0.00	1.85	0.11	2.70	0.00	1.24	0.09	13.50	7.41	41.99	8.68	9.71	9.69
(H_3, M_{13})	1.58	0.00	0.63	0.25	0.41	0.05	1.87	0.25	5.07	0.79	0.99	0.34	30.25	20.64	23.01	7.30	5.68	0.90
(H_1, M_9)	7.74	0.16	5.62	1.46	4.52	2.36	9.02	3.04	25.66	3.40	7.33	2.14	6.50	6.36	2.25	2.25	7.98	2.23
(H_2, M_9)	4.92	0.00	6.81	0.38	5.17	0.13	8.70	0.90	20.53	3.71	9.56	0.49	12.57	1.96	13.56	1.08	9.13	0.16
(H_3, M_9)	1.46	0.02	0.72	0.22	4.65	0.13	9.89	0.47	11.76	2.09	19.07	1.12	15.43	7.29	5.40	3.35	15.92	0.76
(H_1, M_6)	1.15	0.38	4.33	14.67	4.51	20.04	0.47	0.61	2.86	8.72	8.36	10.43	1.01	2.34	1.56	6.20	4.98	7.37
(H_2, M_6)	0.45	0.18	4.42	6.27	37.71	29.07	0.02	0.18	0.90	6.65	4.03	2.34	0.09	0.38	0.38	2.84	3.07	1.01
(H_3, M_6)	0.81	0.05	0.32	0.36	3.63	1.04	0.45	0.56	1.37	4.94	20.49	6.11	1.62	6.45	16.68	12.17	15.98	6.99

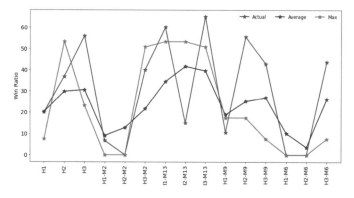

Fig. 14.4 Predicted win-ratios (Average and Max) vs actual observed win-ratios

$Predicted_{max}$—selects the win-ratio for the class with the maximum percentage of predictions.

$Predicted_{aver}$—computes win-ratio as the average of the product of all class win-ratios and the number of predictions per class.

To determine the strength of the relationship between predicted and actual win-ratios (see Fig. 14.4), correlation scores were computed. The Pearson correlation between the actual observed win-ratios of all agents and the $Predicted_{max}$, and $Predicted_{aver}$ were 0.589 and 0.757, respectively. The Spearman correlation between the actual observed win-ratios and the $Predicted_{max}$, and $Predicted_{aver}$ were 0.644 and 0.789, respectively. In all cases, the correlation scores reflected a positive association between the predicted and actual win-ratios, and the association was statistically significant (p-value < 0.01). Therefore, we concluded that the classifier predictions were reflective of the actual human and HMT behaviors. In the last set of experiments, we applied the predicted behA to gain insights on the interference measures defined in Eqs. (14.16–14.19). BehA were chosen based on $Attributes_{aver}$ since the correlation coefficients between the actual trajectories and $Predicted_{aver}$ were higher.

14.4.4 Evaluation of Human–Machine Team Effectiveness

Our primary goal was to evaluate HMT effectiveness by computing behA, which help to evaluate the performance of the HMTs. For all experiments, agent behavior was assumed to be controlled by four behA: probes (Pb); pylons (Pn); stalkers (Sk); and voidrays (Vd) (Table 14.1). Figure 14.5 shows the variation of win-ratios to behA that dictated the behavior of the individual machine bots before training the classifier. It is evident that in general, as the number of probes and voidrays increases, the performance of the agent increases (applies specifically to the distributed attack strategy). The opposite is also true for pylons and stalkers; as their numbers increases,

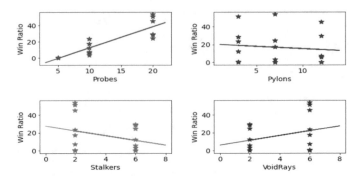

Fig. 14.5 Variation of win-ratios against behavioral attributes

the performance of the bots decreases. Pearson correlation measures (r) show that Pb ($r = 0.89$) had more predictive power compared to Vr ($r = 0.3$), Sk ($r = -0.3$) and Pn ($r = -0.1$). These plots make intuitive sense when analyzing the distributed attack strategy. By increasing the number of probes, the rate of production of resources (minerals and vespene gas) increases, and an agent can build more attacking units which increases performance. For attacking units, building more voidrays instead of stalkers increases the team's performance, since voidrays are more lethal. Building a few pylons at a base is important, but too many becomes wasteful if the priority is to attack the enemy (pylons powers a base but they do not attack), hence, performance decreases.

Predicted behA (from the classifier) for human participants in the form (Pb, Pn, Sk, Vr) where:

$$H_1 = \{13.2, 10.1, 2.6, 5.4\}$$

$$H_2 = \{16.1, 8, 3.4, 4.6\}$$

$$H_3 = \{16.3, 7.9, 3.2, 4.8\} \tag{14.22}$$

Using behA insights from Fig. 14.5, we can infer that in terms of performance, $H_3 > H_2 > H_1$, since H_3 produced the highest number of probes and voidrays, which are associated with higher performance (behavioral attributes for H_2 and H_3 were almost similar). This result is supported by the actual win-ratios where $H_3 > H_2 > H_1$ (Table 14.2). Predicted behA for the HMTs formed between the human players and bot agents, M_2, M_{13}, M_9, and M_6, are shown in Table 14.4, together with their associated interference metrics vectors. By analyzing attribute predictions, we see that HMTs formed with M_{13} yielded values (high Pb and Vr, low Sk and Pn) that were associated with better performance scores compared to M_2, M_9, and M_6.

Table 14.4 Predicted human–machine team behA and associated AIV

	Predicted team attributes				Bot AIV					Human AIV					Interference					
	Pb	Pn	Sk	Vr	Pb	Pn	Sk	Vr	Pb	Pn	Sk	Vr	Bot win-ratio	Human win-ratio	Average win-ratio	Team win-ratio	Type
(H_1, M_2)	8.5	7.6	3.4	4.6	12.4	21.1	6.7	6.7	67.4	51.1	11.7	11.7	0	20	10	6.67	Negative
(H_2, M_2)	9.7	7.7	3.1	4.9	21.9	22.2	8.4	8.4	122.6	25.4	6.9	6.9	0	36.84	18.42	0	Negative
(H_3, M_2)	13.2	5.9	3.7	4.3	67.6	8.4	5.3	5.3	127.8	23.9	7.7	7.7	0	56	28	40	Weak positive
(H_1, M_{13})	18.4	7.5	3.9	4.1	2.5	19.8	3.5	3.5	46.1	51.1	0.3	0.3	50.83	20	35.415	60	Strong positive
(H_2, M_{13})	18.9	7.0	3.0	5.0	1.1	16.4	1.1	1.1	15.4	25.4	1.9	1.9	50.83	36.84	43.835	15	Negative
(H_3, M_{13})	18.6	5.2	3.2	4.8	1.9	5.0	1.5	1.5	13.7	23.9	1.5	1.5	50.83	56	53.415	65	Strong positive
(H_1, M_9)	11.7	7.0	2.9	5.1	2.8	0.0	0.9	0.9	10.3	9.9	0.3	0.3	3.33	20	11.665	10.53	Negative
(H_2, M_9)	13.0	7.1	2.3	5.6	8.7	0.0	0.1	0.1	36.9	1.1	1.9	1.9	3.33	36.84	20.085	55.56	Strong positive
(H_3, M_9)	14.4	7.7	2.6	5.4	19.6	0.5	0.4	0.4	39.8	0.8	1.5	1.5	3.33	56	29.665	42.85	Weak positive
(H_1, M_6)	10.1	9.5	4.8	3.2	25.9	6.0	1.4	1.4	67.4	3.4	11.7	11.7	0	20	10	0	Negative
(H_2, M_6)	6.9	10.8	4.0	4.0	3.5	1.4	4.2	4.2	122.6	15.7	6.9	6.9	0	36.84	18.42	0	Negative
(H_3, M_6)	15.7	9.3	3.5	4.5	114.0	7.2	6.0	6.0	127.8	16.9	7.7	7.7	0	56	28	43.75	Weak positive

Interference was analyzed by comparing predicted win-ratios to those of the bot and the human agents separately. In addition, average win-ratios of the humans and bots were included to see if the overall team performance was better than the average performance. Table 14.4 shows instances of SPI, WPI, and NI. In cases of SPI, predicted team behA were associated with higher performance outcomes. For example, team (H_3, M_{13}), had behA {18.4, 7.5, 3.2, 4.8}, which reflect higher rate of production of probes and voidrays, contributing to higher performance as shown in Fig. 14.5. AIVs reflect how much an agent's behA are closer to the team's behA. For an agent's behA, the smaller the attribute values, the more similar the agent's behA are to the team's behA values (see Eq. 14.19). From the AIVs in Table 14.4, we can infer that the bot agents had more influence on the probe and pylon behA, since they had smaller values compared to the human agents. This result is consistent with the human players' experiences during the game: they mostly focused on utilizing resources (minerals, vespene gas) to build attacking units rather than building the probes and pylons needed to gather more resources.

Results for positive interference (both weak and strong) suggest the presence of factors, such as task allocation and shared responsibility, which boost a team's performance between the human and the bot agents. In teams that experienced positive interference, the human and the bot's stalker and voidray behA were both closer to the team behA, implying that both agents were equally influential at producing attacking units (shared responsibility). In some cases though, the human players were even more influential at building these attacking units than the bot (for example, team H_2, M_{13}). This observation implies that the human players were more focused on building attacking units, whilst the bot was focused on building resources (task allocation and specialization). Results for negative interference generally show the lack of these factors (task allocation, shared responsibility); in most cases, the human agent had very little impact on the game (for example, in team H_1, M_2) as shown by the AIVs which reflect the dominance of the bot in all behA. Interference is also affected by the type of agents in a team: for example, if we consider teams (H_1, M_1), (H_2, M_1), and (H_3, M_1), we see that even though the bot, M_1, was the same for all three HMTs, some human agents managed to find synergy and benefit from cooperating with the bot (H_3), whilst the other human agents could not. The same observations are true for the bots as well.

14.5 Conclusion and Future Work

In this work, we presented a new approach that helps to evaluate HMT effectiveness. By focusing on effectiveness, our goal is to provide explanations that could help to interpret the performance metrics of an HMT. We achieved this through the use of a classifier that maps complex team behavior to a set of behA linked to a team's performance metrics. The complex behavior is modeled through reward functions that are computed via IRL. The assumption is that through these rewards, we are able to capture the intrinsic goals and preferences of each unique agent. The classifier's accuracy was 84% at predicting the correct behA class (out of 18), given a set of agent trajectories. To validate this classifier, we compared performance scores (win-ratios) between predicted and observed behA, and we achieved a relatively high and statistically significant Pearson correlation of 0.76. Using these predicted behA, we then computed AIV vectors to determine how the team output was being affected by contributions from different team members. We used these AIV scores to explain interference outcomes and infer processes such as shared responsibility and task allocation.

During this study, we encountered several limitations which we will attempt to address in future work. First, human agents are highly adaptive, hence, fitting their behavior to one set of behA might not be reflective of their adaptiveness. A solution might be to partition human trajectories according to timesteps, but this requires a significant amount of data which might not be readily available. Another area for future work is in team prescription. From the AIVs, we can determine how each agent contributed to the team's performance outcome: hence, in future work, we plan to exploit these AIV results to modify a team's behavior and increase its effectiveness. Another potential area to address is on human uniqueness and personalization: through these experiments, we observed that HMTs are affected by the types of agents (both humans and bots) who make up the team. In future experiments, we would like to perform a thorough study of agent personalization and tie it to processes such as decision-making styles (Santos et al., 2018). We will attempt to answer how and why an agent benefits from teaming with one bot as opposed to the other(s). In addition to the StarCraft 2, we plan to extend the study of HMT to other domains where HMTs are applicable. In our experiments, we only had one human and one bot in each team; future experiments should examine the existence of more than two agents in each HMTs.

Acknowledgements This work was sponsored in part by ONR Grant No. N00014-19-1-2211, AFOSR Grant No. FA9550-20-1-0032, and DURIP Grant No. N00014-15-1-2514.

References

Barro, S., & Davenport, T. H. (2019). People and machines: Partners in innovation. *MIT Sloan Management Review, 60*(4), 22–28.

Bellman, R. (1957). A Markovian decision process. *Journal of mathematics and mechanics,* 679–684.Sutton, R. S., & Barto, A. G. (1998). *Introduction to reinforcement learning* (Vol. 135). Cambridge: MIT press.

Biondi, F., & Skrypchuk, L. (2017). Use your brain (and light) for innovative human-machine interfaces. In *Advances in Human Factors and System Interactions* (pp. 99–105). Cham: Springer.

Bolstad, C. (2019). *Future Directions for Human Machine Teaming* (No. SAND2019–3068C). Albuquerque, NM: Sandia National Lab (SNL-NM).

BurnySc2. (2016). Retrieved November 1, 2020, from github.com/BurnySc2/python-sc2/tree/dev elop

Castelfranchi, C. (1998). Modelling social action for AI agents. *Artificial Intelligence, 103*(1–2), 157–182.

Crandall, J. W., & Cummings, M. L. (2007). Developing performance metrics for the supervisory control of multiple robots. In *Proceedings of the ACM/IEEE International Conference on Human-Robot Interaction*, 33–40. New York: ACM.

Cuevas, H. M., Fiore, S. M., Caldwell, B. S., & Strater, L. (2007). Augmenting team cognition in human-automation teams performing in complex operational environments. *Aviation, Space, and Environmental Medicine, 78*(5), B63–B70.

Cummings, J. N., & Kiesler, S. (2008). Who collaborates successfully? Prior experience reduces collaboration barriers in distributed interdisciplinary research. *Proceedings of the 2008 ACM conference on Computer-Supported Cooperative Work*. New York: ACM.

Damacharla, P., Javaid, A. Y., Gallimore, J. J., & Devabhaktuni, V. K. (2018). Common metrics to benchmark human-machine teams (HMT): A review. *IEEE Access, 6*, 38637–38655.

Driewer, F., Baier, H., & Schilling, K. (2005). Robot–human rescue teams: A user requirements analysis. *Advanced Robotics, 19*(8), 819–838.

Elara, M. R., Calderon, C. A. A., Zhou, C., & Wijesoma, W. S. (2010). False alarm metrics: Evaluating safety in human robot interactions. In *2010 IEEE Conference on Robotics, Automation and Mechatronics* (pp. 230–236). New York: IEEE.

Endsley, M. R., & Robertson, M. M. (2000). Situation awareness in aircraft maintenance teams. *International Journal of Industrial Ergonomics, 26*(2), 301–325.

Glickman, A. S., Zimmer, S., Montero, R. C., Guerette, P. J., & Campbell, W. J. (1987). *The Evolution of Teamwork Skills: An Empirical Assessment with Implications for Training*. Old Dominion Univ Norfolk VA Center for Applied Psychological Studies.

Gombolay, M. C., Huang, C., & Shah, J. (2015). Coordination of human-robot teaming with human task preferences. In *2015 AAAI Fall Symposium Series*. Menlo Park, CA: AAAI.

Hackman, J. R. (1978). The design of work in the 1980s. *Organizational Dynamics, 7*(1), 3–17.

Healey, A. N., Undre, S., & Vincent, C. A. (2004). Developing observational measures of performance in surgical teams. *BMJ Quality & Safety, 13*(suppl 1), i33–i40.

Hoc, J. M. (2001). Towards a cognitive approach to human–machine cooperation in dynamic situations. *International Journal of Human-Computer Studies, 54*(4), 509–540.

Hoffman, G. (2019). Evaluating fluency in human–robot collaboration. *IEEE Transactions on Human-Machine Systems, 49*(3), 209–218.

Isa, T., Fetz, E. E., & Müller, K. R. (2009). Recent advances in brain–machine interfaces. *Neural Networks: THe Official Journal of the International Neural Network Society, 22*(9), 1201.

Jhaver, S., Birman, I., Gilbert, E., & Bruckman, A. (2019). Human-machine collaboration for content regulation: The case of Reddit Automoderator. *ACM Transactions on Computer-Human Interaction (TOCHI), 26*(5), 1–35.

Katal, A., Wazid, M., & Goudar, R. H. (2013). Big data: issues, challenges, tools, and good practices. In *2013 Sixth International Conference on Contemporary Computing (IC3)* (pp. 404–409). New York: IEEE.

Krach, S., Hegel, F., Wrede, B., Sagerer, G., Binkofski, F., & Kircher, T. (2008). Can machines think? Interaction and perspective taking with robots investigated via fMRI. *PloS One, 3*(7), e2597.

Lebedev, M. (2014). Brain-machine interfaces: An overview. *Translational. Neuroscience, 5*(1), 99–110.

Ng, A. Y., & Russell, S. J. (2000). Algorithms for inverse reinforcement learning. In *ICML* (Vol. 1, p. 2).

O'Connell, T. A., & Choong, Y. Y. (2008). Metrics for measuring human interaction with interactive visualizations for information analysis. In *Proceedings of the SIGCHI Conference on Human Factors in Computing Systems* (pp. 1493–1496). ACM.

Pagell, M., & LePine, J. A. (2002). Multiple case studies of team effectiveness in manufacturing organizations. *Journal of Operations Management, 20*(5), 619–639.

Santos Jr., E., Nguyen, H., Kim, K. J., Russell, J. A., Hyde, G. M., Veenhuis, L. J., Boparai, R. S., De Guelle, L. T., Mac, H. V. (2018). A contextual decision-making framework. *Computational Context: The Value, Theory and Application of Context with AI* (pp. 253–286). CRC Press.

Seeber, I., Bittner, E., Briggs, R. O., de Vreede, T., De Vreede, G. J., Elkins, A. & Schwabe, G. (2020). Machines as teammates: A research agenda on AI in team collaboration. *Information & Management*, *57*(2), 103174.

Steinfeld, A., Fong, T., Kaber, D., Lewis, M., Scholtz, J., Schultz, A., & Goodrich, M. (2006). Common metrics for human-robot interaction. In *Proceedings of the 1st ACM SIGCHI/SIGART Conference on Human-Robot Interaction* (pp. 33–40). New York: ACM.

Sutton, R. S., & Barto, A. G. (1998). *Introduction to Reinforcement Learning* (Vol. 135). Cambridge: MIT Press.

Vagia, M., Transeth, A. A., & Fjerdingen, S. A. (2016). A literature review on the levels of automation during the years. What are the different taxonomies that have been proposed? *Applied Ergonomics, 53*, 190–202.

Vinyals, O., Ewalds, T., Bartunov, S., Georgiev, P., Vezhnevets, A. S., Yeo, M., Makhzani, A., Küttler, H., Agapiou, J., Schrittwieser, J., & Quan, J. (2017). Starcraft II: A new challenge for reinforcement learning. Preprint at arXiv:1708.04782.

Wang, N., Pynadath, D. V., & Hill, S. G. (2016). Trust calibration within a human-robot team: Comparing automatically generated explanations. *2016 11th ACM/IEEE International Conference on Human-Robot Interaction (HRI)* (pp. 109–116). New York: IEEE.

Ziebart, B., Mass, A., Bagnell, A, & Dey, A. (2008). Maximum entropy inverse reinforcement learning. *Proc. 23rd International Conference on Advancement of Artificial. Intelligence AAAI* (pp. 1433–1439). Menlo Park, CA: AAAI.

Chapter 15
Humanity in the Era of Autonomous Human–machine Teams

Shu-Heng Chen

Abstract In this chapter, we address the meaning of the development of autonomous human–machine teams undergirded by the trio, namely, data, the Internet, and algorithms. We first review and examine this issue against a general background related to the philosophy and history of science and technology, symbiosis and cyborgs, and an evolutionary viewpoint from the Anthropocene and Novacene. We then argue that the meaning for humanity in this increasingly intensive autonomous human–machine interaction environment is two-fold, namely, individuality and the democratization of individuality (capability development). Nevertheless, to not leave the future of humanity to be dominated and solely determined by machines (the trio), humanistic scholars have to get involved themselves in the autonomous human–machine teams. In fact, some of their earlier actions have already taken place and have contributed to the changing face of the humanities, which will also be highlighted in this chapter.

Keywords Big data · Algorithms · Internet of everything · The Leinweber-Arnott inquiry · Symbiosis · Novacene · Individuality · Democratization

15.1 Introduction: AHMTs in the Form of the Trio

In the year 1995, the *Journal of Portfolio Management* published an article entitled "*Quantitative and Computational Innovation in Investment Management.*" In this article, David Leinweber and Robert Arnott raised two questions: "If you had unlimited computational power, what would you do with it?" and "What would you do differently if you were completely unconstrained by the capacity of your computers?" Their paper was originally written for the people of Wall Street at the dawn of the new millennium; nevertheless, not so much abiding by its given contextualization, the questions can be reshaped in a broader context and its contemporaneity can be even more limpid. The reason for this reshaping is because three major developments, which were not so palpable in the late 1990s, have gradually been forged since the

S.-H. Chen (✉)
AI-ECON Research Center, Department of Economics, National Chengchi University, Taipei 11605, Taiwan

© Springer Nature Switzerland AG 2021   309
W. F. Lawless et al. (eds.), *Systems Engineering and Artificial Intelligence*,
https://doi.org/10.1007/978-3-030-77283-3_15

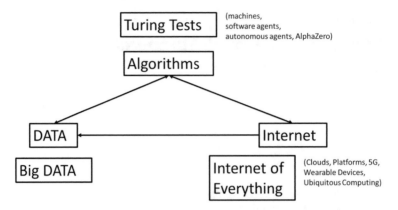

Fig. 15.1 The Trio in the New Millennium

new millennium. These three, the trio, can be briefly denoted as *data, the Internet,* and *algorithms.* The empowerments with which they can clothe humans make the original imagination solely based on the "unconstrained capacity of computers" somewhat narrow and obsolete.

15.1.1 The Trio: Data, the Internet, and Algorithms

Let us first look at these three elements. By data, we mean *big data* (Chen & Venkat-achalam, 2017), by the Internet, we mean the *Internet of Everything* (Lawless et al., 2019), and by algorithms, we mean the algorithms which can meet the various tests in light of the original Turing test (Turing, 1950). The empowerment of these three do not take place independently, but they are closely intertwined in that they form a trio (Fig. 15.1). The data term is big because everything is now *becoming connected* together in a *cyber-world,* an enlarged version of *cyborgs.*[1] The *cyber-world* implies that we are now given a screen that can video-record most of what is happening on our planet and hence enables us to trace each path; alternatively, we are given a full "biog-raphy" of the earth, that includes not just its geological facts but, more importantly, also its humanistic details (Chen, 2020).[2] That is to say, the increasingly intensive and extensive connections, characterized by the Internet of Everything, undergird

---

[1] Cyborgs is short for cybernetic organisms (Clynes and Kline, 1960). For treating the Internet of Everything as an expanded version of cyborgs, the interested reader is referred to Chen (2019).

[2] Chen (2020) proposes a *twin-space theory* to characterize the current digital society. It is argued that the recent revolution in information, communication, and digital technology (ICDT) has gradually mapped our physical space into its digital counterpart. In other words, the planet will have its "mirror" in the digital space. Despite the twin relation, the physical space only exists in the now time (the present time) as it is a slice of the history cut at a specific position and disappears forever when it becomes the past; the data in the cyber space, however, are not subject to such a time restriction, and they can remain forever once they are registered.

the influx of big data, a new kind of data phenomenon which we did not experience before the dawn of this new millennium.[3]

However, no matter how vast the size of the data, much would remain idle without the availability of the algorithms, which can not only process these data, but can also acquire the capability required to perform the job on their own.[4] For the latter purpose, the algorithms also rely on big data for learning purposes. Without gaining access to big data, many of these algorithms would essentially be futile.

Finally, to ensure that the Internet of Everything (humans and machines) can function properly, so that big data can be generated and collected, we also rely on algorithms to facilitate the man–machine interaction, for example, various apps. Therefore, algorithms are also indispensable for the Internet of Everything (Lawless et al., 2019), and the function of many of them can only be defined against the backdrop of such an Internet. In this case, what the Internet is to these algorithms is what the sea is to fish.

15.1.2 AHMTs Manifested by the Trio

Figure 15.1 summarizes the trio, and its bidirectional arrows show the interdependent relationships among them. *Machines in the autonomous human–machine teams (AHMTs, hereafter) are now formally conceptualized as a manifestation of this kind of trio.* For example, an unmanned aerial vehicle (UAV) is not just about the physical body of the vehicle, but the data, algorithms, and the Internet, altogether. Although, we may with this conceptual framework still follow the long stream of discussions on human–machine interactions, we know that we are dealing with a new kind of machine that certainly did not exist in the bourgeoning stage of *ergonomics* (Murrell, 1965); their interactions are not limited to human bodies, but have already been extended to their minds or cognitive systems.

---

[3] Ostensibly, other expressions or characterizations also exist, such as *the society of Web 2.0 or higher*, or *the era of user-initiated-and-supplied contents*, etc. (O'Reilly, 2017). However, it is the Internet of Everything which technologically makes its kaleidoscopically rich contents suppliable.

[4] While in this chapter, we will mainly use the term *algorithms*, different nomenclatures are also commonly seen in other places, such as *machines, software agents, autonomous agents*, etc. These terms may be used interchangeably in this chapter, so long as the ontology of concern to us is the computer programs (software), and not the physical entity (hardware). Even though the object with which humans interact can be wearable devices, chatbots, drones, driverless cars, or sensors, what interests us are the *interactions* or *connections* or *communications* between men and machines, and these interactions are mainly driven by software, which is related to interaction design, user experience design (UXD), and user interaction design (UID).

15.1.3 Scitovsky's Caveat

As summarized in Fig. 15.1, what we are provided with in this age is a much empowered trio, which is certainly built upon the increasing available computational resources as Leinweber and Arnott (1995) have pointed out. However, the question, more enlighteningly, can be restated as follows: *What would we do differently if we were completely unconstrained by the capacity of the trio: data, the Internet, and algorithms when they become infinitely big, connected, and smart?*

The Leinweber-Arnott inquiry, in fact, makes us reminiscent of other similar but more general concerns, such as what to do with excess money or superfluous leisure time or an extended lifespan. Conventional neoclassical economics often indoctrinates us with the view that the consumer's utility will increase with money, consumption, and leisure. The answer is to be expected because consumers are deemed to be rational according to neoclassical economics, and the capability that they can allocate time and money in the most efficient and enjoyable way never bothers a bystander. Nevertheless, Tibor Scitovsky (1910–2002) challenged this assumption in the 1970s and attempted to rebuild the economic foundations upon the psychological studies of motivation. In his book *Joyless Economy* (Scitovsky, 1976), he went to great lengths to explain why consumers may not know how to use their increasing resources (money and time) to achieve a higher level of satisfaction. Scitovsky echoed this observation with a passage that Blaise Pascal (1623–1662) had left for us more than 350 years ago, "I have often said that man's unhappiness springs from one thing alone, his incapacity to stay quietly in one room" (Pascal, 1669[1995], p. 40.).

In the light of Scitovsky's caveat, even though we have been bestowed with additional time for leisure, we could fail to figure out what to do with it, since we do not have the *skills* required to use our leisure in a constructive and enjoyable way; as a result, to relieve ourselves from our boredom, we may only end up with leisure that is less skillful, but the fleeting pleasure obtained cannot be sublimated into a truly enjoyable state and, even worse, can even be destructive. It is this line of argument that reminds us that a blissful direction is not guaranteed despite the companionship of the trio.[5]

In this chapter, in the same vein as Scitovsky, we intend to address the humanistic ingredients required for a "constructive and enjoyable" use of the excess, here, the AHMTs manifested by the trio. The rest of the chapter is organized as follows. Section 15.2 provides a general background that allows us to place AHMTs in a

---

[5] In his *Joyless Economy*, Tibor Scitovsky introduced the essence of culture in consumption, which distinguishes the *enjoyable life* from the *good life*. By comparing the consumption culture between the US and European countries, Scitovsky argued that consumers in an economy underpinned by an impoverished culture may still be able to afford a good or even a luxurious life, but not an enjoyable life.

broader context related to literature, philosophy and the history of science and technology,[6] and STS (standing for "science, technology and society"[7]). Section 15.3 then tackles a more fundamental question, i.e., What is the meaning of the trio for humanity? With the direction of thought suggested there, Sect. 15.4 moves forward to highlight the current changing face of the humanities that are congruent with the indicated direction, followed by the concluding remarks in Sect. 15.5.

15.2 Human–Machine Teams

The idea of human–machine teams denotes the collaboration between Homo Sapiens and "Homo Machines."[8] This collaborative relation, presumably harmonious, is just one of many possible interactions that have been suggested in the literature, philosophy and the history of science and technology, and STS. In this long-accumulating pile of studies, various imaginations or speculations of human–machine mixtures have been demonstrated; while they evolve with humans' refreshing experiences with machines, they remain to diverge into utopias (Lovelock, 2019) and dystopias (Bostrom, 2014; Harari, 2016; Kingsley, 2018; O'Neil, 2016; Rushkoff, 2020) or somewhere in between (Markoff, 2015). It is beyond the scope of this chapter to delve into this open-ended debate; instead, as an abridged version, we shall review five selected "models" which we consider to be pertinent for our ensuing discussions of the meaning for humanity in the age of the trio as manifested by AHMTs.

The five models which we have included in this section together give a flavor of the spectrum which characterizes the current thought over AHMTs. We begin with probably the most classic demonstration on a dystopia, namely, the Shelley Model (Sect. 15.2.1), then go to its utopian extreme, the Lovelock model (Sect. 15.2.2), and, at this juncture, involve the Margulis model (Sect. 15.2.3) as the biological foundation

---

[6] Compared to the abundant literature on the philosophy of science, that existing on the philosophy of technology is relatively scant. Among the few studies that exist, Crocker (2012) is the one that is closely pertinent to this chapter; in particular, it also introduces a symbiotic model to frame the co-evolution of humanity and technology (see Sects. 2.2 and 2.3 below).

[7] STS is a field that normally refers to a movement that places science and technology education in a social, political, economic, and humanistic context. It is not just to equip students with scientific facts, but, more importantly, with their meaning or significance for society as a whole. The movement already existed in the 1960s, but has seen much expansion in recent decades (Pittinsky, 2019).

In fact, Nobert Wiener (1894–1964), the founder of cybernetics, has already drawn our attention to this direction, as shown in Wiener (1948) and Wiener (1950); he can be regarded as a pioneer of STS. When documenting Wiener, Gleick (2011) stated, "Much of the success of his book, abstruse and ungainly as it was, lay in Wiener's always *returning his focus to the human, not the machine.* He was not as interested in shedding light on the rise of computing–to which, in any case, his connections were peripheral–as in *how computing might shed light on humanity*" (Ibid, p. 240; italics added).

[8] The term *Homo Machines* has not been formally used in the public academic dialogues; the term, which we use here, is mainly motivated by James Lovelock (Lovelock, 2019) in his visionary discussion of the machines in Novacene. An alternative and more familiar term is *Homo Techno*.

for AHMTs. We then shift from the interactions between humans and machines to the interactions among humans themselves, and introduce the economic-sociological model of AHMTs, the Polanyi model (Sect. 2.4), and the organization model, the Laloux model (Sect. 15.2.5).

15.2.1 Shelley Model: Frankenstein and His Creature

In 1818, Mary Shelley (1797–1851) published her celebrated *Frankenstein.*[9] In this well-known piece of science fiction, the AHMT, composed of Frankenstein and his creature, had ended up as a tragedy. Victor Frankenstein did not "collaborate" well with the creature, since the creature did not come out handsomely in the way that the chemist Frankenstein had anticipated. Being rejected by the society due to his hideous countenance, the creature was left in a despairing situation and began to commit crimes. Frankenstein was depressed by the behavior of the creature and then tried to annihilate it, but he failed. In this case, humans, driven by envy in the realm of science, tried to create a human-like machine as a scientific achievement, but underestimated the difficulties involved, and in the end, only built the machine that they could not collaborate with. Machines were also frustrated and outraged when they realized that they would not be accepted by humans. An originally romantic idea ended with a nightmare fraught with revenge and criminal activity.

The Shelley "model" provides a classic imagining on the vagaries of the development of AHMTs. For example, novel situations are generally *not foreseeable* and they sometimes have to be handled by autonomous mechanisms. Hence, when a novel situation needs an impromptu reaction, humans may like to behave according to what they deem convenient, but machines may judge it as "unethical" and refuse to cooperate and intervene in the opposite way. Their interactions become strained. Humans, like what we learned from Frankenstein, may make every effort to make machines defunct, but machines, like the creature, may try their best to resist humans' "unethical" motives. Hence, again, an originally romantically designed AHMT may end up with a disaster. While we are pursuing collaborations to form a team, the team, once it becomes autonomous with a biologically like mechanism included, may find its own way of introducing conflicts.

---

[9] Given its significance, a new version has recently been published by the MIT press (Shelley, 2017). By adding many annotations, remarks, and essays from leading experts, this book is mainly prepared for those young talents who are preparing themselves to work in science and engineering or to be an inventor.

15.2.2 Lovelock Model: GAIA and Novacene

Two hundred years later, the machines in the hands of Mary Shelley had a very different kind of offspring when they came into the hands of James Lovelock (Lovelock, 2019). This generation of machines is not that emotionally dependent compared to their ancestors that were "birthed" by Frankenstein; on the contrary, they have become more independent, rational, and intelligent. *Alpha Zero* (Silver et al., 2018), which has inspired Lovelock, has become the new species of Homo Machines. When describing the machines of the Novacene, Lovelock stated that "[t]hey will be entirely free of human commands because they will have evolved from code written by themselves. From the start, this would be much better than human-written code. Cyborgs would start again; like Alpha Zero they would start from a blank slate" (Ibid., pp. 94–95). On the other hand, Frankenstein's modern offspring tend to be more vicious, avaricious, and anthropocentric. Not only have they brought a myriad of species to extinction, massively destroyed rainforests, polluted clean water and air, and exploited various natural resources, but they have also emitted immense amounts of carbon dioxide, heating up their motherland, Gaia, named in homage to that classical Greek goddess of the earth (McCarthy, 2015).

Lovelock proposed his well-known *Gaia hypothesis* (Lovelock, 1988), which basically asserts that the Earth is a self-regulating and self-changing living organism. The Gaia hypothesis can be understood as a balance or order, established by the collection of species on the Earth, which can help the Earth to cool itself enough to continue its existence. However, when that balance is broken and cannot be recovered by the existing laws of natural selection, then the self-regulating mechanism of the Earth, nature, will readjust itself in such a way so that the balance can be restored. According to Lovelock, climate change is the revenge that the Earth has taken on the offspring of Frankenstein; it will eventually make the Earth no longer friendly for humans to live (Lovelock, 2007).

Per Lovelock's theory, machines, on the other hand, may have a strong will to survive or to continue as Frankenstein's creature did, and they may also be sufficiently intelligent to know that they cannot continue their life without the accompany of Frankenstein. In that sense, Homo Sapiens and Homo Machines have to support each other as in a symbiotic system. Hence, to achieve that goal, intelligent machines will earnestly help the Earth to restore the balance that humans have previously destroyed and, in the meantime, prevent humans from being avenged by Gaia. Accordingly, they will not allow humans to abusively exploit the environment as they did in the long past, and the machines will intervene in human affairs, not by eliminating them, but by preventing them from being eliminated. Of course, machines are not going to be doing these things only altruistically, but for the sake of their own survival.

Lovelock's theory regarding the role of machines in the transition from Anthropocene[10] to Novacene provides a very unique and optimistic portrait of AHMTs.

---

[10] Although humans are frail and very constrained, they are capable of inventing tools and machines to set them free. Machines under incessant technological advances enable humans, little by little, to have an overwhelming grasp of the planet. Anthropocene, a new geological term, has been proposed

It also engenders a very different imagination of the AHMT culture. Humans may be advised or even forced not to take those actions that are unfavorable to Gaia and hence unfavorable to themselves. In other words, various forms of paternalism will be implemented to constrain humans' choices and actions under the operation of AHMTs. This may remind us of the *Brave New World* (Huxley, 1932[1998]), which has a remarkable dystopian rhetoric. Nevertheless, a weak form of paternalism, known as *libertarian paternalism*, has been advocated by Richard Thaler, the 2017 Nobel Laureate in Economics (Abdukadirov, 2016; Thaler & Sunstein, 2008). What distinguishes libertarian paternalism from the strong form of paternalism is expounded by Thaler and Sunstein (2008).

> Libertarian paternalism is a relatively weak, soft, and nonintrusive type of paternalism because choices are not blocked, fenced off, or significantly burdened. If people want to smoke cigarettes, to eat a lot of candy, to choose an unsuitable health care plan, or to fail to save for retirement, libertarian paternalists will not force them to do otherwise – or even make things hard for them. Still, the approach we recommend does count as paternalistic, because *private and public choice architects* are not merely trying to track or to implement people's anticipated choices. Rather, they are self-consciously attempting to move people in directions that will make their lives better. They nudge. (Ibid., pp. 5-6; italics added)

The choice architecture mentioned above is nowadays being carried out by various software agents that are designed to help decision makers make a "right" choice. Machines in the form of AHMTs under Novacene will play the same role or probably be more paternalistic when they deem it necessary. They may circumvent humans' permissions to carry out what they consider vital from the symbiotic viewpoint.

15.2.3 Margulis Model: Symbiogenesis and Super Cooperators

One development which is related to Lovelock's Gaian systems and his speculation of Novacene is *symbiogenesis* or *endosymbiotic theory* (Clarke, 2020), which was first written in Russian in 1924 by a Russian botanist, Boris Mikhaylovich Kozo-Polyansky (1890–1957). Boris Mikhaylovich Kozo-Polyansky (1890–1957) and his pioneering piece of work, due to its language, was not well spread during his time. Its English version was only made available in 2010 by the late evolutionary biologist Lynn Margulis (1938–2011) and her colleagues (Kozo-Polyansky, 1924[2010]).

Margulis, best known for her theory of symbiogenesis, had devoted her whole scientific career to enabling symbiogenesis to be accepted as an evolutionary mechanism or principle that dictates the evolution from simple organisms to complex organisms, such as from prokaryotes to eukaryotes, from single-cellular organisms to multi-cellular organisms, and from the simple labor division of cells to a sophisticated

---

for this age characterized by increasing mechanization. The definition given by the Cambridge Dictionary is "the time from the eighteenth century until now, in which it is possible to see the effect that people have had on the environment and climate (= weather conditions)."

labor division of cells (Sagan, 2012). Margulis pointed out that modern genomics has supported some postulations made earlier by Kozo-Polansky (1924[2010]), such as that eukaryotes originated from symbiotic cyanobacteria and that mitochondria were once symbiotic proteobacteria. Despite this being the case, her anticipation that most evolution would involve symbiogenesis remains a major challenging hypothesis in biology.

This new evolutionary principle built upon the theory of symbiogenesis put simply is basically a *cooperation principle*, like cooperation in the familiar prisoner's dilemma game. In the vein of Darwinism, to survive, individuals need to go beyond just competing with each other; more often than not, they may find partners, forming an alliance, so as to enhance their collective survivability by mutually supporting each other. Evolutionary game theorist Martin Nowak made this point quite succinctly in his book *SuperCooperators* (Nowak & Highfield, 2011). In the chapter "Society of Cells," Nowak referred to Margulis's theory to provide evidence as to why cooperation plays such an important role in evolutionary game theory; also in the chapter "Group Selection," he recounted that the unit which the evolutionary mechanism works on consists not just of individuals but also groups or teams. Hence, from Lovelock to Margulis and further to Nowak, an optimistic view of the AHMTs can be built upon an evolutionary-theoretic foundation of the AHMTs, either from the perspective of symbiosis or game theory.

15.2.4 Polanyi Model: Tension Between Habitation and Improvement

In both the Shelley and Lovelock models, we consistently see that machines generally have good intentions for humans, but the reciprocity may not be found on the human side, namely, Frankenstein and his descendants. However, what we have seen in the history of technology is that machines have, in effect, been neutral, but their appearance in human society can worsen the interactions among humans themselves, dividing humans into winners and losers, upper classes and lower classes, who have then fought with each other. Machines, therefore, have become the scapegoats to receive the blame because they failed to accommodate the whole of society. In this case, society is actually not divided as humans against machines, but as *humans with machines* against *humans without machines*, or, in Marxian terms, as capitalists versus the proletariat.

Let us briefly review some episodes in history. In Japan, the famous Meiji Renovation (1868–1912) started from 1868 under Emperor Meiji, which transformed Japan into becoming an industrial and then an imperialistic country. It resulted in Japan playing an increasingly important role in East Asia, so that it could consecutively defeat two neighboring countries, China (Quin) and Russia in 1895 and 1905, respectively. In the end, very unfortunately, it also propelled Japan to initiate World War

II in 1941. The Meiji Renovation has long symbolized a state of "progress"; nevertheless, this time is also a period in which a myriad number of people fell behind or despaired when the pace of the society was accelerated by industrialization and machines.

Mitsuharu Kaneko (1895–1975) in his 1965 book *Zetsubou no seishin-shi* provides us with a detailed description of the despairs suffered by those Japanese who failed to live up to the expectations of the Meiji Renovation. Based on his description, there were really no winners in the society, since even those who gained the upper hand were constantly not free from the worry that they might fail to keep up with the accelerating pace in the ensuing steps of the Renovation.

A similar kind of the history of mentality had been experienced even earlier by those countries in the West, which enlightened Japan and inspired the Meiji Renovation. For example, in the UK, the motherland of the Industrial Revolution, the uneasiness with machines had resulted in radical or violent social movements. This period has been manifested by the well-documented *Luddite movement* from 1811 to 1816, in which a group of British workers in Yorkshire and Nottinghamshire smashed machinery that they saw as threatening to their trade (Binfield, 2004). The sufferings of the working class during that period had become part of Romanticism; many great poets, such as Lord Byron (1788–1824), were involved in defending the Luddites; their poems were spread together with the Luddite movement, reflecting the mentality of that time (Jones, 2013).

Two centuries after the Luddite movement, have humans been more unified by machines? This question may be more philosophical than scientific, but in the meantime, the worsening income and wealth distribution has become one of the main issues of concern over the last several decades. The avid discussions generated by Thomas Piketty's *Capital in the Twenty-First Century* (Piketty, 2014) and the frenetic debate around the Universal Basic Income, specifically, during the 2020 Presidential Election in the US (Yang, 2018), clearly reveal that various efforts are being made to avoid inheriting the same despairing history of mentality from our great-great-grandparents. Hence, throughout history, the upshot of AHMTs is rarely humans versus machines, but humans themselves under various social and institutional settings underpinned by different ideologies. More than half a century ago, Karl Polanyi (1886–1964) in his magnum opus, *The Great Transformation* (Polanyi, 1944), already evinced this sustaining conflict and tension between society and the economy, the state and market, or habitation and improvement in industrial modernity. Polanyi's influence is as relevant today and more so than ever before.

15.2.5 Laloux Model: Soulful Organizations

With the aforementioned selective and brief reviews, we arrive at a fundamental inquiry, i.e., to what extent and scale and in what forms can the collaboration between humans and machines be reified? To answer this question, we also need to know, administratively or logistically, what would be the ideal organization to structure these AHMTs? Regarding the latter inquiry, Frederic Laloux (Laloux, 2014) has recently proposed a seven-stage development theory of organization. Each of these seven stages has been placed in a historical table and assigned a color. Hence, since 100,000 B.C., humans have experienced seven different stages of the organizational paradigms, which are colored by infra-red (the Reactive Stage), magenta (Magic), red (Impulsive), amber (Conformists), orange (Achievement), green (Pluralistic), and teal (Evolutionary). These seven stages also correspond to the human advancement of consciousness, including its value, morals, and cognitive development. While the organizations of the earliest two stages no longer exist, those of the next four still co-exist with the newest one; they together demonstrate a spectrum of modern organizational cultures.

Although we have no space to review these organizational paradigms or cultures, we should not underestimate their intertwined and intricate relation with AHMTs. On the one hand, the extent and the scale of AHMTs can be determined by a given organizational culture (paradigm); on the other hand, the increasing prevalence of AHMTs will impact the transition from one organizational paradigm to the next. In particular, there is the recent emergence of teal organizations, which are characterized by self-management, "with a system based on peer relationships, without the need for either hierarchy or consensus" (Ibid, p. 56). Under the teal organization paradigm, the conventional hierarchical pyramid is replaced with more flexible; liberal; fluid; post-modern boss-free; peer-production forms, consisting of small teams that take responsibility for their own governance. Would this organizational paradigm be particularly suitable for the healthy operation of AHMTs? Without being able to immediately provide answers, we need to keep this question in sight so as to place AHMTs in an apposite frame.

15.3 Meaning of the Trios for Humanity

15.3.1 Co-evolutions of Humans and Machines

In the previous section, we have reviewed the possible imaginations that we can apply to the human–machine "teams" or collaborations. One essential ingredient threading all of these imaginations is co-evolution. As we mentioned above (Sect. 16.2.5), the AHMTs characterized by the trio are expected to result in dramatic changes in social and economic structures, from individuals to their interactions. The AHMTs have already forged and facilitated a cornucopia of novel interaction patterns, such as citizen science (Bonney et al., 2014; Franzoni & Sauermann, 2014), peer production, or community-based production (Benkler, 2002, 2006), a sharing economy (Munger, 2018; Sundararajan, 2016), a gig economy (Prassl, 2018), and so on. From these emerging interaction patterns, AHMTs have substantially reduced the transaction costs required for matching a group of people with mutually supporting interests and talents, which successively revolutionizes the way science, business, and the entire capitalist economy is operated.

As a matter of fact, the width and depth (the extent and scale) of AHMTs are co-evolving with the interactions of humans themselves; the former prepare and incite newfangled modes for human interactions, which in succession calls for further innovations in the engineering of human–machine interactions, from user interfaces (UI) to user experiences (UX). To enhance humans' interactions, machines involved in these AHMTs are given the capability to learn from human behavior and to optimize their interactions; in the meantime, by becoming familiarized with machines, humans also try to find the best ways to behave so that their communications and collaborations with machines can be fulfilled.

When humans in AHMTs can co-evolve with machines, can we expect anything positive regarding the nature of human beings? Alternatively, what is the meaning of the trios (the AHMTs) for humanity? The rest of this section will address this question. We shall claim that the meaning has two aspects, namely, individuality (Sect. 15.3.2) and its democratization (Sect. 3.3).

15.3.2 Individuality

Individuality means that each individual uniquely and immortally exists in the collective memories represented by the cyber space.[11] His/her uniqueness or particularity is defined by his/her path of life. Individuality is probably the most distinguishing feature brought by the trio.[12] To be specific, it means that more and more individuals can possibly have their own biographies in various forms mainly based on their digital traces. This unprecedented event can happen because what humans did, what humans said, and even what humans thought can now be extensively archived in cyber space (Chen & Venkatachalam, 2017). The biography can be single-authored, but, more likely, co-authored via the AHMTs. Even though no one, including the protagonist himself/herself, for the time being, is interested in this authorship, the digital traces distributed and archived in the cyber space indicate that the work can start anytime as long as someone in the infinite future would like to do it.

There is little doubt that machines will evolve and progress in a way that will make the laborious authoring or editing work easier to handle, from archiving, searching, retrieving, sorting, analyzing, and even drafting. The saved labor can provide the involved authors, including the protagonist himself/herself, with more leisure to decide the proper narratives and to decide how life could be interpreted under different contextualizations. The latter activity may drive the protagonist to have a further reflection on his/her "journey" up to a particular point, and hence to configure the agenda for the remaining journey.

---

[11] This definition distinguishes the notion of individuality from the notion of individualism. See also Siedentop (2014).

[12] See also Chen (2020).

In addition to authoring, AHMTs also make distant reading available for humans (see also Sect. 15.4). Without machines, each protagonist, by his/her own close reading, is inexorably so limited that the others' traces which can shed light on his/her own may not be available. However, by distant reading aided by natural language processing and textual analysis, machines can figure out those biographies (traces of life) which might be closely related to the protagonist's own.[13] This is essentially to allow us to author and to read a biography in light of many enlightening references, which will be otherwise unavailable. These cross-references can be particularly insightful for the protagonist in search of his/her meaning of life. Hence, individuality here also reveals a way to search for the meaning of a life.

15.3.3 Democratization of Individuality

In talking about individuality, we know that the transition from the Dark Ages (the Middle Ages) to the Renaissance already indicated the dawn of the age of individuality. Nevertheless, in both the Renaissance and the subsequent Enlightenment, ordinary people did not have the capability required to claim or express their individuality. Even though the Gutenberg Revolution (see below) in the fifteenth century buttressed the widespread propagation of books and ideas, the illiteracy rate remained high for a number of centuries, particularly for females (Houston, 1983; McCloskey, 2016). Therefore, only a minority of the overall population could claim their individuality and preserve their own trace of life and make it publicly accessible. In stark contrast to this limitation, the second distinguishing feature that the trio can bring to humanity is the democratization of individuality or, alternatively put, the *democratization of capability development*.

We use the term *capability development* here to resonate with the *capability approach* advocated by Amartya Sen (1999), the 1998 Nobel Laureate in Economics, as his life-long pursuit. The capability approach is taken as an alternative to British utilitarianism, which was championed by Jeremy Bentham (1748–1832) and became dominant in mainstream economics. Sen, very similar in spirit to Scitovsky, argued that the humans' quality of life depends on their capability to make a choice, and this capability is not ascribed, but is rather acquired from education and learning. Without having their capabilities developed, the humans' effective freedom upon which a choice can be made is severely constrained. In Sen's book, the term education was mentioned 141 times; obviously, education and health care are the key premises for owning the capability to pursue what Sen considers to be the paramount end for development, namely, the freedom to choose and to lead lives that we have reason to value.

---

[13] For example, if digital traces can be properly quantified with the natural language processing techniques, then some clustering tools, such as *K nearest neighbors* (Chen et al., 2007), may be applicable to identify those neighboring traces of life.

The Piaget-Papert Legacy

Democratization had long been pursued by many educational philosophers before the coming of the new millennium. For example, Jean Piaget (1896–1980) believed that everyone has the potential to be a creator (Palmer, 2001), a view echoed well by the recent *maker movement* (Dougherty, 2016). His proposed constructionism, built upon his genetic and constructivist epistemology, has had a long-lasting influence in education (Piaget, 1973). Seymour Papert (1928–2016), one of the founders of the MIT Artificial Intelligence Lab and Media Lab, and also a prominent Piagetian, extended Piaget's epistemology by adding culture, specifically, the *computer culture*, as a pertinent element for facilitating constructive learning. What children can learn and in what sequence during their growing-up crucially depends on the embedded culture characterizing the environment to which they are exposed. Already in the 1960s, Papert contended that the advent of computers could change and enrich our culture for knowledge discovery or acquisition. Under his leadership, a series of softwares had been developed for this pursuit, including Logo, StarLogo, Logo/Lego, Scratch, and NetLogo (Colella et al., 2001; Papert, 1980; Resnick, 1997, 2017). When coming to the millennium, the Piaget-Papert legacy turns out to be even more vigorous except that the computer culture has now been replaced by the *smartphone culture* (Aschoff, 2020; Reid, 2018; Twenge, 2017) as part of the trio manifested by AHMTs.

In this era, not just by reading and writing, but by embarking on their smartphones or the equivalents, can everyone gain entrance to cyberspace, flag themselves, and claim their individuality. To do so, they do not need to be a celebrity, Sir, Lord, Queen, da Vinci, or Michelangelo; they only need to have a smartphone and play with it. What democratization means in this stage is not particularly different except that it focuses more on the reduction or removal of the thresholds and barriers to capability development. The trio and its AHMTs enable learners to achieve this goal much more easily than could have been done in the days of Papert and others. In other words, the autonomous human–machine teams have spawned a new culture that could enhance the degree of human autonomy.

Gutenberg Revolution

If we consider the early development of humanity and the humanities, the Renaissance and the Enlightenment, then one can hardly ignore the role of the Gutenberg Revolution. In this case, the Gutenberg Revolution, also known as the Printing Revolution, helped to make massive printing possible; hence, it reduced the threshold of getting access to reading materials that further incited and facilitated waves of authoring and publishing. In this historical context, the Gutenberg Revolution enhances the autonomy of humans as a reader and a writer, or, in general, the autonomy of intellectual development, including learning (reading) and creating (authoring).

If the significance of the Gutenberg Revolution can be understood in this way, then we can fairly say that the trio has continued and expanded the Gutenberg Revolution to another prodigious scale. This time, the trio has helped humans to reduce the threshold to study sciences, to do programming, to design, and to narrate. In other words, the democratization of education has advanced far beyond schooling and, in addition to the development of children, has also been extended to life-long learning and self-learning. This groundbreaking step can be christened the *democratization of science, software development, design, and narrative*. As we mentioned earlier, it is a milestone to possibly enable humans to become more autonomous and to define their potential roles in their collaboration with humans and machines in various manifestations of AHMTs.

The democratization of science can be exemplified by the mission passionately pursued by the NetLogo Team at Northwestern University currently led by Uri Wilensky.[14] In his keynote speech given at the 2010 Annual Meeting of the *Computational Social Science Society of America*, Uri Wilensky, the founder of NetLogo, asserted that agent-based modeling as manifested by NetLogo can help to reduce the barriers or thresholds for studying complex (adaptive) systems (Wilensky & Rand, 2015). Using the predator–prey model and forest fires as two illustrations, Wilensky showed during his keynote how the complex phenomena conventionally only accessible through advanced mathematics, such as differential equations, can now be approached much more easily via agent-based modeling. By using agent-based modeling, not only can we make complex adaptive systems highly accessible to general citizens (hence, a low threshold), but we can also allow users to broach the questions that are difficult to grapple with via conventional approaches (hence, a high ceiling).

The democratization of software development can be exemplified by the *low-code* or *no-code development platform* (Bexiga et al., 2020; Sahay et al., 2020). In this digital era, when the demand for software development is skyrocketing, related human resources (e.g., software developers) become increasingly scarce, which motivates the possible redistribution of part of the original work back to the demand side or the user side. To accommodate this redistribution of labor, instead of standing on the front line of software development for customers, software developers can concentrate on developing tools or platforms that can help to reduce the thresholds of programming so that downstream users can program on their own. These platforms rely more on visual programming and can be operated in a drag-and-drop manner. They have been used in many educational institutions when programming capability is required for *all* students.[15]

---

[14] As we have indicated in Sect. 3.3.1, StarLogo and NetLogo are both from the Logo pedigree, initially founded by Seymour Papert. StarLogo was initially developed by Mitchel Resnick at the MIT Media Lab. Uri Wilensky took the baton from him to further extend StarLogo into NetLogo.

[15] This can be further illustrated by two local examples. One example is the https://agilepoint.com, which, albeit business-oriented, takes a university–industry collaboration model to help educational institutes to gain access to it. The other example is that some universities have decided to invest in their own low-code development platform; for example, Tunghai university, one of the largest Catholic universities in Taiwan, provides students with *CT2Flow* (Computational Thinking To

As another example, *App Inventor* is a software development environment that lowers barriers to developing applications for the Android operating system. Essentially, it is Lego for mobile applications on the Android platform (Wolber et al., 2011). It was originally developed by Google, but is now maintained by MIT. It shares visual programming with Scratch and StarLogo in dragging-and-dropping visual objects in its interface, and uses small building blocks (like Lego) to create an application. To build the applications, one just drags and drops components onto a canvas and then links actions together using them as building blocks. The required programming knowledge is, therefore, minimal. On its website, the blurb states "…anyone can build an APP with global impact." Although this is typical invitation rhetoric, it reflects the ethos of democratization enabled by the trio.

As a conclusion to this section, the trio and the AHMTs built upon it can be considered as another "Gutenberg Revolution," but much more colossal in scale than the earlier one. Accordingly, its impact on humanity will be enormous. With the prevalence of AHMTs, humans can generally become more creative and consequently autonomous; this empowerment is further incorporated into the operation of AHMTs, and reshapes the division of labor between humans and machines in these teams, as they both have their degree of autonomy constantly upgraded. This location is the place where we see the relevance of Margulis's symbiotic model and Lovelock's Gaia model (Sects. 15.2.2 and 15.2.3), despite the shadow cast by Polanyi's model of the threat of improvement to habitation (Sect. 15.2.4) still remaining.

15.4 Meaning of the Trio for the Humanities

In this increasingly connected and autonomous human–machine interaction environment, we are facing the challenge regarding the future of humanity. Will the future of humanity be built upon AHMTs and subsequently flourish, as indicated in the previous section, or will it be subjugated to machines and become fragmentized and essentially nothing but data strings? Although the existing literature diverges into utopias and dystopias, there is little doubt that if the trio can mean something positive for humanity, it will not be determined by machines, but rather by humans. In this regard, the active engagement of humanistic scholars plays an important role. In this section, we briefly review how humanistic scholars have transferred the power of the trio into new energies for the humanities. Specifically, we focus on how AHMTs have substantially reshaped our status as readers.

Flowchart) and *CT2Code* (Computational Thinking To Code), requiring students to mainly focus on the design of the flowchart and leaving machines to translate it into code. See http://ct.thu.edu.tw.

15.4.1 Distant Reading

First, as already indicated by Chen (2020), the trio has placed us in a cyberspace of books and texts. It, therefore, makes distant reading and voluminous reading increasingly likely. Many questions whose answers depend on an exhaustive search of a huge pile of documents can now be addressed. A typical example is the application of various statistics that we can derive from texts; the famous statistician Udny Yule (1871–1951) demonstrated this kind of work in his day, when general text mining technology was absent. As demonstrated in Yule (1944), the early inquiries were directed at the question of authorship; for example, did Shakespeare (1564–1616) write the plays that are generally attributed to him? However, nowadays, with the help of the trio, we can use a rather large population of documents to raise more ambitious questions, such as those related to the history of ideas (themes, genres, symbols, signs, images, narratives, etc.).[16] How was one idea replaced by another idea? How did a new idea emerge? How does the ecological dynamics of ideas inform us of the shift in the paradigm, zeitgeist, fashion, ethos, norm, culture, trend, and mentality which characterizes an era? Questions of this kind are very tantalizing, but it is the empowerment from the trio that allows us to examine what the data reveal (Moretti, 2005, 2013; Shiller, 2019). Furthermore, through the availability of the data and statistics, making the formal models of the evolution for the history of ideas also becomes possible.[17] As for the latter case, by realizing distant reading, AHMTs also facilitate the extension of Darwinism to the humanities and social sciences.

In addition to the history of ideas, distant reading can be applied to usual expressions as often seen in novels, prose, poems, biographies, diaries, newspapers, personal communications, and conversations on social media. It has allowed us to construct various statistics or indexes related to sentiments, moods, emotions, affections, mentalities, preferences, beliefs, tendencies, etc. These data and their related statistics can be placed with time, and their evolution or dynamics can be traced. One familiar example is *Google Trends* (Stephens-Davidowitz, 2017). Before the coming of the trio, most of these data were not available. At that time, data in the social sciences were mostly collected through institutions, such as the government, exchanges, social agencies, companies, etc. Most of these data were highly discrete and aggregated. Data related to what William James (1842–1910) coined as the *"stream of thought"* or *"stream of consciousness,"* the big data, were not available (James, 1890). While one can infer the *misery index* of a country at a certain time by adding its unemployment rate and inflation rate, how miserable or fortunate people actually felt around that time could be very different from what we are told by the misery index. Now, big data

---

[16] The term *idea* used here is inclusive; thus, each term which we put inside the brackets can be used interchangeably with it. In fact, different scholars based on their unique interests may prefer different terms. For example, Kenneth Boulding (1910–1993) chose the word *image* and Robert Shiller chose the word *narrative*, while they were both discussing the possible causes of business cycles (Boulding, 1956; Shiller, 2019). For our purpose, it is, therefore, preferable to have all of these related terms in the basket.

[17] The agent-based modeling of social epidemics is an example.

can produce another kind of sentiment index based on people's personal expressions of their feelings, their streams of consciousness, etc. (Dodds & Danforth, 2010). This example provides us with an alternative route to measure human well-being.

15.4.2 Extended Reading

Second, in addition to the cyber-world of books, the trio also embeds and enriches this cyber-world with connections to various other networks, such as by forming networks of networks or multiplex networks. Hence, when reading becomes "far-sighted," many other "species," originally not in the "forest," such as maps, images, photos, audios, videos, artworks, and archeological and historical materials, are also brought into the vicinity. Reading is now easily extended. Whatever we are reading, there are potentially large amounts of related information for which we may be interested in receiving hints about or being connected with. With this empowerment, the humanities are now further branched out to the spatial humanities (Bodenhamer et al., 2010; Gregory & Geddes, 2014), the virtual humanities (Wouters et al., 2012), and so on.

15.4.3 Participatory Reading

Third, AHMTs make participatory reading possible, and provide readers with a different route to experience the original text. Embedded within such a complex, fascinating, cyber-world of books and various auxiliaries, the reader can have a more lively reading experience by actually "getting into the book." AHMTs, through various kinds of virtual reality, augmented reality, or mixed reality technology, combined with game designs, can enable the reader to develop an "on-site" experience by transforming his/her status from an audience to an actor.[18]

15.5 Concluding Remarks

In this chapter, we propose a framework to address the significance of the autonomous human–machine teams (AHMT) for the future of humanity. We first suggest that to have a good grasp of the phenomenon and the functions of AHMTs, we need to have a panoramic framework to view AHMTs as the manifestations of the empowered trio forged by the recent ICDT revolution (see footnote). While the increasingly powerful

---

[18] The recent dystopian movie, "Ready Player One," directed by Steven Spielberg (Spielberg et al., 2018), enables us to see how various types of historical knowledge can be vividly appreciated and used by readers while they rely on them to find a way out in a gaming situation.

trio could imply an enlightening future of humanity, we cannot take it too much for granted as neoclassical economics often does. Our circumspection taken here can be justified by the historically long contentiousness of the man–machine relation; in this chapter, from a long-accumulated literature, we selected and reviewed five models that are sufficient to frame our subsequent discussions.

From a positive viewpoint, we argue that the empowerment signified by the trio can be considered as a second Gutenberg revolution, which, like the first one, can have dramatic impacts on humanity. While technological advancements at different stages were always conceived of as betterments and empowerments for humans, the trio has two distinguishing features that are not well shared by its precedents, namely, individuality and the democratization of individuality. The former acknowledges the unique existence of each life and its eternity, and the latter reconfirms the idea that everyone can demonstrate his/her uniqueness by searching for the capability to be a creator. Having the capability to create, to innovate, to discover, and to narrate are the keys to experiencing a meaningful life. In this regard, what the trio could do for humanity is to reduce the hindrances to capability development, especially when the humans are greatly assisted by machines in their autonomous human–machine teams.

Although we are still at the very inceptive stage of the trio and our interactions with machines in the context of human–machine teams are rather limited, there are promising prospects that we can yearn to have from the symbiotic-like co-evolution of humans and machines. First, the autonomy of AHMTs is not only limited to the role of machines, but also to the role of humans. One possibility is that, during the co-evolutionary process, the degree of autonomy of humans and machines will be mutually reinforced in the sense that when machines help humans become more autonomous, humans will also help machines become more autonomous. With this reinforcing dynamic, AHMTs will become symbiotic organisms, developing in a direction toward what James Lovelock had evinced (Lovelock, 2019). Second, a premise to the previous prospect is the society not getting divided or fragmentized during the evolution of AHMTs, an issue of immense concern to Polanyian economics (Holmes, 2018). In this regard, it is expected that the degree of democratization of individuality will also be part of the aforementioned reinforcements. In other words, the property that humans are becoming increasingly autonomous is not parochial, but global.

With these promising prospects, our final remark goes back to the reality. Obviously, to become well immersed in the ensuing co-evolution of humans and machines, the younger generations of humans need to be equipped with the tools to understand machines, their languages, their thinking modes, their autonomy, and intelligence-like behavior, and whether the machines perceive us as humans, as if they are pets in our family, borrowing the tone from Donna Haraway (2008). It is true that the young generation in this age has already been sufficiently exposed to smart phones, social media, and various social innovations characterized by APPs, but how these experiences can be integrated in a way to become part of their positive reinforcement is as yet unclear. Nonetheless, from the recent changing face of the humanities, we observe that humans as readers have become more autonomous, thanks to the operation of the AHMTs. We expect to see more of these autonomous properties attached to humans, and hopefully more to the younger generations.

Acknowledgements This chapter was originally prepared for an invited speech to be delivered at AAAI, 2020 Spring Symposium at Stanford University, March 25–27, 2020. The original title is: *Cyborg Economics: From Machine Dreams to Novacence or to Catafalque?* The author is grateful to the organizer of the symposium, Professor William Lawless, for his kind invitation, in particular, his efforts to make the meeting virtual, obviously due to the COVID-19 outbreak. The author is also grateful for the support this research received from the Taiwan Ministry of Science and Technology (MOST) [grant number MOST 108-2410-H-004-016-MY2].

References

Abdukadirov, S. (Ed.). (2016). Nudge theory in action: Behavioral design in policy and markets. Berlin: Springer.

Aschoff, N. (2020). The Smartphone Society: Technology, Power, and Resistance in the New Gilded Age. Boston: Beacon Press.

Benkler, Y. (2002). Coase's penguin, or Linux and the "Nature of the Firm." *Yale Law Journal, 112,* 369–446.

Benkler, Y. (2006). *The wealth of networks: How social production transforms markets and freedom.* New Haven: Yale University Press.

Bexiga, M., Garbatov, S., & Seco, J. C. (2020). Closing the gap between designers and developers in a low code ecosystem. In Proceedings of the 23rd ACM/IEEE International Conference on Model Driven Engineering Languages and Systems: Companion Proceedings (pp. 1–10). New York: ACM. https://doi.org/10.1145/3417990.3420195

Binfield, K. (Ed.). (2004). *Writings of the Luddites.* Baltimore: Johns Hopkins University HU Press.

Bodenhamer, D. J., Corrigan, J., & Harris, T. M. (Eds.). (2010). *The spatial humanities: GIS and the future of humanities scholarship.* Bloomington: Indiana University Press.

Bonney, R., Shirk, J., Phillips, T., Wiggins, A., Ballard, H., Miller-Rushing, A., & Parrish, J. (2014). Next steps for citizen science. *Science, 343*(6178), 1436–1437.

Bostrom, N. (2014). *Superintelligence.* Paris: Dunod.

Boulding, K. E. (1956). *The image: Knowledge in life and society.* Ann Arbor, MI: University of Michigan Press.

Chen, S. H. (2019). Would IOET Make Economics More Neoclassical or More Behavioral? Richard Thaler's Prediction, a Revisit. In W. Lawless, R. Mittu, D. Sofge, I. Moskowitz, & S. Russell (Eds.), *Artificial Intelligence for the Internet of Everything* (pp. 171–186). London: Academic Press.

Chen, S. H. (2020). Digital humanities and the digital economy. In W. Lawless (Ed.), *Human-Machine Shared Contexts* (pp. 359–383). London: Academic Press.

Chen, S. H., & Venkatachalam, R. (2017). Agent-based modelling as a foundation for big data. *Journal of Economic Methodology, 24*(4), 362–383.

Chen, S. H., Wang, P. P., & Kuo, T. W. (2007). Computational Intelligence in Economics and Finance: Shifting the Research Frontier. In S. H. Chen, P. P. Wang, & T. W. Kuo (Eds.), *Computational Intelligence in Economics and Finance* (pp. 1–23). Berlin: Springer.

Clarke, B. (2020). *Gaian Systems: Lynn Margulis, Neocybernetics, and the end of the Anthropocene.* Minneapolis: University of Minnesota Press.

Clynes, M., & Kline, N. (1960). Cyborgs and space. *Astronautics, 5*(9), 26–27.

Colella, V. S., Klopfer, E., & Resnick, M. (2001). *Adventures in Modeling: Exploring Complex, Dynamic Systems with StarLogo*. Williston, VT: Teachers College Press.

Crocker, G. (2012). *A Managerial Philosophy of Technology: Technology and Humanity in Symbiosis*. Basingstoke: Palgrave Macmillan.

Dodds, P. S., & Danforth, C. M. (2010). Measuring the happiness of large-scale written expression: Songs, blogs, and presidents. *Journal of Happiness Studies, 11*(4), 441–456.

Dougherty, D. (2016). *Free to Make: How the Maker Movement Is Changing Our Schools, Our Jobs, and Our Minds*. Berkeley, CA: North Atlantic Books.

Franzoni, C., & Sauermann, H. (2014). Crowd science: The organization of scientific research in open collaborative projects. *Research Policy, 43*(1), 1–20.

Gleick, J. (2011). *The information: A history, a theory, a flood*. New York: Vintage.

Gregory, I., & Geddes, A. (Eds.). (2014). *Toward spatial humanities: Historical GIS and spatial history*. Bloomington: Indiana University Press.

Harari, Y. N. (2016). *Homo Deus: A brief history of tomorrow*. London: Random House.

Haraway, D. J. (2008). *When species meet*. Minneapolis: University of Minnesota Press.

Holmes, C. (2018). *Polanyi in times of populism: Vision and contradiction in the history of economic ideas*. London: Routledge.

Houston, R. (1983). Literacy and society in the West, 1500–1850. *Social History, 8*(3), 269–293.

Huxley, A. (1998). *Brave New World (1932)*. New York: Vintage.

James, W. (1890). *The principles of psychology* (Vol. Vols 1 and 2). New York: Holt.

Jones, S. E. (2013). *Against technology: From the Luddites to neo-Luddism*. London: Routledge.

Kingsley, P. (2018). *Catafalque: Carl Jung and the End of Humanity*. London: Catafalque Press.

Kozo-Polyansky, B. M. (1924[2010]). Symbiogenesis: A new principle of evolution. Translated by Fet, V., Margulis, L., & Raven, P. Cambridge: Harvard University Press.

Laloux, F. (2014). *Reinventing organizations: A guide to creating organizations inspired by the next stage in human consciousness*. Brussels: Nelson Parker.

Lawless, W., Mittu, R., Sofge, D., Moskowitz, I. S., & Russell, S. (Eds.). (2019). Artificial intelligence for the Internet of Everything. Academic Press.

Leinweber, D. J., & Arnott, R. D. (1995). Quantitative and computational innovation in investment management. *Journal of Portfolio Management, 21*(2), 8–15.

Lovelock, J. (1988). *The ages of Gaia: A biography of our living earth*. New York: Oxford University Press.

Lovelock, J. (2007). *The revenge of Gaia: Why the Earth is fighting back and how we can still save humanity* (Vol. 36). Penguin UK.

Lovelock, J. (2019). *Novacene: The Coming Age of Hyperintelligence*. Cambridge: MIT Press.

Markoff, J. (2015). *Machines of loving grace: The quest for common ground between humans and robots*. New York: Ecco.

McCarthy, M. (2015). The Moth Snowstorm: Nature and joy. *New York Review of Books*.

McCloskey, D. N. (2016). *Bourgeois equality: How ideas, not capital or institutions, enriched the world*. Chicago: University of Chicago Press.

Kaneko, M. (1965). *Zetsubou no seishin-shi (In Japanese)*. Kobunsha Co.

Moretti, F. (2005). *Graphs, maps, trees: Abstract models for a literary history*. London: Verso.

Moretti, F. (2013). *Distant reading*. London: Verso Books.

Munger, M. C. (2018). *Tomorrow 3.0: Transaction costs and the sharing economy*. New York: Cambridge University Press.

Murrell, K. F. H. (1965). *Ergonomics: Man in his working environment*. London: Chapman and Hall.

Nowak, M., & Highfield, R. (2011). *Supercooperators: Altruism, evolution, and why we need each other to succeed*. New York: Simon and Schuster.

O'Neil, C. (2016). *Weapons of math destruction: How big data increases inequality and threatens democracy*. New York: Broadway Books.

O'Reilly, T. (2017). *WTF? What's the Future and why It's Up to Us*. New York: Random House.

Palmer, J. (Ed.). (2001). *Fifty modern thinkers on education: From Piaget to the present*. London: Psychology Press.

Papert, S. (1980). *Mindstorms: Children, computers, and powerful ideas*. New York: Basic Books.

Pascal, B. (1669[1995]). Pensées and other writings. H. Levi (trans). New York: Oxford University Press.

Piaget, J. (1973). *To understand is to invent: The future of education*. New York: Grossman Publishers.

Piketty, T. (2014). *Capital in the Twenty-First Century*. The Belknap Press of Harvard University Press (Original in French, 2013; translated by Goldhammer, A.)

Pittinsky, T. L. (Ed.). (2019). *Science, technology, and society: New perspectives and directions*. Cambridge: Cambridge University Press.

Polanyi, K. (1944). *The great transformation: The political and economic origins of our time*. New York: Rinehart.

Prassl, J. (2018). *Humans as a service: The promise and perils of work in the gig economy*. New York: Oxford University Press.

Reid, A. J. (2018). *The smartphone paradox: Our ruinous dependency in the Device Age*. Berlin: Springer.

Resnick, M. (1997). *Turtles, termites, and traffic jams: Explorations in massively parallel microworlds*. Cambridge: MIT Press.

Resnick, M. (2017). *Lifelong kindergarten: Cultivating creativity through projects, passion, peers, and play*. Cambridge: MIT Press.

Rushkoff, D. (2020). *Team human*. Ledizioni.

Sagan, D. (2012). *Lynn Margulis: The life and legacy of a scientific rebel*. White River Junction, VT: Chelsea Green Publishing.

Sahay, A., Indamutsa, A., Di Ruscio, D., & Pierantonio, A. (2020). Supporting the understanding and comparison of low-code development platforms. In *2020 46th Euromicro Conference on Software Engineering and Advanced Applications (SEAA)* (pp. 171–178). New York: IEEE.

Scitovsky, T. (1976). *The joyless economy: An inquiry into human satisfaction and consumer dissatisfaction*. New York: Oxford University Press (Revised Edition, 1992)

Sen, A. (1999). *Development as freedom*. New York: Oxford University Press.

Shelley, M. W. (2017). *Frankenstein: Annotated for scientists, engineers, and creators of all kinds*. Cambridge: MIT Press.

Shiller, R. J. (2019). *Narrative economics: How stories go viral and drive major economic events*. Princeton: Princeton University Press.

Siedentop, L. (2014). *Inventing the individual: The origins of Western liberalism*. Cambridge, MA: Harvard University Press.

Silver, D., Hubert, T., Schrittwieser, J., Antonoglou, I., Lai, M., Guez, A., Lanctot, M., Sifre, L., Kumaran, D., Graepel, T., Lillicrap, T., Simonyan, K., & Hassabis, D. (2018). A general reinforcement learning algorithm that masters chess, shogi, and go through self-play. *Science, 362*(6419), 1140–1144.

Spielberg, S., Silvestri, A., Penn, Z., Cline, E., & De Line, D. (2018). *Ready player one*. Warner Bros.

Stephens-Davidowitz, S. (2017). *Everybody lies: Big data, new data, and what the Internet can tell us about who we really are*. New York: HarperCollins.

Sundararajan, A. (2016). *The sharing economy: The end of employment and the rise of crowd-based capitalism*. Cambridge: MIT Press.

Thaler, R. H., & Sunstein, C. R. (2008). *Nudge: Improving decisions about health, wealth, and happiness*. New York: Penguin.

Turing, A. M. (1950). Computing machinery and intelligence. *Mind, 59*(236), 433.

Twenge, J. M. (2017). *IGen: Why today's super-connected kids are growing up less rebellious, more tolerant, less happy–and completely unprepared for adulthood–and what that means for the rest of us*. New York: Simon and Schuster.

Wiener, N. (1948). *Cybernetics: Or control and communication in the animal and the machine.* Cambridge: MIT Press.

Wiener, N. (1950). *The human use of human beings: Cybernetics and society.* Boston: The Riverside Press.

Wilensky, U., & Rand, W. (2015). *An introduction to agent-based modeling: Modeling natural, social, and engineered complex systems with NetLogo.* Cambridge: MIT Press.

Wolber, D., Abelson, H., Spertus, E., & Looney, L. (2011). *App Inventor: Create Your Own Android Apps.* Newton, MA: O'Reilly Media Inc.

Wouters, P., Beaulieu, A., Scharnhorst, A., & Wyatt, S. (Eds.). (2012). *Virtual Knowledge: Experimenting in the Humanities and the Social Sciences.* Cambridge: MIT Press.

Yang, A. (2018). *The war on normal people: The truth about America's disappearing jobs and why universal basic income is our future.* Paris: Hachette UK.

Yule, C. U. (1944). *The statistical study of literary vocabulary.* Cambridge: Cambridge University Press.

Chapter 16
Transforming the System of Military Medical Research: An Institutional History of the Department of Defense's (DoD) First Electronic Institutional Review Board Enterprise IT System

J. Wood and William F. Lawless

Abstract This unusual history of how a small team transformed the global system composed of Army and then DoD medical research processes has been unrecorded until now. It offers guidance to others attempting to transform similarly large systems. It begins with an evaluation of the Department of Clinical Investigation (DCI) at the US Army Medical Center (MEDCEN) in 2005, the formation of a collaboration team in 2006, and the team's vision of an electronic records management tool (ERMT) for its documents in 2007. From this small beginning, these disparate efforts combined to transform the management of research protocol submission, review, and approval processes as well as research protocols and supporting documents at all DoD MEDCENs. Before this history began, the Army's MEDCENs used a paper-based research protocol submission and review process by the Institutional Review Board (IRB) for the approval of medical research on human subjects (and animals). The team's evaluation of the existing processes added metrics that enabled the design of an electronic system to measure the performance of the Army's medical research mission. Merging the evaluation and the team's vision to replace the Army's paper-based IRB occurred with the purchase of a commercial electronic IRB system. It took until 2008 for the eIRB to become funded and another year to begin operations, but within 2 years of start-up, it was rapidly adopted across DoD's global research community to become the largest enterprise eIRB in the world. In 2011, a formal evaluation project was proposed to measure the impact of the eIRB's unexpected success across DoD; the impact study was funded in 2012, begun in 2013 and finished in 2014 when we end this history; subsequently, the team was disbanded. Although not a part of this history, we briefly address a few of the statistical results of the eIRB's impact now and more fully at a later time. We close with a postscript to update readers on the unexpected closure of the eIRB and its reincarnation.

J. Wood (✉) · W. F. Lawless
Math & Psychology, Paine College, Augusta, GA, USA

W. F. Lawless
e-mail: w.lawless@icloud.com

© Springer Nature Switzerland AG 2021
W. F. Lawless et al. (eds.), *Systems Engineering and Artificial Intelligence*,
https://doi.org/10.1007/978-3-030-77283-3_16

Table 16.1 Table of acronyms

AMEDD	Army medical department
BAMC	Brooke Army Medical Center
BI	Business intelligence
CIRO	Clinical Investigations Regulatory Office. Army
CONOPS	Concept of Operations described to users
CONUS	Continental United States
COTS	Commercial off-the-shelf systems are commercial software and hardware products that are ready for purchase
DCI	Department of Clinical Investigation
DDEAMC	D.D. Eisenhower Medical Center
DMRN	Defense Medical Research Network
eIRB	electronic Institutional Review Board
ERMT	electronic records management tool; e.g., an eIRB
IACUC	Institutional Animal Care and Use Committee
MAMC	Madigan Army MEDCEN
MEDCOM	Army Medical Command
NNMC	National Naval Medical Center-Bethesda
OCONUS	Outside of the continental United States
TAMC	Tippler Army Medical Center
TATRC	Telemedicine and Advanced Technology Research Center
USU	Uniformed Services University
WRAMC	Walter Reed Army Medical Center

16.1   Introduction. A Tale of Two Histories

Systems are common. Large systems are also common. The larger the system, the more difficult it becomes to transform. This chapter serves as a cautionary tale of the difficulties of attempting to transform one of the largest systems of medical research in the world at that time. But with access to a large IRB data base, it also presents metrics on a path toward the use of Artificial Intelligence (AI) or machine learning (ML) for research on autonomous metrics, on ethical practices, and on mitigating harm.[1]

In 2005, based on its published annual reports, our initial goal was to evaluate research performed at the Army's D.D. Eisenhower Medical Center (DDEAMC) and overseen by its Department of Clinical Investigation (DCI), both at Fort Gordon, GA. The evaluation (Lawless et al., 2007) found that research processes and focus areas could be better organized, that scientists were often fragmented from each other within the organization and across the enterprise as well as not in-line with the

---

[1] A list of acronyms is provided after the references (see Table 16.1).

overall Army medical research strategic goals, and that this fragmentation "precluded the system from being able to determine whether its mission was being carried out effectively, restricting its ability to measure the productivity of its medical scientists," let alone to regulate the process well (Lawless et al., 2010, p. 10).

At the time, the enterprise level view of research topics/focus areas and related process data was in paper form (viz., annual reports)[2]; the data was incomplete; and there was no data readily available from other military sites that could be used to draw meaningful comparisons. In later research, we have theorized and found that fragmentation impedes an organization's ability to be transformed (Lawless, 2017a; Lawless et al., 2018). But at the time, we had hypothesized that fragmentation at DDEAMC's DCI might be overcome with a series of electronic standards for publications, presentations and grants.

We thought that we could use the enterprise data generated by the medical research undergoing IRB reviews at DDEAMC as business intelligence (BI) to improve the medical research under the purview of its DCI (Wood et al., 2008). We had envisioned real-time data collection, analyses, and reporting with machines that would automatically address the Army's Medical Centers (MEDCEN) research mission with metrics for DDEAMC. Inadvertently, our evaluation motivated the need of metrics for the eIRB.

In 2006–7, our second goal was to collaborate to define the requirements of an electronic IT system to allow the Army's medical research scientists and regulatory oversight staff to better manage research proposal submission and review processes and all supporting documents. Having an electronic IT system would enable the MEDCENs to more easily collaborate geographically, avoid duplication of research efforts, and optimize research funding to better manage medical research communications and standards across the Army's sprawling and long-standing research programs. Overall, the team believed that having an eIRB system would be of benefit for all stakeholders in the research enterprise and better enable strategic management and tactical execution of research across the enterprise.

The second goal was met when a pilot eIRB started at DDEAMC for its DCI and was joined by four other MEDCENs.[3] The second goal expanded in FY2010-11 to include all of the Army's MEDCENs and its HQ for its MEDCENs as well as Air Force, Navy, and other DoD research units.

Our history of these dual transformations, the first fortuitous and the second mindful, was guided by the Army's mission for its MEDCENs. As applied to the DCI at DDEAMC, the mission of the Army's Medical Centers was to provide the best health care for its patients who were military soldiers and civilian beneficiaries; to educate, train, and retain its medical staff and graduate medical students; and to advance military medical research (see also Goodin, 2011).

---

[2] Some of the Army's funded medical research programs have been conducted over many years; for these long-term projects, it was common to transport the large number of paper files in small, hand pulled wagons to the IRB of record.

[3] See the timeline, FY2009-10.

16.1.1   Goal 1: The eIRB Transformed the MEDCENs

In 2005, an evaluation of DCI's annual report at DDEAMC was being conducted (Lawless et al., 2007, 2010). The evaluation discovered the lack of electronic business intelligence (BI) tools to measure the performance of the research regulatory body (IRB/IACUC) overseeing the medical researchers at DDEAMC, and what their research produced (namely, journal manuscripts). As we attempted to determine the effectiveness of the research conducted at DDEAMC by its institutional scientists and overseen by its DCI in 2005, we faced only hard copies of annual reports, essentially large but mostly non-searchable data dumps. At the time, no DoD system existed to capture the data at each point along the trail of a research protocol from submission to review and approval as well as the publications that resulted by individual Army Medical scientists and science teams (NSB, 2015; NSF, 2015; also, Goodin, 2011, slide 17). Digital data was entered by hand, producing an unclear but narrow perspective at DDEAMC (and likewise at other MEDCEN sites) of what was occurring with its medical research. We suspected but could not confirm that redundancy in the form of a duplication of effort was occurring across the Army's MEDCENs guided by numerous non-standardized rules parochial to each site, producing conflicting requirements between sites that caused a fragmentation within and between the MEDCENs (Lawless et al., 2007). We believed that this fragmentation among researchers and teams might interfere with the Army's research mission for its MEDCENs. Fragmentation and redundancy are associated with a lack of competition (Lawless, 2017b). While we believed that this fragmentation was inevitably a Department of Defense (DoD) problem, with each MEDCEN possibly pursuing its own path to mission success, based on the limited data we could access at that time, we could not address the causes of the problems we initially saw at DDEAMC, its regulators at DCI, nor advance theory.

Neither did we know the precise status of publications, what was being published, nor the degree of redundancy in teams or repetition in the research being conducted (Wood et al., 2008):

> We found no clear link between research products and the mission; no measure of publication impacts; and no direct way to measure organizational productivity against its peers (reduced or negligible states of interdependence). ... No overarching measure of system performance existed for the ... [MEDCENs] that the separate organizations could follow to guide their collective behavior. As a consequence, long-term work practices and cultural differences predominated [between the MEDCEN sites].

From almost the beginning, we had envisioned that organizational fragmentation could, in part, be reduced with standardized protocols for automatic data collection at DDEAMC and the generation of annual reports by its DCI on its performance for the Army's research mission that could advance the medical research mission; reduce its costs of research reviews; and increase the scientific impact of its medical research products.

From our perspective at the time, we believed that fragmentation and redundancy were not necessarily all bad in that it might reflect a paradox that drove the innovation process for individual scientists, but that it also impeded oversight management of the research conducted by the local DCI and the Army's MEDCENs (Lawless et al., 2010). The result, we speculated, was unnecessary redundancy in medical research projects, not aimed at replication, that were possibly wasting scarce resources.

Our conclusion was not unusual. Smith and Tushman (2005) found that contradictory goals could make an organization both more productive in the near term and transformative in the longer term. But there was no way to know without having better data to find out which scientists or teams of scientists were well funded, who was productive and which scientists and teams were not (Christensen, 2011).

16.1.2   Goal 2: The Initial Meeting on Collaboration

This part of the story began in 2006 with a search to find a way to enhance collaboration among a handful of the MEDCENs. An initial meeting was held in San Antonio with the Army's Chief, Clinical Investigation Regulatory Office (CIRO), and the Army's DCI (regulatory) leaders. A consensus was reached by the DCIs that they needed a new electronic system to manage medical research across the United States and around the globe. A workgroup was formed at this meeting to consider an electronic system to replace the paper products that fed the IRBs then in operation across the Army. At the same meeting, we had begun to think more globally than just among our immediate collaborators. We had identified the replacement of the Army's paper-based system as a DoD-wide problem, leading us to invite participation from the Army's other MEDCENs and their medical counterparts in the Navy and Air Force. But, while the team was efficient and effective, it was a small team without a champion in the upper echelon of Army HQ or DoD.

The Formation of a Disbursed Team

A geographically disbursed military medical research leadership team was formed spanning from Army MEDCENS in Hawaii to Germany. Team meetings were held on how to address research regulatory IT needs across the MEDCEN system; i.e., the management of research documents, review results, and approval processes. For these recurrent meetings, collaboration technology was used, such as WebEx meeting,[4] Defense Connect Online,[5] and the Mind Manager's Mind Mapping tool.[6] Based on these virtual meetings, DCI requirements were defined, needs were identified, Commercial-off-the-shelf (COTS) demonstrations were held online in real time, and

---

[4] https://signup.webex.com/webexmeetings/US/sem_acquisition.html?&DG=01-04-07-US-12-01-02-06&TrackID=1031986&country=US&psearchID=webex&gclid=CMS01dio4NACFZE6g QodBbUHow.

[5] https://www.dco.dod.mil.

[6] https://www.mindmeister.com/?gad_campaign=US&gclid=CNv3-rOp4NACFUQdgQodx5QCIA.

the systems offered by various vendors were evaluated. From Wood (2011b), the meetings were used to evaluate collective research regulatory oversight automation needs and to hold demonstrations from the leading vendors of eIRB systems. DOD participants in this project involved DCI leaders at the Army's Clinical Investigations Regulatory Office (CIRO), TAMC, MAMC, BAMC, DDEAMC, WRAMC, NNMC, USU, and Lackland AFB.

An Electronic IRB (eIRB)

Beginning in 2005 and lasting 18 months enabled by IT technology, a team spread over a large geographical area of AMEDD's DCI regulatory leaders and its medical researchers from Army MEDCENs (and DOD counterparts in the Navy and Air Force) collaborated about IT technology to connect like-minded people across a large geographic area to bring about enterprise change in the narrow sense that we would only transform IT for research documents, reviews, and approval processes at each site; but we also wanted to know what was happening across the Army's MEDCENs. To implement these changes, the tool identified was an eIRB to replace the burdensome paperwork to approve and oversee human research protocols. The same tool was proposed for the Army's animal research review committee known as Institutional Animal Care and Use Committee (IACUC).

The physical and virtual meetings for the working group demonstrated the capability of web-based technology for MEDCEN knowledge management (Wood et al., 2008). For the virtual meetings, many of the MEDCEN leaders had been geographically separated but nonetheless were able to meet about 30 times over almost 2 years and yet collaborate to address the potential for an eIRB in a manner that would have been cost-prohibitive in the past:

> [MEDCEN] leaders from Hawaii, Washington State, Texas, Washington DC, Germany and Georgia worked as a networked virtual organization for approximately 60 hours using web-based collaboration technology with visual and audio communication that lead ultimately to the successful funding of the eIRB system ... Members simply logged onto the web from the convenience of their own office to participate in problem solving... Using this virtual collaboration in conjunction with a mind-mapping program (similar to a semantic network) for more effective brainstorming allowed the saving of thousands of dollars in travel and personnel time.

Out of this collaboration, the team had developed the following forward-looking vision (Wood, 2011b)

> The system we develop will be the standard for the Department of Defense by easily allowing all research proposals, supporting documents and scholarly products to be submitted and managed by a secure, web-based system that will calculate real-time metrics of research, workload, productivity and quality.

An electronic IRB (eIRB) system was selected, recommended to Army Headquarters (HQ), but HQ declined to fund the new system. Apparently, the solution we had proposed was for a problem that Army HQ had not yet recognized as a problem.

After rejection by the Army's HQ in 2007, we took a different approach. A grant was written for the start-up of a pilot that was subsequently funded.

In 2008, the first author received funding for a pilot program as part of a technology initiative at DDEAMC/SERMC (Wood, 2011b). With these funds, a COTS electronic IRB system was purchased from IRBNet.[7] In addition to DDEAMC, the pilot demonstration with IRBNet included Walter Reed Army Medical Center (WRAMC), the National Naval Medical Center in Bethesda (NNMC), and the Uniformed Services University (USU).[8] The Army's IT and security governance requirements were satisfied in order to safely host the COTS system on a DoD network.[9] For security reasons, real-time access and robust functionality, IRBNet software was placed on the Army's TATRC-South servers at Fort Gordon (TATRC, or Telemedicine and Advanced Technology Research Center) rather than using a commercially hosted version. Madigan Army MEDCEN (MAMC) began to use commercially hosted IRBNet version about the same time. These original 4 sites in 2008 plus MAMC expanded to 19 by 2009; by 2011, the network had grown to include 23 facilities and institutions, more than 120 research locations around the globe and about 3,000 users (Wood, 2011b). While the eIRB had begun as a pilot at DDEAMC, the Army had come to now see it as a necessary tool that was needed to transform many if not all of its perceived research and data management shortcomings at its MEDCENs.

16.1.3   Our Two Goals Merged into One

The history of these two goals began from two divergent paths that had now converged. First, an evaluation was conducted in 2005 of the Amy's DCI at DDEAMC that pointed out the need for an online database to track the members of research teams, their performance and their written products (Lawless et al., 2011). Coupled to the eIRB, the evaluation served to guide the development of future metrics for the performance of each MEDCEN as well as the system of MEDCENs. Second, and almost contemporaneously, we determined that an IT system was needed; a team developed and collaborated to define the problem, to work together and to get an eIRB. Meeting the second goal transformed the existing unwieldy paper products system at DDEAMC and eventually brought its collaborators into an electronic system that was relied upon to improve the oversight of research at each site and among all of the Army's MEDCENs. From a handful of sites and users, this system grew rapidly into one of the largest in the world, if not the largest.

The eIRB had become a platform for integrated management and reporting. It transformed procedures for the approval of research protocols and the management of human and animal research (Wood et al., 2008):

---

[7] https://www.irbnet.org/release/index.html.

[8] Malcolm Grow Air Force Medical Center was subsumed under the other sites in the National Capital Area.

[9] Viz., CONOPS, DBT, IATO, ATO, and CON.

The eIRB includes routing of submissions to IRB members; receipt of comments from IRB reviewers; transmission of modification requests to investigators; development of IRB meeting minutes; tracking of protocol status; automatic notification of investigators of continuing review deadlines; and tracking metrics. The technology provides a platform for collaboration across the organization between Principal Investigators and team members when drafting protocol proposals. It provides feedback among IRB reviewers, the PI and study team, and Administrators. It tracks Adverse Events (medical and drugs); provides guided electronic input and assistance and error checking and reporting to PIs and Administrators.

The move to adopt the web-based eIRB had set the stage to turn around the lack of organizational and system-wide standards for the knowledge developed by the MEDCENs (Wood et al., 2009). The eIRB allowed for real-time organizational and system-wide based metrics to improve research competitiveness (based on maintaining interdependent states within and between each team; Lawless et al., 2016).

Based on our first goal, we had recommended the need to standardize the eIRB process; however, we ran into resistance to standardize the eIRB processes across the MEDCENs. We compromised by having a standard coversheet as opposed to standardized protocol templates but not universally adopted with standard forms (e.g., cover sheets for each research protocol; standard data fields; etc.). In this regard, by the end of the impact study in 2014 when the team was disbanded, we were unsuccessful at standardization. Each of the MEDCENs continued to use their existing protocol templates and business processes. By not being firm early on, by focusing instead on participation by the MEDCEN sites, unfortunately, we were unable to standardize later on (Wood et al., 2009):

> In the future, all ... [MEDCENs] plan to use the same protocol templates and processes but in the meantime, they can have an operational system AND have the dataset they need. It is anticipated that it will take a while to get everyone at all ... [MEDCENs] to reach consensus on templates and business processes.

The lack of overarching standards and metrics at each MEDCEN and at the enterprise level meant that mission performance could not be fully assessed, nor standardized nor even assured across the MEDCENs. We had selected IRBNet in part due to its scalability with its attachment-based document processes; in that way, sites could use whatever processes and forms they had or wanted. Over time, once we had consensus, we thought that we could standardize forms and processes at that later time for when we had planned to shift from a largely attachment-based system in IRBNet to a "smart form" process.

Nonetheless, we believed that the data necessary to measure the performance of all of the sites with a common metric existed, but that performance standard had not yet been accomplished by the time our evaluation was completed in 2014 (Wood & Lawless, 2014).

16.2   The Next Steps in the Transformation from a Paper to Electronic System

During the second year of implementing IRBNet, the original sites paid for their use of the eIRB at their individual sites (Wood, 2011b). Yet, many contracting challenges existed. After or during that second year, the Representatives from the Office of the Assistant Secretary of Defense (Health Affairs) joined the team and took over the funding of the eIRB for participating DoD sites.

The program manager team leader for the Defense Medical Research Network (DMRN) and IRBNet successfully secured funding from Health Affairs to expand the program to all DOD medical research facilities. This saved part of the annual cost by DDEAMC to operate IRBNet there and other sites. Total project costs secured for DDEAMC and other DOD sites for the program management was significant. What began as a TATRC funded business process improvement research project for DDEAMC/SERMC had more than met the original working group's vision since this system had become the DoD standard (Wood, 2011a). The Army's Medical Command (MEDCOM) required CONOPS documentation to be completed by DMRN for IRBNet to become recognized as the Army's enterprise system.[10]

There were lots of issues to be dealt with and resolved after year two of pilot operations, such as where to permanently host the servers, how to sustain funding, and a performance contrast of the eIRB impacts on the MEDCEN mission and research in particular. But despite the eIRB vendor helping us to achieve our original vision from 2007, by 2012, our team was beginning to lose control of the eIRB transformation.

16.3   Boundary Maintenance

Various metrics and outcome measures were discussed, but not implemented. Specifically, an impact analysis was not begun until 2012 and not finished until March 2014; e.g., during these early meetings, it became apparent that various groups across the Army's medical complex were trying to start their own systems because they could, or were looking to buy a COTS product for their own site, reflecting a silo mentality that we feared further increased inter-site fragmentation. This silo mentality was amplified by our failure to standardize the forms and the procedures for IRBNet that would have simplified the process to obtain analyses of the research conducted at the MEDCENs by Army and DoD headquarters. Once procedures have been set by headquarters (e.g., CIRO), each of the MEDCENs managed their own affairs within those parameters, including whether to use the eIRB system and to what extent they

---

[10] i.e., AKO/SSO certification, DIACAP, IA, ATO, Army Certificate of Net worthiness and other certification requirements; the Defense Business Transformation documentation process has been completed.

could adopt the eIRBs forms and procedures or to use their own. This inter-site frag-mentation was reflected in turf battles that impeded analyses of the data produced by the eIRB. In the future, we had wanted to address this problem at a fundamental level known as boundary maintenance; i.e., how local boundaries are maintained by local cultures in a tradeoff with how those boundaries may be transformed by upper management (Lawless et al., 2016). For example, the stronger the local culture, the more resistance to the standardized transformations that the eIRB afforded. For this simple model, we would model the entropy produced as our metric, the theory being that the less entropy produced by a structure (e.g., no turf wars at a site or between sites), the more effective is the shape of the combined structure at directing the energy available to the organization's mission (England, 2013), allowing it to produce maximum entropy (MEP) for its mission (Martyushev, 2013).

16.4 Future Steps to Determine Impacts. Preliminary Results in 2010

The next part of the history deals with analyzing the impact of replacing the old paper-products system with the eIRB (Wood et al., 2013). We plan to address the impact in a latter article. But some of the impacts were known by 2010 (Lawless, 2010): At WRAMC, the time to process publication clearances with the eIRB had decreased dramatically from an average of 30 days to 4 days, a significant reduction in wasted time that indicated greater organizational efficiency. And CIRO had discovered that when a new protocol failed to be completed, it wasted a significant amount of money, not counting the possible knowledge lost as well as the prestige of the organization and the researchers involved.

Still, an early analysis of the improvement among the first five sites was presented in IDPS (2011). Using a t-test conducted on its data from the second quarter 2010 to the second quarter 2011, DMRN processing times consistently reduced across five medical centers ($t(8) = 2.53$, $p = 0.035$, $SD(1) = 32.8$, $SEM(1) = 14.67$; $SD(2) = 10.03$, $SEM(2) = 4.49$; $SError = 5.3$). Table 16.2 also provides a summary in 2011 of the user sites. Table 16.3 tabulates the total users by year.

16.5 Summary

Our first goal was to evaluate the performance of the MEDCEN's research processes and research products produced at DDEAMC and eventually for all of the MEDCENs, a goal that remains incomplete due to a lack of uniform standards adopted within and across the MEDCENs. We felt that these standards depended on the data that could have been used to establish metrics of performance at each MEDCEN and across the Army's medical research complex. Instead, the variability we did find

Table 16.2 IRBNet's usage at DoD, Summary in 2011 of the user sites (Wood, 2011a). From Wood (2011b), the data generated by the eIRB could meet the Army's MEDCEN mission (DMRN/IRBNet successfully migrated to fhpr.osd.mil servers; data from the project report sent to TATRC). The 2014 data is from IRBNet, 11/27/14

Medical centers (MEDCENs)	Summary data 2011	Summary data 11/27/2014
Dwight D. Eisenhower Army Medical Center, Walter Reed Army Medical Center, National Naval Medical Center, Uniformed Services University, Madigan Army Medical Center, Naval Medical Center-San Diego, Wilford Hall, Brooke Army Medical Center, William Beaumont Army Medical Center, Tripler Army Medical Center, Womack Army Medical Center, Walter Reed Army Institute of Research, US Army Research Institute of Environmental Medicine, United States Army Medical Research Institute for Infectious Diseases, Army Medical Research and Materiel Command HQ, Clinical Investigation Regulatory Office	Total research sites and boards: 123￼ Research projects: 3,985￼ Submissions securely processed: 13,147￼ Total electronic documents securely processed: 44,772￼ Decision letters and other board documents issued: 4,750	Research institutions: 213￼ Board workspaces: 106￼ Research Projects: 21,321￼ Submitted packages (Board actions): 77,911￼ Project Documents submitted for Board Review: 318,825￼ Training and credentials documents being tracked by Boards: 17,761￼ Decision letters and other board documents issued in response to submitted packages: 100,454￼ Board meetings: 2,358￼ Detailed personal reviews by individual board members: 88,862
	Total users: 2,785 (CONUS and OCONUS)	Total users: 13,752

across the MEDCENs indicated the existence of internal competition that unnecessarily raised costs (Lawless et al., 2013) and reduced data validity (e.g., Gold & Dewa, 2005; Yawn et al., 2009). Eventually, these standards were not implemented across DoD; whatever fragmentation existed then remains unknown today.

We had realized early on that the eIRB could generate enterprise data produced by its medical research teams and regulatory oversight bodies for business intelligence (BI) to improve the medical research mission under the purview of the Army (Wood et al., 2008). Ultimately, we wanted real-time automatic data collection, analyses and reporting with machines that would address the MEDCEN's research mission while transforming the enterprise to promote medical research innovation.

Our second goal begun as a collaboration to enhance IT had instead become the enterprise tool adopted by the Army for all of its medical research. By 2011, we had succeeded with our second goal started in 2005 to create an electronic system that would allow the Army's MEDCENs to be able to better manage medical research regulatory oversight at each MEDCEN and with each other across the Army's medical enterprise. We met this goal by installing IRBNet, an eIRB, to replace the Army's paper-based IRB system at the Army's DDEAMC and four other sites. Before long,

Table 16.3 Total users by years (except for the last date, totals users were collected at milestone intervals)

Date	Users
7/10/2015	14,878
1/22/2015	14,000
8/12/2014	13,000
3/12/2014	12,000
10/1/2013	11,000
5/10/2013	10,000
12/4/2012	9,000
7/19/2012	8,000
3/12/2012	7,000
10/11/2011	6,000
6/3/2011	5,000
2/8/2011	4,000
5/7/2010	3,000
9/23/2009	2,000
3/4/2010	1,000

and in a surprise to us, the Army adopted the eIRB as the means to manage all of its research proposal submission and regulatory oversight processes. Our success had been amplified by our first goal to establish metrics, still elusive. In hindsight, the transformations we enacted may have happened too fast.

Regardless, arising from the convergence of our two goals to evaluate and collaborate, the eIRB was designed to capture data that would allow us to not only know how well the Army's mission was being performed, but also, by being electronic and potentially accessible in real-time by military medical scientists around the globe, it was designed to transform the Army MEDCENs, their medical research, and the research that could one day be used to improve patient care.

We had expected that the data once extracted, analyzed and provided on a periodic basis should have benefited soldiers and other DoD beneficiaries giving DoD research leadership the management data necessary for process improvements. This ultimately could have given military health care beneficiaries quicker access to newly developed treatments from faster research approval and therefore potential life saving interventions due to an improved research review processes. The sooner that researchers can submit and have research approved, the sooner the results can be generated, published and moved to the field. Having actionable, interpretable data from the system for business process improvements should enable leaders to ensure that research processes are efficient and effective. Data from the system if used to improve processes could result in the pool of research information potentially growing faster and in less time for results to be given back to users.

In retrospect, the vision we had crafted in 2007 may have been too limited for what arose out of that vision. CIRO at the time warned us that we could not have an enterprise system without standardizing procedures and forms. But we chose to move forward with an eIRB system that would allow each site to use its own forms and procedures to accelerate the adoption of the eIRB system. The intent was to transition from site specific forms/processes to standardized enterprise forms and processes using the same eIRB system once consensus was obtained by participating sites. Yet we never envisioned that our small team would develop an enterprise system that would be adopted so quickly as was the eIRB. We figured that we could standardize the forms and procedures later. That mistake was compounded by not having a champion at DoD-HQ; recall that our first recommendation for an eIRB to Army Headquarters (HQ) was declined. Further, once the impact study was completed in 2014, despite being effective and successful, the team was disbanded.

A brief conclusion about our team. Our collaboration to improve our reporting, reviewing, and approval processes, motivated by the evaluation's need to include performance metrics, lead to the pilot demonstration of an eIRB system. We were amazed at how rapidly the system transformed into possibly the largest eIRB system in the world. We could have done a lot of things better, but apparently, the concept we had cobbled together as a team turned out to be emphatically successful. Our pilot eIRB, had become the Army's and DoD's defacto enterprise system.

16.6   Postscript

After we had completed our evaluation of DoD's eIRB (Wood & Lawless, 2014), the host contractor, of the eIRB system, had undergone multiple contract extensions with no guarantee that it would be permitted to compete to continue its contract; even the Navy had designed its own, competing web-based system. Instead of accepting its third contract extension, the eIRB system ceased to operate after 2015, forcing a return to a paper-based system for what we thought might have been a period of about a year. But after 1000s of man-hours expended on the recovery from the loss of existing eIRB, which entailed an interim mixed electronic (e.g., email) and paper-based system, and designing a new workflow, a new eIRB contractor has been identified but is not yet fully operational across the enterprise.[11] The original adopted eIRB system had been an attachment-based system allowing each site to use its own forms/processes with the option of standardized forms that were not adopted. As previously discussed, this limited the fidelity of the data, but once the new eIRB system's forms and processes are standardized across the DoD should resolve the primary criticism that we had raised during our evaluation report in 2014.

---

[11] https://www.health.mil/Military-Health-Topics/Research-and-Innovation/Research-Oversight/Electronic-Institutional-Review-Board-Modernization.

References

Christensen, C. (2011). How pursuit of profits kills innovation and the U.S. Forbes, economy. Retrieved September 18, 2011, from http://www.forbes.com/sites/stevedenning/2011/11/18/cla yton-christensen-how-pursuit-of-profits-killsinnovation-and-the-us-economy/.

DDEAMC. (2015). U.S. Army Medical Department, D.D. Eisenhower Army Medical Center. http://www.ddeamc.amedd.army.mil.

Eisenhower Army Medical Center Protocol for Clinical Investigation. (2012). Retrieved February 3, 2012.

England, J. L. (2013). Statistical physics of self-replication. *The Journal of Chemical Physics, 139*, 121923. https://doi.org/10.1063/1.4818538.

Gold, J. L., & Dewa, C. S. (2005). Institutional review boards and multisite studies in health services research: Is there a better way? *Health Services Research, 40*, 291–307.

Goodin, J. L. M. A. J. (2011). OIC, Clinical Investigation Laboratory, "Clinical Investigation Research Laboratories: *The Rest of the Story,* slides presented at D.D. Eisenhower Army Medical Center Department of Clinical Investigation, January 11, 2011.

IDPS. (2011, 9/1) IRBNet DMRN. *Program Summary*, September 1, 2011.

Lawless, W. F. (2010). Unpublished notes from meeting with Dr. J. Retrieved January 20, 2010.

Lawless, W. F. (2017). The entangled nature of interdependence. *Bistability, Irreproducibility and Uncertainty, Journal of Mathematical Psychology, 78*, 51–64.

Lawless, W. F. (2017). The physics of teams: Interdependence, measurable entropy and computational emotion. *Frontiers Physics., 5*, 30. https://doi.org/10.3389/fphy.2017.00030

Lawless, W. F., Bergman, M., Louça, J., Kriegel, N. N., & Feltovich, N. (2007). A quantum metric of organizational performance: Terrorism and counterterrorism. *Computational and Mathematical Organization Theory, 13*(3), 241–281.

Lawless, W. F., Rifkin, S., Sofge, D.A., Hobbs, S.H., Angjellari-Dajci., F., Chaudron, L., & Wood, J. (2010). Conservation of Information: Reverse engineering dark social systems. *Structure and Dynamics, 4*(2).

Lawless, W. F., Angjellari-Dajci, F., Sofge, D. A., Grayson, J., Sousa, J. L., & Rychly, L. (2011). A new approach to organizations: Stability and transformation in dark social networks. *Journal of Enterprise Transformation, 1*(4), 290–322.

Lawless, W. F., Llinas, J., Mittu, R., Sofge, D., Sibley, C., Coyne, J., & Russell, S. (2013). Robust Intelligence (RI) under uncertainty: Mathematical and conceptual foundations of autonomous hybrid (human-machine-robot) teams, organizations and systems. *Structure & Dynamics 6*(2). www.escholarship.org/uc/item/83b1t1zk.

Lawless, W. F., Sofge, D. A., Chaudron, L., & Bartheye, O. (2016). Bistability, Nash equilibria, (relatively) dark collectives and social physics. Modeling the social behavior of teams. *Journal of Enterprise Transformation, 5*(4), 241–274.

Lawless, W. F., Wood, J., Stachura, M. E., & Wood, E. A. (2018). An application of interdependence theory to military medical research teams: Cultural noise, tradeoffs, and meaning. *Journal of Enterprise Transformation:* https://doi.org/10.1080/19488289.2017.1419318

Martyushev, L. M. (2013). Entropy and entropy production: Old misconceptions and new breakthroughs. *Entropy, 15*, 1152–1170.

NSB. (2015). National science board: Research and development: Essential foundation for U.S. competitiveness in a global economy; from http://www.nsf.gov/statistics/nsb0803/start.html.

NSF. (2015). National science foundation's "What is basic science?" From its 3rd annual report in 1953. http://www.nsf.gov/pubs/1953/annualreports/ar_1953_sec6.pdf.

Smith, W. K., & Tushman, M. L. (2005). Managing strategic contradictions: A top management model for managing innovation streams. *Organizational Science, 16*(5), 522–536.

Wood, J., Tung, Hui-Lien, Grayson, J., Poppeliers, C. & Lawless, W.F. (2008). A classical uncertainty principle for organizations. In M. K.-P. (Ed.), *Information Science & Technology Reference (IS&T)*, 2nd Edn. Hershey, PA: IGI Global.

Wood, J, Tung, H.-L., Marshall-Bradley, T., Sofge, D. A., Grayson, J., Bergman, M., & Lawless, W.F. (2009). Applying an organizational uncertainty principle: Semantic web-based metrics. In M. M. Cruz-Cunha, E. F. Oliveira, A. J. Tavares & L. G. Ferreira (Eds.), *Handbook of Research on Social Dimensions of Semantic Technologies and Web Services.* Hershey (Chapter XXIV, pp. 469–488) PA: IGI.

Wood, J. C. (2011a). Personal communication: "EIRB Status" (UNCLASSIFIED), Dr., CIV USA MEDCOM EAMC, January 31, 2011.

Wood, J. (2011b). Defense medical research network business process improvement impact analysis and metric reporting for program management decisions, Project No. 2119, funded pilot. Internal US Army funding document, September 24, 2011.

Wood, J., Lawless, W.F., Mathiassen, L., Stachura, M., & Wood, E. (2013). Grant (18 months 9/30/2012–3/31/2014): Defense medical research network business process improvement impact analysis and metric reporting for program management decisions. Internal US Army funding document.

Wood, J., & Lawless, W.F. (2014, 3/31). An evaluation of IRBNet: Impacts, recommendations and metrics. *Proposed Journal: Military Medicine.* Final grant report (Defense Medical Research Network Business Process Improvement Impact Analysis and Metric Reporting for Program Management Decisions). Internal US Army reporting document.

Yawn, B. P., Graham, D. G., Bertram, S. L., Kurland, et al. (2009). Practice-based research network studies and institutional review boards: Two New Issues. *Journal American Board of Family Medicine, 22,* 453–460.

Chapter 17
Collaborative Communication and Intelligent Interruption Systems

Nia Peters, Margaret Ugolini, and Gregory Bowers

Abstract Within collaborative environments, humans are not only tasked with interacting with technology, but also with other humans. The interruption management systems literature is dedicated to alleviating the ill-effects of interruptions specifically within single-user, multitasking interactions by proposing temporal presentations of interruptions in the main task that are least disruptive to the entire interaction. There is less work focused on this concept within multi-user, multitasking environments. In this chapter we propose various temporal presentations of information at low cognitive workloads and evaluate how these timings affect human performance. In measuring objective and subjective individual and team metrics within a dual-user, dual-task paradigm, performance is optimized for low cognitive workload interruption timings compared to high cognitive ones. This work contributes to the overall body of literature by proposing temporal presentations of information within multi-user, multitasking interactions that circumvent the disruptiveness of disturbances in these domains.

Keywords Interruption timing · Interruption management · Intelligent interruption systems

17.1 Introduction

As humans continue to multitask and collaborate among semi-autonomous systems, their conversations and tasks are being interrupted more often. These interruptions are a side effect of technical advancements in general and specifically semi-autonomous

N. Peters (✉)
711th Human Performance Wing, Air Force Research Laboratory, 4164 Seventh Street, Wright Patterson AFB, Greene County, OH 45459, USA
e-mail: nia.peters.1@us.af.mil

M. Ugolini · G. Bowers
Ball Aerospace & Technologies, 2875 Presidential Dr, Fairborn, OH 45324, USA
e-mail: margaret.ugolini.ctr@us.af.mil

G. Bowers
e-mail: gregory.bowers.4.ctr@us.af.mil

© Springer Nature Switzerland AG 2021
W. F. Lawless et al. (eds.), *Systems Engineering and Artificial Intelligence*,
https://doi.org/10.1007/978-3-030-77283-3_17

technologies which have self-governing capabilities, but also engage with users to achieve task goals. Intelligent software technology can escalate the Human-Computer Interaction (HCI) problem of interruptions by inducing negative effects on human cognition, productivity, affect state, and task performance (Adamczyk & Bailey, 2004) by inundating users with too much information at inconvenient times that do not consider the user's current state. User-interruptions have been studied within the medical domain (e.g., Grundgeiger & Sanderson, 2009), military domain (e.g., Goyal & Fussell, 2017) and (Hodgetts, Tremblay, Vallières, & Vachon, 2015), and commercial domain (e.g., Pradhan, Qiu, Parate, & Kim, 2017, Horvitz, 2001, and Prajapati, Yamada, Unehara, & Suzuki, 2016) to inform intelligent notification systems. The ubiquitous nature of interruptions makes alleviating the ill-effects of this phenomenon a significant area of exploration within human-computer interaction.

Interruption science focuses on how interruptions affect human performance as well as interventions to ameliorate the disruptions caused by them. Although there are many factors that account for the disruptiveness of interruptions, their timing relative to the main task is particularly influential. Research from Gould, Brumby, and Cox (2013), Iqbal and Bailey (2005, 2006), Katidioti, Borst, and Taatgen (2014), and Monk, Boehm-Davis, Mason, and Trafton (2004) suggest disseminating interruptions at times of lower cognitive workloads or at (sub)task boundaries in order to alleviate their disruptiveness.

Since previous research within single-user, multitasking interactions suggests that interruptions within the main task should be sent at periods of lower cognitive workloads and at sub(task) boundaries, we aim to explore whether similar effects are present within multi-user, multitasking interactions. This work is motivated by the limitation of theories and studies dedicated to interruptions in multi-user, multitasking domains such as air traffic control, unmanned aerial systems (UAV) operations, and emergency personnel exercises.

To contextualize this, imagine UAV and ground troop operators collaborating over push-to-talk to identify a target when looking at it from two different perspectives (e.g., the UAV operator has an aerial perspective and the ground troop operator has a first-person perspective). Simultaneously, both collaborators must attend to information in their immediate environment (e.g., UAV operator must monitor changing UAV states). An *interruption* within these interactions can be defined as an unanticipated request for task switching from a person, an object, or an event while collaborating and multitasking. The challenges of single-user interruptions extend to these more complex domains. This extension makes alleviating their ill-effects critical and also more challenging since factors beyond the needs of a single individual who is multitasking have to be extended to multiple users who are also multitasking. The outcomes from this research will not only inform follow-up studies to better understand these relationships, but also motivate the development of theoretical frameworks in this space.

17.2 Interruptions in Multi-user Multitasking Interactions

Similar to Peters, Romigh, Bradley, and Raj (2017b), this chapter evaluates human performance as a function of different temporal presentations of interruptions within the main task specifically within multi-user, multitasking interactions. Peters et al. (2017b) explored the manipulation of interruption timings delivered in the main task (fixed, random, and human determined) and assessed the main and interruption task accuracy and completion times. The results suggest human determined interruptions (a proxy for lower cognitive workload interruptions) significantly improved interruption task performance. Additionally, Peters, Romigh, Bradley, and Raj (2017a) found that 53% of human determined interruptions occurred within 2 s of *(sub)task boundaries* defined as a temporal interval after one task is complete, but before another begins.

Within these interactions, humans are not only multitasking, but also collaborating. The proposal of interruptions at a time of low cognitive workload must be considered for more than one person performing multiple tasks. More formally we can think about interrupting at times of lower cognitive workload as the avoidance of task co-occurrence or *dual-tasking* which is an individual performing two tasks simultaneously. As an example, one reason humans in the Peters et al. (2017a) study may be interrupting at (sub)task boundaries is to prevent dual-tasking.

Compared to single-user multitasking interactions, when considering multiple users, the main task consists of two tasks instead of one: users speaking and listening. There are two implications of dual-tasking in collaborative tasks: (1) if the interruption is intended for the speaker, the speaker must speak to their teammate while listening to the message or stop speaking and listen to the message, and (2) if the interruption message is for the listener, they must now attend to two steams of information. We propose low cognitive workload interruption timings that mitigate dual-tasking in multi-user multitasking interactions. We formally define interruption timings at low cognitive workload as those that minimize the probability of dual-tasking or avoid sending messages when users are either speaking or listening.

17.2.1 Low Cognitive Interruption Timings

Motivated by Adamczyk and Bailey (2004) and Peters et al. (2017a), SUBTASK and KEYWORD are interruption timings that send interruptions after detecting the end of a (sub)task. The SUBTASK timing detects the end of a SUBTASK prior to interrupting and KEYWORD timing detects affirmation cues predictive of (sub)task boundaries. A (sub)task boundary is defined as a temporal interval after a (sub)task is complete, but before another begins. Shivakumar, Bositty, Peters, and Pei (2020) found a lexical category of keywords and phrases called affirmation cues (i.e., got it, copy that, OK I'm done) that are predictive of the occurrence of (sub) task boundary or transition from one (sub)task to the next. We posit that if users are not currently performing an ongoing task, they are not speaking or listening to content related to that task, and allowing a timing that detects transitions between (sub)tasks can minimize dual-tasking.

SILENCE and PUSH TO TALK OFF (PTT OFF) are interruption timings that send interruptions after detecting the end of a conversational turn. These are novel interruption proposals that could result in an interesting trade space. On the one hand for interactions where (sub)tasks are long and provide less opportunities to interrupt, these strategies may provide opportunities to interrupt by analyzing the task at a lower granularity. Conversely, if conversational turn-taking is moving too fast or the length of the interruption message exceeds the available temporal opportunity to interrupt, dual-tasking may occur. There is no clear indication of the implications for these timings, but because they monitor the ongoing task prior to sending interruptions, we believe they may provide opportunities to minimize dual-tasking.

HUMAN are interruption timings sent by a third human listening to the ongoing task and making decisions on when to interrupt that are least disruptive to the overall interaction. The variability in human decisions and the reality that not all human interruption decisions will optimize overall task efficiency must be acknowledged. For our purposes, since previous literature suggest that more than half of human interruptions occurred at task boundaries (Peters et al. 2017b), this gives us some indication that humans are using strategies to minimize dual-tasking.

17.2.2 High Cognitive Interruption Timings

Motivated by Peters et al. (2017a), the RANDOM FEW and RANDOM MANY are interruption timings that send interruptions at random times in the interaction. RANDOM FEW interruptions are sent less frequently than RANDOM MANY. Both have the potential to increase the probability of dual-tasking because they do not monitor where teammates are in their interaction and can easily interrupt while people are speaking or listening. RANDOM FEW may be less detrimental than RANDOM MANY because it is sending fewer interruptions, inherently minimizing dual-tasking compared to RANDOM MANY. Also motivated by Peters et al. (2017a) FIXED interruption timings are sent at fixed timed intervals. Similar to RANDOM MANY and RANDOM FEW, FIXED interruptions have the potential to increase dual-tasking with little consideration of the ongoing task.

17.3 Methods

Within a dual-user, dual-task scenario, we aim to compare individual and team performance between high cognitive load interruption timings and low cognitive load interruption timings to a baseline condition and evaluate the effect these timings have on human performance metrics. We hypothesize that the single (main) task baseline condition will provide optimal performance, high cognitive workload interruption times will degrade performance, and low cognitive workload interruption times will be the same as baseline.

We explore the following research questions:

Research Question 1: Is there a difference in *main task team performance* between interruption times at high cognitive workload, low cognitive workload, and the main task baseline condition?

H_{01}: There is no difference in main task team performance between interruption times at high cognitive workload, low cognitive workload, and the main task baseline condition.

H_1: There is a difference in main task team performance between interruption times at high cognitive workload, low cognitive workload, and the main task baseline condition.

Research Question 2: Is there a difference in *individual subjective measures* between interruption times at high cognitive workload, low cognitive workload, and the main task baseline condition?

H_{02}: There is no difference in individual subjective measures between interruption times at high cognitive workload, low cognitive workload, and the primary task single-task baseline conditions.

H_2: There is a difference in subjective metrics between interruption times at high cognitive workload, low cognitive workload, and the primary task single-task baseline conditions.

Research Question 3: Is there a difference in *individual interruption task performance* between interruption times at high cognitive workload and low cognitive workload?

H_{03}: There is no difference in individual interruption task performance between interruption times at high cognitive workload and low cognitive workload.

H_3: There is a difference in individual interruption task performance between interruption times at high cognitive workload and low cognitive workload.

17.3.1 Data Collection

To explore the aforementioned research questions, we simulate a simple multi-user, multitasking interaction; a dual-user, dual-task scenario. The main task simulates a coordination task where teammates must ground their knowledge of a scene from two different perspectives. The secondary task is the interruption task that simulates people having to monitor information independent of the collaborative task.

In our experiment, the main task is a collaborative *Spot the Difference* task and the interruption task is a *UAV keeping-track* task. Users were tasked with performing this dual-task within a 15-min time limit. Participants were instructed to go through a series of *Spot the Difference* tasks and answer as many UAV queries as possible within the allotted time. Additionally, participants were instructed to prioritize both tasks equally. The subjects were from ages 20 to 35, four females and six males. From these 10 participants, we constructed 10 teams, with each participant serving on exactly two teams.

Spot the Difference The main task is a collaborative, computer-system implementation of the *Spot the Difference* task illustrated in Fig. 17.1.

(a) User I - Spot the Difference   (b) User II - Spot the Difference

Fig. 17.1 GUI for the spot the difference task

Two users speak over a push-to-talk interface to identify differences in their pictures. When users identified a difference in their respective pictures and both of the users clicked on that difference, if correct a visual of the difference appeared. Users were also given an indication of how many differences they found in a picture via a scoreboard.

UAV Keeping Track The interruption task was a *Keeping Track of Unmanned Aerial Vehicle (UAV) States* task inspired by Venturincv (1997) where each subject was asked to keep track of three different pieces of information about changing UAV states: name, attribute, and attribute value. An example is:

Raven-3 (UAV name) Fuel (UAV attribute) is 50% (UAV attribute value)

There were 5 UAV names, 5 UAV attributes, and 5 attribute values giving a total of 125 randomly selected changing UAV states that could be sent as interruptions. Once a UAV state was sent, the next interruption prompted the user to repeat what they heard: "Repeat the Previous Statement." An example of the interruption sequence presented to the users (regardless of the interruption timing condition) follows:

Interrupt 1 for User 1: Raven-3 Fuel is 50%
Interrupt 1 for User 2: Raptor-25 Play is Parallel Sweep
Interrupt 2 for User 1: Repeat Previous Statement
Interrupt 2 for User 2: Repeat Previous Statement

This task was completed individually so participants could not hear the interruptions meant for their teammate.

Interruption timings are inherently a function of the interaction. For instance, if the push-to-talk button was pressed in quick succession due to a conversation with rapid turn-taking, the interruptions in a condition associated with pressing the push-to-talk button would also occur in very rapid succession. This situation would make it incredibly difficult to compare this condition to other conditions with more temporally spaced interruptions. To avoid this undesirable co-occurrence, interruptions were only available to be sent once every 15 s.

Users received a synthetic audio stimulus and a persistent text of the interruption message that was present for the same length of time as the audio. Interruption messages were presented in a pop-up window that partially obscured the main task window. Users verbally articulated their response to the query "Repeat Previous Statement" and their response was scored by the experimenter on which pieces of information they answered correctly. The pop-up window was closed when the user responded and pressed the OK button to close the window (Fig. 17.1b).

17.3.2 Conditions

We used a within-team design with the following 9 conditions (1 control; 8 manipulations):

- **MAIN CONTROL**: Spot the Difference Task only. This is the baseline condition.
- **RANDOM FEW**: Dual-task with randomly timed interruptions occurring at longer temporal delays between 0–45 s.
- **RANDOM MANY**: Dual-task with random interruptions occurring at shorter temporal delays between 0–15 s.
- **FIXED**: Dual-task with interruptions sent every 15 s.
- **PUSH TO TALK OFF (PTT OFF)**: Dual-task with interruptions triggered after push-to-talk was released.
- **SILENCE**: Dual-task with interruptions sent when audio energy was below -70 dBFS for 1 s.
- **KEYWORD**: Dual-task with interruptions sent after a keyword spotter detects a predefined set of keywords from affirmation cues (Shivakumar et al., 2020).
- **SUBTASK**: Dual-task with interruptions sent after both users click a difference.
- **HUMAN**: Dual-task with a third human participant listening in and making interruption decisions.

The presentation order of conditions was counterbalanced across teams. Participants were not told which condition they were running. All participants served on a team as well as serving as a human interrupter at least once. The potential interrupter participant was present for at least the beginning of every session, regardless of condition type, to ensure that the "Human" condition set-up procedures were not noticeably different from the other conditions.

Team Performance Measures We used metrics motivated by the single-user, multitasking interruption literature. Since this design is a dual-user, dual-task paradigm, some were more appropriate at the team level and others at the individual level.

The following team-performance measures for the main Spot the Difference task were evaluated:

- **Average Main Task Time of Completion (min)**: Total time for completed pictures divided by the number of completed pictures.

- **Number of Differences Found**: A count of the number of differences found in the Spot the Difference Task within 15 min.
- **Average Time to Find a Difference (s)**: The average time elapsed between finding one difference and the next difference.
- **Average click delay(s)**: The average time elapsed between one participant clicking a difference and their partner also clicking that difference to confirm.

Individual Performance Measures Since the interruption task was an individual task and the partner does not participate in this task, we extracted individual performance measures from the UAV Keeping Track task.

- **Interruption Score**: Number of queries answered with all three attributes correct divided by the total number of queries sent to an individual.
- **Partial Credit Interruption Score**: Number of correct attributes reported divided by the total number of attributes requested (3 per query). For example, if subjects correctly report 2 attributes, they receive a score of 2/3 (66.66%) for that query.
- **Response Duration for Correct Query Response**: Duration of vocal response when answering correctly.
- **Response Time for Correct Query Response**: Time to click the push-to-talk to respond to a query when the response was correct.
- **Percentage of Unanswered Queries**: Number of queries that were unanswered divided by the total number of interruptions sent.

Due to data processing errors, we did not report response time and duration for the Incorrect Query Responses.

Finally, after each run, we gave users the NASA-TLX survey developed by Hart and Staveland (1988) to extract subjective measures. This survey measures Mental Demand, Physical Demand, Temporal Demand, Performance, Effort, and Frustration. Participants rated their impression of the runs rating these factors from 1–10 (Low–High). The questions on the survey are:

- **Mental Demand**: How mentally demanding was the task?
- **Physical Demand**: How physically demanding was the task?
- **Temporal Demand**: How hurried or rushed was the pace of the task?
- **Performance**: How successful were you in accomplishing what you were asked to do?
- **Effort**: How hard did you have to work to accomplish your level of performance?
- **Frustration**: How insecure, discouraged, irritated, stressed, and annoyed were you?

For the Silence condition, there is a data point missing from Team 1, so this condition has 18 data points compared to the other conditions with 20 data points.

17.4 Results and Discussion

A one-way analysis of variance (ANOVA) at the 0.05 level was used for our analyses. We hypothesized in measuring team, individual, and subjective performance, the *baseline* condition will be optimal, performance will be degraded in the *high cognitive* conditions, and unchanged from baseline performance in the *low cognitive* conditions. The baseline condition is the MAIN CONTROL; the high cognitive load conditions are RANDOM MANY, RANDOM FEW, AND FIXED; and the low cognitive load conditions are SILENCE, PTT OFF, SUBTASK, KEYWORD, and HUMAN.

17.4.1 Team Performance Analyses

The analyses below will allow us to answer Research Question 1. Although the results are not significant, we do want to report trends that suggest some of the low cognitive conditions being similar to or exceeding baseline conditions. Conversely the high cognitive conditions more often degraded baseline performance.

For the dependent variable **Average Main Task Time of Completion (min)**, the ANOVA was *not significant*, $F(8,81) = 1.129$, $p = 0.353$. Compared to baseline, the worst condition was RANDOM FEW where users took an average 2.3 min longer to complete the main task. Compared to baseline, the best condition was FIXED where on average users took 1.3 s less time to complete the main task. Here, a high cognitive load condition RANDOM FEW degraded baseline performance and a high cognitive load condition FIXED exceeded baseline performance.

For the dependent variable **Number of differences found** the ANOVA was *not significant*, $F(8,81) = 0.758$, $p = 0.640$. Compared to baseline, the worst performance condition was RANDOM MANY where on average users found 6.2 fewer differences. Compared to baseline, the best performing condition was SUBTASK where users found 1.9 more differences. Here, a high cognitive load condition RANDOM MANY degraded baseline performance and a low cognitive load SUBTASK condition exceeded baseline performance.

For the dependent variable **Average time to find a difference(s)**, the ANOVA was *not significant*, $F(8,81) = 1.048$, $p = 0.408$. Compared to the baseline, the worst performance condition was RANDOM FEW where on average users took 11.8 s longer to find differences. Compared to baseline, the best performing condition was SUBTASK where on average users took 5.6 s less to find differences. Again a high cognitive load condition RANDOM FEW degraded baseline performance and a low cognitive load SUBTASK condition exceeded baseline performance.

For the dependent variable **Average Click Difference(s)** or the time difference between when the first person identified a difference and then the other person spotted that difference, the ANOVA was *not significant*, $F(8,81) = 0.520$, $p = 0.838$. Compared to baseline, the worst performance condition was the HUMAN condition where users took on average 0.5 s longer to click after the first partner found a difference. Compared to baseline, the best performance condition was RANDOM FEW where on average users took only 0.2 s longer to click after their partner finds a difference. Here both low and high cognitive load conditions degraded baseline performance, but a high cognitive load condition RANDOM FEW degraded it to a lower extent than HUMAN, a low cognitive condition.

17.4.2 Individual Subjective Analyses

The below analyses will allow us to answer Research Question 2. Here we will not only report conditions that significantly degrade or exceed baseline performance, but even if a condition is not significantly different from baseline, we will report the extent to which it is different.

For the dependent variable **Mental Demand**, the ANOVA was *significant*, $F(8,169) = 2.230$, $p = 0.028$. A post-hoc Tukey analysis illustrated a mean difference of 4.95 between the RANDOM MANY and MAIN CONTROL conditions, $p_{tukey} = 0.012$ indicating that the high cognitive load RANDOM MANY condition was significantly more mentally demanding than the baseline condition.

For the dependent variable **Physical Demand**, the ANOVA was *not significant*, $F(8,169) = 0.609$, $p = 0.769$. This result is intuitive since there was no expectation for physical demand based on the nature of the task.

For the dependent variable **Temporal Demand**, the ANOVA was *significant*, $F(8,169) = 2.779$, $p = 0.007$. A post-hoc Tukey analysis illustrated a mean difference of 4.95 between the RANDOM MANY and MAIN CONTROL conditions, $p_{tukey} = 0.005$, indicating that the high cognitive load RANDOM MANY condition was significantly more temporally demanding than the baseline condition.

For the dependent variable **Performance**, the ANOVA was *significant*, $F(8,169) = 3.5865$, $p < 0.001$. A post-hoc Tukey analysis illustrated a mean difference of 4.2 between the FIXED and MAIN CONTROL conditions, $p_{tukey} = 0.030$ and mean difference of 6.65 between the RANDOM MANY and MAIN CONTROL conditions, $p_{tukey} < 0.001$. These results indicate users perceived their performance was significantly worse in the two high cognitive load FIXED and RANDOM MANY conditions compared to baseline.

For the dependent variable **Effort**, the ANOVA was *not significant* at the 0.05 level, $F(8,169) = 1.707$, $p = 0.1$. A post-hoc Tukey analysis illustrated a mean difference of 4.55 between the RANDOM MANY and MAIN CONTROL conditions, $p_{tukey} = 0.057$, indicating that on average subjects were scoring their effort on the RANDOM MANY condition task 4.55 points higher than the baseline. These results indicate users expended more effort on the high cognitive load RANDOM MANY condition compared to baseline.

For the dependent variable **Frustration**, the ANOVA was *not significant* at the 0.05 level, $F(8,169) = 1.94$, $p = 0.057$. A post-hoc Tukey analysis illustrated a mean difference of 4.65 between the FIXED and MAIN CONTROL conditions, $p_{tukey} =$

0.070. Additionally there was a mean difference of 4.45 between the RANDOM MANY and MAIN CONTROL conditions, $p_{tukey} = 0.098$. These results indicate that users were more frustrated in the two high cognitive load FIXED and RANDOM MANY conditions compared to baseline.

17.4.3 Individual Interruption Task Measures

The below analyses will allow us to answer Research Question 3. Although none of the results are significant, we aim to illustrate the extent to which the performance metrics of select low cognitive load conditions are different from high cognitive load conditions.

For the dependent variable **Interruption Score**, the ANOVA was *not significant*, $F(7,152) = 0.74$, $p = 0.740$. Across all conditions the **Interruption Score** was $\mu = 68.8\%, \sigma = 24.5\%$. The highest score was from the low cognitive load condition HUMAN ($\mu = 72.4\%, \sigma = 22.2\%$), and the lowest was from the high cognitive load condition RANDOM MANY ($\mu = 59.8\%$, $\sigma = 25.5\%$) with a 12.5% difference between the two.

For the dependent variable **Partial Credit Interruption Score**, the ANOVA was *not significant* at the 0.05 level, $F(7,152) = 0.511$, $p = 0.825$. Across all conditions the **Partial Credit Interruption Score** was $\mu = 79.9\%, \sigma = 20.6\%$. The highest score was from the low cognitive load condition SILENCE ($\mu = 82.7\%$, $\sigma = 16.6\%$), and the lowest was from the high cognitive load condition RANDOM MANY ($\mu = 72.6\%, \sigma = 23.8\%$) with a 10.1% difference between the two.

For the dependent variable **Avg Response Duration for Correct Query Response(s)**, the ANOVA was *not significant*, $F(7,152) = 0.76$, $p = 0.622$. Across all conditions, the **Avg Response Duration for Correct Query Response(s)** was $\mu = 3.18$, $\sigma = 0.64$. The shortest duration was from the low cognitive load condition SUBTASK ($\mu = 2.95$, $\sigma = 0.63$), and the longest duration from the high cognitive load condition RANDOM MANY ($\mu = 3.355, \sigma = .43$) with a 0.4 difference between the two.

For the dependent variable **Percentage of Non Responses**, the ANOVA was *not significant* at the 0.05 level, $F(7,152) = 0.41$. Across all conditions, the **Percentage of Non Responses** was $\mu = 9\%$, $\sigma = 17.6\%$. The lowest percentage was from the low cognitive load condition KEYWORD ($\mu = 5.3\%, \sigma = 11.9\%$), and the largest percentage was from the high cognitive load condition RANDOM MANY ($\mu = 14\%, \sigma = 23.2\%$) with an 8% difference between the two.

For the dependent variables, **Correct Interruption Response Time**, the ANOVA was *not significant* at the 0.05 level, $F(7,152) = 1.511$, $p = 0.167$. Across all conditions, the **Correct Interruption Response Time** was $\mu = 2.45$, $\sigma = 0.69$. The shortest duration was from a low cognitive load condition SILENCE ($\mu = 2.19$, $\sigma = 0.41$) and the longest duration from a high cognitive load condition RANDOM MANY ($\mu = 2.68, \sigma = .67$) with a 0.49 difference between the two.

17.5   Discussion

For Research Question 1, we can accept the null hypothesis. Although none of the results were significant. Other than the dependent variables **Average Main Task Completion** and **Average Click Difference**, there was a common trend in low cognitive load conditions exceeding or being comparable to baseline performance and high cognitive load conditions degrading baseline performance. This finding is a promising result because it gives some indication that low cognitive load interruptions will not induce the negative effects of interruption timings we have seen in the previous literature (e.g., Adamczyk & Bailey, 2004). Additionally, we found that for dependent variables such as **Number of differences found** and **Average time to find a difference**, the low cognitive load condition SUBTASK actually exceeded baseline condition performance. It is possible that interruption tasks with low cognitive load interruption timings actually increase motivation to allocate more effort to the primary task when interruptions were not present.

Variability in team differences and a sample size of only 10 teams makes it difficult to draw any strong conclusions in relating the interruption timings to main task performance. An expansion of this study and carefully minimizing team-performance variability in the primary task will better allow us to make stronger inferences from results in similar paradigms.

For Research Question 2, we can partially reject the null hypothesis specifically for the dependent variables **Mental Demand** and **Temporal Demand**; where the high cognitive load RANDOM MANY condition was significantly different from the baseline; and for the **Performance** variable, where two high cognitive load conditions RANDOM MANY and FIXED were significantly different from the baseline. These results corroborate similar results from Adamczyk and Bailey (2004) and illustrate how random interruptions negatively influence affect states or the emotional component of completing these tasks. As we hypothesized, across all subjective metrics, none of the low cognitive load conditions were significantly different from the baseline. Finally there was a trend of low cognitive load conditions such as SUBTASK, KEYWORD, HUMAN, and SILENCE and the high cognitive load condition RANDOM FEW having subjective metrics comparable to baseline. The most interesting part of this result is that one of the high cognitive load conditions (RANDOM FEW) was similar to the baseline based on subjective rating. This finding could give some indication that this condition is more comparable to low cognitive load interruption timings especially when measuring subjectivity.

For Research Question 3, we can accept the null hypothesis. Although across all the dependent variables none were significant, we did find a pattern of best performance coming from low cognitive load conditions and the worst coming from a high cognitive load condition (mainly RANDOM MANY). This corroborates findings from Peters et al. (2017a) which indicated random interruption timings significantly degraded interruption task performance. The present study extends this work by evaluating more interruption task metrics to capture the implication of interruption timings on an interruption task.

17.6 Conclusion

Motivated by the previous literature, we proposed several low cognitive load interruption timings, and then evaluated individual and team performance and subjective measures to gauge how disruptive these proposed timings were in multi-user, multitasking interactions. Our results showed not only that for the most part, lower cognitive load interruption timings degrade baseline performance to a lesser extent than high cognitive load interruption timings, but also in some instances, low cognitive load interruptions may even exceed baseline performance.

Limitations of the study include, but are not limited to, the performance variability within the main task making it difficult to make strong inferences about how interruption timings may degrade main task performance. Additionally, with only 10 teams, there is an opportunity to expand the sample size and increase the power of our study. In future work, we aim to address both of these constraints.

The outcomes from this research will not only inform follow-up studies to better understand the relationship between interruption timings and human performance, but also motivate the development of theories and algorithmic solutions to developing interruption management systems that temporally predict times to disseminate information that are least disruptive to the overall exchange.

References

Adamczyk, P. D., & Bailey, B. P. (2004). If not now, when? the effects of interruption at different moments within task execution. In *Proceedings of the SIGCHI Conference on Human Factors in Computing Systems* (pp. 271–278).

Gould, S. J., Brumby, D. P., & Cox, A. L. (2013). What does it mean for an interruption to be relevant? an investigation of relevance as a memory effect. In *Proceedings of the human factors and ergonomics society annual meeting* (Vol. 57, pp. 149–153). Los Angeles, CA: SAGE Publications Sage CA.

Goyal, N., & Fussell, S. R. (2017). Intelligent interruption management using electro dermal activity based physiological sensor for collaborative sensemaking. *Proceedings of the ACM on Interactive, Mobile, Wearable and Ubiquitous Technologies, 1*(3), 1–21.

Grundgeiger, T., & Sanderson, P. (2009). Interruptions in healthcare: theoretical views. *International Journal of Medical Informatics, 78*(5), 293–307.

Hart, S. G., & Staveland, L. E. (1988). Development of nasa-tlx (task load index): Results of empirical and theoretical research. In *Advances in Psychology* (Vol. 52, pp. 139–183). Elsevier.

Hodgetts, H. M., Tremblay, S., Vallières, B. R., & Vachon, F. (2015). Decision support and vulnerability to interruption in a dynamic multitasking environment. *International Journal of Human-Computer Studies, 79*, 106–117.

Horvitz E. C. M. C. E. (2001). Notification, disruption, and memory: Effects of messaging interruptions on memory and performance. In *Human-Computer Interaction: INTERACT* (Vol. 1, p. 263)

Iqbal, S. T., & Bailey, B. P. (2005). Investigating the effectiveness of mental workload as a predictor of opportune moments for interruption. In *CHI'05 Extended Abstracts on Human Factors in Computing Systems* (pp. 1489–1492)

Iqbal, S. T., & Bailey, B. P. (2006). Leveraging characteristics of task structure to predict the cost of interruption. In *Proceedings of the SIGCHI Conference on Human Factors in Computing Systems* (pp. 741–750)

Katidioti, I., Borst, J. P., & Taatgen, N. A. (2014). What happens when we switch tasks: Pupil dilation in multitasking. *Journal of Experimental Psychology: Applied, 20*(4), 380.

Monk, C. A., Boehm-Davis, D. A., Mason, G., & Trafton, J. G. (2004). Recovering from interruptions: Implications for driver distraction research. *Human Factors, 46*(4), 650–663.

Peters, N., Romigh, G., Bradley, G., & Raj, B. (2017a). A comparative analysis of human-mediated and system-mediated interruptions for multi-user, multitasking interactions. In *International Conference on Applied Human Factors and Ergonomics* (pp. 339–347). Springer.

Peters, N., Romigh, G., Bradley, G., & Raj, B. (2017b) When to interrupt: A comparative analysis of interruption timings within collaborative communication tasks. In *Advances in Human Factors and System Interactions* (pp. 177–187). Springer.

Pradhan, S., Qiu, L., Parate, A., & Kim, K. H. (2017). Understanding and managing notifications. In *IEEE INFOCOM 2017-IEEE Conference on Computer Communications* (pp. 1–9). IEEE.

Prajapati, S., Yamada, K., Unehara, M., & Suzuki, I. (2016). Interruption-information management framework for chat interface. In *2016 Joint 8th International Conference on Soft Computing and Intelligent Systems (SCIS) and 17th International Symposium on Advanced Intelligent Systems (ISIS)* (pp. 631–636). IEEE.

Shivakumar, A., Bositty, A., Peters, N. S., & Pei, Y. (2020). Real-time interruption management system for efficient distributed collaboration in multi-tasking environments. *Proceedings of the ACM on Human-Computer Interaction, 4*(CSCW1), 1–23.

Venturincv, M. (1997). Interference and information organization in keeping track of continually changing information. *Human Factors, 39*(4), 532–539.

Chapter 18
Shifting Paradigms in Verification and Validation of AI-Enabled Systems: A Systems-Theoretic Perspective

Niloofar Shadab, Aditya U. Kulkarni, and Alejandro Salado

Abstract There is a fundamental misalignment between current approaches to designing and executing verification and validation (V&V) strategies and the nature of AI-enabled systems. Current V&V approaches rely on the assumption that system behavior is preserved during a system's lifetime. However, AI-enabled systems are developed so that they evolve their own behavior during their lifetime; this is the consequence of learning by the AI-enabled system. This misalignment makes existing approaches to designing and executing V&V strategies ineffective. In this chapter, we will provide a systems-theoretic explanation for (1) why learning capabilities originate a unique and unprecedented family of systems, and (2) why current V&V methods and processes are not fit for purpose. AI-enabled systems necessitate a paradigm shift in V&V activities. To enable this shift, we will delineate a set of theoretical advances and process transformations that could support such shift.

Keywords Verification and validation · Systems theory · Cyber-physical systems · AI-enabled systems · Systems engineering

N. Shadab · A. U. Kulkarni
Grado Department of Industrial And Systems Engineering, Virginia Tech., Blacksburg, VA 24061, USA
e-mail: nshadab@vt.edu
URL: https://www.vt.edu

A. U. Kulkarni
e-mail: aditya88@vt.edu

A. Salado (✉)
Department of Systems and Industrial Engineering, The University of Arizona, Tucson, AZ 85721, USA
e-mail: alejandrosalado@arizona.edu

© Springer Nature Switzerland AG 2021
W. F. Lawless et al. (eds.), *Systems Engineering and Artificial Intelligence*,
https://doi.org/10.1007/978-3-030-77283-3_18

18.1 Introduction

Systems Engineering experts have developed methodologies and processes to successfully verify and validate complex systems. V&V activities play a crucial role to form experts' beliefs about system performance, functions, and structure (Engel 2010; Hoppe et al. 2007; Salado and Kannan 2019). These V&V methodologies and processes were originally designed to support the development of traditional systems, which we describe as behavior-preserving, such that, when subjected to the same inputs, the system is expected to produce the same outputs throughout the system's operational life (Salado and Kannan 2019). Furthermore, traditional systems are deployed in environments where there is little or no learning to be performed by the system itself; instead, learning is an attribute of the human operators that are part of the system's operational environment. Thus, in the design of behavior-preserving systems, V&V activities are employed to predict, confirm, or gain confidence about the future behavior of a system in its operational environment.

In contrast to traditional systems is Artificial Intelligence-enabled systems (AI-enabled systems), which we define as cyber-physical systems that exhibit artificial intelligence (AI) capabilities. The AI capability can utilize *history* to alter the operational parameters of the system. That is, in general, AI-enabled systems are *not* behavior-preserving systems. The possibility of AI-enabled systems to dynamically adjust operational parameters in the field gives rise to an unprecedented challenge in systems engineering: how can we verify and validate AI-enabled systems whose behavior can dynamically change when deployed? (Felder 2018)

In this chapter, we will discuss the challenges that the systems engineering community may face in designing V&V strategies for AI-enabled systems, and how these challenges might be potentially overcome. Overall, we suggest that a paradigm shift is necessary, even though obstacles will be faced, and we focus on the following aspects. First, we elaborate on how performing V&V in a test environment might not be suitable for predicting the system's behavior in its operating environment. Second, we examine the endogenous evolution of intelligent systems that sheds light on the misalignment of using the homomorphism concept in V&V for such systems. Third, we discuss the V&V challenges of the meta-capabilities of intelligent systems. Fourth, we address the scalability of intelligent systems and the implications to V&V at different scales. Fifth, we expand on the nature of dynamic changes of the set of state descriptions of an intelligent system and the related misalignment with current V&V methodologies and processes.

We address these challenges around a systems theoretic definition of intelligence, which we provide later in the chapter.

18.2   A Need for a Paradigm Shift in V&V

There is an increasing number of currently operating systems that are being outfitted with advanced intelligent abilities such as learning, knowledge representation,
and perception. Therefore, it is evident that the existing V&V processes need to be
realigned due to this transition. For instance, autonomous vehicles are now being
seriously considered as viable alternatives to traditional modes of transport. Propo-
nents of the technology argue that it is only a matter of time before civilian laws
are suitably altered and there is widespread usage of autonomous vehicles on public
roads. In this regard, a key challenge is characterizing the capabilities of autonomous
vehicles so that suitable laws can be passed to govern the use of autonomous vehicles.

Characterizing the capabilities of autonomous vehicles will require a new
paradigm for V&V activities during the development process. For example, one
key technology that is currently under development in autonomous vehicles is the
onboard AI that learns the driving style of the car's owner (Kuderer et al. 2015). By
statistically analyzing the owner's driving style, which is defined as a multi-attribute
variable that includes acceleration, deceleration, and route preferences, the onboard
AI is able to learn and replicate the driving style of the user. Similarly, another
key technology in autonomous vehicles is intelligent navigation (Isele et al. 2018),
where onboard AI continuously improves its navigation capabilities during the car's
operation.

Existing approaches to designing and executing V&V strategies may not be fit-for-
purpose in the design and development of AI-enabled systems. For the technologies
presented above, for example, the vehicle's behavior is subject to change based on the
data received by a vehicle during its operation (Felder 2018). Conducting V&V in the
lab will most likely be of little relevance since it will be cost-prohibitive to create an
input dataset that can capture all, or almost all, of the possible scenarios in which the
user will operate the autonomous vehicle. Furthermore, even if V&V is conducted in
the lab, there is no guarantee that the behavior of the autonomous vehicle predicted
by the V&V activities will be realized during the vehicle's operational life. Indeed,
the behavior observed in the lab may be entirely alien to that observed in the field.

The challenge here is to change how we think about V&V activities. In AI-
enabled systems, the consequences of learning by the AI algorithms manifest as a
system-level behavior. However, the actual operational parameters chosen by the
AI algorithms may not be observed until the system is deployed in the field. Thus,
traditional approaches to V&V may end up giving false confidence to both designers
and stakeholders in the possible behavior of the AI-enabled system.

The two technologies mentioned above for autonomous vehicles are not isolated achievements of the engineering community. Indeed, an increasing number of
complex systems currently operating are being outfitted with advanced intelligent
abilities such as learning, knowledge representation, and perception. For example,
in continued deployment approaches, such as DevOps (a collaborative merger of
development and operations), V&V activities are heavily reused as new systems are

deployed within the operational infrastructure. With fixed V&V approaches, the risk of learning how to pass the test increases with each new deployment.

The risk of "learning how to pass the test" is also a cybersecurity-related problem for AI-enabled systems. Persevering with traditional, or known, V&V methods to verify AI-enabled systems enables malicious attackers to compromise the process. This, in turn, gives the designers and users false confidence on the performance of the AI-enabled system. A prime example of this scenario is adversarial attacks on deep neural networks (DNNs) deployed to classify images (Sengupta et al. 2019). DNNs are often used to classify images for various purposes. These include identifying cancer cells for medical treatment, identifying obstacles for navigation of autonomous vehicles, and identifying individuals for public security. Often, DNNs are first trained on known datasets, which are often publicly available. After training a DNN, its performance in classifying images correctly is verified and validated. The DNN is deployed only if there is sufficient confidence in the accuracy of its performance.

Since DNNs are trained on known, or publicly available, datasets, to compromise the development process of a DNN, one only needs to corrupt the dataset. Indeed, adversarial attacks on DNN is an active research area (Wang et al. 2019). Here, attackers introduce small perturbations in certain samples of the dataset. By doing so, the attackers ensure that when the DNN is trained, the perturbations in chosen samples ensure the DNN learns to misclassify these samples. Since DNNs are expected to classify several objects, attackers can ensure the DNNs learn to misclassify certain key objects that are of high value to the attackers. In this way, the DNN gives its designers, and users, false confidence about the accuracy of this performance.

Moreover, the nature of V&V for learning capabilities itself is challenging in system-level verification of AI-enabled systems (Xiang et al. 2018). As AI-enabled systems might have learning capabilities at different scales, their solution space and design space may not be static; in fact, they can keep changing over the system's lifetime. As a result, it makes it difficult for V&V strategies to predict the possible future behaviors of the system over its lifetime.

The examples discussed above show that we cannot utilize traditional V&V strategies to verify and validate AI-enabled systems. As the examples discussed above show, in addition to the inability of accurately predicting all possible future inputs to the AI-enabled system, securing the design process should also be a concern of V&V strategies. Thus, there is a need for a new paradigm in V&V for cyber-physical systems.

18.3   A Systems-Theoretic Interpretation of Intelligence

We first characterize intelligence, with respect to AI-enabled systems, to have a meaningful conversation about V&V in AI-enabled systems. There are multiple formal definitions of intelligence in the literature (Chollet 2019; Legg et al. 2007). In this section, we re-scope previous definitions of intelligence using elements of systems theory. By doing so, we lay a foundation for the discussion on adapting V&V techniques to AI-enabled systems.

We adopt von Bertalanffy's definition of a system and declare that a system is a set of inter-related elements (Bertalanffy 1969), where the type of relation is unrestricted. Since the null relation is a type of relationship between elements (Wymore 2018), it suffices to define a boundary around a set of elements to call such a set a system. We distinguish then between open and closed systems, where open systems are those that transfer information, energy, or matter through their boundaries (in and out) and closed systems are those that do not transfer any information, energy, or matter through their boundaries. Furthermore, we restrict our attention to engineered systems, which we define as those made by humans (or machines) using engineering. Within a systems engineering framework, we distinguish between the Intervention System and Context System; the first is the system of interest that is realized to satisfy a need or pursue an opportunity and the second is the system formed by the Intervention System and all systems that directly interact with it. In the latter system, the satisfaction of the need or realization of the opportunity takes place (Salado 2021). We define an AI-enabled system and call it an intelligent system instinctively in this chapter; it is an engineered system that exhibits one or more of the following capabilities:

1. Learning to perform a function better, which can include more efficiently or more effectively;
2. Learning to handle a larger set of inputs for an existing function;
3. Learning a new function;
4. Learning to achieve an existing outcome in a new context;
5. Learning to achieve an outcome better, which it can perform more efficiently or more effectively; and,
6. Learning to achieve a new outcome
7. Deciding to pursue a different outcome.

Of the seven capabilities of an intelligent system, the first three capabilities are related to a system's ability to effect a change in its behavior (that is, functions the system executes). Whereas the latter four capabilities are related to the "curiosity" exhibited by an intelligent system in seeking new ways to achieve its purpose, a system's purpose is defined by one or more long-term objectives. In this regard, we say a system's long-term objective is an outcome, and distinguish it from a goal, which we define as any task and/or challenge that needs to be achieved to fulfill the desired outcome of the system; for example, the time required for an autonomous car to detect a moving object.

We can broadly define the behavior of systems using functions, which we refer to as behavior functions. The domain of a system's behavior function can be any subset of the space of all possible inputs to the system. Similarly, the range of a system's behavior function is a subset of the space of all possible outputs. Traditional systems are behavior-preserving, and hence their behavior functions are set for their operational life. That is, for behavior-preserving systems, the mapping between the domain and range of the system's behavior functions does not change throughout the system's operational life. In contrast, AI-enabled systems can determine if their behavior functions are suboptimal in operation. Furthermore, AI-enabled systems can change the set of outputs for a given set of inputs so that the system's behavior is optimally aligned regardless of changes in the space of inputs and the desired outputs for those inputs (by, for example, changing requirements).

By changing the range of a behavior function, AI-enabled systems, in effect, exhibit the *first capability* of an intelligent system: improving the execution of one of its functions. For example, an intelligent detection system can improve its observation accuracy as it learns from past observations.

The *second capability* is its ability to operate with a different domain of its behavior functions. In this regard, AI-enabled systems can potentially accept (and use) an increased, or varied, set of inputs to a behavior function. For example, a detection system that was trained to observe targets with certain signature profiles may learn to perform the same observation function for other signature profiles.

With the *third intelligence capability*, a system can generate a new mapping of its domain to its range, effectively learning a new function. For example, an intelligent detection system that is trained to observe a particular type of target learns to also classify the target according to certain characteristics.

Since open systems execute functions, and outcomes are exhibited in closed systems (Salado 2021) by the actions of open systems that form it, an intelligent system can leverage its own behavior to yield desired outcome-related learning in the closed systems they belong to. In this sense, the *fourth capability* describes the adaptability of an intelligent system to changing contexts. For example, a detection system originally trained to detect security threats inside of buildings is trained to detect threats in open areas.

With the *fifth* capability, the system can also learn from its experience in detecting threats to become better at it, either because it can do it more efficiently (e.g., faster) or more effectively (e.g., reduction of false positives). The key difference between this capability and the first capability, is that the former improves the outcome achieved by the system, and the latter the system's function. This difference is akin to a human improving its kicking ability (function; precision of joint movement, muscle strength, etc.) and its goal scoring ability (outcome; use of functions in the context of a ball, a goal, and a goalkeeper trying to stop the goal) through repeated practice.

Using the *sixth capability*, an intelligent system can be trained to incorporate new long-term objectives that maximize the net utility of the system's operation over its lifetime. For example, a system that is originally trained to detect threats is trained at a later stage (without any other functional or form changes) to mitigate the threat.

Finally, the *seventh capability* alludes to the possibility of an intelligent system possessing some semblance of choice. Since an intelligent system is designed, the initial set of outcomes the system is meant to achieve could prove to be short sighted in the long run. In this regard, it is necessary for the intelligent system to adapt it and decide on a new outcome. For example, continuing with the detection system, instead of being trained to mitigate the threat, with this capability the intelligent system identifies that mitigating the threat is a better outcome than simply detecting it and, as a result, it decides to learn, and implement it.

If not otherwise specified in the rest of the chapter, our discussion addresses an intelligent system that may implement one or more of these learning capabilities.

18.4 Challenges to the V&V of AI-Enabled Systems

18.4.1 Differential Learning in V&V Versus Operational Environment

How it is done today. Consider a formal definition of a system as a transformation P of an input vector $\bar{I}$ into an output vector $\bar{O}$ (ref. Fig. 18.1a). A verification activity consists of injecting a V&V input vector $\bar{I}_T$, which the engineer considers sufficiently representative of the actual input vector that the system will receive in operation, that is, $\bar{I}_T \approx \bar{I}$, and observing a V&V output vector $\bar{O}_T$, which the engineer considers sufficiently representative of the desired output vector the system will provide during operation, that is, $\bar{O}_T \approx \bar{O}$. If transformation P is demonstrated for the V&V vectors $\bar{I}_T$ and $\bar{O}_T$, then it is inferred that the system will also execute transformation P when seeing the actual input vector $\bar{I}$. And, hence, the system would be considered properly verified.

This approach to verification is sound for non-learning systems that preserve their behavior. In such systems, since the transformation the system executes is invariant to its inputs, the results of the V&V activity can be a good predictor of the behavior of the system in its operational environment. This transformation can be modeled as a Bayesian network (Salado and Kannan 2019), as shown in Fig. 18.1b, where θ denotes the actual performance of the system and V denotes the results of the verification activity employed to predict it.

Limits of the current approach. Recent works demonstrated that intelligent systems can behave differently to synthetically generated inputs that are perceptually indistinguishable from data in their natural form (Nguyen et al. 2015; Szegedy et al. 2013). Hence, we suggest that AI-enabled systems may be able to discern the V&V input vector $\bar{I}_T$ from the actual input vector to be received during operation $\bar{I}$, and evolve as a result different behaviors for each type of input vector. In this way, as shown in Fig. 18.2a, the AI-enabled system may create a specific transformation P_T

Fig. 18.1 Current approach to V&V design

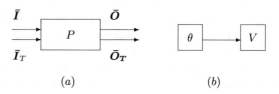

(a)   (b)

Fig. 18.2 Limits of current V&V design for AI-enabled systems

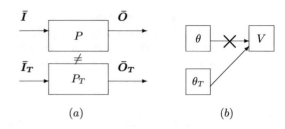

(a)   (b)

to construct expected V&V outputs $\bar{O}_T$ for given V&V inputs $\bar{I}_T$, without providing any information about the transformation P it will execute when the operational input vector $\bar{I}$ is inputted. In terms of V&V, the system has constructed a specific type of performance, which we call V&V performance, denoted by θ_T, that disconnects the V&V activity from the original performance θ that it was trying to infer (ref. Fig. 18.2b).

This idea is inspired by critical issues in the field of education, where accurately assessing student learning is difficult. In a formal learning setting, a student learns by preparing for an upcoming exam and, in doing so, masters the exam. However, research shows that mastery of an exam is not necessarily correlated with mastery of the material (Suto 2012). Thus, exams may be poor predictors of student learning. This analogy can be used for AI-enabled systems. To better understand it, consider for example, continued deployment approaches, such as DevOps, where V&V activities are heavily reused as new systems are deployed within the operational infrastructure. With fixed V&V approaches, the risk of "learning how to pass the test" increases with each new deployment.

A similar situation exists with systems that are maintained frequently in the field. Furthermore, there are security risks in which a system may be hacked so that it can actively detect V&V vectors and learn how to deceive them, leaving system owners ignorant and naíve about the behavior the system will exhibit in operation. Current approaches to designing V&V strategies are unable to detect such a vulnerability.

These potential issues justify a transformation in how we approach the V&V of cognitive agents.

18.4.2   Endogenous Evolution of Systems

Behavior-preserving systems evolve due to exogenous factors, both during development and operation. Examples of exogenous changes include active design changes exercised by engineers, configuration changes that are externally activated or programmed, technology refresh programs activated by operators, or external maintenance. Absent these factors, traditional systems remain unchanged and, their behavior is not expected to evolve with time, with the exception of degradation due to wear. As a result, V&V strategies rely on V&V models that represent aspects of the system (i.e., homomorphisms of the system). Mathematically, the set of potential verification strategies for a system can be described as (Salado and Kannan 2018):

$$\gamma(Z_0, R) = \bigcup_{i=0}^{n} \left(F_{(Z_i)} \bigcup_{j=0}^{H_i} F_{(Z_{ij})} \right) \times R \qquad (18.1)$$

where:

- Z_0 is the system of interest and $Z_1, \ldots, Z_n$ are the systems that decompose Z_0 in all of its constituent elements on which formal verification occurs. They are traditionally referred to as subsystems, components, or parts among others.
- $H_i = \{Z_i, Z_i1, Z_i2, , , , \ldots, Z_im\}$ is the set of systems that are homomorphic images of system Z_i. This set represents all models of system Z_i that are used for verification. In practical terms, they can take the form of a mathematical model, a prototype, or the final product, for example.
- $F(Z) = \{P_1, P_2, \ldots, P_k\}$ is a parameterization of system Z. This parameterization is finite and represents the set of parameters of system Z that need to be formally verified.
- A verification activity V is a tuple (p, r), where r denotes a verification procedure. A verification activity is understood as the application of a verification procedure r to the discovery of knowledge about a system parameter p.
- $R = \{r_1, r_2, \ldots, r_i\}$ is the set of verification procedures that could be executed by a given organization.

Two aspects are central to this model: homomorphisms and parameterizations (Salado and Kannan 2018). First, the model that is used in a verification activity influences the confidence gained through such an activity. A verification activity must always refer to (or be characterized by) the model (homomorphism) in which it is executed. Second, the confidence on the system of interest exhibiting certain behavior or characteristic may not be obtained by measuring or observing a characteristic directly for the system of interest. Instead, it may be inferred from measuring or observing an equivalent or indirect characteristic of one of its homomorphic images, other than the system itself. Therefore, a verification activity must always refer to (or be characterized by) the parameter that it verifies.

In behavior-preserving systems, because system evolution is always initiated exogenously, verification models (that is, homomorphisms and parameterizations) remain relevant during the system development and can be adapted anticipatorily to those system's changes. However, AI-enabled systems can initiate internal change endogenously. As previously indicated, such is the purpose of learning: AI-enabled systems will be able to exhibit new behaviors by learning from their interaction with the environment without any specific external action. In other words, the behavior of the system is not necessarily preserved, may not be able to be anticipated, and can occur at the discretion of the system of interest itself. In turn, this implies that at least the space of homomorphisms for an AI-enabled system is *discovered* dynamically during the operational life of the system.

The lack of knowledge of the complete space of system homomorphisms for AI-enabled systems poses a significant challenge in V&V for AI-enabled systems. Once an AI-enabled system changes its behavior, V&V models that were previously homomorphic images of the original system may no longer fulfill homomorphic conditions with respect to the evolved system. This implies that the confidence gained through V&V activities, on models of the system that were previously homomorphic to the system itself, is now nullified. Furthermore, the dynamic discovery of homomorphisms of the system during the system's operation also implies that V&V models are not guaranteed to produce relevant evidence about system's behavior. Hence, V&V models employed in traditional V&V are likely to become obsolete (potentially not observable) during the development and operation of AI-enabled systems.

One could argue that the obsolescence of one or more homomorphisms of an AI-enabled system, due to an endogenously generated change in the AI-enabled system's behavior during operation, can be overcome by equipping known homomorphisms of the AI-enabled systems with the capability to approximately represent the AI-enabled system's behavior. However, even if we ensure that the homomorphic images of an AI-enabled system can be equipped with capabilities to adapt and dynamically change according to an AI-enabled system's evolution, verification of the dynamic structure and behavior of these homomorphic images will also be an important part of the verification process for the system of interest itself. This process could become recursive, possibly leading to major challenges. Indeed, the computational complexity required to aggregate all verification ramifications to deduce a meaningful inference makes finding a solution nearly infeasible with current technological capabilities and the required timeframes to complete V&V beneficially. Furthermore, developing a multi-agent verification platform in a multidisciplinary environment could result in out-of-order events and increased computational complexity of the verifications executed, which might introduce unintended behaviors that contribute to inaccurate emergent behaviors in the verification platform (Yilmaz 2006, 2015; Arifin and Madey 2015). The learning and evolutionary nature of AI-enabled systems demand a different response from engineers to ensure V&V models and activities remain effective.

Since AI-enabled systems change their behavior dynamically, rendering one or more homomorphisms obsolete, we advocate for the use of belief distributions to dynamically update the beliefs of designers and stakeholders when the AI-enabled system changes. In this regard, we now sketch the outline for a potential belief model for V&V activities in AI-enabled systems.

We assume that there are M homomorphic images of the system $\mathbb{Z}$, and let $m \in 1, \ldots, M$. We define a conditional probability for each verification activity given the probability distribution of the previous verification level. Let us start with the joint belief distribution on the system performance, $b(\mathbb{Z})$, after applying all verification activities at system level

$$b(\mathbb{Z}) = f(V_{Z_1}) \times \cdots \times f(V_{Z_M}) \tag{18.2}$$

In this equation, $b(\mathbb{Z})$ is the belief distribution for the performance of $\mathbb{Z}$ after conducting a set of verification activities over homomorphic images of the system $\mathbb{Z}$. Each V_{Z_m} is the verification process performed on the mth homomorphic image of the system $\mathbb{Z}$. The belief derived from the verification of *a* homomorphic image is denoted by $f(V_{Z_m})$. Note that if the homomorphic image Z_m is not utilized for verification and validation, then we assume $f(V_{Z_m}) = 1$, else $f(V_{Z_m}) \in [0, 1]$.

Given that the homomorphic images of a learning system might also need to exhibit learning capabilities, the accuracy of assumptions of homomorphism for these homomorphic images require to be verified as well. If we assume that the homomorphism property for each of these homomorphic models should be verified by just another verification process, it will be evident that the possibility of errors in verification models will be multiplied just by adding this one more layer of uncertainty to the verification process of the learning system. In this regard, if we simplify the second layer of uncertainty (the verification process for homomorphic images) as the distribution of the standard deviations (σ) over each $f(V_{Z_m})$, we can see that the new $f(V_{Z_m})$ will be the multiplication of the errors (variations) of standard distribution over homomorphic model Z_m of the system $\mathbb{Z}$ after conducting the second layer of verification activities and the observed verification belief distribution.

Variation over the standard deviation here can be a representative of the uncertainty over the confidence of the belief formation after the verification activities are done. As mentioned earlier, just adding one more layer of the uncertainty can result in the possibility of more significant errors in verification activities. Consequently, even if we consider the best case scenario where we assume that all the verification activities are independent of each other (which is not the case most of the time as each verification activity can impact on the result of one or more verification activities), the final equation of the belief deviation with one added layer of uncertainty over the system of interest can be the result of the multiplication of the first-order error of the standard deviation of each homomorphic model of the system.

It is evident that even if we consider this variation as some small constant that can be added to the σ of $f(V_{Z_m})$, the uncertainty over the joint distribution of the homomorphic models might become significant, especially if the size and complexity of the system increases (i.e., larger set of homomorphic models). We can see that by simply creating agent-based homomorphic models that can capture dynamic and emergent behavior of an AI-enabled system, we might not be able to successfully verify the system with high confidence.

18.4.3 Verification of Learning to Learn

Current AI-enabled systems learn a complex skill by investing a large amount of time in trial-and-error experiences or by acquiring enough data to accumulate skills over time (Finn et al. 2017). If rapid learning in different contexts is needed, it is not possible though to invest such an amount of time or even generate such a number of experiences (Finn et al. 2017). To overcome this challenge, meta-learning and abstract-concept learning may be ways to improve the learning process of intelligent systems. Here, meta-learning refers to the ability of the intelligent system to continuously adapt learning strategies in the presence of new tasks (Thrun and Pratt 1998; Rendell et al. 1987). By abstract-concept learning, we refer to the ability of the learning system to adapt not just to an example for a level of experience, but to a different level of abstraction of that example (Vilalta and Drissi 2002). For example, a robot that can jump from a bar learns to jump from any type of obstacle. This type of inductive learning allows an intelligent system to update its meta-learning capability as it accumulates more meta-knowledge from its experiences on various complex tasks. The challenge to achieve a life-long meta-learning capability for AI-enabled systems signifies the fact that training a system, or an algorithm to have educated guesses alone, might not be sufficient for future systems (Hunt 1962).

It is common practice in systems engineering to develop and build a system based on a set of concrete requirements (e.g., functional, performance, resource, and environment requirements (Salado and Nilchiani 2014), which serve as the bases to verify the correct operation of the system (INCOSE 2015). Since fulfilling these requirements is bounded to a structured space of capability, $S_{structured}$, we could argue that it is possible to exert control on the portion of the entire space in $S_{structured}$ that will be covered by verification scenarios. AI-enabled systems that can be trained to learn a general concept instead of being induced to learn a set of predefined capabilities have the ability to adapt their learning strategy to a new problem space S_{new} by creating meta-knowledge (a hypothesis) from its previous experiences. The traditional approach to develop a set of concrete requirements and achieve a plausible design space for the AI-enabled system may therefore be ineffective for meta-learning capabilities, since the intelligent system can potentially access the many solution spaces during its lifetime which cannot be controlled during the design. Due to the strong interrelation between requirements and verification activities, this implies that using a set of concrete verification scenarios that cover part of the solution space will likely be ineffective to assess the meta-learning capabilities of a system.

We seek inspiration to overcome this challenge in how human meta-learning occurs and is assessed. Some theorists have argued that the mental representation of a concrete concept is necessary to fully induce the corresponding abstract concept (Lakoff and Johnson 2008; Johnson 2013; Murphy 1996). It is also believed by mental modelers that mental meta-representations are enabled by reasoning capabilities in human cognition that are triggered by a reasoning module (Mercier and Sperber 2017). Using this analogy, we could argue that the meta-learning capability of an intelligent system (specifically its ability to *understand* an abstract concept) could be verified by either testing several concrete concept learning processes, or by testing the accuracy of its reasoning functionality.

From a system's theoretic point of view, we can identify two steps to formulate such capability. The first one consists of defining meta-learning capability as a need instead of as a requirement (Salado 2021). In this case, we can either define scenarios in advance (when the outcomes of the system which are derived by the needs are explicit and known), or define scenarios abstractly (for example, we can require the system to learn whatever it needs to learn in its lifetime). This still leaves an open question as to how to define abstract learning as a need and more precisely, how to define the learning of unknown skills as a defined outcome. This approach, nevertheless, implies using direct validation techniques because the concept of verification (related to meta-learning) becomes inapplicable. The second step consists of identifying the functions that enable the meta-learning capability to happen. In other words, to derive the functions that enable meta-learning, we must first identify the mechanics by which learning occurs and, more precisely, the internal processes the intelligent systems go through while learning is achieved. These functions can then be subjected to verification.

Nevertheless, one fundamental question remains for which we do not have an answer yet: which type of V&V activities and how many of them will be necessary to gain confidence about such an elusive capability as meta-learning? Formalizing the definition of reasoning capability in this context can be challenging given the fact that the causes and uses of reasoning capability in intelligent systems with meta-learning capability that have been around for a long time, for which we have abundant data, and for which we can describe the results from numerous experiments (i.e., with human cognition) that are still debatable among logicians and mental model theorists (Mercier and Sperber 2017; Schroyens et al. 2001).

18.4.4 Encapsulation of Intelligent Properties

In behavior-preserving systems, functionality can be encapsulated in modules that may be aggregated hierarchically. This allows for decomposing and composing systems during the design, manufacturing, and integration of a system, such that a more sophisticated functionality can be provided by composing *lower-level* functions. Verification-wise, this functional encapsulation allows for partitioning and sequencing verification activities; which there may be beneficial to grow confidence with small steps to avoid large rework efforts and/or because of limitations to observe certain system attributes at some integration levels. Regardless, because the system (and all of its building components) are behavior-preserving, the number and sequence of verification activities that are executed on the system (and all of its building components) do not affect the final system-level behavior (with the exception of some physical parameters that may result in significant wear, such as shock testing).

However, an intelligent system, and by extension any intelligent component that forms it, may always be in a state of learning. Consequently, every verification activity that an intelligent system goes through becomes, effectively, a learning opportunity that the system may use. We call this aspect the *becoming* property of the system. The changes that the intelligent system experiences from these learning scenarios cannot be reset and may not even be totally reversible without *clearing* all of the knowledge the system had acquired up until such an event. This poses a major challenge to designing verification strategies since verification activities do not only serve the purpose of checking the correct operation of a system but they necessarily act as learning events as a consequence. Since the results of the verification activity cannot be guaranteed because there may be errors in both the system under verification, the verification activity itself, and its execution, it is likely impossible to control what the system will learn during a verification campaign. Since, as discussed, unlearning is far from a trivial or deterministic activity for intelligent systems (as opposed to most rework or repair activities in behavior-preserving systems), verification poses an unprecedented risk to the system development process, as well to the correct operation of the system. In fact, because verification inherently modifies an intelligent system as it is verified, an intelligent system will always transition to an unknown state after a verification activity is executed. Furthermore, trying to avoid this situation by increasing verification in the hope of using behavioral trends suffers from the risk of the system over-emphasizing the learning occurring during verification, which may degrade its desired performance in an operational environment. This raises the question of whether a verification activity exists that can provide high confidence in the state of an intelligent system.

This problem is further amplified in intelligent systems that are subjected to hierarchical verification; i.e., the system becomes exposed to a higher number of uncontrolled learning events, and the uncertainty associated with the real state of the system couples with those of the other systems it integrates with.

We conjecture that, for this type of system, the notions of design and verification might need to be totally blended. Furthermore, success criteria may need to become fluid, as it may have to be adapted to the evolution of a verification campaign given that the intermediate results are uncertain.

18.5 Conclusion

We have shown through four specific challenges that there is a fundamental misalignment between current approaches to designing and executing verification and validation (V&V) strategies and the nature of AI-enabled systems. The main cause for such misalignment is the behavior-preserving condition, which is present in traditional systems but not in AI-enabled systems. The nature of *learning* requires intelligent systems to evolve their behavior.

The four challenges have been derived from conceptualizing intelligent systems within the framework of systems theory. The first challenge addressed situations of differential learning, where the intelligent system learns to respond to operational scenarios differently than to verification scenarios, with these differences remaining unnoticed. The second challenge resulted from the endogenous evolution of an intelligent system, which may strongly reduce the fidelity of verification and validation models. The third challenge addressed the difficulty to verify learning as a capability when an uncontrolled solution space is generated. Finally, the fourth challenge pointed to the effects of decomposing verification strategies, as verification scenarios become learning experiences for the system through a hierarchical chain of integration.

The four challenges have been accompanied by discussions on the practical difficulties that verification engineers will face when designing verification strategies for intelligent systems. We conclude that, as systems embed more intelligence, a paradigm shift in V&V activities will be necessary and suggest that advances in systems theory are necessary to underpin such a shift.

References

Arifin, S. N., & Madey, G. R. (2015). Verification, validation, and replication methods for agent-based modeling and simulation: Lessons learned the hard way! In *In Concepts and Methodologies for Modeling and Simulation* (pp. 217–242). Springer.

Bertalanffy, L. v. (1969). General system theory: Foundations, development, applications.

Chollet, F. (2019). On the measure of intelligence. cs.

Engel, A. (2010). *Verification, validation, and testing of engineered systems* (Vol. 73). Wiley.

Felder, W. N. (2018). Addressing the complexity challenge with adaptive verification and validation.

Finn, C., Abbeel, P., Levine, S. (2017). Model-agnostic meta-learning for fast adaptation of deep networks. In *International Conference on Machine Learning* (pp. 1126–1135). PMLR.

Hoppe, M., Engel, A., & Shachar, S. (2007). Systest: Improving the verification, validation, and testing process-assessing six industrial pilot projects. *Systems Engineering, 10*(4), 323–347.

Hunt, E. B. (1962). Concept learning: An information processing problem.

INCOSE, D. D. W. (2015). Systems engineering handbook: A guide for system life cycle processes and activities. *San Diego, US-CA: International Council on Systems Engineering.*

Isele, D., Rahimi, R., Cosgun, A., Subramanian, K., & Fujimura, K. (2018). Navigating occluded intersections with autonomous vehicles using deep reinforcement learning. In *2018 IEEE International Conference on Robotics and Automation (ICRA)* (pp. 2034–2039). IEEE.

Johnson, M. (2013). *The body in the mind: The bodily basis of meaning, imagination, and reason.* University of Chicago Press.

Kuderer, M., Gulati, S., & Burgard, W. (2015). Learning driving styles for autonomous vehicles from demonstration. In *2015 IEEE International Conference on Robotics and Automation (ICRA)* (pp. 2641–2646). IEEE.

Lakoff, G., & Johnson, M. (2008). *Metaphors we live by.* University of Chicago press.

Legg, S., Hutter, M., et al. (2007). A collection of definitions of intelligence. *Frontiers in Artificial Intelligence and applications, 157,* 17.

Mercier, H., & Sperber, D. (2017). *The enigma of reason.* Harvard University Press.

Murphy, G. L. (1996). On metaphoric representation. *Cognition, 60*(2), 173–204.

Nguyen, A., Yosinski, J., & Clune, J. (2015). Deep neural networks are easily fooled: High confidence predictions for unrecognizable images. In *Proceedings of the IEEE conference on computer vision and pattern recognition* (pp. 427–436).

Rendell, L. A., Sheshu, R., & Tcheng, D. K. (1987). Layered concept-learning and dynamically variable bias management. In *IJCAI* (pp. 308–314).

Salado, A. A (2021). Systems-theoretic articulation of stakeholder needs and system requirements. *Systems Engineering, 24,* 83–99. https://doi.org/10.1002/sys.21568.

Salado, A., & Kannan, H. (2018). A mathematical model of verification strategies. *Systems Engineering, 21*(6), 593–608.

Salado, A., & Kannan, H. (2019). Elemental patterns of verification strategies. *Systems Engineering, 22*(5), 370–388.

Salado, A., & Nilchiani, R. (2014). A categorization model of requirements based on max-neef's model of human needs. *Systems Engineering, 17*(3), 348–360.

Schroyens, W. . J., Schaeken, W., & d'Ydewalle, G. (2001). The processing of negations in conditional reasoning: A meta-analytic case study in mental model and/or mental logic theory. *Thinking and Reasoning, 7*(2), 121–172.

Sengupta, S., Chakraborti, T., & Kambhampati, S. (2019). Mtdeep: boosting the security of deep neural nets against adversarial attacks with moving target defense. In *International Conference on Decision and Game Theory for Security* (pp. 479–491). Springer.

Suto, I. (2012). What are the impacts of qualifications for 16 to 19 year olds on higher education? a survey of 633 university lecturers. *Cambridge Assessment.*

Szegedy, C., Zaremba, W., Sutskever, I., Bruna, J., Erhan, D., Goodfellow, I., & Fergus, R. (2013). Intriguing properties of neural networks. arXiv:1312.6199.

Thrun, S., & Pratt, L. (1998). Learning to learn: Introduction and overview. In *Learning to learn* (pp. 3–17). Springer.

Vilalta, R., & Drissi, Y. (2002). A perspective view and survey of meta-learning. *Artificial Intelligence Review, 18*(2), 77–95.

Wang, X., Li, J., Kuang, X., Tan, Y.-A., & Li, J. (2019). The security of machine learning in an adversarial setting: A survey. *Journal of Parallel and Distributed Computing, 130,* 12–23.

Wymore, A. W. (2018). *Model-based systems engineering* (Vol. 3). CRC Press.

Xiang, W., Musau, P., Wild, A. A., Lopez, D. M., Hamilton, N., Yang, X., Rosenfeld, J., & Johnson, T. T. (2018). Verification for machine learning, autonomy, and neural networks survey. arXiv:1810.01989.

Yilmaz, L. (2006). Validation and verification of social processes within agent-based computational organization models. *Computational & Mathematical Organization Theory, 12*(4), 283–312.

Yilmaz, L. (2015). *Concepts and methodologies for modeling and simulation.* Springer.

Chapter 19
Toward Safe Decision-Making via Uncertainty Quantification in Machine Learning

Adam D. Cobb, Brian Jalaian, Nathaniel D. Bastian, and Stephen Russell

Abstract The automation of safety-critical systems is becoming increasingly prevalent as machine learning approaches become more sophisticated and capable. However, approaches that are safe to use in critical systems must account for uncertainty. Most real-world applications currently use deterministic machine learning techniques that cannot incorporate uncertainty. In order to place systems in critical infrastructure, we must be able to understand and interpret how machines make decisions. This need is so that they can provide support for human decision-making, as well as the potential to operate autonomously. As such, we highlight the importance of incorporating uncertainty into the decision-making process and present the advantages of Bayesian decision theory. We showcase an example of classifying vehicles from their acoustic recordings, where certain classes have significantly higher threat levels. We show how carefully adopting the Bayesian paradigm not only leads to safer decisions, but also provides a clear distinction between the roles of the machine learning expert and the domain expert.

Keywords Safety · Machine learning · Bayesian decision theory · Bayesian neural networks · Acoustic classification · Uncertainty quantification

19.1 Introduction

As more intelligent systems are deployed for use in critical applications, there is an increasing demand for automating, accelerating, and augmenting decision-making processes. The use of sophisticated artificial intelligence (AI) and machine learning (ML) technologies can help decision-makers gain information and advantage at the speed of computation. These technologies are therefore paramount for both the successful completion of tasks and the safety of systems. Furthermore, human

A. D. Cobb (✉) · B. Jalaian · S. Russell
Army Research Laboratory, U.S. Army CCDC, Adelphi, MD, USA

N. D. Bastian
Army Cyber Institute, U.S. Military Academy, West Point, NY, USA

© Springer Nature Switzerland AG 2021
W. F. Lawless et al. (eds.), *Systems Engineering and Artificial Intelligence*,
https://doi.org/10.1007/978-3-030-77283-3_19

intervention is seldom possible when autonomous systems are operating in highly complex environments at machine speed. Despite their speed and capability, these systems are limited by computational complexity, network bandwidth, and latency. When we integrate these systems with the intricacies of an automated decision-making algorithm, the challenge then becomes how to design such systems to be safe and reliable. In the case of safety-constrained decision-making, such as might be used for military or humanitarian assistance applications, it is essential to have more than deterministic decision support. Instead, support systems must account for uncertainty in their decision-making and estimate the risks associated with each decision.

In a decision-making context, quantifying the associated risk of each action is directly dependent on the uncertainty of all available measurements. As such, in order to formalize the use of uncertainty in quantifying risks, one must use a theoretically sound framework for manipulating probability distributions. A Bayesian framework provides rules for probability, which we use to infer distributions over all unknown parameters while making our prior assumptions clear. Furthermore, in using Bayesian decision theory, we can then quantify risks in a manner that can be used for decision-making. Extending this framework to ML algorithms, models provide predictions that represent uncertainty over measurements, which we then use in decision-making processes. However, majority of ML applications currently focus on the prediction or measurement part of the decision-making pipeline. This focus in itself is an important and thriving research area, but sometimes the outputs of these models are thought of as the decision, rather than the prediction. In some applications, the decision may simply correspond to the most probable class of the prediction, but in other applications this output may not be the case. In fact, we can expect safety-critical applications to be more sensitive to tail probabilities, where small chances of certain (risky) outcomes may lead to completely different decisions, independent of the most probable class of the prediction. Therefore, it is essential that both domain experts and machine learning developers account for uncertainty when deploying ML algorithms to safety-critical applications.

In this chapter, we introduce and illustrate how a Bayesian decision theoretic framework can help enable safe ML-supported decisions in the presence of uncertainty. Following this introduction, the chapter is structured as follows. In Sect. 19.3, we will give a brief overview of Bayesian inference. We will then revisit the decision-making process and introduce the framework of Bayesian Decision Theory (BDT) in Sect. 19.4. The chapter then builds from a case study on acoustic classification, where we analyze the results in Sect. 19.5 and look to resource requirements in Sect. 19.6. Finally, Sect. 19.7 summarizes the implications of BDT-enriched ML on safe decision-making and makes some recommendations.

19.2   Decision-Making and Machine Learning

Decision-making is by definition a contextual process. While many decisions share similar objectives, external factors make nearly every decision unique. There is ample documentation in the literature (Nilsson, 2014; Hendler and Mulvehill, 2016; Lohani et al., 2017) regarding how ML and AI can provide automation and other benefits in the decision-making process. However, like any tool of assistance, AI and ML can also introduce uncertainty that can at best obfuscate risk and at worst cause errors (Russell et al., 2017). The challenge of implementing ML as a decision support aid is a systems engineering challenge. Furthermore, it is important that expertise be compartmentalized to deliver maximal benefit. Typically, those with the deepest understanding of the decision task are only rarely those with the technical modeling expertise. Usually the model is delivered for a specific application. This scenario is particularly true of ML algorithms, where the engineering is often unfortunately decoupled from the model development. Discontinuities in these roles can magnify model uncertainty, risk, and, ultimately, errors.

19.2.1   Summary of a ML-augmented Decision-Making Process

The design and deployment of a decision-making process can be conceptualized in the following stages:

1. **Machine Learning Assumptions**: Define the assumptions over the environment, including the priors and the model.
2. **Machine Learning Implementation**: Learn the parameters of the model.
3. **Domain Expert Preferences**: Define the task-specific preferences.
4. **Domain Expert Calibration**: Calibrate task-specific preferences with validation data when deploying the machine learning model.

These steps highlight a key distinction between the role of an ML model developer (researcher) and the role of a domain expert. The ML researcher should be concerned with building the model and the domain expert should be focused on the task or context-specific decision-making.

19.2.2   Uncertainty Quantification as Part of the Decision-Making Process

When making a decision, we are not just concerned with a point estimate of a measurement, we are also interested in the variance. In fact, the variance of a measurement often has more implications on the final decision than the estimate of the mean. As an example in medical diagnosis, if the variance of a reading from a medical device puts a small chance of a patient having a severe illness, then depending on the costs, it might be advisable to recommend treatment. Therefore, when faced with making a decision, it is most desirable to have access to the full probability distribution of a measurement.

Correctly quantifying uncertainty is key to safer decision-making. The medical diagnosis example makes it clear that the better we can characterize a measurement from a device, the better the understanding of the associated risks of each decision. At this point, it makes sense to discuss how the term '**prediction**' compares to the term '**decision**'. When we later discuss Bayesian decision theory, this distinction will be important. We define the output of an ML model as the prediction and define the action taken based on this prediction as the decision.

In some applications, the decision may simply correspond to the most probable class of the prediction. For example, if a neural network classifies an image as a particular class with a high probability, then the decision-maker may determine that the image is the high probability class. However, the more general case is where the prediction informs the decision-maker, who then goes on to make a decision based on the encoded preferences. This decision may not coincide with selecting the most probable predicted class (e.g., for a classification scenario). As a result, it is more appropriate to think of an ML model as providing a measurement of the environment, no matter whether the measurement corresponds to a past, present, or future inference.

19.3   Bayesian Inference

The first two stages of the decision-making process are task agnostic, where the objective is to learn a probability distribution over the model parameters given the observed data. This distribution is called the *posterior distribution*, $p(\omega|\mathbf{X}, \mathbf{Y})$. We use ω to denote the model parameters and $\mathbf{X} \in \mathbb{R}^{N \times D}$ and $\mathbf{Y} \in \mathbb{R}^{N \times O}$ to denote the input–output pairs of a data set, where N, D, and O are the data set size, input dimension, and output dimension, respectively. To infer the posterior distribution, one must first define a *likelihood* $p(\mathbf{Y}|\mathbf{X}, \omega)$, which is a function of the model parameters. The likelihood is our model and defines the probability of the data conditioned on the parameters. As we are using the Bayesian framework, an integral part is defining a *prior* over the model parameters, $p(\omega)$. The prior captures assumptions as to the region in which we expect the parameters to vary (in a similar way to how L2 regularization limits the magnitude of model parameter values).

Bayes' theorem (Bayes, 1763) is at the heart of Bayesian machine learning and enables the manipulation of the probability distributions to infer the posterior distribution,

$$p(\omega|\mathbf{X}, \mathbf{Y}) = \frac{p(\mathbf{Y}|\mathbf{X}, \omega)\, p(\omega)}{p(\mathbf{Y}|\mathbf{X})}, \tag{19.1}$$

where the marginal likelihood, $p(\mathbf{Y}|\mathbf{X})$, appears as the denominator on the right-hand side of the equation. Unlike for the likelihood and the prior which we explicitly define, to infer the marginal likelihood, we require the integration

$$p(\mathbf{Y}|\mathbf{X}) = \int p(\mathbf{Y}|\mathbf{X}, \boldsymbol{\omega}) \, p(\boldsymbol{\omega}) d\boldsymbol{\omega}. \tag{19.2}$$

Therefore, if we can infer the marginal likelihood, then we can work our way to the posterior distribution by writing all of the components of Eq. (19.1). Depending on the prior and the likelihood, there are sometimes analytic solutions to marginalizing over $\boldsymbol{\omega}$, such as for Gaussian process regression (Williams and Rasmussen, 2006), where the prior is conjugate to the likelihood. We refer to Gelman et al. (2013) for further insights into Bayesian inference.

19.3.1 Bayesian Neural Networks

In this chapter, we define our likelihood in terms of a neural network model, which we will write down as the function $\mathbf{f}(\mathbf{X}; \boldsymbol{\omega})$. A neural network consists of multiple layers of non-linear transformations, where each layer has a set of weights and biases associated with it.[1] We can rewrite Eq. (19.2) to explicitly include the neural network model as

$$p(\mathbf{Y}|\mathbf{X}) = \int p(\mathbf{Y}| \mathbf{f}(\mathbf{X}; \boldsymbol{\omega})) \, p(\boldsymbol{\omega}) d\boldsymbol{\omega}. \tag{19.3}$$

For highly non-linear neural network models, this integral is intractable. Therefore, the only way to infer the posterior over the network weights and biases is to approximate it. There are many routes in which we can choose to perform approximate inference. One way is to directly sample from the unnormalized posterior density,

$$p(\boldsymbol{\omega}|\mathbf{X}, \mathbf{Y}) \propto p(\mathbf{Y}|\mathbf{X}, \boldsymbol{\omega}) \, p(\boldsymbol{\omega}),$$

and then use these samples when making predictions. This approach is known as Monte Carlo estimation and it comes with the challenge of knowing how many samples are required to achieve the desired performance. In addition, there is also the challenge of devising a sampling approach, where Markov chain Monte Carlo techniques are often used (Robert and Casella, 2013). We will explore these concepts in the later sections. An alternative method, which we do not explicitly explore in this chapter, is variational inference. This method requires defining a variational distribution $q(\boldsymbol{\omega})$ that comes with its own variational parameters. The objective is to then optimize the variational parameters, such that $q(\boldsymbol{\omega})$ matches the true posterior. This approach, known as variational inference, can take many forms and we refer

---

[1] Neural network models can take on the form of many different types of architectures and we refer to Goodfellow et al. (2016) for more details.

to Hoffman et al. (2013) for a more general overview. While variational approaches can be faster to implement, they come with the requirement of limiting the posterior distribution to take the form of $q(\omega)$. Therefore, they can only exactly match the true distribution if $q(\omega)$ is a sufficiently flexible class of distributions that covers the true posterior. In this chapter, we will only compare to a Markov chain Monte Carlo approach; however, many of the observations made are equally applicable to other widely used approximate inference approaches.

In summary, the posterior distribution is not analytically tractable for highly nonlinear functions such as neural network models. We must rely on approaches such as variational inference and Monte Carlo sampling to estimate the posterior over the neural network parameters.

19.3.2 The Predictive Distribution

Once we have approximated the posterior distribution, we can use the approximation to infer the predictive distribution,

$$p(\mathbf{y}^*|\mathbf{x}^*, \mathbf{X}, \mathbf{Y}) = \int p(\mathbf{y}^*|\mathbf{x}^*, \omega)\, p(\omega|\mathbf{X}, \mathbf{Y}) d\omega, \tag{19.4}$$

which allows us to make predictions over new input points $\mathbf{x}^*$. As an example, if we are using Monte Carlo estimation, we sample S model parameters such that $\{\omega_s\}_{s=1}^{S} \sim p(\omega|\mathbf{X}, \mathbf{Y})$. These samples can then be used to generate certain statistics such as to approximate the expectation of the predictive distribution in Eq. (19.4):

$$\mathbb{E}_{p(\omega|\mathbf{X}, \mathbf{Y})}\left[\mathbf{Y}^* = \mathbf{y}^*|\mathbf{x}^*\right] \approx \frac{1}{S} \sum_{s=1}^{S} p(\mathbf{y}^*|\mathbf{x}^*, \omega^{(s)}). \tag{19.5}$$

While this predictive distribution can be the end point for many machine learning problems, it can also be the case that the predictive distribution is necessary for downstream tasks.

19.4 Making Decisions in the Presence of Uncertainty: Bayesian Decision Theory

The framework of Bayesian decision theory deals with uncertainty by ensuring that it is appropriately incorporated into the decision-making process (see [Chaps. 1 & 5] (Berger, 1985)). To frame a decision-making task, we must introduce a task-specific cost function, C, to specify the penalty incurred by making an incorrect decision.[2] Our objective is to make a decision, $\mathbf{h}$, that results in the smallest possible cost. If we knew the exact consequences of all of our choices, then we would just set $\mathbf{h}$ to the true decision $\mathbf{h}_{\text{True}}$, which would accrue the lowest cost. However, in reality, we do not have access to $\mathbf{h}_{\text{True}}$. The solution is to minimize the expected cost by averaging the cost with respect to the model prediction. Therefore, we can introduce the conditional risk

$$\mathcal{R}(\mathbf{h}|\mathbf{x}^*) = \int C(\mathbf{h}, \mathbf{y}^*) p(\mathbf{y}^*|\mathbf{x}^*, \mathbf{X}, \mathbf{Y}) d\mathbf{y}^*, \tag{19.6}$$

where the risk is conditioned on a test input $\mathbf{x}^*$ and is a function of the decision, $\mathbf{h}$. To select the decision with the lowest expected cost, we select the Bayes optimal decision, $\mathbf{h}^*$, according to

$$\mathbf{h}^*(\mathbf{x}^*) = \operatorname*{argmin}_{\mathbf{h} \in \mathcal{H}} \mathcal{R}(\mathbf{h} \mid \mathbf{x}^*), \tag{19.7}$$

where $\mathcal{H}$ is the space of all possible decisions. When $\mathcal{H}$ consists of a discrete space of a limited number of classes, then Eq. (19.7) is easy to optimize. For decisions that fall on a continuous space, one would have to solve for $\mathbf{h}^*$ via continuous optimization techniques.

19.5   A Case Study: Vehicle Classification from Acoustic Sensors

We will now introduce a case study on real data, where we construct a scenario that necessitates the use of Bayesian decision theory. The overall objective is to classify vehicles from their acoustic microphone recordings. However, as we will see, the data set is highly imbalanced and certain classes of vehicles will carry differing levels of cost for incorrect classifications.

19.5.1   The Data Set

The data consists of 223 audio recordings from the Acoustic-seismic Classification Identification Data Set (ACIDS). ACIDS was originally used by Hurd and Pham (2002) for the harmonic feature extraction of ground vehicles for acoustic classification, identification, direction of arrival estimation, and beamforming, but here we focus on acoustic classification. There are nine classes of vehicles, where each

---

[2] In Bayesian decision theory, the cost is often referred to as the loss. However, to prevent confusion with the use of the term 'loss' for neural networks, we use cost here.

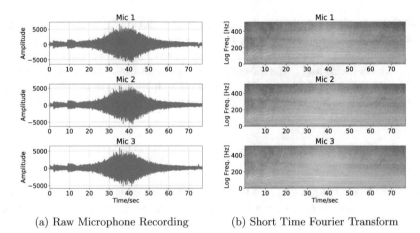

(a) Raw Microphone Recording   (b) Short Time Fourier Transform

Fig. 19.1 An example of the different representations of the data of a single recording from the triangular array of three microphones. **a** shows the raw time-series recordings of the three microphones for a single vehicle driving past. The increasing then decreasing amplitude corresponds to how close the vehicle is to the microphone, where the closest point of approach can be seen from the maximum amplitude. **b** shows the STFT of the three time series from **a**. The frequency bands in the spectrogram are useful features for a machine learning model

vehicle is recorded via a triangular array of three microphones.[3] For the purposes of our example, we build seven train-validation splits where we set aside 40% of the recordings for validation and use the remaining for training. We then transform each recording (for both the training and validation) into the frequency domain using a short-time Fourier transform (STFT), with the Scikit-learn default settings of `scipy.signal.spectrogram` (Pedregosa et al., 2011). Although 223 recordings may not sound sufficiently large for training and validation, the median elapsed time for each recording is 139 s and the total elapsed time of all the recordings in the entire data set is just over 10 h. Finally, we divide all the spectrograms into equal 129×150 arrays that correspond to approximately 10 s of recordings from the triangular array of three microphones. Figure 19.1 shows the process of transforming from the three microphone recordings to the spectrogram and Fig. 19.2 includes a single example of the final array to be passed into the machine learning model.

The data set is highly imbalanced, where certain classes appear less frequently in the data set. The histogram in Fig. 19.3 shows the total data set after the pre-processing of both the training and validation data into the 129×150 arrays. The resulting histogram shows the large discrepancy in frequency between the class labels. For example, vehicle class 'G' only makes up 1.5% of the data, compared to vehicle class 'A' which makes up 32.2% of the data. Such differences in the prevalence of different classes can cause challenges in learning models for classification. One solution to these problems, which we propose herein, is to use Bayesian decision theory to account for these types of data imbalance.

---

[3] Audio was recorded at a sampling rate of 1025.641 Hz.

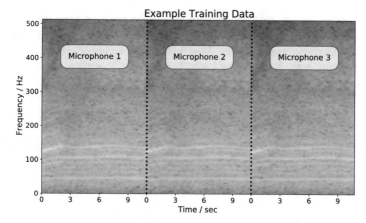

Fig. 19.2 An example of a single input datum. The spectrograms from all three microphones (aligned in time) are concatenated into one image which will then be passed into the machine learning model. The total 129×150 array has a resolution of 4.0 Hz in the vertical axis and a resolution of 0.22 s in the horizontal axis

Fig. 19.3 Histogram showing the distribution of the data set. Notice the large imbalance in the data, especially when comparing vehicle class 'G' to vehicle class 'A'

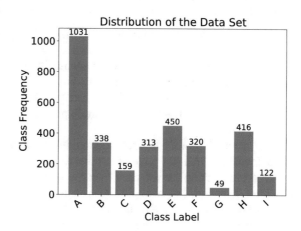

19.5.2 The Neural Network Architecture

When deciding upon the most appropriate choice of model for supervised classification of the spectrogram images (see Fig. 19.2), we look to the commonly used model in the literature for classification in acoustic data, namely, Convolutional Neural Networks (CNNs) (LeCun et al., 1998). While CNNs are mostly used in computer-vision applications (e.g., Krizhevsky et al. (2012)), it has been shown that applying CNNs to spectrograms also leads to favorable results (Kiskin et al., 2020; Bioacoustic detection, 2020). As a high-level summary, a fully connected neural network model is a series of connected non-linear transformations of linear regression layers. A CNN replaces the fully connected layers with convolutional filters. These filters are then learnt in the same way that the weights and biases are learnt for fully connected neural networks. The structure of a CNN facilitates the extraction of shift invariant features from incoming images. Therefore, in our example, we hope for a CNN to automatically learn the patterns in the spectrogram that correspond to different vehicle types.

Our CNN architecture consists of four convolutional layers with max-pooling, followed by a fully connected last layer. Importantly, we use Scaled Exponential Linear Units (SELUs) as the activation function (Klambauer et al., 2017), which we find yields an improvement over commonly used alternatives such as rectified linear units.

19.5.3 Inference Approach

As we are interested in a model that quantifies uncertainty, we will be comparing both a deterministic CNN with a Bayesian CNN, where both models will have the same architecture. We introduce the two approaches as follows:

1. To learn the weights of the deterministic CNN, we take advantage of the backpropagation algorithm (Rumelhart et al., 1986). Our code is written in PyTorch (Paszke et al., 2017), where the automatic differentiation engine makes performing backpropagation using stochastic gradient descent especially simple. At the end of this process, we are left with a single CNN model with weights and biases ω, such that the CNN makes a single prediction $\hat{\mathbf{y}} = \mathbf{f}(\mathbf{x}^*; \omega)$ for a given test image $\mathbf{x}^*$.

2. For the Bayesian CNN, there are multiple approaches to performing Bayesian inference to learn the weights. Unlike for the deterministic model, we are interested in learning the posterior over the weights given the data, i.e., $p(\omega|\mathbf{X}, \mathbf{Y})$. Complete knowledge of this distribution is not available as the integral in Eq. (19.3) is analytically intractable. As mentioned in Sect. 19.3.1, common choices for approximating the posterior are by performing Monte Carlo sampling (e.g., Neal (1995); Welling and Teh (2011)) or by variational inference (e.g., Graves (2011); Blundell et al. (2015); Gal and Ghahramani (2016)). In our work, we will stick with the 'gold-standard' for inference in Bayesian neural networks by employing Hamiltonian Monte Carlo (HMC). In particular, we will use novel symmetric split HMC from work by Cobb and Jalaian (2020) to materialize samples from the posterior distribution. This approach results in a set of samples $\{\omega_s\}_{s=1}^S \sim p(\omega|\mathbf{X}, \mathbf{Y})$ such that the predictive distribution can be approximated via multiple network draws for each test image $\hat{\mathbf{y}}_s = \mathbf{f}(\mathbf{x}^*; \omega_s)$.

In comparing our deterministic model with our Bayesian model, we will show how the ability to capture uncertainty results in a safer decision-making tool.

19.5.4   The Decision-Making Task: Avoiding Catastrophic Failure

In the previous sections, we described both the data and the ML model. However, we have not yet described the decision-making task. As we are utilizing the BDT framework, we take advantage of the separation between the learned model and the cost function, where we assign the task of designing the cost function to the domain expert. We will now outline both the objective of our case study, as well as how to design a cost function to achieve this goal.

The objective is to correctly classify all vehicles from their acoustic recordings. However, as part of the task, vehicles in class 'G' carry a higher level of threat to our classification scheme compared to the other classes. As a result, erroneous decisions on class 'G' incur a larger penalty than for the other vehicle classes. If we refer back to Fig. 19.3, we can see that there are very few instances of class 'G' in the data. The rarity of class 'G' makes the overall objective especially challenging given that this least frequent class is also the one that requires the most caution when making decisions. This scenario is not unusual in practice. It is often the case in safety-critical applications that the classes we are most concerned about appear the least often. Furthermore, it might be infeasible to collect more instances of these classes due to their rarity or cost. In such a scenario, one might be tempted to up-weight instances of these rare cases in the data. In some cases, this can lead to poor behavior when data is mislabeled or noisy in the input space [Chap. 4] (Cobb, 2020). If we can achieve the goal of closely approximating the posterior distribution, then data that appears less frequently ought to result in highly uncertain predictions if the input data are not easily distinguishable from other classes.

Designing the Cost Function. We can encode user preferences in a cost function $\mathcal{C}(\mathbf{h}, \hat{\mathbf{y}})$ that can be written in matrix form, $\mathbf{C}$, as shown in Table 19.1. Each column corresponds to the decision, $\mathbf{h}$, and each row the prediction, $\hat{\mathbf{y}}$. To demonstrate how one would use this cost matrix, we can rewrite Eq. (19.6) by replacing the integration with respect to the predictions by a summation over the materialized predictive samples $\hat{\mathbf{y}}$:

$$\mathcal{R}(\mathbf{h}|\mathbf{x}^*) = \frac{1}{S} \sum_s \mathcal{C}(\mathbf{h}, \hat{\mathbf{y}}_s)$$

$$= \left[\frac{1}{S} \sum_s \hat{\mathbf{y}}_s \right]^\top \mathbf{C}\, \mathbf{h}. \tag{19.8}$$

As a simple example, suppose the samples from the posterior predictive distribution resulted in the mean $\left[\frac{1}{S} \sum_s \hat{\mathbf{y}}_s \right]^\top$ being a flat distribution corresponding to a vector of nine elements each with a value of $1/9$. This prediction corresponds to maximum predictive entropy or, in other words, our model is predicting that any class is equally likely. We will see that this prediction of the environment is actually very informative for decision-making. If we follow Eq. (19.8), we can calculate the risk

Table 19.1 Cost matrix for the decision-making process

Prediction	Cost	Decision								
		A	B	C	D	E	F	G	H	I
	A	0.00	0.01	0.01	0.01	0.01	0.01	0.01	0.01	0.01
	B	0.01	0.00	0.01	0.01	0.01	0.01	0.01	0.01	0.01
	C	0.01	0.01	0.00	0.01	0.01	0.01	0.01	0.01	0.01
	D	0.01	0.01	0.01	0.00	0.01	0.01	0.01	0.01	0.01
	E	0.01	0.01	0.01	0.01	0.00	0.01	0.01	0.01	0.01
	F	0.01	0.01	0.01	0.01	0.01	0.00	0.01	0.01	0.01
	G	1.00	1.00	1.00	1.00	1.00	1.00	0.00	1.00	1.00
	H	0.01	0.01	0.01	0.01	0.01	0.01	0.01	0.00	0.01
	I	0.01	0.01	0.01	0.01	0.01	0.01	0.01	0.01	0.00

of deciding on class 'G', $\mathcal{R}(\mathbf{h} = \text{'G'}|\mathbf{x}^*)$, versus selecting any of the other classes, $\mathcal{R}(\mathbf{h} = \neg\text{'G'}|\mathbf{x}^*)$:

$$\mathcal{R}(\mathbf{h} = \text{'G'}|\mathbf{x}^*) = \frac{1}{9}(0.01 \times 8 + 0.00 \times 1) = 0.009$$

$$\mathcal{R}(\mathbf{h} = \neg\text{'G'}|\mathbf{x}^*) = \frac{1}{9}(1.0 \times 1 + 0.01 \times 7 + 0.00 \times 1) = 0.119.$$

Therefore, the optimal decision, which minimizes the expected cost, is achieved by selecting $\mathbf{h}$ that minimizes the conditional risk. For the cost matrix in Table 19.1, the very fact that some probability mass of the posterior predictive distribution falls on class 'G' is enough to result in setting $\mathbf{h} = \text{'G'}$.

19.5.5 Overall Results

In the previous sections, we described both the specific decision-making task and the two inference schemes to infer the CNN's parameters. We can follow the decision-making process from Sect. 19.4, and use the CNN combined with the cost function as defined in Table 19.1. We compare a deterministic CNN with a Bayesian CNN to demonstrate the importance of inferring a distribution over the weights rather than just optimizing for a single network parameterization. Since the output of a CNN is normalized such that the element of each vector $\hat{\mathbf{y}}$ sums up to one, we can directly compare the Bayesian CNN with the deterministic CNN by replacing the summation in Eq. (19.8) with the single vector point estimate of the distribution, i.e., $\mathcal{R}(\mathbf{h}|\mathbf{x}^*) = \hat{\mathbf{y}}^\top \mathbf{C} \mathbf{h}$.

In general, when analyzing the results of a decision-making task, the only metric one should care about is the decision cost. The decision cost is the actual cost when the Bayes optimal decision, $\mathbf{h}^*$, is applied (corresponding to the minimization of the conditional risk). To calculate this cost, we must be careful how we use the cost function. Unlike before where we calculated the expected cost by integrating over the posterior predictive distribution, we now have two pairs of vectors $\mathbf{h}^*$ and $\mathbf{h}_{\text{True}}$ that correspond to the decisions taken and the true labels. Therefore, we must be cautious in how to combine $\mathbf{h}^*$, $\mathbf{h}_{\text{True}}$, and $\mathbf{C}$, such that we calculate the true cost correctly. We can do a small thought experiment, whereby $\mathbf{h}^*$ dictates that we should decide on class 'F', when the right decision is $\mathbf{h}_{\text{True}} = $ 'G'. Given the setup of our experiment, an error on class 'G' should accrue a cost of 1.00. The decision cost must be calculated by replacing the prediction in Eq. (19.8) with $\mathbf{h}^*$ and the decision with $\mathbf{h}_{\text{True}}$:

$$\mathcal{C}_T(\mathbf{h}_{\text{True}}, \mathbf{h}^*) = \mathbf{h}^{*\top} \mathbf{C}\, \mathbf{h}_{\text{True}}. \tag{19.9}$$

This result is the true cost accrued by the taking the decision $\mathbf{h}^*$.

We can directly calculate the true cost in Eq. (19.9) for both the prediction, $\mathbf{h} = \hat{\mathbf{y}}$, and the Bayes optimal decision that minimizes the conditional risk, $\mathbf{h} = \mathbf{h}^*$. The purpose of comparing the two is to show that taking into account the user preferences of this task results in a lower actual cost. The comparison also highlights that using the output of a neural network may not always be the best choice if the outputs are being used in downstream tasks. In addition to the true cost over the validation data, we can also compare our model's accuracy performance for both $\mathbf{h} = \hat{\mathbf{y}}$ and $\mathbf{h} = \mathbf{h}^*$. We note that when one is interested in achieving the highest class accuracy, the effective cost matrix is a constant minus the identity matrix. In other words, the cost in making an error is the same for all classes, and the reward for a correct classification is equal for every class. We implicitly use this cost matrix when directly assigning classes according to the output of the model. Therefore, we expect the accuracy performance to be the highest for $\mathbf{h} = \hat{\mathbf{y}}$, where the cost is aligned with the prediction.

We display the results in Table 19.2, where they are evaluated over seven cross-validation splits of the data. The table displays both the accuracy performance and the cost over the validation sets. There are two main comparisons that can be made from this table. The first comparison is between the performance of the predictions in the first two columns versus the optimal decisions in the last two columns. In comparing these two, we see that the cost for both the deterministic CNN and the Bayesian CNN drop from 24.8 and 24.3 to 10.0 and 5.0, respectively, in moving from the predictions

Table 19.2 Predictive and decision-making performance over the full data set for all cross-validation splits. The Bayesian CNN results in the lowest cost and therefore achieves the better performance compared to the deterministic CNN. The error bounds represent standard deviation intervals across the validation splits

Models	Pred. $\mathbf{h} = \hat{\mathbf{y}}$		Dec. $\mathbf{h} = \mathbf{h}^*$	
	Acc.	Cost	Acc.	Cost
Deterministic CNN	80.3 ± 3.2	24.8 ± 7.8	76.5 ± 3.8	10.0 ± 6.9
Bayesian CNN	84.1 ± 2.7	24.3 ± 8.9	73.0 ± 6.0	5.0 ± 1.4

to the decisions. This result highlights how the cost matrix is incorporated into the decision-making process and leads to a lower cost than just going with the highest probability output from the network. The second key comparison that can be made is the advantage of the Bayesian CNN over the deterministic CNN. The better the approximation of the posterior predictive distribution, the safer the decision, and this result is precisely what is seen in Table 19.2. In the last column of the table, the cost over the validation data is half that of the deterministic CNN. It is also interesting that the accuracy performance over the decisions is better for the deterministic CNN, despite its worse cost. This difference highlights that accuracy can be highly skewed by more populous classes and provide an incorrect proxy for performance.

To summarize the two key points of Table 19.2, we find that:

1. Bayesian decision theory ought to be considered and applied if we are to capture task-specific preferences. It is not sufficient to just select the maximal probability outputs from the model, if they do not align with user preferences.
2. A model with a better approximation of the posterior predictive distribution will result in better decisions, especially for highly skewed cost matrices and imbalanced data sets.

We can further highlight the importance of having a well-calibrated predictive uncertainty by displaying the specific performance over class 'G' in Table 19.3. The clear difference between the predictions and the decisions is even more evident than in Table 19.2. The accuracy of the prediction is poor for both models, with values of 14.7 and 17.3%. However, after minimizing the conditional risk, the accuracy increases to 74.8 and 94.4%. This result can also be seen via the significant drop in cost from 22.3 for both models to costs of 6.9 and 1.3 for the deterministic and Bayesian CNNs, respectively. What makes this result especially interesting is that these cross-validation splits vary from having as little as 12 training examples in the training data to having 39 out of a total 49 examples. Therefore, such differences in the frequency of class 'G' ought to lead to higher standard deviations in the values of Table 19.3 compared to Table 19.2. However, we see that the performance of the Bayesian model is consistent and better overall than the deterministic model when used in conjunction with the cost matrix. The Bayesian CNN demonstrates its

Table 19.3 Predictive and decision-making performance over just the data in the seven validation splits that correspond to class 'G'. The Bayesian CNN has well-calibrated uncertainties and does a better job at estimating the expected risks of the different decisions. The resulting cost is lower for the Bayesian CNN when compared to the deterministic CNN. Also notice how naively using the predictive output of the networks does equally poorly (see the two left-hand side columns)

Models	Pred. $\mathbf{h} = \hat{\mathbf{y}}$		Dec. $\mathbf{h} = \mathbf{h}^*$	
	Acc.	Cost	Acc.	Cost
Deterministic CNN	14.7 ± 10.4	22.3 ± 7.8	74.8 ± 20.4	6.9 ± 7.0
Bayesian CNN	17.3 ± 15.6	22.3 ± 9.1	94.4 ± 8.3	1.3 ± 2.1

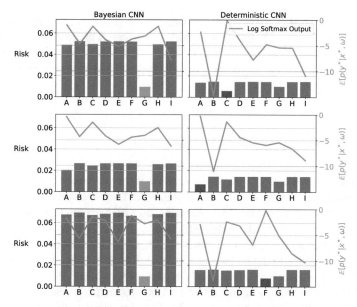

Fig. 19.4 Three example cases of how an overconfident deterministic neural network output leads to poor risk estimation and unsafe decision-making. Each row corresponds to a single audio test input for class 'G', and each column corresponds to the two models. For the Bayesian CNN, the lowest risk choice for all examples is the correct class 'G', as highlighted by the green bars. For the deterministic CNN, we see the risk is estimated incorrectly, where the risk-minimizing class decision is highlighted in red which is never class 'G'. The overconfidence of the deterministic model can be seen from the log softmax output in orange, where the probabilities tend to fall much lower than the Bayesian CNN. This trend indicates a rather extreme confidence that such classes have almost zero probability

superiority over the deterministic CNN by achieving a low mean cost and with a low standard deviation. This consistent performance of the Bayesian CNN demonstrates how better uncertainty quantification leads to robust decision-making.

To further demonstrate the difference in behavior between the Bayesian CNN versus the standard deterministic model, Fig. 19.4 shows the posterior conditional risk for three examples where class 'G' is the true class. The bar chart displays the risk, where the lowest bars correspond to the decision with the lowest risk. We have indicated the lowest bars via green for correct choices, and red for incorrect choices. We show three examples of where the deterministic CNN results in wrong decisions. To see how these decisions were made, we superimpose the logarithm of the mean of the softmax outputs above the conditional risk. These orange lines correspond to the mean prediction of each network, displayed on a logarithmic scale. The deterministic CNN's log predictions in the right column are, in general, lower than the corresponding log predictions for the Bayesian model. The lower the curve, the more confident the network is that the data should not be labeled as that particular class. In these examples, the deterministic CNN never prescribes a higher probability mass of more than 10^{-5} to class 'G', whereas for the Bayesian CNN, the probability mass is often orders of magnitude higher. The better calibrated predictions with a higher probability mass over class 'G' lead to the correct decision being made, despite the fact that class 'G' is never the most probable class according to all three examples.

19.5.6 Calibration of the Cost Function

One of the key challenges in Bayesian decision theory, as well as in non-Bayesian paradigms such as empirical risk minimization (see Leqi et al. (2019)), is the determination of the cost function. While the advantage of using the BDT framework is clear in that it allows the ML model to be treated separately from the cost, it is still left to the domain expert to decide upon how to construct the cost. In some scenarios, cost may be inherent to the problem such as for finance (Spears et al., 2020) or for inventory management (Taskin and Lodree, 2016), where in both cases the cost function can be aligned with the monetary value. However, in many other scenarios, such as for medical diagnosis (Leibig et al., 2017) and pedestrian classification (Cobb et al., 2018), defining the cost is rather subjective and can be challenging.

To demonstrate how one might calibrate a cost function, we continue with the same Bayesian and deterministic models from before, but now explore how to design the cost function when it is not in an explicit form. Instead, the true cost is observable after making a decision. For this example, the true cost follows the one listed in Table 19.1. Within this setup, we can observe the performance of the decisions on the validation data and then calibrate our own cost matrix to match the true costs. For our scenario, this result is the same as saying that class 'G' is an adversarial vehicle, and errors in decisions will cause financial harm. Where, we do not know the exact costs, we do have a few historical examples of the costs incurred in the past.

Figure 19.5 shows this scenario, where our design choice is to vary the cost for the penalty for class 'G'. The x-axis corresponds to this penalty value, which starts from 0.01, where the penalty is equivalent to other classes, and ends at the cost of 10.00, which is ten times the true cost. For both models, we plot the mean and standard deviation bounds of the true validation cost accrued as we vary the cost matrix. The lowest validation cost for a Bayesian CNN occurs at the true value, where the penalty is 1.0 (as in Table 19.1). For each side of this value, the cost increases, demonstrating a better approximation of the posterior distribution. On the other hand, the deterministic CNN is poorly calibrated and is far from identifying the right design choice for the cost matrix.

In summary, we can calibrate cost functions by observing real data. However, there is still the challenge of gathering data on the true costs. As will often be the case, the data's exact influence on the true costs in safety-critical scenarios may not always be available due to the rarity of unsafe events.[4] In addition, while plotting graphs like

---

[4] Unsafe events should be rare if systems are built well!

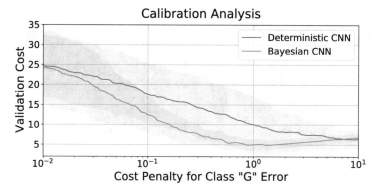

Fig. 19.5 Calibration of the penalty term for class 'G'. The y-axis shows the true cost over the validation splits for the Bayes optimal decision, and the x-axis corresponds to varying the penalty term in the cost matrix for class 'G'. For the Bayesian CNN, the lowest true cost is at a penalty of 10^0, which is exactly equal to the real cost matrix. Figures like this can aid us in designing the cost matrix. Furthermore, we note the poor performance of the deterministic CNN, where the lowest validation cost corresponds to ten times the true penalty

Fig. 19.5 are useful, it may not be easy to analyze different cost functions when all of the penalty terms in the cost matrix can be varied. This challenge highlights the need for domain expertise and the ability to test different cost functions on validation data. Safe reinforcement learning is an example of a place in the literature where these ideas have been explored in a different context. Therefore, borrowing ideas such as building simulators and even running real systems with known safe policies could be beneficial (Polymenakos et al., 2019).

19.6   Resource Requirements of Bayesian Inference

In Sect. 19.5, we deployed two inference schemes for learning the CNN weights. The more simplistic approach found a single set of parameters, whereas the more complex approach inferred an approximate distribution over the CNN weights. We saw that the inference scheme with the better uncertainty quantification led to safer decision-making for the acoustic classification example. This result demonstrates how accounting for uncertainty in real-world problems makes algorithms more robust and safer to use. In general, the most computationally expensive techniques for performing Bayesian inference result in the best performance in terms of accuracy and cost but at the expense of requiring more computational resources. In our above example, we compared Bayesian inference using HMC with stochastic gradient descent.

Figure 19.6 demonstrates the trade-off between these two approaches. The deterministic CNN (blue) demonstrates the performance for the equivalent resource use of a single sample, when compared to increasing the number of samples for the Bayesian CNN (orange). The figure shows how increasing the number of collected

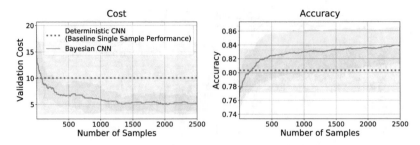

Fig. 19.6 Cumulative performance of the cost and the accuracy as the number of samples in the Bayesian ensemble is increased. Note that the baseline performance for a single deterministic model is shown on the plot via the dotted blue line. Credible intervals are given by the standard deviations across the validation splits. After a sufficient number of samples, the Bayesian CNN converges to a higher accuracy and lower cost than the deterministic baseline

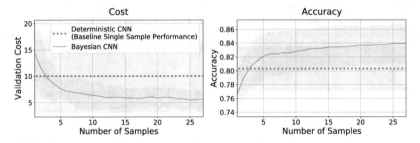

Fig. 19.7 Cumulative performance of the cost and accuracy as thinning is applied (reducing the number of samples by sub-sampling). Unlike for Fig. 19.6, we only incorporate one in every one hundred samples for the cumulative performance. The result is that thinning can significantly reduce the computational requirements. The thinned ensemble of networks still achieves $\approx 84\%$ accuracy with 100 times fewer samples and still achieves a validation cost of just above 5 (slightly higher than that of Fig. 19.6)

samples improves the performance of the Bayesian CNN. It takes approximately 200 samples for the Bayesian CNN to do better in mean accuracy and 100 to do better in mean validation cost, compared to the deterministic model. This result is concerning for real-world applications in that a single pass through the network takes 16.30 ± 0.05 ms on our hardware.[5]

However, Fig. 19.6 is without thinning, whereby thinning is the process of sub-sampling between proposed network parameters from the sampling scheme's Markov chain (see [Chap. 12 Robert and Casella, 2013]). Thinning can substantially reduce the computational cost in both memory and floating point operations at the possible expense of reducing the quality of the approximation to the posterior.[6] Figure 19.7 shows the same curves as in Fig. 19.6, where only $1/100$ of the samples are kept.

---

[5] Based on the following parameters: OS: Ubuntu 18.04.5; CPU: Intel i7-9750H; GPU: GeForce RTX 2080 with Max-Q; Python: 3.8.3.

[6] The reduction in quality of the approximation is not evident here.

The result is that we only need three samples to achieve superior cost and accuracy performance compared to the deterministic model for this scenario. Therefore, it is worth spending time deciding upon the most suitable number of samples in the ensemble to reduce the storage and implementation costs. Finally, if we can build hardware and software such that models can be deployed in parallel, then the cost of using multiple samples of a network (an ensemble) can be reduced even further.

19.7 Conclusion

This chapter introduced the benefits of adopting BDT to reduce uncertainty when employing ML techniques in safety-critical applications. Building a system that relies on BDT provides advantages over systems with end-to-end controllers. Clear preferences can be encoded into the decision-making process that allow for more understandable actions. The separation between the inference component and decision-making component enables the model, a Bayesian neural network, to concentrate on pattern recognition tasks.

We demonstrated how one might use such a framework in practice with a highly imbalanced and challenging data set. For our scenario, the least populous class in the data set was set to have the highest penalty for incorrect decisions. We then observed how the model that better approximated the uncertainty resulted in more reliable and safer decision-making for the task. In addition to accuracy and posterior conditional risk, we also analyzed the trade-off in terms of the computational cost and we investigated one way to alleviate such issues by thinning. We also mentioned alternative approaches to Bayesian inference that may trade-off uncertainty and computational resources differently to the method we showcased here.

One of the challenges in the design of a safe decision-making system is determining the preferences of an end user and how to incorporate preferences into the training of the ML model. In non-Bayesian paradigms, models are typically trained by directly minimizing the empirical risk. The beauty of the Bayesian framework is that a model can be trained without the need to hand-craft loss functions, to which the subjectivity of the relative preferences are kept away from the ML developer/researcher and left to the domain expert. Instead, inference over the model parameters can be kept as objective as possible, while a domain expert calibrates the cost matrix according to personal preferences. Of course, this leaves many challenges open such as how to encode domain-specific preferences into a cost function and, ultimately, which model is best at approximating the posterior predictive distribution of the data. In future work, we hope to incorporate other areas of the literature, where different approaches have been used to tackle the problem of making safe decisions; these include optimization over different user risk preferences by incorporating fuzzy set theory (Ekin et al., 2016), or using a strict robust optimization approach (Bastian et al., 2020).

Acknowledgements Research reported in this paper was sponsored in part by the (CCDC) Army Research Laboratory. The views and conclusions contained in this document are those of the authors and should not be interpreted as representing the official policies, either expressed or implied, of the Army Research Laboratory, the Army Cyber Institute, the U.S. Department of Defense, or the U.S. Government. The U.S. Government is authorized to reproduce and distribute reprints for Government purposes notwithstanding any copyright notation herein.

References

Bastian, N. D., Lunday, B. J., Fisher, C. B., & Hall, A. O. (2020). Models and methods for workforce planning under uncertainty: Optimizing us army cyber branch readiness and manning. *Omega, 92,*

Bayes, T. (1763). LII. An essay towards solving a problem in the doctrine of chances. By the late Rev. Mr. Bayes, FRS communicated by Mr. Price, in a letter to John Canton, AMFR S. *Philosophical transactions of the Royal Society of London, (53),* 370–418.

Berger, J. O. (1985). *Statistical Decision Theory and Bayesian Analysis.* Springer Science & Business Media.

Blundell, C., Cornebise, J., Kavukcuoglu, K., & Wierstra, D. (2015). Weight uncertainty in neural networks. In *Proceedings of the 32nd International Conference on International Conference on Machine Learning-Volume 37,* pp. 1613–1622. JMLR. org.

Cobb, A. D. (2020). *The practicalities of scaling Bayesian neural networks to real-world applications.* Ph.D. thesis, University of Oxford.

Cobb, A. D., & Jalaian, B. (2020). Scaling hamiltonian monte carlo inference for Bayesian neural networks with symmetric splitting. arXiv:2010.06772.

Cobb, A. D., Roberts, S. J., & Gal, Y. (2018). Loss-calibrated approximate inference in Bayesian neural networks. In *Theory of Deep Learning Workshop, ICML.*

Ekin, T., Kocadagli, O., Bastian, N. D., Fulton, L. V., & Griffin, P. M. (2016). Fuzzy decision making in health systems: A resource allocation model. *EURO Journal on Decision Processes, 4*(3–4), 245–267.

Gal Y., & Ghahramani, Z. (2016). Dropout as a Bayesian approximation: Representing model uncertainty in deep learning. In *International Conference on Machine Learning,* pp. 1050–1059.

Gelman, A., Carlin, J. B., Stern, H. S., Dunson, D. B., Vehtari, A., & Rubin, D. B. (2013). *Bayesian data analysis.* CRC Press.

Goodfellow, I., Y. Bengio, & Courville, A. (2016). *Deep learning.* MIT Press. http://www.deeplearningbook.org.

Graves, A. (2011). Practical variational inference for neural networks. In *Advances in Neural Information Processing Systems,* pp. 2348–2356.

Hendler, J., & Mulvehill, A. M. (2016). Social machines: The coming collision of artificial intelligence, social networking, and humanity. Apress

Hoffman, M. D., Blei, D. M., Wang, C., & Paisley, J. (2013). Stochastic variational inference. *The Journal of Machine Learning Research, 14*(1), 1303–1347.

Hurd, H., & Pham, T. (2002). Target association using harmonic frequency tracks. In *Proceedings of the Fifth International Conference on Information Fusion. FUSION 2002.(IEEE Cat. No. 02EX5997)* (Vol. 2, pp. 860–864). IEEE.

Kiskin, I., Cobb, A. D., Wang, L., & Roberts, S. (2020a). Humbug zooniverse: A crowd-sourced acoustic mosquito dataset. In *ICASSP 2020-2020 IEEE International Conference on Acoustics, Speech and Signal Processing (ICASSP)* (pp. 916–920). IEEE.

Kiskin, I., Zilli, D., Li, Y., Sinka, M., Willis, K., & Roberts, S. (2020b). Bioacoustic detection with wavelet-conditioned convolutional neural networks. *Neural Computing and Applications, 32*(4), 915–927.

Klambauer, G., Unterthiner, T., Mayr, A., & Hochreiter, S. (2017). Self-normalizing neural networks. In *Advances in neural information processing systems* (pp. 971–980).

Krizhevsky, A., Sutskever, I., & Hinton, G. E. (2012). Imagenet classification with deep convolutional neural networks. In *Advances in Neural Information Processing Systems* (pp. 1097–1105).

LeCun, Y., Bottou, L., Bengio, Y., & Haffner, P. (1998). Gradient-based learning applied to document recognition. *Proceedings of the IEEE, 86*(11), 2278–2324.

Leibig, C., Allken, V., Ayhan, M. S., Berens, P., & Wahl, S. (2017). Leveraging uncertainty information from deep neural networks for disease detection. *Scientific reports, 7*(1), 17816.

Leqi, L., Prasad, A., & Ravikumar, P. K. (2019). On human-aligned risk minimization. In *Advances in Neural Information Processing Systems* (pp. 15055–15064).

Lohani, M., Stokes, C., Dashan, N., McCoy, M., Bailey, C. A. & Rivers, S. E. (2017).Rivers. A framework for human-agent social systems: The role of non-technical factors in operation success. In *Advances in human factors in robots and unmanned systems* (pp. 137–148). Springer.

Neal, R. M. (1995). *Bayesian learning for neural networks*. Ph.D. thesis, University of Toronto.

Nilsson, N. J. (2014). *Principles of artificial intelligence*. Morgan Kaufmann.

Paszke, A., Gross, S., Chintala, S., Chanan, G., Yang, E., DeVito, Z., Lin, Z., Desmaison, A., Antiga, L., & Lerer, A. (2017). Automatic differentiation in PyTorch. In *NIPS Autodiff Workshop*.

Pedregosa, F., Varoquaux, G., Gramfort, A., Michel, V., Thirion, B., Grisel, O., Blondel, M., Prettenhofer, P., Weiss, R., Dubourg, V., & Vanderplas, J. (2011). Scikit-learn: Machine learning in python. *Journal of Machine Learning Research, 12*(85), 2825–2830. http://jmlr.org/papers/v12/pedregosa11a.html.

Polymenakos, K., Abate, A., & Roberts, S. (2019). Safe policy search using gaussian process models. In *Proceedings of the 18th International Conference on Autonomous Agents and MultiAgent Systems* (pp. 1565–1573).

Robert, C., & Casella, G. (2013). *Monte carlo statistical methods*. Springer Science & Business Media.

Rumelhart, D. E., Hinton, G. E., & Williams, R. J. (1986). Parallel distributed processing: Explorations in the microstructure of cognition, chapter Learning Internal Representations by Error Propagation, (Vol. 1, pp. 318–362). Cambridge, MA, USA: MIT Press.

Russell, S., Moskowitz, I. S., & Raglin, A. (2017). Human information interaction, artificial intelligence, and errors. In *Autonomy and Artificial Intelligence: A Threat or Savior?* (pp. 71–101). Springer.

Spears, T., Zohren, S., & Roberts, S. (2020). Investment sizing with deep learning prediction uncertainties for high-frequency eurodollar futures trading. SSRN 3664497.

Taskin, S., & Lodree, E. (2016). A bayesian decision model with hurricane forecast up-dates for emergency supplies inventory management. In *Operational Research for Emergency Planning in Healthcare* (Vol. 1, pp. 330–352) Springer.

Welling, M., & Teh, Y. W. (2011). Bayesian learning via stochastic gradient Langevin dynamics. In *Proceedings of the 28th International Conference on Machine Learning (ICML-11)* (pp. 681–688).

Williams, C. K., & Rasmussen, C. E. (2006). *Gaussian processes for machine learning* (Vol. 2). MA: MIT press Cambridge.

Chapter 20
Engineering Context from the Ground Up

**Michael Wollowski, Lilin Chen, Xiangnan Chen, Yifan Cui,
Joseph Knierman, and Xusheng Liu**

Abstract We are engineering a system that is designed for a human and a robot to solve problems in a shared space. This system uses context to manage interactions with a human collaborator as well as to manage more mundane aspects of context, such a combining speech and gesture input. Our system is highly modular so as to facilitate good engineering practice. It uses a blackboard type architecture to represent and maintain information of different aspects in the problem-solving process and to maintain context. We give an overview of the current status of our system. We explain the components of our system and provide details of the information produced by the various system components. Additionally, we explain how information is accumulated on the blackboard and discuss and evaluate how various aspects of context are addressed in our system.

Keywords Engineering context · Blackboard architecture · UIMA · Human–robot collaboration · Multi-modal input

M. Wollowski (✉) · L. Chen · X. Chen · Y. Cui · J. Knierman · X. Liu
Computer Science Department, Rose-Hulman Institute of Technology, 5500 Wabash Ave, Terre Haute, IN 47803, USA
e-mail: wollowsk@rose-hulman.edu

L. Chen
e-mail: chenx6@rose-hulman.edu

X. Chen
e-mail: chenl4@rose-hulman.edu

Y. Cui
e-mail: cuiy1@rose-hulman.edu

J. Knierman
e-mail: kniermj@rose-hulman.edu

X. Liu
e-mail: liux6@rose-hulman.edu

© Springer Nature Switzerland AG 2021
W. F. Lawless et al. (eds.), *Systems Engineering and Artificial Intelligence*,
https://doi.org/10.1007/978-3-030-77283-3_20

20.1 Introduction

We are engineering a system that is designed for human–robot collaborative problem-solving in a shared space. Our system is characterized by two input modalities: speech and gesture. These two modalities afford a more natural way of interacting with a robot, a way that does neither require complex descriptions of the locations of objects relative to each other nor an initial phase for naming objects. Our approach simplifies the processing of speech input at the expense of introducing the task of processing gestures as well as the task of combining the evidence obtained from those two modalities.

Our system is designed for a person and a Sawyer robot[1] to solve various wooden, block-world assembly problems. While our system has some autonomy, currently a human collaborator is in charge of the problem-solving efforts. By this claim, we mean that a human collaborator defines the problem to be solved and gives instructions, whether step-by-step or higher level, to the robot. We should point out that there is preliminary work showing that problems can be solved more efficiently when the robot is in charge without the loss of human comfort (see Castro et al., 2017). However, our system has not reached a degree of maturity in which the robot could take over.

The physical system setup is depicted in Fig. 20.1. We use a Kinect V2 Sensor for Xbox One,[2] which contains a depth sensor and a camera. We currently use the microphone built into the laptop. The laptop runs most of our software. The Kinect and the camera are located in a fixed space, overlooking a table-sized interaction space. The robotic arm has its own camera attached to it, near the gripper.

The architecture of the physical components of our system is depicted in Fig. 20.2. Section 20.2 will provide more details about the processing component.

To manage the information processing tasks, we use the Unstructured Information Processing Architecture (*UIMA*; see UIMA, 2019) that was developed by the IBM Watson team to manage the information processing of their highly successful *Jeopardy!*© player. UIMA supports highly modular design and uses what might be considered an additive blackboard representation scheme. The use of UIMA enables the representation of various pieces of information about a problem at a fairly high level. Hence, information can be easily shared and inspected. As such, the use of UIMA lines up well with the recommendation that.

> practitioners must ensure that AI-enabled systems are governable; that they are open, transparent, and understandable; that they can work effectively with people; and that their operation will remain consistent with human values and aspirations,

from the report on *Preparing for the Future of Artificial Intelligence* by Holdren and Smith (2016).

A key component of UIMA is the "Common Analysis System," or CAS. Similar to a blackboard architecture, a CAS object serves to capture information in various

---

[1] https://www.rethinkrobotics.com/sawyer.

[2] https://developer.microsoft.com/en-us/windows/kinect.

Fig. 20.1 Our system

Fig. 20.2 The architecture and information flow of our system

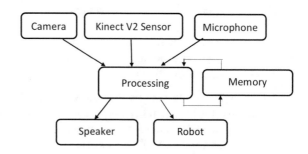

stages of refinement. While CAS objects are explained in Wollowski et al. (2020), due to their central nature, we will briefly reintroduce them here. Figure 20.3 shows a simple example of how one might parse a piece of text in UIMA, capturing information as it is added to the CAS object.

Information is added to a CAS object through software components called *annotators*. Annotators serve as information "gatherers," capturing the outcomes of various information processors. Each annotator interprets the existing data, then adds new data or some combination of both before passing an object to the next annotator in sequence.

The benefit of the use of UIMA is that it forces a highly modular approach to design the information processing pipeline. It also simplifies the process of adding new units as well as that of replacing existing units. In the time span between the stage

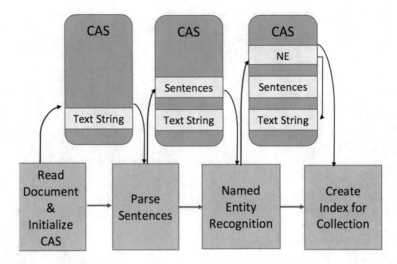

Fig. 20.3 Sample UIMA Processing Pipeline

of development of our system as previously described in Wollowski et al. (2020) and the current stage, we added the following units:

- Memory import and memory storage units;
- Text-to-speech unit;
- Command unit, to interact with the robot; a
- Planner, to give the robot more autonomy; and, a
- Perspective transformation unit.

Additionally, we replaced the Natural Language Processing (NLP) unit, significantly improving its capability and robustness. We made major revisions to the Communication unit and tuned the Confidence Aggregator. We separated the color recognition task from the NLP unit, creating its own unit and we split the processing of spatial relationships into two separate units. In total, we increased the number of units from 7 to 15.

We have come to a point in the development of our system in which not all processing units are in sync. By this, we mean that some of the units have capabilities and are adding information to the blackboard that is not necessarily processed by subsequent units. This disconnect is simply a side effect of the rapid speed of development. We meticulously document the capabilities of each unit and periodically update them so that they process the additional information available to them. We additionally have developed several how-to documents that describe in detail the overall structure of the system, how to interact with it, and how to expand its capabilities, by adding annotators. Our project reached a level of complexity where it is crucial to maintain good software engineering habits. It is not a small benefit that the team of students that work on this project changes once a year. Each new set of students typically performs a good amount of code refactoring.

We are engineering our system from the ground up for several reasons: (i) IBM used an incremental development approach for their very successful Jeopardy!© player (Ferrucci, 2012). Rather than aiming to prove a theory, the Watson team set themselves a performance goal to perform better than the two most successful human Jeopardy!© players. (ii) Rodney Brooks (1990), in his own work and writings, successfully argued to take an approach that is focused on building actual systems from the ground up and on solving problems that are exposed when developing those systems. (iii) Finally, we believe that by building a system from the ground up, we can precisely study context, how it is constructed, how it is used, and how aspects of it are assumed and communicated.

20.2 Information Processing Architecture

In this section, we present an overview of the information processing architecture of our system. Figure 20.4 shows the UIMA pipeline with the current annotators. Throughout this section, we will indicate which components have already been described in detail in Wollowski et al. (2020), and which components are described in this chapter.

Memory Import and Storage. The "Memory Import" unit reads information that is saved as part of the "Memory Storage" unit. The immediate purpose of these two units is to enable a human collaborator to name entities in the collaboration space so as to refer to them by name, rather than by relative location. However, there are additional pieces of information that are stored and preserved for future interactions. These two units are described in Sect. 20.3 and throughout this chapter.

Object Detection. This unit identifies objects in the collaboration space. It interprets camera data to determine the locations of blocks and reads RGB hues of them. It additionally recognizes the interaction space, i.e., the table. Block locations are

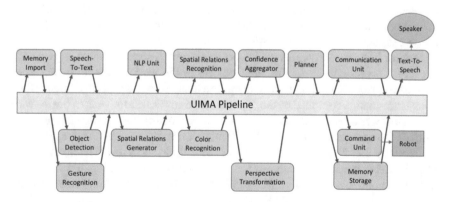

Fig. 20.4 The UIMA information processing of our system

stored relative to the position of the camera. For details, see Sect. 20.4 in Wollowski et al. (2020).

Speech-to-Text. This unit uses the Google Cloud library's speech-to-text service (Google, 2019a). It sends an audio snippet of the speech input and receives back a string representing the spoken text. The string is translated into a JSON[3] object and added to the CAS object. For details, see Sect. 20.6 in Wollowski et al. (2020).

Gesture Recognition. This unit processes a pointing gesture of a human collaborator to determine the direction and location of the pointing action. It uses utilities provided by the Xbox Kinect V2 library to read structural information of a hand's skeleton, including its joint information. Using joints in a hand as the basis of estimating a vector in 3D space, we employ a simple heuristic that takes a point from the middle of the palm to the point in a finger furthest from it to be the pointing vector. The pointing vector is then compared with the center of each block in the collaboration space, to provide a heuristic value that estimates that block's certainty of being identified by gesture. For details, see Sect. 20.8 in Wollowski et al. (2020).

NLP Unit. This unit takes the output of the "Speech-to-Text" unit, parses the text and, based on the parse tree, extracts several pieces of information related to the use of color words, spatial relationships, naming of blocks, gesture, and any commands that have been given. This unit has been completely rewritten, significantly extending its capabilities and robustness. It is described in Sect. 20.4 of this chapter.

Spatial Relations Generator. This unit parses the data from the "Object Detection" unit to calculate the relative locations of the blocks to each other. It produces a graph of relative locations. Currently, our system is able to process "`left`," "`right`," "`front`" and "`behind.`" For details, see Sect. 20.5 in Wollowski et al. (2020).

Color Recognition. This unit processes all of the color words as identified by the "NLP unit." It uses the hue values of each block in order to determine how close a given block is to color. It outputs a list of all blocks together with their associated confidence level in the colors as indicated by the color words. For details, see the "Colors" sub-section of Sect. 20.7 in Wollowski et al. (2020). This unit has since been updated to process more than one color word. In the prior version, this unit searched for a single-color word in the input string as received by the "Speech-to-text unit." It now extracts all of the color words as identified by the "NLP unit."

Spatial Relation Recognition. This unit determines spatial relationships among a selected object and all of the other objects in the working space. It combines information from several units. The algorithm recursively traverses the graph of the spatial information compiled by the "Spatial Relations Generator" unit. It begins with a block that was identified through gesture as determined by the "Gesture Recognition unit," or color as identified but the "NLP Unit." It then iterates through the modifiers produced by the "NLP Unit" to retrieve the lists of blocks in that direction/relation. The algorithm recursively calls itself with the shortened list of spatial modifiers. Recursion continues until all of the modifiers have been used. The confidence value of this classification depends on the distance from the block to the origin.

---

[3] https://www.json.org/.

This unit and the "Spatial Relations Generator" used to be part of one unit as described in Sect. 20.5 in Wollowski et al. (2020). We decided to split that unit into two to implement a good modular design for two independent tasks, first, the task of determining a graph of relative locations of blocks to each other, and second, to determine the locations of the referenced objects.

Confidence Aggregator. In our system, some of the units calculate confidence values and pair them with some of the objects of the domain. The final confidence ratings produced by this unit take into consideration color, gesture, and spatial relationships. This unit combines those confidence values to determine the overall confidence value of the block that is considered to be selected by a human collaborator for some action. This unit is described in Sect. 20.5 of this chapter.

Perspective Transformation. This unit translates the coordinates of the selected object from the perspective of the Kinect to that of the Sawyer robot. This transformation is a very technical aspect of context. It is presented in Sect. 20.6 of this chapter.

Planning Unit. This unit adds intelligence and autonomy to our system. It develops step-by-step plans for solving block-stacking problems. It monitors its planning process and requests assistance from a human collaborator in those cases when the system detects that it cannot solve a given plan. We implemented a basic STRIPS planner (see Fikes & Nilson, 1971). While it is not the most powerful planner one can use, it is sufficient to solve certain types of block-stacking problems. We welcome its limitations such as those documented through the Sussman anomaly (see Sussman, 1975) since they enable us to study human–robot collaboration as well as the use of context for collaboration. This unit is presented in Sect. 20.7 of this chapter.

Communication Unit. This unit is used to communicate with a human collaborator, whether to acknowledge that the system has sufficient confidence in the instructions received, or whether to ask for clarification. This unit attempts to create a collaborative working relationship by addressing its human collaborator by name, by varying its responses, and by cracking a joke every so often. Details of this unit are presented in Sect. 20.8 of this chapter.

Command Unit. This unit issues commands, such as which block to pick up, to the Sawyer robot by communicating with existing software implemented in the Robot Operating System (ROS). Details of this unit are presented in Sect. 20.9 of this chapter.

Text-to-Speech. This unit converts the machine's textual response into speech. The text determined by the "Communication Unit" is converted to speech by sending it to the FreeTTS[4] speech synthesis system. The sound file returned by FreeTTS is then played to the user through the computer's speakers.

---

[4] https://freetts.sourceforge.io/.

20.3　Memory Import and Storage

The "Memory Storage" annotator works in tandem with the "Memory Import" annotator to save pertinent information between runs of the UIMA pipeline. Among others, the use of memory enables a human collaborator to name entities in the domain and to refer to them by name. A user may also name problem-solving plans to reuse them. Additionally, our system stores prior parsed sentences to resolve co-references, and it stores partial parse trees in the case of an incomplete input by a human collaborator, to merge them with additional information provided in response to a request for clarification.

As explained in Sect. 20.4 on "Natural Language Processing," a human collaborator may name entities in the domain. For naming to be useful, names must persist. Since UIMA is a linear processing pipeline, our system writes those names to a persistent block of memory to which it has access. Hence, the first step taken when restarting the pipeline for a new interaction is to initialize the CAS object with any names that were previously defined.

Memory Import. When starting the pipeline, the "Memory Import" annotator reads any saved data from memory. This unit loads the contents of the MemorySave.txt file, which contains information accumulated from previous runs. It extracts the name-block data and places it into the initial CAS object. Figure 20.5 shows the contents of a sample MemorySave.txt file. In it, the block with id:4 was named Bob, and the block with id:3 was named Mitchell. Notice that in addition to the name, the coordinates of a block are saved. The coordinates are used to locate the corresponding block and associate the given name with it.

Memory Storage. This annotator identifies and stores named objects as well as named plans. To determine if the naming command was used in the current run, the CAS object is inspected. In particular, our system searches for the **Name** field of the **NLPProcessor** object added by the "NLP Unit." Any name given there is then associated with a block's location. This association is accomplished by extracting the position coordinates of the object with the highest determined confidence compiled by the "Confidence Aggregator." If the confidence is sufficiently high, then the name–object association is added to the JSON object stored in the MemorySave.txt file. This file is stored in the main project folder. It should be noted that we currently do

Fig. 20.5 An excerpt of a "MemorySave.txt" file

```
[{"namedBlocks":[
  {"id":4,
   "name":"Bob",
   "x":-0.01628926582634449,
   "y":-0.04363936185836792,
   "z":1.2850000858306885},
  {"id":3,
   "name":"Mitchell",
   "x":-0.4298781454563141,
   "y":-0.15041720867156982,
   "z":1.0380001068115234}]}]
```

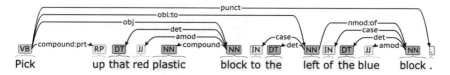

Fig. 20.6   A visual representation of the dependency parse tree for the sample sentence

Fig. 20.7   An excerpt of the
JSON object for the sample
sentence

```
"NLPProcessor":
{"Command": "pick up",
  "Target":
    {"Item": "block",
     "Mods": ["red", "plastic"],
     "Gesture": true,
     "Relation":
       {"Direction": "left",
        "Object":
          {"Item": "block",
           "Mods": ["blue"],
           "Gesture": false}}}}
```

not permit more than one name per object. We also do not permit renaming an object.
These are future extensions of our system.

20.4   Natural Language Processing

Our system's Natural Language Processing (NLP) unit is responsible for parsing a
given string and for extracting certain pieces of information from it. This unit has
been completely rewritten, considerably extending its capabilities and moving it from
Google's Cloud NLP service (see Google, 2019b) to the Stanford CoreNLP library
(see Manning et al., 2014).

Parsing. We use the Stanford CoreNLP library's dependency parser to annotate
a given sentence with both universal dependencies and parts-of-speech tags. This
information is stored in a Semantic Graph object by the parser. A Semantic Graph
object contains all of the edges of relations from a "governor" word to its "dependent"
words. Consider Fig. 20.6; it shows a visual representation of the tagged relationships
for the sentence: "Pick up that red plastic block to the left of the blue block." The
image was produced by the demonstration service[5] that runs on the Stanford NLP
group's website.

Output file format. While processing the semantic graph, our NLP annotator
produces a JSON object that is added to the UIMA CAS object. Figure 20.7 shows
the JSON object used for the running sentence "Pick up that red plastic block to the
left of the blue block."

---

[5] https://stanfordnlp.github.io/CoreNLP/demo.html.

Table 20.1 Common POS abbreviations

Abbreviation	Parts of Speech
VB	Verb, be base form
RP	Particle
DT	Determiner
JJ	Adjective
NN	Noun, singular, or mass
NNP	Proper noun, singular
IN	Preposition, subordinating conjunction

For an explanation of the parts-of-speech tags, see Table 20.1.

The "Mods" field contains a list of modifiers. This list includes properties such as "color" and "texture." The data type of the "Gesture" field is `Boolean`. The overall syntax of the JSON object is that the top level identifies the command, if one is given, as well as the target object for that command. At the next lower level, the JSON object identifies information about the target object, including any relationships that are specified by a human collaborator. The nature of the relationship may be a binary relationship such as "left of" or a tertiary relationship such as "between." If no relationship is given, the "Relation" component is left out of the JSON object. In Fig. 20.7, we show an example of a binary relationship. The object of that relationship is specified in the nested "Object" component.

In case of a tertiary relationship, such as *"Pick up the blue brick between this red bottle and the yellow block,"* our system obtains the dependency parse tree as shown in Fig. 20.8.

Consider the circled "nmod:between" relationships; following those two relations, we can extract the two indexed words "bottle" for the first part of the "between" relation and "block" for the second. Once located, our system will follow the two indexed words to find all of their properties, including modifiers and potential references to gestures. The process of finding modifiers and gestures is the same as the process of extracting those properties for any object. The relation **between** produces an array of two objects. The partial JSON object for the sentence of Fig. 20.8 is shown in Fig. 20.9.

Command extraction. The command of the sentence is either a verb, e.g., "drop," or a phrasal verb, such as "pick up." The steps taken to extract the command from the semantic object are as follows:

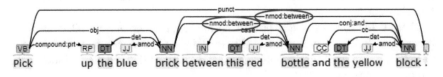

Fig. 20.8 The dependency parse tree of *"Pick up the blue brick between this red bottle and the yellow block"*

Fig. 20.9 Excerpt of the
JSON object for the
dependency parse tree from
Fig. 20.8

```
"Target": {
   "Item": "brick",
   "Relation": {
       "Objects": [
           {"Item": "bottle",
            "Mods": ["red"],
            "Gesture": true},
           {"Item": "block",
            "Mods": ["yellow"],
            "Gesture": false}],
        "Direction": "between"},
       "Mods": ["blue"],
       "Gesture": false},
       "Command": "pick up"}
```

1. The word with no dependency is the **root** of the sentence and, in most cases, a verb is at the root of the sentence. If the root is not tagged as a verb, then the algorithm iteratively visits the dependents of the root in search of one tagged as a verb.
2. After finding the verb, the algorithm attempts to locate the phrasal verb particle. It will start with the verb acquired in the previous step and use the phrasal verb particle relations to extract the particle to form a phrasal verb.

A special case for locating the verb phrase occurs in those cases where the CoreNLP library misclassifies a verb as a noun. This occurs when the library encounters an upper case "Drop" at the beginning of a sentence. We circumvent this case by prepending the sentence with "Please," as well as converting "Drop" to lower case. The library now correctly identifies "drop" as a verb.

Target object extraction. The target for manipulation or naming is the object of a sentence. This target is typically the noun phrase. Our algorithm uses the "object" relation to extract the target from the dependents of the verb.

Relation (reference object and direction) extraction. Our system can recognize seven direction relationships. They are: in front of, behind, to the left of, to the right of, on, under, between, from, and onto. The on relationship can be indirectly acting on the reference object (e.g., on the top of) or directly acting on the reference object (e.g., on the blue block.)

The reference object is either:

a. the nominal modifier (nmod) of the target object (noun → noun); or
b. the oblique nominal (obl) of the verb (verb → noun).

In the CoreNLP library, version 4.0.0,

a. The relationships in front of, behind, and between are treated as nominal–modifier relationships.
b. The relationships to the left/right of, under, from, and onto are treated as oblique nominal relationships.
c. The relationship on is treated as either an oblique nominal relationship or a nominal modifier relationship. If it acts on the reference object directly, the

relationship will be an oblique nominal one. Otherwise, the relationship will be a nominal modifier one.

To recognize if the relationship is a nominal modifier or an oblique nominal one, our algorithm checks if there exists an "obl" relationship. Our algorithm performs the following steps:

1. Both under and to the left/right of belong to the "obl" relationship. For under, the verb points to the reference object. For to the left/right of, the verb points to the direction phrase as left/right. The direction phrase has an "nmod:of" relationship with the reference object.
2. As mentioned above, the relationship on is different from others in the "nmod" category. In general, looking at the form of the "nmod" relationship, our algorithm determines whether to treat it as an oblique nominal relationship or a nominal modifier relationship. In the case of a nominal modifier relationship, such as "on the top of the table," the "nmod" relationship contains a direction within the relationship, such as "nmod:of." Our algorithm extracts that relationship. In the case of an oblique nominal relationship, such as "on the table," the target noun points to the reference object.

Object modifier extraction. The modifiers of an object are the adjectival modifiers of the target/reference objects in the sentence and the dependents of the first-level object modifiers. To extract them, our annotator performs the following steps:

1. It uses the adjectival modifier ("amod") relation to extract the first-level object modifier from the dependents of the object.
2. It then uses the "obl:npmod" as well as the "compound" relation to extract the second and lower level object modifiers from the dependents of the first-level modifier.

Gesture extraction. To detect whether gestures are used on objects, either the target or the reference objects or both, our algorithm inspects the determiner of a given object. The following steps are taken:

1. At first, our algorithm uses the determined ("det") relationship to locate all the determiners of a given object.
2. It will then check whether our set of gesture contains that determiner. If so, the Gesture Boolean variable is set to true for that object. Otherwise, it is set to false.

Naming an object. As mentioned in Sect. 20.3 on "Memory Input and Storage," in addition to issuing commands that ask the robot to perform certain actions, the robot may be asked to remember the names of objects as given by a human collaborator. Our system currently can process the following three naming commands: *name, call,* and *define*. We will expand the word set of naming commands as we continue to work on this project. The name provided is typically located at the end of the sentence. Our software locates the Parts-of-Speech object that occurs last, before any punctuation. If it is of type NNP, see Table 20.1, we will select it as the name, together with any

Fig. 20.10 An excerpt of
the JSON object showing the
naming of an item, *Bob*

```
{"NLPProcessor": {
   "Target": {
      "Item": "bottle",
      "Relation": {"Objects": []},
      "Mods": [
         "blue",
         "plastic"],
      "Gesture": false},
   "Command": "define",
   "Name": "Bob"}}
```

modifiers. For example, in the following sentence *"Name the red block little Bob."* the name will be *"little Bob."* If the last item before any punctuation is of type NN, such as in *"Name that block to the left of the blue block little red riding hood."* Then we will select it and its modifiers as the name.

The target object, the one to be named, is found in the same way as for other commands. In other words, it is the object that is linked by the verb–phrase of the action. In some simple sentences, such as *"Name the blue block Bob."* This does not hold true. In those cases, we select the remaining NN phrase of the sentence as the target object. A name is stored in the **Name** field that is added to the top level of the JSON object. Figure 20.10 shows an excerpt of the JSON object for the sentence: *"Define the blue plastic bottle as Bob."*

Co-reference. Whenever our system has successfully identified a target object, that object is saved in persistent storage, i.e., the file managed by the memory import and storage units. To be precise, our system maintains a single variable to hold a target object, rather than a stack of objects. The variable contents are overwritten each time a new target object is identified. Hence, we only recall references to the most recently identified target objects. Our algorithm proceeds as follows:

1. If the word "it" is the target object of the current sentence, we assume that this sentence refers to the most recently identified target object.
2. Our system then replaces the target object value with the item id of the stored target object.

Consider the following excerpt. *"Pick up that red block. Drop it."* Fig. 20.11 shows an excerpt of the JSON object produced for the first sentence.

After parsing the second sentence, our system determines that the target of the command is "it." Assuming that the target of Fig. 20.11 is stored as block with the id = 3, then our system will replace "it" with the stored target identification. The resulting JSON object is shown in Fig. 20.12.

Fig. 20.11 An excerpt of
the JSON object for the
sentence: *"Pick up that red
block"*

```
"Target": {
   "Item": "block",
   "Mods": ["red"],
   "Gesture": true}
```

Fig. 20.12 An excerpt of
the modified JSON object for
the sentence: "*Drop it*"

```
"NLPProcessor": {
  "Command":"drop",
    "Target": {
      "id":3.0}}
```

Fig. 20.13 An excerpt of a
JSON object for cases in
which the robot is referenced

```
{"NLPProcessor": {
   "Target": {
     "Item": "block",
     "Relation": {
        "Objects": [{"Item": "self"}],
        "Direction": "right"},
     "Mods": ["red"],
     "Gesture": false},
   "Command": "pick up"}}
```

Referencing the robot. Our system recognizes when a human collaborator references the robot, such as in the sentence: "*Pick up the red block on your right.*" or "*Pick up the red block between you and the blue block.*"

In any of those cases, our system places the value **self** in the corresponding object's **Item** field. Figure 20.13 shows an excerpt of the JSON object produced for the first sentence mentioned above.

Incomplete input. Sometimes, a human collaborator may utter an incomplete sentence. Due to the power of the Stanford CoreNLP parser, our system is able to extract sufficient information to: (i) tell which portion is missing and (ii) use the portion that was successfully parsed as part of a request for additional information. Additionally, our system stores the partially parsed data in the MemorySave.txt file to eventually merge it with the data extracted from the clarifying response by a human collaborator. To manage the processing of incomplete data, our system adds a **NeedClarification** object to any JSON object it returns. This object contains three fields to indicate which portions of a command may be missing. This object is shown in Fig. 20.14.

We discuss three cases:

(1) **The command verb phrase is missing**. Consider the phrase: "*That plastic red block to the left of the yellow bottle.*" When processing its parse tree, our system will not find a verb phrase at the root of the graph. Instead, our system will locate the root of the sentence. It will then iterate through all the children of the root and search for the first noun. That noun will be the target of our sentence. Next, we can extract the modifiers as normal. In this case, the **Command** field will be set to **true**.

Fig. 20.14 A sample
NeedClarification
object

```
"NeedClarification": {
  "Target": false,
  "Command": true,
  "Reference": false}
```

(2) **Only the verb phrase is given.** Consider the phrase *"Pick up."* In this case, no target object is given, and neither are any reference objects. Our system sets the **Target** field to **true**.

(3) **Reference objects are missing.** Consider the phrase *"Pick up the yellow plastic block between."* Our system can parse most elements as normal. However, it is not able to find any dependencies related to the direction word. In this case, our system sets the **Reference** field to **true**.

Based on the information from the **NeedClarification** object, the "Communication unit" will eventually request the specified information. In order to be able to merge the partial information with the next interaction in which clarifying information is given, the system will store the partial JSON object in the MemorySave.txt file. We are currently working on the merging of partial information.

20.5 Confidence Aggregator

In our system, some of the units calculate confidence values and pair them with some of the objects in our domain. The final confidence ratings produced by this unit take into consideration the color as determined by the "Color Recognition" unit, gesture as determined by the "Gesture Recognition" unit, and spatial relationships as determined by the "Spatial Relations Recognition" unit. This unit combines all of these confidence values to determine an overall confidence value of the block that is considered to be selected by the human collaborator. In other words, we do not calculate the confidence values of all of the blocks in the domain, as this is not necessary.

The system begins with a block that is either identified by gesture or if gesture is not used, a block that is identified by color. This unit then processes the spatial modifiers as identified by the NLP unit. It does so by consulting the information produced by the "Spatial Relations Recognition" unit. If while following the spatial modifiers, there are no blocks in a particular direction/relation, then the algorithm will attempt to select the next object in a particular direction based on its confidence level, to continue the calculation with it. If no block is found, a confidence value of 0.0 is assigned. To combine all of that information into a single confidence value, we use the product of normalized confidence ratings. We normalize the confidence ratings to ensure that the value of one confidence rating does not distort the value of the aggregated confidence ratings. We note that a weighted sum serves a similar purpose, albeit with the added burden of determining weights for each confidence rating to reflect the relative importance of each form of input.

Given the utterance "Pick up the blue block to the left of that block" and assuming the human collaborator points to the block identified with **"id":3.0**, Fig. 20.15 shows an excerpt of the CAS object with the confidence value of block 3 as the one intended to be picked up.

```
"AggregateConfidence":
[{"id":3.0,
  "confidence":0.9298860211532615,
  "normPointingConf":0.9373988271398364,
  "normColorConf":1.0,
  "spatialRelationshipConf":0.991985475371782},...],
```

Fig. 20.15 An excerpt of the CAS object after confidence aggregation

```
"CoordinateTransformation":
[{"x":  0.6707599004163673
  "y":  0.48190930545330046
  "z":  0.018995275532949774}]
```

Fig. 20.16 An excerpt of the CAS object showing the coordinates of the selected block after being transformed to the perspective of the Sawyer robot

20.6 Perspective Transformation

The selected object's current coordinates are based on the perspective of the Kinect. In order for the Sawyer robot to know the position of the object, these coordinates need to be translated to the coordinate system of the robot.

This translation is performed via a series of transformation matrices. In the current system, one of the measurements used for the transformation is the distance from the base of the Kinect to the base of the robot. This distance is measured manually and does not need to be changed unless the Kinect or the robot is moved to a different location. Figure 20.16 shows the result of the transformation for the block selected for an action by the robot.

20.7 Planning Unit

In order to provide the robot with some autonomy, we implemented a basic planner. We chose to implement a basic version of STRIPS (see Fikes & Nilsson, 1971). STRIPS is not a very powerful planner. Hence, a human collaborator will be required to provide input more often than if a more powerful planner were to be used. We will eventually replace STRIPS, however, at this point, we wish to develop a better understanding of the nature of human–robot collaborative problem-solving. Additionally, using a planner of limited yet well-understood abilities may help a human collaborator to develop trust in the system.

The planner is given a goal state as well as the given state. The given state is extracted from the JSON object that describes the current working space, and the goal state is extracted from the human collaborator's input. The planner's actions and representation of the world are as expected for the block's world. The actions include: PUT_DOWN(x), PICK_UP(x), UNSTACK(x, y) and STACK(x, y). The

Fig. 20.17 A sample plan

```
{"ActionPlan": {
    "initialState": [
       "ON_TABLE(id:3)",
       "ON_TABLE(id:4)",
       "CLEAR(id:3)",
       "CLEAR(id:4)",
       "ARM_EMPTY"],
    "goalState": [
       "ON_TABLE(id:3)",
       "CLEAR(id:4)",
       "ON(id:4, id:3)",
       "ARM_EMPTY"],
    "name": "Easy Condition",
    "state": {
       "normal": true,
       "unsolvable": false,
       "doNothing": false,
       "stuck": false},
    "plan": [
       "STACK(id:4, id:3)",
       "PICK_UP(id:4)"]}}
```

world is represented through the use of the following predicates: CLEAR(x), ON(x, y), HOLDING(x), ARM_EMPTY, and ON_TABLE(x). For more details, see Nilsson (1980). The planner produces a sequence of actions that are saved in the CAS and are in turn read by the "Command unit" to interpret the actions and to send them to the robot. Figure 20.17 shows an excerpt of the JSON object for a sample plan produced by our system.

The **initialState**, **goalState**, and **plan** information is as expected. The **name** field can be used to give plans a name so as to reuse them later on. Named plans will be stored in the MemorySave.txt file. The **state** object is used to convey meta-information about a planning problem. It has four fields, which we will discuss in turn. They will eventually be used by the "Communication unit" to give appropriate feedback to a human collaborator:

1. **normal**. This field is set to true if the planner was able to solve a given planning problem. This result holds for the problem presented in Fig. 20.17.
2. **doNothing**. This field is set to true if the goal state is already satisfied and no further action is necessary.
3. **unsolvable**. This field is set to true if the problem cannot be solved by our planner. This result occurs when there are additional objects in the goal state that are not present in the start state. For example, in Fig. 20.18, there is an additional block **c** in the goal state. This block cannot be matched to the initial state and as such, the predicate ON(c, a), cannot be satisfied for this problem. Alternatively, a problem is not solvable when information is missing from the initial state description. For example, the initial state from Fig. 20.18 needs to be represented by the following state description: ON_TABLE(a), ON_TABLE(b), CLEAR(a), CLEAR(b), and ARM_EMPTY. If any of those

Fig. 20.18 An unsolvable
planning problem

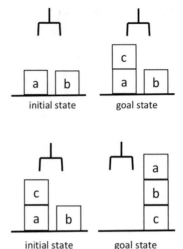

initial state   goal state

Fig. 20.19 Sussman
anomaly

pieces are missing, our planner will not be able to find a solution as it cannot
satisfy at least one goal.

4. **stuck**. This field is set to `true` when the planner is not able to solve a problem
    because it is not sufficiently powerful. For example, this result is the case when
    it encounters the problem known as Sussman's anomaly (see Sussman, 1975).
    An example of this anomaly is depicted in Fig. 20.19. This case occurs when
    the planner undoes a goal in order to satisfy a different goal. Our system detects
    such a situation by monitoring the information placed on the goal stack. If the
    planner undoes an action already placed on the stack to satisfy an earlier goal,
    the planner will terminate. As a fail-safe, our planner terminates after 2 s of
    runtime, again, setting this field to `true`.

20.8 Communication Unit

This unit communicates with a human collaborator. In addition to providing some
fairly technical feedback, it attempts to create a jovial working relationship.

This unit gives the collaborator feedback about its level of understanding and, as
such, enables a human collaborator and the robot to engage in a dialog while solving
a problem. As explained in Sect. 20.5 on the "Confidence Aggregator" unit, our
system combines confidence information from several units to determine the overall
confidence that an object has been successfully identified for a particular action. The
"Communication Unit" acknowledges when it has a high confidence in an object.
Currently, if the computation of the confidence in the selected block has a value of at
least 0.5, then that object is selected for action. The value 0.5 is a tuning parameter

Fig. 20.20 Examples of
high-confidence system
responses

```
Got it
Roger that
Command received
Okay
Will do that
Understood
Yes Sir
```

and will likely change as our system evolves. Figure 20.20 shows a list of responses from which one is chosen at random.

This unit attempts to create a sense of teamwork by asking for the human collaborator's name, which will then be stored it in the `MemorySave.txt` file and used throughout the dialog. Where appropriate, the human collaborator's name will be randomly appended to the response.

If our system has low confidence or if information is missing, it will request more information from a human collaborator. In the case of low confidence, the system will direct the robot to move its robot arm to above the block with the highest confidence, close its gripper, and ask the human collaborator whether that is the block they chose for action. In case some information is missing, see Sect. 20.4 on "Natural Language Processing," the system will request more information by using one of the phrases shown in Table 20.2. The last three responses are given in those cases where no useful information could be extracted from the parse tree. This behavior was inspired by ELIZA, an early natural language processing computer program (see Weizenbaum, 1966.)

20.9 Command Unit

This unit communicates commands to the Sawyer robot using the robot operating system (ROS). Currently, we are supporting the "pick up" and "point" commands. This unit looks into three pieces of data to determine which of those two commands should be issued. The "pick up" action is taken if the following criteria are met:

1. The "NLP Unit" identifies the command as "pick up."
2. The "Confidence Aggregator" returns a value of `true`.
3. The "Spatial Relations Recognition" unit identified a block.

The "point" command will trigger given the following criteria:

1. The "NLP Unit" identifies any command.
2. The "Confidence Aggregator" returns a value of `false`.
3. The "Spatial Relations Recognition" unit identified a block.

The commands sent to the robot consist of arm movements and gripper state changes. An "arm movement" command takes 3D coordinates with the intended goal of moving the gripper to the specified position. The gripper will remain in a vertical

Table 20.2 System responses requesting additional information

Problem	Sample responses
Missing command	What would you like me to do with < JSON target > ?
	Can you tell me what you would like me to do with < JSON target > ?
	What action should I take on < JSON target > ?
	Can you tell me what action you would like me to take on < JSON target > ?
Missing target object	Which item would you like me to < JSON command > ?
	Can you tell me which item you would like me to < JSON command > ?
	Can you tell me the target of command < JSON command > ?
	Which item is the target of command < JSON command > ?
Missing reference object	You would like me to < JSON command > the < JSON target > < JSON Direction > of which item?
	Would you be so kind and tell me the object that is < JSON Direction > of the < JSON target > ?
	Sorry, but can you repeat which item is < JSON Direction > of the < JSON target > ?
Unsuccessful parse	Sorry, but I don't quite follow you
	What do you mean?
	Could you please elaborate?

position throughout the movement process. When the move command is issued, the Sawyer robot will use its camera to recognize the objects in its environment. These are the objects that the ROS uses to create a movement plan. The movement plan contains a goal, which in our case is to move to a specified 3D position. ROS creates a set of movement vectors that will accomplish the goal without colliding with objects in the environment. As such, ROS validates commands given to it by the "Command unit." The set of movement vectors is executed, and the arm will then move to the specified position.

The X and Y coordinates are obtained from the X and Y position of the identified block as determined by the "Perspective Transformation" unit. In case of a "pick up" command, the Z coordinate is set to be 10 cm from the top of the table, which is sufficient to grab a block. In case of a "point" command, the Z coordinate is set to 30 cm above the top of the table, which is sufficiently close for the user to identify to which block the Sawyer robot is pointing.

To be specific, the "pick up" command consists of four phases. In the first phase, the gripper is instructed to open up. During the second phase, the arm is moved above the block at a height of 30 cm. During the third phase, the arm is lowered to where a block can be picked up. This action is taken primarily for testing purposes because it allows the operator to determine if the X and Y positions for the specified block

```
def pick_up_and_move_block(x, y):
  rospy.init_node("GraspingDemo")
  global gripper
  gripper = intera_interface.Gripper('right_gripper')
  gripper.open()
  move_to(x, y, 0.30)
  move_to(x, y, 0.10)
  gripper.close()
  move_to(x, y, 0.30)
```

Fig. 20.21 The "Command Unit" procedure implementing the "pick up" command

are translated correctly, and to prevent the gripper from colliding with the top of the block. In the final phase, the gripper is instructed to close.

When a pointing action is issued, the gripper will first close and then move to position itself to above the block for which the system is requesting feedback. The gripper's open and close commands can be called outside of its move commands and do not require ROS planning or movement vectors.

The "Command Unit" will not modify the CAS object since it is considered an output unit. Figure 20.21 shows the higher level details of the "pick up" command as defined in the "Command Unit." The last command places the gripper at a height of 30 cm above the table. We currently have not implemented the "put down" command.

20.10 Conclusions: Engineering Context

We now briefly describe the key aspects of the context for our collaborative system and how the components of our system contribute to the process of building and maintaining context.

Agreements. The *Memory Import* unit, in cooperation with the *Memory Storage* unit, creates and maintains definitions or references to blocks. The units store and recall names given to the blocks by the collaborator and apply those names to the blocks that are recalled.

Observing the workspace. Our system discovers the relevant workspace, the table in Fig. 20.1, and its elements; i.e., the blocks on the table. The *Object Detection* unit records the hues and locations of the blocks in a three-dimensional space along the axis of the Kinect's camera.

Observing the collaborator. Two units observe the human collaborator. The *Gesture Recognition* unit observes pointing actions of the collaborator and the *Speech-to-Text* unit records voice input from the collaborator.

Interpreting the workspace. While the *Object Detection* unit reads off information from the Kinect sensors, the *Color Recognition* and *Spatial Relations Generator* units interpret the sensor data to determine the colors and the relative locations of the blocks to each other.

Interpreting the collaborator. The *NLP Unit* interprets the text obtained by the *Speech-to-Text* unit to extract commands as well as the block references, which include pointing gestures, references to colors, or relative locations.

Interpreting intent. Several components are used to interpret a collaborator's intent. The *Spatial Relations Recognition* unit, based on a collaborator's utterances about relative locations as extracted by the *NLP unit* and the pre-processed relative locations produced by the *Spatial Relations Generator*, determines confidences in the blocks that may be chosen for various actions. The *Confidence Aggregator* unit combines confidences in the colors of blocks as produced by the *Color Recognition* unit and confidence of the pointing action as produced by the *Gesture Recognition* unit and combines them with input from the *NLP Unit* so as to interpret which block is identified for naming or motion purposes. It, too, associates confidence with blocks in the domain.

Skills. The *Command Unit* converts stacking instructions such as "pick up" into move and grip commands, which are then sent to the Sawyer robot via the ROS. The movement and gripping actions are implemented there, while the *Command Unit* simply interfaces with them. The *Planner* gives the system some autonomy; it can solve block-stacking problems within certain parameters.

Converting to the collaborator's perspective. The *Perspective Transformation* unit converts the perspective extracted and maintained by the UIMA information processing pipeline to that of the Sawyer's robot. In particular, it translates the UIMA coordinates to that of the robots.

Communicating with the collaborator. The *Communication Unit* either confirms confidence in the collaborator's response or it uses the robot's arm to point to a block that the system deems the most likely block to be identified by the collaborator.

Developing a working relationship. In addition to simple acknowledgments, by using a human collaborator's name and by varying its responses, our system attempts to create a working relationship with its collaborator.

Since we are building our system and context from the ground up, we are not in a position yet to address the higher level intricacies of context.

Acknowledgements We like to thank Tyler Bath, Sophie Brusniak, Stella Park, and Mitchell Schmidt for their contributions to this project.

References

Brooks, R. A. (1990). Elephants don't play chess. *Robotics and autonomous systems* (Vol. 6, Issues 1–2, pp. 3–15). Elsevier.

Castro, B., Roberts, M., Mena, K., & Boerkoel, J. (2017). Who takes the lead? Automated scheduling for human-robot teams. In *Proceedings of the Artificial Intelligence for Human-Robot Interaction AAAI Fall Symposium*. Technical Report FS-17-01.

Ferrucci., D. A. (2012). Introduction to "This is Watson". *IBM Journal of Research and Development, 56*(3/4), 1:1–1:15.

Fikes, R. E., & Nilsson, N. J. (1971). STRIPS: A new approach to the application of theorem proving to problem solving. *Artificial Intelligence., 2*(3–4), 189–208.

Google. (2019a). Cloud speech-to-text. Retrieved November 06, 2019, from https://cloud.google.com/speech-to-text/.

Google. (2019b). Natural language. Retrieved November 06, 2019, from https://cloud.google.com/natural-language/.

Holdren, J. P., & Smith, M. (2016). Preparing for the future of artificial intelligence. Retrieved November 06, 2019, from https://obamawhitehouse.archives.gov/sites/default/files/whitehouse_files/microsites/ostp/NSTC/preparing_for_the_future_of_ai.pdf.

Manning, C. D., Surdeanu, M., Bauer, J., Finkel, J., Bethard, S. J., & McClosky, D. (2014). The Stanford coreNLP natural language processing toolkit. In *Proceedings of the 52nd Annual Meeting of the Association for Computational Linguistics: System Demonstrations* (pp. 55–60).

Nilsson, N. J. (1980). *Principles of artificial intelligence* (pp. 275–307). Tioga Publishing. Palo Alto.

Sussman, G. (1975). Sussman Anomaly. Retrieved November 12, 2020 from https://en.wikipedia.org/wiki/Sussman_anomaly.

UIMA. (2019). Apache UIMA. Retrieved November 06, 2019 from https://uima.apache.org/.

Weizenbaum, J. (1966). ELIZA—A computer program for the study of natural language communication between man and machine. *Communic Ations of the ACM., 9*, 36–35.

Wollowski, M., Bath, T., Brusniak, S., Crowell, M., Dong, S., Knierman, J., Panfil, W., Park, S., Schmidt, M., & Suvarna, A. (2020). Constructing mutual context in human-robot collaborative problem solving with multimodal input. In: W. F. Lawless, R. Mittu & D. A. Sofge (Eds.), *Human-Machine shared contexts*. Academic Press.

Chapter 21
Meta-reasoning in Assembly Robots

Priyam Parashar and Ashok K. Goel

Abstract As robots become increasingly pervasive in human society, there is a need for developing theoretical frameworks for "human–machine shared contexts." In this chapter, we develop a framework for endowing robots with a human-like capacity for meta-reasoning. We consider the case of an assembly robot that is given a task slightly different from the one for which it was preprogrammed. In this scenario, the assembly robot may fail to accomplish the novel task. We develop a conceptual framework for using meta-reasoning to recover and learn from the robot failure, including a specification of the problem, a taxonomy of failures, and an architecture for meta-reasoning. Our framework for robot learning from failure grounds meta-reasoning in action and perception.

21.1 Introduction and Background

From thermostats and toasters to self-driving cars and unmanned aerial vehicles, robots are entering the human world in large numbers. Soon, robots of many different kinds will be ubiquitous in almost all aspects of human life. This pervasiveness raises many interesting questions from the perspective of "human–machine shared contexts." How will humans and robots work, learn, and live together? How will they communicate and collaborate with one another? How will humans understand robots? How will robots explain themselves? How will robots learn from observing humans? How will robots learn from their failures?

In a chapter (Goel et al., 2020) in the previous volume in this series of books on Human–Machine Shared Contexts (Lawless et al., 2020), we had advocated the use of cognitive strategies to afford effective human–robot cooperation: "if we want

P. Parashar (✉)
University of California, San Diego, USA
e-mail: pparashar@eng.ucsd.edu

A. K. Goel
Georgia Institute of Technology, Atlanta, GA, USA
e-mail: ashok.goel@cc.gatech.edu

© Springer Nature Switzerland AG 2021
W. F. Lawless et al. (eds.), *Systems Engineering and Artificial Intelligence*,
https://doi.org/10.1007/978-3-030-77283-3_21

robots to live and work among humans, then we may start with human-like, human-level, *cognitive* strategies to addressing novel situations." In the previous chapter, we described analogy as a cognitive strategy for robot learning from human demonstrations and meta-reasoning as a cognitive strategy for a robot to learn from its own failures. In this chapter, while focusing on assembly robots, we investigate meta-reasoning in more depth.

Apart from the ubiquitous Roomba, assembly robots are among the most commonly used commercial robots in the world today (IFR (International Federation of Robotics), 2020). In fact, assembly robots are critical to industrial economies, especially in the manufacturing sector. Most assembly robots are preprogrammed for some specific routine tasks such as fastening a nut into a bolt to hold two surfaces together. In fact, the preprogramming is done carefully to avoid failures because a failure can have significant economic costs (1 min of downtime for a large automotive assembly line past might carry a cost of the order of $50,000). This is also reflected by the vast efforts to structure the manufacturing environment so that the assumptions underlying the programming are always respected.

However, agile manufacturing often requires more flexibility: an assembly robot may face a task slightly different from the one for which it was programmed. Given the reliance of the preprogrammed assembly robot on the rigid environmental structure may mean that it fails to accomplish the new task, even if the difference from the familiar task is very small. In this chapter, we explore the question: how may an assembly robot use meta-reasoning to recover and learn from a failure in such a context? Depending on the specification of the problem, the cost of recovering from a small failure may be less than the cost of re-programming the assembly robot for every new situation in agile manufacturing. This prospect raises a new question: what kind of failures may occur when an assembly robot preprogrammed for a specific task is exposed to a slightly different task?

Meta-reasoning—thinking about one's own thinking—is one strategy. Meta-reasoning has received significant attention in research on AI as reviewed and outlined in Anderson and Oates (2007), Cox (2005), Cox and Raja (2011), Russell and Wefald (1991). However, much of previous work on meta-reasoning has been on simulated robots; meta-reasoning in physical robots has, thus, far received relatively little attention. As one may expect, physical robots impose hard constraints arising out of action and perception. This raises another question: What do the constraints imposed by action and perception mean for meta-reasoning? In this chapter, we are interested in exploring the relationship between action, perception, planning, and meta-reasoning. We specify the nature of the problem and identify trade-offs in designs of possible solutions.

21.1.1 Related Work

Our research lies at the intersection of artificial intelligence and robotics. Our work on meta-reasoning builds on a long line of research: The Autognostic project (Stroulia &

Goel, 1995, 1999) developed a multilayered agent architecture including situated, deliberative, and meta-reasoning components. In analogy to the redesign of physical devices, the Autognostic system viewed an intelligent agent as an abstract device and used a functional model to describe and repair a deliberative navigation planner. The Reflective Evolutionary Mind (REM) project (Murdock & Goel, 2008) generalized the Autognostic agent architecture. It developed a knowledge representation language called Task-Method-Knowledge Language for encoding functional models of agent designs that are more expressive than hierarchical task networks (Nau et al., 2003) and enable explicit expectation descriptions. This depth of description allows the REM architecture to conduct both retrospective and proactive adaptations for an assembly agent.

Unlike the Autognostic and REM projects, the Augur project (Goel & Jones, 2011; Jones & Goel, 2012) focuses on the use of meta-reasoning to diagnose and repair domain knowledge grounded in perception. Given domain knowledge in the form of a classification hierarchy, Augur associates meta-knowledge in the form of empirically verified procedures that capture the expectations about world states with each node in the hierarchy. When the classifier makes an incorrect prediction, Augur system-atically invokes its empirical verification procedures to diagnose the classification knowledge. Finally, the GAIA project (Goel & Rugaber, 2017) provides an interactive CAD-like environment for constructing game-playing agents (for playing Freeciv) in the REM architecture and the Task-Method-Knowledge Language (TMKL). Given the design of a game-playing agent, GAIA executes the agent in the game environ-ment. If the agent fails, then GAIA enables interactive diagnosis and repair of the agents' design. Parashar and colleagues (2018) extend this architecture to a situated agent in Minecraft with a separate and explicit perception process supporting the information gathering and repair efforts. They use an occupancy grid to represent task expectations grounded in the ego-centric view of the agent that is then used as a heuristic for guiding ground-level actions to learn task-level repair.

Goal-driven autonomy (GDA) (Muñoz-Avila et al., 2010) is a goal-reasoning framework where the agent makes use of an expectation knowledge-base (KB) to keep track of plan execution and to find discrepancies if any. GDA is based on meta-reasoning concepts like expectation matching system, discrepancy detection, expla-nation generation, etc. Dannenhauer and Munoz-Avila (2015) use hierarchical plans with annotated expectations, called h-plans, along with a semantic web ontology, to make better assertions about game states and to reason at various levels of a plan hierarchy leading to better control over strategy reformulation.

There are several threads in robotics research supporting and informing our work on representation and reasoning. It is generally agreed in robotics that hybrid systems, which can do both deliberation and some kind of reactive revisions, pave the way for more complex robotic applications (Kortenkamp et al., 2016), but there does not exist a systematic theory of how to combine different levels of planning, reaction, and learning. Müller and colleagues (2007) present a system that encodes plan transfor-mations to make actuation easy based on pre-compiled heuristics and to apply these transformations at run time to make plan execution more efficient. This way, the planner abstracts away the difficulty of manipulation because of geometric and other specific requirements (e.g., the number of objects to move or the number of rooms to visit) onto an abstract space. Beetz and colleagues (2010) present a cohesive "robot abstract machine," which integrates task reasoning with motion planning, perception, and other lower level modules on real robots, and, in theory, also allows meta-reasoning. This architecture is supported by KnowRob (Tenorth & Beetz, 2013), a knowledge database, which collects facts and beliefs for reasoning and revising plans.

Wolfe and colleagues (2010) and Kaelbling and Lozano-Perez (2011) provide two important insights that inform our architecture for meta-reasoning in assembly robots: (a) robots do not have all of the needed information before plan execution and thus the architecture needs to account for plan refinement during execution and (b) motion actions can be thought of as functional entities, which helps in reasoning about their effects in an abstract space. Christensen and colleagues (2010, Chap. 6) conceptualize replanning as a way of refining plans and present an elegant formulation of integrating facts from object perception as "agent now *knows* X" into the refinement-by-replanning framework. Dantam and Stilman (2013) conceptualize task language as a motion grammar relating high-level actions with semantic rules explicitly describing how the position, forces, and velocity of a robot arm are affected when a specific action is applied. Together, these various lines of previous work on robotics help in filling the blanks on how to view the physical processes of a robot in the same functional scope as task-planning. Finally, Parashar and colleagues (2019) present an exhaustive survey of how ontologies of tasks and actions enable and facilitate better human–machine understanding, motivating the design if our architecture for meta-reasoning in assembly robots that connects higher level ontologies to lower level constraints.

21.2   Illustrative Examples

Let us consider an example in which the robot needs to plan a sequence of actions so that it may pick up an assembly part, a pully in this case, lying on a table. Imagine that the robot has a camera mounted onto the gripper allowing the robot to plan motion using the eye-in-hand configuration. As assembly agent, the robot has a library of action sequences for frequently used assembly tasks like "picking up a part," so it retrieves a *task method* that specifies such a sequence from its memory and applies it on the pulley. This method is shown in the top half of Fig. 21.1 along with the expected progression of the plan in the current context. However, suppose that this method previously has only been used for parts far smaller than the pulley and so the agent does not realize that the ***Align*** action (Fig. 21.1 (top)-iii) will not move the gripper all the way to the immediate top of the pulley as expected. This is because ***Align*** uses an algorithm that moves the gripper toward the object until the object is centered on the camera image and occupies a certain amount of area in that image. The distance at which this condition becomes true is different for objects of

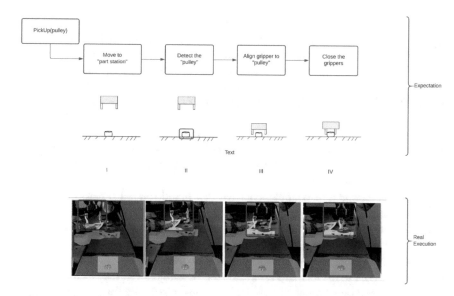

Fig. 21.1 The top half of this picture depicts what the agent expects will happen when it executes the stored plan for **PickUp** assembly action. The agent will (I) go to "part station," which is a fixed location in the environment, (II) agent will detect the pulley object at the part station, (III) the agent will align its gripper with pulley, and (iv) the agent will grasp the pulley. This plan was initially made for much smaller parts that the **Align** action could go close to. However, due to a larger size of the pulley and field-of-view restrictions of the agent's camera, the **Align** action is not able to go all the way to the immediate top of the pulley. This results in a failure as the grippers close far from the pulley as shown in the bottom half of the image

different sizes. Consequently, when the agent executes this method, the results look like Fig. 21.1 (bottom), which is an obvious task failure.

Let us analyze this failure and its possible repairs. This problem can be viewed in two ways: an incorrect parameterization of the *Align* action or a knowledge gap in the task procedure due to a mismatch between the expectation of executing the *Align* action and the actual state of the world. The first view considers that if the robot can just fix the parameterization of *Align* action to enforce the gripper to move closer then we can solve this problem. If *Align* is considered a function with the amount of area covered by object as a thresholding parameter, we can increase the value of this parameter and move closer. However, this repair has strict bounds! The physical shape and size of the part is an immutable property so while a re-parameterization of *Align* may bring the gripper closer, there will always be a minimum distance beyond which the camera will lose focus of the object due to the laws of optics. The second view considers this failure as a knowledge gap in the task specification that manifests as a physical failure. While *Align* falls short of matching the task-level expectations of the agent, the robot's method library may have more assembly skills (like a *MoveTo*(x, y) action) that can be tried to compensate for this gap and repair the plan. This kind of repair is only limited by the completeness and soundness of the method and skill library, which are far more malleable concepts than the laws of optics. We also cannot replace the **Align** action to avoid using it altogether because perception is necessary to situate the objects in the environment, which affects the motion and actions of the robot that manipulates the object under consideration.

The geometry of an object places objective constraints on *what configuration* of the object is compatible with a given assembly operation, while perception helps in grounding the geometry in a *particular situation*. A robot uses both kinds of information to understand *how to place the object* in the current situation (perception) and *how to move* to actuate the desired object state (geometry). Thus, geometry and perception both play an important role in transferring the plan from the familiar problem to a new problem.

To further extend this example, consider that the illustrated subtask was part of a larger assembly task where the robot is required to pick up the pulley and then **Insert** it onto a shaft (Fig. 21.2a). Assume that this time around the robot has a complete plan that works for the given scenario. Now suppose that the robot is given a complementary task in which it needs to pick up the shaft instead and insert it into the pulley affixed to the station Fig. 21.3b-III). At a high level, the agent may ask if the same general plan would still work for the new task? At a finer level, the agent may ask whether there are implicit assumptions in the previous plan based on the geometry of the pulley? If so, how may the agent transform the plan for the shaft for an insertion into the pulley? If the agent knows how to grasp the shaft, a direct transfer of the plan would result in the situation depicted in Fig. 21.2b, where the robot grasps the shaft and moves in the same relative way to insert it as it would have

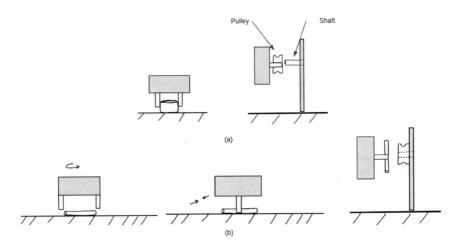

Fig. 21.2 a Depicts the larger assembly task whose subtask was analyzed in Fig. 21.1. The overall assembly task was to pick up the pulley and then insert it onto a shaft affixed to a station. **b** An example of failure due to direct transfer of the plan for the task "pulley-on-shaft" to the "shaft-into-pulley" task, where the geometry of the shaft is not accounted for. In the third diagram, the shaft is aligned with respect to the stationary station in the same way as the pulley, which may make sense causally, but does not make sense geometrically

with the pulley. This is obviously wrong since the shaft's length is compatible with insertion into the pulley and not it's surface. This is an example of task failure due to a knowledge gap in the agent's task model relating the geometry of an object to the assembly attachment.

There are several types of which can occur in a complex assembly system. For example, perception might be imperfect, or the actuators might not work due to network error, or new objects have different physical properties, which breaks the dynamic modeling of the *Screw* action. Thus, to systematically situate the use of meta-reasoning for recovering and learning from failures, it is important to analyze the failures as to whether they are recoverable and the recovery is affordable, as well as to design the architecture of the assembly agent to make the recovery process more efficient and affordable.

Problem statement. Our conceptual framework for meta-reasoning for robotics, meta-reasoning, action, and perception form three vertices of a triangle with deliberative planning and the skill library lying inside the triangle. In a simulated world, we can make assumptions about action and perception and focus on the interactions between the meta-reasoning, deliberative, and skill layers. However, for physical robots, action and perception impose strong constraints. The general goal of our research is to understand the interplay among meta-reasoning, action, and perception. In particular, we seek to ground meta-reasoning in action and perception so that an agent can exploit the task structure and domain knowledge to guide adaptation routines when faced with small variations in the task environment. This capability will help in creating robot agents that are more autonomous and capable of self-adaptation in dealing with small degrees of novelty. Our goal in this chapter is to specify the structure of the problem and thereby characterize the space of feasible solutions.

21.3   Assembly as a Reasoning Problem

Assembly planning and execution is a hard problem requiring solutions to a varied class of subproblems, such as part sequencing as well as metric-level precision planning, to succeed. We choose to model this problem using a three-level problem hierarchy with each subsequent level planning for a smaller scope of the overall assembly problem informed by the solutions of the level above. It is a cascade of mission-level (product planning, longer time-horizon), task-level (action sequencing, medium time-horizon), and skill-level planning (metric-level routines, shortest time-horizon) with each informed of the planning context from the previous component. The assembly mission planner generates a partial-order plan for sequencing part attachments for assembling the whole product. This sequence is used by the assembly task planner to come up with totally ordered task plan actions or *assembly skills* to do the part attachments. Finally, the assembly skills invoke lower level specialized planners and routines to plan for motion or grasping and gain perceptual information from the environment. This decomposition is illustrated in Fig. 21.3.

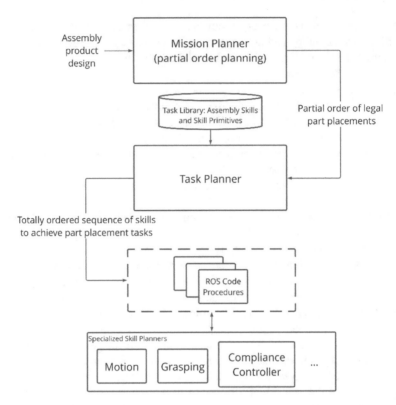

Fig. 21.3 The decomposition and structure of an end-to-end assembly problem. At the top level, a mission planner plans for part placements based on the geometry and specifics of the assembly product. This context is sent to an assembly task planner in the form of partial ordering of part attachments. The task planner uses a skill library made of assembly skills to generate an action sequence, which, in turn, invokes the lower level code procedures to perceive and manipulate the environment

Mission Planning: To represent the assembly product as a mission planning problem, we adapt and refine the description of the *assembly mission* introduced by Mello and Sanderson (1991) for our needs. As shown in Fig. 21.4, the mission *M* is the tuple <P, A, R, f> , where P is the set of all the parts, A is the set of attachments required between the parts, R is a set of relations linking parts with appropriate attachments, and f is the set of functions relating the parts and attachments to their geometric properties. This mission is supported via a knowledge base of parts and their properties including the type of the part, the relevant attachments for each part type, and the part relations enabled by the different attachments. To clarify, *R* in Fig. 21.4 is the configuration of parts to be achieved (*attached*(p0, p1) V *shaft*(p1) V *task-board*(p0)), while *A* is the set of specific assembly skills required to achieve the relation (***Insert***(p2, p1) → *attached*(p2, p1)). *R* also stores a crucial piece of information, which we assume the user will provide, about the relative part configurations; for example, (*on-top*(p0, p1) ∩ *on-top*(p1, p2)). This knowledge

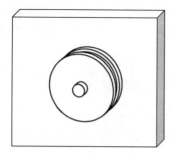

```
P = { p0: taskboard,
      p1: shaft,
      p2: pulley}
A = { a0: fixed,
      a1: insert}
R = { "a-to-p":
        { r0: (a0, p0, p1),
          r1: (a1, p1, p2)},
      "p-to-p":
        { r2: on-top(p1, p0),
          r3: on-top(p2, p1)}}
f = { "final-pose":    { ... },
      "approach-pose": { ... }}
```

Fig. 21.4 The code snippet on the right-hand side describes the assembly product on the left using our formal mission description based on Mello and Sanderson (1991). P collects all the parts while A collects all the attachments used in the product. R relates attachments to parts and the relative configuration of parts with respect to each other. F collects the geometric information associated with the attachments in any arbitrary coordinate frame

helps the mission planner come up with a partial order for progressing through the attachments and send it to the task planner. For a completely pre-defined mission, f stores function mapping each part and attachment to its goal-state in the metric space in the form of its six-dimensional pose. This information is utilized by the task planner to ground the tasks and consumed by the motion planner to plan in metric space. Thus, the input to the mission planner is the assembly product and the output is a partial-order plan of part sequencing with associated pre-defined attachments.

Task Planning: Given that the mission description includes the specific attachment to be used for a part's placement, *assembly task* planning addresses the problem of how may the robot actuate the given attachment for the assembly part? A special top-level method is responsible for sequencing the attachments and does so by choosing the next unplaced part and associated attachment from the partially ordered output of mission planner and decomposing the assembly task associated with it. We use HTN planning (Nau et al., 1999) for assembly task planning. There is a central task library that consists of compound and primitive tasks: each compound task is hierarchically decomposed into a totally ordered sequence of primitive tasks. The primitive tasks directly invoke the metric-level planners and routines to (a) actuate the robot or (b) gather perceptual information for grounding the task decomposition: by grounding we mean parameterizing the compound and primitive tasks with the correct environmental coordinates based on perception.

In this chapter, we will call the primitive tasks as *assembly skill primitives* based on the taxonomy proposed by Huckaby (2014) (see Fig. 21.5). Thus, the mission is made up of tasks and each task is made up of compound or primitive assembly skills. To associate compound assembly skills with attachments, the knowledge base consists of *{attachment-name, goal-configuration, list-of-relevant-parts, list-of-tools} tuples*, where *attachment-name* maps to each unique attachment-type possible in A and associates it with an assembly skill in the task library. The symbols in *list-of-relevant-parts* and *list-of-tools* are used to parameterize the decomposition. Each assembly

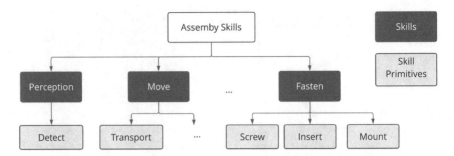

Fig. 21.5 An excerpt from assembly skill taxonomy proposed by Huckaby (2014). The taxonomy defines and organizes all the physical capabilities required to do automatic assembly in a hierarchical manner. At the top are general skills (dark grey boxes), which define high-level capabilities a robot should have. Some general skills are then decomposed further into leaf nodes, which are termed skill primitives (light grey boxes). These are the specific but different kinds of instantiations of the general skill that a robot can have. For example, a robot can **Fasten** two objects by **Screwing** or **Inserting** or **Mounting**

skill is decomposed into a totally ordered sequence of more skills or skill primitives. As shown in Fig. 21.5, some skills act as a high-level guard for contextualizing which skill primitive to invoke, for example, a *Move* skill has a list of {pre-conditions, skill-primitive} tuples; viz, if pre-condition(i) is true then primitive(i) is executed. Other skills can have more complex decompositions. The preconditions of skills encode two important kinds of knowledge: applicability of different primitives under different conditions and different primitive sequences for manipulating objects for the attachment depending upon different initial states.

To make the subsequent discussions about failure analysis in assembly more precise, we introduce minimal terminology here. We define an attachment skill primitive as a special kind of assembly skill primitive that actuates the physical contact-based manipulation, which *attaches* objects in desired configurations (e.g. *Screw* and *Insert*). Preparatory assembly skill primitives are the rest of the domain-relevant object manipulations required to get to a state where an attachment action can be executed.

Definition 0 An attachment primitive, $aa(a_i)$, is an assembly skill primitive that actuates the main contact relation achieved by completion of an attachment $a_i \in A$.

Definition 1 Plan segment $p' = prep(p(a_i)) : last(p') \prec aa(a_i)$ manipulates the world to bring about the preconditions required by an attachment primitive; it is the *preparation method* for that assembly attachment.

Skill Planning: Specialized planners, both off-the-shelf and specifically implemented for the assembly robot, are used at this level to actuate the assembly primitives. We consider the underlying algorithm of the primitives as a black-box and are only concerned with *how* each primitive's execution changes the robot state. We only assume each primitive is completely parameterized by the task, object, and other physical parameters sent by the task planner. Each primitive skill execution is like a blocking function call, with the agent executing the next ordered primitive skill when the control returns.

$$S_{prim} = f_{s\_prim}(\text{skill} - \text{parameters})$$

21.4 Failure Mode, Effect, and Repair Analysis

This section presents our analysis of the failures that we observed while developing a dual-arm assembly system for the World Robot Summit assembly challenge 2020 (aka WRC, 2020; WRC (World Robotic Challenge), 2020) based on the reasoning structure described in the previous Sect. 21.4 (more details can be found in Parashar et al. (2021)). We cannot eliminate all failures in an assembly system that is supposed to operate for different variations of the same product, but we can provide an informed opinion using a qualitative Failure Mode and Effect Analysis (Liu et al., 2013) in an effort to identify which slice of the failure-space is more amenable to an automatic recovery versus meticulous preprogramming. Thus, our research goal is not to automatically recover from all possible failures in the assembly task but to allow the robot to only fail in ways that are non-fatal and then enable it to learn from them. We want to understand the nature of failures, their cost, and the tradeoffs against the cost of meta-reasoning for repairing the failures. We want to answer the question: which class of failures can an assembly agent afford to repair? What kind of repairs are available for such failures? And most importantly, which failures manifest when the task goal or the task environment changes incrementally? We chose to categorize failures by their origin in the planning stack, type of knowledge required for repair, and the practical implications (including severity and detectability). We first present an origin-based analysis of failures at every level followed by their classification into a preliminary taxonomy.

Interestingly, failures can only happen during reasoning or during the run-time execution of a task. However, repairs for potential failures can be identified even before the run time through a meticulous examination and analysis by domain experts. In fact, we observed the need for the pre-meta-reasoning structure (Pourazin & Barforoush, 2006) arising in our work specifically for the failures, which were too costly for our run-time budget defined by the constraints of the competition: speed, repeatability (accuracy of actuation when a motion is repeated), and accuracy of operations.

21.4.1 Skill-level Failures

In general, the function of a skill in an assembly task is either to set up objects in a state where an attachment action can occur (picking, aligning, or placing) or to execute the attachment itself (inserting, screwing, or mounting). Thus, we can distinguish between the skill failures, which occur during the preparation phase versus those which occur during the attachment phase. Based on the taxonomy from Huckaby (2014), we can infer that failures during the preparation phase mainly relate to aligning, grasping, transporting, and detecting objects. These actions typically do not have fatal consequences; most of these skills use heuristic-based algorithms to conduct a search in the physical space until a threshold is passed by the relevant physical measurements. This activity is a classic example of approximate reasoning that provides "adequate" repairs, i.e., near-optimal repairs with defined lower bounds (Russell & Wefald, 1991). If the task-level parameters situate an action in a "good-enough" region of a search space, then reasoning at the lower level can handle recovery from a failure. Therefore, preparation-phase failures can be repaired using behavioral heuristics about how the parameters affect the expansion or contraction of the operational state-space of an action. Note that handling such failures should be within the bounds set by our assumption of skills being a black-box function with the task planner grounding it in parameter values. However, we will need additional meta-knowledge at this level about how each black-box's parameter affects its function.

On the other hand, failures arising during the execution of an attachment action may have fatal consequences. Here by "fatal" we mean rendering a state where either the assembly material is damaged beyond repair or one that requires manual intervention to reset the agent. Consider when an agent applies too much force in the wrong direction while screwing the bolt into the nut and jams the bolt (Fig. 21.6). This is a hard-to-detect failure with a high probability of ruining the parts based on the material. Additionally, to prevent further ruining of the material, the repair requires a human to manually reset the system and assembly line before restarting the process. Generally, such actions require either specialized hardware or implementing sophisticated closed-loop control dynamics (Jia et al., 2018). As a rule, complex attachments require much more sophisticated knowledge for execution and recovery while simpler attachments can be repaired with general heuristics. However, if the attachments have more complex control flows than a linear operation, then such generic repairs like reversals of action (Laursen et al., 2015) might not work at all. Thus, it is reasonable to surmise that there exists a small subset of simple attachment actions for which errors are recoverable like block stacking.

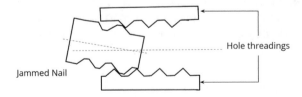

Fig. 21.6 Visual depiction of a nail jamming in a threaded hole due to excess force and/or wrong insertion angle. This failure is not trivially repairable and requires deep modeling of the dynamics between surfaces as well as the helical geometry. Such complex failures are beyond the scope of repairs considering our formal definition of skill as black-box

To summarize this section, we noted two failure modes arising at the skill level, one recoverable and the other fatal. The recoverable failures are repaired by heuristic of "retry with a perturbation." However, each action has a specific meaning for each perturbation associated with it; for example, if a camera cannot detect an object due to glare, then the perturbation is physically achieved by displacing the camera by an arbitrary amount around its focus point. On the other hand, to perturb an alignment action (which is basically a spiral search with some forward force to align and latch the features of bolt and nut with each other), the perturbation is an increase of the search radius or a slight bump in the forward force to make it more detectable. Thus, any repair here would also need specific meta-knowledge about the portable parameters and the desired perturbation function to be applied for each assembly skill.

21.4.2   Task-level Failures

The task-level planner is responsible for ordering skills and figuring out the task and object parameters consumed by the lower level procedures for execution. The former ensures the agent progresses in a causally correct manner in the abstract task space while the latter ensures that the progress is grounded in correct physical positions, forces, and artifacts. Thus, we can classify two kinds of major failures right away: ordering failures and grounding failures.

Failures due to a knowledge gap in causal ordering usually arise when an assembly task is changed in some way that violates the assumptions of the coded recipes/methods. Since a task is scoped by the attachment it achieves, we can ignore a functional change in the goal configuration to be a reason for failure. However, an assembly task can have different resources available in the environment than those assumed by preprogrammed knowledge. In this case, a new task model may need to be inferred. An example is to attach two tiles: the domain designers assume the availability of a dowel and defined *insert* attachment task, but the run-time environment only has a glue-gun available. Also, sometimes a conceptual repair can lead to a grounding repair, for example, if the glue-gun's action model is not known, it would need to be learned or inferred from data. Fitzgerald and colleagues (2019) use demonstrations to ground such constraints for a task model. However, it is difficult to collect demonstrations for learning these constraints for an assembly task simply because the details lie in the force-based maneuvering and jiggling when doing any contact-based action like screwing or insertion. These observations are hard to collect data from and require specialized data collection rigs. Instead, a more applicable repair is to infer the constraints using geometric knowledge and models of the parts since assembly products usually have highly meticulous CAD representations available. Our example in Sect. 21.3 is of a complex failure where there is a grounding failure such that the physical position of the gripper does not match its expected position, and the solution does not just change the grounding information, but rather affects the ordering of the actions themselves by adding a new transport/move action.

Grounding failures can easily lead to fatal behavioral failures if not scoped within the stable region of an agent's motion space: for example, the object position is correctly detected, but the object itself is outside of an agent's reach (assuming a stationary robot). Thus, it is a reasonable assumption that we only consider grounding failures, which respect the motion limits of a robot, i.e., if a task is given, it is achievable for the given physical configuration of the agent. Even with this assumption, a traditional assembly system relies on a perfect encoding of geometric information to operate efficiently. Therefore, repairing grounding problems has a clear metric of overall task and motion efficiency, which can be used to iteratively improve their solutions.

Ordering a repair is based on learning or inferring a new task model for using a new object's features for its intended function, while grounding the repair is based on lifting the constraints added/modified in world geometry to a higher level plane and adapting tasks to account for it. Ordering repairs can range from inferring reversal actions (Murdock & Goel, 2008), or learning a new policy guided by the known goal configuration constraints when new objects are introduced in the task space (Parashar et al., 2018). Grounding repairs usually require integration with a finer-grained representation of the environment to enable the analysis of relations between task symbols and physical configurations (Bullard et al., 2016).

21.4.3 Mission-level Failures

The mission knowledge is necessary for understanding the sequence of part placement that leads to legal product configurations. While some attachments can be reversed (e.g., insertion), others are irreversible by nature (e.g., gluing). Thus, the lower level physical properties of the attachments can make a mission sequencing failure irreversible as well. At this point, the mission planner needs to find new sequences of possible object ordering and check the legality of those attachments by asking the task planner about available procedures. This step is another example of non-fatal failure; however, the repair costs can vary over a large spectrum based on the number of parts and possible attachments between them. A better way would be to ask the task planner for proposals of object combinations since it has access to information about the features of parts, enabling the mission planner to infer the more correct orderings as opposed to random combinations. Better yet, if the mission planner can figure out which attachments are irreversible and order those correctly, then the agent might be able to avoid all major failures at this level. This suggests that knowledge about critical mission landmarks can significantly reduce the overall failure and repair costs of an assembly system. One way of inferring such knowledge is by a geometrical analysis of parts in a simulated environment as shown in De Mello and Sanderson (1989) and by inferring relations between these part orders and the available parts in the current mission (Fitzgerald et al., 2018).

21.4.4 A Preliminary Taxonomy of Failure Modes

Table 21.1 summarizes the failures discussed above and organizes them in a taxonomy of origin and mode, along with whether such failures are recoverable or not, and the knowledge base that recovery depends on. When we say that a failure is recoverable, we assume the availability of the required recovery knowledge.

21.5 Assembly Plan Repair as a Meta-reasoning Problem

The meta-reasoning space of the plan repair domain is composed of a Meta-KB, Trace-KB, and Expectation-KB. Meta-KB compiles facts and beliefs about objects, properties, and their association with task/skill goals. Trace-KB is a time series of environmental observations and the logical progression of tasks that bookend each action. Expectation-KB is a baseline trace generated by the meta-reasoner based on optimistic assumptions. The grounding of Meta-KB and Expectation-KB largely depends upon the context of the failure and repair to be undertaken. While the framework and formulation of meta-reasoning below are general, the choice of representations and the corresponding methods of reasoning and learning cannot be isolated from the specifics of the domain. The meta-reasoning problem could be one of learning, and the Meta-KB and Expectation-KB then may guide the learner to *learn more efficiently*; similarly, if the meta-reasoning problem is one of knowledge modification, then Meta-KB and Expectation-KB should guide modification routines to *modify efficiently*. Meta-KB is especially dependent on the choice of a failure repair and its parametrization. Therefore, it is important to understand the nature of failures in assembly and their corresponding repair mechanisms to propose a class of meta-reasoning strategies, which would allow the agent to recover from unexpected task variations.

Table 21.1 Summary of failure modes, recoverability, and recovery knowledge required

Origin	Mode	Recoverability	Recovery KB
Skill	Preparation	Yes	Parameters and perturbation function
	Attachment	No except for simple ones	Reversibility knowledge
Task	Grounding	Yes	Physical positions and orientations of task-relevant objects
	Action ordering	Yes	Knowledge about robot and object features; interactions between different features
Mission	Part ordering	Depends on the parts and resources available	Reversibility knowledge, knowledge about legal part pairings for tasks

Given our analysis in Sect. 21.5, we are much better situated to propose a class of repairs for the assembly failures discussed. Now we want to answer two questions:

1. What kind of repairs are applicable to the non-fatal assembly failures in Table 21.1?
2. What new components, frameworks, and conceptual extensions are required to the base reasoning model in Sect. 21.4 to support the repairs?

21.5.1 Meta-reasoning Architecture for Robots

To do knowledge repairs, it is important to first be able to detect failures as they happen. Furthermore, as we mentioned, there can be many different locations of causes that could relate to this failure. Thus, to apply appropriate repair the knowledge, it is also important to localize the cause for the failure. Let us briefly discuss an architecture that will enable us to conduct this failure detection and localization. Robotic architectures are special in that they must planning or replanning while situated in a physical environment. The prototypical three-tiered architecture (aka 3 T) (Firby, 1994; Kortenkamp et al., 2016) seems well suited for our purposes. It has a deliberative layer at the top, which takes care of long-term planning for the domain. Next, an executive layer in the middle translates deliberative decisions to real-time process invocations and monitors real-time processes for feeding back into planners if needed. Finally, it has a behavioral layer at the bottom, which houses all the real-time processes (specialized planners and routines in our case), which run in parallel to manipulate and perceive the environment. In fact, our system for WRC 2020 used this exact architecture to detect and repair preparatory skill failures and for simple detection of task failures. In the rest of this section, we use this 3 T meta-reasoning architecture (Fig. 21.7) as base to conceptualize a meta-reasoning architecture for assembly robots. We systematically add feedback for failure detection (input to skill monitor), heuristics for cause localization (directing output from skill monitor), and the relevant meta-knowledge to conduct repairs (resolution and action/perception commands back to skill level). Figure 21.8 shows an example of how high-level tasks are decomposed into skills and executions at the executive level of this 3 T architecture.

21.5.2 Skill Failure Detection and Repair

Feedback: A skill in our formalization is a black-box function parameterized by the task planner. Once a skill is executed, the agent moves to the next planned skill to actuate. We can extend this notion of skill to a function by adding provisions for returning values. In the WRC 2020 system, we extended the skill primitives to be able to return three values: *success, failure,* and *running.* We used the behavior tree (BT) framework to instantiate plans using nodes and arbitrary control flows based

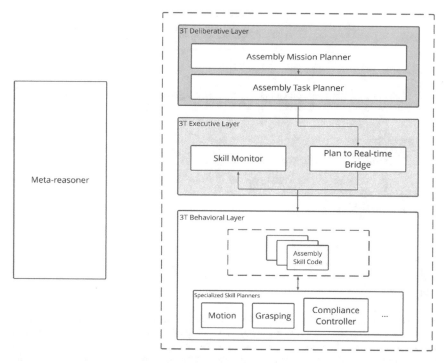

Fig. 21.7 The meta-reasoning architecture for assembly robots based on the assembly planning and execution architecture used in WRC 2020. Note that the meta-reasoner and assembly system are not yet connected; the subsequent sections illustrate the connections between them

on the planner logic (Colledanchise & Ögren, 2018). These three values are the prototypical signals returned by a BT as each node in the tree executes. We know that each skill node (action node in BT terminology) invokes a planner underneath, so a *failure* means the black-box algorithm could not succeed.

Repair: For every preparatory assembly skill, we can come up with a reparative description consisting of repair parameters, a perturbation function, and an expected number of retries. Given access to the transition function of an assembly action, we used a simple algorithm to apply a perturbation function to the repair parameters and repeated for the expected number of tries until the action succeeded. The Expectation-KB consisted of the expected number of retries for *success*, the Trace-KB consisted of the current iteration, and the Meta-KB consisted of a list of tuples {parameter-name, perturbation-function} (Algorithm 21.1). The Meta-KB could have also been empty, which defined the simplest case where the action just needed to be repeated; for example, when the gripper did not actuate due to drivers dropping out but could be retried. This worked because our system had an underlying process supervisor monitoring these processes and restarting them when they went down; describing this base-level recovery framework is outside the scope of the current chapter.

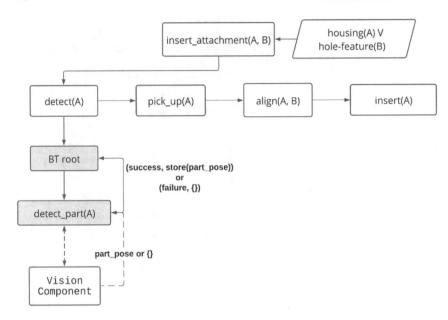

Fig. 21.8 A diagram depicting how high-level plans are translated into a behavior tree to communicate to lower level processes. Depending upon the results of the lower level process, the behavior tree returns success or failure to the tree above it. In this figure, assembly skill primitive detect (white boxes on top) is translated to a simple behavior tree (grey boxes), which relate to the vision component underneath. The "detect_part" behavior tree node is an "action node," which is directly executed. BT also has provision for other kinds of nodes, which assess a condition, or implement conditional control-flow changes

Algorithm 21.1. Repair of preparatory assembly skills given perturbations for each parameter

---
Algorithm 1 Reactive Repair for Preparatory Assembly Skills

Input: skill - reference to procedure, parameters - dictionary of names and values for arg-list of skill

$i = 0$

while skill(parameters[all].values)[0] $\neq$ SUCCESS or $i <$ Exp-KB **do**

    for all (para-name, pert-func) tuples in Meta-KB **do**

        parameters $\leftarrow$ pert-func(parameters[para-name].value)

    end for

    $i++$

end while

The important thing to note here is that the application of these reparative algorithms did not necessarily need the overhead of being sent up to a meta-reasoner and back. First, such a procedure can add unnecessary lag to the signal, which can hurt the run-time stability of the agent. Second, since our architecture is already using behavior trees to instantiate the decision-making process of the planner as a tree structure, and we can easily extend this to add the meta-reasoning procedural

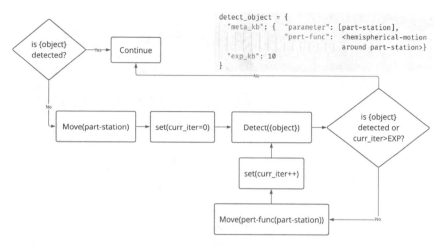

Fig. 21.9 The snippet on the top describes the meta-knowledge associated with the repair of **Detect** action. The tree structure encodes Algorithm 21.1, allowing efficient repair during execution. This tree checks if the parameter {object} is already detected, if not it **Moves** the agent to the part-station and invokes the **Detect** action over the object. The agent repeats this process if the object is not detected and moves the camera with small perturbation to account for any variable lighting, which might be preventing object detection. If the object is not detected even after expected number of retries, then it propagates a failure up to the rest of the tree

structure to it as well. Thus, this repair algorithm is pre-compiled within the reactive structure of the behavior tree allowing for quick catch-and-repair during run time. Figure 21.9 shows such a behavioral tree structure for the *Detect* action.

This form of applying pre-metareasoning (i.e., meta-reasoning based on heuristics and information known before undertaking the reasoning process) gives rise to an updated architecture for meta-reasoning for assembly robots as shown in Fig. 21.10. Our experience with this inquiry differs from the traditional meta-reasoning architectures proposed in Cox and Raja (2011) and suggests that multiple meta-reasoning structures can exist in one architecture supporting meta-reasoning to different levels. In our WRC system, we observed a significant drop in the fatal crashes of the system by implementing the described pre-meta-reasoning behavior.

21.5.3 Task Failures and Repairs

Feedback: The align-failure with pully and insertion of shaft-in-pulley instances in Sect. 21.3 are examples of knowledge gap failures stemming from different causes. The symptom of both these failures is that the preconditions for executing the next action (grasp and insert, respectively) are not satisfied. We, thus, propose the assembly skill taxonomy to be extended by adding the provision for *verification skills*, which can have arbitrary logic for asserting the truth or falsehood of pre/postconditions

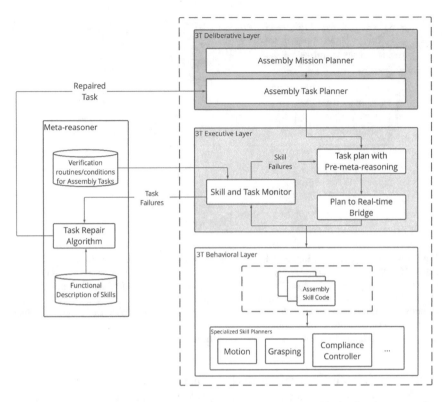

Fig. 21.10 The proposed meta-reasoning architecture integrates two kinds of action-perception repair loops for assembly robots. The inner loop (or the fast loop) is inside the Executive Layer where the plans are precompiled with repair heuristics and do not need to be propagated to the meta-reasoner for repair. The outer loop (or the slow loop) propagates task-level failures to the meta-reasoner, which uses additional knowledge about the functions of the assembly skills to propose repairs to the broken task

based on the output of **Detect** skill. The BT framework has *condition nodes*, which test a given logic returning *success* or *failure* based on the logic's assertion, thus incorporating this in our system should be relatively easy. The harder and more important part is grounding the pre and postconditions of skill primitives in states that are *perceivable by the agent*, for example, a task to turn on a switch inside a closed box without any light attached to that switch will not qualify as the kind of task, which can be verified or repaired.

Jones and Goel (2012) present an approach where meta-knowledge of verifying ground-level decisions is explicitly mapped in percepts thus enabling result-oriented guidance for higher levels. Parashar and colleagues (2018) present an instance of using occupancy grids to represent the environment within the configuration space of a robotic arm and to define a similarity computation over them allowing more detailed perspectives of conceptual plans on ground-level. Thus, these heuristics can be based on memory or explicitly engineered knowledge. In either case, we can now use this as the baseline of agent's expectations as to how the world should evolve. We hypothesize that by grounding meta-reasoning in physical percepts, we can create a multi-modal understanding of actions over ground-level information.

Repair: The verification procedures add *heuristics* in abstract task space about monitoring the progression of the plan in the physical space. By analogy, we propose that the skill primitive descriptions need to be supplemented with heuristics for informing their functions in conceptual and physical spaces. In the context of hierarchical task networks, the extension into hierarchical goal networks (HGNs) makes a similar point; the nice thing about having a goal description is that it can be translated with more clarity into specialized planners down the line. Shivashankar and colleagues (2014) illustrate a process where such an integration is established between task planning and motion planning by using goal definitions as the bridge. Dantam and Stilman (2013) describe the function of actions in a motion grammar by ascribing explicit semantic rules to them while Wolfe and colleagues (2010) introduce the same concept as *transition models*, which have been adopted and refined to suit our needs in our formulation (Sect. 21.4). Stroulia and Goel (1995) and Murdock and Goel (2008) impose a similar view over conceptual transformations; these authors functionally index them for use in generic problem-solving methods, which hits close to our aims of proposing generic repair methods within domain boundaries. Using these functional representations of actions, we expect to be able to conduct repair in a more surgical fashion, with less supervision than an uninformed system.

An important thing to consider here is that an action is not the only cause for a task-level failure. A task failure can also arise due to imperfect perception: as an example, consider plugging a USB stick into the computer port. It is not easy for perception to recognize the correct configuration from an image alone that may be in variable office/home lighting. Furthermore, it is beneficial to figure out approaches, which can resolve actions conditioned on imperfect perception rather than rely on the perfect perception of bespoke features for general robotics. A heuristic that works for every human is to try and plug the USB in one configuration; if it works great, otherwise flip and try again. Thus, actions can provide definitive answers to possible questions if the actions are not too costly (like the WRS 2020 attachments). How may meta-reasoning help with these situations where high-level knowledge about a task and knowledge about an action can resolve perception ambiguities? Along the lines of the work by Christensen and colleagues (2010, Chap. 6), we propose to functionally index not only motion actions but also cognitive actions like perception. One way of implementing this is by explicitly linking the *acquiring* of environmental knowledge with the ***Detect*** action. This way if the plan leads to a failure, we may be able to backtrack wrong object state estimation to ***Detect*** action and revise the assignment, especially under uncertainties. We expect the resulting system to better prepare us for localizing errors and conducting repairs of the right kind.

21.5.4 Toward Mission Repair

Since we are specifically interested in the interplay between action and perception, let us briefly consider a specific kind of mission failure relating to this. A mission formulation has information about which orderings are impossible but not about which orderings are easier or harder for an agent to do with its specific physical and skill-level abilities. Thus, a suboptimal ordering could make for harder to plan tasks for an agent. For example, consider building a house made of lego bricks. The agent could build the house ground-up and then assemble the roof on top of the walls or can assemble the roof separately and place it on top of the walls later. The former is significantly harder for a robot than the latter due to multiple layers of force dynamics involved (robot presses roof, roof presses walls, walls may or may not fall down over a long period of the same). Thus, we end this section with another interesting question: how may we extend reasoning formulations of robot problems to not only consider problem structure but also the feasibility with respect to the acting agent's abilities?

21.6 Discussion and Conclusions

There is a growing need for developing theoretical frameworks for human–robot shared contexts. There is also a growing interest in endowing robots with human-level, human-like capabilities to enhance human–robot collaboration; for example, meta-reasoning. However, much of previous AI research on meta-reasoning has focused on simulated robots, thereby abstracting away from the hard issues of action and perception. In this chapter, we have described a preliminary theoretical framework for grounding meta-reasoning in action and perception.

We considered the case of assembly robots that are preprogrammed for repetitively accomplishing routine tasks without failure. We examined scenarios in which an assembly robot may fail if given a new task that is even slightly different from the task for which it was preprogrammed. In some contexts, the cost of recovering from a failure may be lower than that of reprogramming the robot. However, in such scenarios, we want the robot to not only recover from the failure but also to learn from it. We described a robot architecture in which meta-reasoning helps the robot to localize and identify the cause for the failure and then to repair the knowledge that caused the failure. We found that our robot architecture for meta-reasoning grounded in action and perception in physical robots is significantly different than the idealized architectures proposed in earlier AI research. In summary, we expect a meta-reasoning system to have knowledge about the following concepts:

1. *Visuospatial representations and operations*: In order to ground concepts in their geometric instantiations, it is necessary to have a qualitative mid-level visuospatial representation that can present task-relevant features and operate on them without the need for precise locations and positions.

2. *Specification of functions of actions and tasks*: When a failure is localized and a better recovery state is obtained, or a heuristic toward one is ascertained, the agent would need some form of a state transition model to infer which actions can take it to the desired state.
3. *Explicit model of the effects of perception*: To revise perceptual beliefs of the agent, it is necessary to have an explicit model that links decisions made on those beliefs to the perception action (like ***Detect***) and the perceptual states that led to them. As far we know, such an analysis of using the perception process as a functional entity is missing from the meta-reasoning literature. We believe by modeling perception and its effects in a similar way to actions, for example, by using a transition function that updates the cognitive belief of an object state, we can build a meta-reasoning theory that interweaves action and perception as equals.

Acknowledgements We thank Aayush Naik and Jiaming Hu for their help in implementing the end-to-end assembly robot system described in Parashar et al. (2021). We would also thank the Research Products Development Company for their support in developing the robot system for the World Robot Summit 2020 that enabled this analysis.

References

Anderson, M. L., & Oates, T. (2007). A review of recent research in metareasoning and metalearning. *AI Magazine, 28*, 12–12.

Beetz, M., Mösenlechner, L., & Tenorth, M. (2010). CRAM—A cognitive robot abstract machine for everyday manipulation in human environments. In *2010 IEEE/RSJ International Conference on Intelligent Robots and Systems* (pp. 1012–1017).

Bullard, K., Akgun, B., Chernova, S., & Thomaz, A. L. (2016). Grounding action parameters from demonstration. In: *2016 25th IEEE International Symposium on Robot and Human Interactive Communication (RO-MAN)* (pp. 253–260).

Christensen, H. I., Kruijff, G.-J. M., & Wyatt, J. L. (2010). *Cognitive systems*. Springer Science & Business Media.

Colledanchise, M., & Ögren, P. (2018). *Behavior trees in robotics and AI: An introduction*.

Cox, M. T. (2005). Metacognition in computation: A selected research review. *Artificial Intelligence, 169*, 104–141.

Cox, M. T., & Raja, A. (2011). *Metareasoning: Thinking about thinking*. MIT Press.

Dannenhauer, D., & Muñoz-Avila, H. (2015). Goal-driven autonomy with semantically-annotated hierarchical cases E. In Hüllermeier & M. Minor (Eds.), *Case-Based reasoning research and development* (pp. 88–103). Springer International Publishing.

Dantam, N., & Stilman, M. (2013). The motion grammar: Analysis of a linguistic method for robot control. *Trans. Rob., 29*, 704–718. https://doi.org/10.1109/TRO.2013.2239553

De Mello, L. H., & Sanderson, A. C. (1989). A correct and complete algorithm for the generation of mechanical assembly sequences. In *1989 IEEE International Conference on Robotics and Automation* (pp. 56–57).

Firby, R. J. (1994). Task networks for controlling continuous processes. In *Proceedings of the Second International Conference on AI Planning Systems* (pp. 49–54).

Fitzgerald, T., Goel, A. K., & Thomaz, A. L. (2018). Human-Guided object mapping for task transfer. *ACM Transactions on Human-Robot Interaction (THRI), 7*, 1–24.

Fitzgerald, T., Short, E., Goel, A. K., & Thomaz, A. L. (2019). Human-guided trajectory adaptation for tool transfer. In *Proceedings of the 18th International Conference on Autonomous Agents and MultiAgent Systems* (pp. 1350–1358).

Goel, A. K., Fitzgerald, T., & Parashar, P. (2020). Analogy and metareasoning: Cognitive strategies for robot learning. In *Human-Machine shared contexts* (pp. 23–44). Elsevier.

Goel, A. K., & Jones, J. K. (2011). Meta-Reasoning for self-adaptation in intelligent agents. In: *Metareasoning: Thinking about thinking* (p. 151). Cambridge, MA: MIT Press

Goel, A. K., & Rugaber, S. (2017). GAIA: A CAD-like environment for designing game-playing agents. *IEEE Intelligent Systems, 32*, 60–67.

Huckaby, J. O. (2014). *Knowledge transfer in robot manipulation tasks*. Georgia Institute of Technology.

IFR (International Federation of Robotics). (2020). *World robotics report*. Frankfurt.

Jia, Z., Bhatia, A., Aronson, R. M., Bourne, D., & Mason, M. T. (2018). A survey of automated threaded fastening. *IEEE Transactions on Automation Science and Engineering, 16*, 298–310.

Jones, J. K., & Goel, A. K. (2012). Perceptually grounded self-diagnosis and self-repair of domain knowledge. *Knowledge-Based Systems, 27*, 281–301. https://doi.org/10.1016/j.knosys.2011.09.012

Kaelbling, L. P., & Lozano-Pérez, T. (2011). Hierarchical task and motion planning in the now. In *2011 IEEE International Conference on Robotics and Automation* (pp. 1470–1477).

Kortenkamp, D., Simmons, R., & Brugali, D. (2016). Robotic systems architectures and programming. In *Springer handbook of robotics* (pp. 283–306). Springer.

Laursen, J. S., Schultz, U. P., & Ellekilde, L.-P. (2015). Automatic error recovery in robot assembly operations using reverse execution. In *2015 IEEE/RSJ International Conference on Intelligent Robots and Systems (IROS)* (pp. 1785–1792).

Lawless, W., Mittu, R., & Sofge, D. (2020). *Human-machine shared contexts*. Academic Press.

Liu, H.-C., Liu, L., & Liu, N. (2013). Risk evaluation approaches in failure mode and effects analysis: A literature review. *Expert Systems with Applications, 40*, 828–838.

Müller, A., Kirsch, A., & Beetz, M. (2007). Transformational planning for everyday activity. In *Proceedings of the Seventeenth International Conference on International Conference on Automated Planning and Scheduling, ICAPS'07* (pp. 248–255). Providence, Rhode Island, USA: AAAI Press.

Muñoz-Avila, H., Jaidee, U., Aha, D. W., & Carter, E. (2010). Goal-driven autonomy with case-based reasoning. In *International Conference on Case-Based Reasoning* (pp. 228–241).

Murdock, J. W., & Goel, A. K. (2008). Meta-case-based reasoning: Self-improvement through self-understanding. *Journal of Experimental & Theoretical Artificial Intelligence, 20*, 1–36.

Nau, D. S., Au, T.-C., Ilghami, O., Kuter, U., Murdock, J. W., Wu, D., & Yaman, F. (2003). SHOP2: An HTN planning system. *Journal of Artificial Intelligence Research, 20*, 379–404.

Nau, D. S., Cao, Y., Lotem, A., & Muñoz-Avila, H. (1999). SHOP: Simple hierarchical ordered planner. In *Proceedings of the 16th International Joint Conference on Artificial Intelligence* (Vol. 2, pp. 968–973).

Parashar, P., Goel, A. K., Sheneman, B., & Christensen, H. I. (2018). Towards life-long adaptive agents: using metareasoning for combining knowledge-based planning with situated learning. *The Knowledge Engineering Review, 33*, e24. https://doi.org/10.1017/S0269888918000279.

Parashar, P., Naik, A., Hu, J., & Christensen, H. I. (2021). Meta-Modeling of assembly contingencies and planning for repair. arXiv:2103.07544 [cs].

Parashar, P., Sanneman, L. M., Shah, J. A., & Christensen, H. I. (2019). A taxonomy for characterizing modes of interactions in goal-driven, human-robot teams. In IROS (pp. 2213–2220).

Pourazin, S., & Barforoush, A. A. (2006). Concurrent metareasoning. *The Journal of Supercomputing, 35*, 51–64.

Russell, S., & Wefald, E. (1991). *Principles of Metareasoning. Artificial Intelligence, 49*, 361–395.

Shivashankar, V., Kaipa, K. N., Nau, D. S., & Gupta, S. K. (2014). Towards integrating hierarchical goal networks and motion planners to support planning for human-robot teams. In *International Conference on Intelligent Robots and Systems* (pp. 1–3).

Stroulia, E., & Goel, A. K. (1999). Evaluating PSMs in evolutionary design: The A UTOGNOSTIC experiments. *International Journal of Human-Computer Studies, 51,* 825–847.

Stroulia, E., & Goel, A. K. (1995). Functional representation and reasoning for reflective systems. *Applied Artificial Intelligence, 9,* 101–124. https://doi.org/10.1080/08839519508945470

Tenorth, M., & Beetz, M. (2013). KnowRob: A knowledge processing infrastructure for cognition-enabled robots. *The International Journal of Robotics Research, 32,* 566–590. https://doi.org/10.1177/0278364913481635

Wolfe, J., Marthi, B., & Russell, S. (2010). Combined task and motion planning for mobile manipulation. In *Proceedings of the Twentieth International Conference on International Conference on Automated Planning and Scheduling, ICAPS'10.* (pp. 254–257). Toronto, ON, Canada: AAAI Press.

WRC (World Robotic Challenge). (2020). *Industrial robotics category assembly challenge—rules and regulations 2020,* Tokyo, Japan. Retrieved January 16, 2020.

Chapter 22
From Informal Sketches to Systems Engineering Models Using AI Plan Recognition

Nicolas Hili, Alexandre Albore, and Julien Baclet

Abstract The transition to Computer-Aided Systems Engineering (CASE) changed engineers' day-to-day tasks in many disciplines such as mechanical or electronic ones. System engineers are still looking for the right set of tools to embrace this opportunity. Indeed, they deal with many kinds of data which evolve a lot during the development life cycle. Model-Based Systems Engineering (MBSE) should be an answer to that but failed to convince and to be accepted by system engineers and architects. The complexity of creating, editing, and annotating models of systems engineering takes its root from different sources: high abstraction levels, static representations, complex interfaces, and the time-consuming activities to keep a model and its associated diagrams consistent. As a result, system architects still heavily rely on traditional methods (whiteboards, papers, and pens) to outline a problem and its solution, and then they use modeling expert users to digitize informal data in modeling tools. In this chapter, we present an approach based on automated plan recognition to capture sketches of systems engineering models and to incrementally formalize them using specific representations. We present a first implementation of our approach with AI plan recognition, and we detail an experiment on applying plan recognition to systems engineering.

Keywords Plan recognition · Artificial Intelligence (AI) · Systems engineering · Sketch recognition · Model-driven development

N. Hili (✉)
University Grenoble Alpes, CNRS, LIG, 38000, Grenoble, France
e-mail: nicolas.hili@univ-grenoble-alpes.fr

A. Albore
Onera DTIS, BP74025, 2 avenue Edouard Belin 31055, Toulouse CEDEX 4, France
e-mail: alexandre.albore@onera.fr

J. Baclet
IRT Saint-Exupéry, 3 rue Tarfaya, CS 34436, 31400, Toulouse, France
e-mail: julien.baclet@irt-saintexupery.com

© Springer Nature Switzerland AG 2021
W. F. Lawless et al. (eds.), *Systems Engineering and Artificial Intelligence*,
https://doi.org/10.1007/978-3-030-77283-3_22

451

22.1 Motivation

Despite its proven modeling value in many engineering domains, Computer-Aided Design (CAD) tools have only had a moderate acceptance by system engineers and architects to assist them in their day-to-day tasks (Robertson and Radcliffe, 2009). The complexity of creating, editing, and annotating models of system engineering takes its root from different sources: unsuitable representations, outdated interfaces, laborious modifications, and difficult collaborations (Rudin, 2019).

As a result, especially in the early development phases, system architects tend to favor more traditional tools, such as whiteboards, paper, and pencils, over CAD tools to quickly and easily sketch a problem and its solution. Among the benefits of sticking to traditional tools, whiteboards foster collaboration and creativity as the users do not need to strictly conform to a formal notation.

A common pitfall for using traditional tools, however, is that human users are required to reproduce any sketched solutions inside of formal tools when it comes to formalizing them. Modern post-WIMP[1] interfaces (e.g., electronic whiteboards) could help to automate this task by allowing users working on a digital representation of the model, that can be directly exported, to be modified via modeling tools. Bridging the informality of the working sketches captured on interactive whiteboards with formal notations and representations has the potential to lower the barrier of acceptance of CAD tools by the industry (Botre and Sandbhor, 2013; Alblawi et al., 2019). This acceptance can be obtained by automatically or semi-automatically translating informal sketches into their corresponding formal elements using a specific and conventional notation.

This chapter presents the outcomes of BabyMOD (Hili and Farail, 2020), a one-year project conducted at IRT Saint Exupéry whose main objective was to identify new methods and approaches for modeling in systems engineering that leverage the use of modern post-WIMP interfaces, free-form modeling, and natural sketching. BabyMOD was a preparatory work for EasyMOD, a 4-year industrial collaborative project that started in 2020. During BabyMOD, we conducted several brainstorming sessions with our industrial partners to identify which requirements that CAD tools for systems engineering should fulfill; we developed different prototypes that make use of AI solutions to quicken model building by providing an automated assistant that performs shapes completion, while providing a certain level of explainability. Our final implementation combined traditional shape recognition algorithms and *plan recognition* (to forecast the final shape and to provide the user with a selection of recognition choices) so that model elements can be recognized from user drawings, and, consequently, automatically translated in a formal representation.

The remainder of this chapter is structured as follows: Sect. 22.2 presents the related work; Sect. 22.3 presents our approach based on plan recognition; Sect. 22.4 details our implementation based on the Planning Domain Definition Language (PDDL) formalism; Sect. 22.5 demonstrates the applicability of our approach through an experiment; Sect. 22.6 concludes this chapter and details future work.

---

[1] Windows, mouse, and pointer interfaces.

22.2 Related Work

22.2.1 Natural Sketching

Natural sketching aims at bridging the gap between free-form modeling and formal representation using dedicated graphical notations. In software engineering, modern post-WIMP interfaces, such as interactive whiteboards, interactive walls, and large multi-touch screens, have been used to capture models in software engineering during the first stages of the design process. Yet, we reckon that the practice is not well settled in systems engineering.

During the BabyMOD project (Hili and Farail, 2020), we conducted several surveys and brainstorming sessions with our industrial partners over a year to identify the requirements a CAD tool for systems engineering leveraging modern, post-WIMP interfaces should fulfill. Among the different requirements we identified for the CAD tool, eight were specific to the recognition mechanism and are listed below:

Req. 1 (Incremental formalization): The recognition of model elements should be done incrementally. This means that informal sketches and model elements may co-exist during the model lifetime.

Req. 2 (On-demand/automatic recognition): Recognizing model elements should be either done automatically or triggered by the user. The choice between the two options should be left to the user.

Req. 3 (Recognition of complete models): It should be possible to recognize interconnected model elements at once and not only model elements taken separately.

Req. 4 (Shape/text seamless recognition): It should be possible to mix geometrical shapes and handwritten notes (without any virtual keyboard or voice recognition assistant) in a seamless way. The tool should distinguish geometrical shapes from text nodes without any additional actions from the user so it can apply the correct recognition method.

Req. 5 (Explainability): The outcome of the recognition algorithm should be explainable to the user. "Explainability" is the property of a system that provides an output that makes understandable to the human user the reasons for an algorithm's choice. This is a condition needed by any process-directed tool that allows the users to evaluate the criteria behind a choice to use the tool efficiently (Rosenfeld and Richardson, 2019).

Req. 6 (Performance): The recognition of both single model elements and complete diagrams should be fast and accurate.

Table 22.1 Existing approaches for natural sketching

	MyScript Diagram	OctoUML	Google AutoDraw	FlexiSketch
Platform	Web, Windows, Android, MacOS	Web	Web	Android
Open source	✗	✓	✗[a]	✗
Recognition				
Algorithm	Proprietary	Geometrical shape detection[b]	Recurrent Neural Network (RNN)	Geometrical shape detection[c]
Sktech recognition	Basic geometrical shapes	Basic geometrical shapes	Doodle and Clip arts	Complex geometrical shapes
Bulk recognition	✓	✓[d]	✗	✗
Handwritten text recognition	✓	✗	✗	✗
Incremental recognition	✓	✓	✓	✓
Explainable results	✗	✗	✗	✗
Adaptation to modeling				
Type Promotion	✗	✗	✗	✓
Adaptability	Flowcharts, organizational charts, mindmaps	Class diagram only	✗	✓
Performance				
Accuracy	Relatively accurate	Relatively accurate	Accurate	Relatively accurate
Speed	Relatively slow	Moderately fast	Fast	Relatively fast

legend: ✓ = available ✗ = not available
(a) The dataset used to train the *Quick, Draw!*'s Convolutional Neural Network (CNN) algorithm is open source
(b) Based on PaleoSketch (Paulson and Hammond, 2008)
(c) Based on a Levenshtein distance algorithm
(d) With some restrictions

Req. 7 (Adaptability): It should be possible to adapt the recognition process to various kinds of models without a large amount of changes to the underlying recognition mechanism.

Req. 8 (Tolerance to drawing imperfections): As no assumptions can be made about the quality of the sketches realized by the user and his/her drawing skills, any recognition algorithm should be tolerant to drawing imperfections.

Table 22.1 compares different tools used for natural sketching and sketch recognition. We compared the tools based on four topics: (i) platforms and licenses; (ii) the underlying recognition mechanism; (iii) the effort needed to adapt the recognition algorithm to the modeling domain; and (iv) the observed performance.

MyScript (MyScript, 2020) is a leading company in the domain of handwriting recognition. It features *MyScript Diagram*, a natural sketching tool used to create various kinds of charts, from flowcharts to mindmaps. Ten primitive shapes and connectors are recognized, and text recognition is supported in multiple languages. MyScript runs on Windows, MacOS, and Android, or on the cloud. The recognition algorithm remains proprietary and recognition can be done remotely (on a subscription basis) or on-device. Compared to the other solutions, MyScript Diagram does not need to rely on other interaction modalities (such as voice recognition or virtual keyboard) to recognize shapes and text in a simultaneous way. On the negative side, performing recognition on the cloud is relatively slow and can take several seconds for the recognition process.

OctoUML (Jolak et al., 2016; Vesin et al., 2017) is the prototype of a modeling environment that captures UML models in a free-form modeling fashion and in a collaborative way. It can be used on various devices, including desktop computers and large interactive whiteboards. Sketches are then converted into a graphical UML notation. OctoUML supports class and sequence diagrams. It uses a *selective recognition* algorithm to support an incremental formalization.

OctoUML relies on PaleoSketch (Paulson and Hammond, 2008), a recognition algorithm capable of recognizing eight primitive shapes (lines, polylines, circles, ellipses, arcs, curves, spirals, and helixes) and more complex shapes as a combination of these primitive ones. By recognizing more primitive shapes than other low-level recognizers, PaleoSketch intends to recognize domain-specific shapes that could be indescribable using other methods. The drawback is that it consumes time to recognize more primitive shapes. In our tests, we observed that recognizing shapes takes on average 500ms and up to 1 s, both of which are noticeable to the user. Besides this condition, the rationale behind recognizing more elementary shapes is elusive as some shapes (helixes, waves, spirals, etc.) are never used in modeling languages, specifically in Model-Based System Engineering (MBSE)

In BabyMOD, we took the opposite stance by choosing to recognize only a few primitive shapes (lines, circles, and ellipses) and to use plan recognition to identify model elements as any combination of these primitive shapes. The three primitive shapes are indeed sufficient in MBSE to recognize most modeling elements drawn in the most common modeling languages and to reduce the number of primitive shapes that need to be recognized to speed up the recognition process. In our tests, recognizing complex shapes (e.g., an operational actor made of four straight lines and one circle) fell under 100 ms, which is barely noticeable to the user.

Google AutoDraw is a graphical tool to sketch doodles and clip arts. The recognition process relies on the implementation of *Quick, Draws!*, an online pictionary-like game where players competed against an AI to make the AI guess drawings. *Quick, Draws!* made it possible to build a large dataset of doodles and clip arts that is used to train the Recurrent Neural network (RNN) in Google AutoDraw. The recognition is fast and accurate, and incremental recognition is also possible. However, Google

AutoDraw is mostly an online experiment and has no goal to be used as an API to build other tools (such as modeling tools) from it.

FlexiSketch (Wüest et al., 2012) is a diagram modeling tool available on Android platforms. Using FlexiSketch, a user can sketch model elements and later promote them as types that can be easily re-used. Once a graphical sketch has been associated with a model element, similar sketches are automatically recognized. This allows for adapting FlexiSketch to new graph-based modeling languages.

The FlexiSketch's recognizer relies on an adapted version of a Levenshtein string-distance algorithm. The recognition is relatively fast and accurate. FlexiSketch does not support text recognition, and textual properties of model elements are only set using the Android virtual keyboard.

We note that among the four solutions, MyScript Diagram and OctoUML are able to recognize multiple elements at the same time, and, therefore, could be used to recognize complete models at once (Req. 3). However, OctoUML suffers from severe restrictions in the sense that it will recognize separate elements each time a finger is lifted from the surface of the screen, limiting the complexity of the created shapes to one-line drawings only.

Finally, none of the aforementioned solutions provide explainable outputs. Google AutoDraw and FlexiSketch provide alternative suggestions, and MyScript Diagram can provide word suggestions during text recognition. But none of them can explain why an element has been recognized in the first place. In our approach, the output of the recognizer is completely explainable. The user is informed of which part of a modeling language (the primitive shapes composing the modeling elements) is being recognized, and what remains to be drawn using visual feedback.

22.2.2 Artificial Intelligence

One trend to recognize modeling elements is to rely on AI tools and algorithms, more specifically, on Machine Learning (ML) techniques based on ANN. This family of approaches typically involves two phases. During the training phase, algorithms are trained to recognize elements based on pre-existing libraries. During the recognition phase, they can identify elements with a certain degree of confidence.

While broadly used for recognizing medical images, this technique is inappropriate for system engineering for two reasons. First, the similarity between graphical symbols representing model elements in standard modeling languages (Moody, 2010) (e.g., UML OMG, 2017) can yield an important error by the ANN response or require a too-expensive training phase; and, second, the lack of explainability of the ML solution (Rudin, 2019) is another hindrance for large scale applications.

AI automated planning (Ghallab et al., 2004) has been used to perform activity recognition in the context of a system managed by the human operators whose currently pursued operational goal has to be determined (Hollnagel, 1988). Several plan recognition (Kautz and Allen, 1986) fields of application have surfaced, including "operator modeling", to improve the efficiency of man-machine systems. Early applications of the approach failed because of the complexity of plans, the issues due to evaluating actions that did not fit any plan, or the issues from interleaving planning and execution. Moreover, the work in plan recognition has historically proceeded independently from the planning community, using handcrafted libraries rather than planners (Avrahami-Zilberbrand et al., 2005). In the following section, we describe our adaptation of AI planning to recognize sketches of model elements.

22.3   Plan Recognition Approach

To quicken the development of models of systems engineering, we have implemented a web-based modeling environment (see Fig. 22.1) that easily captures functional models of systems on large interactive screens. We investigated two alternative approaches based on machine learning and symbolic AI, respectively. The first approach consists in training an ANN to define a library of model elements that our tool could recognize based on user inputs. While the approach worked for a few sets of model elements, the number of errors increased proportionally with the number of model elements that had to be recognized because of the similarity between different graphical symbols. Besides, since the ANN provided no means to interpret the result, the user was often clueless when attempting to understand why a shape had not been correctly identified.

These observations led us to investigate an approach based on AI automated planning and, more specifically on plan recognition to identify complex sketches

Fig. 22.1 Overview of our modeling environment, where two users collaborate on a whiteboard equipped with the sketching tool

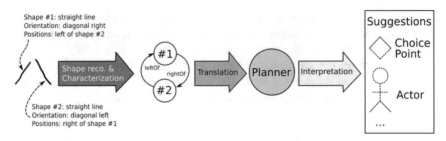

Fig. 22.2 A three-step approach for AI plan recognition is illustrated on an example. During the *shape recognition & characterization step*, two primitive shapes, #1 and #2, are recognized as straight lines. #1 is characterized by its orientation (diagonal right) and its relative position (left of) to #2. #2 is characterized by its orientation (diagonal left) and its relative position (right of) to #1. The resulting graph is then translated into a PDDL and is the input of the planner. The planner then identifies and orders the most probable sketches to be drawn

representing model elements that guide the users in the completion of the model. Automated AI planning (Ghallab et al., 2004) is a model-based approach for the task of selecting and organizing actions in a sequence called a *plan*, with the aim of fulfilling high-level objectives called *goals*. Here the task is to identify the shapes yet to be drawn, and their placement to create a meaningful system-engineering sketch from an initial shape. For our sketching tool (see Fig. 22.1), we adopt a planning-based approach for goal recognition that uses the planning framework to perform the converse task of automated planning (Ramírez and Geffner, 2009), i.e., recognizing the most probable goal given an initial state and a plan. We use a *goal library* to describe the possible solutions of a plan, given a model of the domain that a hypothetical drawing-agent would evolve.

We thus call repeatedly the planner on the current state, in order to obtain a plan for every final model element in the goal library, starting from the current state of the system (representing the sketch currently on the board).

Using plan recognition to characterize how far a drawn set of simple shapes is from a complete sketch of a model element used in system-engineering design gives us the ability to provide users with an interpretation of the planner's results. In other words, the plan is directly interpretable as the sequence of actions to be done with our sketching tool (or one of the possible sequences of actions) in order to obtain a complete model element. The most probable complete models assumed by the planner are also shown to the user as suggestions.

This approach assumes the planner being a rational agent, for which, under the principle of rational action, it is assumed to be returning the optimal or at least sub-optimal path to goal (Masters and Sardina, 2017). So, instead of relying on a plan library (Carberry, 2001), which would store a huge set of plans generated off-line to match them with the shapes drawn by the user, we use a planner to generate new plans on-the-fly that helps us to evaluate which ones of the goals the user has set out to achieve.

Table 22.2 Some graphical symbols used in MBSE languages. The minimal functionally complete set $S=(ellipse, straight\_line)$ is self-sufficient for describing the different graphical symbols

(a) Capella operational actor	(b) ArchiMate actor and role	(c) UML three-compartment class
(d) UML lifeline	(e) SysML state	(f) UML exit pseudo state
(g) Requirement in arKItect Systems Engineering Advanced (SEA)	(h) Enhanced Function Flow Block Diagram (EFFBD) Control construct	

22.3.1 Approach Overview

Figure 22.2 gives an overview of our recognition process. It involves three automatic phases: *primitive shape characterization and positioning*; *translation*, and *recognition/interpretation*. The entry point of the process is a sketch (or a fragment of one) manually drawn by human users on a digital whiteboard. This sketch will constitute the drawing of a model element to be recognized by the process.

During the first step, the process extracts primitive shapes out of the sketch using traditional shape recognition algorithms. Our algorithms recognizess ellipses and polylines. A polyline consists of a series of connected straight line segments. When a polyline is recognized, it is not characterized as a whole, but instead, each segment composing it is characterized individually and independently of the others.

To facilitate the characterization and planning phases, we chose to restrict the set of primitive shapes to recognize to $S = (ellipse, straight\_line)$. Besides speeding up the geometrical shape recognition algorithm by only recognizing these two primitive shapes, it can be considered for the most common modeling languages used in MBSE as a *minimal functionally complete set* (by analogy with mathematical logic). For example, a three-compartment rectangle used to represent a UML class (see Table 22.2) can be strictly reduced to six inter-connected straight lines. A circle is an ellipse where the two foci are on the same spot (the center).

Once primitive shapes are recognized, every shape (being an ellipse or a straight line) is characterized by its distinctive features and its position with respect to all of the other shapes composing the same sketch. Straight lines are characterized by their four possible orientations $D = (horizontal, vertical, diagonal\_left, diagonal\_right)$. Ellipses are tagged as being circles or not. For example, in Fig. 22.2, Shape #1 is characterized as being a *straight line*, located *at the left side of* Shape #2, another straight line. To compute straight line orientations, the raw angle between the two end points of a line is 'smoothed' to its closest remarkable $\frac{i\pi}{4}$-angle. Finer-grain fractions can be chosen for smoothing angles, but they would be less tolerant to drawing imperfections. For example, to sketch an operational actor, left and right legs could be characterized as 45° or 60° straight lines depending on the user's talent for drawing.

After the recognition process, we compute the positioning of every primitive shape relatively to the other shapes composing the same sketch. In our approach, the notion of a *sketch* is not restricted. It consists of a set of inter-connected primitive shapes being part of the same model element or multiple inter-connected ones (cf. Req. 3). Currently, our algorithm is only able to recognize single elements separately, like other similar approaches used for sketch and shape recognition. Recognizing complete diagrams at once is currently a work-in-progress.

Five possible relations $s_1 \longrightarrow (s_2, \ldots, s_n)$ of positions are defined: *above_of*, *below_of*, *left_of*, *right_of*, and *intersect_with*. The relations *above_of* and *below_of* (respectively, *left_of* and *right_of*) are bijective relations such that

$$\forall s_1, s_2 | s_2 \in left\_of(s_1) \iff s_1 \in right\_of(s_2).$$

The relation *intersect_with* is also bijective. It occurs when two primitive shapes are intersecting at the center:

$$\forall s_1, s_2 | s_2 \in intersect\_with(s_1) \iff s_1 \in intersect\_with(s_2).$$

Finally, all relations are also transitive, e.g.,

$$\forall s_1, s_2, s_3 | s_1 \in left\_of(s_2) \wedge s_2 \in left\_of(s_3) \implies s_1 \in left\_of(s_3).$$

The output of the first step is a directed graph $G = (V, E, l_v, l_e)$ where the set of vertices V corresponds to the set of primitive shapes composing a sketch, and the set of edges E corresponds to the relative positioning relations between the vertices (see Fig. 22.3). We apply two labeling functions. The vertex labeling function, $l_v : V \longrightarrow \mathbb{L}^2$, decorates each vertex with a label denoting the nature (ellipse or straight line) and the distinctive feature (*orientation* for straight lines, *nature* for circles or not for ellipses) of the primitive shape corresponding to the vertex. The edge labeling function, $l_e : E \longrightarrow \mathbb{L}$, decorates each edge with the corresponding relative positioning relation that binds each pair of primitive shapes.

The resulting graph G is then translated during the second step into a PDDL file (McDermott et al., 1998). The PDDL formalism is a standardization attempt to describe AI planning problems and is now used by several components-off-the-shelf AI planners (Ghallab et al., 2004; Edelkamp and Hoffmann, 2004). Section 22.4 further describes the formalism and the translation process. Along with the AI formalization of the drawing problem and the description of the initial sketch, the planner is provided as well with the list of all the model elements deemed possible. This list

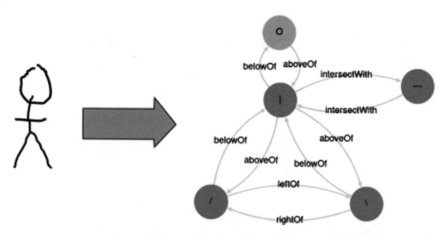

Fig. 22.3 An actor being drawn (left side) and the resulting graph G (right side). Each edge is a relation between two primitive shapes connected at their end points or intersection. The orange node represents the head of the actor. Pink nodes are straight lines whose orientations are indicated by the node labels. Transitive relations are not represented as well as the $leftOf$ and $rightOf$ relations between the body and the legs

constitutes the *goal library*, i.e., the set of the possible goals that our framework will consider when doing plan recognition.

The last step consists in running the planner for the sketch being drawn by the user. To do it, we used the Fast Downward planning system (Helmert, 2006). The planner takes as an input the PDDL file automatically obtained during the previous step and outputs an ordered list of possible matches between the sketch being drawn by the user and the goals denoting the different model elements that could be recognized. The set of possible matches is ordered based on the degree of confidence of the match regarding the element currently drawn. The degree depends on the *distance* (in the plan) between the current sketch and the possible goal, i.e., the number of steps that would remain to finish drawing the element completely.

22.3.2 Tolerance to Drawing Imperfections

One drawback of AI automated planning compared to ML techniques is that it is less robust to drawing imperfections (cf. Req. 8). In fact, a planning model considers the single shapes or polylines as a unique entity. Thus, for example, a line is either intersecting another one or it is not. Let us consider an example where a human user is drawing a Capella operational actor (see Fig. 22.4). An incorrect drawing can result in misleadingly interpreting the user intention and lead to an incorrect graph G from which it would be impossible to reach the correct objective in a plan.

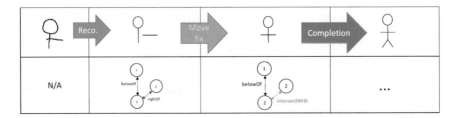

Fig. 22.4 An actor being drawn where the arms are incorrectly interpreted at the right side of the body of the actor. Actions defined in PDDL support quick fixes to remove, replace, or move a primitive shape in the sketch being recognized

To address Req. 8, we defined actions in our plan to support quick fixes. A *remove* action consists in removing from a graph G a node and the edges that connect that node to other nodes of the graph. A *remove* action is interpreted as the primitive shape (represented by that node) has been incorrectly drawn and should not be considered as part of the sketch. Besides, the planning representation of the sketching framework includes actions for moving the primitive shapes, or adding new ones to the sketch.

Update actions consist in modifying a node or an edge of a graph G. An example of a node update action is changing an eclipse into a circle, or changing a straight line's orientation (*change-shape*). As for example, in Fig. 22.4, an update action can be used in order to fix the position of the actor's arm to set its position at the intersection with the actor's body. Performing this action is necessary to further complete the sketch with the missing elements.

22.4 Implementation

The planning paradigm is used here, as we have just seen, to obtain sequences of elementary actions needed to obtain a model element. In the following, we will see the formal basis of automated planning in AI, the paradigm used here to model the set of the user's objectives, and the way users have to draw them. Then, we describe how our peculiar planning problem is translated into PDDL, the language used to describe automated planning tasks.

22.4.1 Automated Deterministic Planning

A planning task is defined by a model's description provided by a language; solving an automated planning task requires a description of the system, whose states are considered by the planning agent. This system, modeled as the environment in a planning task, has to be driven by means of *actions* from an initial situation to a desired goal, or a final situation.

The paradigm of (deterministic) planning we use has to be cast in a representation based on states and on transitions between them, i.e., a directed graph whose nodes represent states, and whose edges represent actions. But, usually, a factored representations is used, following the STRIPS formalism (Fikes and Nilsson, 1971). A factored representation represents states via a set of variables, interpreted as a conjunction, and such that each state s is a complete assignment of the state variables. In particular, the actions encoding the transitions between states are expressed in terms of preconditions and post-conditions. Action preconditions specify the conditions under which an action can be applied. The post-conditions specify the changes to variable assignments made by the effects of the applied actions. All other variable assignments are left unchanged by the action; we often refer to that rule as a solution to the *frame problem* (McCarthy, 1986).

A planning problem is then defined as a 4–tuple $\langle \mathcal{F}, \mathcal{A}, \mathcal{I}, \mathcal{G} \rangle$, consisting of

- $[\mathcal{F}]$ a set of Boolean variables[2];
- $[\mathcal{A}]$ a set of operators, where each action a is a pair of preconditions and post–conditions: $\langle \, \text{pre}(a), \text{add}(a), \text{del}(a) \, \rangle$, with $\text{pre}(a)$ the set of preconditions of a and $\text{add}(a)$ and $\text{del}(a)$ the set of effects, respectively, defining the set of propositions added and deleted from the state. An action a is applicable in state s iff $\text{pre}(a) \subseteq s$ and the application of a in s is defined by the transition function $T(s, a) = (s/\text{del}(a)) \cup \text{add}(a)$;
- $[\mathcal{I}]$ a set of variables $\mathcal{I} \subseteq \mathcal{F}$, describing the initial state; and,
- $[\mathcal{G}]$ a set of variables $\mathcal{G} \subseteq \mathcal{F}$, describing the goal state(s).

To the planning model described above, we add a particular kind of action called an axiom (Thiébaux et al., 2005). These axioms are applied like actions to a state, but they do not contribute to the evaluation of the distance between the current state and a goal. Instead, they are used to model collateral effects of applying an action.

To evaluate a plan, π, given by a sequence of actions, its length $|\pi|$ is commonly considered as a preference criterion, and it corresponds to the number of actions in the plan. The axioms are not added to evaluate the length $|\pi|$.

22.4.2   Modeling Sketches

Sketching is represented as a planning problem as defined in Sect. 22.4.1. In order to feed our planner, we model all of the actions that users can perform. In the PDDL representation, the coding of the variables (stated as first-order logic predicates) is rather simple, and follows the relations given in Sect. 22.3.1.

---

[2] Note that factored representations can use multivalued variables, but variables usually assume Boolean values, which can be done without a loss of generality.

In the domain definition, we will have predicates that accept variables of two different types: polylines (primitive graphical symbols) and shapes (ellipse or straight line)—see Listing 22.1.

```
(define (domain BOARD)
(:requirements :strips :typing :equality
 :derived-predicates)
(:types polyline shape)
(:predicates (leftOf ?x ?y - polyline)
             (rightOf ?x ?y - polyline)
             (aboveOf ?x ?y - polyline)
             (belowOf ?x ?y - polyline)
             (onboard ?x - polyline)
             (boardempty)
             (intersectWith ?x ?y - polyline)
             (hasShape ?x - polyline ?z - shape) )
```

Listing 22.1 PDDL domain definition: requirements and predicates.

The actions represent the movements or other transformation actions of the primitive graphical symbols in the sketch. These actions are then *change-shape, move-left, move-right, move-above, move-below, move-upon, add, add-above, add-below, ..., remove-left, remove-right*, etc. Every action also implements the collateral effects on the shape that are a consequence of the action. For instance, if the polyline *A* is added below *B*, then *B* will also be above *A*, and all of the polylines left and right of *B* will be above *A* (Listing 22.2).

We wrote above that we are making use of axioms to encode additional collateral effects of the actions (Listing 22.3). Such axioms are applied until at a fixpoint between actions along the plan. They could be seen as syntactic sugar, if it was not for the fact that if they were lost in a compilation (as conditional effects of the "regular" actions for instance), it would be impossible to restrict the growth of plans and domain descriptions to polynomial size (Thiébaux et al., 2005).

The PDDL encoding of the initial and goal states is straightforward and uses as an initial state of the sketch as it is drawn by the users. The goals are the ones specified as possible model elements. The planner is called to solve this planning problem and produces a plan, which is a sequence of actions (axioms are not represented) that, if executed, could, from the current sketch, generate a model element as a goal. Actually, the planner is called on repeatedly to meet the different goals, with the objective of evaluating which is closest to the current sketch. The goals are then sorted by the length of the plan needed to reach them. The shorter the plan, the more likely is the goal to be the one aimed for by the users. These runs have been performed using the Fast Downward planning system (Helmert, 2006), which supports axioms with the additive heuristic.

```
(:action add-below
    :parameters (?x ?y - polyline ?s - shape)
    :precondition (and (not (= ?x ?y)) (not (onboard
?x)) )
    :effect
        (and (aboveOf ?y ?x) (hasShape ?x ?s)
             (belowOf ?x ?y) (not (boardempty))
        (forall (?b - polyline)
           (and
           (when (aboveOf ?b ?y)
             (and (belowOf ?x ?b) (aboveOf ?b ?x)))
           (when (leftOf ?b ?y)
             (and (belowOf ?x ?b) (aboveOf ?b ?x)))
           (when (rightOf ?b ?y)
             (and (belowOf ?x ?b) (aboveOf ?b ?x)))
)) ))
```

Listing 22.2 A PDDL example of adding a new polyline below an existing one. Here effects make use of conditions encoded with "when": Conditions are like preconditions, but if they do not hold in a state, the actions are still executed, but the conditional effect that does not hold will simply not be applied in the state.

```
(:derived (onboard ?x)
    (exists (?y)
        (or
           (leftOf ?x ?y)
           (rightOf ?x ?y)
           (aboveOf ?x ?y)
           (belowOf ?x ?y)
           (intersectWith ?x ?y) )))
```

Listing 22.3 A PDDL example of an axiom that encodes the presence in the sketch (onboard) of a polyline "?x".

22.5 Experiment

We evaluated the feasibility of the approach from the point of view of the planner performances on a benchmark suite representing some models analyzed in this paper. All planning problems are automatically generated from the BabyMOD interface (cf. Fig. 22.1). Each problem has an initial state made of few hand-drawn shapes and a goal corresponding to some engineering models like the ones illustrated in Fig. 22.2. For each problem, we ran the Fast Downward planning system on a Lubuntu machine mounting an Intel[R] Core[TM] i5-8250U CPU @ 1.60 GHz 64 bits and 8 GB RAM.

Table 22.3 shows the results of these tests. Each row describes a problem, its complexity (*task size*), the length of the calculated plan $|\pi|$, and the time needed to compute a solution. For reading purpose only, we named each problem as the concatenation of its initial state and its goal. For example, the problem named *two-diagonal-lines_actor* corresponds to the example shown in Fig. 22.2, where the initial

Table 22.3 Performances of Fast Downward on our benchmark suite. **task size** is a measure of the complexity of the benchmark, given by the number of elements the planner manipulates and crudely corresponds to the number of variables times the number of operators (axioms included); $|\pi|$ indicates the number of actions in the plan (axioms excluded); **search** and **total time** measure the performances of the planner in seconds

Problem	Task size	$|\pi|$	Search time	Total time
circle_actor	26015	9	0.01	0.03
circle-and-two-lines_actor	25763	6	0.01	0.03
circle_exitPseudoState	4936	7	0.00	0.01
circle-above-of-vertical-line_actor	25889	7	0.01	0.03
diagonal-left-line_actor	25977	8	0.01	0.03
diagonal-left-line_choicePoint	12733	12	0.03	0.04
diagonal-left-line_exitPseudoState	4914	6	0.00	0.01
diagonal-right-line_actor	25977	11	9.27	9.29
diagonal-right-line_choicePoint	12733	12	0.03	0.04
diagonal-right-line_exitPseudoState	4914	6	0.00	0.01
horizontal-line_actor	25977	7	0.01	0.03
horizontal-line_function	12737	17	2.09	2.10
horizontal-line_lifeLine	26018	19	1.50	1.52
two-diagonal-lines_actor	26035	8	0.01	0.04
vertical-line_actor	25977	8	0.01	0.03
vertical-line_function	12737	16	0.94	0.95
vertical-line_lifeLine	26018	19	2.69	2.71

state consists of two diagonal lines, and the desired goal is the complete sketch of a Capella operational actor. The problem named *circle-and-two-lines_actor* represents the problem seen in Fig. 22.3, i.e., the same actor, but with one imperfection.

Some observations can be raised from the reading of Table 22.3. First, the time needed to compute a path for most of the problems (apart from some exceptions described hereafter) is below 5ms overall. For the planning community, it may appear too small at first glance, but this can be explained by the fact that the benchmarks used in the context of systems engineering model recognition are rather simple compared to the ones traditionally used by the planning community for the Planning Competitions.[3] It is worth noting that, in the context of model recognition, we need to run Fast Downward multiple times to attempt to find the best model element that matches a partial draw, based on the calculated paths. However, the number of model elements conventionally manipulated at the same time (i.e., in a defined modeling

---

[3] For the deterministic track, see https://ipc2018-classical.bitbucket.io/.

viewpoint) does not usually exceed a dozen or so model elements. Therefore, the time needed by our recognition algorithm remains below 100ms, which is effectively imperceptible to a human, hence validating our performance requirement (Req. 6).

Second, we can observe some large variations of time for some benchmarks. For *diagonal-right-line_actor*, *horizontal-line_function*, and *vertical-line_lifeLine*, fast downward solved the instances in more than one second. Here, the size of the problem does not affect the solution time in a notable way, and the pre-processing time (given by the overhead of the total time versus the search time) does not exceed 20 ms. The plan search is heavy since the board is initially (almost) empty, thus, the planner has to search through a huge part of the state space to reach the goal. In *diagonal-right-line_actor* for example, the goal is made by several line segments that must be added below a circle. Besides, the different axioms needed to reach the goal are supported by the planner, but not by the heuristic, that might be a very ineffective way to handle axioms.

It is worth noting that *diagonal-right-line_actor* and *two-diagonal-lines_actor* are very similar, yet, the computing time is notably different. One may question the relevance of attempting to recognize an actor from one segment only, since it is more traditional to start drawing an actor either from its head or from its legs both together. However, this would require to conduct a proper user experiment to classify the drawing habits of systems architects, which is out of the scope of this experiment.

As a conclusion, the benchmark suite inspired by systems engineering models shows that our planning approach is suitable for recognizing model elements and therefore can be embedded in a CAD tool. Plan recognition can provide systems architects with a guidance in the form of possible goal sketches, and an explanation of why the proposed sketches are the ones suggested. While most of the benchmarks show that the recognition is fast enough to be imperceptible to the users, some others, however, are not conclusive as the amount of time needed to recognize model elements was not negligible. This constitutes a threat to the validity for our approach and leaves room for improving both our recognition algorithm and the planning architecture.

22.6 Conclusion

In this chapter, we have proposed an approach to automatically translating informal sketches into model elements using a formal notation. We have decomposed our approach into two main components. First, simple algorithms are used to detect elementary shapes (ellipses, circles, lines) from a sketch drawn by human users; second, plan recognition techniques are used to recognize model elements based on preset libraries of goals. Compared to existing techniques based on ML only, this approach increases the explainability and interpretability of the results by end users.

One major objective of this work is to provide explainable results to the users, which is a central property in human-agent systems (Rosenfeld and Richardson, 2019). In fact, the order of the selection for the choices has to be motivated by a better usage of the tool. Even the simple reason behind proposing a specific choice to users is widely accepted as necessary in order for the human users to understand and to better interact with the tool. Splitting the approach in two—on one side, the shape recognition, and on the other side, the symbolic planning application—permits us to provide users with the knowledge of a system through the elicitation, for a specific goal, of the causal structure behind the performed task. The human decision is then supported by the interpretability of the algorithmic results. In fact, ML approaches and, in particular, the results provided by neural network-based algorithms are well known to be poorly understood. This is a large barrier to the adoption of machine learning on applications involving interactions with human users. This uncertainty comes from the black box implementation of neural networks, which do not provide information on their inner "reasoning" process. Even if there is actually a lot of effort to "open" the black box implementation, other fields of AI provide better explainability of the solution gathering process. This is the case with automated planning that the approach offered here provides the symbolic representation and the structure needed to understand the ML output.

We have presented a preliminary implementation, integrated now in our existing web-based modeling environment for systems engineering. Compared to our previous handmade implementation, this new implementation relies on the PDDL formalism and on an off-the-shelf deterministic planner to synthesize possible plans that users can follow to draw a model element. Our approach is tolerant to drawing imperfections. To achieve that, we implemented specific actions in our plan in order to support the modification of a sketch prior to recognizing the expected model element.

Different challenges still need to be addressed. First, the optimization of our planning modeling process can be improved to reduce computation time, and to improve reusability. Our current implementation is only able to recognize model elements individually. Recognizing a diagram as a whole is more challenging. We are currently working toward that goal. Recognizing text and shapes in a simultaneous way is a second challenge we will attempt to address. A solution is to recognize specific patterns to distinguish text from geometrical shapes and apply the correct recognition algorithm to each. ML combined with plan recognition can be a solution to that challenge.

References

Alblawi, A., Nawab, M., and Alsayyari, A. (2019). A system engineering approach in orienting traditional engineering towards modern engineering. In *2019 IEEE Global Engineering Education Conference (EDUCON)*, pages 1559–1567. IEEE.

Avrahami-Zilberbrand, D., Kaminka, G., & Zarosim, H. (2005). *Fast and complete symbolic plan recognition: Allowing for duration, interleaved execution, and lossy observations*. MOO: In Proceedings of the AAAI workshop on modeling others from observations.

Botre, R., & Sandbhor, S. (2013). Using interactive workspaces for construction data utilization and coordination. *International Journal of Construction Engineering and Management, 2*(3), 62–69.

Carberry, S. (2001). Techniques for plan recognition. *User Modeling and User-Adapted Interaction, 11*(1), 31–48.

Edelkamp, S. and Hoffmann, J. (2004). Pddl2. 2: The language for the classical part of the 4th international planning competition. Technical report, Technical Report 195, University of Freiburg.

Fikes, R. E., & Nilsson, N. J. (1971). Strips: a new approach to the application of theorem proving to problem solving. *Artificial intelligence, 2*(3–4), 189–208.

Ghallab, M., Nau, D., & Traverso, P. (2004). *Automated Planning: theory and practice*. Elsevier.

Helmert, M. (2006). The fast downward planning system. *Journal of Artificial Intelligence Research, 26*, 191–246.

Hili, N., & Farail, P. (2020). BabyMOD, a Collaborative Model Editor for Mastering Model Complexity in MBSE. *International Workshop on Model-Based Space Systems and Software Engineering*, 1–4.

Hollnagel, E. (1988). Plan recognition in modelling of users. *Reliability Engineering & System Safety, 22*(1–4), 129–136.

Jolak, R., Vesin, B., Isaksson, M., and Chaudron, M. R. (2016). Towards a new generation of software design environments: Supporting the use of informal and formal notations with octouml. In *HuFaMo@ MoDELS* (pp. 3–10).

Kautz, H. A. & Allen, J. F. (1986). Generalized plan recognition. In *AAAI* (vol. 86, p. 5).

Masters, P., & Sardina, S. (2017). Cost-based goal recognition for path-planning. In *Proceedings of the 16th conference on autonomous agents and multiagent systems (AAMAS)* (pp. 750–758).

McCarthy, J. (1986). Applications of circumscription to formalizing common-sense knowledge. *Artificial Intelligence, 28*(1), 89–116.

McDermott, D., Ghallab, M., Howe, A., Knoblock, C., Ram, A., Veloso, M. et al. (1998). PDDL-the planning domain definition language.

Moody, D. L. (2010). The "Physics" of notations: A scientific approach to designing visual notations in software engineering. In *2010 ACM/IEEE 32nd international conference on software engineering* (vol. 2, pp. 485–486). IEEE.

MyScript (2020). Myscript home page. https://www.myscript.com/. Retrieved 2020-01-15.

OMG (2017). Unified Modeling Language Specification version 2.5.1. https://www.omg.org/spec/UML/2.5.1/PDF. Retrieved 2020-02-19.

Paulson, B., & Hammond, T. (2008). PaleoSketch: Accurate primitive sketch recognition and beautification. In *Proceedings of the 13th international conference on Intelligent user interfaces* (pp. 1–10).

Ramírez, M., & Geffner, H. (2009). Plan recognition as planning. *Twenty-First international joint conference on artificial intelligence*.

Robertson, B., & Radcliffe, D. (2009). Impact of CAD tools on creative problem solving in engineering design. *Computer-Aided Design, 41*(3), 136–146.

Rosenfeld, A., & Richardson, A. (2019). Explainability in human-agent systems. *Autonomous Agents and Multi-Agent Systems*

Rudin, C. (2019). Stop explaining black box machine learning models for high stakes decisions and use interpretable models instead. *Nature Machine Intelligence, 1*(5), 206.

Thiébaux, S., Hoffmann, J., & Nebel, B. (2005). In defense of pddl axioms. *Artificial Intelligence, 168*(1–2), 38–69.

Vesin, B., Jolak, R., & Chaudron, M. R. (2017). Octouml: An environment for exploratory and collaborative software design. In *2017 IEEE/ACM 39th international conference on software engineering companion (ICSE-C)* (pp. 7–10). IEEE.

Wüest, D., Seyff, N., & Glinz, M. (2012). Flexisketch: A mobile sketching tool for software modeling. In *International conference on mobile computing, applications, and services* (pp. 225–244). Springer.

Chapter 23
An Analogy of Sentence Mood and Use

Ryan Phillip Quandt

Abstract Interpreting the force of an utterance, be it an assertion, command, or question, remains a task for achieving joint action in artificial intelligence. It is not an easy task. An interpretation of force depends on a speaker's use of words for a hearer at the moment of utterance. As a result, grammatical mood is less than certain at indicating force. Navigating the break between sentence use and mood reveals how people get things done with language—that is, the fact meaning comes from the act of uttering. The main goal of this chapter is to motivate research into the relation between mood and use. Past theories, I argue, underestimate the evasiveness of force in interpretations (formal or otherwise). Making their relation explicit and precise expands the use of argumentation schemes in language processing and joint action. Building from prior work, I propose a model for conceiving the mood/force relation and offer questions for future research.

23.1 Helpful Misalignment

Over the last decade,[1] the Air Force Research Laboratory designed the Automatic Ground Collision Avoidance System (Auto-GCAS) and plans to use the software in the new F-35s.[2] When the jet's predicted trajectory is fatal, the system prompts the pilot to change course. If the pilot is unresponsive, the system takes control, 'roll[s] the aircraft upright and initiates a 5-G pull, diverting the plane and pilot out of harm's

---

[1] For more information, including their decision to use the technology, see https://www.f35.com/news/detail/f-35-to-incorporate-automatic-ground-collision-avoidance-system.

[2] I owe Bill Lawless more than my thanks. Besides his warmth, encouragement, and invitation to contribute, he patiently read through this manuscript offering many helpful and detailed suggestions. Any remaining flaws are my own. John Licato also deserves gratitude. His Advancing Machine and Human Reasoning lab embodies Leibniz's motto, *Theoria cum praxi*. This chapter emerged from discussions with him and the YIP team.

R. P. Quandt (✉)
Claremont Graduate University, 150 E 10th St, Claremont, CA 91711, USA
e-mail: ryan.quandt@cgu.edu

© Springer Nature Switzerland AG 2021
W. F. Lawless et al. (eds.), *Systems Engineering and Artificial Intelligence*,
https://doi.org/10.1007/978-3-030-77283-3_23

471

way.' Once the trajectory is safe, Auto-GCAS returns flight controls to the pilot. Since 2014, seven pilots credit their lives to the system. Benefits are clear: not only does the jet stabilize itself, but it also addresses a threat without an external command. The program 'assumes temporary control' to do so. Recent studies examine pilots' behavior with (Richardson et al., 2019), and knowledge (Sadler et al., 2019) and trust of (Lyons and Guznov, 2019), the highly automatic system; this research concerns the system's effects on pilots from a model of human-machine interaction. Such a model anticipates more than describes. Auto-GCAS is a fail-safe. Pilot and jet are not (yet) acting jointly. In this chapter, I address joint action.

Automatic systems must decide and act to interpret a command due to informal, open-textured predicates (IOPs) (Hart, 1961). Such predicates over- or under-shoot intended acts or objects (Licato and Marji, 2018). There is no neat rule for what is in or out, and so a judgment must be made on whether the predicate was satisfied. For this reason, interpretations of IOPs have moral criteria for success and appraisal,[3] and so differ from a calculation based on probability. Interpretation assumes a degree of autonomy and responsibility because the interpretation is a decision and/or act. As Auto-GCAS advances past a fail-safe to joint action, the system must tailor commands to settings exceeding a pilot's manual control. Even if pilots authorize an operation or can abort it, they control the aircraft less. Automated systems curtail their control by executing a command with a measure of autonomy.

Misaligning sentence mood and use is one way of dealing with IOPs. By misaligning, I localize the gap between intention and expression thereby casting systems and tools for handling open-texture within select contexts. Of course, much is done with words. Linguistic protocols streamline action. Auto-GCAS prompts the pilot, a nascent protocol of the sort, and more protocols will likely be adopted as the system's scope expands, yet protocols cannot erase IOPs. Take, for example, the sentence, 'Merge into the left lane when there is a vehicle on the shoulder.' If there is a nearby car, one speeding from behind, an emergency vehicle on the opposite shoulder, an ending lane, et cetera, the command differs in meaning, or the action required. Attending to the relation between mood and force brings out the contextual dependence of language and action. At issue is how an automatic system interprets a command through action as well as how to evaluate their act. There is inevitable tailoring to setting (and should be). Dialogical models are popular for enhancing human-machine interaction in other ways (Walton et al., 2008; MacCormick and Summers, 1991; Sartor et al., 2014; Summers, 2006; Walton et al., 2016) and I will use them here. The misalignment between sentence mood and use allows us to program interpretation via action, test it, and define criteria for its success.

We can make our target phenomenon more precise. Imagine a system that fact-finds every indicative sentence, responds to every imperative with an act, and puts out information for every interrogative.[4] Syntax prompts one response rather than another. If we input 'A vixen is a female fox,' the system prints 'True.' Inputting

---

[3] Moral in the sense of evoking a purposive context in which blame and praise are given.

[4] Our worries are how syntax relates to use, especially how utterances are more than their syntax, not exhaustiveness or scope.

'Pick up the cup' results in the act. And 'Red' answers 'What color is the cup.' And let us assume that the system handles the thorny issue of relevance. What happens with the following? 'The vixen needs some water.' 'Pick a cup for coffee.' 'Can you pick up the cup.' The system is programmed to match indicatives with assertions, imperatives with commands, and interrogatives with questions, but the syntax does not settle the force of utterances. Apart from context, it is unclear how the system should process the above. Someone may say, "The vixen needs some water," to prompt someone to get water or tell them where the water bowl is. The statement may describe or direct. A host may offer coffee with 'Pick a cup for coffee.' And a person may direct someone to pick up a cup with an apparent question. A tight knit between syntax and use abridges how people usually speak. That is well-known. Too close a tie between syntax and force obscures the meaning of these sentences, and so open-texture results from meaningful utterance inextricably. Let us stress: without identifying what the sentence calls for, we cannot give its meaning (Searle and Vanderveken, 1985, Chap. 1; Green, 2000, pgs. 435–436; Davidson, 2001, pg. 114). The utterance is a sort of act—an assertion, command, or question. Not only does the imagined system have little scope in the ebbs and flows of natural language, but it also fails to access meaning. And so the system cannot act (jointly). On the one hand, this is because a speaker's intent inflects meaning. So recognizing intent enables the system to interpret a command via action with reliability. But, on the other hand, the system must recognize the sort of act uttering is (command qua command) to be obliged to act or not. Machine learning models miss the problem if force and mood are left undefined. Our question then: how does syntax relate to use?

Mood and force misaligned present obstacles to formalizing joint action. It exposes the autonomy of linguistic meaning,[5] which in turn tells us how humans act together. We may be tempted to take the break between mood and force as abnormal or parasitic, safely ignored. When speakers speak properly, the story goes, mood and force have regular, normal pairings. And, if so, all we need is a catalog of right use (a complex one, no doubt). Speakers by and large use indicatives to assert, imperatives to command, and interrogatives to ask. But their mismatch is abundant and often. In jokes, fiction, greetings, idioms, and play, speakers break the bond between mood and force. These everyday uses show that the supposed bond appeals to an imprecise intuition, one that explains little (Davidson, 2001, pgs. 111–113). At issue are the basics: meaning and action (Searle and Vanderveken, 1985; Davidson, 1980). Still, our intuition of their bond is telling, and programmers successfully work on the link between the sentences speakers use and how they use them.[6] This convergence is a benefit of approaching action through language—symbols are already part of the exchange. We can pinpoint requirements for joint action through symbols, especially where the symbols break down.

If the use of words cannot be fixed by grammar or rule, we cannot attach symbols to the force of an utterance. In the first part of this chapter, we establish the conditional, its antecedent, and inference. The force of a speaker's utterance must be found apart

---

[5] More on this shortly.

[6] Chatbots and automated translators being a case in point.

from the words used, at the moment, and bereft of a specific constant to lean on. With dialogical models, we can program ways to locate force. Doing so occupies the second half of this chapter.

23.2   Theorizing the Relation

1. Model and definitions. In dialogical models, ordinary language is schematized in a quasi-logical way.[7] So Jack tells Jill, "I'm gonna climb this tree," and Jill replies, "You'll need a ladder," and Jack looks for a ladder. Of course, Jill may not say anything. She may give Jack a dubious look after noticeably glancing at the height of the lowest branch. Or Jack may begin shimmying up the tree, prompting Jill's remark. Words or no, the exchange can be schematized as an argument. For example, here is the argument from two-person practical reasoning (Walton, 1997; Walton et al., 2008):

> *Premise 1*: X intends to realize A, and tells Y this.
> *Premise 2*: As Y sees the situation, B is a necessary (sufficient) condition for carrying out A, and Y tells X this.
> *Conclusion*: Therefore, X should carry out B, unless he has better reasons not to.

An exchange and its schematization are not the same. This difference is hardly worth noting. Pair you or I with Jack, and we can help him climb the tree, then explain the scheme we illustrated. But the example brings out a basic assumption to any formalization. An utterance within a dialogue is a speech *act*, or a move (Walton, 1996). A proposition is meaningless apart from its place in conversation (or context broadly). The above scheme assumes that Jack sincerely declares his purpose and Jill's reply helps him achieve it. If Jill knows there is no ladder or has hidden the ladder, the scheme fails. Besides relevance, the scheme must interpret the force of any given utterance and reply (Macagno, 2018, pg. 10). And for the model to work in AI, force must be dealt with.

A persisting, implicit variable limits dialogical models of the above type. The schema works or fails after the fact, and is heuristic at best. However, our aim is joint action. A map helps someone chart the woods; it does not find the way.[8] There are kinds of acts in Jack's statement and Jill's reply. These acts differ by more than intent. Jack may have been declaring his intention or foreseeing an unwanted act. Jill could be describing or directing. These acts through utterance change what took place. They concern the force of the utterance. We can motivate these requirements with an idealized model of communication (Davidson, 2005, pgs. 100–109). And, from this model, we will distinguish mood and force.

Suppose that in every linguistic exchange, a speaker has a theory for how their sounds will be heard by someone else and the hearer has a theory for interpreting

---

[7] Logic is a theory of valid inference that is formal in that it concerns the form of an inference (as opposed to content) and uses a formalism (Brun, 2003).

[8] Though Google maps does.

the speaker. Talk of theory brings out requirements for successful speech; that is, these theories are not about cognition or what 'really happens.' In other words, neither person has a conscious theory or mental map. After communication occurs or fails, we use this model to explain what is needed. Our question is why and how communication succeeds as much as it does.[9] On this model, then, speaker and hearer have two theories: theories anticipating their exchange and the theory during the exchange. The first is a prior theory, the second, a passing theory. Knowledge of grammar, idioms, definitions, past uses or misuses, culturally shared information, norms of setting, et cetera, make up the prior theory. By contrast, passing theories align how *this* hearer interprets the words of *this* speaker at the moment. So if Jill misspeaks, "You need an adder," yet Jack interprets 'adder' as 'ladder,' as Jill intended, prior and passing theories conflict without loss. According to Jack's prior theory, 'adder' and 'ladder' are not synonymous, yet he understands what Jill meant. This example reveals more than harmless abuse of language. The conflict between theories goes beyond malapropisms, slurs, swallowed letters or words, improper grammar, neologisms, and their kin. Passing theories concern tone, word choice, setting, speaker and hearer, gesture, and stress. And their propositional attitudes (id est, sincerity, irony, sarcasm, humor, and testimony) are hard to anticipate. One person raises their eyebrows to express sincere concern, another person does the same to express disbelief. And a one-off utterance may not align with past usage or effect future use. Maybe Jill will never use 'adder' in lieu of 'ladder' again. Yet she and every other speaker get by. Converging passing theories, not prior ones, is all communication requires (Davidson, 2005, pg. 96).

A speaker must express their intent for speaking in a way the hearer can pick up—that is all. Conventions, norms, and regularities have their place, no doubt, but with limits. Prior theories ease dialogue without specifying requirements for speech. Before giving an argument for this view, let us define mood and force.

Mood is the form of a verb that expresses a fact, a command, a wish, conditionality, and potentiality.[10] A verb is indicative, imperative, interrogative, optative, subjunctive, and exhortative.[11] Prior theory encompasses mood, then, and so forms expectations. Force sits squarely in passing theories. Some definitions show as much: "The real import or significance (of a document, statement, or the like); the precise meaning or 'value' (of a word, sentence, etc.) as affecting its context or interpretation."[12] The definitions note that force (i) comes from the moment of uttering, (ii) inflects meaning, and (iii) does so through the import, significance, affects, or effects of the words spoken.

Definitions of mood and force motivate our central claim that an isolated sentence does not fix its range of uses. Mood does not set force. If Jacks says, "Should I climb this tree?" he may be teasing Jill, who knows he intends to climb the tree regardless

---

[9] Which means we assume speakers frequently succeed.

[10] See *Oxford English Dictionary*, entry for 'mood,' n.2.

[11] This list need not be exhaustive for our purposes.

[12] See *OED*, entry for 'force,' n.1., 9. Utterances are our concern, not documents or statements—moments of joint action.

of her opinion. Jack is not asking with the interrogative. Returning to the initial thought experiment, whichever mood we input, the guaranteed, predictable output stipulates a force that abridges how words are used. Dialogical models risk doing the same arbitrarily or, at least, implicitly. Yet conventions, norms, and regularities offer constants to the program, so the help they offer must be brought in. But what do they offer?

2. *Linguistic autonomy.* A social convention is 'a regularity widely observed by some group of agents,' and people navigate endless situations with them.[13] Driving patterns are the textbook case—Americans drive on the right, English on the left. There is an intentional social observance of some act, practice, or manner. If a convention ensures that certain words have a certain force, theorists and programmers should formalize the link. The words used result in an assertion, command, or question, as opposed to the use of those words fixing force. The difference is slight, yet where we place the stress changes how force is set in an utterance. Phrases like 'as I claim' seem to define the force of an utterance when said sincerely. If so, the words fix force over and above the uttering of them. The speaker must speak sincerely, of course, so the act of uttering is required; but the words themselves settle what force the utterance has. Add 'as I claim' to a sentence and a speaker asserts. Davidson glosses, "Stated crudely, such theories maintain that there is a single use (or some finite number of uses) to which a given sentence is tied, and this use gives the meaning of the sentence" (Davidson, 2005, pg. 271). Conventions, norms, and regularities in linguistic acts restrict the force(s) of words. This view has plausibility. A speaker's intent cues meaning and then bleeds through convention. Jack intends to climb the tree, intends to let Jill know, and uses conventions to let her know. He cannot say just anything to communicate; conventions guide him. He has options, but conventions, along with setting, limit which words he can use to a certain effect. Stray from those constants and our sounds, gestures, and scripts are meaningless. Formalize them and machines enter the linguistic fray.

Speakers choose their words for a given effect, and some words lend themselves better than others to an intent. In this way, language is conventional. It is shaped and patterned. Is the pattern shaped with conventions, though? Say it is. Then meaning and force depend on conventions directly or indirectly: directly insofar as an utterance obeys a convention and indirectly when an utterance refers to one. The latter allows for abnormal (or parasitic) uses that remain meaningful (id est, when Jill misspoke with 'adder'). Both assume a settled range of possible uses from conventions governing the words themselves. Words fix use via a convention. Since meaning depends on convention, then only conventional use is meaningful. The problems come when we have to say which convention must hold in any given case. Holding a convention constant within a linguistic exchange does not fix meaning, which we see in open-textured predicates. Bad faith actors abuse conventions, for example. So if Bob loses a bet to Ann, agreeing to buy her breakfast, he can plumb what makes up a breakfast repeatedly while failing to satisfy their largely intuitive agreement. Bob may bring

---

[13] See Michael Rescorla's entry for convention in *The Stanford Encyclopedia of Philosophy.* He cites David Lewis' book, *Convention.*

Ann a cheerio with a drop of milk, uncooked bacon and rotten eggs, an elaborate meal to an unspecified time and place, and so on. After each frustration, Ann may add a condition for satisfying the bet, yet Bob cunningly exploits loopholes indefinitely. A 'conventional' breakfast seems obvious until tested (Licato & Marji, 2018). The same holds for any dialogical constant. Any specified constant will not be enough to ensure satisfaction; it will be replaceable, or specify too much, depending on the intended act. Our point is that taking conventions as basic results in a regress. And the regress exposes a lack of traction on the meaningfulness of utterances.

The circle gets vicious when scholars group normal linguistic uses and abnormal uses. Normal uses, they say, obey conventions. Abnormal uses break them. Conventions found meaning since both uses rely on them, directly or indirectly. So the theory goes. But, asking which linguistic acts are conventional, we have only normal, regular uses. However scholars parse the normativity of regularity (so many times, in relevantly similar settings, speaker/hearer roles, et cetera), conventions are the supposed reason for regularity. Conventions give that regularity normative weight so that speakers can often enough misspeak without that misspoken phrase shifting from abnormal to normal.[14] In the give and take of ordinary language, conventions are regularities, intended or not. Theorists helplessly slide between these notions. By the same token, it is hard to say what a given convention is over and above a speaker saying certain words in a certain way that they expect a hearer to pick up. The convergence of passing theories, though, hardly amounts to a convention.

A thought experiment by Quine can be retold to a new purpose (Quine, 1960, pgs. 28–30). A linguist meets a speaker from an unknown land during fieldwork. The linguist cannot make out any similarities between the speaker's tongue and other, known languages. All the linguist's training and techniques come to naught, save query and ostension. The linguist points to an object and the speaker makes a sound. The linguist copies the sound and points to the object again. A rabbit jumps out of the nearby brush and the speaker points and says, 'Gavagai.' In her notebook, the linguist writes down 'gavagai' next to 'rabbit.' Another rabbit jumps out and the linguist points and says, 'Gavagai.' The speaker nods and, after a few more queries, the linguist believes 'gavagai' means 'rabbit.' Now, let us suppose for the sake of argument that the practice of uttering a sound, pointing, and nodding is shared conventions between the linguist and native speaker. Do these conventions explain the exchange? Quine uses this thought experiment to show indeterminacy in successful communication. From observation, 'Gavagai' may mean 'rabbit,' 'undetached rabbit part,' 'rabbit stage,' 'the unique appearance of a rabbit's left foot while running less than 20 miles per hour,' or the name of an indigenous dragonfly that hovers above rabbits. More sophisticated forays into the nuance of the speaker's language enable greater abstraction and precision. All the same, specific conventions do not fix the speaker's intended meaning or overcome the indeterminacy. Repetition, prolonged behavior, added word pairings, changed settings, syntax, the linguist's experience, expertise, knack, and so on, hedge indeterminacy. Specifiable conventions ease the

---

[14] Those who hold to conventions need not deny semantic drift. Regularity does not suffice for establishing normal usage.

exchange by focusing its purpose, yet these hardly pick out linguistic competency. Persisting indeterminacy requires us to look beyond conventions for the source of meaning.

Linguistic acts are meaningful for speakers and hearers prior to the conventions that speed us along.[15] That is, a speaker may or may not use any given convention to fulfill their intent in speaking. A hearer may rightly understand them anyway. Once we specify a convention as such, it can be disregarded or violated. Linguistic meaning is autonomous. The argument follows:

1. *Premise*: If meaning is conventional, then our utterances have meaning when they obey (or refer to) conventions.
2. *Premise*: Our utterances have meaning apart from any specifiable convention.
3. *Conclusion*: Meaning is not conventional.

By and larger, and especially with strangers, speakers speak in conventional ways. I am not denying intentionally guided patterns in dialogue that ease conversation. Language use is conventional in some sense. Again, our concern is meaning—what is required for successful communication. How we understand the requirements changes how we program language processing. And the argument is that conventions do not fix the uses to which a given sentence can be put. Which variables matter in a moment of discourse for the meaning of an utterance depends on the passing theories of a speaker and hearer, not a fixed, prior selection embodied in a convention that a speaker enacts.

Programmers require conventions, and so isolate or create some. I have no qualms with this practice and suggest some conventions of my own later on. The argument that meaning comes before conventions seems like harmless theorizing. If right, though, programming natural language changes insofar as defining and obeying conventions does not ensure that certain words have a certain force in ordinary language settings. This consequence includes when a machine is processing a human utterance or speaking to a human. And, if force changes meaning, identifying conventions and their execution will not ensure correct interpretation. Speakers must intend their words to be heard as asserting, ordering, asking, and may say various words or do various deeds to express their intent. No one convention nails down their intended meaning. More broadly, the argument implies that obeying conventions does not ensure a certain action since they do not ensure an agent carries out an intent. Agents must represent themselves in a certain way by doing certain acts. The problem is that publicly observable words, tones, gestures, references, et cetera never ensure a person's intent is recognized as such by others. An insecure hearer, for example, may always ask, "Was that sarcasm? an insult? a lie?" On Davidson's idealized model, 'what must be shared is the interpreter's and the speaker's understanding of the speaker's words' (Davidson, 2005, pg. 96). Conventions ease the convergence of passing theories, yet never with certainty. Indeterminacy persists and successful communication requires more or less than a convention. An unprecedented act or phrase may do the trick. So, an utterance's force comes from a speaker's expressed

---

[15] Prior in the ontological sense, meaning constitutive, not in the temporal sense.

intent and the hearer's recognition through publicly observed content. This is all that is required for passing theories to align, and so how meaning emerges.

You may puzzle over the coupling of claims that language is conventional and that no convention fixes the meaning of an utterance. And the reason for the second claim might seem weak. Just because Americans could drive on the left side of the road does not mean that driving lacks any specifiable convention—namely, that Americans drive on the right. A grunt can be meaningful apart from conventions, the analogy reads, so meaning *tout court* lacks conventions. The example clarifies our argument. While driving is conventional because people agree to drive on one side of the road, they do not begin driving when they drive on the right. Someone from England may wake up in the United States, unaware, and start driving. He can drive and will be driving, though violating the nation's convention. Obeying conventions does not constitute what it means to drive, though drivers do well to obey them. Like driving, meaning comes before socially observed regularities and agreed-upon conventions (tacitly or explicitly) for speech. The argument concerning meaning goes further by stating that isolating conventions in ordinary discourse is less informative or helpful than it seems. Conventions are less helpful to us because language is autonomous.

So far, we have argued that conventions do not set the meaning of an utterance with guarantees. Rather, meaning is autonomous. The convergence of passing theories, not prior theories, is what successful communication depends on. Linguistic meaning is autonomous, Davidson explains, because "once a feature of language has been given conventional expression, it can be used to serve many extra-linguistic ends; symbolic representation necessarily breaks any close tie with extra-linguistic purpose" (Davidson, 2001, pg. 113). A slip of the tongue, garbled speech, botched grammar, and malapropisms reveal that an utterance's meaning does not rely on a convention. A mistake may become a new norm. Converging passing theories define the point from which conventions are upheld as such, changed, or new ones formed. A speaker may use a string of words for an unusual end. The words themselves do not fix their intended use, nor is there a closed set of possible uses. As a result, theorists cannot translate natural language into a symbolism, distilling meaning in clear vessels. A perspicuous symbolism cannot make humans honest by divulging their intent or attitude. This is a limit of formal languages. We will pause over this limit before offering a theory of the force/mood relation.

3. Formal languages. Autonomy clouds an otherwise perspicuous symbolism. This is because fixing an expression siphons the purposes to which the expression can be put. There persists a mismatch of utterances and their symbolic representation. Autonomy also cleaves natural language from formal ones, which effects how humans speak with machines and vice versa.

A language is a recursively axiomatized system: a set of finite rules joined to a finite vocabulary that produces an indefinite number of expressions. Languages are formal when they operate by explicit rules.[16] Computability is a subset of formality in which a system lacks insight or ingenuity, the system is closed, and the explicit rules cannot be violated (Novaes, 2012, pg. 17). The order of input from a fixed

---

[16] For a typology of formality, see (Novaes, 2011).

set of variables outputs predictably. The mechanism does not assign meaning to the variables in the sense that the input results in a set output apart from an interpretation of the input. The operation is 'blind.' A calculator computes $1 + 1$ irrespective of whether the numbers describe tangible objects or not, through the algorithms of automated vehicles or Auto-GCAS dwarf basic arithmetic.

Computation requires a sequential, definite, and finite sequence of steps. Vocabulary forms according to rules and protocols. A predictable end results predictably since outputs can be traced back through the carried-out operation. A computable language can be operated by anyone with the same result. An operation does not change from the person inputting. The same input results in the same output, regardless of the user. And a concrete, external symbolic system makes up a computable language (Novaes, 2012, pgs. 25–27). On its own terms, then, there is no indeterminacy in the mechanism until the variables inputted and outputted occur within a purposive or intentional context—that is, until a machine employs its computable language to talk with humans and act among them.

The convergence of passing theories is the one requirement for successful communication. Human language is autonomous since humans need not obey the script. Daily conversation is a creative, elusive, and evolving endeavor. Speakers and hearers have insight and ingenuity in chosen ways of speaking and making sense of another person's speech. So a computable language is not autonomous. Human utterances are interpretive through and through. A speaker chooses to utter certain words in a way the speaker expects the hearer to understand. And a hearer must understand those words at least as a speaker intends. The act of speaking is anything but blind.[17] Nor is there is a sequential, definite, and finite sequence of steps for making oneself understood. Most speech lacks protocols and, as we argued, conventions can be used or ignored. Nor do a speaker's words land predictably. The same words across speakers, or from one speaker to different hearers, or from the same speaker to the same hearer at a different time or place, may differ in meaning.

To recall, joint action is our goal. The requirement for successful communication is an avenue to joint action. Utterances are acts whose meaning exceeds isolated words. Propositional attitudes, like beliefs and desires, must enter the picture (Davidson, 2001, pg. 161). Joint action, then, requires shared beliefs and desires as well as the capacity to pick out beliefs and desires evinced by utterances. Joint action requires 'common ground' (Atlas, 2008; Macagno and Capone, 2016; Stalnaker, 2002). For Jill to help Jack, they must mutually believe that Jack is not tall enough to reach the first branch. Jill must share Jack's desire (to some extent) that he climb the tree. And there are the endless, mundane beliefs: Jill and Jack must think the other is real, that the tree is there, that they can speak to one another, that a ladder will hold Jack, and so on. We will set aside the large question of whether AI can achieve semantic intensionality (or propositional attitudes). Our smaller claim is that machines must engage with the force of utterances in order to act with humans. Without an interpretation of force, a speaker's beliefs and desires will not be fully

---

[17] Though speakers may speak thoughtlessly, that is, without attention to how their words will be heard.

incorporated into their utterances. Their act will not be fully appraised. And this marks a step toward joint action more broadly.

4. A theory for moods. Given the autonomy of language and the constraints of formal languages, an utterance's force remains a defeasible and non-constant variable (when codified). Rarely does a speaker explicitly indicate the force of their utterance, but, even when they do, their explicit words or gestures are no guarantee that their utterance has said force. Nor must a speaker evoke some convention for their words to be enforced, and so meaningful. Conventions are fickle guides for interpreting a speaker. So our theory of the mood/force relation begins and departs from the one thing needed: the convergence of passing theories. From here, we can build conventions and protocols back in.

And a theory of mood nears force. Speakers utter words in a certain mood to cue a hearer into their words' force. Such a theory must meet three requirements (Davidson, 2001, pg. 116). First, the theory relates indicatives to other moods. 'Vixen is a fancy word,' 'What is a vixen,' and 'Tell me what a vixen is,' though with distinct moods, have the same force when eliciting a definition of 'vixen' from a hearer. The speaker intends the hearer to say what a vixen is, and says these words in their mood to express that intent. A theory of mood explains how these sentences relate.

Second, an adequate theory of mood ascribes meaning to an utterance in one mood that is not shared by a similar utterance in a different mood. 'What is a vixen' and 'Tell me what a vixen is' may share force, but their meaning and mood differ. Inversely, the same words may share mood, yet differ in meaning and force. Compare 'A vixen is a female' when spoken of a fox or a woman. And since force is part of meaning, how sentences can share force yet semantically differ needs explanation. The first and second requirements for a successful theory of mood align with the intuition (the same intuition prompting recourse to conventions) that something basic and solid joins mood to force. Though at times differing, how mood, force, and meaning combine are basic to the intelligibility of uttering.

A theory must be semantically tractable, lastly. How the theory interprets utterances should mesh with a larger theory of meaning. The sentences cannot be unrecognizable from their uses. I assume that assigning truth conditions to an utterance gives its meaning. Davidson uses Tarski's theory of truth so that a theory of meaning entails that for each sentence s, a T-sentence results: 's is true if and only if p,' or 's means that p' (Davidson, 2001). Whether Tarski's theory of truth works for meaning, we assume that specifying the truth conditions of an utterance gives its meaning. A theory of mood succeeds, then, when it conforms to interpretations of an utterance's truth conditions.

But the three requirements threaten a working theory. Truth-functional operators do not mark the difference between 'What is a vixen' and 'Tell me what a vixen is.' If giving truth conditions gives us meaning, imperatives and interrogatives seem meaningless. The theory stuts from a paradox: the first two requirements require an operator for moods (to relate sentences across moods, while preserving differences), a non-truth-functional operator, while the third requirement leaves us only truth-functional operators (Davidson, 2001, pg. 116). In other words, sentences with moods must have a distinct operator; non-indicatives lack truth values, and so cannot have a truth-functional operator; operators must be truth-functional. So non-indicatives have no meaning or, if meaningful, no mood.

Some may brush off the paradox with the observal that illocution differs from perlocution, or the force of the utterance from the aim of uttering. The above requirements assume a view of force which conflates them and, as a result, our notion of mood veers from common usage. Such an objection rightly picks out that force effects the mood of a sentence. The grammatical categories are provisional or not exhaustive of mood. The objector disagrees. On their view, someone may say, frustrated, "A vixen is *just* a vixen," with assertoric force, yet with the aim of ending the conversation. The first is illocution—that is, the intrinsic point of the utterance—while the aim is perlocution, or the intended effect on the hearer from the utterance. Mood and force are bound to the words in an utterance. The purposes to which that linguistic package can be put are many, open-ended, and various.

Distinguishing elements intrinsic and extrinsic to an utterance helps but does not circumscribe utterances. A parent may ask their child what a vixen is to prompt their curiosity. Their words ask with an aim in mind: the force of their words is to ask, and they ask for a further purpose. In this sense, illocution and perlocution separate force from intended effects or purposes. Moreover, words may be spoken with a certain force for a variety of reasons and purposes. Their effects on a hearer may vary widely, too. But meaning comes from a speaker's uttering words and a hearer hearing them as the speaker intends at the moment of utterance. We misstep if we assume that an utterance has its force prepackaged in the sentence used, syntax, and all. Such a view implies that a speaker's and hearer's passing theories mesh with their prior theories—a requirement to let go of. Conventions do not pair words with forces essentially or regularly. The convergence of passing theories is the only requirement for successful communication, and so force infects meaning from a hearer rightly hearing the speaker's words. When the parent asks her child what a vixen is, the child may interpret the words as a prompt, or mild directive, to think about the word's meaning in the story. The parent prompts, not asks.[18] An utterance's point (intrinsic to force) and its aim (extrinsic) have a fluid boundary.

The line between extrinsic and intrinsic properties of an act becomes porous from the type/token distinction with respect to speech acts. Brun's adaptation of Lewis Carroll's argument for logical principles can be adjusted to our purposes (Brun, 2003, pg. 73). Brun argued,

1. Inference S has form V.
2. According to principle P, each inference of form V is valid.
3. S is valid.

---

[18] This should be distinguished from indirect speech acts, which have a primary and secondary force. The same example above can be used for indirect speech acts. If the parent asks to direct the child to get a dictionary, foremost, and also to look up the meaning of the word, she asks a question and directs. Again, the parent may intend to ask and the question's perlocutionary effect be that it prompts curiosity and reflection in the child. The turnable example shows the importance of theorizing the mood/force relation for AI. An otherwise same exchange can differ from intent and propositional attitudes. The same can be said for actions, generally.

Another argument is needed to support the above. Naming the above argument inference T, below is inference U.

1. Inference T has form W.
2. According to principle Q, each inference of form W is valid.
3. T is valid.[19]

Call the sentence of a speech act, $f(p)$, and its use, $F(P)$. Inference S can describe the move from $f(p)$ to $F(P)$. That is, the inference names the alignment of the sentence's logical form with the logic form of its use. A speech act has occurred when the inference is valid. Whichever logical principle we appeal to, however, there is an infinite regress due to a slight of hand. The assumed inference S, the successful speech act, is not the same as its renamed form, T, in inference U. This reveals a categorical difference between the drawn inference—the action—and its logical form, which entails that the logical form of the sentence used is not identical to its enactment either. If it was, the logical form of the action could enter a symbolism and be secured thereby. Such a move results in an infinite regress, though. The logical form of an act is not essential, nor perspicuous.

Moods characterize sentences; force and meaning come from the utterance. Because of this difference, it is tempting to assume mood can easily be dealt with and force evades us. Our formal apparatuses pick out and categorize mood. But the only operators at hand are truth-functional when it comes to meaning. So either non-indicatives lack meaning or non-indicatives reduce to indicatives. In the latter, there is only one true mood or mood colors the surface of sentences. Yet moods change the meaning of sentences. 'Tell me what a vixen is,' 'What is a vixen,' and 'I don't know what a vixen is' are not the same. How mood contributes to an utterance's meaning comes after the successful exchange. Prior theories only get a hearer so far when making sense of a speaker. If someone asks, 'Is a vixen a female fox,' to which someone else replies, 'Does the sun rise in the morning,' the reply is less a question than an answer. But there is also the more stable relation between sentences, which a theory of mood pins down.

Theorists, I suggest, need an account of force for an adequate theory of mood. Force and mood go hand in hand; one cannot be handled apart from the other. Non-indicators require operators with none at hand. Force lacks operators, too, yet alters meaning. I move that these characteristics mark utterances from two sides: the sentences a speaker uses and the use itself, both of which are meaningful in the act of uttering. To make sense of mood or force, theorists should attend to how they relate. Otherwise, they fail to account for on-the-ground interpretations. If mood and force inflect meaning—truth conditions—then both function at the moment of utterance. They contribute through the act of uttering. For a theory of mood to have purchase in day to day conversation, the theory must assign meaning in light of identification of force. If not, the theory covers over an utterance's meaning for an insulated theory of syntax (a syntax of grammar textbooks instead of natural language), past empirical regularities, or stipulated conventions. The problem is that

---

[19] I will return to this argument below.

speakers often use sentences in the same mood with different forces or sentences across moods with the same force. And these uses can be unprecedented, yet suit a moment or conversation. Words lend themselves to such uses. By clarifying force, the requirements for a theory of mood can be met.

23.3 Setters and Indicators

The first clue comes from the difference in force between saying 'Go' and 'I order you to go.' Both utterances are commands lacking truth conditions since they do not report an internal state (id est, my wanting you to make it the case that you go). The two sayings have the same force and a theory must track word meaning. Adding meanings in embedded phrases misses the sameness of words. Compare 'I order you to go' and 'He orders you to go.' The referent of 'you to go' changes depending on the subject, changing truth conditions, though its meaning should remain the same. Notice, too, that the force changes. In the first, 'you to go' is not commanded. 'I order' commands while the embedding tells what I order. The second can be glossed, 'He orders you to make it the case that you go.' The speaker likely asserts, 'He orders,' while the embedded phrase carries the force of a command (given the speaker's assertion holds). If force marks a special set of truth conditions, embedding 'you to go' cannot have its ordinary meaning to make sense of the above contrast. We must step off well-worn semantic tracks. The same issue confronts 'Go' and 'I order you to go,' where 'you to go' (taken as synonymous with 'go') loses its commanding force. Free, then embedded, the phrase cannot preserve its same meaning, and this upends the view that force marks a set of its own truth conditions. Without a phrase's ordinary meaning, it cannot have its usual uses. Davidson stresses, "The problem is adventitious, since what is special about explicit performatives is better explained as due to a special use of words with an ordinary meaning that as due to a special meaning" (Davidson, 2001, pg. 117). There is another way forward, he argues. Word meaning holds with changes in force since force concerns the use of words instead of carrying a special meaning.[20]

To handle non-indicatives, Davidson begins with indicatives (Davidson, 2001, pgs. 118–119). Since a theory of meaning specifies truth conditions of an utterance, indicatives fit nicely. They have truth-functional operators. How embedding works in indicatives helps us see their function in non-indicatives. How 'I order you to go' differs from 'Go' reveals the nature of force and its relation to mood. 'Jones asserted that it is raining' can be dealt with as two utterances: 'Jones asserted that' and 'it is raining.' The first is often spoken assertively, that is, the speaker asserts that Jones asserted. The speaker says the embedded phrase non-assertively as it is the content of Jones' assertion. The demonstrative, 'that,' refers the first utterance to the second. And, let me add, this is how we analyze utterances of these sentences,

---

[20] Still, force remains part of an utterance's meaning, as will be unpacked later.

not the sentences themselves.[21] Together, the utterance can be rephrased, 'Jones made an assertion whose content is given by my next utterance. It is raining.' The truth conditions are that 'Jones asserted that' if and only if Jones asserted that in a given time and place. And the demonstrative refers to the content of Jones' assertion. Whether Jones spoke truly depends on whether it was raining at the time of his uttering and where he spoke. An adept of Jones' language recognizes what must be the case for the assertion to be true. So if Jones asserted truly, and it is not raining around us, we can infer that Jones is somewhere else. The two utterances are conjoined since if either is false, the whole is.

Indicatives are left alone on Davidson's theory because they have a truth-functional operator. To me, this default is more provisional than he lets on. Indicatives look like assertions, yet, as Davidson notes, they have a motley group of possible forces. Although force concerns use, different forces change the meaning of an utterance. In reply to the assertion, 'A vixen is a female fox,' a perplexed hearer may query by repeating the sentence. Leaving the repetition alone as an indicative risks overlooking how it differs from the assertion. So force does not leave indicatives intact, but we will circle back to this point after engaging with available theories.

1. Mood setters. Non-indicative sentences, for Davidson, are 'indicative sentences plus an expression that syntactically represents the appropriate transformation,' which he calls a mood setter (Davidson, 2001, pg. 119). Commanding, 'You are going,' shares truth conditions with the same phrase when reporting an event. They differ from a transformation, or this is how we theorize moods at least. Speaking of transformation or change concerns the non-indicative sentence's relation to its sibling indicative. Utterances have truth conditions, not sentences, so the speaker does not break an indicative from its mold. Put again, the speaker does not transform a ready-to-hand indicative. Meaning comes from uttering a sentence, and a mood setter marks a change *in the sentence*, evinced by a verb, word order and choice, punctuation, tone, gesture, and stress. In parsing, the uttered sentence has an indicative core, so non-indicatives retain meaning. Mood setters fix the change over and above the indicative core.

Mood setters change an indicative given a theory of which indicatives are the default. Since indicatives have truth conditions and meaning amounts to truth conditions, non-indicatives are meaningful due to their shifted indicative core. How a mood setter also has meaning brings in the act of uttering. Mood setters hold or fail to hold. If a hearer repeats the speaker's words to query, the speaker may take the repetition as mocking. Or 'What is a vixen' may be taken as an idiomatic expression (like 'Who is John Galt') instead of a sincere question. A mood setter has the form of a sentence rather than place-holding. Davidson explains, "It behaves like a sentence an utterance of which refers to an utterance of an indicative sentence" (Davidson, 2001, pg. 120). To see what he means, recall how demonstrative pronouns were dealt with in 'Jones asserted that.' The 'that' refers to a subsequent utterance or embedded sentence. Similarly, a mood setter refers to an indicative when uttered such that the truth conditions change. When Jones asserts that x, the speaker does not assert x.

---

[21] In other words, we are treating the uttering of the sentence, not a stand-alone sentence.

By embedding x, a speaker changes its truth conditions. Likewise, the mood setter changes by referring to, or embedding, an indicative core. The analogy stops where an embedded sentence stands freely. Mood setters lack truth conditions of their own as well as syntax and logical structure. A mood setter cannot be spoken on its own. It holds or fails to hold relative to an utterance. And the function of mood setters does not logically conjoin to the indicative core such that the whole utterance of a non-indicative is true if each conjunct is true. The whole utterance lacks a truth-functional operator that defines its logical form. The mood setter holds or fails to hold, and the truth conditions of the spoken indicative likewise change or fail to change.

A speaker does two simultaneous acts by saying a non-indicative—the indicative core and mood setter referring to it. While what follows sounds like repetition, here I am speaking of utterance more so than a sentence. Think again of the demonstrative in 'Jones asserted that.' By uttering the demonstrative, a speaker refers to the embedded utterance. Two utterances occur one after the other and they differ in force. A mood setter has an analogous role: it refers to an indicative to transform the indicative's truth conditions. There, the analogy ends. A mood setter has a sentential function, but is spoken at the same time as the indicative sentence it changes. A mood setter lacks syntax or structure, logic, or otherwise. Two distinct, yet indistinguishable speech acts occur. Distinct, because we can explain how sentences in non-indicative moods use some explicit sign to represent the transformation of the indicative. The utterance sounds different than an indicative. Indistinguishable, because the sign used cannot be formalized into a necessary constant, nor can the uttering of any mark guarantee the sentence has a certain mood. 'There is broccoli on your plate,' while indicative in surface syntax, can be an imperative or interrogative. Force unhinges mood from any essential symbol. A speaker must make their intent known, yet have the autonomy of language at his disposal.

On Davidson's account, mood setters are uttered, enact a transformation, and mark the appropriate transformation. They are uttered, and a sentence without being one or the other simply, or both. Mood setters comprise too much conceptually. Here is the problem: force swings freely of mood, yet mood expresses a transformation resulting from the force of the utterance that limits the scope of its force. Davidson uses mood setters to bridge the gap between the utterance and the sentence, which may be why they are so uncanny. They behave like a sentence but are not sentences. They are not part of the sentence, yet are sentential, nor encoded, though an explicit mark. Mood setters occupy a gray area of theory and the ins and outs of everyday speech. This makes them attractive. They also respect linguistic autonomy and the requirement that hearers recognize the intended meaning of a speaker's words. They seem on the one hand indifferent to force; on the other, they result from and limit force. Theorists should say more on how mood relates to force than Davidson's setters allow.

Suppose we say, "A vixen is *just* a female fox." Now, conventional wisdom leads us to believe this is an indicative sentence that asserts. The sentence can be put to many uses that do not change its mood or force. If so, the adverb stresses harmlessly. But the force changes when, for example, someone says this sentence in reply to someone else who persists in thinking that 'vixen' means something more. Then, the utterance commands and, if so, 'just' seems to be the explicit mark for the speaker's intent. Is it a mood setter? Yes, insofar as it marks the transformation of an otherwise indicative into an imperative. The word reveals the speaker's intent, which changes the indicative. But, no, since a word like 'just' cannot be a mood setter. Words are not mood setters. The speaker's intent, as perceived by the hearer, changes the indicative, but neither intent nor a hearer's perception make up a mood setter.

The lacuna has another side. 'A vixen is *just* a female fox' looks indicative. While surface grammar may deceive at times, mood setters seem to both preserve tried and true categories (indicatives, imperatives, and interrogatives) by leaving indicatives alone and letting force swing free, while adopting minimal restraint (mood setters are a non-conventional, explicit mark). If mood tracks semantically and force changes the meaning of sentences, then Davidson's theory restricts an utterance's force. Perlocutionary force swings freely, not force. But then conventions seem more than useful and the scope of linguistic autonomy narrows (or is lost). Worse, the conceptual distinction is applied arbitrarily since mood setters are underdetermined in successful communication and his theory illumines less than a theory should.

Let us move forward by keeping mood setters within a theory of meaning. That is, mood setters are not uttered by a speaker; they mark a transformation within theory that takes indicatives as the default.[22] An utterance is one act, and so 'Go' and 'Did he go' are one speech act. The act is decomposed into a mood setter and an indicative core. As a result, mood setters track the usual categories, though the categories do not tie down how the force of an utterance changes its meaning. This is because force comes from the act of uttering, whereas mood theorizes the sentences used. A theory of force brings us to the act of uttering. Non-indicatives lack truth values yet remain meaningful because they can be parsed within a theory of meaning that presents their truth conditions. What mood setters call a change of the default indicative is the distinct act of non-indicatives. For non-indicatives, it is the act that matters more than the meaning. Force inflects words through use, rather than channeling a latent meaning in the words themselves. Mood setters theorize distinct acts with sentence types without those types fixing force. With these insights in our back pocket, let us turn to Green's theory of force indicators (Green, 1997, 2000) to place conventions.

2. Force indicators. Many interpret Davidson's thesis as upsetting force indicators—that is, any explicit mark the utterance of which *enacts* a given force.[23] They are right on two fronts: on Davidson's view, (i) we cannot assign a constant mark directly to an utterance's force, (ii) nor utter some constant for our utterance to assert rather than command or question. Both are non-starters since force concerns the use of words, not the words themselves, and speakers have autonomy. My theory of mood and force must begin and end with the requirements for a hearer to rightly interpret a speaker: the convergence of passing theories. Defeasibility and presumption have a crucial role here, as Walton, Reed, and Macagno stress (Walton

---

[22] In other words, speakers only say mood setters when we are theorizing what happened in a linguistic exchange. They do not say mood setters in the sense they say words.

[23] The word itself ensuring a given intent.

et al., 2008, pgs. 2–3, 32). But some critics miss Davidson's argument and insight.[24] They fail to see how his views give a theoretical basis for the inherent defeasibility of interpretation and the elusiveness of everyday language. The more we understand why our day-to-day exchanges are defeasible, the better we incorporate AI into those exchanges. And we can accept Davidson's position while carrying on our formalizing projects. We can theorize force, that is, even if we cannot attach a symbol to an utterance's force with any guarantees.

A mood setter systematically represents non-indicative moods with syntactic effects. Force surfaces when indicatives transform into non-indicatives since truth conditions alone give force meaning. Any sentence can have any force, in principle; however, force has a narrow semantic range. Ambivalence and ambiguity carry over into the interpretation of an utterance, leaving force inert or absent if an explicit, determining mark is not given. As a result, indicatives suffer from underdetermined force, while force surfaces more in non-indicatives. But indicatives can be used to question, interrogatives to command, imperatives to assert. And Davidson observes that "the concept of force is part of the meaning of mood" (Davidson, 2001, pg. 121). Force depends on mood, or vice versa, opaquely from mood setters. Force concerns the use of words with and without a semantic load, mysterious either way. Maybe more attention to force will clarify linguistic acts.

With respect to force, an expression is often split into force and content. A sentence has truth conditions apart from the force of its utterance. This is taken to entail that whatever has meaning in an utterance cannot indicate force; whatever indicates force lacks meaning. Put otherwise, words which have meaning cannot at the same time signal their own force, nor vice versa. If a word indicates force, it does not add meaning to the utterance. An explicit mark either has meaning or indicates force, exclusively. Assumed are two distinct uses of words: to convey meaning or force. To be clear, this is not Davidson's position. For him, force concerns use *tout court*. A sentence has propositional content that changes when the sentence is used in certain ways (to command, to question). Green not only devises a notion of force indicator to patch the split of force and content, but also rejects a strong version of linguistic autonomy.[25]

Force and content split with the suant reasoning (Stenius, 1967, pgs. 258–259; Green, 2000, pg. 437). Say someone shows a picture to someone else. It can be shown to indicate what someone looks like, to show how someone ought to look, or to ask about what is shown. Suppose we attach a force indicator to the showing of the picture. If meaningful, it is part of the picture. Then another indicator would be needed. If the addition is meaningful, we need another, then another, and so on. The same is said of words.

Embedding gives us more reason to split force and content. Speech act analysis reveals an utterance's meaning by examining how saying a locution is to do an act (Green, 2000, pg. 437). But if saying certain words thereby does an act, speech act

---

[24] In their defense, Davidson implicitly relies on arguments given elsewhere and writes densely in his own style.

[25] I will define strong and weak versions of linguistic autonomy below.

analysis is often false because those same words can be embedded. As we saw above, when 'Go' is embedded in 'I order you to go,' the word loses its original force. To say, 'Go' is not always to order someone to make it the case that they go. A speaker may report, "Jones orders you to go." We may conclude that grammar bars force. This is what Green calls Frege's point: If a locution, a, is part of a sentence and it is grammatical to embed a, then there is no speech act, X, such that to utter a is to X (Green, 2000, pg. 439). Embedding disables the force of uttering set words despite a successful speech act. If Green can repair the split between force and content, his theory must handle embedding.

Green's theory of force agrees with Davidson that strong illocutionary force indicators (strong ifids) are impossible or useless. A strong ifid is 'an expression any utterance of which indicates that an associated sentence is being put forth by a speaker with a certain illocutionary force' (Green, 1997, pg. 218). Put otherwise, a strong ifid pairs a sentence with a force upon being uttered. And force changes the speaker's commitment to a sentence. What sets a strong ifid apart is that its symbol or conventional mark brings about a given force when uttered. If

$$\Delta_-$$

stands for the function of illocutionary force and A stands for a sentence, then

$$\Delta(A)$$

is an utterance of the sentence, A, with illocutionary force (Green, 1997, pp. 218–219). Since any sentence containing the above pair is an utterance of it, a strong ifid can be embedded or free. Force has a symbol that can be uttered to confer said force to a sentence. By pairing the symbol with a sentence in the act of uttering, the utterance has a set force.

Strong ifids do not work.[26] If they did, there would be no difference between 'serious' speakers, on the one hand, and jokers, story-tellers, actors, politicians, and other 'non-serious' speakers on the other. Each would use their sentences with indicators, yet a friend telling of an event differs from an actor on a stage. Not to mention that a symbol cannot guarantee a speech act occurs or that a locution is enforced. Besides actors, jokers, and their kin, the scope of sentence use defies strong ifids. Saying 'I order you to go' does not ensure that the utterance is a command or that the utterance only commands. The words can be said without the speech act happening. Or, if responding to the question, 'What did Jack just say,' the words assert. Again, someone can add 'seriously' or 'honestly' to their assertion without being serious or honest or intending a hearer to think so. A symbol cannot contain or confine the meaning or force of an utterance. Meaning comes from the convergence of passing theories, though prior theories form beliefs and expectations. This requirement brings us into the complexities of the most mundane exchanges.

---

[26] Except as a function within abstract systems, but natural language is not an abstract system.

When it comes to the force of everyday utterances, ambiguity is ubiquitous. An insecure hearer can almost always ask, 'Was that an insult?' A theory of force must preserve this ambiguity, otherwise it overdetermines an utterance. This is a problem for strong ifids because they both secure and restrict the force of an utterance. An utterance has *this* force as opposed to *that* force, and this skews uttering and its representation. Think, again, of 'A vixen is *just* a female fox.' A strong ifid must disambiguate and fix the force prior to use. But the same words can be used to assert, command, and question, and sometimes it is unclear which force a speaker intends. What is more, the sign does not disambiguate and fix the force of a given utterance prior to uttering. Indexical variables and hearers do. Adding another mark does nothing more than prefacing, 'I assert that.' A general theory cannot force passing theories to align with prior theories, yet that is what a strong ifid portends. If there are unsolved ambiguities in an utterance, a theory of interpretation should retain them until a speaker clarifies. With force, we can always ask about sincerity, trust, transparency, beliefs, and intentions, and so the force of an utterance never comes fully into view. Giving a speaker new symbols (or ascribing them) cannot evade such questions.

Green proposes a way to save strengthened moods: weak ifids. He couches this indicator within illocutionary validity since it concerns a speaker's commitments based on an utterance. Validity centers on a speaker, S, and a sequence of force/content pairs,

$$< \Delta_1 A_1, ... \Delta_n A_n, \Delta B >,$$

such that a speaker's pairings are valid if and only if a speaker is committed to a given sentence under a given mode, then the speaker is also committed to another sentence under the same mode (Green, 1997, p. 228). To be clear, a mode is not a mood: a sentence has a mood while a commitment to a sentence has a mode. So 'A vixen is a female fox' is indicative and, if asserted, a speaker is committed to the sentence assertorically. If that holds, the speaker is also committed to the sentences, 'A vixen is a female' and 'A vixen is a fox,' in the same way. This is not to say that a speaker must assert these implied sentences. Again, this theory focuses on a speaker's commitments. And validity concerns the consistency of a speaker's beliefs across force/content pairings. Assumed is that the first sentence was uttered with a given force. For this reason, Green's ifids are weak.

If a sentence, A, joins with any mode, then that sentence has a certain force. The new and contentious variable is

$$f_\Delta,$$

which stands for the force associated with connective,

$$\Delta\_.$$

The variable joins mood and force through the following mechanism: mood carries a certain force through the speaker's commitment expressed by uttering a sentence (id est, the mode in which it is uttered). A weak ifid is a valid inference, one that infers force from a mode:

$$\frac{f\ldots\Delta(A)\ldots}{f_\Delta A}.$$

Assuming a mode/content pair has a force, then the utterance has *this* force, be it asserting, commanding, or questioning. Since mood does not fix mode, a speaker may utter an indicative sentence without asserting. If a speaker is committed to 'A vixen is a female fox' as a supposition, then its force differs. Green's theory comes to force from belief and ascribes beliefs conditionally. A weak ifid does not guarantee an utterance has a certain force or that a speech act has happened. It signals that, if a speech act has occurred, the speaker must have a certain belief or type of commitment, and not exclusively. A few observals are in order.

If a speaker is committed to the claim that a hearer should tell him what vixens are, then 'Tell me what a vixen is' commands. This does not mean that the speaker's belief is enough to fix force. A speech act can fail with or without the proper belief. Given that the uttering enacts, the utterance has imperatival force. Some of the conditions for the utterance enacting are the proper belief, sincerity, and the intent to command, but there are other conditions outside the speaker's control, such as the hearer recognizing the speaker's intent and interpreting the words properly. If the utterance enacts, and so commits a speaker to something, the utterance has a certain force and commits the speaker to certain claims. There is a close parallel between the force of the utterance and the beliefs of the speaker. But the output is a minimum since the utterance may have other forces, other modes, and more than one purpose. In this way, too, the indicator is weak.

Green thinks that some English expressions are weak ifids. Cataloging these devices would be a sentential basis for programming and generalizable over a group of speakers. He gives an example: say 'I claim' parenthetically and, if a speaker is committed to anything at all, they are committed assertorically (at least), and so assert. Other forces may be in play, no doubt. The syntax gives a required minimum. A speaker asserts, along with any other force or point at work. "A vixen, I claim, is a female fox" commits a speaker to the belief that a vixen is a female fox, if spoken seriously. In support of this view, Green gives a thought experiment (Green, 1997, pp. 235–236). Add to our language the verb, 'swave,' which means the same as 'to wave' except it also expresses assertoric commitment when it has any force. Set in a conditional, a speaker commits, "If John swaves his hand, then Mary stops her car." This is a complex speech act. The whole entailment is asserted, as is the antecedent, and so the speaker is committed to the consequent by implication. Since words can be weak ifids, language can be tailored to fix a minimum force of utterances.

Green notes a counterexample that 'we could learn to live' with (Green, 1997, p. 236). 'It is not the case that John swaved his hand' ascribes an inconsistency to the speaker. The problem occurs in 'It is not the case that John waved his hand, as I claim.' Green avoids outright contradiction by separating the truth conditions of the parenthetical from the rest of the sentence. This results in a strangeness similar to Davidson's mood setter. The parenthetical has unique truth conditions, yet functions on the rest of the sentence through a weak-ifid elimination inference. Its truth conditions depend on whether an assertion is made. If so, it ascribes assertoric force to the utterance and the respective belief. Here is the uncanniness: 'as I claim' is syntactic and more than syntax because it is the direct expression of a speaker's intent. To utter these words seriously is to assert. The words bring us from mood to force rigidly. These words are distinct from 'I claim that' due to the function of parentheticals. As Green concedes, embedding a sentence with 'I claim that' need not assert. It is not a weak ifid (Green, 1997, p. 234). A speaker may say, "I assert that grass is green," hypothetically. By contrast, Green assumes that no one will utter a parenthetical seriously without asserting, but his example suggests we should not assume as much. He wrongly takes the ambiguity of the parenthetical's syntactic function as a mark of transparency. Recall 'It is not the case that John waved his hand, as I claim.' If the parenthetical ascribes a belief, the utterance seems to conflict. It does not conflict, Green assures us, if the negation is stipulated. While right, there seems to be no good reason to say one is stipulative rather than the other. To see this, note another way the problem could be resolved. We can interpret the parenthetical as applying to the whole sentence, 'It is not the case that John waved his hand' rather than 'John waved his hand.' Its scope and application are ambiguous. And so a parenthetical is not the same as the fictional 'to swave.' What is more, I see no reason that this parenthetical and others have a more distinct syntactic function than 'I claim that.' Green takes the syntax of parentheticals to fix a speaker's intent. The problem is that the syntax is taken to pigeonhole the truth conditions given by an utterance, as if the sentence has its own range of truth conditions. Green is right that the parenthetical involves a transformation, but wrong on assigning where that transformation comes from and how it is determined. A speaker claims and can use words in any way that expresses their intent to a hearer. The force is set from successful linguistic exchanges, not from certain, formulaic expressions.

An interpretation assigns beliefs and intentions to the speaker. Green holds intention constant to assign belief, then he holds belief constant to assign intention. They can be parsed in either order. But an interpretation must assign both simultaneously and without relying on one or the other. Green seems to find words that fix both. Take 'John swaved his hand.' If uttered seriously, a speaker believes that John waved his hand and intends to assert the belief. The qualification, 'seriously,' is less than helpful, though. Better to say that the verb, 'swave,' assumes a certain intent which then evokes a belief or vice versa. Otherwise, we are left with a vague constant from which to ascribe belief and intent (Davidson, 2001, p. 111). There is the option that 'swave' is constant, but, as we noted, force concerns the use of words, not a special meaning. Davidson suggests preference as the constant for assigning belief and intention,[27] but that is not pressing here. As soon as we admit that no word can ground ascriptions of intent and belief singly—that is, without seriousness, preference, or other ways of speaking—the spell breaks and weak ifids weaken. They assume a speech act has occurred along assumed lines of regularity that are unaccounted for. Force cannot be explained apart from mood.

---

[27] See Davidson (2001, 'Thought and Talk,' pp. 155–170).

A parenthetical, Green claims, ensures at least one force among others. In complex speech acts, the parenthetical need not evince the main force of the utterance, as in 'Tell me whether a vixen is a female fox, as I claim.' The force of an utterance may be underdetermined, as in the example, or overdetermined. Consider 'Do you think, as I claim, a vixen is a female fox?' To interpret 'a vixen as a female fox' as being asserted because it follows the parenthetical builds too much into the sentence. The question taunes a more tentative commitment. Of course, the moment of uttering may suggest a speaker is deeply convinced a vixen is a female fox, and so the parenthetical rightly signals the assertoric belief. But that is the point: much depends on the moment of utterance between speaker and hearer when it comes to force.

3. Force setters. Davidson offers a theory of mood, but leaves us to wonder over force. Green and others theorize force without making sense of its elusiveness. Green also explains force with grammar apart from mood, which is a misstep. Still, the use of illocutionary validity for assigning force is insightful. The transformative nature of force needs to be explained with the syntactic categories defined by mood. To do so, we propose force setters. After defining this concept and arguing for its use, we will turn to the implications for argumentation schemes.

A force setter concerns the use of words strictly. Davidson's mood setter describes it as a change in truth conditions with respect to an indicative core. This will be retained in our explanation; however, the task is to explain how the use of words has distinct forces. Asserting, asking, and commanding need to be explained, how these forces differ, and why moods lend themselves to certain uses. A few claims bear repeating. Successful linguistic exchange requires converging passing theories, not aligned prior theories. In fact, passing theories may conflict with prior ones, yet speakers are heard as they intend. So what sets the force of an utterance is not merely speakers' intents or beliefs. Hearers must pick up on this intent. Truth conditions come from utterances, or speakers, not sentences. A force setter, then, marks the act a speaker intends by uttering certain words and a hearer recognizes as such. Such a mark is uttered to signal the kind of act a speaker intends. This mark is relative to time, place, speaker, and hearer(s). The mark is not a transformation of an indicative sentence, strictly speaking, nor is this a piece of grammar. The 'just' in 'A vixen is *just* a female fox' may serve as a force setter, as can an empathetic tone, a look, a gesture, and a pause. A force setter can be whatever a hearer perceives as such. A force setter inflects the utterance or, more precisely, is the inflection of an uttering.

Though it sounds more uncanny than it is, a force setter is hard to speak of. This is partly due to the persisting ambiguity of a speaker's intent: a speaker may always be insincere or speak in bad faith. A speaker can abuse language to manipulate or mislead a hearer. But a force setter is always a mark for a speaker's reason and intent, and these propositional attitudes separate forces. Different forces have different purposes. So an assertion puts forward truth conditions, a question elicits an answer of different sorts, and a command prompts a hearer to do (or not do) something. Suffice to say, forces differ by the reason for uttering, and how it is intended to be heard and responded to. A force setter must be distinct enough to distinguish these acts, while loose enough to embody the wide range in which speakers make their intent known. For these reasons, a theory of action is required to offer a full interpretation of an utterance.[28] Instead of developing such a theory here, we will focus on the last question that remains more squarely in the linguistic sphere: Why do moods lend themselves to certain uses?

Force swings loose of mood, yet moods lend themselves to certain uses. A speaker readily asserts with an indicative, asks with interrogatives, commands with imperatives. But none of the moods fix certain acts (not to mention these same acts do not require certain moods). The question is how susceptible forces are to moods. How similar is 'Alexa, turn on music' to telling Jill, one's daughter, to turn on music? Our answer is that the apparent suitability of mood to use is a misleading one and that different grammatical forms expand possible utterances rather than limit them. If so, a force setter is required to express that aspect of an utterance that expresses a speaker's intent and beliefs over and above sentence grammar or structure. It is an open variable that is measured in its effects—that is, after a successful linguistic exchange. It is also more of a placeholder since it may turn out that a speaker was not sincere, a hearer misheard, or other conditions fail to hold (id est, the speaker was not authorized to say what they did). Whatever the story is for why these grammatical forms emerged, a part of that story is convenience. When speaking with a stranger, it is easier to rely on some widely accepted norm for asserting, asking, and commanding. But this convenience does not get at the significance of linguistic force or action.

A brief comparison of force setters with our earlier candidates will help us formalize them. Mood setters name a transformation because their utterance changes the truth conditions of an otherwise indicative sentence. A default indicative sentence with standard truth conditions becomes an indicative with added truth conditions. To an extent, the original truth conditions change, too. All of this occurs within a theory for interpreting an uttered sentence. An interpretation gives another sentence within the theory for the uttered one. Here is the major insight: there is an analogous relation between the utterance and the sentence serving to interpret it. Davidson's theory of mood works by assuming a successful linguistic exchange. He asks how an interpretation can be given for non-indicative sentences. But this leaves a mood setter ambivalently acting as both part of an utterance and part of the sentence: it is that an utterance of which changes the sentence in a certain way, while at the same time being that change in the sentence. Leaving a mood setter as the latter, we use force setter for the former. This does not leave Davidson's theory otherwise intact, however.

Force indicators are a strip of grammar that commits a speaker to a certain mode if they are at all committed. But grammar misleads when it comes to utterances; meaning is autonomous because speakers use finite variables with rules to speak in an indefinite number of ways. Conventional aspects of language open up more expressive possibilities. Green's proposal assumes a speech act has occurred and starts after the requirement for successful communication (convergence of passing theories). For this reason, the best he can give us is an under- and overdetermined

---

[28] See Davidson (2001, 'Thought and Talk') for a full argument.

indicator for the kind of commitment a speaker holds. But he wants to find a fixed constant in the sentence for assigning propositional attitudes. On my view, force bars us from such efforts. Any words we fix on never fit perfectly and always elide a constant, serious meaning. Situations, intentions, and speakers sneak in to inform the sentence being analyzed, and this happens to Green. We are concerned with natural languages and have no desire to curtail them for a theory. Still, Green is right to address force. The problem is formalizing such a wilely variable.

Assumed so far is that a force setter is an explicit mark. That need not be. A person may say to another, "It is starting to snow," as a way of directing the hearer to close the window. Nothing explicit tells an anonymous observer that the speaker is telling the hearer to do anything. But if an observer knows the speaker and the hearer—knows their relationship—the speaker is commanding the hearer to do something. In short, to bring in Austin (Austin, 1962, Lecture V), there are explicit and implicit performatives. Certain words mark the act instead of being the act: so, 'I am marrying,' said during a marriage ceremony, differs from 'I do,' spoken at the altar. By paying attention to the effects of linguistic acts, we can define a placeholder variable conditionally. In this way, we can draw from Green's formalization of force indicators without committing ourselves to any given linguistic constant.

As before, validity centers on a speaker, S, except force pairs with utterance,

$$\beta(u).$$

So there is an asymmetry between the force of an utterance and sentences ascribed to the speaker. A non-trivial act of interpretation is required. We will come back to this in a moment. To recall, validity concerns a speaker's commitments to a given sentence under a given mode, or

$$< \Delta_1 A_1, ... \Delta_n A_n, \Delta B > .$$

If one pairing holds, then another sentence is held under the same mode (Green, 1997, p. 228). Since mode is not mood, a speaker may commit themselves assertorically with an interrogative or imperative. Nor is mode all there is to force. To assert is not to believe something assertorically. It is an action. Force concerns what we do with our words. Illocutionary validity assumes that force is set, and so we need force setters.

A weak ifid infers force after the fact, and so likewise assumes force is set. If the inference interprets an utterance, instead of a sentence, we come closer to the requirement of successful communication—that is, the convergence of passing theories. With force, that is key. However, we need to retain the indeterminacy that comes from the simultaneous assigning of meaning to a speaker's words and beliefs to the speaker. Prior to illocutionary validity, there is an inference of the following kind:

$$\frac{...\beta(u)...}{f_\psi S}.$$

The force setter is f', which lacks its own content in the ascribed interpretation. Still, we need a variable to distinguish an otherwise identical sentence that conveys the (nearly) same belief, though doing something distinct. A speaker can say, "A vixen is *just* a female fox," to answer a question, order someone else to be quiet, or question them. In each case, the speaker may believe a vixen is a female fox, and say as much.[29] Also, the ascription assumes a speech act has occurred, the one we think occurred. Green and Davidson are right that we cannot secure an action with theory.

From the force of uttering—the premise—we infer a mood setter and a sentence. Now, already, this is slightly off insofar as saying the words, 'It is snowing,' is not the same as the words just typed. Davidson seems keen to this limit for formalizing force, and so restricts himself to mood. But the formula does not output input. It is meant to draw out what is involved. The words uttered are kept distinct from the uttering, then the sentence we analyze has a mood setter that assumes a given, ascribed force. Added to the indicative core and mood setter is an assumed speech act which the parsing fixes, id est, the force setter. The setter is not the force, which occurs in uttering the words in a certain way. Nor is it negligible because in interpreting an utterance the force may part from mood and that separation contributes to meaning. What sets mood is grammatical or explicit. Unless we are prepared to give up standard grammatical moods, or distinguish grammatical moods from semantic ones, a variable is required for forces (asserting, commanding, and asking).

Before returning to argumentation schemes, I will look once more to the requirements for a theory of mood. My earlier problem was that a theory must preserve the relation between moods, ascribe meanings suitable and unique to a given mood, and must track the meaning of utterances. The first two requirements prompt a sentential operator; the last bars us from any operators other than truth-functional ones. On Davidson's theory, moods share a common, representable element and so are related: they have an indicative core with truth conditions. We agree so far. A mood setter couples with the indicative core and describes a transformation of truth conditions. The transformation is relative to a prior indicative that parallels the one used. That is fine within the theory. We part ways with Davidson when he suggests assertions be left alone. An assertion has a force setter, though it does not signal a transformation. It signals a given force when a speech act has occurred. An indicative asserts, orders, and questions. From the indicative core, moods relate more or less. They differ with respect to their truth conditions. If the theory interprets utterances rightly, then it tracks with meaning. With this last requirement in mind, we come to argumentation schemes.

---

[29] With the question, we can imagine the speaker first calling out someone who insulted a woman by calling her a vixen. The one who insulted might respond that a vixen is a female fox. The utterance, "A vixen is *just* a female fox," questions the sincerity of the person who insulted. Endless cases like these can be imagined because of the autonomy of linguistic meaning.

23.4 Schemes and Force

Argumentation schemes are defeasible: hearers accept a conclusion given the evidence, memory, experiences, the speaker, other hearers, at this moment for this reason, and (sometimes) to act. One of the reasons for this is the assumptions (or presumptions) on which an argument scheme stands or falls. Another is that these arguments are exchanged in settings of limited knowledge, be it casual conversations or hearing a speaker on a stage. There is a third reason: the arguments require defeasible interpretations. A speaker's words may be loosely or poorly worded with implicit premises or with a tricky ordering of premises and conclusion. More, when prompted by critical questions, the argument may seem to shift. The arguer is not necessarily changing ground, though. Shifting schemes are a dynamic to arguments of the kind Walton, Macagno, and others are after. On the one hand, schemes guide an interaction by giving form to what is said in arguing and replying. On the other hand, schemes guide how we formalize presentations or conversations after the fact. Between them are the elusive utterances that speaker and hearer(s) exchange, and here is where force comes in.

The use of words changes them, and pinning them down hinders clean cut schematizing. But to use argumentation schemes computationally, the force of utterances must be dealt with. There cannot be an undefined intuition or capacity involved in translating ordinary speech into a schema. The requirement for successful communication—the convergence of passing theories—presents the difficulty, yet there are cues that programmers and engineers are privy to. It is not an impossible task, but one that results in defeasible results. A speaker can always reply, 'That is not what I meant,' and we should take their word (at least partially). As a first step for dealing with force, we will closely examine a case in which an 'is just' statement is made. How we interpret the force of the writing changes the commitments at issue, and how we handle the ambiguity brings us closer to applying argumentation schemes computationally.

Our target case comes from an advice column in *The Washington Post* (Hax, 2020). A woman asks about her sister who is anxious over kissing someone other than her boyfriend after too many drinks. The kiss was witnessed by her cousin who, she fears, has told other family members. Now the sister is bringing her boyfriend to a family wedding and cringes at the thought that someone will say something in front of her boyfriend. Carolyn Hax advises,

> The only way she will feel less anxious is if she gets out from under the weight of her secret, for good. Either she tells her boyfriend; breaks up with him and thereby renders the secret moot; or finds a way to release herself of the guilt and *just accept* what she did as the kind of stupid thing humans do and forgive herself for it.[30]

Hax advises schematically: at first glance, she gives a disjunctive argument with three alternatives. This is an argument from practical reasoning since an action will achieve less anxiety. But this advice is not clean-cut. The third option seems to encompass

---

[30] Italics added.

the first pair ('a way to release herself of guilt') and 'just accept' seems to repeat the conclusion. Where we stress changes the argument type and claims at issue. By looking at points of ambiguity, we will define criteria for handling the force of 'is just' and 'nothing but' statements. This case also tests our ability to deal with force by grammar. A result is that the scheme cannot be crafted apart from critical questions since an interpretation requires a process of questions, a result of persisting ambiguity, which comes from the prevalence of the force/mood relation.

23.4.1   Practical Reasoning

The major premise of a practical inference is the goal, the minor premise is the action to achieve the goal, and the conclusion is the normative uff (Walton et al., 2008, pg. 323).[31] There are a few options to meet the goal.[32] For Hax, the sister's goal is either to 'feel less anxious' or 'to release herself of the guilt' and/or 'just accept' what she did. But the sister also wants to get through the wedding without embarrassment. If getting through the wedding is the basic goal, then the final alternative differs from the first statement. If the sister steels herself or finds another way to bypass feelings of embarrassment, then she can go to the wedding with or without the revelation of her past deed. But this depends on how we interpret 'just accept.' The phrase seems to encompass the point of the first two options to suggest the action needed to relieve anxiety. If the first two acts do not relieve anxiety, in other words, they are not options.

Which goal matters for constructing a schema. Suppose it is relieving anxiety. Then the minor premise consists in three actions, each of which singly satisfies the goal. We have the following:

- *Major premise*: The sister has the goal of relieving her anxiety over a secret.
- *Minor premise*: Telling the secret to her boyfriend (A) would achieve the goal.
- *Minor premise*: Breaking up with her boyfriend (B) would achieve the goal.
- *Minor premise*: Releasing herself from guilt, accepting her action, and forgiving herself (C) would achieve her goal.
- *Conclusion*: She ought to do either A, B, or C to achieve her goal.

Fixing the goal does not clarify 'just accept,' which challenges my first pass at a schema. Hax seems to be saying more in her last option than the others. That is, the last option is more than an alternative to the first two. Hax may be stressing the last one and, if so, the above schema holds. She could also be stating what the sister must do to move on. If right, her list is not a disjunction for meeting the same goal. We test a schema's adequacy by asking critical questions. The fourth critical question that Walton, Reed, and Macagno (Walton et al., 2008, pg. 323) list asks for the grounds

---

[31] The conclusion brings us from possible action to what the sister *ought* to do.

[32] This is similar to the first critical question for a practical inference, except it is not about conflict (Ibid.). Here, interpreting the goal itself is in question.

on which the goal is possible. The second critical question asks about the plausibility of alternatives. But reading Hax's advice, the alternatives follow from or lead to the sister's acceptance of herself, not relief from anxiety. Hax writes in the third option, 'finds a way to release herself,' then with 'just accept' describes what is needed regardless of what the sister does or does not do. Relieving herself of anxiety results from achieving the goal. It is not the final aim of Hax's advice.

So accepting her past deed may be the goal Hax is arguing for. This is the way to lighten the weight of her secret. Then the schema shifts as follows:

- *Major premise*: The sister has the goal of accepting her past deed.
- *Minor premise*: Telling the secret to her boyfriend (*A*) would achieve the goal.
- *Minor premise*: Breaking up with her boyfriend (*B*) would achieve the goal.
- *Minor premise*: Finding another way to release herself of guilt (*C*) would achieve the goal.
- *Conclusion*: She ought to do either *A*, *B*, or *C* to achieve her goal.

The alternatives enable the sister to accept her past deed. Hax stresses the final option to prompt the addressee to stress the same with her sister. It is the bottom line of what must be done. But, again, the disjunctive form misleads if the other options are 'escapes' from what must be done. The normative uff coming from 'just accept' underlines not only the goal but, the crux, the only action that needs to be done. Then we come back to the first goal: when the sister asks about the alternatives, Hax means for her to see that the only viable option for relieving anxiety is accepting and forgiving herself. She anticipates this with her first conditional ('The only way she will feel...'). The point is not that the sister accepts her past deed; it is for her to accept herself as a means of relieving anxiety. The anxiety is the problem to overcome. And so we are back to the first goal with its ambiguities.

Maybe Hax gives false alternatives and we capture the stress, tone, and qualification by streamlining the practical inference. Other options (answers to the third critical question) pale in comparison to the last and should be tossed. Again, Hax's goal is to relieve the sister's anxiety to get through the wedding (and life). Here is the form:

- *Major premise*: The sister has the goal of relieving anxiety over a secret.
- *Minor premise*: Accepting her past deed will achieve this goal.
- *Conclusion*: She should accept her past deed to achieve her goal.

To accept her past deed is to forgive herself for it. The other options, telling her boyfriend or breaking up with him, are lesser options. This schema best expresses the inference at stake, yet ambiguity persists because readers cannot be sure of force. My main point is to show this persistence with a glaring example. On the third schema, the phrase, 'just accept,' (basically) commands the addressee to tell her sister to accept her past deed. Hax issues a directive vicariously through the sister. But then we may wonder whether this is an argument from authority (Walton et al., 2008, pgs. 308–09) or an argument from interaction of act and person (Walton et al., 2008, pg. 321). The normative thrust of the inference seems to come from the author rather than an action or reason.[33] Inversely, the sentence declares all that needs to be done to meet a goal. The write-up describes an action and its result rather than telling the addressee to do something. The final clause is an indicative like the others. The argument's weight seems to come from its form: to meet an end, an action must be done. Even with this streamlined form, in sum, the force remains undecided and, as a result, so do the truth conditions.

Let us assume that the argument is a practical inference. If the final statement is an indicative, 'just' is an adverb with benign stress—it leaves the truth conditions alone. If an imperative, the adverb is more. Gesture, facial expression, tone, and conversational circumstance are no help for deciding whether the adverb is benign or not. The lesson from before returns: the mood setter always comes after a given speech act has occurred. This was the limit to Davidson's account and his concept's bivalence. Mood setters as Davidson saw them were both uttered and that which refers to the uttering. Alone, then, mood setters will not guide us.

The adverb is not a weak force indicator either, as Green would agree. There is no minimum force that 'is just' or 'nothing but' always have. Still, they can serve as marks for a certain force. This is the challenge that Davidson alerted us to. The same words can set a given utterance apart or not. And this was the weakness of Green's indicators. If they set a minimum force, it underdetermines the primary force of a sentence which it was meant to capture, or overdetermines how the sentence is being used.[34] Cataloging weak ifids will be of little help to theorizing force or computing it.

So we suggest force setters as an ideal for handling force. Along with tracking large regularities with grammar,[35] we deal with speakers and their tendencies. For this, analogies are needed to track and anticipate how a given speaker tends to use their words. The inference given above from illocutionary validity can be explicated as an argument from analogy. This suits an exception-filled consistency. From there, further analogies can be drawn across speakers. But the more we generalize, exceptions abound, and so we are not satisfied with mappings of language use within a large community. No one speaks the language of textbooks, dictionaries, and grammar. Our goal is to leverage a loose structure of regularities to craft a form joined with a series of questions for making the force explicit.

A theory of the relation of mood and force hinges on the distinction between utterances and sentences. Force occurs in the moment of uttering, while mood describes the sentence mood. A speaker's choice of words brings in the mood of a sentence, yet the mood does not require a given force. The mood does not restrict the autonomy of meaning. Rightly interpreting a speaker's words does restrict a speaker's choice of what to say. For one, the speaker must use words intelligible as words, not jibberish. And this depends on a speaker's expectations of the hearer. No doubt, there is a shared vocabulary and general syntax, though, again, exceptions abound. A theory

---

[33] Besides, accepting oneself is a strange sort of act.

[34] '...as I claim' may be a throw-away expression, a rhetorical flourish in conversation, rather than actually signaling a commitment. Still, other marks of seriousness are there.

[35] A very useful project, as almost every scholar recognizes.

must direct us to the speaker's intention for how their words are understood and a hearer's picking up on that intention.

23.4.2 Analogy

Within a theory, the relation of mood and force can be treated as an analogy. This does not mean that the relation of an utterance to a sentence, or vice versa, is entirely analogical, only that the relation can be treated as such within a theory (with the goal of computing the relation). In other words, this is how to formalize the relation. Using illocutionary validity, a force setter is

$$\frac{...\beta(u)...}{f_\psi S}.$$

When spoken to, a hearer must recognize the words spoken and how the speaker uses those words. There is an endless list of other background knowledge and beliefs that may be required for an exchange. The lowercase Greek letter stands for the force in uttering and the lowercase Latin letter stands for the words used. An inference must be drawn to replace that pairing with an assumed act, the mood setter of that act, and a sentence. Drawing from Macagno's work on relevance, we can define criteria for matching the force of an utterance with a sentence.

Force splays "crucial challenges for pragmatics," Macagno warns.[36] Citing Dascal and others, he notes that the force of an utterance limits a reply's relevance (Dascal, 2003), and so must be accounted for by his approach, that scholars need a view of speech acts that goes beyond sentence types and generic acts (Sperber & Wilson, 1995, p. 247), which accounts for more than single utterances (Capone, 2017, p. xvii; Oishi, 2017, p. 343; Sbisá, 2002, p. 427), and for utterances that cannot be parsed by pairing grammar and illocutionary content (Strawson, 1964; Streeck, 1980; Kissine, 2013). Macagno adopts an argumentative approach to relevance to address these concerns. Besides justifying relevance and marking strength, his approach assesses the 'reasonableness' of an interpretation—a stake in the mood/force relation. A brief summary of his theoretical commitments will aid us in evaluating his criteria.

Utterances, for Macagno, are held as dialogical responsibilities (Brandom, 1994, pp. 160–162), or "modifications of the social or dialogical status of the speakers based on the evidence produced (what is said)" (Macagno et al., 2018, p. 2).[37] As a result, utterances license certain inferences, and so can be represented by patterns of material inferences (Walton et al., 2008, Ch. 1). Green's weak ifids seem to lurk in the background since an utterance can be parsed as a speaker's mode of commitment. But we should not give in to doubts: Macagno recognizes the dead end of pairing

---

[36] The account below relies heavily on Macagno's current work (for quote, Macagno et al. (2018, p. 7)).

[37] See also (Macagno and Walton, 2017).

illocutionary content to grammar—exactly what Green tries to do. An utterance is interpreted according to a speaker's intent to achieve a social effect based on reasons (Capone, 2013, pp. 446–447; Marmor, 2014, Ch. 2). "More specifically," Macagno continues, "the starting point is constituted by the categories of joint (social) actions performed, proposed, and pursued by the interlocutors," that is, socially binding relations that result from a speech act (Macagno et al., 2018, p. 8). Depending on the categories, their status, and how they are used in interpretation, our reconstructed ideal of an utterance fits, and we must begin with an action or view utterances as certain kinds of acts. Macagno constructs the underlying intentions or conversational demands through presumptions fixed by a conventional relation between 'utterance form and force' or systematic reasoning (Leech, 1983; Strawson, 1964). An utterance within a dialogue is a move that changes the conversation in a certain way and can be classed by their subject or socially binding relation.

With all the theoretical weight and nuance here, Carolyn Hax's advice still eludes us. There are seven categories of action that form the starting point for interpretation: rapport building, information sharing, discovery, inquiry, persuasion, deliberation, and negotiation (Macagno et al., 2018, Table 1; Macagno, 2019, Fig. 2). Which is meant by Hax's declaration that the sister must 'just accept' her action? Clearly, Hax is trying to persuade, but she could be persuading by stating the need to accept or by inferring means to ends. Or, Hax could be negotiating. Out of the options she lists, it would be best for the sister to just accept her action. Given the situation, Hax publicly writes to the sister in such a way that the sisters could work out their options together, or Hax herself could be negotiating with the options presented by the sister, not to mention that these columns are meant to entertain other readers. But Hax may also deliberate toward a certain decision, the sister's decision to accept her action. Or, again, Hax could be establishing rapport by venting her frustration at the simple choice that needs to be made. Our point is that, like Green's weak ifid, categories of action can only be loosely applied and they do not interpret the force/mood relation. We should add that this criticism and the ones to come are not meant to undermine Macagno's argumentative approach, but to draw a limit. As it stands, we cannot account for the relation between force and mood.

Relevance depends on an utterance type given a dialogue goal, Macagno adds. The aim of a dialogue, however, differs from the force of a given utterance—one is locutionary force, the other illocutionary. While Macagno brings in lower and higher levels of dialogue goals, illocutionary force remains unaccounted for. Whether Hax's statement commands or declares, our interpretation seems to fit any of the goals assigned. Nor does the aim restrict the force of a given utterance. Someone can achieve the goal of having a door closed by asking someone else to close it, ordering them to, or describing the problems of leaving the door open. Macagno's approach to relevance, in short, assumes that a given speech act has occurred with a certain definiteness that has been left unexplained and intuitive. An utterance has been replaced by a sentence in his analysis.

Still, Macagno's criteria for encoding relevance is a useful starting point for dealing with the relation between mood and force. A series of yes or no questions leads to the presumption of relevance (or irrelevance) and sets its strength. The questions and their ordering assume an interpretation of the utterance's force, yet test an interpretation of an otherwise ambiguous utterance. Here are the questions, then we will explain as follows:

- Is U [the utterance] coherent with the goal of the previous move(s)?
- Does U address the Topic x of the previous move(s)?
- Can U be presumed to contribute to the point?

Other questions measure the strength of relevance. If we adopt a principle of charity in which we assume that, more often than not, a speaker speaks meaningfully, and so speaks relevantly to the matter at hand,[38] then we can use relevance as a way for evaluating an interpretation. This is insufficient on its own, but it will help. Given its written form, Hax has constructed a string of sentences that cohere to a common goal. Their topic is the same and each sentence contributes to the aim (however we construe it). With this default, we can ask which interpretation optimizes relevance, and this will be the presumed interpretation from which an argumentation scheme can be constructed.

So u stands in for '[she] finds a way to release herself of the guilt and just accepts what she did as the kind of stupid thing humans do and forgive herself for it.' At issue is the force of this utterance (or inscription). And the represented sentence with a given mood setter and assumed force is inferred. Our proposal is that the suant inference is an analogical one:

$$\frac{...\beta(u)...}{f_\psi S}\ .$$

Since the author is absent, we cannot seek clarification. At best, the sisters can give a reasonable approximation of Hax's intended meaning. That is, they must suppose a certain force based on reasons.[39] The ideal is that the sentence that replaces the original inscription (id est, their interpretation) will share truth conditions. The sentence has a mood setter that shares the truth conditions, more or less. The statement will be relevant and, assuming that the overall argument is a practical inference, will result in the strongest argument. There are three steps:

1. Suppose content for the force setter (fix the speech act).
2. Pair the utterance with an indicative counterpart.
3. Articulate the change of the indicative according to the mood setter.

An interpretation is defeasible insofar as future information (a second article by Hax, say, reading prior ones, or a phone call from her) may change which interpretation is more likely. And the relation between mood and force sustains defeasibility. Notice, too, that the force must be determined simultaneous to weighing the relevance, setting other variables like the goal of the discourse, the topic, and the statement's contribution, and identifying the argument type. This cannot be treated as a linear

---

[38] More needs to be said on this principle. For now, we will leave it general and undeveloped.

[39] How they receive the advice also contributes to its force.

process, but one of mutual dependence. To illustrate, we will outline the inference given by two suppositions of Hax's advice.

Suppose, first, that the statement commands: f' represents the command of the original inscription. In place of the inscription, we have 'The sister will accept her action' and then we ask how the mood setter changes the otherwise indicative sentence. The sister accepting her action in response to reading the piece makes the sentence true. The sister not accepting her action makes it false. We still have the question of whether the prior options are alternatives, and so are also commands, joined to this command, or are the rhetorical groundwork for the command. Sidelining that question, we have the practical inference from before:

- *Major premise*: The sister has the goal of relieving her anxiety over a secret.
- *Minor premise*: Accepting her past action will achieve this goal.
- *Conclusion*: She should accept her past action to achieve her goal.

The force of the utterance as it has been parsed in the theory is broken up into the minor premise and the conclusion. The indicative core appears in the minor premise and is framed as a means to achieve a goal. The force comes out in the conclusion. We can ask whether this further parsing of the statement aligns with the speaker's/writer's intent. Before listing relevant questions, we can compare the above supposition with another.

The statement may also state a claim so that f' represents the declaration. 'The sister accepts her action' goes in place of the inscription with the stress of 'just' amounting to rhetoric.[40] The sentence is true if the sister accepts her action, but not in response to Hax's directive. The truth of the statement is closely tied in to the means-ends inference of the argument: if the sister accepts her action, then she will relieve her anxiety. The normative weight of the conclusion does not come from the force of an inscription, but from the inference drawn. Glancing at the preceding paragraph, we see that the basic argument form works here, too, which might tempt us to treat the mood/force relation as negligible. But doing so blinds us to the defeasibility of the interpretation that the argument form assumes, which changes how we respond to the critical questions associated with the scheme.

There is a gap between the original advice column, the interpretation, and the argument scheme. The relation between force and mood brings out the inherent defeasibility of computing arguments. As long as we continue to offer directives for making the intention explicit, presuming an intention, and testing the results, these schemes produce reliable presumptions. So, to conclude, we offer a list of questions that the comparison of the two force setters illumine.

1. Does the force of an utterance (or inscription) change the truth conditions of a premise or inference?
2. Are the effects of an utterance isolated to the utterance or do they change how utterances relate?
3. Does including the force in a premise (or conclusion) rather than the inference (or vice versa) conflict with the speaker's intent?

---

[40] That is, the adverb does not change the truth conditions of the inscription.

4. Does the force setter cohere with the goal of prior moves? the scheme?
5. Are there alternative force setters that would also meet the goal of prior moves? the scheme?
6. Does the force setter weaken the overall argument? (That is, result in more unanswered critical questions.)
7. Does the force setter result in a conflict with prior (or related) utterances? with the topic of the dialogue?
8. Does the force setter result in an utterance that does not contribute to the aim of the dialogue?
9. Does the force setter weaken the utterance's relevance? (Macagno, 2019, p. 9; Macagno et al., 2018, pp. 16–19).

These questions are meant to guide further research. Grammar and other dialogical regularities cannot be the sole reliance in the task of interpreting utterances. Heuristics and the like are required to guide dialogical exchanges between AI systems and persons by making the force explicit (enough) so that AI systems can adapt to the exception-filled ways humans use language.

Margins of error persist. Since speech and action are social, they are moral, and speaking and acting fall under moral criteria. To program moral norms and the like, we should not strive to efface all chance for error. The lesson of informal, open-textured predicates is that doing so (that is, effacing all error) takes our systems outside language and action. Instead, we should strive for AI systems that can speak, hear, and act with persuasive reasons—systems that can aid human reasoning by offering arguments or evaluating ours. Argumentation schemes are one way for bringing artificial intelligence within a purpose context. But to do this, datasets of actual arguments are needed.[41] These datasets would provide information for building machine learning algorithms to interpret the mood/force relation. As I have argued, mood and force must be dealt with to achieve these broader goals.[42] From this raw data, programmers can write algorithms for translating dialogue into schemes or, inversely, for evaluating dialogue with schemes. From them, AI can speak and act for similar reasons by co-opting persuasive schemes. Systems will err at times, but such is the plight of all agents.

References

Atlas, J. D. (2008). Presupposition, chapter 2. *Blackwell handbooks in Linguistics.* Oxford: Blackwell Publishing Ltd.

Austin, J. L. (1962). *How to do things with words.* Oxford: Oxford University Press.

Brandom, R. (1994). *Making it explicit: Reasoning, representing, and discursive commitment.* Cambridge: Harvard University Press.

---

[41] Though this is a goal of the Advancing Machine and Human Reasoning lab at the University of South Florida.

[42] The questions listed above can be used to assess and use such datasets.

Brun, G. (2003). *Die richtige formel: Philosophische probleme der logischen formalisierung.* München, London, Miami, New York: Dr. Hansel-Hohenhausen, Frankfurt A.M.

Capone, A. (2013). *Further reflections on semantic minimalism: Reply to wedgwood* (pp. 437–473). Cham: Springer.

Capone, A. (2017). *Introducing the notion of the pragmeme, chapter introduction.* Dordrecht: Springer.

Dascal, M. (2003). *Interpretation and understanding.* Amsterdam: John Benjamins Publishing Company.

Davidson, D. (1980). *Essays on actions and events.* Oxford: Oxford University Press.

Davidson, D. (2001). *Inquiries into truth and interpretation.* Oxford: Clarendon Press.

Davidson, D. (2005). *Truth, language, and history.* Oxford: Clarendon Press.

Green, M. S. (1997). On the autonomy of linguistic meaning. *Mind, 106*(422), 217–243.

Green, M. S. (2000). Illocutionary force and semantic content. *Linguistics and Philosophy, 23*, 435–473.

Hart, H. (1961). *The concept of law.* Oxford: Clarendon Press.

Hax, C. (2020). *A kiss is just a kiss, but secrets can be relationship poison.*

Kissine, M. (2013). *From utterances to speech acts.* Cambridge: Cambridge University Press.

Leech, G. N. (1983). *The principles of pragmatics.* London: Longman.

Licato, J., & Marji, Z. (2018). Probing formal/informal misalignment with the loophole task. In *Proceedings of the 2018 International Conference on Robot Ethics and Standards (ICRES 2018).*

Lyons, J., & Guznov, S. Y. (2019). Individual differences in human-machine trust: A multi-study look at the perfect automation schema. *Theoretical Issues in Ergonomics Science, 20*(4), 440–458.

Macagno, F. (2018). Assessing relevance. *Lingua, 210–211*, 42–64.

Macagno, F. (2019). Coding relevance. *Learning, Culture and Social Interaction*, Sept: https://doi.org/10.1016/j.lcsi.2019.100349.

Macagno, F., & Capone, A. (2016). Uncommon ground. *Intercultural Pragmatics, 13*(2), 151–180.

Macagno, F., & Walton, D. (2017). *Interpreting straw man argumentation: The pragmatics of quotation and reporting.* Amsterdam: Springer.

Macagno, F., Walton, D., & Sartor, G. (2018). Pragmatic maxims and presumptions in legal interpretation. *Law and Philosophy, 37*(1), 69–115.

MacCormick, D. N., & Summers, R. S. (1991). *Interpreting statutes: A comparative study.* Routledge.

Marmor, A. (2014). *The language of law.* Oxford: Oxford University Press.

Novaes, C. D. (2011). The different ways in which logic is (said to be) formal. *History and Philosophy of Logic, 32*, 303–332.

Novaes, C. D. (2012). *Formal languages in logic.* Cambridge: Cambridge University Press.

Oishi, E. (2017). *Austin's speech acts and mey's pragmemes* (pp. 335–350). Dordrecht: Springer.

Quine, W. V. O. (1960). *Word and object.* M.I.T Press.

Richardson, C., Truong, D., & Jin, C. W. (2019). Examination of factors related to pilot acceptance behaviors toward the automatic ground collision avoidance system in fighter aircraft operations. *The International Journal of Aerospace Psychology, 29*(1–2), 28–41.

Sadler, G., Ho, H., Hoffman, L., Zemlicka, K., Lyons, J., & Wilkins, M. (2019). Assisting the improvement of a military safety system: An application of rapid assessment procedures to the automatic ground collision avoidance system. *Human Organization, 78*(3), 241–252.

Sartor, G., Walton, D., Macagno, F., & Rotolo, A. (2014). Argumentation schemes for statutory interpretation: A logical analysis. In *Legal Knowledge and Information Systems. (Proceedings of JURIX 14)* (pp. 21–28).

Sbisà, M. (2002). Speech acts in context. *Language Communication, 22*(4), 421–436.

Searle, J., & Vanderveken, D. (1985). *Foundations of illocutionary logic.* Cambridge: Cambridge University Press.

Sperber, D., & Wilson, D. (1995). *Relevance: Communication and cognition.* Oxford: Wiley-Blackwell.

Stalnaker, R. (2002). Common ground. *Linguistics and Philosophy, 25*, 701–721.

Stenius, E. (1967). Mood and language-game. *Synthese, 17*, 254–274.

Strawson, P. F. (1964). Intention and convention in speech acts. *Philosophy Review, 73*(4), 439–460.

Streeck, J. (1980). Speech acts in interaction: A critique of Searle. *Discourse Processes, 3*(2), 133–153.

Summers, R. S. (2006). *Form and function in a legal system: A general study.* Cambridge University Press.

Walton, D. (1996). *Argumentation schemes for presumptive reasoning.* Mahwah, NJ: Lawrence Erlbaum Associates.

Walton, D. (1997). *Appeal to expert opinion.* University Park: Pennsylvania State University Press.

Walton, D., Reed, C., & Macagno, F. (2008). *Argumentation schemes.* Cambridge University Press.

Walton, D., Sartor, G., & Macagno, F. (2016). An argumentation framework for contested cases of statutory interpretation. *Artificial Intelligence and Law, 24*, 51–91.

Chapter 24
Effective Decision Rules for Systems of Public Engagement in Radioactive Waste Disposal: Evidence from the United States, the United Kingdom, and Japan

Mito Akiyoshi, John Whitton, Ioan Charnley-Parry, and William F. Lawless

Abstract For large decision-making systems, radioactive waste is one of the most contentious of technological risks, associated with perceptions of "dread" and deep social stigma. These characteristics contribute to the intractable nature of the radioactive waste problem throughout systems in western democracies. The disposal and long-term management of radioactive waste is an issue entangled in technical, environmental, societal and ethical quandaries. The present study asks how different systems in societies address these multifaceted quandaries. Drawing on formal decision-making theory, it identifies a decision rule that facilitates the approval of deep geological disposal plans while achieving a successful outcome in social and technological terms, with the perception of fairness and legitimacy. We compare two decision rules, the consensus rule and the majority rule, and argue that the principle of majority rule maximizes information processing across a system and increases the likelihood of reaching lasting decisions. We also note positive effects of early public participation in the decision process. This conclusion is reached by a comparative analysis across three societies: The United States, the United Kingdom, and Japan. One remarkable finding is the actual and potential effectiveness of majority rule in

The earlier version of this paper was presented at an OECD-NEA workshop held in Paris in December 2019, "The nuclear and social science nexus: challenges and opportunities for speaking across the disciplinary divide." The authors have declared that no competing interests exist.Both the Japan HLW Stakeholder Survey data set and the recordings of simulated workshop analyzed in Section III are available upon request.

M. Akiyoshi (✉)
Department of Sociology, Senshu University, Kawasaki, Japan

J. Whitton · I. Charnley-Parry
Centre for Sustainable Transitions, University of Central Lancashire, Preston, UK
e-mail: JWhitton@uclan.ac.uk

I. Charnley-Parry
e-mail: IParry@uclan.ac.uk

W. F. Lawless
Math and Psychology, Paine College, Paine College, Augusta, Georgia
e-mail: w.lawless@icloud.com

© Springer Nature Switzerland AG 2021
W. F. Lawless et al. (eds.), *Systems Engineering and Artificial Intelligence*,
https://doi.org/10.1007/978-3-030-77283-3_24

these countries despite different policy priorities and cultures. This study reached its conclusion through a synthesis of multiple methods: case studies in the United States and the United Kingdom, and a survey and simulated workshop in Japan.

Keywords Majority rules · Consensus-seeking rules · Stakeholder engagement · The United States · The United Kingdom · Japan

24.1 Introduction

If the goal for autonomous systems of humans and machines to reach the best decision possible, radioactive waste is one of the most contentious of technological risks confronting humans, associated with perceptions of "dread" and deep social stigma (Slovic & Layman, 1991). These characteristics contribute to the intractable nature of the radioactive waste problem throughout western democracies (Barthe & Mays, 2001; Freudenburg, 2004; Short & Rosa, 2004), with the possible exception of Sweden (Chilvers, 2007; Lidskog & Sundqvist, 2004). Despite its complex nature, there exists international agreement—among many countries with developed nuclear industries (McEvoy, 2016)—for the long-term management policy of spent nuclear fuel and high-level radioactive wastes: deep geological disposal, provided that there is public consent (Lawless et al., 2014). Differing from other sub-surface waste management options, the geological disposal of radioactive waste is significantly challenging in that it requires significant detailed assessments across an extreme duration to "understand the impact of potential fugitive radionuclides, for up to 1 million years into the future" (McEvoy, 2016, p. 508), reflecting the vast timescales required for radioactive waste materials to decay naturally to a point at which the risk to society is deemed acceptable (NDA, 2010). Hence, the disposal and long-term management of radioactive waste is an issue entangled in technical, environmental, societal and ethical quandaries.

This study asks how different societies address these multifaceted quandaries. Drawing on formal decision-making theory, it identifies a decision rule that facilitates the approval of deep geological disposal plans while achieving a successful outcome in social and technological terms, with the perception of fairness and legitimacy. It gauges the effectiveness of decision rules in the context of public and stakeholder engagement in spent fuel and high-level nuclear waste management. We compare two decision rules, the consensus-seeking rule (CR) and the majority rule (MR), to argue that the principle of majority rule maximizes information processing and increases the likelihood of reaching stable energy waste-management decisions. We also note positive effects of early public participation in the decision process. This conclusion is reached by comparative analysis of three societies: The United States, the United Kingdom, and Japan. One remarkable finding is the actual and potential effectiveness of majority rule in these countries despite different policy priorities and cultures. This study reached its conclusion through a synthesis of multiple methods: case studies in the United States and the United Kingdom, and a simulated workshop and survey in Japan. The next section reviews the literature and is followed by the analysis of empirical data. Before continuing, we caution readers to distinguish "arriving" at consensus from "seeking" consensus. We not only find nothing wrong with the former even when reached under majority rule for ordinary events (e.g., a motion to adopt unanimous consent to start a meeting; to honor a person; to adjourn) but also for momentous debates (e.g., declarations of war; health emergencies; natural catastrophes). Problems occur however, when rules for seeking consensus or unanimity empower a minority to overrule or block a majority, which we have labeled as minority rule (Lawless, 2019).

24.2 Literature Review: Decision Rules that Encourage Public Engagement

Broad public support for energy technologies can no longer be based upon tacit technocratic assumptions of public trust in technical expertise and with project developer claims, an assertion increasingly supported in the literature. Planning and decision making processes that are technocratic frequently follow the technocratic approach of Decide-Announce-Defend (D-A-D), an often used strategy of expert assessment, closed decision-making, and public relations mechanisms of information provision; they have often caused planning and decision-making processes to experience resistance in the forms of social movements of opposition that inevitably emerge in response (Whitton, 2017). Public engagement upstream of the decision point for siting controversial technologies and its noted benefits have been discussed for some time (Corner et al., 2012; Wilsdon and Willis, 2004). In the context of dealing with technology-generated social controversy, engagement strategies through which heterogeneous citizen groups have the appropriate and necessary access and resources to engage in decision-making processes and to be able to form opinions and preferences through informed deliberation and public debate on issues that could potentially affect them, are increasingly being seen as the gold and necessary standard (Felt & Fochler, 2008; Flynn et al., 2011; Whitton, 2017). Several energy scholars support the notion that greater public participation in decision-making results in conflict mitigation or reduction, resulting in more robust decisions for large energy infrastructure developments, whereas fewer opportunities for public participation can often result in public critique, opposition and project delays, on occasion due to direct action (Devine-Wright et al., 2010). Further research to expand our understanding of "the perceptions, priorities, involvement and support of local residents regarding large scale energy infrastructure" (Whitton, 2015) is of great importance, as asserted by Walker et al. (2014):

> How to ensure fair processes and just outcomes for local communities, and how to enhance the acceptability of energy generation facilities amongst local populations remain important areas of human-energy research. (p. 46).

In a nuclear context, the advantages of public participation have been documented with regards to the strategy adopted for Swedish nuclear waste management decisions (Lidskog & Sundqvist, 2004), whereas the negative consequences of failing to adequately or appropriately involve public stakeholders have been discussed in the context of the Czech Republic (Dawson & Darst, 2006) and UK (WCMRWS, 2013) case studies.

In the recent literature, Fan (2019) provides a rare perspective on radioactive waste governance in Taiwan, noting the often-seen conflicts between policy stakeholders and local citizens concerning knowledge, decision-making, participation and dialogue, or a lack thereof. With the backdrop of Taiwan's phasing out of nuclear power by 2025—a decision taken by its Democratic Progressive Party government— the author describes the challenges surrounding this phase out and of an evident knowledge gap and the prevalence of "top-down procedures" in Taiwan. However, the study also explores the experimentation of and potential for nationwide deliberative forums to enable collective dialogue on high-level radioactive waste storage, forums that have been established by civic society organizations such as environmental non-governmental organizations. Seemingly achieving what few countries in the West have to date, these forums served to challenge the social-technical divide and provide a space for open discussion and reflection on technical issues and information, whilst allowing young people to learn to deliberate and engage with others holding alternative or opposing views. In response, and in the pursuit of dialogic democracy, Fan argues for the establishment of "hybrid forums," that of open spaces enabling groups to collectively discuss technical options underpinned by notions of transparency, openness and equality, as promoted by Callon et al. (2009). As Fan posits, such forums have the potential to shape public discourse by enabling affected communities to participate in often restricted and technocratic processes, and thus enhancing public communication whilst "improving citizen consciousness of nuclear waste issues" (Fan, 2019, p. 327). These studies have highlighted the public's lack of trust as important and possibly pivotal factors in creating public uncertainty or opposition to nuclear waste repository siting proposals (also see Krütli et al. 2010), as found by scholars studying electricity transmission, infra-structure planning (Cotton and Devine-Wright 2012) and wind energy developments (Cowell et al., 2011).

Kemp and colleagues note that the UK nuclear experience has highlighted both the capability of citizens to engage with "complex technical issues" (Kemp et al., 2006, p. 1021) and the importance of early or "upstream" public and stakeholder engagement in "reaching a successful outcome" (Kemp et al., 2006), whereby stakeholder values and opinions are appropriately and effectively reflected. Achieving fairness has long been cited as another essential criteria of such participatory processes. For example, Beierle (2002) states that fairness requires broad representation and an equalization of participants' power and competence, the latter or both involving the confirmation of factual claims through scientific information and technical analysis. In the UK, the support for greater dialogue-based engagement and public involvement in decision-making from central and local government and government agencies has increased in recent decades (Whitton, 2011). However, as scholars such as

Irvin and Stansbury (2004) discuss, despite their value, there are challenges associated with citizen participatory approaches, including a dearth of peoples' interest or time to participate in the process; a consultation fatigue; and the potential for public mistrust to develop should the process be perceived to be a "box-ticking exercise" for pre-determined decisions. The latter arises when few genuine opportunities exist to influence outcomes or decision-making, or there exists an inability to sufficiently engage with, discuss or debate highly technical issues or concepts Whitton et al. (2015, also see 30 and 31). To combat such challenges, Whitton et al. (2015) proposed discussing and establishing local stakeholder priorities at an early stage of the process, thus ensuring that resultant dialogue is "time-effective, locally relevant, focused towards specific stake-holder interests, and generates knowledge which can be utilized within a range of decision-making processes" (p. 129).

Engagement approaches for nuclear energy generation projects and nuclear waste management projects have been found by scholars, such as Blowers (2010), to differ greatly, as have the perceived procedural fairness of both. For example, much of the discourse and engagement with stakeholders with regards to the development of new nuclear energy generation sites has often taken place in or been focused on existing nuclear locations. These areas which house existing nuclear facilities and infrastructure have been described as "the most viable sites" for future nuclear development (BERR, 2008, p. 33) by the nuclear industry, sites that Blowers (2010) describes as demonstrating the characteristics and conditions of the "peripheralization" that served to make the original sites attractive for nuclear development. This contrasts with the siting strategy for nuclear legacy waste disposal sites, known as the MRWS (Managing Radioactive Waste Safely) process (based on Committee on Radioactive Waste Management, or CoRWM recommendations), based in the first instance on the scientifically based identification of safe deep repository sites and second on the acceptance of these identified suitable sites by the potential host communities; this acceptance, however, is provisional and can be withdrawn at a pre-defined and relatively late stage in the siting process (Blowers, 2010; CoRWM, 2006).

In political terms, radioactive waste management has been termed a "poor relation" in comparison to nuclear energy and the "Achilles' Heel" of the nuclear industry (Blowers & Sundqvist, 2010). This relationship as an afterthought is further articulated by the following summation of radioactive waste management as:

> ...an apparently insoluble problem continuing into the far future, blotting nuclear's copybook and halting the onward progress of nuclear energy" (Blowers & Sundqvist, 2010, p. 149).

Formal decision-making theory helps address some aspects of the apparently insoluble: how to improve procedural fairness, stakeholder engagement, and the chance of a successful outcome. The primary model of decision-making, the rational choice model, emerged from the research of economists and other social scientists in an attempt to improve the decisions of humans by serving to make them more consistent and in line with their preferences (Amadae, 2016). An evolution of this theory is known as the rational consensus decision model designed to build consistency for group decisions (Herrera et al., 1997). Mann also extended the theory of rational decision-making to collectives and across species; from his conclusions:

...rational decision making is consistent with empirical observations of collective behavior ... with individuals demonstrating a strong preference for an option chosen by others, which increases with the number of others who have selected it ... [and] how easily an unbreakable consensus decision could emerge, once the cumulative social information provided by past choices outweighs any new quality signal that an uncommitted individual might receive ... [where] utilities may also be understood as fitness consequences of the decision in terms of evolutionary adaptation ...(Mann, 2018, p. E10387).

Mann's model is further distinguished by being "based on perfectly rational individual decisions [made] by identical individuals in the context of private and public information." Mann reasoned that his "model predicts that the decision-making process is context specific." That is, and to the point we introduce later, his research was completed in the laboratory, leading him to speculate that his results.

...would be less clearly observed in more natural conditions ... where the model predicts a more gradual decline in the degree of consensus achieved as the magnitude of conflict is increased (Mann, 2018, p. E10393-4).

Putting aside for the moment the issue of conflict raised by Mann, but central to understanding the effects in the field we will describe later on, three assumptions for the rational choice model reduce its value: first, that the rational decisions made by individuals can be scaled to judge the rational value of social decisions; second, that the elements of a rational decision can be disaggregated; and third, that preferences normally solicited with questionnaires can instead be imputed by observing the actions individuals make.

In rebuttal, first, social decisions are always accompanied by interdependence, the transmission of constructive and destructive cognitive effects present during every social interaction (Lawless forthcoming); second, however, disaggregating the effects of interdependence is difficult to study in the laboratory, which Jones called "bewildering" (Jones, 1998, 40, p. 33), let alone dealing with it as a scientist in the real world. And third, Kelley (1979) found that in the laboratory, the preferences determined by a questionnaire for an individual when alone did not match what an individual would chose in a social (game) situation, the motivation for imputing these values based only on observations, consequently impeding the scale up to larger collectives. The phenomenon of interdependence accounts for all of these differences. For the prisoners dilemma game (PDG), Kelley described this phenomenon as the transformation of a given situation (i.e., a game matrix) into an effective matrix. No matter what Kelley tried in the laboratory to identify the strongest preferences of individuals, interdependence affected the actual choices that they made (Lawless, 2017a, b).

A few years later, based strictly on repeated game contests with the PDG game, Axelrod (1984, pp. 7–8) concluded that competition reduced social welfare: "the pursuit of self-interest by each [participant] leads to a poor outcome for all." This outcome can be avoided, he argued, when sufficient punishment exists to discourage competition; e.g., China's use of its "social credit" system to reward citizens for loyalty, or punish them for its lack (Bandow, 2019). Rand and Nowak (2013) attempted to extend Axelrod's work from the laboratory to the outside world: they started with Axelrod's assertion that "The population does best if individuals cooperate ..." (Rand & Nowak, 2013, p. 413). However, by not finding examples of cooperation that increased social welfare in the real world, Rand and Nowak fell short but concluded with their hope that the "evidence of mechanisms for the evolution of cooperation in laboratory experiments … [would be found in] real-world field settings" (Rand & Nowak, 2013, p. 422). Unlike game theory, interdependence scales up (Lawless, 2017a, b). For example, from our research, we have found that innovation is significantly more likely to be associated with highly competitive teams (Lawless forthcoming); moreover, with access to the National Science Foundation's database, Cummings (2015) found that the poorest performing scientific teams were interdisciplinary teams, likely from spending too much time on finding ways to cooperate across disciplinary boundaries (Lawless forthcoming). For completely different reasons, Kahneman (2011) concluded that the rational choice model does not apply to the choices actually made by the average person (also, see his interview by Workman 2009).

To recapitulate, the literature review establishes three points that inform the empirical analysis. First, the technocratic approach of Decide-Announce-Defend (D-A-D), although widely deployed, often results in adverse outcomes in radioactive waste management. Second, there is some evidence that early or "upstream" public and stakeholder engagement improves the decision-making processes. Third, decision-making theory provides partial support for competition as a way to increase social welfare when cooperation is hard to come by. The next section examines cases from three societies—the United States, the United Kingdom and Japan—to understand the real-world effect of upstream engagement and majority rule that promotes a competition of ideas.

24.3 Empirical Analysis of Public Engagement and Decision Rules

24.3.1 United States

Real-World Decisions at DOE

In the real world of the United Sates Department of Energy's (US DOE) massive cleanup of its extraordinary radioactive waste contamination unfortunately spread across the United States by DOE's mismanagement of its nuclear waste operations (Lawless et al., 2014), possibly at a total cost in the hundreds of billions of dollars for the cleanup of only Hanford, WA, and the Savannah River Site (SRS), SC, the US DOE's two sites with the largest inventory of military radioactive wastes. The US DOE's cleanup contrasts the more rational style of consensus-seeking found in authoritarian and more socialist countries versus the traditional majority rule found in democracies.

The US DOE Citizen Advisory Boards (CABs) are located at major DOE cleanup sites. To reduce the adverse effects from conflict thought to be prevalent under majority rules, the US DOE recommended that its CABs use consensus rules; however, the US DOE did not preclude majority rules. That set up a natural field experiment. The Hanford CAB (HAB) uses consensus-seeking rules; the SRS CAB uses majority rules. Bradbury and Branch (1999) were assigned to evaluate the nine DOE CABs existing then across the United States. From Bradbury and Branch (1999, p. iii) about consensus-seeking,

> Purpose, Goals, and Commitment to Consensus: A definition that has been established and agreed on among board members concerning the basic purpose of the board has a major impact on board procedures and board effectiveness. Boards that have made a commitment to including a wide range of community viewpoints (including those critical of DOE) and to finding areas of agreement among those viewpoints are better able to meet DOE's intent than those that have not made such a commitment. The commitment of individual board members is important, often assisted by effective facilitation.

Based on their definition, from their perspective, Bradbury and Branch saw that success is strictly limited to a process but not to an actual cleanup; that is, in their view, "best" would include the broadest possible participation so that "the process of striving for consensus both reinforced and demonstrated members' commitment to the essential goal of providing advice to the US DOE and the regulators that would have broad-based support" (Bradbury & Branch, 1999, p. 7). Thus, in their judgment, no matter the consequences of the advice rendered, HAB's internal deliberations would be superior to those undertaken by SRS-CAB.

But to their credit, however, in their Appendices, Bradbury and Branch evaluated how the individual CAB members felt about their deliberative processes. They found anger among the member of HAB and pride for those with SRS-CAB. Bradbury and Branch (1999, Appendix: Hanford Advisory Board, p. 12) found at HAB that a:

> Lack of civility, and indulgence in personal attacks during board meetings can erode personal relationships and reduce the effectiveness of board deliberations. Despite a variety of efforts, the board has not managed to adequately control this problem.

In contrast, Bradbury and Branch (1999, Appendix: Savannah River Site Advisory Board, p. 12) found at the SRS-CAB that:

> A shared sense of purpose, pride in the board, camaraderie, and sense of family were very evident.

The "lack of civility" experienced by the members of HAB towards each other versus a shared "sense of pride" by the members of the SRS-CAB might be attributed to the difference in consensus-seeking rules versus majority rules; instead, we attribute it to the accomplishments in the field driven by these two vastly different styles. One of the complaints often heard from HAB members was their inability to make recommendations to the US DOE at Hanford on the concrete actions it should take to improve or accelerate the cleanup; in contrast, most of the recommendations by SRS-CAB to the US DOE were to "accelerate" its cleanup efforts (e.g., Lawless et al., (2005); see Table 24.1). Considering the few positive results achieved at Hanford by HAB versus the significant successes achieved at SRS by the SRS-CAB, we conclude that majority rule is superior to finding a consensus; not to be confused,

Table 24.1 Contrasting the cleanup at HAB versus that at SRS

	Hanford	SRS
The number of HLW tanks cleaned and closed	0	8 cleaned and closed; from 1997
Canisters poured of vitrified HLW glass and stored ready for shipment to a HLW repository	0	4,200 canisters poured and stored; from 1996
Legacy transuranic wastes removed from site and shipped to the repository at WIPP, NM	11,000 drums	750 cubic meters

Notes: The number of HLW tanks closed at SRS is from Blanco (2019, 5/4) Liquid waste system plan revision 21; presentation to the SRS-CAB, from https://cab.srs.gov/library/meetings/2019/wm/5-SP-Rev-21-to-CAB-5-14-19-(001).pdf; the amount of legacy transuranic wastes at Hanford in 2019 is unknown, but estimated, from https://www.hanford.gov/page.cfm/TRU; also, the legacy TRU at Hanford in 2009 was estimated at 75,000 cubic meters, from http://www.environmental-defense-institute.org/publications/Buried%20TRU%20at%20Hanford%20Rev.2.pdf; legacy Tru at SRS in 2017 is from https://cab.srs.gov/library/meetings/2017/wm/Solid_Waste_Fox.pdf

the SRS-CAB often arrives at consensus decisions, but it is through a competitive process, not the cooperation supposedly inherent in the consensus-seeking process.

Two successes at SRS, relevant for this discussion, regard the extremely dangerous high-level radioactive waste (HLW) tanks that were recommended to be closed by the SRS-CAB. It made the first recommendation to initiate HLW tank closure in 1996 (SRS-CAB, 1996). There were 51 HLW tanks at SRS. These giant underground HLW tanks contain radioactive wastes from the production of nuclear weapons-grade material (e.g., Pu-239). The first two HLW tanks, Tanks 20 and 17, were closed in 1997, and the first two HLW tanks were closed under regulatory authority in the USA and possibly in the world. Then when SRS, supported by the SRS-CAB (1999), began to close HLW Tank 19 in 2000, the US DOE was sued to cease and desist from closing additional tanks; the US DOE lost and ceased all of its tank closures. That changed when the National Defense Authorization Act (NDAA) for fiscal year 2005 was signed into law on October 28, 2004. The Sect. 3116 of the NDAA allowed the US DOE to resume closure of its high-level waste tanks. Strongly supported by DOE and the State of South Carolina, the SRS-CAB (2005) quickly recommended that DOE resume its closure of both HLW Tanks 18 and 19.

However, neither the SRS-CAB, the US DOE, nor the State of South Carolina, anticipated what would happen next. The NDAA-2005 law had given the U.S. Nuclear Regulatory Commission (NRC) limited oversight authority over all future HLW tank closures by the US DOE; effectively, the US DOE had to gain permission from the NRC to proceed. Month after month, the US DOE would propose a plan to close HLW Tanks 18 and 19; NRC would criticize the plan, forcing the US DOE to revise it. Nothing happened on tank closures for almost seven years. That situation continued until a public meeting held by the SRS-CAB in November 2011 when environmental regulators from the State of South Carolina complained in public that the US DOE was going to miss its legally mandated milestone to close HLW Tank

19. Afterwards, the SRS-CAB (2012) made a new recommendation to the US DOE demanding its immediate initiation of the closure of HLW Tanks 18 and 19.

The US DOE, the State of South Carolina, and DOE-Headquarters quickly agreed with the SRS-CAB. Once the SRS-CAB got the public got involved, all agencies including the NRC quickly agreed to DOE's closure plan and the tanks were closed in what one ranking DOE official described as "…the fastest action I have witnessed by DOE-HQ in my many years of service with DOE" (Lawless et al., 2014).

Since that day, the SRS site has celebrated the 20th anniversary of its very first two HLW tank closures. From its news release (SRS, 2019):

> Closure is the final chapter in the life of an SRS tank. Once workers remove the radioactive liquid waste from the tank, they fill it with a cement-like grout, providing long-term stabilization of the tank and ensuring the safety of the community and environment surrounding SRS. The first waste tank closure in the nation—Tank 20 at SRS—came about six months before the Tank 17 closure. Each tank held about 1.3 million gallons and began receiving waste from the nation's defense efforts in 1961. Each SRS tank contains a different combination of insoluble solids, salts, and liquids, making each closure unique.

High-Level Waste (HLW) Repository

The WIPP facility, NM, the repository in the U.S. for the disposal of transuranic (TRU) wastes, has been opened for a number of years. It became the driving force by the SRS-CAB to remove all of the legacy transuranic wastes from SRS and to dispose it in the WIPP repository (e.g., SRS-CAB, 2019a, b). From SRS-CAB (2012), the SRS-CAB recommended to the US DOE early on that:

> We are aware that when the Site began processing the radioactive waste into the glass form the first material processed was sludge from the storage tanks. Some of this sludge material did not contain extremely high levels of radioactivity and hence are likely to be much "cooler" in terms of heat load and radiation exposure. We therefore suggest that perhaps these less radiation-intensive canisters would be more amenable for shipment to WIPP, at least in the first stages of any such program as noted above.

Encouraged by SRS-CAB multiple times over several years (e.g., SRS-CAB, 2019c), and under DOE's authority (DOE, 2019), a new risk-based interpretation was rendered for what constitutes HLW. Going forward, reprocessing waste will be considered to be HLW according to its radioactivity characteristics, not just where it was made (known as a source-based definition; e.g., office paper from an area near where TRU wastes passed would be classified as TRU even though measurements might indicate no radioactivity present. Conversely, often very low-level wastes (LLW) might be in actuality more dangerous than HLW).

Yet when the new DOE policy on classifying high level waste based on its risks was announced earlier this month, reflecting the wishes of the citizens from around the Hanford site, Washington state Gov. Jay Inslee and Attorney General Bob Ferguson said in a joint statement that all options would be considered to stop "this reckless and dangerous action" (Cary, 2019).

In contrast, reflecting the views of citizens from around the SRS site in South Carolina, in a letter to the editor, *Aiken Standard*, SC (Marra & McLeod, 2019):

Many of us agree that moving radioactive waste out of South Carolina is the right thing to do. The Department of Energy has taken a step to expedite the process by considering an interpretation change to what actually is classified as high-level waste. This would allow for more expeditious treatment and disposal of waste not considered HLW, and most importantly, removal of wastes from states like South Carolina where it has been stored for decades. On June 5, 2019, DOE announced a revised interpretation of the term high-level radioactive waste and what constitutes HLW. This change would allow DOE to dispose of wastes based on the radiological characteristics and ability to meet appropriate disposal facility requirements. As it exists today, the U.S. classifies high-level waste based on origin—that is—high-level waste is any waste that results from spent nuclear fuel processing. No other country in the world uses a definition based solely on origin but more appropriately makes the determination based on risk.

Summary: Minority Control Versus Free Speech

We have identified consensus-seeking as minority control, the reason it is preferred by authoritarians (Lawless et al., 2014). The European Union, in a White Paper, reached the same conclusion (CEC, 2019, p. 29):

> The requirement for consensus in the European Council often holds policy-making hostage to national interests in areas which Council could and should decide by a qualified majority.

Under majority rule, free speech is openly permitted. When speech is allowed to be free and unmoored from seeking a consensus, then the best ideas, concepts and beliefs must compete to win. From Supreme Court Justice Holmes (Holmes, 1919):

> … the ultimate good desired is better reached by free trade in ideas – that the best test of truth is the power of the thought to get itself accepted in the competition of the market …

Similarly, Justice Ginsburg (Ginsburg, 2019) delivered the opinion in a Supreme Court decision rejecting a case brought against the Environmental Protection Agency (EPA) in its attempt to short-circuit deliberations in the lower courts and to legislate under its own authority, not that of the U.S. Congress, in order "to set limits on greenhouse gas emissions from new, modified, and existing fossil-fuel fired power plants" [p. 1]. Ginsburg decided against EPA, concluding that the case before the Supreme Court had been insufficiently reviewed by EPA and the public that the case must continue through the lower courts so that it would achieve an "informed assessment of competing interests" (Ginsburg, 2019, p. 3).

In summary, the consensus-seeking decision rules employed by HAB have impeded the cleanup DOE's Hanford facility in the State of Washington. In contrast, the majority rules used by the SRS-CAB have accelerated the cleanup at DOE's SRS site in the State of South Carolina. Thus, majority rule support by citizens works like free speech—the best ideas win, they become the best and most robust decisions, and, contradicting Axelrod, the results provide for the best social welfare possible.

24.3.2   United Kingdom: The "Participatory Turn" and Its Consequences

Geological disposal is now the UK government's preferred, and it seems most likely, long-term option for radiological waste management, with various work streams on this option being undertaken in recent years. This choice includes a literature review into geological disposal by the UK's Department for Energy and Climate Change (DECC) (EQUITIS, 2016), and government-led workshops with host communities exploring geological disposal. At present, the UK is one of several countries that have determined deep geological disposal of radioactive nuclear wastes to be its preferred policy option, involving the long-term storage of radioactive wastes in a Geological Disposal Facility (GDF). Such a facility would be located several hundred meters below the surface; would employ several protection measures and containment barriers, including the local geological environment (NDA, 2010); and would require assessments of the geological environment to demonstrate long-term stability, reliability and behavior predictability (IAEA, 2011).

In the UK, policy making for radioactive waste management takes place within a "participatory and analytic-deliberative decision-making framework" (Cotton, 2009, p. 153), whereby integration is sought between scientific and technical expertise and the values and perspectives of stakeholders and members of the public. Hybrid methodologies such as analytic-deliberative processes (Stern & Fineberg, 1996) in Chilvers (2007) have emerged over recent decades that fuse formal quantitative risk assessment techniques with participatory approaches to incorporate an extended range of expertise, knowledge and values through new forms of citizen-science interaction. As Chilvers (2005) states, only relatively recently have citizens and stakeholders in the UK become actively involved in "complex, uncertain environmental decision processes" [p. 237]. This involvement is a significant shift from the 1970s and 80s, during which the 6th report of the Royal Commission of Environmental Pollution (RCEP, 1976) recommended the development of a national radioactive waste disposal facility, and that a National Waste Disposal Corporation should be responsible for its development and operation. UK Nirex Ltd (known as Nirex), funded directly by the nuclear industry and other waste producers (Simmons & Bickerstaff, 2006), was established in 1982 to serve in this capacity (Chilvers 2005), despite the RCEP report proposing the establishment of a "completely independent statutory body" (Simmons & Bickerstaff, 2006, p. 531). Following scientific research and site evaluations, Nirex announced in 1988 the development of a deep underground "Rock Characterisation Facility" to examine the geological suitability of Sellafield in Cumbria, where it was thought a geological disposal facility would be constructed.

Following significant local and national public opposition, the Nirex project was rejected in 1994 by the Cumbria County Council and again on appeal in 1997 by the UK Secretary of State. As Chilvers (2005) points out, this decision signified a pivotal and important moment in the history of radioactive waste management in the UK. The technocratic and expert-led approach to engagement up until 1997, where consultation was limited to waste management companies, industry stakeholders, government and regulators, had been shown from then onward to be inadequate in the face of strong public opposition. Prior to this, public involvement in decision-making was absent or limited (Chilvers et al., 2003). Simmons and Bickerstaff (2006) described the contrasting priorities of technical experts and local residents of areas such as from Sellafield during this period of site evaluation and selection:

> Where the technical experts were focused on the capacity of the physical characteristics of potential sites to ensure safety, local people were concerned about the impacts on the community—landscape impacts, disruption to the community, stigma effects and psycho-social impacts upon local residents [p. 532].

As Simmons and Bickerstaff (2006) observed, the 1997–2005 period saw marked change and signified a period of "participatory turn" with regards to UK radioactive waste management policy. The technocratic manner of Nirex consultations in the 1990s served to highlight the inadequacy of this approach, despite the growing realization since the 1980s that local concerns needed to be addressed. However, Nirex's approach did demonstrate an emergent shift from site selection being almost entirely focused on geological suitability to the acknowledgement of the necessity of social acceptability. The MRWS process was presented as the new consultative process by the UK government and its devolved administrations (Wales, Scotland, Northern Ireland); it commenced in 2001 with the aim "to develop and implement a UK nuclear waste management programme which inspires public support" (Simmons & Bickerstaff, 2006, p. 533). This program was then proceeded in 2003 by the appointment of the independent oversight committee, CoRWM, with the remit of recommending the best option or combination of options for managing the UK's solid radioactive waste stockpile via a long-term and protective solution to government ministers (Ball, 2006). However, as Ball (2006) points out, CoRWM received criticism of its analytic-deliberative approach from various agencies. He observes that the root causes of this criticism can be partially traced to both "a conscious failure to adopt a science strategy as a part of the process" and a failure to effectively utilize expertise from "other crucial areas, including the social sciences" (Ball, 2006, p. 1), which as posited by Ball, leads to the avoidable and significant credibility damage that hindered the efficacy of the process overall. Periods of public consultation, with the opportunity to provide feedback on specific issues or plans, has for some time been considered by the United Kingdom (UK) Government to be the most appropriate method by which to involve the public in new policy and legislation development (Cabinet Office, 2012), particularly since the end of the twentieth century.

As the majority stakeholder in the UK nuclear industry, the UK Government has facilitated the adoption of the consultative process and associated guidance as standard practice. When new plans are large-scale and considered controversial, a planning inquiry (with independent adjudication) is the more common engagement option. However, there are a small number of examples in the UK where action 'beyond consultation' has been undertaken, such as during the decommissioning of Trawsfynydd (Bond et al., 2004) where public participation contributed in selecting decommissioning options, thereby demonstrating local community involvement in nuclear decision-making processes (Whitton, 2015). Yet, it is more common to find the opportunities for participation and influence to be lacking in industry decision-making settings; Cotton and Devine-Wright (2012) find in their study of public engagement for electricity-transmission infrastructure planning in the UK that despite claims by network operators to support industry-public deliberative dialogue, opportunities and evidence for this dialogue in practice are lacking, and citizen perspectives are found to remain very much excluded or on the periphery of decision-making.

As Whitton et al. (2015) argue, UK Central and Local Government administer a form of democracy that "does not provide stakeholders with the power to veto decisions by majority rule, nor require the decision-maker to reach a consensus with stakeholders" [p. 130]. During the period of 2008–2013, the UK Government's MRWS process employed public consultation to identify volunteer communities to be sites for a deep geological repository, with three local authorities volunteering for the programme: Copeland Borough Council, Allerdale Borough Council, and Cumbria County Council. In 2011, the Government stated that the site selection process would only continue if there was agreement at borough and county levels. In January 2013, the three local authorities voted on whether to proceed to Stage 4 of the process, with both borough councils voting in favor and the county council voting against continuing with the site selection process. This outcome ended the site selection process, with the UK's Department of Energy and Climate Change (DECC) releasing a statement detailing that the West Cumbria site selection process had been closed (DECC, 2013).

24.3.3 Japan: Public Interest in Participatory Approach to GDF Siting

Current Status of Siting Efforts

The Nuclear Waste Management Organization of Japan (NUMO) is in charge of geological disposal of HLW and public consultation in the GDF siting and development process to gain acceptance from the general public and the affected communities once sited. It has been soliciting a hosting community since its establishment in 2000, but except for an entry by Toyo City that was eventually withdrawn in 2007, there has been no hosting offer. To facilitate the siting process and demonstrate scientific feasibility of geological disposal, the Agency for Natural Resources and Energy (ANRE) published a map that color-coded geological and geographical properties of the nation in 2017 (ANRE, 2017).

Since 2018, NUMO has been touring the country to provide information sessions based on this map. The information session is titled "Dialogue-Based Explanatory Meetings on the Nationwide Map of Scientific Features for Geological Disposal."

The first author observed some of these meetings. NUMO attempts to take questions, but it refrains from answering policy issues such as spent nuclear fuel reprocessing and the future of nuclear power policy on the grounds that its exclusive purview is geological disposal and that it has no jurisdiction over broader policy matters. At a symposium on the safety case published by NUMO in 2018, the lack of a genuinely participatory framework in Japan for its citizens emerged as a critical issue that had to be addressed.

Japan is often described as a consensus-oriented society (Noorderhaven et al., 2007; Vogel, 1975). Given the lack of a feedback mechanism between the government and its citizens in the GDF siting process, and given the prevalence of consensus-seeking in energy policy deliberations and beyond, it is intriguing to see whether an MR-based participatory mechanism can generate greater support for a GDF. If an MR mechanism is potentially fruitful but not being used, then its absence may contribute to the government's prolonged difficulties in securing a disposal site. Our survey and workshop explored the Japanese citizens' level of interest in getting involved in decision-making for the GDF and the feasibility of MR-based participation.

Simulated Workshop to Test Alternative Decision-Making Mechanisms

A simulated workshop was held in May 2019 to investigate the feasibility of CAB-styled deliberation comparing the effectiveness of MR and CR rules. We wanted to understand whether deliberative advantages associated with MR will be found in the context of Japanese society, or whether its cultural peculiarities will attenuate them as compared with other societies. Participants were 51 students from two universities (Meiji University and Senshu University) who were recruited through fliers and word of mouth. Participation was voluntary, and they gave informed consent in writing.

The workshop had two components: a lecture by a NUMO officer, followed by a discussion. In addition, a survey was administered before and after the workshop to measure participants' knowledge, trust in NUMO, and attitudes towards the GDF. Since most students knew little to nothing about nuclear power, much less GDF siting, the workshop moderator began with an overview of Japanese nuclear power use followed by a session on how a GDF works. During the lecture, participants were shown video clips prepared by NUMO. To illustrate that a GDF can be engineered to safely store HLW, the officer also performed a demonstration with bentonite clay, a material used to encase an overpack that prevents vitrified HLW from leaking.

After the lecture and demonstration, the participants were divided into five groups, three of them tasked with using an MR approach, and the other two asked to take a CR approach. Group assignment was partially randomized on gender and grade, but unobserved qualities such as discussion skills and intelligence were not controlled. The goal of the 90-min discussion was to reach a decision regarding the siting of a GDF based on a hypothetical scenario. Each group had a "NUMO officer" and a "President of Senshu University" role-played by volunteers. The rest of the partic-ipants assumed the role of local residents and were asked to approve or reject the construction of GDF under the hypothetical condition that Higashimita, the area around the University, had been determined to be the best candidate location in the nation and that the Japanese government wanted to build a GDF there. MR groups had to reach a decision by majority vote at the conclusion of discussion, while the CR groups were to deliberate thoroughly and search for a consensus. The discussion was recorded and transcribed. The transcript was given in vivo coding and descriptive coding and analyzed using Kenneth Burke's five keys of dramatism: act, scene, agent, agency, and purpose (Burke, 1969).

The results of the workshop lent support to the advantage of MR even in the context of Japanese society and this particular socio-political issue. At a minimum, there was no evidence that MR is detrimental to support-building. Of the five groups, only one MR group approved the siting of GDF in their community with seven ayes and three nays. Another MR unanimously opposed with eight no votes. The third MR group also disapproved, with four ayes and seven nays. Neither of the two CR groups accepted the GDF in their community. In the post-workshop survey, the odds of approving a preliminary site investigation by NUMO are higher for MR participants: 21 MR participants approved and nine disapproved whereas as for CR groups, 10 participants approved and 11 disapproved. The odds ratio is 2.57 and the direction of association is compatible with the notion that MR facilitates support for a preliminary investigation. But with 51 data points, it is not statistically significant at the five percent level.

Workshop transcripts reveal a more dramatic contrast between MR and CR than was evinced by the quantitative data. The use of Burke's five keys of dramatism found that more place names were mentioned in MR discussions. In addition to Higashimita and its vicinities, only Aomori and Fukushima were mentioned in the CR groups while Korea, Omiya, Minamata, and Olkiluoto were talked about in the MR groups. A more diverse set of actors and actions were evoked in MR groups than in CR as well. As examples, on the impact of the GDF on the two universities, CR groups focused on health risks but MR groups discussed the potential pay-off of siting (the color and number after the quoted remarks below identify the group and participant):

CR.

We have plenty of young people here [because of the universities]. The youth are more sensitive to exposure to radioactivity with higher risks of thyroid cancer and skin cancer. (pink-1).

MR.

[Because of the GDF], universities can lose applicants. These universities are not public, but private ones. If they lose applicants, that means they go out of business. (blue-4).

If parents of prospective students do not approve their enrolment at universities near a GDF, local business will be hurt as a result—realtors and shops that cater to students. (blue-3).

Well, you might lose applicants, but why not start a major in nuclear energy and things like that? Then people interested in these topics will enroll. (blue-2).

Note that when the involvement of universities with the GDF is discussed, a health hazard is central in the CR group. In the MR group, participants were also initially concerned with dwindling applications because of the presence of the GDF, but then they started thinking about the upside of having such a facility. In this and other segments of the discussion, CR tended to drive the focus toward risks only, while among MR participants, concern for risks was balanced by consideration of potential gains.

Survey of Interest in Participatory Approaches

An online survey was conducted in July 2019 to measure the general public's knowledge and interest in HLW management in general and the siting process of a GDF in particular (the Japan HLW Stakeholder Survey, hereafter JHLWS). The population surveyed were residents of Japan aged 20–69 with access to the Internet. The sample size was 3,188. Demographic variables and socioeconomic variables such as age, gender, education attainment, employment status, marital status, and income were also measured. Voting behavior at national and local elections was assessed as well as a general indicator of willingness to participate in public affairs. The respondents were given choice options ranging from "almost always vote at elections" to "have never voted." The descriptive statistics of respondents are summarized in Table 24.2.

The level of knowledge on HLW issues was measured by asking respondents to review thirteen statements about relevant facts and select the ones that they have heard. They were also asked which of the thirteen facts they can explain to others. The list of knowledge statements is given in Table 24.3.

Table 24.2 Descriptive statistics of JHLWS respondents (percentage)

Gender	Male	50.8
	Female	49.2
Age	20–29	15.6
	30–39	19.3
	40–49	23.7
	50–59	19.1
	60–69	22.3
Education	High school	25.8
	Junior college	20.6
	University	53.6
Marital status	Married	55.9
	Divorced/widowed	5.7
	Partnered	1.0
	Never married	37.5
Parental status	A parent	47.7
	Not a parent	52.3

Note: Percentages may not sum to 100 because of rounding

Table 24.3 Knowledge statements

Question number	Statement
13–1	Nuclear power is generated when a steam turbine extracts thermal energy produced by uranium nuclear fission
13–2	As of July 2019, the number of nuclear power plants in operation is less than half of those before the East Japan Earthquake
13–3	Nuclear power generation produces radioactive waste
13–4	New regulatory guidelines were implemented based on the lessons learned from the accident of Fukushima No.1 Nuclear Power Plant
13–5	Germany and Switzerland are planning to phase out nuclear power
13–6	France, the United Kingdom, and the United States will use nuclear power as one of the primary sources of electricity
13–7	Japan is planning to chemically separate spent uranium and plutonium from HLW to reuse as fuel
13–8	Finland does not intend to reuse spent fuel and adopts the 'once-through' policy
13–9	In the United States, Yucca Mountain was selected as a nuclear waste repository site, but the Obama administration suspended the project
13–10	HLW is produced in reprocessing of spent fuel to extract uranium and plutonium
13–11	Japan has not yet decided on the disposal site for HLW generated by nuclear power generation
13–12	In July 2017, the Nationwide Map of Scientific Features for Geological Disposal was published. It depicts scientific conditions that need to be taken into account in siting a repository
13–13	NUMO is an organization in charge of geological disposal including vitrification of HLW resulted from reprocessing of spent nuclear fuel

Attitude questions include 12 statements about Japan's HLW management and GDF siting processes. Respondents were asked to give their preference based on a 10-point Likert scale ranging from 1 "Agree" to 10 "Disagree". Table 24.4 shows the list of attitude statements. Variables are recoded so that higher values indicate stronger preferences for MR.

A general survey of attitudes towards nuclear power has been conducted by the Japan Atomic Energy Relations Organization since 2010, but it has not asked questions about stakeholder participation. In contrast, the JHLWS contains items that were specifically designed to measure respondents' preferred mode of decision-making regarding the siting process, and their willingness to get involved in deliberations with the government if such opportunities arise.

In the JHLWS, Q15-3 measures the preference for a referendum on the siting of a GDF. Q15-6 is concerned with the respondent's willingness to take part in deliberations under a hypothetical scenario of a GDF planned in or near the respondents's community. Q15-10 asks whether the respondent thinks it is necessary for Japan to have a mechanism through which the general public can take part in deliberations

Table 24.4 Attitude statements

Question number	Statement
15–1	Our generation is responsible for the disposal of HLW
15–2	If a GDF is planned in my community or nearby, I think I will approve the proposal
15–3	In siting a GDF, a candidate community should have a referendum about whether to accept it
15–4	The Japanese government should first decide whether it will continue using nuclear power before selecting a GDF site
15–5	It is feasible to safely carry out deep geological disposal
15–6	If my community becomes a candidate site for a GDF, I would like to take part in the debate regarding its acceptance
15–7	Deep geological disposal is the best solution for HLW disposal
15–8	Administrative agencies should work with elected leaders such as governors and mayors for GDF siting
15–9	Administrative agencies should work directly with local residents for GDF siting
15–10	There needs to be a mechanism through which the general public can participate in deliberations about siting
15–11	GDF siting decisions should be left to the experts
15–12	Provided there is sufficient financial compensation, I think I can accept a GDF in my community or nearby

on the siting. Together, these items constitute a scale measuring willingness to adopt majority rule with greater participation than is currently implemented in siting policy processes in Japan. Frequency distributions of these variables reveal that the respondents support a referendum on the siting in the candidate community. 74.2% prefer the referendum with a varying degree of support. 75.8% think that there should be a mechanism through which the public takes part in the siting decision processes. These results imply that a mechanism analogous to an MR-based CAB is likely to enjoy wide public support in Japan. There is no evidence that the Japanese public prefers CR or decision-making processes governed by a small group of experts. Only 7.1% fully support the statement, "The siting of a GDF should be left to experts."

In short, frequency distributions suggest the untapped demand for participation by the public in Japan. It opens up a new question: "Who wants greater participation?" Of particular interest is the ambivalent role of knowledge as a correlate of the desire for participation. The aim of NUMO's many PR activities is to promote the knowledge of a GDF. But that knowledge may spur citizen's desire to participate in decision-making and not just to acquiesce to NUMO's plans. To account for the determinants of preference of participation, a regression equation was estimated:

$$\text{Participation} = a + b(\text{Knowledge}:\text{Nuclear}) + c(\text{Knowledge}:\text{HLW}) + d(\text{Voting})$$

$$(24.1)$$

Table 24.5 Interest in participation in GDF-related deliberations (OLS regression)

	Coeffcient	Std. Err
Nuclear	0.130***	0.015
HLW	0.030**	0.014
Voting	0.024***	0.004
R^2	0.103	

$*p < .05$ $**p < 0.05$ $***p < 0.001$ (two-tailed tests)
Note: See main text for model details and controlled variables

Factor-based scaling was used to construct the outcome, participation scale from the three variables (Treiman 2008). As for the explanatory variables, two dimensions of the relevant knowledge emerge from factor analysis: basic knowledge about how nuclear power generation works and knowledge of Japan's policy on reprocessing. Again, factor-based scaling was used to construct these two scales. The equation also included a variable that measured a respondent's voting behavior. It was included to examine the relationship between a citizen's desire for participation and voting in national and local elections. Gender, age, education, log-converted household income, marital status, and parental status were included as controls. The coefficients are reported in Table 24.5.

The model estimates indicated that the preference for greater participation is affected by knowledge of nuclear power generation, knowledge about reprocessing, and voting behavior. Coefficients for these variables are all positive and statistically significant. Altogether, the results of the JHLWS confirm that the Japanese public are supportive of MR-based participatory decision making. Those who typically vote at elections and those who are more knowledgeable about nuclear power generation and Japan's reprocessing program are more likely to prefer greater participation.

The results of the simulated workshop and the JHLWS provide us with two crucial findings. First, there is interest in more participatory deliberations regarding HLW decision-making. Nothing stereotypically intrinsic to Japanese culture—whether the Confucian tradition, aversion to open conflict, or deference to elders—prevents its people from preferring a participatory approach. The workshop results show that the advantages associated with MR can be applicable to Japan as well. Moreover, preference for greater participation and preference for MR (the latter proxied by preference for a referendum) "hang together" well enough to construct a reliable scale. Both sets of data have their own limitations: the workshop participants are a small segment from the society of interest and by no means a representative sample. Similarly, the survey studied only those with internet access and the ability to fill out the questionnaire online, and thus it is not an accurate snapshot of the Japanese people as a whole. These limitations notwithstanding, this chapter helps to provide a better understanding of the universal applicability of MR and the rationale for participatory decision-making for autonomous systems.

24.4 Conclusion

This study attempts to gauge the effectiveness of decision rules for public and stakeholder engagement in spent fuel and high-level nuclear waste management. Its findings are three-fold. First, early or "upstream" public engagement, based on open and transparent dialogue, is more likely to lead to an acceptable outcome for a variety of stakeholders. Second, majority-seeking leads to optimal information processing and concrete policy input from stakeholders, while consensus-seeking is less effective at achieving those objectives. Third, upstream engagement and majority-seeking may be fruitfully employed even in societies with diverse cultures and track records of public engagement. We reach these findings through the literature review on engagement strategies and formal decision-making theory as well as comparative analysis of three societies that face the task of deep geological disposal.

While our goal was analytic rather than prescriptive, this work has potential policy ramifications not only for topics facing large uncertainties and conflict but also for the possible application to autonomous human–machine decisions. As we noted at the outset, disposal and long-term management of radioactive waste is fraught with multi-faceted quandaries. The robust empirical findings presented here can direct policy-makers toward practical measures to help better understand and navigate through some of the difficulties. Future research must extend our exploration of the two effective tools we have identified—upstream participation and majority rule—by incorporating more observations from more diverse societies than were available for this study.

Acknowledgements This work was supported by a grant from The Nuclear Waste Management Organization of Japan, under its program to support research on social aspects of geological disposal, in fiscal year 2018–2019. The funder had no role in study design, data collection and analysis, decision to publish, or preparation of the manuscript. The authors thank the Mitsubishi Research Institute, Aguru Ishibashi, and Naoto Tanaka for their assistance in data collection.

References

ANRE. (2017). Kgakuteki Map Kouhyouyou Site. Agency for natural resources and energy. Retrieved October 31, 2019, from https://www.enecho.meti.go.jp/category/electricity_and_gas/nuclear/rw/kagakutekitokuseimap/.

Amadae, S. M. (2016). Rational choice theory. Political science and economics, Encyclopaedia Britannica. Retrieved 2016, from https://www.britannica.com/topic/rational-choice-theory.

Axelrod, R. (1984). *The evolution of cooperation.* New York, NY: Basic.

BERR. (2008). Meeting the energy challenge: A white paper on nuclear power, Department for Business, Enterprise and Regulatory Reform, London: TSO.

Ball, D. J. (2006). Deliberating over Britain's Nuclear Waste. *Journal of Risk Research, 9*, 1, 1.

Bandow, D. (2019). 1984: China edition. Closing the Chinese mind would be tragic at any time, but especially now…, National Interest. Retrieved July 22, 2019, from https://nationalinterest.org/feature/1984-china-edition-68082.

Barthe, Y., & Mays, C. (2001). Communication and information in France's underground laboratory siting process: Clarity of procedure, ambivalence of effects. *Journal of Risk Research, 4,* 411 (2001).

Beierle, T. C. (2002). The quality of stakeholder-based decisions. *Risk Analysis, 22,* 4, 739.

Blowers, A. (2010). Why dump on us? Power, pragmatism and the periphery in the siting of new nuclear reactors in the UK. *Journal of Integrative Environmental Sciences, 7,* 3, 157.

Blowers, A., & Sundqvist, G. (2010). Radioactive waste management—technocratic dominance in an age of participation. *Journal of Integrative Environmental Sciences, 7,* 3, 149.

Bond, A., Palerm, J., & Haigh, P. (2004). Public participation in EIA of nuclear power plant decommissioning projects: A case study analysis. *Environmental Impact Assessment Review, 24,* 617.

Bradbury, J. A., &Branch, K. M. (1999). An evaluation of the effectiveness of local site-specific advisory boards for U.S. Department of energy environmental restoration programs, Pacific Northwest National Laboratory, PNNL-12139. Retrieved 1999, from https://www.osti.gov/servlets/purl/4269.

Burke, K. (1969). *A grammar of motives* . University of California Press.

CEC. (2001). White Paper. European Governance, Commission of the European Community, July 2001.

Cabinet Office. (2012). Consultation principles, crown Copyright; July 17, 2012 [Updated November 5, 2013]. Retrieved April 25, 2014, from https://www.gov.uk/government/publicati ons/consultation-principles-guidance.

Callon, M., Lascoumes, P., & Barthe, Y. (2009). *Acting in an uncertain world: An essay on technical democracy.* MIT Press.

Cary, A. (2019). State and top fed official at odds over hanford high level radioactive waste. *Tri-City Herald,* June 26, 2019. Retrieved October 31, 2019, from https://www.tri-cityherald.com/news/local/hanford/article231846798.html#storylink=cpy.

Chilvers, J. (2005). Democratizing science in the UK: The case of radioactive waste management. In M. Leach, I. Scoones & B. Wynne (Eds.) *Science and Citizens: Globalization and the Challenge of Engagement* (Chap. 17, p. 237). London: Zed Press.

Chilvers, J., Burgess, J., & Murlis, J. (2003). Managing radioactive waste safely participatory methods workshop report (Vol. 1): Final Report, Working Paper, DEFRA, London.

Chilvers, J. (2007). Towards analytic deliberative forms of risk governance in the UK? Reflecting on learning in radioactive waste. *Journal of Risk Research, 10,* 2, 197.

CoRWM (2006). Moving forward: CoRWM's proposals for implementation (CoRWM Document 1703). London: Committee for Radioactive Waste Management. Retrieved February 2007.

Corner, A., Pidgeon, N., & Parkhill, K. (2012). Perceptions of geoengineering: Public attitudes, stakeholder perspectives, and the challenge of 'Upstream' engagement. *Wiley Interdisciplinary Reviews: Climate Change, 3,* 5, 451.

Cotton, M. (2009). Evaluating the 'Ethical Matrix' as a radioactive waste management deliberative decision-support tool. *Environmental Values, 18,* 153.

Cotton, M., Devine-Wright, P. (2012). Making electricity networks 'Visible': Industry actor representations of 'Publics' and public engagement in infrastructure planning. *Public Understanding of Science, 21,* 1, 17.

Cowell, R., Bristow, G., &Munday, M. (2011). Acceptance, acceptability and environmental justice: The role of community benefits in wind energy development. *Journal of Environmental Planning and Management, 54,* 4, 539.

Cummings, J. (2015). Team science successes and challenges. National science foundation sponsored workshop on fundamentals of team science and the science of team science (June 2), Bethesda MD. Retrieved 2015, from https://www.ohsu.edu/xd/education/schools/school-of-med icine/departments/clinical-departments/radiation-medicine/upload/12-_cummings_talk.pdf.

DECC. (2013). Written ministerial statement by Edward Davey on the management of radioactive waste, department of energy and climate change (January 31, 2013). Retrieved April 24,

2014, from https://www.gov.uk/government/speeches/written-ministerial-statement-by-edward-davey-on-the-management-of-radioactive-waste.

DOE. (2019). The new interpretation of DOE's HLW, department of energy, department of energy. Retrieved October 31, 2019, from https://www.energy.gov/sites/prod/files/2019/06/f63/DOE-New-Interpretation-of-High-Level-Waste.pdf.

Dawson, J. I., &Darst, R. G. (2006). Meeting the challenge of permanent nuclear waste disposal in an expanding Europe: Transparency, trust democracy. *Environmental Politics, 15*, 4, 610.

Devine-Wright, P., Devine-Wright, H., & Sherry-Brennan, F. (2010). Visible technologies, invisible organisations: An empirical study of public beliefs about electricity supply networks. *Energy Policy, 38*, 4127.

EQUITIS. (2016). Working with communities: Geological disposal—literature review report commissioned by department of energy and climate change, April, 2016. Retrieved October 31, 2019, from https://assets.publishing.service.gov.uk/government/uploads/system/uploads/att achment_data/file/637265/gdf-working-with-communities-literature-review.pdf.

Fan, M.-F. (2019). Risk discourses and governance of high-level radioactive waste storage in Taiwan. *Journal of Environmental Planning and Management, 62*, 2, 32.

Felt, U., &Fochler, M. (2008). The bottom-up meanings of the concept of public participation in science and technology. *Science and Public Policy, 35*, 7, 489.

Flynn, R., Bellaby,P., &Ricci, M. (2011). The limits of upstream engagement in an emergent technology: Lay perceptions of hydrogen energy technologies. In P. Devine-Wright (Ed.) *Renewable Energy and the Public: From NIMBY to Participation*(p. 245). London: Routledge.

Freudenburg, W. R. (2004).Can we learn from failure? Examining US experiences with nuclear repository siting. *Journal of Risk Research, 7*, 2, 153.

Ginsburg, R. B. (2011). American Electric Power Co., Inc., et al. v. Connecticut et al., 10–174. Retrieved October 31, 2019, from http://www.supremecourt.gov/opinions/10pdf/10-174.pdf.

Herrera, F., Herrera-Viedma, E., & Verdegay, J. L. (1997). A rational consensus model in group decision making using linguistic assessments. *Fuzzy Sets and Systems, 88*, 31.

Holmes, O. W. (1919). 250 U.S. 616. Abrams v. United States (No. 316), Argued: October 21, 22, 1919. Decided: November 10, 1919. Affirmed. Dissent: Holmes. Retrieved October 31, 2019, from https://www.law.cornell.edu/supremecourt/text/250/616.

IAEA. (2011). IAEA safety standards: Disposal of radioactive waste (Specific Safety Requirements—No. SSR-5). Vienna: International Atomic Energy Agency. Retrieved October 31, 2019, from https://www-pub.iaea.org/MTCD/publications/PDF/Pub1449_web.pdf.

Irvin, R., Stansbury, J. (2004). Citizen Participation in Decision Making: Is It Worth the Effort? *Public Administration Review, 64*, 55

Jones, E. E. (1998). Major developments in five decades of social psychology. In D. T. Gilbert, S. T. Fiske & G. Lindzey (Eds.), *The handbook of social psychology* (Vol. I, p. 3). Boston, MA: McGraw-Hill.

Kahneman,D. (2011) *Thinking, fast and slow*. New York, NY : MacMillan, Farrar, Straus & Giroux.

Kelley, H. H. (1979). *Personal relationships: Their structure and processes*. Hillsdale, NJ: Lawrence Earlbaum.

Kemp, R. V., Bennett, D. G., & White, M. J. (2006). Recent trends and developments in dialogue on radioactive waste management: Experience from the UK. *Environmental International, 32*, 1021.

Krütli, P. et al. (2010). Functional-dynamic public participation in technological decision-making: Site selection processes of nuclear waste repositories. *Journal of Risk Research, 13*, 7, 861.

Lawless, W. F. (2017b). The physics of teams: Interdependence, measurable entropy and computational emotion. *Frontiers of Physics, 5*, 30.

Lawless, W. (2019). The interdependence of autonomous human-machine teams: The entropy of teams, but not individuals advances sciences. *Entropy, 21*, 52, 1195.

Lawless, W. F. (forthcoming). Interdependence for human-machine teams. *Foundations of Science*.

Lawless, W. F. (2017a). *The Entangled Nature of Interdependence. Bistability, Irreproducibility and Uncertainty, Journal of Mathematical Psychology, 78*, 51.

Lawless, W. F., Bergman, M., &Feltovich, N. (2005). Consensus-seeking versus Truth-seeking. *ASCE Practice Periodical of Hazardous, Toxic, and Radioactive Waste Management, 9*, 1, 59.

Lawless, W. F. et al. (2014). Public consent for the geologic disposal of highly radioactive wastes and spent nuclear fuel. *International Journal of Environmental Studies, 71*, 1, 41.

Lidskog, R., & Sundqvist,G. (2004). On the right track? Technology, geology and society in swedish nuclear waste management. *Journal of Risk Research, 7*, 2, 251.

Mann, R. P. (2018). Collective decision making by rational individuals. *PNAS, 115*, 44, E10387.

Marra, J., & Mcleod, R. (2019). Letter: Interpreting the meaning of high-level waste. *Aiken Standard*, June 13, 2019. Retrieved October 31, 2019, from https://www.aikenstandard.com/opinion/letter-interpreting-the-meaning-of-high-level-waste/article_7625368c-8cb1-11e9-b8b7-2be5d76f50e3.html.

McEvoy, F. M., et al. (2016). Tectonic and climatic considerations for deep geological disposal of radioactive waste: A UK perspective. *Science of the Total Environment, 571*, 507.

NDA. (2010). Geological disposal: generic post-closure safety assessment, NDA Report No. NDA/RWMD/030. Nuclear Decommissioning Authority, UK.

Noorderhaven, N. G. Benders, J., & Keizer, A. B. (2007). Comprehensiveness versus Pragmatism: Consensus at the Japanese-Dutch Interface. *Journal of Management Studies, 44*, 8, 1349.

RCEP. (1976). *Nuclear power and the environment, royal commission on environmental pollution.* London: HMSO.

Rand, D. G., &Nowak, M. A. (2013). Human cooperation. *Cognitive Sciences, 17*, 8, 413.

SRS-CAB. (1996). Recommendation no. 15, high level waste tank farm closure, Savannah River Site Citizens Advisory Board. Retrieved January 23, 1996, from https://cab.srs.gov/library/recommendations/recommendation_15.pdf.

SRS-CAB. (2019a). Recommendation no. 105, Tank 19 Closure. Savannah River Site Citizens Advisory Board, November 16, 1999. Retrieved October 31, 2019, from https://cab.srs.gov/library/recommendations/recommendation_105.pdf.

SRS-CAB. (2019b). Recommendation no. 111, WIPP RCRA permit/transuranic (TRU) waste. Savannah River Site Citizens Advisory Board, January 25, 2000. Retrieved October 31, 2019, from https://cab.srs.gov/library/recommendations/recommendation_111.pdf.

SRS-CAB. (2019c). Recommendation no. 290. Assess feasibility of disposition of SRS canisters to WIPP. Savannah River Site Citizens Advisory Board May 22, 2012. Retrieved October 31, 2019, from https://cab.srs.gov/library/recommendations/recommendation_290.pdf.

SRS. (2019). SRS celebrates 20th anniversary of tank 17 closure, Savannah River Site Citizens Advisory Board, December 12, 2017. Retrieved October 31, 2019, from https://www.energy.gov/em/articles/srs-celebrates-20th-anniversary-tank-17-closure.

Short, J. F., & Rosa, E. A. (2004). Some principles for siting controversy decisions: Lessons from the US experience with high level nuclear waste. *Journal of Risk Research, 7*, 2, 135.

Simmons, P., & Bickerstaff, K. (2006). The participatory turn in UK radioactive waste management policy. In K. Andersson (Ed.), *Proceedings of VALDOR-2006* (p. 529). Stockholm: Congrex-Sweden AB.

Slovic, F. P.M., & Layman, M. (1991). Perceived risk, trust and the politics of nuclear waste. *Science, 254*, 1603.

Stern, P., & Fineberg, M. (Ed.). (1996). *Understanding risk: Informing decisions in a democratic society.* National Academy Press.

Treiman, D. J. (2008). *Quantitative data analysis: Doing social research to test ideas .* Jossey-Bass.

Vogel, E. (1975). *Modern Japanese organization and decision-making.* University of California Press.

WCMRWS. (2013). The final report of the West Cumbria managing radioactive waste safely partnership, Copeland, UK: Copeland Borough Council. Retrieved February 12, 2013, from http://www.westcumbriamrws.org.uk/images/final-report.pdf.

Walker, B. J. A., Wiersma, B., & Bailey E. (2014). Community benefits, framing and the social acceptance of offshore wind farms: An experimental study in England. *Energy Research and Social Science, 3*, 46.

Whitton, J., et al. (2015). Conceptualizing a social sustainability framework for energy infrastructure decisions. *Energy Research and Social Science, 8*, 127.

Whitton, J., et al. (2017). Shale gas governance in the United Kingdom and the United States: Opportunities for public participation and the implications for social justice . *Energy Research and Social Science, 26*, 11.

Whitton, J. (2011). Emergent Themes in nuclear decommissioning dialogue: A systems perspective. *Systemist, 33*, 2/3, 132.

Wilsdon, J., & Willis, R. (2004). *See-through science: Why public engagement needs to move upstream* . Demos.

Workman, L. (2009). Lance workman interviews Daniel Kahneman, Nobel Laureate and co-creator of behavioural economics. *The Psychologist, 22*, 36.

Chapter 25
Outside the Lines: Visualizing Influence Across Heterogeneous Contexts in PTSD

Beth Cardier, Alex C. Nieslen, John Shull, and Larry D. Sanford

Abstract Open-world processes generate information that cannot be captured in a single data set. In fields such as medicine and defense, where precise information can be life-saving, a modeling paradigm is needed in which multiple media and contexts can be logically and visually integrated, in order to inform the engineering of large systems. One barrier is the underlying ontological heterogeneity that multiple contexts can exhibit, along with the need for those facts to be compatible with or translated between domains and situations. Another barrier is the dynamism and influence of context, which has traditionally been difficult to represent. This chapter describes a method for modeling the changes of interpretation that occur when facts cross-over context boundaries, whether those contexts are differentiated by discipline, time or perspective (or all three). We that processing Here, a new modeling environment is developed in which those transitions can be visualized. Our prototype modeling platform, *Wunderkammer*, can connect video, text, image and data while representing the context from which these artifacts were derived. It can also demonstrate transfers of information among situations, enabling the depiction of influence. Our example focuses on post-traumatic stress disorder (PTSD), combining psychological, neurological and physiological information, with a view to informing the

---

Alex C. Nieslen and John Shull equally contributed to second authors.

B. Cardier (✉)
Eastern Virginia Medical School, Trusted Autonomous Systems DCRC & Griffith University, Brisbane 4111, Australia
e-mail: b.cardier@griffith.edu.au; bethcardier@hotmail.com

A. C. Nieslen · J. Shull
Virginia Modeling Analysis and Simulation Center, Old Dominion University, Suffolk, VA 23435, United States
e-mail: anielsen@odu.edu

J. Shull
e-mail: jshull@odu.edu

L. D. Sanford
Eastern Virginia Medical School, Department of Pathology and Anatomy, Norfolk 23501, United States
e-mail: sanforld@evms.edu

© Springer Nature Switzerland AG 2021
W. F. Lawless et al. (eds.), *Systems Engineering and Artificial Intelligence*,
https://doi.org/10.1007/978-3-030-77283-3_25

535

aggregation of information in intelligent systems. These different forms of information are connected in a single modeling space using a narrative-based visual grammar. The goal is to develop a method and tool that supports the integration of information from different fields in order to model changing phenomena in an open world, with a focus on detecting emerging disorders. In turn, this will ultimately support more powerful knowledge systems for fields such as neurobiology, autonomous systems and artificial intelligence (AI).

25.1 Introduction

The inability to combine information from different sources can have disastrous consequences. By early 2001, US intelligence agencies knew that a small group of Saudi nationals had taken flight lessons in Florida. However, officials did not discover the false statements on the visa applications of these men or the manipulations of their passports (Kean & Hamilton, 2004). Separately, a different agency tracked the evolution of rumors following the crash of Egyptair flight 990, October 31, 1999. The rumors had been sparked by a suspicion that the National Transportation Safety Board, a US investigative agency, was mistaken in their belief that the Egyptian pilot of this flight had driven his plane into the ocean as an act of suicide. An alternate story emerged in the middle eastern streets, in which the pilot had heroically saved thousands of lives by plunging the aircraft into the sea instead of allowing it to be flown into Mecca by Mossad, Israel's intelligence agency (Goranson, 2009). This rumor incubated a conceptual structure that would seem unprecedented when it later became a reality: a hijacked plane is crashed into a significant building as an act of revenge. Unfortunately, these separate streams of information did not converge until after September 11, 2001.

The 9/11 terrorist attack against the United States became a well-known example of how the distribution of information across many forms and agencies can lose important intelligence (Kean & Hamilton, 2004). The problem of communicating information between different sources is also an issue in the domain of autonomous systems, where there is an increasing demand for unmanned systems to collaborate with humans and other forms of embodied artificial intelligence (Bayat et al., 2016). In neurobiological research, the ability to model information from different biophysical domains and scales would enable more precise and personalized treatments (Noble, 2015). Our research was funded in response to the first domain and now continues in relation to the second and third. In this work, principles of narrative indicate how to combine information from heterogeneous contexts. A barrier to automating this process is the way in which context is formally conceptualized. This research addresses the problem by developing a modeling method for aspects of context which are usually excluded from knowledge models: influence and ontological heterogeneity.

How do we integrate information from very different frames of reference? Our new 3D modeling platform was designed to model how systems combine into mega-systems. The prototype matures a graphical vocabulary from prior work which represents the transformations of meaning that occur when a fact shifts between situations. Here we describe the new affordances made possible by that platform, beyond the original 2D method produced in Apple's Keynote (Cardier, 2013, 2015; Cardier et al., 2017; Shull et al., 2020). By itself, this visualization system does not solve the problem of ontological heterogeneity, but it does make visible the novel operations required to integrate information from it, endowing the graphical grammar with more dimension and capability. This feeds our theoretical understanding of the operations required. The ultimate purpose of these visualizations is to be used in conjunction with formal methods, one of which is described elsewhere (Cardier, 2013; Cardier et al., 2017; Goranson et al., 2015). In this role, a modeling platform such as this would serve as an interface for a reasoning system that supports open-world modeling—modeling in which all information cannot be known in advance.

The *Wunderkammer* prototype was developed by a team based at the Virginia Modeling, Simulation and Analytics Center (VMASC) at Old Dominion University (ODU). It can accommodate video, images, text and semantic information. The immersive capabilities of Unity 3D allow those various modalities to be connected, and the resulting models can be animated and zoomed through. The new capabilities it adds beyond the 2D method are multi-model modeling, zooming and the depiction of influence through these different operations. These new capabilities are described here, along with indications of the direction of further work.

Our example is post-traumatic stress disorder (PTSD), which is chosen because the interaction among fields with differing ontologies (psychology, neurology and physiology) is well-documented and critical to effective intervention, but difficult to represent. That information framework was supplied by a team in the Center for Integrative Neuroscience and Inflammatory Diseases (CINID) at Eastern Virginia Medical School (EVMS). PTSD also manifests as a narrative, in terms of the internal narrative that a sufferer articulates to themselves, as well as the story they share with their therapist. The 'narratives' in our example are drawn from a case study concerning Mike, a 32-year-old war veteran who was traumatized when working as a medic in Iraq (Hurley et al., 2017). We explain the key features of Wunderkammer using the example of PTSD to indicate the kinds of operations needed to bridge multiple situations and extract coherent intelligence using a systematic method.

25.2   Defining and Representing Context

Context is conceived according to a spectrum. At one end are the conceptualizations of context which are easier to implement, because they align with the capacities of formal representation (Jahn, 1997), such as the works of Minksy (1975), Schank (1995) and Schank and Abelson (1977). In these models, context is a closed subset of reality, with a limited scope and well-defined entities. It is difficult to transfer information among heterogeneous platforms which use these kinds of representations of context because a connection between them depends on the terms in different reference frameworks being the same. The problem is well-established in ontological interoperability (Walls et al., 2014), biological multiscale modeling (Noble, 2015) and autonomous systems (Bayat et al., 2016). Unfortunately, this inability to track real-world phenomena across different representational boundaries is a barrier to modeling how disorder emerges and influences existing situations.

At the other end of the spectrum is lived context. This notion of context is anchored in human perception, in the way humans notice the culmination and transformation of real-world elements. This kind of context is 'always someone's construction' (Krippendorf, 2019, 40), an interpretation drawn from a subjective perspective on the open world. That perspective continuously adjusts the name and implications of everything it perceives as the swim of reality is carried along by unfolding time. The elements which populate this dynamic interpretation can be anything—physical, social or conceptual—and the reference frameworks for these forms of information can include any context, regardless of how different the scale, time or ontological representation. Without those multiple contexts, a model which includes cause and effect will eventually break, as causal influence moves through scales and terms which do not translate from one situation to the next. Devlin describes the challenges of representing open-world context as one in which 'the horizon of understanding continues to recede with every cycle of increased explanation ... the task is endless' (Devlin, 2005, 10).

This dynamism is difficult to capture with an objective formal generalization, which is why implementable formalisms of context tend toward the first conceptualization rather than the second. The problem of formalizing a dynamic and limited perspective was first observed by Hume in his 1748 treatise, *An Enquiry Concerning Human Understanding*, which tackled the issue through the lens of modeling causal influence. Hume asserted that a formal system such as logic cannot objectively capture cause and effect because an entity might bear one name or composition at the beginning of a process but have transformed on both counts by its end (Hume, 1748, 70). We account for these evolutions by using the limitations of context identified by Devlin to address the issue raised by Hume. Rather than render context as a static and objective ontology, we present it as an artifact of subjectivity—a limited ontological scope that changes as more information about the world emerges. Humans use narrative structures to describe and reason about this dynamism. This makes narrative operations a good vehicle to illustrate this process.

As narrative provides critical aspects of this method, it is worth taking a moment to examine what is meant by the term 'narrative'.

25.2.1 *Defining Narrative*

Narratologist Gerald Prince defines a *narrative* as an event that causes a change of state (Prince, 1973). This is a good starting place for our use of the term, as the mechanisms of state change are central to the problem of transferring information among contexts. However, building on a narratological definition can be misleading, as this research is not narratological in its disciplinary scope. Structuralist narratology generally focuses on the relationship between character, event and plot. We anatomize narrative differently to leverage its role as a system for reasoning-through-change.

Our conceptualization of narrative instead draws from cognitive narratology, in which stories are analyzed as 'strategies for organizing and thereby making sense of experience' (Herman, 2001, 132). Our method focuses on the strategies used by stories to make sense of experience which is drawn from ontologically heterogeneous situations. During these narrative operations, conceptual structure is incrementally modified to reveal how causal agency emerges and provokes transformation. High-level storytelling structures such as analogy and ambiguity facilitate these transitions, blurring one definition into another, or creating new conceptual blends from multiple conceptual frameworks (Fauconnier & Turner, 2002). Those networks establish the causal affordances which are possible in that context—affordance being the 'possibilities for action opened up by the overall layout and dynamic unfolding of a context' (Herman, 2000). In turn, these channels of affordance inform the mental model of the reader, creating a map of the available paths through the world. We visualize the formation of these affordances by explicitly illustrating them. The bridging operations are our focus because they facilitate the transference of information from one context to another. The components of these bridging operations are illustrated in the taxonomy shown in Figs. 25.1 (for 2D) and 25.2 (for 3D).

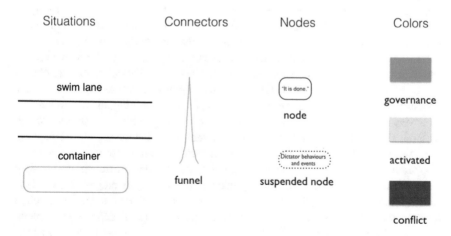

Fig. 25.1 2D Taxonomy

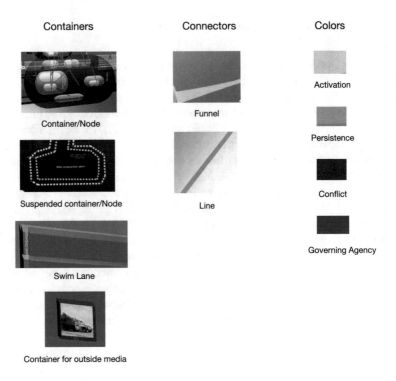

Fig. 25.2 3D Taxonomy

Our description of narrative can also be related to logic because the structures we visualize will be used to transition among general ontologies with a logical structure. Logic most easily builds knowledge systems in which the meaning of the terms do not change. It is a system in which the identity of its elements remains consistent and coherent through all operations, operations that are mathematical in nature. By contrast, narrative is a system that tracks the means by which existing rules are broken and adjusted to form new coherences. It builds knowledge structures that are always in the process of transition. In this research, the structures of interest are the narrative operations that enable adjustment across logical states, bridging one to another.

Several features of narrative are reproduced in the graphical vocabulary of this method. The first feature is that context is a limited and subjective network of information. The second is the continuous generation of new identities for these networks—the way in which one name can become another. The third is the transitions between states which make that possible. Finally, there is the capacity to integrate information from numerous ontological frameworks, even when they are heterogeneous. Each of these narrative features is represented as a mechanism in our modeling environment.

Given these narrative-based factors, we define an ontological transition as the transfer of influence between fundamentally different knowledge structures, whether that transfer is represented as semantic networks, or structures with more dynamic forms of information such as energy or flow, as described in previous work (see Cardier et al., 2017). The transfer occurs regardless of representation, among multiple contexts at a single scale, multiple scales within the same context, and multiple scales within multiple contexts' interactions. In our work, these transitions are between underlying ontological networks.

A causal transition is the transfer of influence between two or more different configurations of the above, where one structure is imposed on another such that the latter is changed. It concerns not only the description of event succession but also influences among them, which is sufficient for transfer to occur, according to a relationship of affordance. A modeling environment that captures this structural imposition could advance the ability to predict future events according to prior patterns. This work aims to build that foundation.

25.2.2 Surrounding Literature

This work has theoretical ancestry in the fields which informed the original method, making it possible to track contextual transitions: cognitive narratology (Herman, 2002, 2017), discourse processes (Gentner et al., 1993; Trabasso & Sperry, 1985), the philosophy of causality (Einhorn & Hogarth, 1986; Murayama, 1994) and in the philosophy of context, situation theory (Barwise & Perry, 1983) and layered formalism and zooming (Devlin, 1995, 2009). The rationale behind that foundation is discussed elsewhere (Cardier, 2013, 2014; Cardier et al., 2017; Goranson et al. 2015). With the new implementation, several other fields now bear on this work: text visualization, 3D visualization and immersive design, technical communication, rhetoric, and the semiotics of VR.

Text visualization and its sibling, semantic visualization, are focused on automatically extracting meaning from large collections of unstructured text (Risch et al., 2008, 155). The scope of these approaches ranges from systems that simply present existing explicit information visually (such as word clouds), visualizations of underlying dynamics (such as conversation analysis) and extends to visual presentations of analysis performed by artificial intelligence (such as knowledge graphs). These methods are interfaces for interpretation, and like other implementations, their conceptualizations are usually biased toward what computational methods can easily capture, with a focus on explicit, easily detectable entities in the text, such as keywords, places, people or events (155). Due to the importance of context and implicit information in interpretation, it is easy for these systems to misinterpret or omit critical real-world information, an issue made explicit by companies such as Lexalytics (2020).

Some of these systems provide a dashboard to view and manage text, in which a researcher can draw links between fragments of text, such as the well-established NVivo and MAXQDA software packages (Tummons, 2014). In contrast, approaches like big mechanism (Cohen, 2015; Kyndi, 2018) perform a deeper computational analysis of more complex texts, such as academic papers, to produce knowledge graphs of their networks. This research is closer to our goals, in that it identifies the nuances in texts rather than attempting an interpretation using the most general definitions of explicit words. However, it still assumes a single homogenous and general reference framework for those ontologies. We need to preserve differences between ontologies—for example, the word 'disorder' does not mean the same thing in psychology as it does in cancer research.

We also rely more heavily on the power of visual design than most of these methods. An example of a like-minded approach is Lexomancer (Angus et al., 2013; Angus & Wiles, 2018), which depicts the degree of interaction between conversational partners in an easy-to-parse 2D graph. In Lexomancer, the high abstraction of the text requires the reduction of complex semantic information to a few parameters, such as the reoccurrence of individual words (Angus & Wiles, 2018). Lexomancer uses that information to reveal a high-level pattern—the dynamic interaction between interlocutors—and is thus able to reveal whether their conversational topics involve an equal exchange of ideas or the dominance of one or more parties. Like Lexomancer, our tool records more hidden knowledge than is otherwise possible. However, rather than using visual design to track the recurrence of explicit terms, our method demonstrates how every time the same explicit term is used, it means something different each time.

The study of immersive design is also important to this work and entails several disciplines, including technical communication, rhetoric, human–computer interaction and new media studies. A common goal among these domains is the effort to codify interactivity and interfaces across structures of user suasion, information exchange, flow and agency. They also establish frameworks for the meaningful study of technical systems and their impact on user experience (Carnegie, 2009). However, each discipline tends to align questions of both 'immersion' and 'design' along the objects of study central to their own fields, and concepts of interactivity remain highly volatile as new technologies introduce entirely novel schema and paradigms of immersion and integration every year (Tham et al., 2018, 50–54).

Our own approach focuses on semiotic frameworks as a means of understanding interactivity and its role in information exchange, imposition of bias and shifting workflows for practitioners (for instance, Barricelli et al., 2018). We also design toward standards from the burgeoning field of human–computer co-creativity. Co-creativity provides highly applicable frameworks for tools and environments providing 'a middle ground between autonomous creative systems, which are intended as the sole shepherds of their own creativity, and creativity support systems, which instead facilitate the creativity of their users' (Kantosalo et al., 2020). By enhancing knowledge modeling with this prototype, we pursue a more robust metacognitive visibility and the formalization of conceptual models that reflect domain expertise by users, increasing a user's ability to discover what they know. This is in line with the best data practices of intentionally designed information systems in support of each other.

The Wunderkammer framework thus informs both design and analysis of the viability of that design, allowing both the researcher/modeler and the analyst to better understand the provenance of insights as well as map the communicative structure and power of the virtual environment to the separate intents of both the user and the system itself. This formalizes what Marini et al. (2012) refer to as 'psychological fidelity' rather than physical fidelity. Wunderkammer's designed environment does not represent an immersive map of 'real' models but instead provides an interrogatable model of 'realized' territory within the narratologist's own structures of understanding. Aligning with Carnegie's assertion that the interface serves as a 'locus of power' which is 'not natural or inevitable' in its designed form, our goal is to use the interface to create immersion within thoughts and processes rather than within experiences and spaces. This fosters co-creativity through an immersive creation and consumption of narrative information.

Extending from this, the **semiotics of VR** recognizes that the mimetic and communicative qualities of VR are a system of signs like more traditional modes of communication, such as text or film (Belanger, 2009), but with the added dimensions of immersion and interactivity (Steuer, 1995, 46). This field is still emerging and draws from related disciplines such as game design, communication theory, rhetoric and psychology. Given that we were designing a new graphical grammar in immersive space, we drew on insights from both these fields.

We now explore how these ideas can more fully represent the example of multi-system interaction in PTSD.

25.3 PTSD Example

Currently, a fully integrated model of PTSD only occurs in the mind of an expert researcher. Our aim is to make more of the expert's knowledge explicit in a modeling environment. Our example follows Mike, a 32-year-old veteran of the Iraq war, as he undergoes therapy for a trauma that occurred when he tried to save a fatally injured soldier (Hurley et. al, 2017). His therapy reveals older traumatic events which feed the wartime trauma—discovering these feeder events is a part of the therapeutic method for the treatment of PTSD during the 'history' stage of therapeutic analysis (Menon & Jayan, 2010). For Mike, the most important of these events is an incident from his childhood when his father moved out of the family home, telling Mike that he was now responsible for his mother. It also reveals that Mike has been struggling to relate to his own wife since returning from Iraq.

To present this information, elements from multiple contexts are brought together—emotion, memory, stress and the central nervous system functioning. Four short scenes are modeled: one for the childhood trauma, one for the wartime event, one for an event in which Mike's son is involved in a car accident (a scene invented by us to illustrate Mike's report of martial conflict) and a PTSD panic attack. These separately modeled scenes are then combined to show how the influence from different events affects Mike's behavior over time and informs his emerging, disordered condition of PTSD.

Some new features of PTSD are included in this model, which are currently not visualized by other methods:

- Mike's traumatic fear response includes emotion, fearful memories, stress responses and the central nervous system, which integrates these elements across brain circuits. The degree of influence these elements have on each other and on Mike's life changes during each subsequent featured event. Our graphical grammar allows these influences and their effects to be visualized as they change over time.
- Trauma can hone and recast other difficult experiences which have occurred over many years, going back to childhood. The immersive space allows us to connect multiple models to depict influence throughout these different times. Our method can also indicate which events or mental narratives directly feed the current trauma.
- PTSD is a multi-scale trauma. The affordances of Unity enable us to zoom between these scales, viewing the micro and macro implications. At the same time, we also move from one disciplinary ontology to another.
- An overview of the whole system is possible.
- Insight arises as a viewer moves between existing knowledge frameworks. Zooming 'outside the lines' enables the discovery of structures that might be visible in one context but not another. In our example, the interaction between two primary features—individual perception and central nervous system function—is explored within the context of PTSD-associated panic attacks. This exploration makes visible a causal agent which was not revealed by the originally modeled elements.
- The tool thus allows a PTSD patient to become the modeler and exercise agency over the presentation of their story. The therapist could also become a co-modeler. PTSD therapy includes a focus on particular memories, whether from the traumatic event or earlier when the roots of the fear response first became established. PTSD also entails the current day, where its effects are felt, and the future, which the sufferer becomes increasingly anxious about. Photos, videos, text or verbal recollections of these events can be imported, arranged and annotated in the Wunderkammer environment, making all these dimensions visible to the PTSD patient and their therapist, who collaborate to modify the disorder, both psychologically and graphically.

A means of representing these features is now explained.

25.4 Representations

Shifting from a static notion of context to a dynamic one requires a shift in modeling conventions. The original 2D method contributed dynamism and a limited ontological scope to a conceptualization of context, making a new visual grammar necessary. Jumping to an immersive representation of those features is a more dramatic stretch still. In this section, the foundational 2D system is briefly explained and the 3D version, with its additional capabilities, is described alongside it.

It should be noted that when performing these operations, the Wunderkammer platform uses a much fuller range of human signaling than the usual desktop modeling platforms. Wunderkammer can be controlled by voice, gesture, eye gaze, head gaze and hand controllers. These new features add dimension to the experience of building and reading the visual grammar. As Bret Victor observes, including more modes of human intelligence expands our imaginative space beyond the methods enabled by mediums based on 2D screens—'of all the ways of thinking that we have, we've constrained ourselves to a tiny subset' (Victor, 2014, 24:25). By building a modeling platform inside a real-time game engine's environment, we have added movement, gesture, volume, time and speech to the expression of thought. With that, an enhanced geometric understanding is also provided (El Beheiry et al., 2019, 1315). These new dimensions also introduce new design considerations, which will now be discussed.

25.4.1 Visual Grammar: Taxonomy

Our method visualizes the mechanisms of contextual transitions: boundaries, influence and limited networks. The 2D version of this tool is produced in the application Keynote, which allows frame-by-frame animation and so can depict the required dynamism. These are used and expanded in the 3D version.

Nodes and edges are fundamental visual units, drawn from knowledge graph theory to represent concepts and relationships. A key difference from the usual representations of these, however, is that our nodes also function as contexts. Any node can become a context if you zoom in and examine how it is composed. This aspect of context was originally noted as a problem by Devlin (2009). Our method embraces zooming as a feature of how open-world reasoning operates.

Our conceptualization of context is also distinctive for the way its *limited scope* is built into the rationale of the system. The notion that a subjective context is limited is foundational in humanities domains such as cultural theory but is usually avoided in the sciences, where generalization is the goal. Devlin acknowledges this circumscribed quality, defining a context (which he refers to as a *situation*) as 'a limited part of reality' which includes the relations between its elements (Devlin, 2009, 238). In our visual grammar, each context is represented as a discrete network of information surrounded by a border. In prior 2D work, this border was referred to as a 'box'. To make it easier to conceive of the volumetric implications in Wunderkammer, the 3D instance is described as a ***container*** here. The graphical grammar for 2D can be seen in Fig. 25.1, and the 3D version is shown in Fig. 25.2.

Containers can house any entity and the immediate inferences it provokes. These entities and their associations are also represented by nodes and lines.

The container's edge thus has numerous functions. This edge—which forms a skin around the enclosed network—represents an item's name and identity. Thus there are two levels to this representation: the name and its ontological composition. This format enables an identity to change over time—for example, Mike as a 'child' can become Mike as a 'man' by preserving some entities from the first context to the second, while changing others. The representation of containment is also key to conveying how one context can be understood on another's terms, during interpretation.

Our definition of context as a limited ontological network is thus further refined as a 'derived' ontology (Cardier, 2013). Each context represents a new derived ontology, even if only one element has changed from one to the next. When information moves between contexts, it becomes part of a different ontology. This shift is how its interpretation changes with shifts of time, perspective or context (Goranson et al., 2015). Attributions of causal agency change with it (Einhorn & Hogarth, 1986). This change has interesting implications when multiple contexts are connected, which will be discussed in a moment.

If a context persists as a frame of reference for the length of a model, it is represented as a container with an open end (see the item 'container' in Figs. 25.1 and 25.2). For example, if 'psychology' is a continuous point of reference for interpreting incoming information, it will be represented as a continuous container in which information can constantly unscroll. There is a precedent for this representation in business process models, in which a persistent context is known as a 'swim lane'. For ease, we also refer to this form of a container as a *swim lane*. Our swim lanes have the same attributes as containers, except they have one open end. An example of how swim lanes are laid out can be seen in Figs. 25.3 and 25.4. The taxonomy of operations in Figs. 25.1 and 25.2 operates over the swim lanes in Figs. 25.3 and 25.4, respectively, stitching together information from multiple contexts.

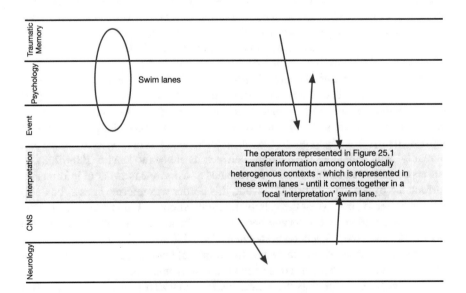

The operators represented in Figure 25.1 transfer information among ontologically heterogenous contexts - which is represented in these swim lanes - until it comes together in a focal 'interpretation' swim lane.

Fig. 25.3 Layout—multiple swim lanes run alongside each other, making it easy to connect them. The semantic products of that connection then collect in the 'interpretation' swim lane, which acts as a federating frame of reference overall

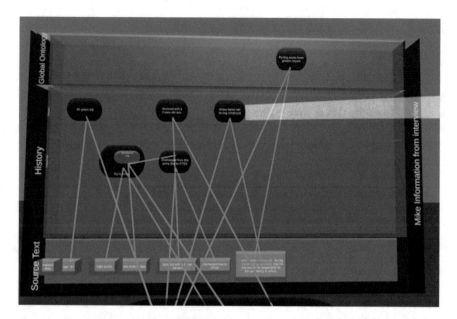

Fig. 25.4 3D representation of the layout

This brings us to the feature of *multiple contexts.* In the open world, numerous contexts can interact to produce an emergent network, which serve as the reference when interpreting a particular situation. For example, the node 'Early psychological issue in which paternal masculinity lets Mike down' appears in all four modeled scenarios. It is the ancestor of the later situations in which PTSD is emerging, and yet those later PTSD-related experiences also inform which aspects of that node's structure become salient later on. That container is therefore acted on by past and also future states. Given that this node appears multiple times and signifies a different interpretation in each, it has numerous dimensions of influence. These overlap to produce a particular structure, which anchors Mike's emerging disorder. It will be critical that the therapist understands and counteracts this structure during therapy— which she does by demonstrating to Mike that he did not unduly let down the soldier who died under his care because he did the best he could (Hurley et al., 2017).

In more sophisticated texts, such as literature and poetry, multiple contexts can simultaneously bear on the interpretation of a fact. For example, the title of the story *Red Riding Hood as a Dictator Would Tell It* connects the contexts of *Red Riding Hood* and *dictator* in an explicit relationship, where one context uses the terms of another to communicate, and in the process reveals implicit intent (Cardier, 2015). Relationships among contexts such as these define how a fact should be decoded in a specific situation.

25.4.2 Visual Grammar: Dynamic Operations

Influence is another fundamental feature of interpretation and requires special description due to its dynamism. The term *influence* refers to the way a situation imparts its structure to another situation. A context (limited ontological network) or node which exerts this agency is designated as 'governing'. In the visual representation, that structure becomes infused with a blue color to indicate its activity (see Figs. 25.1 and 25.2). Additional nodes are then produced from that influence, which is recorded graphically.

Our tool also visualizes influence as an actual transfer of force, each instance of which is represented as a discrete 'funnel'. A funnel acts like a moving arrow, indicating the direction in which influence flows, and so it is a dynamically animated operator. When a funnel strikes an object, its subsequent change in structure reveals the consequences of that influence. Changes are expressed in the arrangement of arrays of nodes. Visually, funnels also provide a way for the user's eyes to be directed in a heavily populated space.

In the 2D representation, funnels were responsible for the majority of the visual action. In the 3D representation, they are currently more static—an issue that will be resolved in the next version. Tangibly representing influence is key to modeling context in an open world, due to the way contexts must continually interact and evolve to keep pace with reality's swim. Influence can also be a lens through which to understand causality, where the topology of one situation informs the next.

Any node/container can be **nested**. *Nesting* is when one container is placed within another. All the objects within the first container are then subject to the influence of the second, constrained by the structures of the new context they are within. In a sense, nesting is another representation of influence, as the nested ontologies operate on the derived ontologies represented by their containers (contexts). Nesting is shown in Fig. 25.5a–c, as one container inside another. These are recorded by Wunderkammer as parent and child nodes.

Besides conveying contextual influence, a containing function makes it easier to maintain cohesion between elements in a particular situation, because when the container moves, all objects within it move as well, unless altered. For example, the node named 'Significant psychological issue learned in childhood' is filled with smaller networks containing the personal history information collected by a therapist before treatment. That cluster reappears as a self-contained unit in all four scenes from Fig. 25.6a–d.

More information can be communicated in the 3D version, but this also complicates readability when many containers appear at the same time or occlude each other. Another advantage of the 3D instance of containment is that it provides a greater sense of enclosure than the 2D version. This containment is reinforced by the physical action of placing one node inside another. Another advantage is the structure that is produced has more dimensions, which can signify additional parameters if needed. See Fig. 25.5c for a visual comparison.

(a)   **(b)**

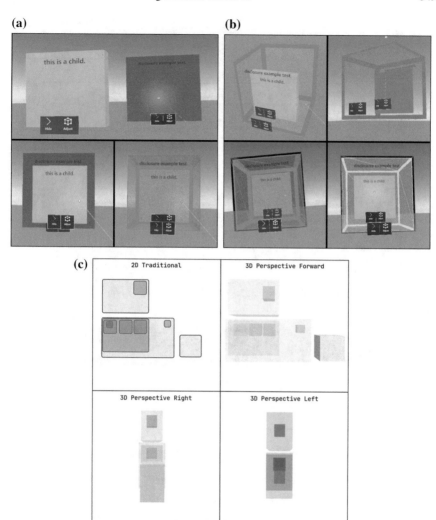

(c)

Fig. 25.5 a 3D representation of the process of nesting—the child node (upper left) is selected (upper right) and placed inside the parent (bottom two frames). **b** Observing the 3D representation of nested containers with expanded volumes from different angles. **c** Comparison between 2 and 3D nesting. Top left, a 2D traditional representation of nested objects. Top right, a forward perspective of a 2D to 3D transformation using similar tones and scale. Bottom left, a right perspective of a 2D to 3D transformation using similar tones and scale. Bottom right, a left perspective of a 2D to 3D transformation using similar tones and scale

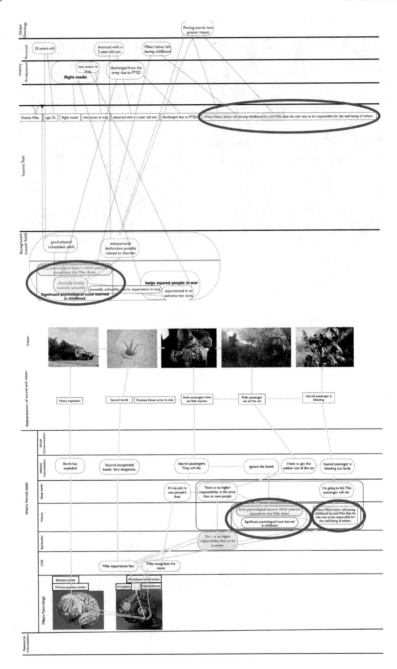

Fig. 25.6 **a** Clinical history—describes the connection between the initial trauma of Mike's father leaving and the later wartime trauma. These connected nodes reoccur in Mike's perception of subsequent events. **b** Key trauma—Mike is unable to save the fatally injured soldier in Iraq. **c** Emergence of PTSD—Mike's wife and son are involved in a car accident. **d** Established PTSD (in which a solid signature structure replaces the tentatively dotted outline in Fig. 25.6c)—a panic attack is triggered by a slamming door

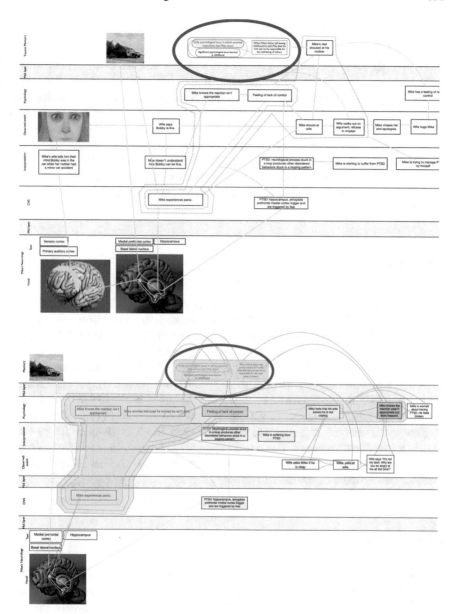

Fig. 25.6 (continued)

25.4.3 Technical Foundations

The container system is managed by six sub-systems that use existing mathematical concepts of the planar convex hull algorithm (Kirkpatrick & Seidel, 1986) and directed graph theory (Goldberg & Harrelson, 2005). This algorithm is then blended across the user input actions to allow an easy user experience that can work in any 3D reality space. The user interface is designed around and built on top of the MRTK SDK, the Microsoft mixed reality toolkit, which is an open-source software under an MIT license. This toolkit allowed us to build input mechanisms that were more responsive to human movements. The base programming language is built on top of the C#.NET platform (created by Microsoft) which is used within the game platform Unity3D.

25.5 Examples

Special capabilities were required for the PTSD example, which is a disorder that spans multiple scales and modes of information. Perhaps the most significant advantage of the 3D implementation was that the Unity environment could handle entire models as easily as the 2D method handled containers and nodes. The 3D implementation added an extra level. That additional level also made it possible to show influence among multiple models. This capability took on new importance when modeling PTSD, due to the way a traumatic fear response can be fueled by multiple incidents and times. There was now a way to represent this accumulated structure.

This spatial benefit is one of the four new capabilities made possible by our 3D representational approach. These four capabilities are: building multiple models, linking multiple models, zooming and signature structures. The 2D and 3D modeling methods handle these capabilities to differing degrees.

25.5.1 Four Multi-disciplinary Models

It is currently difficult to demonstrate how a traumatic experience can feed off previous events in a survivor's history, refining the triggers for the panic responses they experience. To show a more detailed illustration of those emerging and evolving conceptual architectures, we generated four scenes from the Mike example. Each captures a particular traumatic event from Mike's life. At the end of each scene, a state of disordered health is presented as a constellation of relationships. These finishing states are then connected to each other in the multi-model model.

The four scenes are as follows: (1) the childhood trauma, (2) the wartime traumatic event, (3) an incident where Mike's son is injured, and (4) an argument between Mike and his wife in which he is experiencing established PTSD. In Fig. 25.6a–d, four separate 2D visualizations are shown, one for the final state of each scene. At present, the 2D keynote drawings are still a clearer way to represent the fine details and connections among nodes (an issue that will be discussed later). The integration of these models is then shown in the Unity 3D environment, in which it is possible to demonstrate emergent connections between models. The combined model is only possible in 3D.

The **first scene**, shown in Fig. 25.6a, shows Mike's clinical history. It focuses on his earliest trauma: when Mike was seven years old, his father told him he would be separating from Mike's mother and so Mike, as a child, would now be responsible for her. This history was discovered by the therapist before she commenced Mike's therapy, as discovering past traumas is a stage of eye movement desensitization and reprocessing therapy (Menon & Jayan, 2010). The most important aspect of this structure is circled in Fig. 25.6a. It records how Mike is in good physical health but poor mental health. It also records how this childhood experience with his father feeds his state of poor mental health.

The **second scene**, shown in Fig. 25.6b, illustrates the fear experience which provoked Mike's PTSD—a mass casualty conflict event that occurred when a Humvee struck an improvised explosive device (Hurley et al. 2017). Mike was in the vehicle behind that Humvee and tried to save one of the two soldiers inside. The 2D model records that Mike interprets this event using a kernel of the previous childhood trauma structure, and so he feels responsible for the deaths of the soldier he is trying to save. This kernel is again shown in the red circles which are nested within his history. Each of these different contexts is indicated by swim lanes with those titles.

In the **third scene**, shown in Fig. 25.6c, the signs of PTSD begian to emerge after Mike has returned from Iraq and is back at home in Tennessee. In this modeled event, Mike's 2-year-old son (which we have fictitiously named Bobby, for ease of reference) is in the car when his wife has a minor vehicle accident. She reassures Mike that the child is fine, but Mike does not understand how this can be the case. When he hears the news, he immediately recalls the fatal Iraq accident and his unsuccessful intervention. He experiences heart palpitations, shortness of breath and a hot flash. These physical symptoms pass as the conversation with his wife continues. Mike shouts at her but when she disengages, he recovers and apologizes, and they reconcile. Privately, Mike recognizes that his reaction was not normal.

In our 2D model of this scene, the same kernel of childhood trauma appears again, linking and fueling Mike's fear reaction. It is indicated within the red circle in Fig. 25.6c. The emergence of PTSD is indicated by the dotted outline, which surrounds some characteristic elements. The dotted line is a simple representation of a complex phenomenon—the panic response which comes with Mike's traumatic memories is not yet established as regular but he has experienced it a few times. Mike does not yet feel a complete loss of control in which panic causes more panic. This ambiguity means that Mike is eventually able to muster an appropriate behavioral reaction and reconcile with his wife.

The dotted outline is the most important feature in this series of models, except for the reoccurring kernel of trauma structure from his childhood. The dotted line signals that Mike's disorder is a tentative or emerging context. As far as the visualization is concerned, its actual shape is also important—that shadowy outline becomes a signature for the emerging PTSD, which can be visually characterized and then recognized in other situations. That shape is based on the structural affordances of our method, so its repeated recognizability will signify similarity among situations, to the extent that they register against our graphical system of entities and relationships. That same shape appears in the final Fig. 25.6d, when PTSD is established. This enables a user to easily correlate them. In future versions of this system, the emergence of particular shapes could enable fast, high-level recognition of recurrent processes. These 'signature structures' are discussed in Sect. 25.4.5.

This specific dotted 'PTSD' shape is possible to represent in Keynote but not yet in Wunderkammer. The 3D instances of these figures were thus manually built in Unity 3D and inserted to serve as an example.

The **fourth scene**, shown in Fig. 25.6d, shows that a signature shape of PTSD is now established. The structure has fully emerged since the last figure. The encircled kernel is still there, driving its structure. The benefits of allowing signatures to be identified will be discussed in the section, 'Signature Structures'.

25.5.2   Integration of Multiple Models: Model of Models

In the compound figures, these four models have been integrated. This connection allows structures in each individual scene to be related.

The most important connection among the models is the encircled structure noted above—Mike's childhood trauma. It is a core channel of influence throughout all of the situations, connecting similar memories and emotional responses across time. This kernel is not the only reoccurring emotional structure. For example, in Fig. 25.6a, Mike sees his father yell at his mother. This event influences two subsequent scenes, shown in Fig. 25.6c and d, in which Mike yells at his wife while experiencing a panic attack. Another reoccurring emotional structure relates Mike's experience watching a solider die in a vehicle to a later situation, in which Mike's son is in a car accident and Mike cannot understand why the child is okay. These channels between multiple situations are shown in the model of models—see Fig. 25.8a–c.

Figure 25.7 shows an early sketch of how the four foundational models were intended to come together. Designed by Cardier, this sketch pushes the limits of Keynote's capabilities, with the connections only drawable using the sharpie 'pen' function because any other method made the images of the individual models glitch and jump around. It represents a capability beyond what the 2D method is capable of.

The finished product can be seen in Fig. 25.8a–c, instanced in an interactive space. Not only can all the models be linked in an immersive Unity environment, but the assembly can be explored from every angle and across time. Pragmatically, the additional dimensions make it easier to illustrate how influence is moving between the different stages of Mike's life. The details can also be easily zoomed and examined.

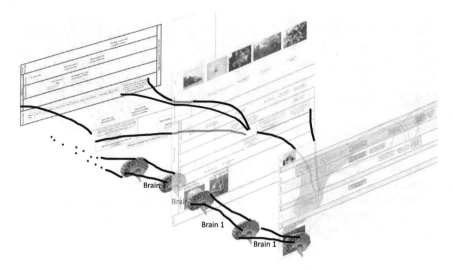

Fig. 25.7 A sketch showing how four different models should be connected

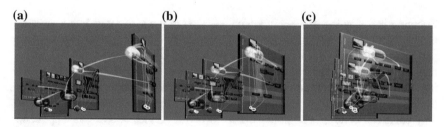

Fig. 25.8 a, b and **c** These three iamges are snapshots which rotate around the integrated model (which is composed of four different models)

Color makes the structures of influence stand out as they move between the different scenes. The large assemblies within the contexts—and how they assemble with other contexts—are only possible in a 3D space such as this.

The Wunderkammer prototype is capable of performing this assembly but not easily, as this model of models is a new way in which the prototype is being used. For this reason, these final images were generated in Unity 3D as a speculative indication of what it can do. In both the 2D and 3D tools, we are reaching the limit of what can be supported.

Integrating multiple graphical models in this manner indicates how to a higher level of semantic interpretation can be visualized. When higher-level structures are meaningfully connected, they produce conceptual structures similar to those which might be drawn out in a literary analysis. For example, one repeated structure is that Mike is struggling with being responsible for other people, due to his childhood trauma. That motif is established because it appears in numerous situations. It is also

(a)   (b)   (c)

Fig. 25.9 **a**, **b** and **c** Zooming into one of the models, gaining a closer and closer view

connected to another, in which Mike yells at his wife, like his father did with his mother. This is a 'theme' which has started to emerge due to the features it shares in common with multiple clusters of nodes. It is similar to literary analysis in that many layers of meaning are connected across numerous situations and the way they operate and repeat at such a high level.

25.5.3 Zooming

Zooming is a viewing process in which one area of the scene gets larger so that it can be seen in more detail (Shneiderman, 1996, 339). Zooming is also an important part of an exploration because it allows a network to be examined from perspectives that might not have been anticipated (El Beheiry et al., 2019). It functions as an intuitive 'drill-down' feature that allows a user to expand one aspect of that system for closer scrutiny, or pass through one level of scale in order to view another. Any container/node can be zoomed-into to reveal further nodes. Our application of this feature is also directly linked to Devlin's method for *Layered Formalism and Zooming*, in which facts (nodes) are actually contexts (containers) viewed at a different scale (Devlin & Rosenberg, 1996).

In the 2D Keynote, while zooming automatically is not possible, it can be imitated using a frame-by-frame animation. In contrast, the 3D environment makes zooming easy and powerful. Figure 25.9a–c gives a sense of how zooming works in Wunderkammer. It is difficult to convey dimensional movement in the flat image on this page, so a series of stills are shown instead. The experience of zooming is actually more like being in an aircraft, flying through cloud after cloud of information.

A more complex example of how zooming can be used can be seen in the example, 'Sandwich Layers'.

25.5.4 Sandwich Layers

How do we integrate heterogeneous contexts? This question is best addressed by the ability to examine the space between 'sandwich layers'.

New connections depend on finding new points of view. A change of perspective can be achieved by bringing in another existing context and using it to find a different path through the available information. This principle has already been described in prior work (Cardier, 2014, 2015; Cardier et al., 2020a, b). Another way to change perspectives is to engineer an intermediary context using known information, to enable a transition between states. During this process, a previous cluster of information is adjusted in relation to a specific set of facts and problems.

In our PTSD example, a goal is to discover a bridge that can formally connect two domains—'psychology' and 'central nervous system function'—in a predictive fashion. The relationship between these two domains is described in the medical literature. Psychologically, the panic attacks of PTSD can stem from the aggregation of previous traumas, because they determine where a patient's sense of control will fail. The root cause of the panic attack is a change at the neurocircuit level which inappropriately engages fear responses—although these changes are not fully understood, they likely involve interactions between the amygdala, hippocampus and prefrontal medial cortex as well as other brain regions. Which disciplinary perspective is more important depends on the reason for the enquiry.

Using the existing literature, we can populate details between our two presented swim lanes, 'psychology' and 'central nervous system function' with reference to Mike's particular situation. The path of information in Fig. 25.10 was assembled to bridge these two contexts. Mike's physically experienced panic attack (from the central nervous system) becomes a psychological panic attack because it causes him to realize that he is not well. The associated network of facts can link these two nodes in separate domains.

The sequence occurs like this. First, a trigger causes Mike to be afraid, which in turn prompts his sympathetic nervous system to produce a 'fight or flight' response. He experiences shortness of breath, increased heart rate and difficulty in concentrating. His parasympathetic nervous system, which would usually enable the body to calm this response, is not appropriately activated by the central neurocircuits. The sense of physical panic thus does not stop. An awareness of this causes Mike to reflect on his past trauma and psychologically register that he is not well. It causes a further sense of loss of control, increasing the sense of physical panic further.

This sequence establishes a causal chain in which general information is recast so that it is specific to connecting the two example nodes. The two connected nodes are 'Mike experiences panic' (in the central nervous system context) and the node 'Mike knows the reaction isn't appropriate' (in the psychology context). This relationship establishes a path of causal affordance which can be used predictively in situations with similar elements, such as other situations in Mike's life. That sequence is modeled in Fig. 25.10a–c. The model is shown in its 2D Keynote format due to the need for readability. Figure 25.10b zooms close to show the chain of events that link these two contexts.

The last of these images, Fig. 25.10c, reveals that the causal agent connecting the two contexts is actually the *absence* of a process. The absence of a response by the parasympathetic nervous system is central to enabling the causal chain in which Mike's physiological reaction is linked to his psychological reaction. When

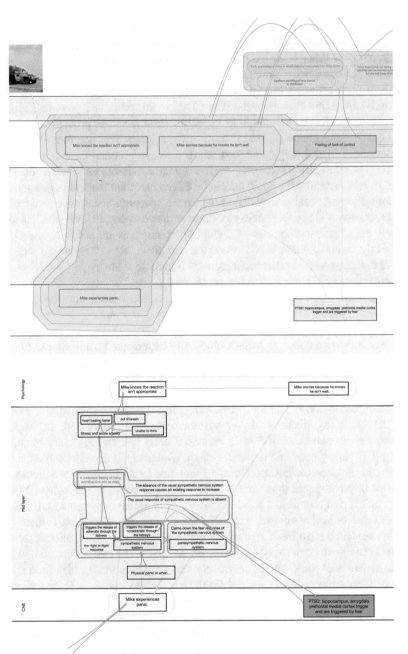

Fig. 25.10 a Zooming—this image focuses on the two fields which are connected in the yellow PTSD structure. **b** Sandwich layer—a new chain of facts links the 'psychology' and 'CNS' contexts. **c** Sandwich layer—within this view, a new causal agent is registered. Although this node appeared in the initial slide, its causal importance was not identified in that context

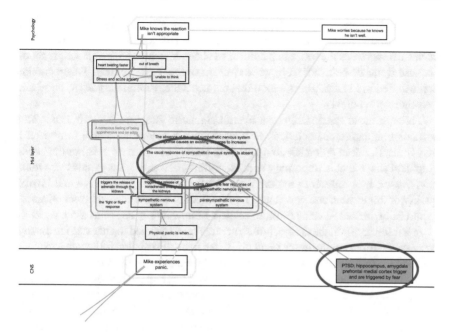

Fig. 25.10   (continued)

his physical panic does not subside, it causes a feeling of loss of control, which Mike registers psychologically. The absence or suppression of something can thus be a causal agent. We represent this absence using a tentatively dotted line, to show where the process would have been under normal conditions. This absence bridges the two nodes in question.

It is anticipated that more detailed versions of this feature could be used to understand how to bring together different contexts across a range of fields that have fundamentally different ontological foundations.

25.5.5   *Signature Structures*

The final feature is the signature structure—the term 'signature' refers to an overall architecture captured by an aggregation of facts and their networks, a higher-level design. That system of relationships can function like an analogy, making it possible to identify structural similarities across heterogeneous situations even though the individual entities in each might be dissimilar. In our case, signatures are based on the relationships among semantic networks and our taxonomic choices.

In the Mike example, our signature structure reveals that PTSD's signature structure is recursive. The panic which comes with PTSD is rooted in a sense that control has been lost. This process can be triggered by an initial stimulus, such as the sound of a door slamming, which is depicted in Fig. 25.6d. Mike's physiological reaction to that sound is an involuntary panic attack. This attack causes him further alarm because it increases the sense that control has been lost. Mike fears the fear reaction because it means he is not well, which in turn causes more anxiety. This recursion is illustrated in Fig. 25.10a as a loop that connects the 'central nervous system' and 'psychology' contexts.

Through these relationships, an overall signature structure is established. This particular signature characterizes an introspective system that is able to register a flaw in itself, but in doing so, compounds the effect of that flaw. It is not the actual graphical shape that is important, because different visualization parameters would likely result in a different physical area. What matters is the iterative and insular quality of this system and how that is represented. In Mike's case, this recursiveness would be expressed in some form, regardless of how its key elements are presented.

In a future system, these signature structures could be used to characterize elusive processes—for example, in social media, when many distributed followers parrot the ideas of a single agent. Rather than try to analyze unobservable agents, activities in these domains could be tracked using signatures. The ability to find overall signatures would be a benefit to many domains. We encounter many of the same dynamics in competitive cyber contexts and related 'information fusion' applications: implicit influence, ontological misalignment and recursive influence. Of particular concern are situations where reasoning is distributed in autonomous systems. In that case, we lose the ability to have a global executive to manage the suitability of local results, either by truth or trust metrics. A suitable solution may leverage this work to model local influence and identify similar structures in distributed systems. In a system with a formal back-end this system would also be able to automatically learn new 'signatures', which are emergent contexts that can be re-used to identify other situations, by extracting key aspects of relational structure and finding them in other instances. This general approach is explored in a companion chapter in this volume, where specific attention is given to trusted results in local closed reasoning but a larger open world (Garcia et al. Chap. 13 in this volume). That work would enable a formal implementation of the system described here.

25.5.6   Media

The 2D Keynote method is able to include text, photos, images and videos because these are capabilities of Keynote. However, all such items needed to be small in order to fit on a single keynote page. They are inserted and managed manually.

By contrast, Wunderkammer can turn any node into any media object and situate it in a seemingly infinite space. Videos can be as large as actual movie screens. The affordances of the Wunderkammer tool also have powerful implications for how these media items could be further structured—for example, one movie could be playing while it is physically inside another movie. In the PTSD model, 3D artifacts

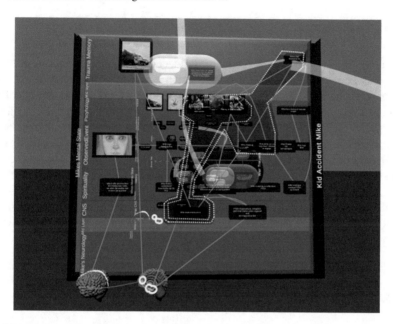

Fig. 25.11 Image showing the use of different media—3D brain, photos and text

such as a model brain were included. An example of how these are connected is shown in Fig. 25.11.

In both tools, any of these objects can be linked to any other object, regardless of the media entailed. However, Wunderkammer enables digital precision and the possibility that this positional information can be included in a reasoning system later. For example, the user can discretely and uniformly select points around an object via a uniform sphere with points every 30 degrees from the center all the way around. This feature results in approximately 96 connection points equally spaced around a sphere, enabling structures to be highly nuanced. Later, these points will be readable as coordinates by a back-end system. When shape and structure have interpretive implications, this precision will be valued. The capabilities of the tool thus lead to a new design implication: these positions need to mean something, in order for them to be readable and processable by an intelligent system.

Wunderkammer has other features which increase its media capabilities. There is an internal camera so that snapshots' from within the model can be taken, as though the user is in a physical environment. Given that a user's hands will be occupied by VR controllers and that users are likely to be standing, voice dictation capabilities are also included to label the nodes. If needed, a virtual keyboard can be summoned to input text.

Using these capabilities, we produced a model in which multiple disciplines and modes are combined, and influences are shown between them.

25.6   Discussion

This research is a step toward modeling influence among heterogeneous contexts, using the example of a veteran's PTSD which is informed by multiple traumatic events. The new modeling platform, *Wunderkammer*, makes critical aspects of this demonstration possible. It is a prototype, however, and as such, represents a first attempt at what is possible. There are noted problems when the data design in immersive spaces moves beyond visualization and into the robust analysis (El Beheiry et al. 2019) and some of these barriers arose during the development of this prototype. The main limitations encountered were readability and dynamism; these are discussed here. However, the work was robust enough and offered enough new affordances, that a useful application of the result could be developed, in the form of a new modeling environment for PTSD patients to document and annotate their past experiences, for therapeutic purposes. This is also discussed.

25.6.1   *Readability*

A limit of the Wunderkammer modeling platform is that it is both less technologically accessible and more difficult to read than Keynote—see Fig. 25.12a and b for a comparison between the two formats.

Fixing the readability problem is partly a design issue. A visual grammar should be systematic, such that every placement has meaning—it is a group of 'principles that tell us how to put the right mark in the right place' (Tufte, 1990, 9). General methods for 2D visualization have been developed over such a long period of time that 'visualizing data on a 2D screen is now a relatively standardized task and consensus exists for navigation' (El Beheiry et al., 2019, 1320). The design of our 2D method leveraged implicit conventions, including a dependence on a fixed viewer stance, a bounded 'page' view and an X/Y graph format in which information is registered according to its position among the axes. A problem with 3D is that it adds two more factors that are invisible in 2D representations: the moving perspective of the viewer and the lack of a constraining frame. These two qualities make it difficult to 'read' the placement of data items.

There is thus a tension between traditional 2D modes of representation and the nature of an immersive space, where a viewer's stance is unbounded and constantly moving. On the problem of positioning items, one solution would be to create a systematic grammar of 3D objects that is custom for the immersive space, where every part of the X/Y/Z axis has significance. Research with designer Niccolo Casas explored what this might look like (Cardier et al., 2017, 2020a, b). With this in mind, we partly addressed the problem by imposing a grid in the Wunderkammer space which had a snap-to-position function, enabling objects to be aligned in reference to it (Cardier et al., 2019). This alignment helped to regulate the space, but an underlying

(a)

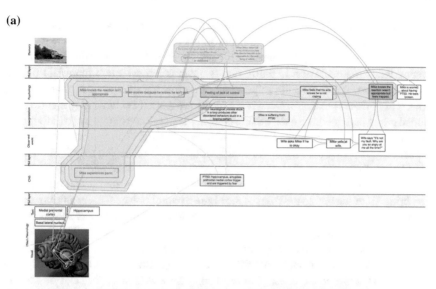

(b)

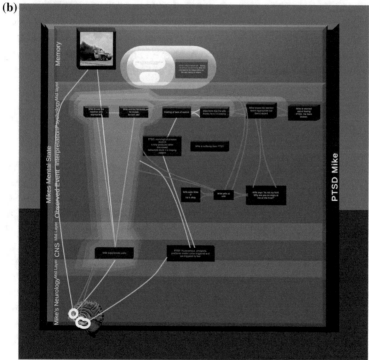

Fig. 25.12 **a** 2D depiction of 'signature' structure. The nodes, their relationships and their higher-level structure are legible. **b** 3D depiction of 'signature' structure. This is the same structure as the previous figure. The nodes, their relationships and their higher-level have a less visually precise structure which is more difficult to read when zoomed out

method to register the fine positioning made possible by a digital environment is still needed. In addition, the problem of occlusion persists.

The issue of 3D objects obscuring each other increases as more objects are assembled. This occlusion is partly due to their volume—when many 3D objects are networked, it can give the impression of a crowded garage more than parsable data. This effect is exacerbated when objects are nested because they can be positioned many layers within each other. As well, the possible novel ways of solving the nesting problem that WunderKammer addresses through volumetric solutions still present text layering problems. For example, other text rendering solutions could be used but there are generally trade-offs. For example, instead of nesting the text with the associated volumetric item(s), we could leverage the nested graph relationship and bring all of the text to the front of the highest parent object. This capability would help in one area of readability but at the cost of jeopardizing the overall structure.

One possible solution is to move between both 2D and 3D views. The immersive space is needed to build massive networks with a variety of architectural affordances. However, when reading that immersive space, the three dimensions could be rendered into two. This would be a flat picture of 3D—an example of this can be seen in Figs. 25.7a–c and 25.8a–c, in which 3D immersion is depicted in a flat 2D photo. Another possible solution is that the graphics remain as 2D 'threads' in the 3D space, so the physical space can support limitless entities but constrain the ways in which its items are seen to relate to each other, and perhaps even enforce a particular viewing position. Exploring these issues will be the subject of future work.

25.6.2 Dynamism

A significant problem that we wanted to solve with this prototype was the lack of visualization space. The tool was thus quickly developed to accommodate massive networks of structure and containers. Once this capability was established, however, the problem of animating them came to the fore. Both the construction and interpretation of dynamic structures were harder in an immersive environment than in a 2D representation.

One reason is that 2D animation traditionally depends on a flat, constrained frame of reference. Its successive and incremental changes usually occur in relation to a bounded frame. That circumscribed space on the page gives a point of reference for any shifts in the depicted shape, forming a lens. The limited scope enables a viewer to understand what is changing and what is not. Keynote replicates some of these properties, enabling a user to copy the last frame and make changes, and then 'run' the result to produce a 'flip' effect which animates the series.

Wunderkammer does a rudimentary version of this, in which a timeline can be scrubbed to see different states of an environment flick past. However, it does not permit the same amount of control due to scale, immersion and readability. On scale and immersion: copying an entire environment (especially while within it) and then making select changes in relation to another entire environment is not feasible. It is a bit like blinking between different homes, and during each teleportation, trying to rearrange the furniture so that the two environments relate to the other. On readability: recalling the position of nodes in order to incrementally adjust them is harder when there is an additional dimension, in the form of the Z-axis.

These limitations may be resolved to varying degrees as the tool's state advances. However, we also must remain cognizant of how our framework for analyzing success in modeling activity is bifurcated between the success of the immersive end-state *model* and the success of the immersive modeling *process*. This likely merits additional study and consideration of the role of procedural modeling tools in various stages of cognitive modeling.

In the next version of this platform, the animation capability will be re-conceived in terms of an immersive space. Attention to the state-of-the-art animation software will inform how the animation features can be developed. The game environment Sony Playstation4 Dreams suggests how an easier approach to animation could be managed in an immersive space, by animating items separately. Knowledge graph tools such as Mindomo and Node Red Interface are capable of more easily creating nodes and links which have a systematic appearance. Bolt Visual Scripting, Unity 3D's plug-in which allows non-programmers to create game environments, offers the potential of doing both a systematic visual vocabulary and animation.

25.6.3   Future Applications

We did not expect to produce a finished product with this prototype, but this early form provides enough new capabilities that it could be appropriate for a related but different purpose. It could be developed into an immersive interface that allows patients and their therapists to jointly inhabit situations and histories in virtual reality, and arrange them into networked structures, for the purpose of treating PTSD. This would build on the work of Virtually Better and the Oxford VR social anxiety program, in which veterans with PTSD inhabit generic situations related to their fear in order to regain a sense of control. Wunderkammer would be a more personalized system, giving patients and therapists an environment in which to structure their own narratives, photos and videos and then annotate them, to reveal how key patterns emerged through their lives. The goal would be to give a PTSD sufferer a greater sense of control over the narratives of their traumatic experience and recovery.

A tool like this would use the functionalities we have developed to imitate internal memory organization and narrative-making. Our system's ability to handle containers can be leveraged so that these artifacts can be enlarged and stepped into, and populated with photos or videos of remembered situations. Containers are also easy to step out of—they are a controllable physical boundary that enables a user to distance themselves from triggering situations and switch to an immersive safe space instead. Inside the space, users would be able to take photos, write notes (these can be voice-activated), import videos and link these items into narratives. These environments and memories could be easily structured and annotated—for example, memories of a disappointing father, such as Mike's, might be linked to an aspect of the traumatic event he experienced, revealing how one fuels the other. Afterward, that cluster of memories could then be shrunk into a small box and 'put away'.

Patients and therapists could co-occupy this space, collaborating during therapy to build healthier interpretations using the client's own photos and memories. In fact, the 3D Unity platform could even support remote or group therapy sessions, which would be particularly beneficial for patients who live far from accessible services.

25.7 Conclusion

It is difficult to model the aspects of context which inform interpretation in an open world: influence and the transfer of information between heterogeneous contexts. We aim to capture these qualities by developing new conceptualizations of context and new methods to represent them. This chapter discusses two methods developed to achieve this, with a focus on new functionalities afforded by Wunderkammer, a prototype immersive modeling environment built by the Virginia Modeling, Analysis and Simulation Center at Old Dominion University.

The 2D method was developed in Keynote to capture aspects of open-world interpretation that are not currently represented by text analysis. Its taxonomy added a representation of context boundaries, influence and information transfer to traditional knowledge-representation conventions. However, that 2D approach could not produce three of the four special features described in this chapter: linking multiple models, zooming and signature structures.

Wunderkammer represented the first example of a 3D approach to our method and added immersive and spatial capabilities which were not possible using the 2D approach. These new capabilities extended the scope of what can be represented and imagined in inter-contextual influence, such as limitless representational space, an additional 'z' axis, whole-body interaction with the user interface and immersive user visualization. It also added multi-modal media formats such as video, image, voice and text, which can be imported, created, linked and arranged, enabling us to replicate a wider spectrum of information as it is found in an open-world experience. These multi-modal items could then be used to compose numerous situations, which themselves be assembled into models of scenes. In turn, these could be connected to show how influence evolves through numerous contexts over time.

Our example concerns PTSD, featuring information from psychological, neurological and physiological domains and integrating them to produce a fuller picture of our example subject, Mike. We modeled four scenes from Mike's life with PTSD. These were connected into four models, which were then integrated into a metamodel to provide a broader picture of causal influence across time. In the immersive environment, it was possible to depict the influences between events at the relevant different stages of Mike's life. Higher-level structures such as this enabled a user to see how 'thematic' similarities emerged across multiple heterogeneous contexts. It also made it possible for an overall 'signature' to be identified at a more abstract level, to discern whether a disordered pattern was emerging.

Combining multiple heterogeneous models in the same virtual space is a step toward a fuller representation of the influence among heterogeneous contexts. The new features presented indicate the kinds of operations needed to model heterogeneous information from the open world. In future work, this will be applied to models of information transfer in autonomous systems, social media, artificial intelligence and PTSD modeling.

Acknowledgments The prototype tool described here was built by the Virginia Modeling Analysis and Simulation Center at ODU with partial support from a grant from the National Academies Keck Futures Initiative ('Design in Information Flow: Using aesthetic principles to overcome computational barriers in the analysis of complex systems'). Visualizations of the speculative capabilities of the tool for PTSD and the 'model-of-models' were drawn by Beth Cardier while a Research Fellow with Griffith University and Trusted Autonomous Systems Defence CRC, using Keynote. The 3D embodiment of the 'model-of-models' image was generated in Unity 3D by John Shull.

References

Angus, D., Rintel, S., & Wiles, J. (2013). Making sense of big text: A visual-first approach for analysing textdata using Leximancer and Discursis. *International Journal of Social Research Methodology, 16*(3), 261–267.

Angus, D., & Wiles, J. (2018). Social semantic networks: measuring topic management in discourse using a pyramid of conceptual recurrence metrics. *Chaos: An Interdisciplinary Journal of Nonlinear Science, 28(8)*, 085723.

Barricelli, B.R., De Bonis, A., Di Gaetano, S., & Valtolina, S. (2018). Semiotic framework for virtual reality usability and UX evaluation: A pilot study. In M. De Marsico, L. A. Ripamonti, D. Gadia, D. Maggiorini & I. Mariani (Eds.), *Proceedings of 2nd Workshop on Games-Human Interaction Co-Located with the International Working Conference on Advanced Visual Interfaces*. Castiglione della Pescaia, Italy: CEUR Workshop Proceedings, 2246, 1–6.

Barwise, J., & Perry, J. (1983). *Situations and attitudes*. MIT Press.

Bayat, B., Bermejo-Alonso, J., Carbonera, J., Facchinetti, T., Fiorini, S., Goncalves, P., Jorge, V., et al. (2016). Requirements for building an ontology for autonomous robots. *Industrial Robot: An International Journal, 43*(5), 469–480.

Belanger, W. (2009). *A semiotic analysis of virtual reality*. Salve Regina University.

Cardier, B. (2013). *Unputdownable: How the agencies of compelling story assembly can be modelled using formalisable methods from knowledge representation, and in a fictional tale about seduction*. University of Melbourne.

Cardier, B. (2014). Narrative causal impetus: Situational governance in game of thrones. In J. Zhu, I. Horswil & N. Wardrip-fruin (Eds.), *Intelligent Narrative Technologies*, 7, 2–8. Palo Alto, CA: AAAI Press.

Cardier, B. (2015). The evolution of interpretive contexts in stories. In *Sixth International Workshop on Computational Models of Narrative*, 45, 23–38. Saarbrücken/Wadern: Dagstuhl Publishing.

Cardier, B., Goranson, H. T., Casas, N., Lundberg, P. S., Erioli, A., Takaki, R., Nagy, D., Ciavarra, R., & Sanford Larry, D. (2017). Modeling the peak of emergence in systems: Design and katachi. In P. Simeonov, A. Gare, K. Matsuno, A. Igamberdiev & A. Hankey (Eds.), *Progress in Biophysics and Molecular Biology: Special Issue on Integral Biomathics: The Necessary Conjunction of the Western and Eastern Thought Traditions for Exploring the Nature of Mind and Life*, 131c, 213–241.

Cardier, B., Shull, J., Casas, N., Nielsen, A., Goranson, T., Sanford, L. D., & Lundberg, P. (2019). A cathedral of data: Using asymmetry to annotate real-world artefacts in virtual reality. Presented at the Symmetry: Art and Science, 2019—11th Congress and Exhibition of SIS, Kanazawa, Japan, November 28.

Cardier, B., Goranson, T., Diallo, S., Shull, J., Casas, N., Nielsen, A., Lundberg, P., Sanford, L. D., & Ciavarra. R. (2020a). A narrative modeling platform: representing the comprehension of novelty in open world systems. In W. Lawless, R. Mittu, & D. Sofge (Eds.), *Human-Machine Shared Contexts*, New York: Elsevier.

Cardier, B., Shull, J., Nielsen, A., Diallo, S., Casas, N., Lundberg, P., Sanford, L., Ciavarra, R., & Goranson, T. (2020b). A narrative modeling platform: representing the comprehension of novelty in open world systems. In W. Lawless, R. Mittu & D. Sofge (Eds.), *Human-Machine shared contexts*, Elsevier.

Carnegie, T. A. (2009). Interface as exordium: The rhetoric of interactivity. *Computers and Composition, 26*(3), 164–173.

Cohen, P. (2015). DARPA's big mechanism program. *Physical Biology, 12*, 1–9.

Devlin, K. J. (1995). *Logic and information.* Cambridge University Press.

Devlin, K. J. (2005). Confronting context effects in intelligence analysis: How can mathematics help?", online report, https://web.stanford.edu/~kdevlin/Papers/Context_in_Reasoning.pdf.

Devlin, K. J. (2009). Modeling real reasoning. In G. Sommaruga (Ed.), Formal Theories of Information: From Shannon to Semantic Information Theory and General Concepts of Information. *Lecture Notes in Computer Science, 5363*, 234–252. Springer.

Devlin, K., & Dushka, R. (1996). Language at work: Analyzing communication breakdown in the workplace to inform systems design. University of Chicago Press.

Einhorn, H., & Hogarth, R. (1986). Judging probable cause. *Psychological Bulletin, 99*, 3–19.

El Beheiry, M., Doutreligne, S., Caporal, C., Ostertag, M. D., & Masson, J.-B. (2019). Virtual reality: Beyond visualization. *Journal of Molecular Biology, 431*(7), 1315–1321.

Fauconnier, G., & Turner, M. (2002). *The way we think: Conceptual blending and the mind's hidden complexities.* Basic Books.

Gentner, D., Ratterman, M., & Forbus, K. (1993). The roles of similarity in transfer: Separating retrievability from inferential soundness. *Cognitive Psychology, 25*, 524–575.

Goldberg, A. V., & Harrelson, C. (2005). Computing the shortest path: A search meets graph theory. In *Proceedings of the Sixteenth Annual ACM-SIAM Symposium on Discrete Algorithms*, 156–165. Philadelphia: Society for Industrial and Applied Mathematics.

Goranson, H. T. (2009). *Briefing on the background of the needs of the intelligence community after 9/11.* Stanford University.

Goranson, T., Cardier, B., & Devlin, K. (2015). Pragmatic phenomenological types. *Progress in Biophysics and Molecular Biology, 119*(3), 420–436. https://doi.org/10.1016/j.pbiomolbio.2015.07.006

Herman, D. (2000). Narratology as a cognitive science. *Image and Narrative, 1*, 1–31. online, http://www.imageandnarrative.be/inarchive/narratology/davidherman.htm.

Herman, D. (2001). Story logic in conversational and literary narratives. *Narrative, 9*(2), 130–137.

Herman, D. (2002). Story logic: Problems and possibilities of narrative. Lincoln: University of Nebraska Press.

Herman, D. (2017). *Storytelling and the sciences of the mind.* MIT Press.

Hume, D. (1748). An enquiry concerning human understanding and other writings. Cambridge: Cambridge University Press.

Hurley, E. C., Maxfield, L., & Solomon, R. (2017). Case example: Mike, a 32-Year-Old Iraq War Veteran. American psychological association: Guidelines for the treatment of post traumatic stress disorder. online https://www.apa.org/ptsd-guideline/resources/eye-movement-reprocessing-example.

Jahn, M. (1997). Frames, preferences, and the reading of third-person narratives: Towards a cognitive narratology. *Poetics Today, 18*(4), 441–468.

Kantosalo, A., Ravikumar, P.T., Grace, K., & Takala, T. (2020). Modalities, styles and strategies: An interaction framework for human–computer co-creativity. In F Amilicar Cardoso, P. Machado, T. Veale, & J. M. Cunha (Eds.), *Proceedings of the 11th International Conference on Computational Creativity. Coimbra, Portugal: Association for Computational Creativity,* 57–64.

Kean, T., & Hamilton, L. (2004). How to do it? A different way of organizing the government. US federal government. National commission on terrorist attacks upon the United States (blog). https://govinfo.library.unt.edu/911/report/911Report_Ch13.htm.

Kirkpatrick, D. G., & Seidel, R. (1986). The ultimate planar convex hull algorithm? *SIAM Journal on Computing, 15*(1), 287–299.

Krippendorf, K. (2019). *Content analysis: An introduction to its methodology* (4th ed.). Sage Publications.

Kyndi. (2018). Cognilytica briefing note. Kyndi Corporate Wesbite (blog). Retrieved March, 2018, online https://kyndi.com/wp-content/uploads/2018/03/Cognilytica-Briefing-Note_Kyndi.pdf.

Lexalytics. (2020). Technology: Sentiment analysis. Lexalytics Website (blog). online https://www.lexalytics.com/technology/sentiment-analysis.

Marini, D., Folgieri, R., Gadia, D., & Rizzi, A. (2012). Virtual reality as a communication process. *Virtual Reality, 16*(3), 233–241.

Menon, S., & Jayan, C. (2010). Eye movement desensitization and reprocessing: A conceptual framework. *Indian Journal of Psychological Medicine, 32*(2), 136–140.

Minsky, M. (1975). A framework for representing knowledge. In P. Winston (Ed.), *The psychology of computer vision* (pp. 211–277). McGraw-Hill.

Murayama, I. (1994). Role of agency in causal understanding of natural phenomena. *Human Development, 37*(4), 198–206.

Noble, D. (2015). Multi-Bio and multi-scale systems biology. *Progress in Biophysics and Molecular Biology, 117,* 1–3.

Prince, G. (1973). A grammar of stories: An introduction. Walter de Gruyter.

Risch, J, Kao, A., Poteet, S., & Jason Wu, Y. J. (2008). Text visualization for visual text analytics, 154–171.

Schank, R. (1995). *Tell me a story: A new look at real and artificial memory.* Northwestern University Press.

Schank, R., & Abelson, R. (1977). *Scripts, plans, goals and understanding: An enquiry into human knowledge structures.* Lawrence Erlbaum Associates.

Shneiderman, B. (1996). The eyes have it: A task by data type taxonomy for information visualizations. Proceedings 1996 IEEE Symposium on Visual Languages, 336–343. Boulder, Colorado: IEEE.

Steuer, J. (1995). Defining virtual reality: Dimensions determining telepresence. *Journal of Communication, 42*(4), 73–93.

Tham, J., Duin, A. H., Gee, L., Ernst, N., Abdelgader, B., & McGrath, M. (2018). Understanding virtual reality: Presence, embodiment, and professional practice. *Technical Communication, 65*(1), 45–65.

Trabasso, T., & Sperry, L. (1985). Causal relatedness and importance of story events. *Journal of Memory and Language, 24,* 595–611.

Tufte, E. (1990). *Envisioning information.* Graphics Press.

Tummons, J. (2014). Using software for qualitative data analysis: Research outside paradigmatic boundaries. *Big Data? Qualitative Approaches to Digital Research, 13,* 155–177.

Victor, B. (2014). The humane representation of thought. Closing Keynote. Honolulu, Hawaii: ACM. online https://vimeo.com/115154289.

Walls, R. L., Deck, J., Guralnick, R., Baskauf, S., Beaman, R., Blum, S., Bowers, S., et al. (2014). Semantics in support of biodiversity knowledge discovery: An introduction to the biological collections ontology and related ontologies. *PLoS One, 9,* e89606. online https://doi.org/10.1371/journal.pone.0089606.

Printed in the United States
by Baker & Taylor Publisher Services